A Transcendental DIARY

Travels with His Divine Grace A.C. Bhaktivedanta Swami PRABHUPĀDA

VOLUME ONE

NOVEMBER 1975 - APRIL 1976

Hari Śauri Dāsa

H S BOOKS

Readers wishing to correspond with the author may write to the following address:

Lotus Imprints
P.O. Box 2280
Alachua, FL 32615-2280, USA

Volume 1 first published in 1992; 3,000 copies
Volume 1 reprinted in 1995; 2,000 copies
ISBN 0-9633355-1-0 (Volume 1; paperback)
ISBN 0-9633355-0-2 (Volume 1; hardcover)
Volume 2 first published in 1994; 5,000 copies
ISBN 0-9633355-4-5 (Volume 2; paperback)
ISBN 0-9633355-3-7 (Volume 2; hardcover)
Volume 3 first published in 1994; 5,000 copies
ISBN 0-9633355-6-1 (Volume 3; paperback)
ISBN 0-9633355-5-3 (Volume 3; hardcover)
Multi-Volume Set
ISBN 0-9633355-2-9

Published by Lotus Imprints
Printed in India at Indira Printers, New Delhi-110020.

Front cover photo: Vṛndāvana, India; April 4th, 1976

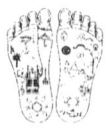

Celebrating the 100th Anniversary of
His Divine Grace
A. C. Bhaktivedanta Swami Prabhupāda
Founder–*Ācārya* of the
International Society for Krishna Consciousness

Śrīla Prabhupāda Centennial
1896–1996

"He built a house in which the whole world can live."

DEDICATION

This book is humbly offered at the lotus feet of His Divine Grace Śrīla Prabhupāda, by whose mercy this dog has been made to dance. May he be pleased to be present within each and every page.

"What is not possible to achieve in thousands of lives can be achieved in one moment if there is an opportunity to meet a saintly person. It is therefore enjoined in Vedic literature that one should always try to associate with saintly persons and try to disassociate oneself from the common man, because by one word of a saintly person one can be liberated from material entanglement."

Śrīmad-Bhāgavatam 3:22:5, Purport.

TABLE OF CONTENTS

ACKNOWLEDGEMENTS vii

INTRODUCTION—An Overview ix

FOREWORD xiii
Dr. E. Burke Rochford, Jr.
Middlebury College, Vermont

PREFACE—Setting the Scene xvii

CHAPTER ONE—New Delhi and Kurukṣetra 1
November 26th–December 1st, 1975

CHAPTER TWO—Śrī Vṛndāvana Dhāma. 29
December 2nd—December 12th, 1975

CHAPTER THREE—New Delhi 105
December 13th—December 15th, 1975

CHAPTER FOUR—Bombay 115
December 16th—December 24th, 1975

CHAPTER FIVE—Sanand; Bombay 153
December 25th—December 31st, 1975

CHAPTER SIX—Madras **175**
January 1st–January 2nd, 1976

CHAPTER SEVEN—Nellore **191**
January 3rd–January 8th, 1976

CHAPTER EIGHT—Bombay; Calcutta **245**
January 9th–January 16th, 1976

CHAPTER NINE—Śrī Dhāma Māyāpur **265**
January 17th–March 21st, 1976

CHAPTER TEN—Calcutta, New Delhi, Modinagar and Aligarh **481**
March 22nd–March31st, 1976

CHAPTER ELEVEN—Śrī Vṛndāvana Dhāma ... **507**
March 31st–April 11th, 1976

CHAPTER TWELVE—Bombay **537**
April 11th–April 18th, 1976

APPENDIX A—Chart of Days of the Week **567**

ABOUT THE AUTHOR **569**

GLOSSARY **571**

GENERAL INDEX **585**

ACKNOWLEDGEMENTS

There are so many devotees who have given me encouragement to write this book that it is not possible to mention them all here individually. However, it is with deep gratitude that I acknowledge the well-wishes of each and every one of them.

Many devotees stepped forward with practical help, both financial and service-wise. Some of them donated their hard-earned funds, some their labor and some provided materials and services at cost or at reduced rates. Accordingly, I want to give particular mention and thanks to the following persons and organizations, without whose help this project could not have been possible.

My sincere thanks go to Abhirām dāsa, Balabhadra dāsa, Bhāgavat Āśraya dāsa, Bhaktivedanta Book Trust Australia, Los Angeles, and UK, Bhagavān dāsa, Bhakta Barry (NZ), Brahmatīrtha dāsa, Bhāva dāsa, Bhavānanda dāsa, Bṛghupati dāsa, Danavīr dāsa, Indulekhā dāsī, ISKCON North Sydney, Īśvara dāsa, Jaya Gopāla dāsa, Kārṣṇa dāsa, Mādrī dāsī (NZ), Madhusevita dāsa, Mahātmā dāsa (Australia), Mandukini dāsī and Aravinda dāsa, Matsya Avatāra dāsa, Nareśvara dāsa, Palace Press, Param Brahma dāsa, Purujita dāsa, Śākṣī Gopāla dāsa (Australia), Śyāmasundar dāsa, Tamal Krishna Goswami, Tīrtharāja dāsa, Trāṇa Kartā dāsa, and Viśvambhara Swami.

On the editing side, I can honestly say that without the enthusiasm of the following editors this book would not have made it to print. I am deeply indebted to Riktānanda dāsa and Sītā dāsī, who, between them, did the bulk of the work. Kuṇḍalī dāsa also provided willing work at short notice.

I am extremely grateful to Śrīkānta dāsa for an excellent job of copy editing and proofreading, and Rakṣana dāsa for proofreading at short notice. Grahila dāsa provided a first-rate index. Jaya Balarāma dāsa did the Sanskrit editing and Kuśakratha dāsa the Sanskrit proofreading.

The beautiful design work is to the credit of Yamarāja dāsa, for the photo-pages layout, Śākṣī Gopāla dāsa (UK), who very kindly did the front and back cover design, and Locan dāsa, who provided the art work for the end covers.

I also want to acknowledge the hard work of Āditya dāsī, who made the first typed version of my original handwritten diary in 1977, and Gopa-mātā dāsī, who put it all on computer disk.

Special mention and thanks go to the devotees at the Bhaktivedanta Archives—Parama Rūpa dāsa, Ekanātha dāsa, Raṇajit dāsa, and Dulāl Candra dāsa—who were ever willing to provide good advice and many valuable materials that were essential to make this presentation complete. BBT Archives also did the typesetting and layout.

Finally, my wife Śītala dāsī deserves an accolade for providing constant support and encouragement and many hundreds of hours of labor. She edited, typed, corrected, and advised without complaint, and is as much responsible for the successful completion of this book as I am.

I humbly apologize to anyone I have inadvertently omitted from these credits, and I ask them to please be satisfied with the result, which, I think, is worth far more than my few words of thanks.

INTRODUCTION

For a period of sixteen months, from late November, 1975 to the end of March, 1977, I had the great fortune to travel with His Divine Grace A. C. Bhaktivedanta Swami Prabhupāda as his personal servant.

Although the initial period of my tenure was to be only two or three days, by the grace of Lord Kṛṣṇa I immediately recognized the unique opportunity in my being able to personally associate with Śrīla Prabhupāda. Thus, on the first night, I purchased a blank notebook in which to keep a diary of my experience. I was thinking that ten or twenty years hence I would be able to read those notes and relish the brief time spent in his association. When my position in his entourage was more firmly fixed, I continued to update the diary on a daily basis.

At the same time, I was very aware that Prabhupāda's words—especially his conversations on the daily morning walks and with his visitors—were being recorded on tape. I considered these to be another kind of diary.

This book, then, represents an expanded form of my personal written diary coupled with snippets and segments of the electronically recorded one. Added to this are selections of His Divine Grace's correspondence.

This is one small attempt to bring to the attention of the world the greatness of Śrīla Prabhupāda, his person and his message. I have attempted to present an accurate and detailed historical record of the activities and pastimes of

Śrīla Prabhupāda—Śrīla Prabhupāda *as he is*—during the latter part of his stay with us. It is then, a partial biography.

This should not be taken as the personal memoirs of a former servant, although certainly I have expressed some of the feelings and emotions I experienced at the time. Nor is it a retrospective analysis. It is a simple, factual account of times, places, and events, which I, as his personal servant, was in a unique position to observe.

My purpose in presenting this material is two-fold. Firstly, I wanted to glorify Śrīla Prabhupāda in whatever small and humble way I could. Such a brilliant figure has rarely been seen on the stage of human life, and I was keen that, before we are robbed by passing time of the clear memory and appreciation of his pure and transcendental nature, this material be made as widely available as possible. Secondly, I wanted to give the devotees of Lord Kṛṣṇa, in particular, the opportunity to associate with Śrīla Prabhupāda in the same intimate and daily way that I did. All scriptures emphatically declare the incalculable benefit of association with a saintly person, yet that opportunity is normally only available to a limited few. However, through the printed word, it can be expanded unlimitedly.

I readily admit to my limitations in making this presentation. I am neither a writer nor a devotee. The only qualification I can claim is to say that I was there. Somehow or other Kṛṣṇa gave me sufficient presence of mind to record the events, and thus, with whatever little humility I possess, I now present this material for the pleasure and edification of all devotees of Śrīla Prabhupāda, the future followers of His Divine Grace, historians, scholars, and the public at large.

The Bhaktivedanta Archives is gradually making the complete versions of all of Prabhupāda's conversations, letters, and lectures available in both tape and book form. That being the case, one might question the need for the inclusion of extracts from these sources here. The answer is simple: within these pages the reader will find the circumstances surrounding particular events, and thus the words of Śrīla Prabhupāda will take on fresh and deeper relevance.

One may also question the inclusion of names and incidents that may be less than flattering to the individuals concerned. To this I should state my reasoning in doing so. It is certainly not my intention to cast anyone in an embarrassing light. Nevertheless, things did happen, which, due to our immaturity in devotional service or our lack of comprehension, created problems that only His Divine Grace could resolve. Great profit can be derived from understanding how Śrīla Prabhupāda dealt with difficult situations, how he corrected problems, and how he settled disputes between his spiritual children. For us, this was all part of the process of growing up in our spiritual lives, and to whatever degree we accepted Śrīla Prabhupāda's advice, and sometimes chastisement, to that extent or more, we profited in our Kṛṣṇa consciousness.

We can take these incidents in the same spirit that Śrīla Prabhupāda himself did; he didn't condemn anyone because of his or her sometimes negative behavior. Rather he worked to improve both the situation and the person involved, to the benefit of all. He was corrective and supportive in every situation, and these incidents should be viewed from that perspective.

I pray for the blessings of all the devotees and followers of Śrīla Prabhupāda and hope my humble attempt will serve to increase their appreciation and understanding of the personality and teachings of His Divine Grace.

As Śrīla Prabhupāda himself noted as we traveled on the overnight train from Allahabad to Calcutta in January, 1977, "History will mark this period, how the Kṛṣṇa consciousness movement changed the world." He left a great legacy to the world, and this is one very small attempt to make it known.

Again, referring to the books written by himself, Śrīla Prabhupāda said that if a person reads "one verse, one line, one word," his life will be changed.

I am confident that the same effect will be had by reading books written about him. And that is the purpose of Srīla Prabhupāda's appearance: to change our lives from the dull and mundane to the transcendental realm of spiritual enlightenment and unlimited happiness, where all difficulties and contradictions are automatically resolved in the light of their common relationship to Lord Śrī Kṛṣṇa, the cause of all causes, and the center of all existence.

Hari-śauri dāsa
Completed on the Holy Occasion of Śrī Gaura Pūrṇimā
March 18th, 1992, Vṛndāvana, India

FOREWORD

In 1965 an elderly man from India came to the United States to fulfill a promise to his Spiritual Master to preach Krishna Consciousness in the West. Unbelievably, in a matter of only a few short years, he and his followers had built a worldwide religious movement of nearly 5000 initiated disciples and tens of thousands of followers and supporters. Moreover, many millions of books and other pieces of spiritual literature had been distributed in every corner of the globe. With success came controversy, however, as a well-organized anti-cult movement sought to limit the influence of Hare Krishna. Charges of brainwashing provided the media and the general public with a quasi-theory to account for the growth of "menacing cults" like Hare Krishna. Yet in uncritically accepting false claims about "mind control," many never came to understand the social and cultural significance of new religious groups such as the International Society for Krishna Consciousness (ISKCON), more popularly known as Hare Krishna. Nor did most members of the public understand the legitimate appeals of ISKCON; the richness and authenticity of its spiritual tradition, its lifestyle of "simple living and high thinking", and, perhaps most importantly, the charisma and spiritual potency of its founding leader, A.C. Bhaktivedanta Swami Srila Prabhupāda.

It has been almost fifteen years since the disappearance of Śrīla Prabhupāda in November, 1977. While much has happened to Prabhupāda's disciples and his movement during this time, his memory and inspiration live on forever. Most, of course, immediately think of the legacy represented by Prabhupāda's translations and commentaries on the Vedic literature, or his movement, with communities of devotees located throughout the world. Yet there is another part of this legacy that lives on in the individual and collective memory of his disciples. In this first volume of Hari Śauri's *Transcendental Diary* the reader comes to understand the man who has touched the hearts and minds of so many people around the world.

Some might point to good luck, others Krishna's arrangement, but by whatever means, Hari Śauri found himself in the enviable position of serving as Prabhupāda's personal assistant over a sixteen month period from November, 1975, until March of 1977. By way of Hari Śauri's diary we gain a personal and detailed understanding of Prabhupāda the man, as well as the spiritual leader. Hari Śauri provides us with a window into the activities, thoughts, and concerns of Prabhupāda. In this volume we travel with Prabhupāda throughout India between November, 1975, and April, 1976. One comes away from this book with a personal connection to Prabhupāda, appreciating his love for Krishna as well as his many disciples. We witness Prabhupāda's sadness as his young followers faced personal and spiritual problems; his never-ending joy and delight as book distribution simply exploded in 1975 and 1976; and, the purpose of his chastisement for the occasional errant disciple, including the author.

Yet we learn more about this remarkable man and his ability to inspire his followers. We join Prabhupāda and his disciples on many morning walks. On these occasions, we see the intellectual as well as the spiritual side of Prabhupāda. He debates with his disciples often challenging the logic and theory of evolutionary science and the "rascal scientists." We see Prabhupāda's mastery of argument and his commitment to doing Krishna's work no matter what the calibre of the opposition. It is clear, as well, that these debates with his disciples help sharpen their own philosophical understanding and preaching skills.

The value of this volume and the ones to follow can not be overstated. To the disciples of Prabhupāda, the accounts contained here are a spark bringing to light endless stories and emotions that only further their connection to the Spiritual Master. To those devotees who had no personal contact or association with Srila Prabhupāda, this book serves a particularly important purpose; it becomes the basis for "knowing" Prabhupāda in a more intimate way. It allows new disciples and aspiring disciples to connect with the purity and inspiration of Prabhupāda and the mission of Chaitanya Mahaprabhu. Through Prabhupāda's example of full surrender to his own guru one also learns how to approach and serve the Spiritual

Master. To the average reader—with no direct involvement in Prabhupāda's movement—this book is also a source of inspiration. It is nothing short of miraculous that one man could inspire so many people throughout the world to become God-conscious. We learn here how and why this has happened.

For scholars and students of religion the material presented represents a critically important historical record. Anyone seeking to understand Prabhupāda's movement specifically, or the centrality of charismatic leadership to the development of religious movements, will want to consider this book. The use of a diary to record and present Prabhupāda's life has helped assure that the material presented is richly detailed and an accurate reflection of unfolding events. Hari Śauri has given the reader a clear and rather straight-forward presentation of events rather than engaging in historical reconstruction meant to serve partisan or theoretical interests. As such, it will be of great interest to historians and sociologists of religion who seek to understand the cultural and social significance of Prabhupāda and the broader Hare Krishna movement.

In 1976, I had the good fortune of seeing Srila Prabhupāda during his final stay at ISKCON's Los Angeles community. At the time I was new to my research and could only vaguely understand the significance of Prabhupāda as a man and spiritual leader. Over the years it has become clearer to me that Prabhupāda was and is the lifeline of the Hare Krishna movement. While no longer physically present, his example and teachings still inspire those who are touched by him and his movement. Hare Krishna.

Professor E. Burke Rochford, Jr.
Middlebury College, Vermont.
Author of *Hare Krishna In America* (Rutgers University Press)

PREFACE

Setting the Scene

In late November of 1975 Śrīla Prabhupāda returned to Delhi after completing a tour of South and North Africa and Mauritius. He arrived via Bombay accompanied by only one personal servant, Harikeśa das, and Ambariṣa das, great-grandson of Henry Ford, the founder of Ford Motor Company. He was joined by Hansadūta das, his Governing Body Commissioner (GBC) for northern Europe, who flew in from Germany to be his personal secretary for the month of December.

Prabhupāda's intention was to spend a day or two at his ISKCON center in Bengali Market, while arrangements could be made to go to Kurukṣetra and then to spend some time at our temple in Vṛndāvana.

* * *

Location-wise our ISKCON center in New Delhi was well placed. Bengali Market is a small commercial area just southeast of Connaught Circus in the heart of New Delhi. Within easy walking distance lay some of the most prestigious landmarks and properties of India's chief city. The nearby Mandi House traffic roundabout was the distributor for most of the traffic in the area, forming the confluence of seven important arteries.

Many prestigious buildings were dotted about the area. There were the National Research Center for Social Sciences, the National Museum of Natural History, the Nepali Embassy, the Japan Cultural and Information Center, the Soviet House of Culture, various *bhavāns* or meeting halls, and *kalā-kendras* or auditoriums for cultural programs of every description. Wide, tree-lined roads with large houses were set back in secluded gardens, and the homes of the very wealthy could be found within only a few minutes' proximity.

A little farther away lay Curzon Street [now Kasturba Gandhi Marg]. Stretching away toward the famous India Gate, flowers and lush parks formed a wide, green expanse. There was not much evidence of the image popular in much of the West of a poverty-stricken India. It was the showpiece area of the capital.

However, the building ISKCON New Delhi was renting didn't match its surroundings. It was situated at 19 Todar Mal Lane, a short, less busy, residential street cut off at one end by the intersection of a railway line. Number nineteen was a slightly ramshackle building and the odd man out in the otherwise neatly terraced urban street. Single-storied and squat, it was a rather uninviting place that looked like an afterthought of the builders to fill in a gap they really hadn't planned to leave. A few plants heroically fought for life in a small and barren patch of dirt that passed for a front garden. If the word *temple* implies something quite grand, then such a appellation for the tiny house was a misnomer. For any devotees visiting the home of the International Society for Krishna Consciousness in the capital city of India, this place came as a bit of a disappointment.

Nevertheless, it had the same kind of sacrosanctity of any ISKCON center in the world. The small number of devotees were hard at work, visiting and preaching to important men, making Life Members, and establishing a firm basis for the future growth of the Society. Devotional service was the only activity, and the Deities of Śrī Śrī Rādhā Pārtha-sarathī were the most important residents. In this respect it was a typical ISKCON temple, and thus it was a haven for spiritual life in a city rapidly divorcing itself from its traditional spiritual roots.

Opposite our temple, at the end of the road on the corner, there was Nathu's Sweets and Restaurant—white-tiled, somewhat rundown, a little grubby, but accommodating. Across from this stood the Bengali Sweet Shop, selling *rasagullās, gulabjamuns,* and every other traditional sweet delicacy imaginable. Fifty yards farther was a small traffic roundabout with a colorful variety of modest shops and vendors sweeping round its periphery. This connected to Tansen Marg which in turn led the short distance to Mandi House.

Śrīla Prabhupāda wasn't actually staying in our temple. Due to the lack of amenities he, Harikeśa, and Hansadūta were occupying a small, four-room, second-floor apartment at number 9.

* * *

On November 25th I had come in to Delhi from Vṛndāvana, only for the day, on some unexpected personal business. I had been a resident at our Kṛṣṇa Balarāma temple and guesthouse complex since August, serving as the temple commander. Along with several others I was midway through a major cleaning of the temple in preparation for Śrīla Prabhupāda's visit. However, I was pressed by Gopāla Kṛṣṇa das, the local GBC, to stay on in Delhi to help clean Śrīla Prabhupāda's quarters and to guard his door for the few days he was scheduled to be there.

ISKCON Delhi had a manpower shortage. There was only a handful of devotees: Temple President Tejīyas dāsa and his wife, Madirā, both Americans; Oṁkāra dāsa, the French *pūjārī,* and his wife, Nirmalā, and their young daughter and son; an English *brahmacārī,* Tribuvanātha dāsa; and one Indian devotee. Gopāla Kṛṣṇa therefore decided that some extra help was needed. Although I was eager to get back to help with the preparations for Śrīla Prabhupāda's arrival in Vṛndāvana, I was more than happy to take advantage of the sudden and unsought opportunity to do some service for His Divine Grace.

* * *

At 4:00 p.m. I eagerly reported to Śrīla Prabhupāda's apartment for his afternoon *darśana.* I sat at the door and listened attentively as Prabhupāda played host to a small gathering of devotees and guests. With so few present it was a rare opportunity for me to associate with Śrīla Prabhupāda in a setting far more intimate than possible during his visits to larger ISKCON centers. Sitting behind a small, low table in the main room, Śrīla Prabhupāda spoke animatedly on a variety of topics until about 7 p.m. To the visitors as they left, I handed freshly made sweets from the Bengali Sweet Shop.

Next morning, on November 26th, I cleaned Prabhupāda's apartment while he took his usual walk. And on Gopāla Kṛṣṇa's request I dutifully sat outside the door in the stairwell during the morning as a guard.

Meantime, Śrīla Prabhupāda and Harikeśa were discussing how to arrange for Prabhupāda's regular massages. There was apparently no one available, although at least four former personal servants had been present in India when Śrīla Prabhupāda returned from his African tour. When he got back to India he had given *sannyāsa* to Navayogendra and Nanda Kumāra in

Bombay and sent them with Brahmānanda Swami to help rectify some major problems in North Africa. The other two, Upendra and Nitāi dāsa, were also not available: Upendra, although in Delhi, was on his way overseas, and Nitāi had to get his visa renewed in Bombay.

This was all unknown to me. I was happy just to be in Delhi at the same time as Śrīla Prabhupāda. I could not know what Providence had in store for me.

CHAPTER ONE

New Delhi and Kuruksetra

November 26th, 1975

**ISKCON, 19, Todar Mal Lane,
Bengali Market, New Delhi.**

At 11:30 a.m. I was sitting alone in the tiny temple room chanting in front of the Deities when Harikeśa walked in. Stopping at the open door he peered at me intensely through his thick glasses. "Do you know how to massage?" he asked.

"No, I've never done it in my life."

"Well, go up on the roof of Prabhupāda's apartment and watch how Upendra massages Śrīla Prabhupāda. Upendra is leaving tomorrow, so someone else will have to give Śrīla Prabhupāda his massage."

Hardly daring to believe what I had just heard, I didn't wait around. I immediately ran down the street to number nine, a small, two-story building, and quickly climbed the steep steps, past the ground-floor apartment of the building's owner, Mr. B. N. Mukherjee, past the mezzanine, past Śrīla Prabhupāda's flat, and up the final flight to the roof.

It seemed too good to be true; things like this just don't happen! But sure enough, as I came out of the covered stairwell, I found His Divine Grace dressed in his *gamsha,* sitting on a straw mat in the sunshine. His eyes were closed, and Upendra was kneeling behind him, massaging his back with mustard oil. I offered my obeisances and sat down to watch.

After a minute Śrīla Prabhupāda opened his eyes and looked at me inquiringly. With a slight tip of his head, and raising his eyebrows, he asked, "Hm? What is that?"

I explained that Harikeśa had sent me to learn how to render the massage. "All right," he said simply, and again closed his eyes until the end of the massage. When it was over, Prabhupāda returned to his rooms downstairs to bathe and eat his lunch.

Upendra took just two minutes to explain to me some of the finer techniques of massage—the amount of time to spend on each part of his body, the correct order to do it in, and the two types of oil to be used. Upendra confirmed that he would be leaving tomorrow for a preaching assignment in Fiji. And since Nitāi, Prabhupāda's other servant, had gone to Bombay to renew his visa, Śrīla Prabhupāda would need someone to give him his noon and evening massages, at least while he remained in Delhi. Harikeśa was fully engaged in transcribing Śrīla Prabhupāda's tapes and cooking, so he was unable to do it. Under the circumstances, it seemed I was the only one available to execute this personal service.

Apparently, early this morning, Śrīla Prabhupāda and Harikeśa had discussed how to arrange for his morning massage. His Divine Grace had noticed me guarding the door and, remembering me from Australia, thought I might be able to do it. Harikeśa apparently had strong reservations about my suitability. He saw me in action as the temple commander in Vṛndāvana two months ago, when I had a somewhat violent exchange with a young Bengali man. It was only resolved through Śrīla Prabhupāda's personal intervention. Despite this, Prabhupāda has decided to give me a chance.

I returned to the temple quite unable to comprehend my good fortune. I am apprehensive but utterly ecstatic at the extraordinary turn of events. As requested, I went back to Śrīla Prabhupāda's quarters at 9:00 p.m. It was the first time that I had ever been in Prabhupāda's rooms at such a late hour. To see him smiling and relaxed, sitting back and chatting with his servants (to be part of it!), was a privilege I had never even dreamed of.

After a few minutes Śrīla Prabhupāda retired to his bedroom, and Upendra signaled for me to follow.

As Upendra stood at the side of the bed massaging Śrīla Prabhupāda, I looked on through the semi-darkness of the room. Upendra explained that if the bed was large enough Prabhupāda allowed his servant to sit cross-legged beside him. With this bed that was not possible.

Prabhupāda dozed lightly as Upendra carefully kneaded and squeezed his calves, thighs, and feet. After a few minutes, he turned on his side, and Upendra worked on his left hip. This hip sometimes becomes numb due to poor blood circulation.

Upendra whispered to me that once, while he was massaging at night, Prabhupāda began to snore, so he stopped massaging and began to tiptoe out of the room. Just as he reached the door, Prabhupāda's voice came from out of the darkness, "Oh, you are finished already?" He had Upendra return to continue the massage.

There is no set duration. One simply keeps going until, on awakening, Prabhupāda tells the servant he may leave. Then he generally turns over and goes back to sleep again for a short while before getting up to begin his nighttime writing.

After only ten minutes Śrīla Prabhupāda gave a gentle "Hm," signaling that the session was over. We left the bedroom, and Harikeśa escorted us out of the apartment and locked up for the night.

I never expected that such an opportunity would actually ever come my way. In *śāstra* it says that even a moment's association with a pure devotee is enough to bestow upon one the perfection of life and that such association is rarely achieved. I never dreamt I would be the recipient of such good fortune, even after lifetimes of rendering devotional service. Everything has occurred simply by Śrī Kṛṣṇa's arrangement and Śrīla Prabhupāda's causeless mercy.

Excited and elated, I immediately rushed to the New Janata Book Depot, a small shop on the corner next to Nathu's Sweet Shop, and purchased a blank, lined notebook. Although my new engagement is to last only the next couple of days while Prabhupāda remains in New Delhi, I have decided to keep a diary of events so that in the future I will have something with which to remember this rare chance to personally serve His Divine Grace.

November 27th, 1975

While Prabhupāda took his morning walk, I cleaned his apartment. It is a small residence, with four rooms—very basic, but adequate quarters. The entry from the stairwell brings one into the main room, measuring about twenty feet by ten. I dusted off the sparse furnishings, including Prabhupāda's sitting place and the small, low desk at which he spends most of his time either receiving guests or translating during the night. I went through the back and straightened up the servants' room, where Harikeśa and Hansadūta are staying.

Prabhupāda's bedroom, about the same size as theirs, runs off from the side of it. It didn't take long to change the sheets on the small single bed and scrub out the tiny, cramped attached bathroom. Going back through the servants' room I came through a narrow passageway to the very small kitchen. I cleaned its unpolished stone benches and white ceramic tiled walls and swept off the narrow back veranda where Harikeśa seems to do most of the cooking on a coal-fired bucket stove. Finally, I wiped the floors, all standard yellow mosaic stone and marble chip, mostly uncovered except for the thin, cotton rug, or *dhuri,* in the sitting room. I finished well before His Divine Grace returned from his daily walk.

* * *

At 11:00 a.m. I reported to the flat for my first day's duty as masseur. I walked in just as Śrīla Prabhupāda was giving his blessings to Upendra for the success of his new preaching assignment in Fiji. After receiving Prabhupāda's garland, Upendra left for the airport. Looking at me, Prabhupāda casually tipped his head from side to side and signaled that it was time for his massage.

Prabhupāda went up to the roof and changed into his *gamsha.* I was already wearing mine. As he sat on the straw mat, all the instructions Upendra had given me began to whirl through my mind. Now I was on my own. There was no trial, no practice session, no comment from Śrīla Prabhupāda—nothing. I was in at the deep end! I had to concentrate hard to overcome my nervousness and remember what to do. I had never massaged anyone before, what to speak of even touch His Divine Grace. So I mentally prayed to Kṛṣṇa to please give me sufficient intelligence to do it nicely for Śrīla Prabhupāda's pleasure.

In order to ensure a proper service attitude, I first offered Śrīla Prabhupāda my humble obeisances before touching him. Prabhupāda sat cross-legged as I fought my nervousness and knelt upright before him. I took hold of the bottle of sandalwood oil, poured a few drops into the palm of my hand, and began to massage Prabhupāda's head. Sandalwood has cooling properties and is therefore good for the brain.

After only a minute my thumbs and finger joints became suddenly, and severely, sore. Every knuckle ached so much I thought my hands were going to seize up. It was a sensation I hadn't foreseen. My mind flooded with signals of protest, which I fought to transcend. I prayed to Kṛṣṇa for the determination not to fail at my first attempt. By concentrating on trying to please Śrīla Prabhupāda I was able to keep the motion of my hands going without interruption. Thankfully, the pain soon disappeared, my hands loosened, and I pressed and rubbed Prabhupāda's smooth, shaved head without difficulty.

Not knowing any particular techniques, I simply tried to think what it would be like to receive the massage, how each stroke of thumb or finger would feel, and then I acted accordingly.

I took great care not to jerk, scratch, or poke him, yet at the same time give him a firm and smooth massage, working the oil into his skin thoroughly. It wasn't a question of merely rubbing in some oil. The trick, I realized, was to apply pressure, moving my fingers and thumbs backward and forward, while holding his head steady and balanced. I was extremely cautious when massaging his temples, forehead, and around his eyes, for the oil could easily make the thumbs slip.

After fifteen minutes I moved around to Śrīla Prabhupāda's back and switched to mustard oil, which is used on the rest of his body. Mustard oil vitalizes and tones the skin, giving warmth to the body. I spent another fifteen minutes squeezing, pressing, and rippling the supple muscles of his neck, shoulders, and back. With both circular and up-and-down motions of my thumbs, I gave his lower back and spine a firm workover.

Next, moving to his right side, I sat cross-legged and massaged his chest and stomach. These motions were all circular, made with the flat of my hand, all the time directing the massaging motion toward his heart.

Concentrating intensely on what my hands were doing, I failed to notice that I was sitting extremely close to His Divine Grace, breathing directly into the side of his face. I was embarrassed when Prabhupāda suddenly leaned away from me, half turning his head and giving me a sidelong look. He cautioned me, and I mentally made a note to remember to look away in the future.

After ten minutes I moved to his right arm. With his arm outstretched and hand resting palm down on my right knee, I worked his biceps, forearm, wrist, and the joints of his hand. I noted that his hands were very refined, his palms especially soft and smooth. I was extremely apprehensive when it came to popping his joints by pulling each finger, as I had to tug quite hard. Horrible thoughts of dislocation rushed through my mind, but Prabhupāda didn't seem to mind at all. After twenty minutes on his right side I moved to his left arm and repeated the procedure.

Then I moved to his front. He stuck his legs out, and I spent about fifteen minutes on each one, first his left leg, and finally his right. Prabhupāda warned me not to touch his knee that is still bruised from his recent car crash in Mauritius. He is treating this with a poultice of hot ghee and neem leaves.

I carefully massaged his thighs, calves, and ankles and finished with his feet, which I made a special effort to massage as nicely as possible. Rubbing my thumbs up and down his high arches and pressing the joints in the ball of each foot, I ended by pulling each individual toe, giving a slight squeeze to the soft, fleshy end portions. This made my thumb and forefinger snap together as they came up over the tips of his toes. Now I have some practical understanding of the meaning of "lotus feet," as Prabhupāda's feet are surprisingly soft and delicate, just like the petals of a flower.

After an hour and a half, I reluctantly concluded my service by again offering obeisances. Śrīla Prabhupāda stood up, took a little mustard oil in his palm, and applied it to the various gates of his body—ears, nostrils, genital, and anus. He then went downstairs to bathe and take his lunch.

Throughout the massage he hadn't said a word but sat silently with his eyes closed and his body relaxed, glistening and golden in the gentle winter sun. Later, I was relieved and elated to find out that Prabhupāda had commented I gave a good massage.

* * *

In mid-afternoon I took an auto-rickshaw to the flower stands in Chandni-chowk in Old Delhi and bought the biggest garland I could find, just as I had done yesterday. It took over an hour to go there and back in the noxious, noisy, dirty Delhi traffic, but it was worth it. I waited to present it to Śrīla Prabhupāda at the beginning of his *darśana* at 4:30 p.m.

He was pleased to receive it, and this gave me an excuse to remain in the *darśana* and spend more time with him. By now news of his arrival had spread, so a number of well-wishers and Life Members came to see him.

Śrīla Prabhupāda also met with several potential English-Hindi translators. He is eager to see his books published in the Indian languages, but in ISKCON so far we have no trained translators among our devotees. Thus, Gopāla Kṛṣṇa has been publicly advertising for qualified Hindi translators.

Śrīla Prabhupāda personally interviewed all the applicants who responded, carefully checking their philosophical understanding as well as their scholastic abilities. He wants to be certain that the translator is capable of conveying precisely the same meaning as the original text and that no tinge of impersonalism creep into the translation of his books. Unfortunately, India is teeming with false interpretations of *śāstra,* contaminated primarily with the *māyāvāda* notion that God is impersonal. So to find someone who is free from such impure influence is no easy task.

Darśana ended around 7:00 p.m. After the guests left, His Divine Grace sat with his secretary and the local ISKCON managers. He discussed their preaching activities, giving advice and suggestions.

Harikeśa asked me to also leave along with the guests. He wanted to make the point that although I am massaging Śrīla Prabhupāda for the next day or two, I should not consider myself a member of Prabhupāda's personal party. It seemed a bit pointless to me since I had to return at 9:00 p.m. for his evening massage, but I wasn't disappointed. In these past two days I have already experienced more personal association with Śrīla Prabhupāda than at any time in the last nearly four years as a devotee. So I have no complaints. I'm just eager for whatever bits of nectar I can get.

When I returned I presented Śrīla Prabhupāda with some thick, hole-proof, knee-length socks from Australia. It's getting cold in the mornings, and I had two new pairs I hadn't worn. Prabhupāda looked inquiringly from behind his desk. "Are they wool?" he asked.

I looked at the labels. "No, Śrīla Prabhupāda."

"Oh." His reaction was one of mild disappointment, and without saying anything more, he continued with his work. Thinking that Prabhupāda didn't want the socks, Harikeśa prabhu told me to keep them.

* * *

The evening massage, which had appeared to be easier than the morning session, was actually more difficult. The house was quiet, the lights were out, Śrīla Prabhupāda dozed lightly, and I was left to massage with only my restless, wandering mind to keep me company. Were it not for the ache in my legs, which developed from standing in one spot, I might easily have succumbed to fatigue. Yet I managed to keep going, steadily and gently compressing and squeezing through Prabhupāda's thin *dhotī*, up and down, up and down. After twenty minutes his faint "Hm" was a signal that my first day as his masseur was over.

I went back to the temple to rest, feeling satisfied with my first attempts to personally serve his Divine Grace, and completely enlivened from the intimate contact I had had with him.

November 28th, 1975

At six o'clock this morning Harikeśa came panting in to the small *brahmacārī āśrama* exclaiming, "Where are the socks? Prabhupāda's asking for them!" His face fell when he saw I was already wearing one pair. Naturally I couldn't give him those. Fortunately the other pair was still unused. He gratefully took them to Prabhupāda. They fit perfectly, and he wore them on his walk.

* * *

Śrīla Prabhupāda attended a morning program at the Jorbagh Colony organized by Mr. Susil Ansal, the son-in-law of the owner of the Tiger Lock Company, Mr. S. K. Saigal. Jorbagh is a fairly prestigious neighborhood next to Lodi Gardens, one of New Delhi's historical landmarks. The program was held at the local community hall—a large, ugly, concrete building, featureless and uninviting, with a cavernous interior reminiscent of a school hall.

A small but interested audience gathered to hear Śrīla Prabhupāda deliver an excellent lecture from the Fifth Canto of the *Śrīmad-Bhāgavatam* on King Ṛṣabhadeva's instructions to His one hundred sons. As always, whether speaking to one man or ten thousand, Prabhupāda's speech was earnest and grave. He applied himself fully to the great task of cutting through the clouds of illusion that keep every living being firmly bound up in material existence.

Śrīla Prabhupāda explained that our real problem is this body. "*Nūnaṁ pramattaḥ kurute vikarma yad indriya-prītaya āpṛṇoti.* We have now become mad after sense gratification. *Mattaḥ* means mad, and when the prefix *pra* is added it means *sufficiently* mad. Not only mad, but *sufficiently* mad, and we are engaged in activities which are forbidden.... This is called *vikarma.*"

He explained that the knowledge to free oneself from this madness depends upon which authority one accepts. One can accept the atheistic views of materialistic scientists, which are based on nothing more than mere speculation. Or one may accept *śāstric* knowledge, which is practical, authoritative, and accepted by all the great thinkers and saintly persons.

Challenging those who accept the views of the scientists, Prabhupāda cited an example from *śāstra* that describes the moon as farther way from earth than the sun. According to the *Bhāgavatam* it's some 1,600,000 miles higher than the sun.

Scientists say that the sun is 93,000,000 miles away from earth, he said, which, if we accept, means that the moon is almost 95,000,000 miles distant. "So," he asked, "how could the astronauts have journeyed there in only four days? You may say that you have not practically experimented; but what you have experimented? You also hear from others. You believe that they have gone to the moon planet. You have not gone. You have heard from somebody in the newspaper, that's all. That is your authority.

"So if you can believe in the newspaper, then I cannot believe in *śāstra?* It is a different source of knowledge, but one takes one source, another takes another source. Our source of knowledge is Kṛṣṇa, or Kṛṣṇa's disciples. This is the source of knowledge—*avaroha-pantha,* knowledge coming from higher authorities."

Prabhupāda gave a concise conclusion, frankly telling his sophisticated and somewhat Westernized audience what their real business in life is. "You have to accept this process of austerity by which you purify your existence. Then you will get deathless life, eternal. This is science. This *Bhāgavata* literature, this Vedic literature, is giving you information how you can revive your original, eternal life.

"That is the business of human life; not to become mad like hogs and dogs and simply work very hard, 'Where is stool?' and eat it and get some strength and then enjoy senses. This is not life. In the human form of life if we do not purify our existence, if we do not realize God, if we do not understand what is my relationship with God, then we are simply wasting time living like cats and dogs. These things should be stopped. And our Kṛṣṇa consciousness movement is meant for stopping this rascal civilization and giving you life. Thank you very much. Hare Kṛṣṇa."

Prabhupāda couldn't have spoken Lord Caitanya's message more lucidly, establishing it clearly that he himself is the indisputable spiritual authority for this age. His powerful lecture filled us with renewed conviction and enthusiasm to practice Kṛṣṇa consciousness. The audience responded altogether favorably, although some of the questions showed a rather dismal lack of attentiveness. Still, Prabhupāda patiently answered them in his own inimitable style, always respectful, but candid.

His first questioner asked, "And what do you think about the factor in reincarnation? Do you think it has got any significance?"

"I do not think anything," Prabhupāda stated frankly. "I have already explained. We do not think, 'perhaps, maybe'."

The man persisted. "Do you think reincarnation is there?"

"Yes, that is stated in the *śāstra.*"

"What is your opinion about it?"

"I have no opinion. I take *śāstra* as it is."

"After all, you are writing—"

Seeing he wasn't getting anywhere, Śrīla Prabhupāda didn't bother any more. Cutting him off, he took another question.

"I accept the goal is self-realization, but my general difficulty is that the soul is so difficult to turn about, but—"

"It is very difficult, undoubtedly," Śrīla Prabhupāda said, "but if you train from the very beginning of life.... That is stated by Prahlāda Mahārāja. He was child, five years old. In tiffin hours the other children of the demons, they were playing, and Prahlāda Mahārāja was asking to sit down and hear him. He was preaching, 'My dear friends, don't spoil your life by playing. Now this is the period of understanding *bhāgavata-dharma.*' *Bhāgavata-dharma* means to understand God and our relationship with God and act accordingly. "We might have done mistakes in our life, but if we train our children in the *brahmacārī* system and gradually they understand the *bhāgavata-dharma,* at least their life becomes perfect. And in the *Bhāgavata* it is ordered in this Ṛṣabhadeva's instruction: *pitā na sa syāj jananī na sā syāt svajano na sa syāt gurur na sa syāt:* 'One should not become guru, one should not become kinsman, one should not become father, one should not become mother ...' *na mocayed yah samupeta-mṛtyum,* if one cannot give lesson to the children how to avoid death.'

"This is the duty of the guardians, of the government, how to avoid death. Where is that education? So that is the defect of the modern education. There is no training. It is going on, very risky civilization."

The man was looking for something more immediate though. "Swamijī, I was asking point in a different way, that we are so helpless. We are born as human being with inherent weaknesses and shortcomings, like *kāma, krodha, moha, lobha* [lust, anger, illusion, greed]."

"Yes, that I know." Prabhupāda assured him. "But you can rectify it provided you like. But if you don't like to rectify yourself, how it can be done? If you are thinking that you have got so many defects, you rectify your defects. Just like these European, American boys. They were all illicit sex hunters and intoxicators and meat-eaters. That is their daily affair. How they have given up? They have decided that, 'We shall rectify ourself.' You rectify yourself and you will be able to do. Are you prepared to rectify yourself?"

Still unable to grasp that rectification was his own choice, the man answered, "Why nature has given us—"

"Nature has made you a dog. Why should you remain a dog? You should become a human being. That is your duty."

After another question Prabhupāda stopped. The audience was well satisfied, and Mr. Ansal concluded the program with a final speech in praise of Śrīla Prabhupāda. His Divine Grace then returned to the temple in time for his massage.

* * *

It was during Prabhupāda's noon massage that I made my first major mistake as his servant. Because of his weak heart Śrīla Prabhupāda requires to bathe in warm water, which, unlike the West, is not usually available on tap in Indian houses.

Upendra had shown me how to set up a bucket of water and a portable immersion heater in the *varṣati,* the small room on the roof, at the beginning of the massage. It takes about twenty minutes for the water to heat up, so the servant must remember to switch it on halfway through the massage in order that the water is hot by the end. Then I am supposed to take it downstairs to the bathroom, where Śrīla Prabhupāda mixes it with another bucket, of cold water, according to his liking.

Concentrating on massaging him nicely, I completely forgot about heating the water until the very end of the massage. Thus, Prabhupada had to wait. I was embarrassed at my own stupidity and very regretful that Śrīla Prabhupāda had to wait around because of my foolishness. He was slightly annoyed, but kindly did not reproach me. I think this was both because I was new to the service and because of my remorse.

* * *

Harikeśa usually tries to time things so that lunch is ready just at the moment His Divine Grace finishes his bathing and dressing. And although yesterday Harikeśa prabhu made it quite clear that I am allowed into Prabhupāda's apartment only during massage and *darśana* times, today he was too busy cooking to usher me out after the massage. So, by lingering for a few minutes, I got the chance to help Harikeśa serve Śrīla Prabhupāda his *prasādam*.

Prabhupāda ate his meal on a *choṅki,* a small wooden table about a foot high, in his bedroom. I first served his *thali,* a full plate with various preparations of *sabji,* rice, *dahl,* chutney, and a sweet, all in their own small bowls. After five minutes Prabhupāda rang a small hand bell.

Harikeśa, squatting out on the balcony before the small bucket of hot charcoal, immediately tossed a piece of flat, rolled-out dough onto the coals. By expertly manipulating it with a pair of tongs, he allowed it to cook on both sides. As it puffed into a kind of organic hot-air chamber, he carefully retrieved it and dropped it on a small plate, which he then handed to me. Hot *chapatis* were then brought in to Śrīla Prabhupāda, as required, fresh from the stove. Fresh and hot is the Madwari *dhawa* style of eating, and Śrīla Prabhupāda ate three *chapatis* like this.

Acting as the waiter, I found it exciting to run in, bow down, and then drop the hot *chapati* on Prabhupāda's plate. He deftly prodded it with delicate and aristocratic movements of his first and middle fingers to release the hot air. After flattening it, he tore off a small piece using only his right hand, gathered up some *sabji,* and popped the morsel into his mouth.

After eating, Śrīla Prabhupāda went into the bathroom, while I removed his plate and cleaned the *choṅki*. Prabhupāda then sat in his *darśana* room for a brief interval before retiring for his afternoon nap. Meanwhile, Hansadūta, Harikeśa, and I happily shared the remnants of Prabhupāda's meal.

* * *

During the afternoon *darśana* Prabhupāda had me stand at the door to distribute sweets to each guest as they departed. Śrīla Prabhupāda was insistent that every visitor must receive some *prasādam*. Because there are no devotees available to prepare the sweets, Prabhupāda has given Tejīyas permission to buy them from the Bengali Sweet Shop on the corner. He said those sweets may even be offered to the Deities, as they are cooked with pure ingredients.

* * *

These few new engagements have enabled me to remain in Śrīla Prabhupāda's quarters for most of the day, albeit seemingly against Harikeśa's better judgement. Nevertheless, Harikeśa has given me some helpful guidance on how to serve Śrīla Prabhupāda properly. Today he explained to me that obeisances should be offered each time one enters or leaves Śrīla Prabhupāda's presence, whether by his coming and going or by one's own.

From the past few days' experience I am beginning to understand that humility is everything, the essential basis on which all other service is built. Being humble is the only means to counteract offenses and is the key to a good service attitude. Śrīla Prabhupāda is tolerant of ignorance, if one is eager to serve.

This whole experience is tremendous. It is extremely blissful to be so close to the vital essence of what Kṛṣṇa consciousness is all about—association with and service to the pure devotee of the Lord.

November 29th, 1975

For his morning walk Prabhupāda followed a route that took us along Tansen Marg, across Mandi House, up Feroz

Shah as far as Curzon, then left, almost to India Gate, before turning along Tilak Marg and then returning.

During the course of the walk the conversation was lively, with the science-versus-religion dialogue predominating. Śrīla Prabhupāda commented on the numerous *kalā-kendras* in the area. *Kalā* means "art" or "culture," and in Bengali *kalā* also means "cheating." Prabhupāda pointed out that although their presentations are supposed to be cultural for the upliftment and refinement of human life, they are not culture at all. He said that real culture means to understand that everything comes from the soul.

People give attention to the activities of the body, such as the vibrations produced by the tongue, without really understanding the cause. When the body is dead, there is no more singing, although the same tongue and ears are present. They don't know who is the person singing and hearing. Materialistic scientists claim that it is all chemical reaction, but they cannot produce such a chemical.

When Ambarīṣa prabhu said the scientists were simply bluffing, he agreed. He humorously emphasized his point by declaring that the scientists should be "kicked on the face." They were offering the public "postdated checks" by promising to deliver proof of their claims in the future, but an intelligent man should not be cheated in this way.

Harikeśa suggested the scientists should receive their own treatment. "They should have their salaries paid by postdated check."

"No, they will not accept that. That they will not accept," Prabhupāda smiled.

"In the future we will pay you!" Harikeśa joked.

And Tejīyas added, "When you find the chemicals!"

Prabhupāda stopped and entertained everyone with an amusing parody of a dependant scientist and his boss. "Now you starve. In future I shall pay!" he said, imitating the boss. Then, taking the part of the scientist, "How shall I eat?"

"Now, you starve. In future, you'll get payment!"

He had everyone laughing as he walked on, continuing to expose the folly of modern man in accepting such false promises.

Defending the scientists, Harikeśa cited some of their advances. In Russia, for example, they claim to have grafted an extra head onto a dog.

Prabhupāda had a quick answer for him. He pointed out that Rāvaṇa had ten heads, and still he could not save himself from the hands of Rāma. "Rāvaṇa was thinking, 'Who can be more intelligent than me?' But, still Lord Rāmacandra proved 'Yes, I am better intelligent than you!'"

A Punjabi devotee, Caitya-guru, observed that in India people now regard their own philosophies to be outdated and are showing increasing interest in Russian books and Soviet philosophy. Prabhupāda asked what the basis of Marxist philosophy was.

A devotee replied, "Matter is supreme."

"If matter is supreme," Prabhupāda argued, "why don't you combine matter and let it move? What is that Supreme which is moving this matter? If they do not know, then again a rascal, in spite of so much philosophy and so much communism. Why when Stalin and Lenin died, they simply remained matter? Why it was not moving? Where is that matter?"

Harikeśa tried to argue that Marxism is actually a social philosophy. He explained that the main point of Marxism is to eliminate the unfair conditions in the world, whereby a few people are very wealthy while others remain poverty stricken like in India. The communist tries to abolish the poor by taking money from the rich.

"Again that, 'We are trying to abolish,'" Prabhupāda mocked. "The post-dated check again!"

Ambarīṣa, a multimillionaire in his own right, added his own pertinent observation. "In Russia, everyone is poor."

"But at least they are equal," Harikeśa answered.

Again Prabhupāda shot him down. "Well, when you become poor, then naturally it is equal. There is no rich man. If everyone is fool, then everyone is equal, that's all."

Prabhupāda recalled how the taxi drivers in Moscow were so poor they were begging for something extra. Most people were so poor they couldn't afford a taxi. They were walking on the street.

"Yes," Harikeśa argued. "But why should somebody be rich, and I be poor? What gives him the right to have money?"

"That is everywhere," Prabhupāda answered. Tipping his head toward Ambarīṣa, he continued, "He is born in a rich family, I am born in a poor family. So why this is happening?"

"Yes, that's unfair," Harikeśa said. "I mean, I should take his money."

"No, no, not unfair. This is nature's arrangement, *uccavācca*. Why one has become animal? Why one has become man? The same living entities?"

"Chance!" Harikeśa declared.

Prabhupāda stopped. "Chance! Who is making this chance? Can I make you by chance a dog? That is not possible. There is no such chance. It is by *karma-phala* [the fruit of one's past activities]. Just like you infect some disease, you suffer from that disease. So this happens to the rascal. One who is intelligent, he does not infect. He is always cautious. Therefore this chance of infection is not there. Actually you cannot say, 'chance.' It is your ignorance. You create 'chance.' Because you do not know what will happen after something, on account of ignorance it is 'chance.' But if you are fully aware, there is no question of chance. An intelligent student, he does not think, 'By chance, I may be passed.' He reads properly. He appears in the examination, gives the proper answer. It is not chance. And if he thinks, 'All right, by chance I will be passing the exam,' is it very intelligent?

"These rascals are talking like that. There is no question of chance. On account of ignorance they commit something infectious and they suffer. And because they cannot explain, they say it is chance. It is not chance. It is due to some cause."

Hansadūta said Marx had philosophized that capitalist systems would eventually collapse on themselves, and communism would be the natural outcome.

Even if that were true, Prabhupāda wouldn't give Marx any credit. He said that when there is no capital, naturally they will be communistic. That was already predicted by Vyāsadeva. "That is not a communistic idea. That is the future of *Kali-yuga*. That is mentioned in the Bhāgavatam. *Ācchinna-dāra-draviṇā yāsyanti giri-kānanam.* They will be harassed by famine, taxation, and starvation. Naturally they will be disappointed, *ācchinna.* That is already told."

He noted how in Communist countries people must queue for hours just to obtain basic commodities. That is all due to Godlessness.

Going down as far as the Indian Transport Offices we turned left on Sikhandra Road, gradually making our way back to Todar Mal Lane by crossing over College Road and coming down Barbar Road. As we made our way along the dirty footpaths, Prabhupāda intermittently drew our attention to the deteriorating state of India's capital. He said that people are starving, and yet they are building museums of natural history and so forth to show heaps of dead stones and bones. This cheating and bluffing is going on, he said, at the cost of the poor man's blood. "There are so many buildings, but there is not a single building where spiritual culture is discussed, although it is the real basis of life."

As we arrived back at the temple, Prabhupāda ended the conversation on an ominous note. "Civilization will collapse very soon, all over the world. It will collapse. Either you may bring this 'ism' or that 'ism,' this civilization will collapse. People will become mad, being harassed in so many ways. When one is harassed in so many problems, he commits suicide. So that position is coming."

"Or he starts a war," Harikeśa said.

"Yes." Prabhupāda agreed. "When the government cannot adjust, they start a war."

* * *

Ambarīṣa has come here to Delhi for a special purpose. He plans to finance a new development in Kurukṣetra, and he has already donated $150,000 for the project. Prabhupāda wants to build a Varṇāśrama University there, as well as a temple of Kṛṣṇa and Arjuna. To this end he has been in contact with Gulzarilal Nanda, a former home minister and twice the acting prime minister of India. Gulzarilal Nanda is now in charge of a special trust set up to develop the Kurukṣetra area for pilgrims.

Nandajī arrived at the temple at noon and came up on the

rooftop. As Prabhupāda sat on a straw mat in his *gamsha* receiving his massage, Nandajī perched on a chair. They discussed the Kurukṣetra project.

They talked first about the work Nandajī has done to restore and develop the Kurukṣetra area and what Prabhupāda's requirements would be for his proposed college. Then they gradually ranged on to more general topics. At the end, they agreed to meet once again on December 1st, in Kurukestra. Prabhupāda will examine the land and continue the discussions on his plans for development at the site.

* * *

Later, around 9:00 p.m., Prabhupāda finished eating a little *prasādam* and then asked me take his plate, along with a basket of fruit that had been given to him earlier in the evening, down to the temple. The fruit was to be given to the Deities, and Śrīla Prabhupāda's plate was to be washed off and cleansed. Picking up his plate in one hand and the fruit in the other, I started for the door, but Prabhupāda immediately stopped me. He pointed out that the plate, having been eaten from, was dirty. I had picked it up, contaminating myself by touching it, and then I touched the fruit to be offered to the Deity. He told me to wash my hands and take the items separately. We all smiled at his thoughtfulness and my dullness.

From my point of view as a disciple, both guru and God were to be worshipped on the same level. Foremost in my mind was the thought that every little opportunity to render some service was for my own benefit. In other words, I thought that I was becoming purified simply by touching the plate that Śrīla Prabhupāda had personally eaten from.

He, however, thought of himself as a humble servant of Kṛṣṇa; thus he saw the plate as being contaminated. Because he has such a high standard of purity, and because the fruit was to be offered to the Deity, Śrīla Prabhupāda could therefore not accept the mixing of the two items.

In Prabhupāda's presence it is becoming quite clear how little I have learned in almost four years in the movement. Being with Śrīla Prabhupāda is opening up a whole new perspective on devotional service to me. As Prabhupāda's assistant, one has to learn to see matters from his point of view, and that takes precedence over one's own.

November 30th, 1975

As Śrīla Prabhupāda took his massage on the roof, Hansadūta prabhu came up to join him. After sitting for a while and reading from the Fifth Canto of *Śrīmad-Bhāgavatam,* he expressed to Śrīla Prabhupāda his appreciation of the newly published volume. Prabhupāda chatted a little with him, extolling the pleasures of sitting in the sunshine. He said the *rājarṣis* of former ages all made their capitals in India on account of the pleasant, sunny weather. Even during winter the days are warm and sunny, and in the summer the evenings are very pleasant and mild.

Hansadūta asked Śrīla Prabhupāda about the possibility of opening a center in Kabul. He explained that the residents there have shown interest in our Society. And a good number of young Westerners pass through the area, many of whom are receptive to learning about spiritual life.

Śrīla Prabhupāda positively declared that it is his desire to see a center in every city of the world. He encouraged Hansadūta to go ahead and try to establish something.

Gopāla Kṛṣṇa joined us on the roof to finalize arrangements for tomorrow's journey to Kurukṣetra. When he asked who would accompany His Divine Grace on the trip, Śrīla Prabhupāda, with an upward tip of his head, immediately indicated me. "He may go."

Gopāla Kṛṣṇa registered mild surprise, since I am only a temporary fill-in. "Hari-śauri, Śrīla Prabhupāda?"

To which Prabhupāda responded, "Well, I have to have my massage."

So by Prabhupāda's grace, and to my great satisfaction, my tenure as his servant has been extended, and I will get my first chance to travel with His Divine Grace.

* * *

Unfortunately I blundered with the hot water for his bath again today. I remembered to place the immersion heater in the bucket of water, but I foolishly forgot to switch it on. This time Śrīla Prabhupāda became exasperated and reprimanded me because he had to wait until the water heated up. I had nothing to say. I hung my head, feeling terrible. It was the second time in three days, and there was no excuse.

Now I can understand that although Prabhupāda is very tolerant of mistakes arising from inexperience, he expects us to learn from our errors. Simple carelessness does not sit well with him at all. He wants us to act with clear intelligence, seeing this as the symptom of our Kṛṣṇa consciousness.

* * *

After taking lunch *prasādam* Prabhupāda sat at ease in his sitting room for a short while. Then he walked through the servants' room to his bedroom to retire for his afternoon nap. Hansadūta, Harikeśa, and I were in the servants' room, taking our lunch. As he came in, we offered our obeisances. I was sitting on the floor eating from a bowl with a spoon, and as I knelt back, I put the spoon down and rested my hand on my knee.

Immediately Prabhupāda looked at me and said, "Oh, you are eating and then?" He put his hand on different places of his body as if to illustrate a child contaminating his clothes with a dirty hand.

My instinct was to say, "Well, Śrīla Prabhupāda, my *hand* isn't dirty. I'm eating with a spoon." But I thought better of it and checked myself. Prabhupāda could obviously see that. I realized that Prabhupāda simply had a better understanding of what constitutes cleanliness. He laughed. As he walked past us into his bedroom, he shook his head and said, "You are all brought up *mlecchas.*"

Then again in the evening, without first washing my hands, I picked up a water jug after handling Śrīla Prabhupāda's plate. Śrīla Prabhupāda immediately noticed and corrected me. He laughed and told me not to mind. It is the position of the guru, he said, to find out the faults in the disciple and rectify them.

It was simultaneously embarrassing and pleasurable to be on the receiving end of Prabhupāda's reproof. His standard of purity is so much higher than ours. By his keen observation and objective criticism he is training us to the highest levels, making us fit for serving Kṛṣṇa. I feel very fortunate that Prabhupāda is very patiently training me. Even though he sometimes calls us *mlecchas,* he is actually very proud of his Western disciples. He constantly points out to his visitors how we have been transformed.

These incidents have made me realize that Śrīla Prabhupāda has unlimited patience in training his disciples. Although he must have given these instructions hundreds of times during the last ten years, he is still prepared to patiently teach the same things again and again to any new disciple, provided that student has an attitude of humble service and is eager to learn.

* * *

Śrīla Prabhupāda's schedule is finally fixed for him to go to Kurukṣetra on December 1st and to Vṛndāvana the following day. Gopāla Kṛṣṇa informed me today that as soon as Prabhupāda gets to Vṛndāvana, I have to leave immediately for Calcutta to help with the management. Harikeśa has also made it quite clear that he has already arranged for someone else to assume the role of masseur in Vṛndāvana.

So my short sojourn is, sadly, coming to an end. But still, I have a feeling of overwhelming gratitude for having been allowed in His Divine Grace's personal service these past few days. It is something I never expected nor deserved, truly the causeless mercy of Śrīla Prabhupāda and Kṛṣṇa.

December 1st, 1975

Kurukṣetra

At morning's first light, Śrīla Prabhupāda and his party set out in two cars for the famous *tīrtha* of Kurukṣetra, the site where Lord Śrī Kṛṣṇa spoke the *Bhagavad-gītā* to Arjuna some five thousand years ago. Prabhupāda rode in the first car with Harikeśa, Gopāla Kṛṣṇa, and Hansadūta prabhus. Caitya-guru, Ambarīṣa, and I brought up the rear. Leaving New Delhi we drove due north for about three hours to reach our destination.

Kurukṣetra is still a popular pilgrimage site, as it was even thousands of years before Lord Kṛṣṇa's appearance. It is a small town, but there are many temples. Every year, especially during an eclipse of the sun or moon, millions of pilgrims gather to bathe in the large lakes and to visit the site of the famous battle between the Pāṇḍavas and the Kurus.

Gulzarilal Nanda received Śrīla Prabhupāda at a nearby guest house. They took breakfast together, then Nandajī took him on a tour of the area known as Brahma-sarovara.

This particular site is the main pilgrimage center. It consists of a very large lake, approximately half-a-mile wide and two-thirds of a mile long. Nandajī has established a Trust called Manava Dharma for the purpose of developing the area, and to date they have spent one and half crores of rupees (about one and a half million dollars) doing this. The money has all come from government grants.

The lake was impressive, with exceptionally clean water. All around, at regular intervals on its shored-up banks, there were *ghāṭas* for bathing, with separate enclosed facilities for women. Nandajī's plan is to eventually create steps leading into the water along the entire length of the shoreline. Across the expanse of water we could see a line of buildings and temples on the opposite bank, one of which was a Gauḍīya Māṭha.

Nandajī took Prabhupāda around to one end of the tank where he pointed out some plots of land that were available for development, as well as some land along the side of the lake. It became clear he wanted Śrīla Prabhupāda to purchase a parcel of land, although Prabhupāda would have preferred that Nandajī donate something to ISKCON. Prabhupāda didn't appear too impressed with the offer. He inquired about the low elevation of the land and the possibility of flooding during the rainy season. All in all Prabhupāda seemed somewhat doubtful but still expressed some interest.

Nandajī has gathered quite a coterie of men who all glorify him and consider him a spiritual leader as well as a statesman. Around the end of the tank we noticed a very large statue of Nandajī had been erected. And, as we continued our tour, his secretaries praised him constantly. Indeed, his efforts to develop the area are impressive.

In addition to the Brahma-sarovara development he also showed Prabhupāda a new irrigation system. This fed off a small pump station with locks constructed on a small canal running alongside Brahma-sarovara. It was designed to supply water to the entire district. Then he took Prabhupāda to a small *go-śālā* and finally to a recently established Ayurvedic pharmacy. We returned to the Guest House at noon.

As Prabhupāda took his massage in the sunny back garden, Nandajī sat in a chair and talked about his future plans for improving the area. He also expressed his ideas for strengthening the moral and spiritual lives of the Indian people, especially the young. He feels that their sense of values are being eroded away by the forces of materialism and atheism. The conversation centered on the philosophy of the *Bhagavad-gītā* as the basis for achieving positive changes. Although Nandajī began the speaking, he ended up hearing; initiating the dialogue but gradually winding down as Śrīla Prabhupāda took over.

The *Bhagavad-gītā,* Prabhupāda pointed out, must be properly understood and assimilated before it can be given to others. Therefore it has to be accepted exactly as Kṛṣṇa spoke it, first to the sun god, Vivasvān, and then later to Arjuna here in Kurukṣetra.

At the mention of the sun god, Nandajī expressed some doubt as to how this should be understood. It seemed to him somewhat symbolic. But Śrīla Prabhupāda explained that Vivasvān actually exists and that everything in the *Gītā* is factual, not symbolic.

Nandajī leaned back as Prabhupāda elucidated the Vedic descriptions of life on other planets such as the sun and moon. He cited the statement of Lord Kṛṣṇa in the *Gītā* that the living entities are both *nitya,* eternal, and *sarva-gataḥ,* all-pervasive. This meant, he said, that they are unaffected by any material condition and are therefore found everywhere in the universe. Śrī Kṛṣṇa specifically points out that the *ātmā* is not burnt by fire, so Kṛṣṇa's statement that He spoke the science of *Bhagavad-gītā* to the sun god must be taken as it is, literally, and not as something symbolic.

At Nandajī's prompting, Prabhupāda also described the position of the sun, the moon, and other planets according to the *Śrīmad-Bhāgavatam.*

Apparently Nandajī had never considered that the *Gītā* should be accepted literally. Nevertheless, he continued to listen attentively as Śrīla Prabhupāda skillfully guided the discussion. Prabhupāda didn't create a controversy, even though the subject matter could have prompted one. He kept things on the level of a pleasant *tete-a-tete.* He allowed his companion to reveal his position and then gradually drew him closer to the Kṛṣṇa conscious viewpoint. He encouraged Nandajī to study the *Gītā* and even suggested that, as he was now retired from politics, he should consider taking *sannyāsa* and preach the message of Kṛṣṇa full time.

Nandajī visibly balked at this. The very thought of entering the renounced order of life literally made him fidget in his seat. Tactfully, Prabhupāda didn't press the point. And after a few minutes more Nandajī courteously took his leave, allowing Prabhupāda to bathe and eat his lunch.

Prabhupāda is fascinating to hear and watch, especially when dealing with persons who are prominent in the common man's eyes. He talks with such total conviction and realization, and quotes so many references from the *Vedas,* that it is very difficult to dispute what he says.

Yet, mundane men in India, despite their professed attachment to the Vedic way of life and the teachings of the *Gītā,* seem to have great difficulty in accepting the *Vedas* literally. They accept only that part that fits within their own limited viewpoint and either interpret or avoid that which does not tally with their own sense of what is logical.

Śrīla Prabhupāda, however, never covers over the statements of Śrī Kṛṣṇa, or any Vedic authority, with speculation. He accepts the *Bhagavad-gītā* as it is. Consequently he is always very effective in changing people's lives for the better. He has such presence, learning, and conviction that men like Nandajī are naturally respectful. Whether they actually take his advice, though, is another matter.

Immediately after lunch Nandajī took Prabhupāda on a tour of Kurukṣetra University. Prabhupāda made certain that his books were left there for further examination. Then Prabhupāda returned to the Guest House and said good-bye to his host. He declined to give any immediate decision on the land purchase but assured Nandajī that he would be in touch with him in the near future.

Śrīla Prabhupāda rested for an hour, then we prepared for our return to New Delhi. After some discussion, however, Prabhupāda decided to visit another, less developed, area of Kurukṣetra called Jyotisar. This area has not been within the focus of attention of Nandajī's Manava Dharma Trust, although it is reputed to be the actual place where the *Bhagavad-gītā* was spoken.

We drove through the town, past the sites of the morning's tour. About seven miles on, we turned off down a narrow, dusty track to an unimpressive clutch of buildings. By the side of a modest lake with curving banks we saw several small shrines. One housed a deity of Sarasvatī, and in another Kṛṣṇa stood with a conch in His right hand and *cakra* in His left.

But the main feature was out in the open, under the spreading arms of a large banyan tree. The tree is said to have been there since the time of the battle five thousand years ago. There, we came upon a half-life-sized, white-marble Deity of Śrī Kṛṣṇa and Arjuna in a chariot, encased in a metal-and-glass house. Arjuna was sitting cross-legged on the back of the chariot with his palms together. And Kṛṣṇa, who was painted blue, sat on the front, half-turning to Arjuna. His left hand held the reins to the four horses, and His right hand was raised, with the thumb and forefinger forming a circle in the classic *mudrā* signifying the exchange of spiritual knowledge.

Prabhupāda walked about and gave the entire area a thorough inspection. After ten minutes he asked us what we thought about it. Free from the previous constraints imposed by our status as guests, everyone expressed their enthusiasm. We unanimously concluded that it seemed as if this was the main pilgrimage site. We all sensed the spiritual vibrancy of the area. A deep sense of timeless wisdom and serenity seemed to permeate the atmosphere.

Harikeśa put it very succinctly. "The other place was like the heavenly planets, but this place is Vaikuṇṭha!"

Prabhupāda smiled and said that we should build a temple

of Kṛṣṇa and Arjuna here. At Brahma-sarovara he suggested that another temple could be built for Kṛṣṇa, Balarāma, and Subhadrā, because They went there to bathe during the solar eclipse.

Caitya-guru was chosen to negotiate with Nandajī for the land. Prabhupāda also requested him to try to get land donated at Jyotisar.

On the way back, Prabhupāda candidly remarked about the Kurukṣetra development. "They call it *mānava-dharma* [religious actions for humanity]; I call it *paśu-dharma* [animal life]. One-and-a-half crores of rupees spent, and they erect a big statue for birds to pass stool on. But they have installed not one single Deity."

* * *

New Delhi

It was about nine in the evening when we arrived at No. 9 Todar Mal Lane. As he sat in his room, Prabhupāda inquired about the day's mail. Generally, Prabhupāda's mail is handled exclusively by his secretary. But, since Hansadūta had gone off to get something to eat at Nathu's, Śrīla Prabhupāda sent me to the temple to collect his mail. When I handed him the letters, to my great surprise, he asked me to open them and read him the contents. It was a privilege that I eagerly although nervously accepted. Tearing open the envelopes one by one, I read out the messages. Prabhupāda also opened a few and inspected them.

Puṣṭa Kṛṣṇa Swami sent one from South Africa, describing his plans to purchase a Mercedes in Germany and drive it here for Prabhupāda's use in India. One was from Kīrtirāja dāsa in Los Angeles. He is moving to Europe in order to begin preaching in Poland. Another, written by Gopīparāṇadhana dāsa, contained a translation of the first chapter of Śrīla Bhaktivinoda Ṭhākura's work *Śrī Caitanya-śikṣāmṛta.* There were several other letters as well.

Just as Prabhupāda was finishing his reading, Harikeśa came in. Shocked to see me reading Prabhupāda's mail, he proceeded to chastise me, disregarding the fact that Śrīla Prabhupāda was present right in front of us. "This is to be done only by the secretary," he said angrily, "You have no business even touching the mail!"

Śrīla Prabhupāda did not say a word. He merely stood and walked quietly into his bedroom to take rest. Harikeśa meanwhile continued to emphasize his point. "If Brahmānanda was still the secretary, you'd never get away with this!" He cooled off, however, when I explained that Śrīla Prabhupāda himself had asked me to read to him. Harikeśa conceded that under the circumstances I had no choice but to do it.

In one sense Harikeśa was right. Prabhupāda's mail *is* private and is not to be dealt with whimsically. From Harikeśa's point of view I am just a temporary helper, and thus I should be careful not to tread on the more exclusive domain of Śrīla Prabhupāda's regular servants. Otherwise Prabhupāda himself will be disturbed in his daily activities.

Nevertheless, we both understood that, while recognizing a certain preeminence of his senior men, in the aggregate Prabhupāda doesn't discriminate. If the right man is not around, he employs whoever is available. To him we are all his disciples in the service of Kṛṣṇa, and he engages anyone who is willing and available, according to necessity and the devotee's own capacity. Accepting my action as an innocent response to a direct request from Śrīla Prabhupāda, Harikeśa relented. Then I joined Śrīla Prabhupāda to give him his massage.

After a few minutes' silence in the gentle darkness, as I carefully massaged his legs and feet, he softly asked me how I liked the idea of having a temple at Jyotisar.

I said, "Yes, it would be very nice."

He smiled and replied, "Yes, Kṛṣṇa spoke His *Bhagavad-gītā* there." Then he closed his eyes and went to sleep.

CHAPTER TWO

Sri Vrndavana Dhama

December 2nd, 1975

After a short early-morning walk, our party left New Delhi, following the main Agra road as far as the District of Mathurā, a two-hour trip. Just before the Vṛndāvana turn-off, Prabhupāda was pleased to see a newly erected sign on the Agra Road advertising our ISKCON Kṛṣṇa Balarāma International Guest House. As his car turned left onto Chattikara Road, Guṇārṇava dāsa, eagerly waiting at the roadside on a motorcycle, sped ahead to inform the devotees of His Divine Grace's imminent arrival.

We drove the last few miles down the narrow road, past open fields and roadside trees and bushes, until Vṛndāvana village finally came in sight. It brought a strong feeling of attainment, as if we were arriving home. Vṛndāvana is not an ordinary village. Even a neophyte devotee such as myself can perceive how different its spiritual atmosphere is from anywhere else.

As the spires of our ISKCON temple came into view Śrīla Prabhupāda's comments on an enchanting description of *Mathurā maṇḍala* by Rūpa Gosvāmī in *The Nectar of Devotion* ran through my mind. "'I remember the Lord standing by the banks of the Yamunā River, so beautiful amid the *kadamba* trees, where many birds are chirping in the gardens. And these impressions are always giving me transcendental realization of beauty and bliss.' This feeling about *Mathurā-maṇḍala* and Vṛndāvana described by Rūpa Gosvāmī can actually be felt even by nondevotees. The places in the eighty-four-square-mile district of Mathurā are so beautifully situated on the banks of the River Yamunā that anyone who goes there will never want to return to this material world. These statements by Rūpa Gosvāmī are factually realized descriptions of Mathurā and Vṛndāvana. All these qualities prove that Mathurā and Vṛndāvana are situated transcendentally. Otherwise, there would be no possibility of invoking our transcendental sentiments in these places. Such transcendental feelings are aroused immediately and without fail after one arrives in Mathurā or Vṛndāvana."

By Śrīla Prabhupāda's mercy we disciples are realizing the truth of these words. Vṛndāvana invokes and inspires extraordinary devotional feeling. Pilgrims flock from all over the country to bathe in the Yamunā's sanctified waters or simply to spend a day or night within its holy precincts. Especially during auspicious times of the year, tens of thousands of pilgrims crowd Vṛndāvana's nine-mile-long *parikrama* path as they circumambulate the entire area. Some repeatedly cover the entire distance over and over again not by walking, but by continually offering *daṇḍavats.* And then, apart from the visiting pilgrims, there are the residents of Vṛndāvana: old men and widows who've come to live out their last times seeking a release from repeated birth and death rather than a temporary cure for physical ailments. They know that to die in Vṛndāvana means never having to return to this material world again.

There are literally thousands of temples in the greater Vṛndāvana area. They range in size and grandeur from large, custom-built structures, with towering domes and elaborate carvings, to simple homes in which traditional family Deities are humbly worshiped. Most famous are those of the Six Gosvāmīs, Śrī Caitanya Mahāprabhu's intimate followers.

Modern Vṛndāvana has risen and flourished because of the initial efforts of Śrīla Rūpa and Sanātana gosvāmīs some four hundred years ago. They dedicated their lives to the restoration of the once-hidden sites of Śrī Kṛṣṇa's pastimes. Now, by their grace, thousands of pilgrims visit every day, attending temple *āratis* and festivals that celebrate the pastimes of the Lord.

Following in the footsteps of the Gosvāmīs, Śrīla Prabhupāda's special contribution is to broadcast the glories of the *dhāma,* not simply within India, but throughout the entire world.

By providing us with the Kṛṣṇa Balarāma Temple and Guest House, Prabhupāda is giving us firsthand experience of the holy dhāma's transcendental nature. As his most elaborate and expensive project to date, in the most important place in the world for all Vaiṣṇavas, Prabhupāda is paying special attention to its development. Especially because none of his disciples have ever managed such a large project, he is taking great care, personally guiding and overseeing the management's development of the project to assure its success. He is only too aware of the many pitfalls to be avoided here in India. He spent considerable time doing this two months ago, and now he plans to spend the next two weeks to further solidify the high standards he requires.

When the cars pulled up outside the main gates Prabhupāda stepped out to an exuberant welcome. As he moved forward to the temple entrance, I tucked in close behind. It was a completely new and marvelous experience for me, arriving at a temple *with* Prabhupāda instead of being there to receive and welcome him.

My close friends Bhagavat Āśraya and Guṇārṇava both gave me quizzical looks filled with surprise, perhaps even amazement. A few days ago I had left Vṛndāvana for a one-day trip to Delhi, and now I was returning as part of Śrīla Prabhupāda's entourage! But this was only a second's exchange. Śrīla Prabhupāda again absorbed our full attention, and we hurried to catch up as he entered the temple among a crowd of joyous, chanting disciples.

Prabhupāda took *darśana* of the Deities, offering his prostrate obeisances before each of the three altars, housing Śrī Śrī Gaura-Nitai, Śrī Śrī Kṛṣṇa-Balarāma, and Śrī Śrī Rādhā-Śyāmasundara. After tasting the *caraṇāmṛta,* the water that has bathed the Deities, he walked back across the black-and-white checks of the marble floor to the *Vyāsāsana,* the seat reserved for him in the temple, and accepted *guru-pūjā* before giving a lecture from the *Śrīmad-Bhāgavatam.*

Śrīla Prabhupāda spoke on the Seventh Canto, Sixth Chapter, Verse 1, concerning Prahlāda Mahārāja's instructions to his school friends. This section of the *Bhāgavatam* is not yet published, as Śrīla Prabhupāda is still translating it. Thus it is new and exciting to hear.

After the devotees responsively recited the Sanskrit, Harikeśa loudly read the translation. Repeating the verse, Prabhupāda described Prahlāda Mahārāja as our predecessor guru and one of the twelve great authorities, or *mahājanas,* on the science of *bhāgavata-dharma.* He explained that although Prahlāda Mahārāja was born the son of a great demon, his life proved that even birth in a sinful family does not bar one from Kṛṣṇa consciousness, a point very relevant to us.

He noted that Prahlāda instructed his friends about *bhāgavata-dharma* during "tiffin hours," although only five years old. *Kaumāra* means "at a young age," and *prājño* means "sufficiently intelligent." When one is sufficiently intelligent he follows *bhāgavata-dharma,* and this is described by Kṛṣṇa in the *Bhagavad-gītā* as surrender unto Him. Prabhupāda said that Śrī Kṛṣṇa advents once in every four billion years at this very place, Śrī Vṛndāvana-*dhāma,* just to teach us this. Therefore Vṛndāvana is so valuable.

He summed up the purpose of the Kṛṣṇa consciousness movement as teaching that Kṛṣṇa is the Supreme and that there is no one superior to Him. "We are preaching this. In this temple we are asking everyone, 'Here is Kṛṣṇa. Always think of Kṛṣṇa. Chant Hare Kṛṣṇa. Then you will have to think, Hare Kṛṣṇa.' Simply by chanting Hare Kṛṣṇa mantra you become a devotee of Kṛṣṇa."

From his own experience, he pointed out that the results of that devotion are wonderful. "We don't do any business, but we are spending at least twenty five *lakhs* [2,500,000] of rupees every month. Kṛṣṇa is supplying. If you remain Kṛṣṇa conscious, fully dependent on Kṛṣṇa, then there will be no scarcity. I started this Kṛṣṇa business with forty rupees. Now we have got forty *crores* [400,000,000] of rupees and ten thousand men eating *prasādam* daily. So this is Kṛṣṇa consciousness!"

Everyone cheered, "*Jaya!*"

Prabhupāda smiled and continued. "As soon as you become Kṛṣṇa conscious, you simply depend on Him and work sincerely, and then Kṛṣṇa will supply everything. For example, in Bombay: now the land is one *crore* of rupees worth, and when I purchased this land I had, might be, three or four *lakhs.* I was confident that 'I shall be able to pay, Kṛṣṇa will give me.' There was no money. I have got now practical experience that you depend on Kṛṣṇa—there will be no scarcity."

Finally Prabhupāda pointedly reminded his young audience to get on with the task of becoming Kṛṣṇa conscious now, while we still have the opportunity. "*Artha-dam.* You do not know when you will die. At any moment you will die. Therefore before your next death, you realize Kṛṣṇa. *Artha-dam* means even if you live for only a few years, if you take the chance of chanting Hare Kṛṣṇa, still you are benefitted. This chanting of Hare Kṛṣṇa is so important that you can always think that 'Death is coming. Death is at my door. Let me finish my chanting. Let me finish my chanting.' Always you should think like that, that 'Death is already coming, so let me chant.' So this is called *bhāgavata-dharma,* and the Kṛṣṇa consciousness movement means *bhāgavata-dharma.* So you read Prahlāda Mahārāja's instructions very nicely and utilize it in your life. Your life will be successful. Thank you very much."

To the cheers of the devotees Prabhupāda left the temple and disappeared into his quarters with Hansadūta and Harikeśa. I remained outside, feeling happy yet regretful. I had been allowed to travel back to Vṛndāvana with Prabhupāda's party but only to collect my belongings before going on to Calcutta. I reflected on how even a drop of Śrīla Prabhupāda's mercy is so sweet and satisfying, yet it leaves you craving for more.

Others were craving Śrīla Prabhupāda's mercy also. Pṛthu Putra, whom Harikeśa had appointed as my replacement, approached me, expressing his eagerness to take over as Prabhupāda's masseur. I had foolishly forgotten Śrīla Prabhupāda's *gamsha* in the motel bathroom in Kurukṣetra, so I had to go to Loi Bazaar to buy him another. Inviting Pṛthu Putra along, I explained to him what I had learned about massaging Prabhupāda and told him about my experiences in New Delhi and Kurukṣetra as we bumped and bounced our way through the narrow streets on a rickshaw. While at the cloth store I bought myself a new *dhotī* also.

Pṛthu Putra was as excited as I had been at the prospect of personally serving His Divine Grace. My own feelings of regret at losing the opportunity mingled with a deep sense of gratitude for having had the chance at all, and I resigned myself to whatever my new assignment might bring.

Arriving back at the Mandir, however, something unexpected and wonderful occurred. Harikeśa met us on the porch of Śrīla Prabhupāda's quarters with an apology. "Sorry, Pṛthu. Forget it! Prabhupāda doesn't want any change!"

My heart leapt and Pṛthu Putra's fell. Harikeśa looked at me, simultaneously resigned and apologetic. "Śrīla Prabhupāda just told me he doesn't want to keep changing his servant every five minutes. He said you are doing fine so you're to continue, at least while he's here in Vṛndāvana, and he told me that I'm to divide up the duties so that you will have a full day's engagement."

I couldn't believe my good fortune. So far I had only been doing his massage, but now I was being given full responsibilities as Śrīla Prabhupāda's personal servant, at least while he is here in Vṛndāvana. Not only was I being retained, but I was also getting an increase in service.

Harikeśa appeared a little shamefaced, as he didn't like the idea of relinquishing the servant's duties to someone else. He admitted that losing some of his duties had left him feeling uncertain about his future and what Prabhupāda wanted him to do.

Nevertheless, Harikeśa made me feel welcome, and I immediately moved my personal belongings into the small servant's room. The room was bare, save for a glass cabinet and a solitary line drawing on the wall of Jagannātha Miśra and Śacīdevī with baby Nimāi on her lap. It was signed at the bottom 'Devahūti dāsī 11/74.' I felt very privileged to be staying within the sacred precincts of Prabhupāda's personal quarters.

Śrīla Prabhupāda is certainly being very kind, for it seems to me there are many other devotees far more qualified than I, and yet here he is, keeping me on for a few weeks more.

Thus I spent this morning with Harikeśa, as he filled me in on the details of my new service. First, in the bedroom we went through the contents of Prabhupāda's suitcase. Śrīla Prabhupāda has very few personal possessions: everything he owns fills only half of a large, red suitcase. He has three or four sets of cloth—*kurtā, luṅgī,* and *kaupīna;* a couple of sweaters, a few pairs of socks, *gamsha,* heavy, lined winter coat, *chaddar,* and some sundries.

A second suitcase holds various electrical devices used for operating his dictaphone and the large, reel-to-reel tape recorder to record his morning walks and classes. There are two electric bells on long leads, one of which is immediately set up between his desk and the servant's room whenever Prabhupāda arrives at a new place. The other is a spare. The servant also uses this suitcase for his own clothing and other belongings. Harikeśa showed me how to pack the suitcases properly for travel both within and outside India. It's an art in itself.

He revealed the contents of Prabhupāda's bedroom cupboards, which contain his bed sheets, floor covers, bathing *loṭās,* and towels. His servant doesn't necessarily handle these items, but he has to give instructions about them to the cleaning crew that comes in every morning when Prabhupāda takes his walk.

He also showed me the two large, brass buckets Prabhupāda uses for bathing (which require polishing every day) and the straw mat and bottles of oil for massage. After showing me what clean clothes to lay out for Prabhupāda to change into after his bath, he finally left me on my own.

Śrīla Prabhupāda's servant always has to be readily available. If Prabhupāda rings for anything it's the servant who responds, not the secretary. Along with giving the two massages, the servant is expected to see that Prabhupāda's clothes are washed, his rooms cleaned, *prasādam* is on time, and to arrange all the many small items needed to make Prabhupāda's day go smoothly. The art is to see that Śrīla Prabhupāda is not in any way inconvenienced and can go on with his mission of preaching Kṛṣṇa consciousness undisturbed. Prabhupāda's secretary, usually a GBC member, takes care of correspondence, requests for appointments with His Divine Grace, travel arrangements, tour schedules, and the like. Harikeśa transcribes Prabhupāda's translations and nightly revelations and sends them to the Bhaktivedānta Book Trust (BBT) in Los Angeles for editing and publishing. He also cooks for Prabhupāda, although here in Vṛndāvana he has help with this from other devotees.

* * *

At 11:15 a.m. I changed into my *gamsha* and went into the *darśana* room where Prabhupāda was sitting at his desk talking with some devotees. He decided to go up on the roof and sit in the sun.

Prabhupāda climbed the covered back stairs without difficulty, coming out into the bright sunlight. After a quick glance of inspection over the side wall, he walked on through the ten-by-twenty-foot room to the open back section.

Prabhupāda changed into his *gamsha* and sat on the straw mat. As I began to massage him, Hansadūta arrived with the mail. Prabhupāda sometimes replies to his letters at mid-morning, but more often during his massage. Hansadūta read each letter one by one, writing down Śrīla Prabhupāda's replies exactly as he dictated them.

It is instructive and entertaining to hear various ISKCON reports from all over the world, both the problems and the successes, and to hear Prabhupāda's responses to them. He is very punctual in answering, always replying within a day or two of receiving a letter. He answers a letter as if the correspondent is there in front of him. His responses are accompanied by all the same facial gestures that mark his conversations—appreciative raising of his brows and widening of his eyes, a slight tip of his head, bright smiles, scolding looks. He gives each letter his full attention, and his replies are expressive and personal and always to the point.

Today he dealt with the letters received in New Delhi.

To Kirtiraja he wrote an encouraging letter, urging him to preach in Poland. He reminded him of Lord Caitanya's prediction that Kṛṣṇa consciousness will spread to every town and village of the world. Then he expressed his gratitude that so many American and European boys and girls are helping to make this a reality. "It is not bogus like Communism, socialism and so many 'isms' going on in the world today, but it is purely spiritual, authorized by Kṛṣṇa Himself, who spoke this science of life five thousand years ago on the battle-field of Kurukṣetra. The battlefield is still there, and you will be happy to know that yesterday we have been at that very spot where Kṛṣṇa spoke to Arjuna, and we will build a gorgeous Kṛṣṇa-Arjuna temple there. People will come from all over the world to see it and understand the authority and sublime message of Lord Kṛṣṇa." He ended by asking Kirtiraja to send regular progress reports on his mission.

Puṣṭa Kṛṣṇa Swami sent a report on the proposed new Mercedes car. He also enclosed a critical news article from the magazine of a Christian sect, with his reply correcting their misconceptions.

Prabhupāda was pleased by his preaching and told him, "They do not accept the fact of rebirth, and they claim 'Awake' so this is nonsense. Your letter was nice. The whole world is in darkness, and we are bringing it to light by preaching *Bhāgavata-dharma.* Thank you for helping me."

A letter requesting Prabhupāda to accept eleven new candidates for first initiation came from Germany, and he replied to Cakravartī dāsa according to his standard format. "Please accept my blessings. I have accepted the following list of boys and girls as my duly initiated disciples. So you are the president there at Schloss Retterschof, it is your duty to see that the standards of Kṛṣṇa consciousness are always maintained. Especially chanting sixteen rounds daily, observing the four regulative principles: no meat, fish, eggs, no intoxication, no gambling, and no illicit sex life. The students must all attend morning and evening ārati and classes. If we follow this simple program along with regular *saṅkīrtana,* distributing the books and preaching, then there will be no fall down. Just like if one keeps himself clean and properly nourished by eating regularly, he will not infect disease, but if there is neglect, there is room for infection, he becomes weak and falls prey to disease. So Kṛṣṇa consciousness is the medicine for the material disease, and chanting Hare Kṛṣṇa mantra sincerely is the basic ingredient of that medicine."

In accepting new disciples Śrīla Prabhupāda gives each a spiritual name and a new set of beads. Śrīla Prabhupāda has delegated the task of choosing spiritual names to his secretary. The secretary culls the names from books listing the various names of Rādhā and Kṛṣṇa, and they are sent with Prabhupāda's reply. Prabhupāda has also entrusted his *sannyāsīs* and some GBCs with the responsibility of chanting the first round of the *mahā-mantra* on each disciple's new set of beads. Sometimes he chants on the beads himself before sending them in the mail to the new disciple.

Lastly he replied to a letter from Tuṣṭa Kṛṣṇa Swami in New Zealand. Tuṣṭa Kṛṣṇa Mahārāja belongs to a group of devotees who split away from ISKCON several years ago. They disagreed with certain methods of book distribution and the managerial structure within ISKCON. The leader of this group is a former ISKCON *sannyāsī* named Siddha Swarūpānanda Goswami. Although members of this group have their own ideas about spreading Kṛṣṇa consciousness, Tuṣṭa Kṛṣṇa Mahārāja writes to Śrīla Prabhupāda regularly.

Tuṣṭa Kṛṣṇa had previously recommended various people for initiation, but before accepting them Prabhupāda wanted to know if Tuṣṭa Kṛṣṇa Mahārāja himself was following. Tuṣṭa Kṛṣṇa's letter contained positive confirmation, and Prabhupāda wrote back, "Every student is expected to become *ācārya. Ācārya* means one who knows the scriptural injunctions and follows them practically in life and teaches them to his disciples. I have given you *sannyāsa* with the great hope that in my absence you will preach the cult throughout the world and thus become recognized by Kṛṣṇa as the most sincere servant of the Lord. So I am pleased you have not deviated from the principles I have taught, and thus, with power of attorney go on preaching Kṛṣṇa consciousness. That will make me very happy as it is confirmed in the *Guru-aṣṭaka:* '*yasya prasādāt bhagavat-prasādaḥ.*' Just by satisfying your spiritual master, who is accepted as the bona fide representative of the Lord, you satisfy Kṛṣṇa immediately without any doubt."

Prabhupāda also alluded to Tuṣṭa Kṛṣṇa's independent mentality, carefully encouraging him to keep him close. "Keep trained very rigidly, and then you are bona fide guru, and you can accept disciples on the same principle. But as a matter of etiquette it is the custom that during the lifetime of your spiritual master you bring the prospective disciples to him, and in his absence or disappearance you can accept disciples without any limitation. This is the law of disciplic succession. I want to see my disciples become bona fide spiritual master and spread Kṛṣṇa consciousness very widely; that will make me and Kṛṣṇa very happy."

He ended each letter with, "I hope this finds you well" and the epithet "Your ever well-wisher, A.C. Bhaktivedānta Swami."

Each day after taking dictation, Hansadūta types the letters and later, in the evening, places them on Prabhupāda's desk. Each one is clipped to an addressed envelope, a carbon copy, whatever enclosures there might be, and the letter being replied to. In the night Prabhupāda reads and signs them. They are mailed the next day.

Toward the end of the massage Akṣayānanda Swami came up to the roof. He requested Prabhupāda to allow Pṛthu Putra to be initiated into the renounced order of life, joining in the ceremony already arranged for two *brahmacārīs* from the Bombay temple, Lokanātha and Śrīdhara, who are to be awarded *sannyāsa* tomorrow.

Prabhupāda asked, "Why does he want to be a *sannyāsī?*" Akṣayānanda replied very simplistically, "To increase his preaching."

Prabhupāda seemed to find his answer rather trite, so Akṣayānanda Mahārāja assured him that Pṛthu Putra was already living apart from his wife and preaching enthusiastically with the Vṛndāvana *saṅkīrtana* party.

Prabhupāda was still somewhat skeptical and wanted more confirmation of his worthiness for *sannyāsa.* He suggested that Pṛthu Putra travel in America with the Rādhā-Dāmodara party under Tamāl Kṛṣṇa Goswami for a year and get trained up, but Akṣayānanda Mahārāja persisted. He said that Pṛthu Putra had been in India for many years and wasn't thinking of leaving. Because Akṣayānanda Mahārāja attested to his dependability, Prabhupāda finally agreed.

* * *

Since the only bathroom was the one attached to his bedroom, Prabhupāda had to go back downstairs to bathe. Sitting on a small, wooden stool on the marble floor of his bathroom, he mixed hot and cold water in the brass buckets and began to wash off the oil. Meanwhile, I carefully laid a set of clean clothes on his bed: *kurtā, dhotī,* and *kaupina.* I transferred the four gold buttons from his soiled *kurtā* and inserted them in the clean one. After taking care of his dirty clothes and the massage paraphernalia, I went to the sitting room.

On his desk Prabhupāda has a very small silver *lotā* filled with water, together with a matching spoon and lid. Scooping up some water with the spoon I put it on the lid, and next to this I put a small ball of *gopī-candana tilaka* clay and a compact mirror. After dressing, he crossed the black, polished sitting room floor covered with thin, white-sheeted cotton mattresses. These serve as seats for his daily visitors. Sitting at his desk he put on his *tilaka* and then chanted *Gāyatrī* mantra.

Immediately after Harikeśa came into the side room carrying a full *thali* of *prasādam.* Prabhupāda sat down to eat lunch in peace and solitude, eating slowly and deliberately, occasionally glancing out over the back veranda into the back yard.

After lunch Prabhupāda returned to the room on the roof. Walking through the door he turned and gave me my first direct instruction in my new service. "Now your only business is to stay with me twenty four hours. You can remain here," he said, indicating a straw mat outside the door, "and do not leave." Then he went inside to rest.

I happily sat down, feeling very satisfied to have received my first personal directive from him. And what an instruction! To be with him continuously: who could hope for anything more?

He awoke an hour or so later and sat for a while at his desk reading *Śrīmad-Bhāgavatam* as I cooled him with a small peacock fan. Feeling fully satisfied performing this menial service, it occurred to me just how simple and sublime spiritual life can be. Only a few short weeks ago I had been busily engaged as the temple commander here in Vṛndāvana, frantically running around from morning until night (and often in the middle of the night). Always active and energetic, I didn't like to sit idle for even a few minutes. Since I first joined the movement I have had the impression that I wasn't properly conducting my devotional service unless I was constantly physically active and producing some tangible result. But now here I was, in stark contrast, standing quietly fanning Śrīla Prabhupāda, pouring out a little water into his cup, or patiently guarding his door. It seemingly was so little, but because it was directly pleasing to the spiritual master I could understand it to be just as substantial as any major undertaking in devotional life.

It is extremely pleasurable to be with Prabhupāda during these quiet moments. He is gentle and mild in his manner and completely fixed and steady in his devotion to Kṛṣṇa. He has tremendous strength and force but is devoid of passion. His presence is totally dominating without being at all domineering, his mind steady and his senses controlled effortlessly. His intelligence is perfectly clear, and he knows how to act and how others should act in every situation. His presence thus makes spiritual life a reality.

Watching him today, it struck me that he is a living, breathing *Bhāgavatam;* whatever description of Kṛṣṇa consciousness is in his books, he himself is that. Reading his books brings gradual realization, but what is understood in perhaps several lifetimes of study is revealed on a second-to-second, minute-to-minute, and day-to-day basis in Prabhupāda's personal association.

I have therefore resolved within myself to learn as much as I can while I have this matchless opportunity to observe him closely. Simply watching Śrīla Prabhupāda in his daily activities—how he deals with devotees, how he responds to different situations, how he preaches, how he manages the worldwide affairs of his ever-expanding society, how he relaxes, how he continually pushes forward the movement of Lord Caitanya, how absolutely every facet of his being is fully Kṛṣṇa conscious—it is quite feasible to understand the full import of the sacred scriptures. By studying and preaching one may make steady advancement, but at least for me, although I have full faith in Kṛṣṇa consciousness, many ideas and principles are still only intellectually perceived, not yet fully realized. But by observing Śrīla Prabhupāda I can see they are a natural, integral part of his very being.

December 3rd, 1975

First thing this morning Prabhupāda complained that during the night someone's snoring had disturbed him. Prabhupāda translates in his sitting room, which is next to the servants' room where all three of us sleep. Since Harikeśa has not previously drawn any complaint we concluded that the culprit is either Hansadūta or myself, so we now share a Guest House room.

Today I gave Śrīla Prabhupāda a new *tilaka* mirror. His previous one was a converted powder compact given to him in Japan, with an ivory design on the lid and a mirror inside. The face powder had been removed and replaced with a picture of Rādhā and Kṛṣṇa.

In September I had asked a local craftsman to make a new compact as a Vyāsa-pūjā gift for Śrīla Prabhupāda, but I received it just last night, over two months late. It is made of solid silver with a peacock embossed on the bottom and a gold relief depicting Kṛṣṇa and Balarāma in Vṛndāvana forest on the lid. Although it is considerably heavier than the one it replaces, Prabhupāda seemed to like it very much. I was surprised and pleased when he offered me his old one.

* * *

During Śrīla Prabhupāda's last visit in August-September he spent the three weeks from Janmāṣṭamī through Rādhāstami painstakingly supervising every aspect of the temple management, and he is continuing to do so on this trip as well. He is personally inspecting the temple, guest house, and restaurant. He ensured that we were maintaining proper standards of Deity worship, such as overseeing the quality of the *bhoga* offerings and scrutinizing the flowers we purchased for Their Lordship's garlands. He was aware of the devotees' attendance at the programs and would speak out whenever our standards of cleanliness and punctuality fell short. He was even concerned with the hired laborers' attention to their work. The plans for the new *gurukula* building and many other important features of life in the large and important temple compound all received his concerned attention.

This trip is no different. Most of his disciples here are raw recruits, with little or no experience in managing affairs in India. Therefore Prabhupāda is personally checking on everything—correcting, advising, and sometimes chastising.

Viśāla dāsa got a taste of Prabhupāda's chastisement this morning. Viśāla is in his mid-thirties, a rotund, early devotee from America. He is likeable and eager to please, but with an eccentrically humble manner that can border on the onerous. Prabhupāda generally receives Viśāla's overwrought praises with good humor and appreciation, but this morning he decided it wasn't the time for eulogies.

As Prabhupāda strode out of the front gate for his morning walk, Viśāla emulated the Vedic *brāhmaṇas* by chanting some verses from the *Śrīmad-Bhāgavatam* in praise of Prabhupāda: "We think that we have met Your Goodness by the will of Providence—."

Gripping the spiral-tapered walking stick that Viśāla himself had given him for this year's Vyāsa-pūjā gift, Prabhupāda poked its silver tip at some puddles in the temple entrance way and interrupted caustically, "It is the grace of Providence you do not see that it is properly cleansed?"

Unexpectedly cut short and somewhat taken aback, Viśāla stammered apologetically, "I ... I'm sorry. I will see to that, Your Divine Grace. That is my fault."

Prabhupāda remained deadpan. "Why there is water? This water means the shoes—dirt; it will be dirty. So you have no eyes to see?"

"I am blind. I'm sorry. I will see that it is cleaned for you."

"Then become with eyes. Simply praying, what you will do? Do something practical!"

Leaving Viśāla agape he strode strongly off down the road with his amused disciples following.

Harikeśa perceived some irony in Prabhupāda's remarks. "This is the argument people always throw against us," he said. "'Simply praying, what will you do? Do something practical.' People often criticize the devotees in this way."

Prabhupāda answered that Kṛṣṇa consciousness *is* the practical side of yoga. He said that it isn't a system of simply "pressing the nose." Kṛṣṇa consciousness is not mere sentiment and an excuse for doing nothing, nor are devotees incapable of real achievement.

He explained that the real problem is that people are not following Kṛṣṇa's instructions properly. If one practically surrenders to Kṛṣṇa, He makes everything successful.

"Practical," he said, "means it will be done by Kṛṣṇa. Your only business is to surrender to Kṛṣṇa. You cannot do anything. And as soon as you think, 'I shall be able to do it,' then you are a rascal. Immediately you are rascal."

"So only a fully surrendered soul can do everything perfectly?" Harikeśa asked.

Prabhupāda answered, "He cannot do anything. Everything is to be done by Kṛṣṇa. But he has to apply his intelligence by Kṛṣṇa consciousness. Even if he is intelligent, he cannot do anything."

Harikeśa added, "Except surrender."

"Yes. He can surrender, and Kṛṣṇa will do everything. You have to act very sincerely under the direction of Kṛṣṇa, and then the war will be successful, as Arjuna did."

Harikeśa wanted more clarification. "So imperfect activity is a sign of lack of surrender?"

"Yes," Prabhupāda said. "You work sincerely, devoutly, and have faith that Kṛṣṇa will save me from all dangers. *Rakṣiṣyati iti viśvāsa-pālanam.* 'I have surrendered to Kṛṣṇa sincerely. Now Kṛṣṇa will give me all protection.' This faith, that is the beginning of devotional life—faith."

"So is this faith *śraddhā* or *niṣṭhā?*" Harikeśa wanted to know.

"*Sraddhā.* Beginning, *śraddhā.* Then, when he is advanced, then he becomes fixed up. 'Yes, Kṛṣṇa is protecting me.'"

Prabhupāda walked briskly, occasionally stopping to emphasize a point, sometimes greeting the local residents with "Hare Kṛṣṇa," and sometimes speaking a little about the surroundings. After exactly half an hour he turned and headed back for the temple.

Upon entering the temple compound Prabhupāda noticed a young Western hippie girl who was staying in the Guest

House. He cautioned the managers that people in such dress should not be admitted to the Guest House simply because they are paying guests. We must use some discretion, otherwise the local residents will consider us no better than our hippie visitors.

Akṣayānanda Mahārāja explained that the hippie girl had agreed to wear a *sari* when she arrived but has now reverted to her old dress.

Prabhupāda said "Yes, that is due to habit."

Akṣayānanda told Prabhupāda that recently one young man had arrived there dressed in a similar way, but after a few days he shaved his head and became a devotee.

Prabhupāda told him that was all right, but meanwhile the temple will become known as a "hippie resort, and the prestige of the temple will be minimized." Nevertheless, he agreed that we must give everyone a chance to become devotees; but if they do not change their habits after three days they should be asked to leave.

* * *

As his Indian, Canadian, and French disciples sat before him, Prabhupāda conducted the fire *yajña* this morning for the *sannyāsa* initiations of Lokanātha, Śrīdhara, and Pṛthu Putra in the temple courtyard. He gave a short talk based on the *sannyāsa* mantra beginning *"etāṁ samāsthāya parātmā niṣṭhām,"* from the *Caitanya-caritāmṛta.* He told them that although they are young men in the midst of the very powerful material energy, if they simply keep full faith in Kṛṣṇa and follow the previous *ācāryas* they will remain fixed up. He advised them to do this by chanting the Hare Kṛṣṇa mantra. He even suggested that as *sannyāsīs* they should chant extra rounds.

Describing the *sannyāsa* initiation as the last ceremonial procedure in the *varṇāśrama* system, and the *sannyāsī* as the guru of the other social and spiritual divisions, he told them to follow the example of Śrī Caitanya Mahāprabhu and preach all over the world.

"Preaching is also not very difficult because you haven't got to manufacture anything. Everything is there, and it is Caitanya Mahaprabhu's order. Caitanya Mahāprabhu also took *sannyāsa* at a very early age, twenty-four years old only. So He has practically shown by His activities how to preach Kṛṣṇa consciousness all over the world. And He gives order to everyone, '*āmāra ājñāya guru hañā tāra ei deśa*': 'In whichever country you may live, it doesn't matter. Try to deliver them by becoming their guru.'

"And how one becomes guru? That is also very easy. Śrī Caitanya Mahāprabhu says, '*yāre dekha tāre kaha kṛṣṇa-upadeśa.*' You haven't got to manufacture anything. Simply you try to repeat the instruction of *Bhagavad-gītā, kṛṣṇa-upadeśa.* Not only *Bhagavad-gītā,* there are many other instructions. Especially *Bhagavad-gītā.* So if you simply carry the message of *Bhagavad-gītā,* then you become guru. Don't manufacture anything. Then it will be spoiled. '*Man-manā bhava mad-bhakto mad-yājī mām namaskuru.*' You can, everyone can, say this. Kṛṣṇa says, 'You always think of Me.' So you can repeat only. You can say to others, 'My dear Sir, please think of Kṛṣṇa.' It doesn't require very much education. Simply just like a peon carry the message, 'Sir, you always think of Kṛṣṇa.' Then you become guru.

"If you follow it strictly, you also think of Kṛṣṇa yourself, and you teach others, 'My dear Sir, my only request is that you think of Kṛṣṇa,' nobody will kill you. If he doesn't follow, he will appreciate you, 'Oh, these *sannyāsīs* are very nice. They are advising to think of Kṛṣṇa.' Then you become guru. Simple thing."

He ended with a reference to the multinational status of his candidates. "This kind of duty was entrusted by Caitanya Mahāprabhu to the Indians. *Bhārata bhūmite haila manuṣya janma yāra, janma sārthaka kari kara para upakāra.* This is Caitanya Mahāprabhu's mission, that every Indian should learn what is this Kṛṣṇa consciousness and preach it all over the world. That is His order. But our Indians are not taking care of it. Therefore it doesn't matter—Indian or European or American. Who will carry the order of Caitanya Mahāprabhu he will be benefitted. He will be glorified. So don't be hesitant, because the soul is neither Indian or American. '*Ahaṁ brahmāsmi.*' Every one of us, we are part and parcel of Kṛṣṇa and our position is Brahman. '*Brahma-bhūtaḥ prasannātmā.*' So from that platform you go on preaching Kṛṣṇa consciousness. By executing the order of Śrī Caitanya Mahāprabhu, you will be glorified, the country will be glorified, the whole world will benefit. Thank you very much."

One by one the three men came forward in their new dress as *sannyāsīs*. Bright faced and enthusiastic, they humbly received their *tridaṇḍas* and the title "Swami" as the assembled devotees loudly cheered, "*Haribol!*", "*Jaya!*" Everyone threw grains into the sacrificial fire to complete the ceremony.

Afterward the three new *sannyāsīs* all came into Prabhupāda's room to receive his blessings. Prabhupāda sat at his desk, next to the fireplace. Giving each a garland, he encouraged them to go out and preach immediately. It clearly delights Prabhupāda to see his disciples commit themselves fully to the service of the Supreme Lord. On the basis of such surrendered disciples he is able to spread Kṛṣṇa consciousness all over the world.

Yet, Prabhupāda is not indiscriminate about awarding *sannyāsa*. Recently, two boys arrived from Germany, Alanātha and Sucandra, asking permission to take *sannyāsa*. Prabhupāda discussed their request with Hansadūta, as well as Bhavānanda and Sudāmā mahārājas, who had just arrived from New York. Prabhupāda indicated that he considered the boys a bit young to accept *sannyāsa*. He warned them that it is very difficult to remain in the renounced order, especially in the Western countries. He cited the example of two of his leading disciples, both GBC men, who had fallen victim to *māyā* after becoming *sannyāsīs*. Prabhupāda explained, "*Māyā* is very, very strong. Butter is sure to melt when there is fire." He artistically gestured, waving his left hand in the air, bringing his right hand to meet it from below. "Even if the butter is here the fire will come. I tried to think of so many ways to keep them separate, but it was not possible. They are spirit soul, of course, but *māyā* is very strong."

Bhavānanda and Sudāmā mahārājas are staying here for a few days before leaving for Bengal. They plan to hire two forty-foot-long boats to travel to all the villages along the Ganges. They want to perform *kīrtana*, distribute *prasādam*, and recruit new devotees. Prabhupāda decided that the two German devotees should go with them for further training.

Not everyone is happy to see a new *sannyāsī*. Since his arrival Hansadūta has also approached Prabhupāda for *sannyāsa*. But his wife, Himavatī, heard about it in Germany and immediately rushed to Vṛndāvana to voice her objection. She was very upset, but Śrīla Prabhupāda pacified her. Nevertheless, she is still adamantly opposed to her husband taking *sannyāsa*. Therefore Prabhupāda is not encouraging him to do so. Hansadūta is somewhat confused about what to do and wants Prabhupāda to decided his fate. But Prabhupāda won't give him a direct instruction. He is leaving it to Hansadūta to make the decision.

* * *

This afternoon while Prabhupāda rested upstairs I noticed that the water pot in his room was empty. I thought of taking it downstairs to fill it but was hesitant, since Śrīla Prabhupāda had instructed me not to leave his presence. I got in a quandary: "If Śrīla Prabhupāda wakes up and I'm not here, that will not be good. On the other hand, if he asks for a drink when he wakes up, then he will have to wait." I wasn't sure what to do, but decided it was best to wait.

Sure enough, though, the first thing Prabhupāda did when he awoke was to sit at his desk and tell me to fill his glass. I diffidently explained there was no water in the pot and that I would have to go downstairs to get some.

He asked me, "Did you not think about filling it while I slept?"

I explained my dilemma, and Śrīla Prabhupāda tipped his head a little. "Hm, all right," but his tone indicated it was second best.

From this incident I can understand that although it is essential to follow the instructions of the spiritual master closely, a little intelligence in the application of those instructions is also required. A first-class servant will anticipate the needs of his spiritual master rather than simply wait to be told everything. One who is expert at pleasing the guru can do many things on his own initiative and still adhere strictly to all instructions. Our intelligence shouldn't be stereotyped or inflexible.

December 4th, 1975

On the walk this morning Akṣayānanda Swami told Śrīla Prabhupāda that people sometimes ask his opinion about a local *bābājī* who is building a big temple on the Vṛndāvana-Mathurā road. Looking across the fields we could see it in the far distance. An unfinished edifice as yet, it is reported that it will house various deities in its lower chambers and the *bābājī's* personal quarters on top. This man is well known for smoking large quantities of cigarettes, thus earning him the nickname "Pagal Baba." *Pagal* means "crazy." Akṣayānanda said that he answers people's queries by explaining that our Guru Mahārāja does not approve of us smoking cigarettes.

Invariably they say, "But Pagal Baba smokes."

Akṣayānanda then responds, "Ah, that's because he is *pagal!*" And they agree. Prabhupāda also agreed. He said that our four regulative principles will expose so many persons as frauds.

This led into a lively discussion about the sometimes confusing difference between following in the footsteps of great personalities and imitating them. Akṣayānanda Mahārāja said that many people eat meat because they claim that Lord Rāmacandra did.

Prabhupāda quickly fired back, "Lord Rāmacandra can eat you and the whole universe! Can you do that?" We all laughed. A few words from Prabhupāda exposes the rascals.

As we walked along in the early morning sunshine he clearly defined the difference between Lord Rāma and the ordinary living beings. Then as a final thought he pointed out that Lord Rāmacandra is not offered meat in any temple. So why should anyone claim that because the Lord ate meat, therefore he can? He explained that Kṛṣṇa also ate the Khāṇḍava fire, but He doesn't say to offer Him fire. He says a little fruit, a flower, some water.

Prabhupāda is expert at exposing the faulty logic of the unscrupulous, who try to justify their lust by misconstruing *śāstra* and the activities of others with whom they cannot compare.

He doesn't take the short and easy route to defeat them. Rather than say simply that Lord Rāmacandra never ate meat, he chose to explain the more difficult to grasp, but ultimately more relevant, point that there is a vast difference between the incarnations of the Lord and ordinary men. Therefore They should not be imitated, but instead Their instructions followed.

Class was very interesting, with Prabhupāda continuing with the second verse from Prahlāda's instructions to his school friends. After chanting the Sanskrit, Harikeśa read out the as-yet-unedited translation. "In this human form of life there is chance to go back to home, back to Godhead. Therefore every living entity, especially in this human form of life, must be engaged in devotional service. This devotional service is natural because Lord Viṣṇu, the Supreme Personality of Godhead, the master of the soul, the Supersoul, is the most beloved being of all other living beings."

Prabhupāda explained that the Vedic literature describes three stages of spiritual development: *sambandha*—to know our relationship with the Lord, *abhidheya*—to act accordingly, and *prayojana*—to attain the purpose for which we establish our relationship. *Sambandha-jñāna* means that first we must understand our relationship with God. Without knowing our relationship we cannot act, even on the material platform. He gave several pertinent examples to show how a sense of relationship motivates a person to act. Similarly, unless we know our relationship with God why would we want to serve Him?

Śrīla Prabhupāda also emphasized the need for proper *gurukula* education. Construction of the *gurukula* is now underway here in Vṛndāvana, and Prabhupāda has high expectations for it. He said every child should be trained in the principles of *bhāgavata-dharma.*

"This should be taught to the children. Otherwise when he is engaged in so many nonsense service it will be very difficult to drag him from this false engagement and again establish him in Kṛṣṇa's service. So when we are children we are not polluted; we should be trained up in *bhāgavata-dharma.* That is Prahlāda Mahārāja's subject matter. We are serving. The birds are serving. They have got small kiddies, children. They are picking up food and working very hard and bringing it in the mouth. And the small kiddies, they are chanting, 'Mother, Mother, give me, give me,' and eat food. There is service. Don't think that anyone is without service. Everyone is serving. A man is working hard day and night. Why? To give service to the family, to the children, to the wife. The service is going on, but he does not know where to give service. Therefore Kṛṣṇa said, 'Give Me service. You'll be happy.' This is this philosophy, *bhāgavata-dharma.* Thank you very much."

* * *

When Prabhupāda returned to his rooms he sat for a few minutes before breakfast, talking about the unfortunate state of the world. Hansadūta and I sat before him. Prabhupāda relaxed, leaning back against the soft bolsters on his seat. He delivered a sharp critique of the leaders of society, the politicians and the educators, for misleading people and creating a thoroughly hellish situation for everyone.

He explained how the entire world is becoming increasingly chaotic and demonic, causing suffering to people. He searched for an appropriate word to summarize it. "They have made it a pan— What is that?" We couldn't figure out the word he was looking for.

"*Pandemonium*! Just look it up."

Prabhupāda's choice of words seemed a bit quaint to me, but when I read out the definition of *pandemonium* in the dictionary, I saw that Prabhupāda had used precisely the correct word to convey his point. It said, "Pandemonium: pan-demonic; abode of all demons; any place of lawlessness, violence and uproar; utter confusion."

We all laughed, and Hansadūta and I looked at each other appreciatively. Prabhupāda has a surprising command of the English language. Day by day new aspects of his extraordinary character are revealed, and we are extremely grateful that Kṛṣṇa has sent us such a wonderful spiritual master.

* * *

After lunch Śrīla Prabhupāda went upstairs to take rest, which is his usual routine. Today he had me put his bed, a simple wood-framed cot crisscrossed with thick, wide, cotton strapping and covered with a thin mattress and sheet, outside on the front terrace of his room. He slept peacefully in the sunshine, with the domes of Kṛṣṇa-Balarāma Mandir towering above, benign and protective.

I remained in the small room on the roof. Feeling a little tired, I sat on the edge of what I thought was a spare wood-base bed in one corner of the room. As one of the Guest House beds with a sponge mattress, it did not appear that Śrīla Prabhupāda had ever used it. The next thing I knew, Śrīla Prabhupāda was waking me up. Rising after his nap, he had come through the door to find me sound asleep on the bed. He gave me a gentle shake, and I jumped up quite embarrassed and apologetic.

Prabhupāda wasn't annoyed, but he did comment very kindly, "If you are fatigued, that is all right. You can rest on a mat on the floor, but whatever is the spiritual master's should never be used."

Moving over to sit at his desk he asked, "So, what is your name?" Certainly he must have already heard it many times over the last few days, so perhaps it was his way of making me feel more comfortable. It relieved my embarrassment, making me feel that he is getting to know me on a more personal basis.

"'Arry Sawry, Śrīla Prabhupāda," I said in my broad Northern English brogue.

"Haree Showree," Prabhupāda corrected in his elegant Bengali accent. Giving me a warm smile he asked for some water.

December 5th, 1975

It is hard to say when Prabhupāda's day begins and when it ends, because he never seems to conclude his activities in the way we do. He only rests for a few hours each day, and even that is intermittent.

Śrīla Prabhupāda maintains a remarkably regulated daily routine. While here in Vṛndāvana his schedule is:

6:00 a.m. — Wash, brush teeth, and take Āyurvedic medicine.
6:30 – 7:30 a.m. — Morning walk.
7:30 – 8:30 a.m. — Greet the Deities, *guru-pūjā,* then *Śrīmad-Bhā-*

	gavatam lecture from the Seventh Canto.
9:00 – 9:30 a.m.	— Breakfast of fruits and *chira.*
9:45 – 11:15 a.m.	— Rest on roof for an hour and then meet people (usually by appointment).
11:15 – 1:15 p.m.	— Massage with oil.
1:15 – 1:45 p.m.	— Bathe.
1:45 – 2:30 p.m.	— Lunch *prasādam.*
2:30 – 3:00 p.m.	— Sit in room or chant *japa.*
3:00 – 4:00 p.m.	— Rest.
4:00 – 5:00 p.m.	— Meet with specific people or devotees, or chant.
5:00 – 6:30 p.m.	— Give public *darśana.*
6:30 – 9:30 p.m.	— Meet public or senior devotees, GBC business or just chat.
9:30 p.m.	— Take hot milk, massage and rest.
12:00 – 1:00 a.m.	— Rise and translate.
5:00 a.m.	— Light rest or *japa.*

Śrīla Prabhupāda's typical routine goes something like today.

After his all-night translation work he stopped at *maṅgala ārati* time and lay back against the bolsters with his feet up. He slept lightly for a short time.

At six o'clock he went into the bathroom to wash, brush his teeth, and freshen up. He came back and sat for a few minutes as he put on *tilaka.* When that was completed, he took a reddish Āyurvedic medicinal pellet called Yogendra-rasa. After I had crushed it with a large, roasted cardamom seed and then mixed it with honey in a small oval mortar, he added a little water. He drank the mixture straight from the mortar, scraping up the residue with the pestle, which he then deposited on his tongue with an elegant twist of his fingers.

Then Prabhupāda prepared to leave for his morning walk. Getting up from his desk he stood patiently as I helped him on first with his *uttarīya* (the saffron top-piece traditionally worn by all *sannyāsīs*) then with his heavy, saffron-colored coat and his woollen hat. I finally hung his bead bag around his neck. All the while he conversed with Hansadūta, Akṣayānanda Swami, and Gopāla Kṛṣṇa.

As he walked toward the door, I rushed ahead to place his

cane directly into his hand. I then positioned his shoes so that he could step into them and out of his slippers in one easy movement, all while I was holding the door open. It is somewhat of an art to manage all this without delaying or interrupting Prabhupāda's steady progress out.

The expectant devotees waiting outside enthusiastically shouted, "*Jaya* Śrīla Prabhupāda!" as he appeared, offering their obeisances and a garland.

Smiling and modest, he returned their greeting with "*Jaya!* Hare Kṛṣṇa!" The privileged few who went on the day's walk gathered closely around him as he made his way up the side of the temple and out the front gate onto Chattikara Road.

Heading west into the countryside beyond the boundary of Vṛndāvana village we walked for exactly half an hour, as far as a solitary house named "Moda Place," and then back. Prabhupāda's gait is surprisingly swift and strong, and by the end we were struggling to keep up.

At precisely seven thirty he entered the temple from the side door and waited patiently as the *pūjārīs* strained to swing back the immense wooden doors on each of the three altars. The conch shells trumpeted their call to the faithful, announcing the imminent appearance of the Deities. The curtains drew back, and the Govindam prayers boomed over the loudspeaker. Śrīla Prabhupāda, followed by all the devotees, offered his prostrate obeisances first to his Guru Mahārāja, Śrīla Bhaktisiddhānta Sarasvatī, and Their Lordships Śrī Śrī Gaura-Nitai, then to the two moonlike brothers Śrī Śrī Kṛṣṇa-Balarāma, and finally to the brilliant forms of Śrī Śrī Rādhā-Śyāmasundara.

After taking a little *caraṇāmṛta,* Prabhupāda walked across the black-and-white checkered marble floor and mounted the steps to his carved marble *Vyāsāsana.* As he sat flanked by ornamental lions, the devotees offered *guru-pūjā.* Chanting the prayers "*śri guru caraṇa padma ...,*" each devotee came forward to offer a flower to his lotus feet and bow before him. Everyone relished this opportunity to glorify Śrīla Prabhupāda in person. It is a daily act of humble submission, an affirmation of our full commitment to his service and a reminder to our flickering minds that without him we are nothing.

As the *kīrtana* ended, Harikeśa moved forward to swing the microphone around in front of Prabhupāda's mouth. Prabhupāda's voice rang out over the loudspeakers, "*Jaya oṁ viṣṇupāda paramahaṁsa parivrājakācārya aṣṭottara-śata Śrī Śrīmad bhaktisiddhānta sarasvatī gosvāmī mahārāja prabhupāda ki jaya!*"

The devotees bowed their heads to the ground in obeisance to the disciplic succession, the Pañca-tattva, the holy *dhāmas,* the Vaiṣṇavas, and all the assembled devotees.

Then Harikeśa passed Prabhupāda his *karatālas.* We sat down to listen and respond to Prabhupāda's sweet and melodious voice as he glorified Śrī Śrī Rādhā-Mādhava:

"*Jaya Ra-dha Ma-dha-vuhhh, kunjavi ha-ri,*
gopi janabal-la-bhaa girivaradha-ri;
Jasodanandana brajajana ranjana,
jamuna tii-raaa banacaa-ri."

His eyes closed in concentration, his face showing the intensity of his meditation on the objects of his love and worship in the groves of Vṛndāvana on the banks of the Yamunā river. He infused new meaning and freshness into the song, though he sings it every day before class. His brass *karatālas* rang out, quickening the pace, and the devotees' voices swelled in response. Just as it came to a heart-filling crescendo, the *karatālas* gave their final three metallic rings, "*dung dung dung,*" and everyone knelt with their heads to the floor as Prabhupāda recited the *prema-dhvani* prayers again.

Harikeśa jumped up again, removed Prabhupāda's *karatālas,* and quickly hung a small microphone around his neck, the other end of which he connected via a two-way switch to the large reel-to-reel Uher tape recorder that he had carried since the morning walk. He handed Śrīla Prabhupāda the *Bhāgavatam,* an Indian Sanskrit edition containing the commentaries of different *ācāryas* that Prabhupāda uses for his evening translation work, already opened to the proper page. He carefully slipped Prabhupāda's spectacles onto him.

Then he sat to lead the devotees in responsive chanting of the Sanskrit verse, loudly reciting the translation before Śrīla Prabhupāda began his lecture. "Prahlāda Mahārāja continued to speak: My dear friends born of demonic families, the happiness which is perceived with reference to the senses can be obtained in any form of life according to one's past fruitive activities. Such happiness is automatically obtained, as sometimes we obtain distress without any endeavor."

Harikeśa also wore a neck microphone plugged into the same small box with the two-way switch as Prabhupāda's. He recorded himself and then threw the switch to record Śrīla Prabhupāda.

Prabhupāda read out the verse: "*Sukham aindriyakaṁ daityā deha-yogena dehinaṁ, sarvatra labhyate daivād yathā duḥkham ayatnataḥ.*"

Sometimes speaking with his eyes closed in complete concentration and sometimes opening them, surveying his audience, he propounded the ancient philosophy of the *Śrīmad-Bhāgavatam* in the modern context. He quoted other Sanskrit verses profusely, cross-referencing each point with other works, such as the *Bhagavad-gītā* and the *Purāṇas* or the *Upaniṣads*. His explanations are always clear and potent. Prabhupāda is amazingly skilled at conveying the most profound and complex philosophical concepts in a way anyone can easily understand and apply. Having grasped the very essence of life, its meaning and purpose, he can present it for the understanding of both ordinary people and intellectuals.

Punctuating his lecture with analogies and vivid practical examples, he told a story to illustrate that the sense of material enjoyment is the same for all living beings, whether dog, hog, or human being. "There was a prostitute called Laksahīra, whose charge was one *lakh* of pieces of diamond. It doesn't matter, a big diamond or a small diamond; that was her charge. So one man was suffering from leprosy, and he was assisted by his wife, a very faithful wife. So still he was morose. The wife asked the husband, 'Why you are morose? I am giving you so much service. You are leper, you cannot move. I take you on a basket and carry you. Still you feel unhappy?'

"So he admitted, 'Yes.'

"'Oh, what is the cause?'

"'I want to go to the prostitute Laksahīra.'

"Just see! He is leper, a poor man, and he is aspiring to have a prostitute who charges one hundred thousand pieces of diamond. So anyway, she was a faithful wife. She wanted to satisfy her husband. Some way or another she arranged. Then when the leper was at the house of the prostitute, the prostitute gave him very nice dishes of food, but everything in two dishes; everything—one in the golden pot and one in the iron pot.

"So while he was eating, he asked the prostitute, 'Why you have given me in two pots?'

"'Because I want to know whether you will feel different taste in different pots.'

"So he said, 'No. I don't find any difference of taste. The soup in the golden pot, the soup in the iron pot, the taste is the same.'

"'Then why you have come here?'"

In the same way Śrīla Prabhupāda explained about distress. "If a man is a millionaire he still suffers the same distress from typhoid fever as a poor man. Happiness and unhappiness are the same in different pots. This is knowledge."

From these simple stories he derived a profound conclusion. "This is foolishness. The whole world is going on like that. They are simply trying to taste the same thing in different pot. That's all. They are not detestful, 'No sir, I have tasted enough.' That is called *vairāgya-vidyā*—no more tasting. 'It is all the same, either I take in this pot or in that pot.' Therefore it is said, *sukham aindriyakhaṁ,* the sense pleasure, whether you enjoy as a dog or a human being or a demigod or as a European or as an American or an Indian—the taste is the same. This is very important. You cannot have a better taste. Better taste is only Kṛṣṇa consciousness. It doesn't matter in which pot I am in at the present moment. *Ahaituky apratihatā.* You can taste Kṛṣṇa consciousness without any hesitation, without any check, without any hindrance."

After half an hour he brought the class to an end. The devotees shouted, "*Jaya,* Śrīla Prabhupāda! Śrīla Prabhupāda *ki jaya!*"

Again Harikeśa sprang into action, deftly removing Prabhupāda's spectacles, the *Bhāgavatam,* and the microphone from his neck and handing him his cane, all as he stepped down from the *vyāsāsana* to go out the door.

At the top of the steps leading out onto the path, I waited with his shoes. Slipping into them, Śrīla Prabhupāda walked the hundred yards past the temple, toward the Guest House. The devotees followed, dancing and chanting, "*Jaya* Prabhu-pāda, *jaya* Prabhu-pāda, *jaya* Prabhu-pāda, *jaya* Prabhu-pāda!"

Śrīla Prabhupāda passed through the open veranda into the small secretary's room and through the door on the right into his sitting room. This is the room that Prabhupāda uses for both giving *darśana* and working. He propped his cane in the corner next to the door and then slipped out of his outdoor shoes into his slippers. (Prabhupāda never walks barefoot, even inside.) I helped to remove his coat and hat.

Prabhupāda sat for a few minutes looking outside, through the three tall, narrow windows barred with ornamental grill work, into the small *tulasī* garden with the solitary tree. Surveying his room, Prabhupāda glanced appreciatively at the large shelves displaying copies of his translations of *Śrīmad-Bhāgavatam* and *Caitanya-caritāmṛta.* He requested that we hang his flower garlands on the various beautiful original oil paintings or the photos of Deities and devotees adorning the walls. The garlands were to be left hanging until dry and then removed. He has complained that in the past the devotees cleaning his room have unnecessarily removed the garlands while still fresh.

As soon as his breakfast was served he walked through the other door to his *prasādam* room. He sat on a seat behind one of the two low wooden tables called *choṅkis.* On his *choṅki* was a silver water tumbler, a packet of toothpicks, and a small hand bell to summon his servant, should he want anything else. From this seat Prabhupāda can look over the small back veranda into his enclosed garden. The original painting of Kṛṣṇa taking *prasādam* in the company of His friends, used for the cover of the first *Hare Kṛṣṇa Cookbook,* smiled down on Prabhupāda as he took his meal.

Kiśorī dāsī and other ladies prepared Prabhupāda's breakfast. It consisted of various cut fruits: seedless grapes, guava, banana, orange, pomegranate, and whatever else was freshly available at the market. With this he had a small bowl of fried *chira* (flattened rice mixed with peas), another of fried cashew nuts, and a small piece of *sandeśa* milk sweet. One item is vital to Prabhupāda's breakfast: ginger soaked in lemon juice. He won't start breakfast without it, as it stimulates his digestion.

Śrīla Prabhupāda ate little and very slowly, as an act of devotion: *prasāda-sevā,* service, rather than indulging the tongue. When he finished, I cleared his plate and wiped the table as he sat and cleaned his teeth. It surprised me to see that his teeth moved apart when he inserted the wooden pick, but Prabhupāda just laughed about it.

When he finished he held out his open palm for me to tip a little Bhaskar Lavan, an Āyurvedic digestive powder, into it. Tilting his head back, he dropped in the powder. Then still maintaining the pose, he poured in some water from the tumbler without touching it to his lips. After washing his mouth and hands in the bathroom he returned to his *darśana* room.

Sometimes, Prabhupāda sits in his *darśana* room after breakfast and chats with his servants for a few minutes, usually commenting on the present state of the world. These moments are especially sweet—to be with Prabhupāda as he sits, relaxed and casual, basking in the warmth of his intimate association.

This morning was particularly memorable. The sun was shining brightly through the tall and narrow windows, casting patches of dazzling light on the clean, white sheets on the floor. He sat comfortably in the middle, his legs crossed, right ankle resting on the left knee. His fingers loosely intertwined, he closed his eyes briefly and enjoyed the warmth of the sun as it danced upon his golden form. Seeing the opportunity, Hansadūta, Harikeśa, and I sat on either side of him, just happy to be with him in a quiet moment. He began to reflect on the unfortunate state of the world's inhabitants. He explained that due to a lack of knowledge about the Supreme Lord people are suffering. Under the false impression of being independent they commit all kinds of sinful acts, not knowing and not caring for the results, foolishly thinking they are free to do as they like. But when the volume of sinful life becomes too great they suffer the consequences in the form of pestilence or war. They think that by politics and meetings they can avoid such things, but that is not possible. They are helpless to prevent them, and therefore they receive their punishment through the three-fold miseries of life. At just the right moment, nature brings the demons together and engages them in war.

To illustrate the point, he gave an amusing but striking example of how *māyā* works. "In my young days we had one teacher. Whenever there was any misbehavior between the boys, the teacher would stop them and bring them out to the front of the class. He would make them stand face-to-face and each take hold of the ears of the other and on his order make them pull. So the one, he is pulling, and the other is hurting, so he pulls back even harder, and each one is pulling and crying. But they cannot let go because the teacher is ordering, 'No, you cannot stop. You must go on pulling!' Similarly, *māyā* brings together one Churchill and one Hitler. 'Now, rascal, pull!' And neither can stop. And the foolish people glorify them."

The thought of the scene so humored him that even before he finished he began to laugh heartily. His shoulders and belly shook, and his brilliant teeth flashed like pearls in the sun. When Prabhupāda smiles the entire room, even the universe, seems to light up. It's a Vaikuṇṭha smile that spreads transcendental effulgence everywhere around. Prabhupāda's mood was so open and congenial it seemed, if just for a moment, that we had joined a picnic with Kṛṣṇa and His cowherd boyfriends, joking and laughing in the forests of Goloka. We laughed with him, glancing at each other in appreciation and wonder as to who this extraordinary personality Śrīla Prabhupāda really is. He is far beyond our comprehension, yet we feel ourselves extremely fortunate to share these intimate moments with him.

It was an entrancing moment, and it occurred to me that Śrīla Prabhupāda must have many friends in the spiritual world with whom he can eternally enjoy happy and carefree days. Yet being extraordinarily merciful he chooses to be here among us. Although the most exalted personality, he appears to like nothing better than to be with his disciples, foolish and neophyte as we are. He gives the impression there is no one in the world he would rather be with and nothing he would rather be doing than sharing whatever he has with us, although we have nothing to give him in return that could possibly be of interest to him. It seems a lopsided relationship, but Prabhupāda doesn't mind. He is not looking for anything for himself, only to see what he can give us. As a result, we have obtained more than any of us can ever have hoped for.

After chatting with us, Prabhupāda took rest upstairs on a mattress in the sun for about an hour.

He reserved the time from 10:00 until 11:15 a.m. for special guests and discussed management of the temple with senior devotees. Sometimes he replies his mail during this period also. Today he dealt with a wide range of people and projects. He is negotiating the offer of a *go-śālā* near Mathurā, the opening of a post office in our future *gurukula* building, and the establishment of a bank branch in the Guest House. These arrangements will provide better facilities for the devotees and guests, which will result in the temple becoming a greater focus of local community activity. When more people come, more preaching can go on, the net result being that Kṛṣṇa consciousness will further increase and more souls will be saved from the clutches of material existence.

Prabhupāda confronted a variety of topics in today's mail, from orchestrating the worldwide production and distribution of his books through the efforts of enthusiastic followers to solving the personal problems of a disciple struggling with *māyā* to encouraging the newly interested—a university teacher in Copenhagen and a distressed young man in Australia. Everyone received his close personal guidance and attention.

Rāmeśvara, head of the American division of the Book Trust, reported a recent new record in book distribution. In a one-day competition, Los Angeles, Chicago, and Atlanta temples distributed 5,406 hardbound books, with some individual devotees selling over two hundred each. Rāmeśvara's report was dramatic. "Our men are willing to do anything to please you, and all of them have dedicated their whole lives to distributing these books. Our only desire is that you may kindly bless us with greater and greater desire to distribute these books all over the world until every home has whole libraries of your books. By Your Divine Grace's blessing we will never stop distributing these books. We are thinking that this is the highest pleasure in all the three worlds."

Prabhupāda's response was equally enthusiastic. "Your report of book sales is over-encouraging. You are all becoming very, very dear to my Guru Mahārāja. I started this movement by book selling. I was never a beggar for money, but I was writing books and selling. My Guru Mahārāja very much liked my writing, and he used to show others in my absence, 'Just see how nicely he has written, how he has appreciated.' He encouraged me, and my Godbrothers, they also liked my writing. After I wrote that poem for Vyāsa-pūjā of my Guru Mahārāja, they used to call me 'Poet.'

"Anyway, I was working writing books and publishing BTG alone, but I could not give the thing shape, so I decided to go to the U.S.A., and now you all nice boys and girls have helped me so much. It is all the mercy of Kṛṣṇa. Thank you very much."

Yaśodānandana Mahārāja and Acyutānanda Swami are touring South India, and Prabhupāda plans to meet them in Nellore in a few weeks. They are arranging programs for him in a large hall in Madras, where their party has met with a good reception. They also sent a favorable report of their book distribution. They are holding *paṇḍalas,* making Life Members, and distributing *The Scientific Basis of Kṛṣṇa Consciousness,* written by Svarūpa Dāmodara, one of Prabhupāda's disciples.

Although each of their men sells only a few copies of one small book and collects 150 rupees per day, Prabhupāda considers this a good beginning and his expectations are high. "There is tremendous field in India for selling books," he wrote. "If you continue this effort you will soon compete with America. Gopāla Kṛṣṇa is arranging to print *Śrīmad-Bhāgavatam* in Hindi, First Canto Vol. 1 15,000 copies, also *Bhagavad-gītā As It Is.* So there is a big field, in India 600,000,000 people. In every home there should be at least one BBT publication, so the field is very big."

Aja, the president of Boston temple, has begun holding lectures at local universities, where he distributes *prasādam* and magazines. The devotees have made applications to teach courses on Kṛṣṇa consciousness in several colleges, and they've established a new center in Amherst, a big college town.

Prabhupāda was extremely happy to hear this, for one of his greatest ambitions is to see his books studied seriously in the schools and colleges of the world. He replied, "I am very pleased to note that you are attempting to preach seriously in the schools and colleges. Prahlāda Mahārāja, a great devotee and authority in our line, said Kṛṣṇa consciousness should be taught from the very beginning of childhood. The defect of modern education is that the children are taught all nonsense things. They do not receive even the first point of knowledge, that 'I am pure spirit soul, part and parcel of God.' This simple fact they have yet to learn, so if you can teach them just this one point it will be a great success, because this is the basic platform of advancing in spiritual understanding. If we want to read and write, then it is essential to learn first of all the ABCs."

A *brahmacārī* in England asked for guidance in his service and *āśrama* after a period of difficulty, and Prabhupāda encouraged him to push on. "From your letter it appears that you are a little confused. This means that the consciousness is not clear, *brahma-bhūtaḥ prasannātmā, na śocati na kāṅkṣati.* The clear stage of consciousness is free from hankering and lamentation. As long as we are on the material platform, bodily conception of life, we will hanker after so many things required for material supremacy. Therefore to clear this cloudy consciousness Caitanya Mahāprabhu has recommended that one should simply chant the holy name of God sincerely and hear it with attention. So chant, dance, take *prasādam* and be happy. Marriage is not recommended. Are you prepared to get a job, live outside the temple in an apartment, provide the wife with bangles, *saris* and sex? Better you concentrate on this chanting and hearing process, then teach others and give them *prasādam.*"

Prabhupāda has attracted the attention of people in all walks of life, and his replies to nondevotees are equally to the point. When Mark Phillips, a young Australian married man, sent a faltering cry of distress, Prabhupāda offered the universal panacea. "Yes, we are eternally related to the Lord as servant, so naturally when we forget our eternal relationship as servants of the supreme master, Kṛṣṇa, we suffer Therefore Kṛṣṇa advises everyone, in *Bhagavad-gītā,* to simply surrender to Him and He will take care of us. In Australia we have got our temples; consult the *Back to Godhead* magazine for the temple nearest you. Please visit the temple and take advantage of the pure, spiritual atmosphere. This will immediately extinguish the burning fire of material suffering in your heart. Meanwhile I humbly request you to chant Hare Kṛṣṇa, Hare Kṛṣṇa, Kṛṣṇa Kṛṣṇa, Hare Hare/ Hare Rāma, Hare Rāma, Rāma Rāma, Hare Hare. This chanting will bring you all perfection of life; please try it."

Dr. Yogi Rāj Dev Swarūp teaches yoga at the University of Copenhagen and has recently obtained an Indian government grant to begin a yoga institute in New Delhi. He wrote a letter expressing his appreciation of Prabhupāda's work and asking how he can help the mission.

Prabhupāda replied, "I thank you very much for your kind appreciation. Because you are a teacher in a respectable university I request you to study some of my books, especially *Bhagavad-gītā As It Is.* As stated in the *Gītā, manaḥ saṁyamya mac-citto, yukta āsīta mat paraḥ.* 'One should meditate upon Me (Kṛṣṇa) within the heart and make Me the ultimate goal in life' (*Bg.* 6.13-14). Western people are now becoming more and more interested in yoga practice, but unfortunately, because they have no authorized source of information, they are being misled by unauthorized teachers and concocted methods of yoga practice. Actually the *aṣṭāṅga-yoga* system practiced thousands of years ago is not practical for this age; therefore Lord Caitanya Mahāprabhu introduced the chanting of the holy name of God: Hare Kṛṣṇa, Hare Kṛṣṇa, Kṛṣṇa Kṛṣṇa, Hare Hare/ Hare Rāma, Hare Rāma, Rāma Rāma, Hare Hare.

"In all our temples we are doing that and we have more than forty big volumes of authorized books: *Śrīmad-Bhāgavatam, Bhagavad-gītā,* etc. Intelligent people are accepting this Movement all over the world, so if you are serious about joining this mission then why not study these books, understand the philosophy and teach."

* * *

Despite his workload, Prabhupāda always adheres to his schedule. At 11:30 a.m. he took his massage, followed by a bath and lunch and then an hour's rest. I've never seen anyone sleep as little as Śrīla Prabhupāda, about three to four hours total, yet he never shows any sign of fatigue.

When he woke around 4:00 p.m. Kiśorī dāsī placed a freshly made garland around his neck, dabbed some freshly ground sandalwood paste on his forehead and temples, and offered him some fresh fruit juice. He then sat at his desk to receive visitors.

At 5:00 p.m. his doors opened for *darśana.* A steady flow of curious and respectful people, fifty or sixty at a time, continuously packed his room either to sit and watch or to ask questions. He sometimes talked specifically with a particular visitor, not minding if the other fifty listened in, and at other times he spoke generally to all.

I was posted at the door to give out *pera,* a milk sweet that is a Vṛndāvana specialty. Prabhupāda is particularly insistent that all visitors receive some Kṛṣṇa *prasādam,* a tangible offering for their spiritual advancement. A discussion of philosophy may be easily forgotten, but *prasādam* will always act to purify. *Prasādam* distribution is also in accordance with Vedic etiquette that a guest must always be offered a place to sit and a little refreshment, no matter who he may be. Thus, as always, Śrīla Prabhupāda was the perfect host.

At 6:30 p.m. the temple conch and bells announced evening *ārati. Darśana* concluded, and Śrīla Prabhupāda sent the devotees and guests over to the temple to chant and see the Deities. Relaxing for a while, he spent the rest of the evening discussing philosophy and matters of practical management, giving advice to his managers and sometimes sitting quietly chanting.

A local devotee, Śrī Viśvambhara Dayal, popularly known as Bhagatjī, arrived at 9:00 p.m. to prepare Śrīla Prabhupāda's hot milk and hold light discussion on the temple management, *gurukula,* and other matters.

Śrīla Prabhupāda drinks a glass of hot milk every evening just before taking rest, sometimes supplementing it with a savory like *kachori, paraṭhā,* or fried *chira.* He gave the cooks clear instructions how to make each preparation. His milk has to be exactly the right temperature—very hot, so that it can be easily digested, but not so hot that it burns.

One previous evening he demonstrated to me how to bring boiling milk to the right temperature for drinking. Calling for another bowl, he poured the milk from his silver cup from a height of about six inches into the bowl and then back again a few times to aerate the milk and reduce the temperature. When it was just right, he drank it.

The evening massage took more than half an hour. Lately the weather has been cold throughout the night until sunrise. Thus Prabhupāda's circulation and joints need more attention. I took rest about eleven o'clock.

As we disciples slept, Prabhupāda arose around 11:30 or midnight to begin his most important work of the day, the translation of the *Śrīmad-Bhāgavatam* and the writing of his transcendental purports. Harikeśa is a light sleeper, and he often awakens as Prabhupāda comes through the servant's room on his way into the *darśana* room. Rolling over in his sleeping bag, he offers his obeisances as Śrīla Prabhupāda passes.

Sitting at his desk Prabhupāda chanted *japa* for an hour or so in complete concentration on the holy names. He prayed to Kṛṣṇa for the ability to serve Him nicely and to present the eternal words of the *Śrīmad-Bhāgavatam* in a manner just suitable for the understanding of the entire world, conscious that his work will form the basis for law and order in the next ten thousand years.

Putting aside his *japa-mālā* he donned his spectacles and clicked on the desk light. He opened the *Bhāgavatams* at the book marks—the green Varanasi edition with the Sanskrit commentaries of previous *ācāryas* and the red Bengali one with commentaries by Śrīla Bhaktisiddhānta Sarasvatī Ṭhākura—leaned forward, and studied them intently. The microphone close to his mouth, he flicked on the tape and began his dictation: "*Śrīmad-Bhāgavatam,* Seventh Canto, Seventh Chapter, verse twenty-five, purport continued...."

December 6th, 1975

Early this morning Prabhupāda sent for the temple managers and angrily chastised them because we have spent fifty *lakhs* of rupees to build such a big temple and guest house, yet he cannot get hot water in the cold season. The past few mornings the water has been so cold that he couldn't even brush his teeth. One after another, Gopāla Kṛṣṇa, Akṣayānanda Swami, Guṇārṇava, and Dhanañjaya were called. No one seemed to want to take responsibility. Śrīla Prabhupāda demanded to know why. Whenever they offered a feeble excuse or explanation, he abruptly cut them off. It was clear he wanted to hear a plan for rectifying the mistakes, not excuses.

Prabhupāda called for Saurabha dāsa, the Dutch devotee and architect who was responsible for supervising the construction and design of the project, but he could not be found. This only increased Prabhupāda's exasperation. Holding Saurabha responsible for the mistake, he sharply rebuked him in his absence.

When the devotees assured him that the problem would be fixed immediately Prabhupāda's mood changed. As quickly as it had arisen, his anger disappeared.

As our spiritual master, Śrīla Prabhupāda is training us in every aspect of devotional service. His praise and criticism are never unreasonable or excessive, but always intended to push us forward in our spiritual progress. He expects us to be conscientious, as attention to the details of our service is the practical manifestation of our seriousness and sincerity. He doesn't like to hear excuses for tasks undone, and he loathes the bureaucratic mentality that in the West we call "passing the buck."

He told us that the British Rāj had introduced this mentality, and it has crippled India. He is determined to see that it not get a footing in ISKCON. "I ask you to do something. You ask him. He asks another. And you go away and forget. Business finished. Simply bureaucracy! If I ask you to do something, it is your responsibility, not his. Even if you give it to someone else, you have to see it is properly completed."

Despite his criticism of the management over the hot-water incident, Prabhupāda is very pleased with the service of Saurabha and the other devotees. More than once he has asked me during massage what I thought of the Guest House and temple. When I responded with appreciation, he looked over the buildings and said, "Yes, I think he has done very nicely. There is no such building anywhere." But he is determined not to allow us to become complacent. Now the facility has to be maintained and managed efficiently, and Śrīla Prabhupāda is personally showing us how to do it. As the representative of Kṛṣṇa, he wants to make sure that whatever resources Lord Kṛṣṇa has provided are used correctly without waste. And he is constantly urging us to develop the same sense of responsibility.

* * *

Prabhupāda is especially fond of Prahlāda Mahārāja's instructions because they are so pertinent to modern society. This morning's verse in particular emphasized the point that economic development is a waste of time. Śrīla Prabhupāda delivered a crushingly negative appraisal of contemporary society that considers progress only in economic terms. He said that no one can obtain more happiness than they are due by *karma.* Just as distress comes without working for it, so happiness also comes. Therefore, we should work only for spiritual advancement.

He told us, "The human life is meant for understanding Kṛṣṇa. Instead of using the energy for understanding Kṛṣṇa, they are spoiling the energy unnecessarily to earn money. This is the modern civilization. The whole Western world, how they are spoiling their life unnecessarily! Prahlāda Mahārāja has begun with the words *durlābhaṁ mānuṣaṁ janma.* This life is very, very important, and after many, many births you have got it.

"Cāṇakya Paṇḍita said, '*āyūṣaḥ kṣaṇa eko'pi na labhya svarṇa-koṭibhiḥ.*' *Svarṇa* means "gold coins," and *koṭi* means "ten millions." So suppose today is sixth December. Now it is seven o'clock in the morning; now passed. Can you bring it back again by paying one *crore* of gold coins? Hm? 'Let me get back seven o'clock, sixth December 1975, again?' No—it is gone forever. So just see the value, that you cannot get back even a moment of your life by paying millions and millions of dollars. How time is valuable! Just calculate."

As he surveyed the eighty or ninety young men and women who have come here to get the special blessings of serving in the holy *dhāma,* he warned us to be attentive to our purpose. "There is no guarantee that I am going to take again a human form of life. But there is a little guarantee for the devotee. Guaranteed in this way, that if he unknowingly commits some mistake, then it is guaranteed. And if he knowingly commits mistake, then he is going to be cat or dog. This is the facility. If one purposefully commits mistake and sinful life, 'Now I am chanting Hare Kṛṣṇa, I can do all sinful life. It will become counteracted,' that rascal will be punished very, very much. *Nāmnād balād yasya hi pāpa buddhiḥ.* 'I am living in Vṛndāvana. Oh, it is *dhāma.* So let me do all nonsense. It will be counteracted.' They'll be these cats and dogs and monkeys in Vṛndāvana. *Dhāmāparādha.* Of course, Vṛndāvana's influence will be there, but at least one life he has to become the hog and dog in Vṛndāvana. As you see, there are many dogs, hogs. But still, Vṛndāvana-*dhāma* is so powerful that next life he will get salvation, even if he has become a dog or hog. But that is not good. Why should we act in such a way that in Vṛndāvana-*dhāma* we shall commit sinful life and become a cat or dog? We should be careful. You simply dedicate your life to serve Mukunda. Kṛṣṇa's another name is Mukunda. *Muka* means liberation. *Mukti.* So *ānanda,* the *mukty-ānanda,* that is real *ānanda,* liberation. So our business is how to surrender fully unto the lotus feet of Mukunda, *mukunda-caraṇāmbujam,* and fully engage in His service. Therefore Prahlāda Mahārāja says, 'Don't try for anything else.'"

* * *

Prabhupāda has given Harikeśa a new service. He wants him to write an essay titled "Experimental Knowledge," explaining the defects of modern science and presenting the scientific basis of Kṛṣṇa consciousness. Prabhupāda has been personally coaching him, calling him in regularly to discuss points of logic. He told Harikeśa not to criticize modern science as such but the misuse of it. Science should not be used as a tool to propagate atheistic theories, and false claims must be exposed. Modern scientists are challenging God, and now Prabhupāda as God's servant and representative is challenging them. "Inventions you can take credit for, but why claim to be God?"

December 7th, 1975

One of Śrīla Prabhupāda's foremost desires is to develop a first-class *gurukula* system. He was personally involved in the development of the school in Dallas, ISKCON's first *gurukula,* and now here.

Recently in Dallas some difficulties have arisen in complying with local Texas laws regarding dormitories. Jagadīśa dāsa, the GBC for that area, was forced to look for another facility that would conform to government standards. In a previous letter Jagadīśa sent Prabhupāda some information regarding a new site for the school in another city. Prabhupāda approved the idea, but today another letter arrived retracting the proposal because of hostile reactions from the local residents. Jagadīśa proposed that the school remain in Dallas and they just build a new dormitory on the existing site. Prabhupāda encouraged him to stay in Dallas, saying that from the beginning he had considered the facilities there to be ample. He is anxious to see the school firmly established and stable, as he doesn't want the children's education disrupted.

Here in Vṛndāvana, Bhagatjī, who lives a few houses away from our *āśrama,* arranged to purchase land for our *gurukula* and gave one *lakh* rupees for building the school. Bhagatjī has also come forward to help manage the temple. Pleased by his efforts, Prabhupāda meets with him almost every day.

On Rādhāṣṭamī, during his last Vṛndāvana visit, Prabhupāda laid the foundation stone for the *gurukula.* Construction of the building on the land next to the temple has already begun. Now he is keenly following developments and regularly discussing the plans.

One of Prabhupāda's favorite quotes is "Child is the father of man," meaning the future of the world lies with its young.

Therefore, good training and education are essential for a peaceful population and trouble-free world. He often expresses his conviction and happiness that the movement he began for respiritualizing the world will go on because "the young people of your country have taken it up."

In this respect, the young Prahlāda Mahārāja's instructions are particularly important for us. This morning's *Śrīmad-Bhāgavatam* verse (7.6.5) spoke precisely on this theme of taking full advantage of one's youth for spiritual attainment. The translation was, "For this reason, a person who is fully competent to distinguish wrong and right while keeping himself in material existence, *bhāvam aśritah,* must endeavor for achieving the highest goal of life so long the body is stout and strong and is not embarrassed by the dwindling condition of life."

Śrīla Prabhupāda commented, "Nobody wants to become old man, especially in this winter season. It is very difficult for old men. So, you have to accept *jarā* and *vyādhi.* Nobody can escape disease. When I am diseased there is a great struggle how to cure myself, go to the doctor, take good medicine, and so on. But we cannot check the diseased condition. Similarly we cannot check our old age, cannot check our birth, death. Therefore here it is said, *kuśalaḥ. Kuśalaḥ* means if you actually want benefit, because this kind of struggling has not given you any benefit, *tato yateta,* then you should endeavor for this. What is that? *Ksemāyā,* for your ultimate benefit. And how long? *Śarīraṁ. Puruṣaṁ yāvan na vipadyeta puṣkalam.* So long you are stout and strong you should try how to become free from this bondage of birth, death, old age, and disease. Not that you keep this business set aside, 'When we shall get old then we shall chant Hare Kṛṣṇa and become Kṛṣṇa conscious.' That is not the meaning. Immediately.

"Prahlāda Mahārāja said that from the very beginning of life, when *kaumāra*—a small child, boy—from that age one should begin this *bhāgavata* life, or Kṛṣṇa consciousness. That is called *brahmacārī,* to teach *brahmācārya* from the very beginning of life. And when you are young, then you should work with more vigor and intelligence. At that time brain is very nice. Young man has got all the facilities. The machine is strong. This is a machine. So old machine cannot so work. So it is a great fortune for the young boys and girls of Europe and America that in this young life they are cultivating Kṛṣṇa consciousness. It is a very good fortune."

There is a quality about Śrīla Prabhupāda that makes him utterly appealing to everyone. He relates perfectly to his youthful disciples although, materially speaking, we are two or three generations apart. Despite the vast difference between our cultural background and spiritual understanding, there are no barriers between us. He is sympathetic and has a seemingly perfect empathy with us. How he is able to relate to us in such a wonderful way was revealed soon after class.

We were talking in his sitting room about growing old, and at one moment Prabhupāda got up from his desk. His eyes shone brightly and he said simply and convincingly, "I am not an old man! I will never grow old!" We laughed. Prabhupāda is a self-realized soul. He does not identify with his body, and he doesn't see us as material entities either. He relates to us as one spirit soul relates to another. We are all meant to serve the Supreme. In that sense he does not perceive himself as superior to us, yet he always keeps the formal guru and disciple relationship intact. Prabhupāda's humble service is to bring us back to Kṛṣṇa, and our humble service to Kṛṣṇa is to serve Śrīla Prabhupāda.

* * *

Prabhupāda derives great inspiration from the life of Prahlāda Mahārāja and often refers to his exemplary behavior when preaching. A recent letter from Yogeścandra dāsa requested Prabhupāda's blessings for a party of eight men who are to collect funds for the Māyāpur temple. "You always have my blessings," Prabhupāda replied. "The father always wishes that the son may be more successful than himself. This is the spiritual conception. If one is doing well, then the materialistic persons become envious and try to check his progress. This was actually so with Prahlāda Mahārāja. He was only five years old, he was preaching Kṛṣṇa consciousness to his school friends, and the father Hiraṇyakaśipu became so envious that he attempted to kill his five-year-old son in so many ways. Kṛṣṇa consciousness is just the opposite. If someone is doing well then the attitude of the devotee is to give him all facility to go on and improve more and more."

December 8th, 1975

Prabhupāda is always concerned about our welfare—not just philosophically, but in many practical ways as well. For example, this morning was very cold; winter is really setting in. He remarked about it on his walk and then asked if the devotees are getting ghee on their chapatis. Akṣayānanda Swami replied that only the guests are given some because it's expensive and not necessary for the devotees.

But Prabhupāda disagreed. He said that it is necessary in this season. In the cold weather the devotees must have a little extra ghee and grains. He recommended a mix of *channa* and *urad dahls* as being both palatable and beneficial—not too little and not too much. "Unnecessary *vairāgya,*" he said, "there is no need. We don't approve that. *Yuktāhāra-vihārasya.* What you require for keeping health—but not to eat too much. But what is absolutely required must be done."

Śrīla Prabhupāda is quite pleased with Harikeśa's article, "Experimental Knowledge." Last night he had him read it aloud. Then this morning as we walked, he asked him to reiterate some points for the other devotees to hear.

He injected some very amusing observations himself. Recalling his trip to South Africa he said there were many factories for chicken killing. "So I suggested that the egg, you can analyze. Find out the chemicals and create one egg. That was my proposal. "Motioning to Harikeśa, he said, "So he is going to create!" We all laughed as Śrīla Prabhupāda continued, "He'll explain how to create egg from—"

"From chemicals," Akṣayānanda Swami suggested.

And Jñāna dāsa added, "And make chicken."

Then Harikeśa described, "Calcium phosphate and a little sulphur for the yellow. Make some color and cover it in plastic and put it in an incubator, and let a chicken grow."

"And you eat!" Prabhupāda concluded.

Akṣayānanda Swami thought that would be a great article.

Prabhupāda stopped and said seriously, "My only regret is that these rascals are going as scientists and big men. Simply talk. They cannot create. It is very simple thing. Put some chemicals together, and if you know the chemicals, then why don't you put it? And incubator put, then you don't require to kill so many chicken."

"Actually it's a wonderful challenge," Harikeśa agreed. "This big, big scientist, big, big brain—"

But Prabhupāda interrupted, "'Big, big monkey, big, big belly. Ceylon jumping—melancholy!' You do not know this? *Baro baro bandolel, baro baro pet. Lanka dingate—matakare het!*"

We were all laughing as Prabhupāda went on, "This translation was done by one big professor of President's College, Professor Rowe. So these professors required to learn Bengali, so he translated, 'Big, big monkey, big, big belly. Ceylon jumping—melancholy!'" Prabhupāda was extremely humorous, and his descriptive analogies perfectly fit.

Scientists are always full of big talk, saying that life comes from matter and that it is just a combination of chemicals. Yet life is occurring everywhere at every moment, and still they can neither say what the combination is, nor can they reproduce it. Similarly, the big monkey companions of Hanuman were full of bravado and boasts, but when it came to jumping across the ocean from India to Lanka they were "melancholy." Only Hanuman by the grace of Lord Rāma could do it. Nevertheless, despite his often humorous critiques and sometimes general condemnations of the modern materialistic scientists, Prabhupāda cautioned us that any attempt to preach on a scientific basis must be done expertly.

When Alanātha, a European devotee, told him of plans to publish a magazine in Sweden with articles challenging the material scientists, Prabhupāda warned him. "Don't write anything nonsense. It must be very solid. Otherwise you'll be laughingstock. One must be confident before challenging others. In all stages he must be able to defend himself from the opposing elements. Then such challenge is all right. We are confident that this soul cannot be manufactured by any material combination.

Therefore we can challenge. And we can defend ourselves in any stage."

In class Prabhupāda continued to speak on the same topic. He said that modern civilization means to increase the killing. By scientific advancement modern man has become expert in killing the less fortunate—chickens, cows, babies—and even their own souls. The government is advertising "One, two, three—*bās!*" advising people to restrict the size of their families to a maximum of three by contraception or abortion. But those who have no control of their senses misuse their lives and everyone else's. Prabhupāda explained how such people cannot imagine a life without sense gratification, wanting to eat, sleep, and have sex almost unlimitedly.

He recalled how in the early days of ISKCON in New York his neighbors would protest at the morning chanting. "In the beginning, in that Second Avenue 26, when our morning prayer was going on at seven, not very early. And so many other tenants, half-naked, would complain to the landlord. 'Mr. Judah, what is this going on? What is going on? Stop it! Stop it! Stop!'

"So Mr. Judah used to say, 'No, no, they'll not stop. I cannot say. You go to the police.'

"So sometimes police were coming to stop us, but we did not stop." This brought a laugh to the assembled devotees.

Śrīla Prabhupāda went on, "So *ajitātmanaḥ*. The human life is meant for gaining victory over the senses. 'No, better be victimized by the senses.' This is modern civilization."

He warned of the danger of becoming too attached to family life, which the *Vedas* compare to a dark well. He told us that in Vedic civilization it was compulsory that at age fifty one must give it up. Otherwise, one becomes an *ātma-ghatam,* a killer of the soul.

There are an increasing number of householders and women with children staying in our *āśrama* now, and many seem to have come here to settle. Living in Vṛndāvana and raising one's children here is certainly very appealing for any devotee, but Prabhupāda warned us that we must be very careful how we conduct our activities in the holy *dhāma.* "So those who do not observe these rules and regulations, they are called *ajitātmanaḥ,* victimized by the senses. Their business is to sleep as much as possible. They are passing their days without any benefit—*niṣphalam,* without any result. If one is not serious about the value of this human form of life, he may waste his time by sleeping. But no. If we follow our predecessors, our Gosvāmīs, who were all ministers, they came to Vṛndāvana to practice—what? *Nidrāhāra vihārakādi-vijitau,* to conquer over sleeping, eating, and mating. And coming to Vṛndāvana, if we indulge in that way, then what is the use of coming to Vṛndāvana? Go to hell and live there."

* * *

Prabhupāda is very eager to begin *go-rakṣa,* or cow protection. This morning he told Akṣayānanda Swami to construct a shed on our spare land and immediately buy some cows. He sees this program as an essential aspect of our preaching work and is encouraging us to establish it on a worldwide basis.

Then, while hearing this morning's mail, the topic of cow protection came up again in Rūpānuga's October monthly GBC report. (All GBC men have to send detailed monthly reports, which His Divine Grace listens to with careful attention). Rūpānuga mentioned that the cows on our Pennsylvania farm are giving forty-eight pounds of milk a day per cow and have even won some awards.

Pleased with this report, Prabhupāda wrote an encouraging response. "Our cows are happy, therefore they give plenty of milk. Vedic civilization gives protection to all living creatures, especially the cows, because they render such valuable service to the human society in the shape of milk, without which no one can become healthy and strong. In your country the dog is protected and the cow is killed. The dog is passing stool and urine in the street, he is considered best friend of man. And the cow is all pure—stool, urine and milk—but they are taken to the slaughterhouse and killed for food. What kind of civilization is this? Therefore we have to preach against all this nonsense."

Prabhupāda also asked him for a report on the newly acquired eleven-story building in New York. He is concerned that this large building be correctly managed, as recent reports have suggested difficulties.

A BBT and zonal report, full of devotional enthusiasm, also arrived from Hṛdayānanda Goswami, the GBC for South America. He is supervising the production of Prabhupāda's books in Spanish and Portuguese, and he enclosed two new publications: *Easy Journey to Other Planets* (Portuguese, 50,000 copies) and *Elevation to Kṛṣṇa Consciousness* (Spanish, 125,000). *Bhagavad-gītā Tal Como Es* has just gone to the printer. They have assembled a team of translators with the aim of publishing at least one hardbound book per month.

Hṛdayānanda Mahārāja requested help from the English-language BBT in Los Angeles for manpower and loans. He also presented a proposal to produce Prabhupāda's books as both a standard publication and a "super cheap" version. This will enable them to distribute books profusely even in the poorest South American countries.

Another idea he proposed was for each GBC man to spend at least three months per year in a zone other than his own. He felt that this arrangement would give Śrīla Prabhupāda relief from the burden of managerial concerns. It also would enable each man to analyze his zone objectively and, by consultation with another GBC member, solve any problems.

Prabhupāda heard the report with great satisfaction and carefully inspected the new books and a photo of Śrī Śrī Rādhā-Madana Gopāla from Mexico. Then he dictated his reply. "Yes, you print all of my books; if you can sell then, why not print? Print as much as possible and store them if necessary. But you must pay regularly the BBT loans; that is not to be neglected.

"Your idea of printing a deluxe edition and an ordinary edition is all right. Everyone should get a book, that is the idea. So do it.

"The idea of GBC changing zones for two-three months of the year is also good. Bring up this point at the Māyāpur meeting and vote on it."

* * *

Each moment in Prabhupāda's association is instructive. Even in the simplest of dealings his every action is exact and proper. He notices the smallest detail.

In mid-morning, when I entered his room, Prabhupāda noted I was wearing a new cotton *dhotī* I had purchased several days ago. He commended the thick quality and asked the price. I told him it was only fourteen rupees. He also asked how I purchased it, and I explained that I had a little money saved. He said he thought it was a good bargain and told me to call in Akṣayānanda Swami. When he came in, Prabhupāda told him about my new *dhotī* and asked him to reimburse me for the money spent. He said that my small savings should be kept for emergency use, and the temple should cover my expenses.

* * *

Over the past few days Prabhupāda has given many small but significant instructions on a variety of issues. For example, a devotee who lost his original beads gave me a new set for Prabhupāda to sanctify by chanting on them. Prabhupāda agreed, but mentioned that this was not really necessary because it is the chanting of the devotee that is sanctified at initiation, not the beads.

During a walk Akṣayānanda Swami told Prabhupāda about a retired gentleman who wants to live in the *āśrama*. The man is very respectful and even offers his obeisances to the *sannyāsīs*. Prabhupāda replied, "If a *sannyāsī* is not offered respect, the punishment is that he must fast for the day. That it is *śastric* injunction." Bhagavat Āśraya asked what the punishment was if one doesn't fast. Prabhupāda said simply, "You must go to hell!"

An astrological researcher wrote from London asking for Śrīla Prabhupāda's time and date of birth. Prabhupāda obliged him. "Regarding your question about my birth. I was born September 1, 1896, Tuesday at about 4:00 in the afternoon. My *raśī* is Mithuna."

Prabhupāda is always anxious to establish new centers in India and build up those that are already existing. He wrote to Mahāṁsa Swami to say that he intends to spend at least one *crore* rupees in Hyderabad. And he authorized Gaura Govinda Swami to open a center in Orissa. The Vṛndāvana devotees are to check the offer of a temple in Kanpur.

Śrīla Prabhupāda is always flexible. Gargamuni Swami is to come to India with five Mercedes vans and twenty men to begin traveling *saṅkīrtana* and standing-order distribution to libraries. Although Prabhupāda had requested him to manage the Calcutta temple again, when he heard his new program of selling books he wrote, "Yes! Your present engagement is more important. Managing Calcutta temple is not so important. I am pleased that you are selling my books; this is superior engagement, so please increase it more and more."

December 9th, 1975

There are problems with the drainage from our Guest House. The septic tanks are inadequate, and there is no room to build larger ones. Neither is the local municipality providing sewage lines to this area. Overflow is polluting the back alley, and there have been complaints from local residents. Prabhupāda has had many discussions with Saurabha, Guṇārnāva, and the other managers aimed at finding a solution.

This morning, instead of his regular walk, he went down the side alley and along the Vṛndāvana *parikrama* path. He came out into an open space of about two acres, said to be the actual Rāman-reṭi area where Kṛṣṇa and Balarāma played with Their cowherd friends. Walking across the soft sands, he looked around at the barren land. A few of Vṛndāvana's many peacocks strutted here and there, and a group of green parrots, like a gang of noisy adolescents, squawked and squabbled overhead. A crow cawed loudly from the top of a high tree, and varieties of birds flitted among the surrounding foliage.

Prabhupāda is thinking of purchasing the land to use as drainage for the Guest House. He also suggested we turn it into a park. As he walked around he said we should "colonize" the area, similar to our Los Angeles community. He didn't stay very long, and after a short walk on the road, he returned to the temple.

* * *

Class this morning was longer than usual. Prabhupāda contrasted the genuine renunciation of Śrīla Rūpa Gosvāmī, the founder of present-day Vṛndāvana village, with that of some of his modern imitators. Such imposter renunciates simply come to beg *chapatis* just to sell them in the market in order to buy *bidis,* a cheap variety of cigarette. Prabhupāda explained that following the rules and regulations of devotional service, *vidhi-bhakti,* is essential. First there is *vidhi-bhakti,* then *rāga-bhakti,* spontaneous service, and at last *prema-bhakti,* pure love of Godhead. In the beginning stage we have not awakened our natural love for Kṛṣṇa, and therefore we should be careful not to act whimsically. He reminded us that by birth we may be at a disadvantage, but not disqualified.

He explained that progress depends on proper guidance. Then he described the vital role that he was playing as the representative of the Six Gosvāmīs. "So in the beginning, neophyte stage, not that because we have come to Vṛndāvana, immediately we have become advanced. No. *Vidhi-bhakti* must be followed—regulative principle—by the injunction of the *śāstra* and the order of the spiritual master. One who is inquisitive to understand *Brahman,* he should be given chance. Just like there is a little fire. Fan it. Fanning, fanning, fanning, and it becomes a big fire. So our process is that. We pick up anyone. Caitanya Mahāprabhu has given open declaration—*kṛṣṇa bhajanete nāhi jāti kulādi vicāra*—anyone who is desirous of becoming Kṛṣṇa conscious, it is open. Anyone can come."

Prabhupāda went on to say that although a devotee is naturally enthusiastic to offer this process of purification to everyone, we should not be disappointed if only a few take it up. Nor should we be complacent, now that we have achieved what many consider to be the goal of Kṛṣṇa consciousness itself—residence in the holy *dhāma.* "Caitanya Mahāprabhu never sat down tightly in Vṛndāvana. He traveled all over India and took so much trouble. So preaching is very important, and you should engage. That will help you. Every one of you should be pure in your activities and try to preach Kṛṣṇa consciousness as far as possible. If you remain pure, then your preaching will be successful and you'll get encouragement. That is the instruction of all Vaiṣṇavas. Thank you very much."

* * *

Back in Prabhupāda's room after breakfast, Hansadūta read out some particularly ecstatic letters from America describing the book distribution. Prabhupāda's enthusiastic response to them was clear evidence that, as he said in class, he is fanning, fanning, fanning to bring back the fire of spiritual consciousness in the hearts of the conditioned souls. He has declared the entire world an open house for the introduction of Kṛṣṇa consciousness. The letters show just how seriously his disciples are applying themselves to the task.

In a BBT report Rāmeśvara informed Śrīla Prabhupāda that this month they'd printed 350,000 English *Bhagavad-gītās,* with 500,000 more planned in hardbound. *Śrīmad-Bhāgavatam* Sixth Canto, Part Two was at the printers, and Part Three was in production. A record number of *Back to Godheads* are also going out. Rāmeśvara concluded enthusiastically, "Our only desire is to surrender our lives to help publish and distribute millions of Your Divine Grace's wonderful books. Here in LA they are selling over 200,000 BTGs this month of December, more than even the entire Rādhā-Dāmodara party combined. Of course Rādhā-Dāmodara is selling more big books than anyone else. Devotees are more enlivened in the USA than I have ever seen for distributing your books. This will be the biggest month ever. Already one million BTGs is not enough for this month."

Nothing pleases Śrīla Prabhupāda more than hearing how his books are being printed and sold. He wrote back, "You keep your enlivened position. I was just talking to Hansadūta about the good fortune of America that Kṛṣṇa consciousness is there; and if you can cover the whole America with Kṛṣṇa consciousness that will be good for the whole world."

Then Hansadūta prabhu read out an ecstatic report by Uttamaśloka dāsa, the president of the Chicago temple, although it was not directly addressed to Śrīla Prabhupāda. It described the efforts of the devotees in the recent, record-breaking, Thanksgiving-day book-distribution competition. Out of 5,000 books sold by the three temples, Chicago, assisted by nine Rādhā-Dāmodara traveling *saṅkīrtana* party *brahmacārīs,* sold over 2,000. The letter was written to Rāmeśvara prabhu and sent on. Hansadūta read it out loud as Prabhupāda listened, eyes sometimes wide with amazement and appreciation at the incredible effort and risk his disciples are taking to distribute his books throughout this world of darkness.

"We took the challenge seriously—not that we were puffed up and over confident of victory—for we knew that anything could happen by Lord Caitanya's mercy. Then the first crew left—16 men and women—they were distributing by about 6:30 a.m. Later a small party went out by about 10:00 a.m. with more books and prasādam, and later on in the day several others came out. Altogether there were about 25 devotees at the airport throughout the day. Śrīpati and I sort of floated about helping in different ways, like you did. There were the 17 regular distributors plus Tripurāri Swami and a couple of weekend regulars and a few more newcomers.

"In the first hour and half most of the distributors had done 15 to 25 books, so by the time we got out (about 11:00 a.m.) they had already done about 300-400 books! The mornings are always good. Things were quiet; not too many announcements and no break ups or hassles. We all met together for lunch at 1:00 p.m. and took a preliminary count: over 750 books—we were close to breaking the world's record half way through the day. By 1:00 p.m. Manusuta dāsa had already done 100!!!!!! Praghoṣa dāsa 80!!!! and Tripurāri Swami 70!!!!! Our hairs began to stand on end a little as we speculated about the potential results and everyone was back distributing by 1:30 p.m.

"Basically we distribute two terminals ... there is a corridor about 25ft. wide that the people funnel through after coming from the 'fingers' ... All of the passengers come through there on their way to the baggage claim and also on their way to a flight. We found out from the paper next morning that over 220,000 people came through the airport that day!!!!

"At about 4:00 p.m a demon worker of the airlines came up to one devotee and punched him in the face; the men were stunned. Then he went up to another devotee and punched him in the face! The men and karmīs began to congregate. Tripurāri Swami came running to see what was happening; the demon punched him in the face!!! All of the devotees immediately jumped on the demon and began beating the stool out of him!!!!!!! There was a huge crowd all around and the devotees were shouting for the police to stop this man. There was blood on his face and on the ground. Praghoṣa's punch had drawn blood and there were drops of blood on Praghoṣa's clothes and drops of perspiration on his face: he was feeling very blissful!!"

Prabhupāda's eyes opened wide at the description of the fight. *"Acchā!"* he said in surprise, shaking his head in wonder at the risks his men were taking on his and Kṛṣṇa's behalf. Hansadūta was laughing and shaking his head in awe, and he read on.

"Half the crowd was in our favor and the other half against. The police came in and the demon said that we had given him a book and then taken it back and started a fight. The police arrested the devotees! This is typical of all the incidents—they attack us and we get arrested! Anyway somehow or another, by Kṛṣṇa's grace, the devotees were released and back distributing in 20 minutes.

"Around 6:00 p.m. I took a preliminary count ... I sat in the phone booth and added the score. As I added my eyebrows began to raise higher and higher! My eyes began to bulge from their sockets!! My mouth dropped open! I was speechless! Tears actually began to flow from my eyes! We had broken 1400 books! I couldn't believe it; I was stunned and took another count to be sure, and sure enough, it was right. I began to shout in ecstasy 'Hari Bol, Hari Bol, Hari Bol!' All the karmīs were looking at me through the phone booth with screwed up faces of bewilderment.

"When I got back there had been another incident.... A couple of plainclothers (cops) had tried to set up one of the women for an arrest and she tried to get one of the men to help her. One of the men tried to intervene and they arrested him and took him downstairs. Another mother went down to find the girl whom they tried to arrest and when the cops saw her they said "Where's the other girl?" "I don't know" she said. "OK, then we'll arrest you instead!" "Hey, let me go! I didn't do anything!" Two small scuffles broke out with the two devotees and the police. Another devotee came in to stop it ... and the police turned on him and the three of them mercilessly beat him up on the floor in front of many bystanders! One of the policemen's guns fell out during the scuffle and books were scattered everywhere. The devotees were then taken to jail downtown (the two men devotees). Of course this knocked at least 100 books off our score."

Prabhupāda was listening with rapt attention to the whole description, occasionally raising his eyebrows in surprise and shaking his head and smiling in appreciation. He was aglow with obvious pride at the determination of his disciples to sell his books despite all obstacles, and he listened to the entire report, blow by blow.

"While we listened to this incident and took prasādam, a demon who had found three books ripped them up and threw them in our midst. Unaffected, a little tired, but undaunted in their determination, the devotees went back to distribute. Meanwhile a huge blizzard began and traffic started jamming both on the roads and in the air.... At 10:30 p.m. I got a report from Śrīpati: over 1700 books—we might break 2,000!!!! This is incredible!! Who can imagine the mercy of Lord Caitanya Mahāprabhu? All but four of the men were coming back at 11:30 p.m.—Manusuta w/191; Praghoṣa w/153; Tripurāri Swami w/135 and Raṅganātha w/120 The first crew returned in the blizzard by 2:00 a.m. and the four others left about 1:30 or 2:00 a.m. Everyone struggled to get up for maṅgala ārati (the four latecomers didn't even go to sleep) and after an ecstatic kīrtana I ran around to get the final scores.... On Thursday we fasted from breakfast and chanted and slept till noon ārati when we had a big ārati, kīrtana and after a nice feast!!!!

"Thank you for inspiring us to compete for the mercy of the Spiritual Master. If it weren't for you we wouldn't know what to do. All glories to Śrīla Prabhupāda!

Your servant, Uttamaśloka dāsa."

Another page carried the totals for each distributor. Two men did over four hundred between them: Manusuta set a new individual world's record with 210 books, Praghoṣa was just behind with 200. Another seven, Tripurāri Swami, Raṅganātha, Romapāda, Buddhimanta, and Preraka prabhus, including two women, Ṣaḍbhuja and Jagaddhātrī dāsīs, broke the one-hundred-book mark. The grand total was 2,042 hardbound books.

At the bottom of the list Uttamaśloka added a note to Rāmeśvara: "My humble suggestion and request is that you read this letter and all of its contents to the assembled devotees of

New Dvārakā Dhāma. Even though it is irregularly composed and full of mistakes and errors, it is still very transcendentally pleasing and will be relished by all."

At the top of the letter Rāmeśvara had written in large, clear capital letters, "THE MOST ECSTATIC SKP NEWSLETTER OF ALL TIME! SHOULD BE READ ALOUD TO ALL OF THE ASSEMBLED DEVOTEES!"

When Hansadūta finished, Śrīla Prabhupāda had a huge smile on his face, clearly pleased and obviously enjoying transcendental ecstasy. He dictated his reply, not to Rāmeśvara but to Uttamaśloka. "Please accept my blessings. I read your *saṅkīrtana* newsletter with great relish. Europe and America are in great danger, this Hare Kṛṣṇa movement is enveloping them. The *saṅkīrtana* devotees are very, very dear to Kṛṣṇa. Because they are doing the field work of book distribution, Kṛṣṇa has immediately recognized them as true servants. Just like during the war time, a farm boy or ordinary clerk who goes out to fight for his country on the front, immediately becomes a national hero for his sincere effort. So Kṛṣṇa immediately recognizes a preacher of Kṛṣṇa consciousness who takes all risks to deliver his message.

"It is called *dhīra bratta*—determination. These boys and girls are *mahātmās—mahātmānas tu māṁ pārtha, daivīṁ prakṛtim āśritāḥ, bhajanty ananya manaso, jñātvā bhūtādim avyayam:*—'O son of Prtha, those who are not deluded, the great souls, are under the protection of the divine nature. They are fully engaged in devotional service because they know Me as the Supreme Personality of Godhead, original and inexhaustible.' This verse is applicable here. If these boys were under the material nature they would not take so much risk. They are *mahātmā,* they are real *mahātmā,* not that long beard and saffron cloth *mahātmā.* They are unswerving in their determination, *dhīra bratta.* All glories to the American devotees!

"I hope this letter finds you and all the *saṅkīrtana* devotees well, Your ever well-wisher, A.C. Bhaktivedanta Swami."

Book distribution is going on enthusiastically all over Europe as well; and devotees there are also taking risks. Yesterday Alanātha told Śrīla Prabhupāda that in some places in Western

Europe the devotees are being arrested simply for selling his books. He wanted to know if they should make some secret arrangement for selling. Prabhupāda replied, "Why secret? Take permission from the courts."

Alanātha said that wasn't possible. Prabhupāda, however, said that if arrested we should use the opportunity to present our case in court. "This is very important book. The government should allow us to sell. Present in court the professors' opinions, how they are giving standing orders. Why the state should restrain distributing knowledge? Do they want to keep their men in darkness? You have to preach like that."

Adversity never daunts Prabhupāda. He has firm conviction in his mission and is prepared to fight to establish Kṛṣṇa consciousness in this God-forsaken world.

Prahlāda Mahārāja's instructions give daily affirmation that Kṛṣṇa consciousness is the prime necessity of life. Therefore Śrīla Prabhupāda wants to give Kṛṣṇa consciousness freely to as many people in as many places in the world as possible, and distributing transcendental literature is the most effective means. Kṛṣṇa is empowering Śrīla Prabhupāda to write the books. He, in turn, is now investing his energy in inspiring his disciples to distribute them.

* * *

This afternoon I spoke with Harikeśa and Hansadūta Prabhus about my service. Prabhupāda is due to leave in a couple of days for Delhi and Bombay, and Gopāla Kṛṣṇa is constantly reminding me that he wants me to go to Calcutta. I confessed to them that I have become extremely attached to serving Prabhupāda, and am not particularly enthusiastic about going to Calcutta.

Harikeśa has changed his opinion about my being on the party, even to the point of telling Gopāla Kṛṣṇa directly to back off from his idea. He told him that Prabhupāda's personal party is transcendental to zonal and GBC considerations. Harikeśa advised me, "You should ask Prabhupāda if you can stay with him."

I told him I was reluctant to bother Śrīla Prabhupāda with personal requests, but he urged me to go ahead. "After all," he said, "it is directly connected to Śrīla Prabhupāda, so it affects him too. You have nothing to lose. At worst he can only say no."

I accepted his words as good advice, and tomorrow I will ask Śrīla Prabhupāda personally.

December 10th, 1975

Morning walks are always fascinating. Devotees often bring up controversial subjects just to get Śrīla Prabhupāda's reaction. Akṣayānanda Swami initiated the discussion this morning by mentioning a questionable statement made by a senior devotee in a class recently. "I was told by one devotee that the *ācārya* does not have to be a pure devotee."

Prabhupāda stopped abruptly. "What?"

"That the *ācārya* does not have to be a pure devotee."

Prabhupāda was annoyed. "Who is that rascal? Who said? Who is that rascal? The *ācārya* does not require to be a pure devotee?"

"Nitai said it. He said that Lord Brahmā is the *ācārya* in the *Brahma-sampradāya,* but yet he is sometimes afflicted by passion. So therefore it appears that the *ācārya* does not have to be a pure devotee. So it does not seem right."

"So who is that rascal? I want to know. Who has said?"

"Nitai. Nitai dāsa."

Prabhupāda was indignant and denounced such a speculative mentality. "He manufactured his idea. Therefore he's a rascal. Nitai has become an authority?"

"No, actually he said that he thought—"

"He thought something rascaldom, and he is expressing that. Therefore he is more rascal."

He walked on again, digging down to the real cause of the comments. "These things are going on. As soon as he reads some books, he becomes an *ācārya,* whatever rascal he may be."

"So there's no doubt that Lord Brahmā is a pure devotee?"

"Whatever he may be, he is *ācārya,*" Prabhupāda answered. Then he stopped again and brought in another example. "Then Kṛṣṇa is also passionate. Kṛṣṇa danced with so many *gopīs;* therefore He is passionate. These things are to be seen in this way, that 'Such exalted person, he sometimes becomes passionate, so how much we shall be careful.' This is the instruction. Then we petty things, petty persons, how much we shall be careful. It is not that '*Ācārya* has become passionate, therefore I shall become passionate. I am strict follower of *ācārya.*' These rascals say like this."

Prabhupāda gave a lengthy critique including commenting on various gurus and writers who, unable to understand Kṛṣṇa's transcendental nature, still want to comment on His words or on the literature that describe Him. They make Him appear an ordinary man, only to imitate Him. There are others who think they can understand Him simply by reading the *Gītā* or *Bhāgavatam,* despite Kṛṣṇa's statement that out of many millions of persons only one may understand Him.

Śrīla Prabhupāda said that a guru, *ācārya,* is essential for proper realization. He referred to his early morning translation work from Verse Thirty of the Seventh Chapter of *Śrīmad-Bhāgavatam.* "You'll find in today's tape that Prahlāda Mahārāja is recommending, 'Spiritual life begins by *guru-śuśrūṣā,* by serving guru.' Rūpa Gosvāmī said, *ādau gurvāśrayam,* 'The first beginning is to take shelter of the bona fide spiritual master.' *Sad-dharma-pṛcchat:* 'Then inquire from him about the spiritual path.' *Sādhu-mārgānugamanam:* 'Follow the previous *ācāryas.*' These are the steps. In *Bhagavad-gītā* Arjuna said, *śiṣyas te 'haṁ śādhi māṁ,* 'Now I become Your disciple. Teach me.' And these rascals are more than Arjuna: 'There is no need of guru.' Hm? He says, *śiṣyas te 'ham.* Why? He was already friend. Why he should submit himself as disciple? That is the beginning of spiritual life."

This conversation eventually led into another controversial subject in which Caitya-guru said, "One Life Member's wife was very upset. She came to see you with that rascal yogi. He said that the *Vedas* mention that we can drink, and that women and men have equal rights." Prabhupāda acknowledged the meeting with a nod of his head.

Caitya-guru went on, "Then as she was also saying the same thing, you answered her: 'Okay, if woman and men have equal rights, why don't you beget children in the womb of your husband?'" Prabhupāda smiled as he recalled the incident.

"She was very upset," Caitya-guru said. "She said, 'Prabhupāda sometimes says things like that which are unreasonable.'"

Everyone laughed loudly.

"No," Prabhupāda said. "I said that if you have equal rights, then make some arrangement. Sometimes you become pregnant, sometimes he becomes pregnant. Why there is not right? Equal right?"

Caitya-guru explained, "She told me, 'Prabhupāda sometimes says these things that we feel all ashamed.'"

"But in speaking spiritual understanding," Prabhupāda boldly pronounced, "we cannot make any compromise. What to speak of in Mauritius, in Chicago I told."

Then Prabhupāda related an exchange he had with a stewardess on a plane journey in America. She had taken exception to a TV show in which Prabhupāda had declared that men and women were not equal.

"I think that was the same stewardess," Harikeśa offered, "who came in the back and asked us why the Swamijī doesn't like women."

Prabhupāda was apologetic for the misunderstanding, but he wasn't about to alter the truth. "No, no. I don't say that I don't like women. But I cannot say that equal rights. How can I say? First of all show equal rights—your husband becomes sometimes pregnant, and then you become pregnant, alternately." Prabhupāda explained that even in Russia, where they had tried to make people equal, still there are managers and workers. So that sort of equality isn't ever possible.

When Harikeśa mentioned that nowadays there are women senators and ambassadors, Prabhupāda still did not concede that this means equality. "That simply requires education," he said. "But by nature the woman's body is different from man's."

However, when Caitya-guru took his comments to imply that this difference means that women are subordinate, Prabhupāda corrected him. "Not subordinate, actually. Their occupations are different That is another mistake. Just like the leg is walking and the head is directing; so although the occupation is different, both of them are important. We require the head and leg also. If simply head is there, if there is no leg, then who'll walk? This is the understanding. Not equal. Everyone must have his separate duties to serve the whole. That is the arrangement; this is real understanding. The most important part of the body is head, but that does not mean the leg is not important. Leg is important in its work, and head is important in its work. So we require both, head and tail both. Not that simply leg or simply head. But when we make comparative study, we can understand that head is more important than the leg. If you cut your leg, you can live, but if you cut your head, you'll die. Therefore the conclusion is: head is more important than the leg. Comparative study. Otherwise, head is also required and leg is also required.

"You collect some flowers, nice flowers, and add with it some green foliage, it becomes more beautiful. Simply flower is not so beautiful. When it is arrayed with some green foliage, then it becomes more beautiful. So we have to take in that sense. But comparatively, the flower is more important than the foliage. But the both of them are required."

Harikeśa added, "The foliage also becomes beautiful because of the flower."

"Yes, that is God's creation. Just like these trees: they are condemned. But still with trees we can make a beautiful garden, and that is very enjoyable. That is God's arrangement."

* * *

For an ordinary man, a life void of family affairs is almost unthinkable. Thus, Prahlāda Mahārāja's instructions to develop detachment from worldly affairs are very difficult to appreciate except by those with a very broad understanding and a genuine desire to seek out the real meaning of life.

Sitting on his *āsana* during class, the perfect representative of the Gosvāmīs, Śrīla Prabhupāda explained how painless this process can be by simply directing the inherent tendency to form bonds back toward Kṛṣṇa. "This is *bhakti* process. Not that we have to bring a separate attachment. It has to be cleansed. That is described in the *Nārada-pañcarātra: sarvopādhi-vinirmuktaṁ tat-paratvena nirmalam, hṛṣīkena hṛṣīkeśa-sevanaṁ bhaktir ucyate.* Consciousness is there, attachment is there, but it is being covered by so many designations. Just like we have got feeling for raising children; attachment, that is attachment.

"So what Mother Yaśodā is doing? She is attached to Kṛṣṇa, and that is Vṛndāvana. The same thing in otherwise: Vṛndāvana life means all attachment to Kṛṣṇa. Mother Yaśodā is attached to Kṛṣṇa, Nanda Mahārāja is attached to Kṛṣṇa, the cowherd boys are attached to Kṛṣṇa, the cows and calves are attached to Kṛṣṇa, Rādhārāṇī is attached to Kṛṣṇa, the trees are attached to Kṛṣṇa, the flowers are attached to Kṛṣṇa, the water is attached to Kṛṣṇa. That is Vṛndāvana. Vṛndāvana means the central attachment is Kṛṣṇa. That is Vṛndāvana.

"So if you can create that central attachment for Kṛṣṇa, then it is Vṛndāvana. Then you can create Vṛndāvana anywhere. Any family, any society, any country—just make the point of attachment Kṛṣṇa, and it is Vṛndāvana. That is required. That is the Kṛṣṇa consciousness movement."

Immediately after class, as Prabhupāda relaxed in his *darśana* room waiting for breakfast, Harikeśa asked some questions about Lord Brahmā. He explained that he had read in the *Śrīmad-Bhāgavatam* that every living entity upon leaving the spiritual world first falls to the level of Brahmā. He wondered whether that means that each *jīva* becomes a Lord Brahmā in charge of his own universe, or, as some devotees have interpreted, that he falls to the planet Brahmaloka?

Prabhupāda confirmed that *each* living being becomes a Lord Brahmā.

A little incredulously I tried to grasp this inconceivable fact. "But that means each and every living being has his own universe?"

Prabhupāda responded rather sharply, "Oh? *Śrīmad-Bhāgavatam* is wrong? You do not think it is possible for Kṛṣṇa to give everyone his own universe? For Kṛṣṇa anything is possible!"

We brought up the statement that at the end of the universe, Lord Brahmā, as a pure devotee and the head of our spiritual lineage, goes back to Godhead. Prabhupāda confirmed that this does not happen to every Brahmā. The living beings begin their entanglement in material life from that status and then fall further down as their material desires increase.

* * *

Today during Prabhupāda's morning massage on the roof, I tentatively asked if I could continue as his servant. I explained that I had become very attached to personally serving him, and had no specific engagement to return to. Although Gopāla Kṛṣṇa wanted me to go to Calcutta to help manage the temple, I frankly admitted that I had no experience with management in India, and thus I didn't really feel qualified.

Prabhupāda thought for a moment, and then asked what my educational background was, in particular whether I knew any foreign languages. I confessed to having no talent for learning foreign languages. In fact, it was my worst subject in school.

He listened to what I said, then sent me to call Harikeśa. "So," he asked Harikeśa, "he wants to remain with me. What do you think?"

"Well, he's doing very nicely. I think it would be a good thing for you to have a steady servant."

"What about Nitai?" (Nitai is in Bombay renewing his visa and is supposed to rejoin Prabhupāda there.)

Harikeśa was forthright. "Well, Nitai joined up with us in America. But when we got here, he wanted to leave and stay to develop the *gurukula*. There's no guarantee he won't want to leave again in another few months. But Hari-śauri can remain as your permanent servant and you won't be disturbed by any more changes."

Śrīla Prabhupāda tipped his head. "All right."

I am ecstatic! I can't believe my good fortune! Three or four weeks ago I was cleaning the temple floors, and now I am to be His Divine Grace's permanent personal servant. This is solely his mercy, because I have absolutely no qualification. Unlike his previous servants I can't cook, type, or do anything useful. Yet he's keeping me on just to purify me. Although I have no particular ability to do any of the servant's duties, I have tried to do my best to perform whatever menial service Prabhupāda has given me. It seems that because of this service attitude, Śrīla Prabhupāda is prepared to keep me on.

GOODWILL
of Silicon Valley

60 S. San Tomas Aquino Rd.
Campbell, CA 95008
(408) 374-0682

www.goodwillsv.org
Store 52 WS 74 Opr melindab
7/31/2018 12:12:02 PM #57

*Books Paperback Book 0.99	0.99
UPC: 010820160001	
Sub Total	$0.99
Total	$0.99
Cash	5.00
Change Cash	**4.01**

Goodwill gladly accepts returns within
30 days of purchase for EXCHANGE only.
Please see store for details.
Return only to the store where purchased.
Original store receipt must be presented.

000005200000074201807310000057

* * * * Customer Copy * * * *

December 11th, 1975

Prabhupāda always begins his morning walk at dawn when the still, fresh morning air and quiet atmosphere are healthy for both body and mind. Few people are out then; only the occasional bullock or buffalo amble slowly past, straining with heavily loaded carts. The drivers peer with somnambulant curiosity from under thick blankets at the "Western" Vaiṣṇavas struggling to keep up with their master, straining to hear his every word as he enlightens and entertains us with his vision of the world seen through the eyes of *śāstra*.

Śrīla Prabhupāda always strictly adheres to the authoritative statements of the Vedic literature. Yet, he expertly assesses our particular time, place, and circumstance and delivers the Vedic conclusions in a way that is easy for us to understand and apply. Despite his obvious success in spreading Kṛṣṇa consciousness without any loss of its true potency, there are those who criticize his adaption of the principles of *sādhana*. These people sometimes confuse the minds of his neophyte disciples with other ideas.

All over India many *bābājīs* and gurus claim to be authorities on spiritual life, yet they find fault with Prabhupāda's honest efforts to rescue the fallen, conditioned souls.

Here in Vṛndāvana, Śrīla Prabhupāda is especially protective of his vulnerable young disciples, always watching to see that we do not become infected with ideas that will poison our spiritual lives. He strictly forbids us to live outside of the temple, and in the past posed strong opposition to the tendency of some devotees to go off to Rādhā-kuṇḍa to live with a particular *bābājī* there. He is very much on his guard to see that his spiritual children are not beguiled by envious or ambitious spiritualists. He knows that such people can easily undermine our faith and cause havoc in our spiritual progress. He constantly insists to the temple leaders that they be alert in this regard.

These impediments to our spiritual lives do not always come from non-*Gauḍīya sampradāya* elements. Prabhupāda is aware that some of his Godbrothers are less than enthusiastic about his achievements. The natural respect for our spiritual elders we've imbibed from him could result in an unsuspecting fraternization with members of their *maṭhas*. This could leave us vulnerable to subtle impurities, derailing our dependency on Śrīla Prabhupāda. So this is also something he is constantly combatting.

During this morning's walk Akṣayānanda Swami sought sastric verification for our standards of chanting *japa*, which some have faulted. "Of course we accept," he said. "When you tell us to chant sixteen rounds, we accept that figure in perfect faith. You're the *ācārya*. But what if we wanted to convince others? Is there any *śāstric* or Vedic verse we can refer to, to corroborate that at least they must chant sixteen rounds? Or that many number of names?"

"No," Prabhupāda answered. "In the *śāstra* it is not said like that. It is said, *saṅkhyā-pūrvaka*. You must fix up in numerical strength ... whatever you can. But I have fixed up sixteen rounds, because you cannot do."

Akṣayānanda Swami confirmed, "That's all we can do."

Prabhupāda smiled and added, with a touch of irony, "Yes. That also is difficult."

Akṣayānanda Swami laughed, "Yes."

Prabhupāda continued, "Otherwise, Haridāsa Ṭhākura was chanting three *lakhs*. So, that is not possible. You should not imitate, but whatever you fix up you must do. That is wanted."

"Yes," Akṣayānanda Swami said. "I was told that in the beginning you asked the first disciples to chant sixty-four rounds?"

Prabhupāda said, "Yes."

"They were unable," Akṣayānanda Swami said, with everyone laughing. Akṣayānanda Swami added, "Then you asked them to chant thirty-two?"

Prabhupāda grinned. "Hm. *Sāṅkhya-pūrvaka-nāma-gāna-natibhiḥ. Sāṅkhya-pūrva*, or numerical strength must be there. And you should follow rigidly."

"So if we are serious and sincere, it means that that sixteen will increase to continuously chanting," Akṣayānanda Swami said.

"You can do also now," Prabhupāda said. "It's not that because I've finished sixteen rounds—You can increase. But that sixteen must be finished."

"Yes," Akṣayānanda Mahārāja agreed. "What I mean is, that's to bring us to the platform of chanting constantly. At least we must do that numerical number. If we're fortunate, we may finally be able to chant constantly day and night."

"Yes," Prabhupāda confirmed.

As we walked on, people began to appear here and there, a few at first, the numbers gradually increasing, going about their morning duties in preparation for another bout of daily labor. A few bicyclists passed us, whizzing silently along under self-propulsion, swerving at the last moment to avoid seemingly certain collision. "More dangerous than cars," Prabhupāda commented.

Śrīla Prabhupāda then initiated a conversation about his favorite subject, materialistic science. He asked whether scientists acknowledge that there is life on the sun globe. Thus a long, animated discussion ensued about the defects of scientific speculation and the inability of the godless scientists to solve the real problems of life—birth, death, disease, and old age.

He walked as far as his halfway mark, a solitary house called "Moda Place," then returned at the same brisk pace.

The temple bell rang as Prabhupāda entered the compound grounds. He walked across the red flagstones and into the temple to greet Their Lordships Kṛṣṇa and Balarāma and give *Śrīmad-Bhāgavatam* class. Just before entering the temple door, he summarized modern society. "Hiraṇyakaśipu civilization. And we are presenting Prahlāda civilization. So this is a struggle, but ultimately Prahlāda will come out triumphant and Hiraṇyakaśipu will be killed. *Jaya!* Hare Kṛṣṇa!"

Prabhupāda seems especially enlivened from his translation work on the history of Prahlāda. Many of his conversations draw graphically from Prahlāda's teachings. His classes are strong and powerful indictments of everything wrong with the modern world. The small child Prahlāda's battle and victory against overwhelming odds by his full dependence on Kṛṣṇa is a fit comparison to Prabhupāda's own single-handed struggle against a world populated with extremely materialistic people.

Today's verse was from the Seventh Canto, Sixth Chapter, Verse Nine. "Who is the person who is too much attached to household life on account of being unable to control the senses and who can liberate himself because he is bound up very strongly with the rope of affection for the family, namely wife, children, relatives, etc.?"

After reading out the Sanskrit, Prabhupāda recalled the morning's conversation and explained the difference between the scientists' approach to life and that of the devotee. The materialists derive enjoyment from killing, not knowing that this only increases their problems; but the devotees solve all problems and attain happiness by cultivating detachment.

He illustrated this by citing an incident from his early days of preaching in the West. "The examples are here. Although you are young boys and girls, you have given up so many nonsense things. This is called *vairāgya,* detachment. Meat eating is the general life of the Europeans and Americans, but at the present moment if someone offers you millions of dollars and he requests you, that you take some meat with me, I think you will deny. This is called *vairāgya.* I've actually seen. Our Gargamuni was sent to his father. I advised him that, 'Your father has big business; just take it for Kṛṣṇa consciousness.' So father was very glad, but he offered meat.

"When Gargamuni said, 'Father, I cannot take meat,' then the father became angry. He drove him away. Hiraṇyakaṣipu father. So Gargamuni came back. The young man, father's property, he refused to take it. This is *vairāgya.* And the whole Kṛṣṇa consciousness movement means *vairāgya-vidya,* the education of detachment."

He referred to Śrīla Rūpa and Sanātana gosvāmīs as examples in recent history of learned and intelligent men who, after having achieved great things materially, practiced the art of detachment to attain the goal of life. "Voluntarily accepting poverty, this is Indian civilization, this is Vedic civilization—not to increase material opulence, but to decrease. The more you decrease, you are civilized. But the Western countries, if you decrease, if you instruct them to decrease this nonsense activities, they'll say, 'Oh, this is primitive.' Primitive. This tendency is present. But actually the primitive civilization—not primitive, that is, very sober civilization—instead of increasing unwanted necessities, decrease it. That is *Śrīmad-Bhāgavatam.*"

He very nicely summed up the meaning of his spiritual movement and the opportunity he is presenting to us by the construction of the Kṛṣṇa-Balarāma Mandir and Guest House. "We are interested to construct a nice temple, but we are not interested to construct a very big skyscraper building. We should live very humbly. Vṛndāvana means everyone is engaged how to keep Kṛṣṇa in comfort. This is Vṛndāvana. Not for personal comfort. The whole Vṛndāvana is engaged, beginning from Mother Yaśodā, Nanda Mahārāja, the young *gopīs,* and the young cowherd boys; that is Vṛndāvana. Kṛṣṇa is the center. So the more we become engaged with the view to giving Kṛṣṇa the comfortable position, that is our aim of life. Then we can be liberated."

Prabhupāda's words are not impractical expressions of idealism. They have the greatest impact because he himself is the very epitome of a Brijbāsī, a resident of the holy *dhāma.* He lived for years in total poverty, without any care except how to preach. He has built a grand temple, a guest house, an *āśrama,* and he is still preaching. He goes on expending his energy for Kṛṣṇa's comfort at the expense of his own, without exhibiting any attachment for sitting down in his spacious quarters in comfortable retirement.

* * *

Harikeśa's article is taking shape, and he read it out this evening, enlivening Śrīla Prabhupāda and instigating a lively conversation. Prabhupāda's idea is to show how everything has a single ultimate cause—life. Scientists look for life within chemicals, but find none. Yet life is there, and the chemicals act and react in exact ways for a purpose. So, according to whose purpose? Understanding that, he said, should be the goal of knowledge.

The moon is also one of Śrīla Prabhupāda's favorite topics. According to the scientists, there is no life on the moon, and they say it is doubtful whether there is life on any other planet in our solar system.

Prabhupāda argued that life is everywhere: on the moon, sun, and every other planet. He said that even on this planet life can be seen everywhere: in water, air, and on land. This is the statement of *śāstra*. Living beings are not material, but spiritual, and exist in all conditions of matter.

Śrīla Prabhupāda detailed the progression of material development as described in the Third Canto of the *Bhāgavatam*. He explained how the individual elements come, one after another, in a systematic chain of cause and effect.

Harikeśa listened attentively in order to incorporate the added information into his work.

"First there is sound," Prabhupāda explained, "and from sound, ether is generated. Then from ether, air. When there is friction in the air, then fire comes—electricity. When excessive heat is there, then water comes. Just like we see how immediately after the heat of the summer the rainy season comes. From water, earth comes. If we examine a drop of water when it dries up, there is some small deposit.

"All the elements have accompanying characteristics and attributes. In this way, by the influence of time, the elements are generated, one after another. All the bodies of the living beings are made from these elements. So why not fire bodies? The scientists cannot perceive. The defect is theirs, but they judge everything by their own standards of imperfection and advertise this as knowledge."

December 12th, 1975

There is an old man with white hair and beard who recently moved into the *āśrama*. When Prabhupāda came out from his front porch to begin his walk, all the devotees offered their obeisances except the old man. He was busy throwing water from a brass *loṭā* onto the *tulasī* plants in the small garden in front of Prabhupāda's house. He wasn't very conscious of Śrīla Prabhupāda's presence, and a few devotees felt he was being offensive. Prabhupāda's mood was different. "This is devotee!" he said, turning to all of us. "Just see how nicely he is watering the *tulasī* tree. You should all do this."

Out on the road, Prabhupāda's thoughts turned to last night's discussion on Harikeśa's science article. He had Harikeśa give a brief summary of the premise to his attentive audience.

As the subdued but rising sun cast its long shadows and steadily increased its fiery and brilliant effulgence, Prabhupāda challenged that our own imperfectness leads us to think there is no life on the sun. He described how the Tata Iron and Steel Works appears from a distance as a mass of flame, but that does not mean there are no people there. Similarly, the sun appears to our eyes as a ball of flame, but that does not mean there is no life. The discussion invigorated Prabhupāda and enlivened the devotees, and the exchange continued throughout the walk.

Early morning walking is a very popular form of exercise in a country where people habitually rise at dawn, and Prabhupāda generally greets familiar faces each morning with "Hare Kṛṣṇa!" and "*Jaya!*" When a couple of local residents approached, he also drew them into the polemic. Presenting his arguments, using the example of the Tata Iron Factory, he solicited their opinions. He encouraged one of them to join in by referring to him as a "*bora-bora* scientist," a big, big scientist. After a minute's conversation they also concluded that *śāstra* must be correct.

Prabhupāda explained that it ultimately comes down to what authority one follows. Scientists quote the findings of other scientists, and we quote the *Bhagavad-gītā.* The real problem is that everyone thinks himself independent and ignores Kṛṣṇa's statement, *vāsudevaḥ sarvam iti,* that He is everything.

To emphasize the foolishness of the materialistic mentality, Śrīla Prabhupāda made a brilliantly funny imitation of a so-called independent man. "He prefers to be controlled by the laws of nature instead of by Kṛṣṇa. That is his misfortune. He is controlled, but he thinks I am free. That is ignorance. *Mūḍha.* Just like I am the state citizen. I am not free. I must work according to the state laws. 'I don't care for the government.' That is my foolishness. You have to care. At home I can say to my wife, 'I don't care for government, I don't care for police.'

But when there is crime, when the police come, then he says, 'Ohhnn!'" Śrīla Prabhupāda made a sad face, making everyone laugh.

Prabhupāda continued, "There is an example that the *murgi*, what do you call? Chicken? The male?"

Someone answered, "Cock?"

"Yes. So when in the morning, it is let loose, he says, 'I don't care for *anywwhawwoone... caawwwcawww*.' Then in the evening when he is pushed into the nest," Prabhupāda became very subdued and humble as he imitated, "'*Caawcaacaacaaw*. Whatever you like you can do. Whatever you like you can do.'"

We all burst out laughing at Prabhupāda's comic impression.

"This is the example, you see. When he's under arrest," (imitated a groveling manner). "'Now sir, whatever you like you can do with me. If you like, you can excuse me.'" Prabhupāda laughed. "And when he's out ..." Then in a loud, boastful voice, "'I don't care for anyonnnne!' *Murgi* intelligence. 'I don't care for anyone. I am God.' *Murgi* logic. *Harāv abhaktasya kuto mahad-guṇā, mano-rathenāsati dhāvato bahiḥ;* if one is not a devotee his only business is to remain on the mental platform and concoct things. And at the end he thinks that I am God. Concoction. If he's not a devotee, he has no good qualification. He is simply hovering on the mental platform."

"The sixteenth chapter describes it very nicely." I ventured, thinking of a verse in *Bhagavad-gītā*.

"Yes. *Pravṛttiṁ ca nivṛttiṁ ca, janā na vidur āsurāḥ:* In which way we have to direct our activities, in which way we shall have to stop our activities—they do not know. *Asurā ajñāna*. Because they don't take direction from God. They make their own way of speculation. Therefore they are animals, or demons. Because they do not take direction during life, therefore at the end Kṛṣṇa comes, *mṛtyuḥ sarva-haraś cāham*. All mental speculation, creation, is taken away. At death. In Bengal it is said, *kṛṣṇa nāma vinā ār sabe miche palaite patha nai yama ache piche:* 'Take to Kṛṣṇa consciousness, don't try to escape. Because behind you there is Yamarāja!' He will finish your all concoction."

* * *

This is Prabhupāda's last day in Vṛndāvana. Tomorrow he goes to Delhi for several days and then on to Bombay.

He gave his final lecture on Prahlāda Mahārāja's instructions in Seventh Canto, Sixth Chapter, Verse Ten. "Money is so dear that one conceives that money is sweeter than honey. And who can give up the desire of accumulating such money, especially in household life? The thieves, the professional soldiers, or the mercantile community try to acquire money by risking the very life."

He explained the foolishness of the materially attached persons. Everything that a person holds near and dear is in fact the very cause of his suffering, and to maintain his household a person may take on all manner of dangerous occupations, even at the risk of death. This is all going on merely because of sexual urges. He pointed out that those who are *brāhmaṇas* never take up such a risky life, preferring instead to engage in the peaceful development of spiritual affairs and to live a simple life free from such desires.

In that respect he said that the "hippie" lifestyle of many Western youths was actually an advantage. It simply had to be directed properly. "Therefore I was saying these Europeans, American boys, they prefer to become hippies; that is another process of desirelessness—don't want. They are coming from rich man's house, but they don't want. That is desireless, but it is not properly utilized. Now they have got this opportunity: how to serve Kṛṣṇa. Therefore they are advancing so quickly."

* * *

During his massage Prabhupāda heard a letter from Jayaśacīnandana dāsa in Los Angeles written on behalf of a group of *brahmacārīs*. In every ISKCON temple in the world the assembled devotees offer their obeisances to the Deities in the morning as the Govindam prayers loudly play. George Harrison recorded it and Yamunā dāsī sings the mantras.

Disturbed by this custom, Jayaśacīnandana quoted Śrīla Bhaktivinoda Ṭhākura (as well as Śrīla Prabhupāda) that if a *brahmacārī* hears and is attracted to a woman singing, it is a subtle falldown. "In light of this," he wrote, "many of the *brahmacārīs* approached the temple president to see if it would be possible that when the Deities are greeted in the morning that instead of listening to Gurudāsa Mahārāja's former wife singing the *Brahma-saṁhitā* prayers, we could listen to Your Divine Grace rather than hear a woman sing. He did not want to change the tape because it had been a standard thing in ISKCON since 1970. So requested by many devotees, I am enquiring from Your Divine Grace if we could play a tape recording of you singing instead of a woman when the Deities of Rukmiṇī-Dvārakādhīśa are greeted in the morning. I am sure that all the devotees would be enlivened to hear you instead of electric guitars, the London symphonic orchestra, etc. etc."

Prabhupāda was not pleased. He said that constantly changing things is "our Western disease." His reply was short and direct. "No! You have made some discovery. All along you have been hearing the recording of Yamunā dāsī, and now you want to change. It is not ordinary singing, it is concert. Many people are singing, so it is not bad. Just like *saṅkīrtana,* many voices are there—men and women; so it is the same thing, *saṅkīrtana.* I approve of it. Here in the Kṛṣṇa-Balarāma temple we are hearing the same recording every morning. So if it is good here, why not there?"

* * *

Every day since Prabhupāda has been in Vṛndāvana Bhagatjī has been making *chapatis* for him. Prabhupāda normally doesn't see anyone while he eats, but he makes an exception for Bhagatjī, who brings the last *chapati* in himself. He then sits and chats with Prabhupāda for five or ten minutes before returning to his home.

Today Bhagatjī came with a donation of 53,000 rupees in cash, given on behalf of his mother for the purchase of land for the *gurukula.* A stone bearing her name as the donor will be placed on the land after its registration. It is a widespread tradition in India to give donations to religious institutions in the name of one's deceased relatives. Thus they get both material and spiritual benefit in their new birth. Prabhupāda is very happy that Bhagatjī has come forward to help with the management of the temple, and he looks to him as an experienced local man to guide and train his Western disciples in the intricacies of Indian management.

* * *

Prabhupāda observed his normal program, while we spent most of the day preparing for three months' travel. He will not be returning until the Gaura Pūrṇimā festival in March. We stored everything not required in his *almirah* and cupboards, while packing everything else to be ready for our early-morning departure. We left his desk paraphernalia, toiletries, and dictaphone. They'll go in at the last minute.

CHAPTER THREE

New Delhi

December 13th, 1975

Prabhupāda likes to travel early in the morning. At 6:00 a.m., he chanted *Gāyatrī-mantra,* donned his coat, gloves, and hat, and headed for the door. In a flurry of activity Harikeśa and I quickly packed last-minute items. Harikeśa placed the dictaphone and *Bhāgavatams* into a black attache case. Meanwhile I hastily filled Prabhupāda's red vinyl briefcase with his desk paraphernalia (a pen case, a golden straw for drinking coconut juice, a jar of ink, a small silver cask filled with cardamom seeds, his glasses, *tilaka* clay, *loṭā,* mirror, mortar and pestle, a small enameled tin full of snuff for his high blood pressure, and a black Revlon manicure case.) Finally, I swiftly stuffed Prabhupāda's indoor slippers and the brass spittoon engraved with his name into my shoulder bag and rushed to catch up.

Before exiting, Prabhupāda turned to the painting of his Guru Mahārāja Śrīla Bhaktisiddhānta Sarasvatī Ṭhākura hanging on the wall. "Hare Kṛṣṇa!" he said out loud, humbly touching his forehead to its base. Then he grasped his cane, slipped on his shoes, and swiftly walked out to the side gate amidst the clamor of the *kīrtana.*

Harikeśa and I climbed into the car following Prabhupāda's, and we sped off, leaving the shelter of the holy *dhāma* for the external parts of Kṛṣṇa's kingdom.

About halfway to Delhi, on a clear stretch of road, our driver suddenly stopped for no apparent reason. Shifting the aging Ambassador's gear stick, he reversed back a hundred yards, not heeding our questions as to what was going on. Then it became apparent. He stopped the car, opened his door, and dragged in the still warm and slightly mangled body of a recent road victim—a dead rabbit. Tucking the rodent's carcass under his seat, he was about to start off again, but our loud and angry protests stopped him. It wasn't for us to question his eating habits, but there was no way we were going to allow him to keep his gruesome potluck prize in the same car. He sheepishly deposited it back on the roadway, and sped off again in pursuit of Śrīla Prabhupāda's car.

ISKCON, Todar Mal Lane,
Bengali Market, New Delhi

Today Prabhupāda talked informally with me for the first time. During his massage, as he relaxed and basked in the friendly sun, he looked out across the rooftops and suddenly asked, "So, you know our philosophy?"

"Yes, Śrīla Prabhupāda. At least I think so."

"So you can explain?"

I was a little nervous at being directly questioned, but did my best. "Everyone in the material world is suffering due to being in illusion, thinking that they are this body. Because the body is temporary, the happiness they get from it is temporary also. Actually they are not this body, they are eternal servants of Kṛṣṇa—"

Prabhupāda immediately corrected me. "First of all you tell them that they are spirit soul. Then later on what is the function of the soul can be brought out."

He seemed satisfied with my explanation, and I felt especially privileged to be personally tutored in the basic ABCs of preaching.

Even when no one is around, Śrīla Prabhupāda's mind never deviates from his mission. He sees every occasion as an opportunity to teach Kṛṣṇa consciousness, either personally or through his disciples.

* * *

One great advantage of traveling with Śrīla Prabhupāda is that you can get answers to doubts and questions very easily. I approached him today with one that has confused me just lately.

"Śrīla Prabhupāda, I have been reading in *The Nectar of Devotion* that unless one has done devotional service in a previous life, it is not possible to take it up in this life. Also, in *Bhagavad-gītā* it states that if one takes up yoga but fails to reach the goal Kṛṣṇa still rewards that person with birth in a good family, wealth, intelligence, or good looks. "So how does that work? At least in my own case, I wasn't born in a good family. They are all just ordinary, working-class people, meat-eaters with no idea of anything spiritual. Nor do I personally have any of the opulences mentioned in the *Gītā*. Yet here I am doing devotional service."

Śrīla Prabhupāda smiled and immediately gave the answer. "It is like Prahlāda Mahārāja. He did not become degraded by his birth in a demonic family. Rather, the family was glorified because of him."

December 14th, 1975

Early this morning Prabhupāda walked his usual route past the *kalā-kendras* and *bhavāns*. Cocks crowed, and occasionally a few cars and trucks passed by. Tejīyas, Hansadūta, Harikeśa, Nayanābhirāma, and I kept close as he strode the littered streets. Noting the dilapidated appearance of New Delhi, Prabhupāda remarked with disapproval, "If this is the capital, what does it indicate about the condition of the country?"

Prabhupāda questioned the wisdom of pursuing economic advancement. Pointing to a tree he challenged Harikeśa, "Where does its food come from? Kṛṣṇa is providing, but these rascals, they cannot understand. The animals have no arrangement for making industry, but nature's food is already there. They are not opening factories. Modern men claim to be more civilized, but they have simply complicated their activities by opening factories. Formerly the sages took fruits from the trees and milk from the cows. Whatever nature supplied, that's all."

Harikeśa mockingly protested, "But it's a lot of fun to drive fast cars and have sex and see movies and, this is fun you know. It's the only way to enjoy!"

Prabhupāda retorted, "Yes. Enjoyment is there in the cats and dogs. When you enjoy sex in a palace or the dog enjoys sex on the street, the value is the same. Taste does not increase or decrease. But you are thinking to enjoy sex in big palace is advancement. This is your foolishness. Actually sex enjoyment in the palace or on the street is the same."

Harikeśa made another pitch speaking for the materialists. "But there is happiness of the senses. When you have sex life—"

"Happiness there is, not for the rascals, but for the intelligent. Happiness there is. Unless there is happiness, how we are seeking for happiness? Unless there is immortality, how we are seeking for immortality? There is. But the way in which we are seeking for these things, that is wrong. That is the whole education. Just like a foolish animal, he is seeking water from the desert because it appears there is water. That is his foolishness. A human being, he knows that there is no water; it is all sand. That is the difference between animal and human being."

To emphasize even further the effects of illusion and its result, Prabhupāda told us two anecdotes of what it means to be an animal: A dog was carrying some bread in its mouth. Seeing its own reflection in a pool of water, it thought there was another dog carrying a piece of bread, and immediately barked to challenge its imaginary competitor, hoping to gain more bread. Thus he lost his bread in the water. Similarly, a lion was once tricked into thinking there was another lion within a well. He gave a roar, and a roar came back. Thus he jumped into the well and lost his life. "Although lions are fabulously strong," Prabhupāda told us, "in spite of so much strength, he's an animal. Similarly, this modern civilization, in spite of so much so-called advancement, they are simply animals. A big animal is eulogized by a small animal, that's all. Animal is animal—big animal or small."

Prabhupāda pointed out one of New Delhi's flea-bitten dogs sniffing in the gutter. The wretched dog was homeless, scratching for food, and suffering without a master. "This is *śūdra,*" he said. "If anyone depends on the master's mercy, he's a *śūdra.* Here in New Delhi, these big, big buildings, big officers, as soon as the government will sell, they will be street dogs, that's all. Now they are plundering by official instrument. So when the government will be finished they will be street dog.

This is your civilization. Immediately, if all of a sudden there is attack on New Delhi, all the people will starve. There is no food at home, and they'll die."

"That's a really important point," Harikeśa responded, "that the government takes more and more, and everybody gets poorer and poorer."

"Yes," Prabhupāda replied. "The government is also poor because they do not know how to govern. *Buddhi yasya balaṁ tasya:* if one has got intelligence, he has got strength."

Harikeśa added, "Change of government means getting poorer."

"Just like they say," Prabhupāda confirmed. "A change of theories by the rascals. Change means rascal. Anything change means it is the domain of rascals. Pandemonium. Just like in *Manu-saṁhitā* it is said that women should not be given independence. Once said, that is fact. If you want to change, you suffer. That's all."

I said, "Any deviation from absolute law means immediate suffering."

Prabhupāda agreed. "*Bās!* Immediately you have to suffer."

"You're painting a pretty bleak picture," Harikeśa suggested.

Prabhupāda didn't immediately catch his idiomatic expression, so Harikeśa elaborated. "The one you're painting of society and the future. There's no hope."

"No," Prabhupāda said. "Unless they take to Kṛṣṇa consciousness, there is no hope; that's a fact. There will be more chaotic condition, and everyone will suffer and perish. *Ācchinna-dāra-draviṇā yāsyanti giri-kānanam* [1]. This is already predicted. I am not painting. It is already there; I am simply repeating. That's all. I am not speculator."

"Actually most of them are aware that they're in a very bad position," I added. "Everybody is expecting another war."

"Yes, just see. This is the capital of India, just see the position. We can now, understand."

Prabhupāda somberly observed an overloaded hand-drawn cart pulled by several dirty, poorly dressed, and barefoot men. Their veins bulged as they strained and sweated to get their

---

1 *"Having their wives and property taken away ... the citizens will flee to the mountains and forests."* S.B. 12.2.8

load to its destination. "Economic development," he mocked. "Where is economic development for these men? When there was no economic development, the same *taila* [cart] and poor people with black cloth were there. And now, the same thing is still there. So where is development? Nature's law you cannot check. It must go on. *Bhāgavata* says, 'Don't try to improve all these things, it is not possible. Improve your Kṛṣṇa consciousness; that will be benefit for your life.'"

Keeping up a brisk pace, Prabhupāda turned his attention to the *kalā-kendras*. Noting their advertisements for *māgha-melā* dances, he said they are simply encouraging illicit sex. "Yet if our men dance, they say we are crazy."

He told Tejīyas that he should immediately hire some of the halls for a week at a time and present plays, *kīrtana*, and *prasādam*. "Five minutes talking and ten minutes *kīrtana*—alternate. Tickets can be given and donations asked for." Because Nayanābhirāma has had previous experience in art and drama, Prabhupāda told him to arrange performances all over Delhi. He said that way we won't require any big arrangement for living, but our propaganda will go on. Prabhupāda seemed certain that this program will attract thousands of people. "Of course," he added with a touch of irony, "I can suggest, but whether you do it is another thing."

Walking back toward the temple, loud train whistles and increasingly noisy traffic signaled the awakening of the city. The conversation turned to another topic. Hansadūta told Prabhupāda about the plight of a former GBC secretary, Śyāmasundara, an early recruit to the Kṛṣṇa consciousness movement. He has fallen into considerable difficulty in a bad business deal, losing a large amount of the Society's money. He is now selling jewelry to repay it, but neglecting his devotional life.

Prabhupāda, the ideal representative of Śrī Caitanya Mahāprabhu, compassionately remarked, "No. He has done a mistake, so he wants to rectify it. He wants to bring money. But if the money is lost, it is lost. Let him come back. A life saved is more important than saving the money. So if I could know the address, then I could write? I wanted to write him a letter."

Harikeśa said Śyāmasundara told him that he wanted to

make millions of dollars for Prabhupāda so that he can make up for his mistake.

Prabhupāda responded with loving concern for his wayward disciple, "Yes, and I am thinking when making millions of dollars he may not be lost. I want one soul saved. That is more than millions of dollars."

* * *

One reason for remaining in Delhi is to see Gulzarilāl Nanda again in a follow-up to the earlier Kurukṣetra trip. Nandajī arrived about midday while Prabhupāda was taking his massage on the roof of number nine. Sitting on a chair as Prabhupāda relaxed in his *gamsha* in the sun, he listened carefully while Prabhupāda revealed his desires for Kurukṣetra. Prabhupāda first requested Nandajī to get as much free land as possible for us at Jyotisar. (Prabhupāda wants between four and ten acres.) As soon as that land is acquired, Prabhupāda said he will immediately begin building a Kṛṣṇa-Arjuna Temple there. But he put him off for now about purchasing property at Brahma-sarovara. After the rainy season he said he would reappraise the land and decide whether to begin a project there.

Nandajī is eager for ISKCON to build a college at Brahma-sarovara as quickly as possible to train up young people. He began to confide how anxious he is about the atheistic influence of the USSR on the country and the present government's close relationship with the Soviets.

But Prabhupāda cut him off. India is in a state of official emergency, and many have been jailed for simply criticizing the government. "We are not interested in politics," he said emphatically, "only Kṛṣṇa."

Nandajī politely took his leave, promising to pursue Prabhupāda's requests.

* * *

During the afternoon *darśana* there was a lively discussion about how to preach effectively. Prabhupāda challenged us to go beyond mere parrotlike repetition and come to the platform of genuine realization. He emphasized that people will be convinced of our philosophy only when we present everything with logic and *śāstra*. Otherwise, they will simply be cheated by so many false yogis and swamis who misuse the *Vedas* for making money. Everyone else is presenting the impersonalist and *māyāvādī* idea, removing Kṛṣṇa from the picture.

He concluded, "Therefore, these rascals they have no clear understanding, and they are swamis, yogis, and *avatāras.* It is a very dangerous position, very dangerous. We have to deal with all rascals and fools. And they have made some position; of course, that position is nothing. Mr. Nanda is also big on this idea, *nirviśeṣa śūnyavādī.* Still, we cannot change our position. We must go on with our conviction, and that is real, reality. So, begin *kīrtana.*"

December 15th, 1975

Bhagavat dāsa, an intelligent and talkative twenty-five year old New Yorker, currently the Calcutta temple president, passed through on his way to renew his visa in the West. He told Prabhupāda that some astrologers and political experts are predicting a big war early in 1976 with China, Pakistan, and America against India and Russia.

Prabhupāda shrugged, saying that an atomic war will be short and severe. "But war or not," he said, "it makes no difference for us. A devotee doesn't care if he lives or dies; he always serves Kṛṣṇa. We shall simply continue to do our duties—chant Hare Kṛṣṇa."

Bhāgavat also asked if he could take *sannyāsa.* Śrīla Prabhupāda's response wasn't one of enthusiasm, but rather noncommittal. Never wanting to dampen anyone's enthusiasm for preaching, he tactfully agreed to consider Bhagavat for *sannyāsa* at next year's Gaura Pūrṇimā festival in Māyāpur.

Bhagavat is a portly, almost overweight, fellow, and later Prabhupāda told us that for *sannyāsa* one should be "fit, not fat."

* * *

Interviews with prospective Hindi translators are still going on, and His Divine Grace has already engaged a Mathurā woman named Dr. Paliwal. Later this evening Mr. Singh arrived and showed Prabhupāda his Ph.D. thesis—a lengthy treatise on Caitanya Vaiṣṇavism.

Impressed with the man's work, Śrīla Prabhupāda said he wanted to spend more time with him, examining the document and testing his ability to translate. This posed a dilemma. It was too late to do anything on the spot, and Prabhupāda has to fly to Bombay first thing in the morning. Prabhupāda asked Mr. Singh if he could come to Bombay. He was immediately agreeable but could not afford to buy a plane ticket.

Prabhupāda thought for a moment and then called in Harikeśa and Hansadūta. "So, what tickets do we have for Bombay?"

"Well, there are four: yours, Hansadūta's, mine, and Harisauri's."

"So give him his," Prabhupāda said, without even a glance in my direction.

Harikeśa gave me a sympathetic smile and shrugged. Within a moment my ticket was handed over to Mr. Singh. The man happily left, and Śrīla Prabhupāda took rest.

CHAPTER FOUR

Bombay

December 16th, 1975

Delhi airport was filled with its usual bustle, and while Hansadūta and Harikeśa dealt with the baggage and other formalities, Śrīla Prabhupāda sat calmly in the boarding area. As he waited, a friendly Bengali gentleman, Mr. M. N. Chaudhuri, talked with him for some time. It pleased Prabhupāda to discover that the man worked in the West Bengal Department of Development and Planning.

Mr Chaudhuri spoke enthusiastically and appreciatively about Śrīla Prabhupāda's worldwide missionary work. He offered to help in any way he could, so Prabhupāda wrote down his name and address. At six o'clock the party, along with the Ph.D. candidate, flew out.

I booked myself on the next flight out at 10:00 a.m. I had a little money saved, just enough for the fare, and by midday I too was in Bombay.

Hare Kṛṣṇa Land
Juhu Beach, Bombay

Hare Kṛṣṇa Land at Juhu Beach is only about half an hour drive from the airport—six rupees by taxi. The site is very impressive. Situated in the heart of exclusive Juhu, only a minute from the beach, it covers more than four acres, with half a dozen three-storied apartment buildings spaciously dotted among the many swaying palm trees.

It surprised me to find that the "temple," at the front of the land, is merely a simple shelter—a small, brick Deity room and a *darśana* area barely large enough to hold fifty people. It is completely open on three sides, covered with a flimsy tin roof balanced on thin, iron poles.

Nevertheless, the worshipable Deities, Śrī Śrī Rādhā-Rasabihārī, are beautifully dressed and meticulously cared for, despite the inadequate facilities.

I am surprised to discover that nondevotees occupy many apartments on our property, several of them even meat-eaters. When Śrīla Prabhupāda obtained the land, six occupied buildings were already there, and according to Indian law their tenancies can't be terminated. Devotees are gradually using those few flats vacated by former tenants.

Śrīla Prabhupāda has arranged to have the third floor built on the top of each building to provide living quarters for his disciples. That work has just been completed, and the foundation is now being laid for the new temple complex. Some used materials left over from the Vṛndāvana temple construction have been trucked in.

A devotee directed me to Śrīla Prabhupāda's quarters in a building at the back of the land. After climbing several flights of steep steps to the top floor, I entered the open receptio-room door at the same moment His Divine Grace entered from the other side. He had just taken his massage.

"Oh, so you are here!" he said in mild surprise as I offered my obeisances. "All right, very good!" he remarked, disappearing into the bathroom.

Nitai appeared next; he had just given Prabhupāda his massage. "Oh, you're here! Okay, I don't mind. I'd rather develop the *gurukula* in Vṛndāvana anyway."

Then Harikeśa came in, also surprised to see me. I found out later that when my ticket was handed over to Mr. Singh, everyone had considered my tenure with the party at an end. They assumed that Nitai would rejoin the party as Prabhupāda's servant. Apparently I was the only one who had not realized it.

But Prabhupāda was pleased that I came. He sent me to find Girirāja, the temple president, and instructed him to repay me the full cost of my air fare. He advised me that I should keep my own money for emergency uses.

* * *

Yesterday Prabhupāda gave Hansadūta permission to buy a bus and start a traveling *saṅkīrtana* party in India. He suggested that they carry Śrī Śrī Gaura-Nitāi in a box. Then wherever they stop, they should take Their Lordships out, sit under a tree, and hold *kīrtana.* Prabhupāda assured him that many people would come. Afterwards *prasādam* could be distributed and a discourse held.

"Do it immediately!" Prabhupāda told him enthusiastically. He went on to explain that he had planned to do this, "But somehow I came to the West; it was Kṛṣṇa's arrangement. Now the Americans are doing."

Hansadūta thus busied himself today investigating prices both here and in Europe for a suitable vehicle.

December 17th, 1975

It was a little chilly this morning, and while getting ready for the morning walk Prabhupāda noticed that I was shivering. I was wearing only a *kurtā.* He called me into his room and gave me a lightly embroidered *chadar.* It had been given to him in Delhi, and he had worn it a few times. I was surprised. It was indeed a special honor. His Divine Grace's thoughtfulness and concern completely endears him to me.

Harikeśa was also surprised, or perhaps shocked would be more apt, when he saw it draped around my shoulders. He asked me, "Why are you wearing Prabhupāda's *chadar?*"

"I didn't have anything warm to wear so Prabhupāda gave it to me," I explained.

In an admonishing tone he said, "There's a standing rule that the servants should never ask the spiritual master for anything."

But when I told him that Prabhupāda had just given it to me without my saying anything, he immediately softened, appreciating Śrīla Prabhupāda's kindness. I value his good advice nonetheless. Harikeśa is excellent association for me because of his complete dedication to pleasing Śrīla Prabhupāda.

* * *

Prabhupāda takes his walks along a beach only half a mile from the temple. He leaves at six-thirty and returns an hour later for Deity *darśana.*

Dr. Chaturbhai P. Patel usually meets him on the beach. He's short, stocky, and always barefoot. With his raucous laugh Dr. Patel seems terribly full of himself; nevertheless, he has developed an attraction for Prabhupāda's association.

He obviously holds Prabhupāda in great respect, although it isn't always the humble and submissive sort that the devotees cultivate. He knows some Sanskrit and has studied Prabhupāda's *Bhāgavatam;* this makes for lively conversation on both topical and philosophical matters. Dr. Patel is known among the devotees for expressing strong, and generally tainted, opinions, although he cushions them with good humor, ultimately agreeing with Śrīla Prabhupāda's pure and unbiased spiritual vision.

This morning they talked briefly about human civilization. Dr. Patel blamed the spoiling of modern civilization on the atheistic communist philosophers: Marx, Hegel, and Engels.

Śrīla Prabhupāda didn't agree. "Everyone is manufacturing his own ideas," he said, "including Indian leaders like Mohandāsa Gandhi and others. But if people take to the movement of Śrī Caitanya Mahāprabhu, the country will change for the better overnight."

As our small group walked along, the Arabian Sea's waves mildly lapped at our feet. By seven o'clock hundreds of people were walking and exercising up and down the flat, sandy shore. Occasional sounds of jets boomed overhead as planes arrived and departed from the nearby Santa Cruz airport. Various vendors gradually set up along the hotel fronts, selling *dobs* (green coconuts), tea, *bidis,* and the like.

Several gentlemen came forward to offer their *praṇāmas* to Prabhupāda. He responded with, "Hare Kṛṣṇa! *Jaya!*"

Dr. Patel introduced one such admirer as a renowned poet from Dvārakā. His name was Bethai, meaning "coming from the Dvārakā-*bet.*" Dr. Patel mentioned that Mr. Bethai only wrote poems about God.

Prabhupāda good-naturedly quoted a Bengali poem that wherever one finds himself he should neither perform religious acts nor sinful ones; he should simply always remember the lotus feet of Kṛṣṇa.

This prompted Dr. Patel to voice a complaint about how

our *pūjārīs* dress the temple Deities. "Sir, lotus feet. These people are actually putting such a long *varga* [dress]. I am trying to see the lotus feet of God here, *arcā-vigraha.* Well, I am unable. Instruct them to put up the *varga* a little, so that we can have *darśana* of His sacred feet. Please tell them. Too long *vargas,* you simply can't see anything."

Girirāja patiently explained that the Deities' feet can always be seen throughout the day; but when They wear Their night clothes, Their feet are not visible. Since Dr. Patel only comes early in the morning, while the Deities are in still in Their night outfit, he never gets to see Kṛṣṇa's feet.

There seems to be a mild acrimony in Dr. Patel's dealings with the devotees. He behaves as if he ought to be given some special entitlement by us as a learned and elderly person, and he tries to play off his relationship with Śrīla Prabhupāda to extract some special attention.

At any rate, in this instance, Prabhupāda didn't take the matter too seriously. His mind was working in a different way. Whether the Lord's feet were visible or not, he was content that after the long, hard struggle to establish the temple on Hare Kṛṣṇa Land, their Lordships were still with us. Prabhupāda's response to Dr. Patel's complaint was thus full of gratitude and appreciation. "How He [Kṛṣṇa] sat tight to call everyone to come and see? Hm? The Municipality came to drive Him away!"

For several years Prabhupāda has fought on Śrī Śrī Rādhā-Rasabihārī's behalf. The previous owner tried to cheat Prabhupāda of the land, while the municipality had presented severe objections to establishing a temple. At one time they had even half-demolished the Deities' temporary shelter. They burned the roof-support poles with oxyacetylene torches and carried the protesting devotees off in a police truck. They even went so far as to begin ripping off the Deity room's roof with Śrī Śrī Rādhā-Rasabihārī still inside! Only a last-second intervention by a few favorable people in local government prevented the total destruction.

Returning to the temple we observed the regular program of greeting Their Lordships, *guru-pūjā,* and class. Then Prabhupāda retired to his quarters for the day.

* * *

During mail time, as Prabhupāda relaxed up on the roof, he dictated a letter to Jayapatākā Swami in Māyāpur. He enclosed an introductory letter for him to meet Mr. Chaudhuri, the gentleman we met at the airport yesterday. Seeing that meeting as Kṛṣṇa's arrangement, Prabhupāda requested Jayapatākā to visit him personally with *prasādam* and flowers and to invite him to Māyāpur. He wants Jayapatākā to try to enlist his help in getting the government to acquire land for our ISKCON Māyāpur development scheme. He also suggested Mr. Chaudhuri might be able to help Jayapatākā Mahārāja, an American, with his application for Indian citizenship.

A letter from Mahāṁsa Swami included a progress report on Hyderabad, where another new temple is steadily being built. Work has already begun on raising the dome. The project is costing 75,000 rupees per month, which the devotees are collecting throughout South India. Mahāṁsa also reported four small books—*Śrī Īśopaniṣad, Rājavidyā, Perfection of Yoga* and *Matchless Gifts*—have been translated into Telegu.

Śrīla Prabhupāda was most happy to hear about a small bullock cart traveling *saṅkīrtana* party. Mahāṁsa wrote, "The bullock cart party (only three devotees) were very successful on their second attempt. They collected lots of rice, distributed *prasādam* and small literatures, evening programs, and sleeping under a different tree everyday. They are thrilled and so enthusiastic. They love this kind of preaching work. Now I am giving them a portable sound system and more equipment and one more devotee and sending them immediately to a massive voyage on bullock cart all the way to the Māyāpur festival!"

Prabhupāda replied enthusiastically, "Naturally the *saṅkīrtana* men traveling with the bullock carts are blissful. It is Lord Caitanya's engagement. Lord Caitanya personally traveled all over India for six years. His program was simply *kīrtana* and *prasādam* distribution. Lord Caitanya never spoke philosophy in public. When He met big scholars like Sārvabhauma Bhaṭṭācārya he spoke philosophy, otherwise for the mass of people, *kīrtana* and *prasādam* distribution. So continue this program, it is very pleasing to Lord Caitanya."

Prabhupāda also received a long letter from Svarūpa Dāmodara dāsa, who holds a Ph.D. in organic chemistry. Svarūpa Dāmodara listed seven major contradictions between the statements of modern astronomers and the *Bhāgavatam*. He wants to present a clear and direct challenge to modern scientists, but because the *Bhāgavatam* statements are so brief, he asked for further information on Vedic astronomy. He especially asked about the distances to the Sun and Moon.

He also presented a comparative chart about the days of the week. He wrote, "According to Encyclopedia Americana, the system of the days of the week, based on the seven planets and their ruling demigods, originated in Europe near the beginning of the Christian era. However, from the *Bhāgavatam* we know that this cannot be true. It has been since the time of the *Vedas*." His chart revealed this very clearly. [See Appendix A]

The seriousness of his disciple's approach to this problem pleased Prabhupāda. He replied, "This scientific book should be done very carefully, so that people in general may not be misled by the over-intelligent scientists. There are so many contradictory things, but we have our authority and they have their authority. Our knowledge is from Vedic scriptures, which we accept as definite and without any mistake. A modern scientist believes that there was no civilization before three thousand years. Our *Bhāgavatam* was spoken by Śukadeva Gosvāmī five thousand years ago, and he is explaining as I have heard it from authority. So we have got *paramparā* system for millions of years. If there was no civilization before three thousand years, then how this subject matter of knowledge could be discussed? How could it be received through *paramparā* system? So there is contradiction certainly. But the statement that there was no civilization three thousand years ago can be adjusted by the conviction that there was civilization millions and millions of years ago."

Prabhupāda advised Svarūpa Dāmodara to consult "any learned astronomer" for astronomical information. In particular he mentioned that Śrīla Bhaktisiddhānta Sarasvatī had been extremely learned in that field.

"The main point," he stressed, "is to prove that life comes from life and not from matter. If we prove this one principle, so many other issues can be brought forward for serious consideration. The scientists' knowledge is imperfect and therefore always changing, but Vedic knowledge is perfect and never changeable."

Prabhupāda mentioned the example in the *Vedas* of the *agni-pok* germ. It lives within fire, even though scientists say life cannot exist there. He said, "There are so many contradictions, but we have our own defense. Why should we blindly accept imperfect scientists? The word 'progress' is used when there is imperfection in the beginning. So this regular changing of standard of knowledge in the name of progress proves that they are always imperfect. It is a fact they are imperfect because they gather knowledge with imperfect senses. At any rate, we cannot deviate from Vedic knowledge."

Prabhupāda ended his letter requesting him to come to the Māyāpur festival because afterwards he hopes to visit Mānipura, Svarūpa Dāmodara's birthplace.

There was also news from a Gujarati devotee, Jaśomatīnandana, who has been in Ahmedabad for the past few days organizing a new ISKCON center. He arranged for Śrīla Prabhupāda to lecture at programs in several nearby villages and towns. The King of Sanand has even invited Prabhupāda to stay in the palace. The Yuvrāj, the king's son who recently became a Life Patron, plans to host Prabhupāda and up to twelve devotees with a big parade when he arrives.

Prabhupāda approved, and is scheduled to fly to Ahmedabad on the morning of December 25th.

* * *

In the evening Prabhupāda had an engagement at the home of Mrs. Gopī Kumāra Birla and her son, Aśoka. She had invited friends from many of the leading business families in Bombay. The Birlas are possibly the richest, and one of the most influential, families in India. Girirāja had previously suggested to her several possible topics for the evening's discussion, and she has chosen "How to Become Successful in Life."

The Birlas had set up an *āsana* on a side lawn of their large, opulent estate. Next to it, on a table, the devotees placed a shrine with small brass Rādhā-Kṛṣṇa Deities.

Śrīla Prabhupāda arrived in the Birla's white Mercedes. He

immediately noticed that his seat was placed higher than that of the Deities. So he had the devotees remove the base of the *āsana,* making his seat lower.

Then, above the muted clamor of Bombay's evening traffic, Prabhupāda addressed his attentive audience on the evening's topic. "Rādhārāṇī and Durgā, both of them are *prakṛtis* of the Supreme Personality of Godhead, but one *prakṛti* is meant for controlling this material world and the other *prakṛti* is meant for blessing the spiritual world.

"Rādhārāṇī, the name has come from the word *ārādhyate. Ārādha* means worshiping, beginning from Rādhārāṇī and her expansion Lakṣmī in Vaikuṇṭha. Here we worship Mother Lakṣmījī, the goddess of fortune, to receive some favor, but in the Vaikuṇṭha world there are many hundreds of thousands of Lakṣmīs, and with great respect they are engaged in serving the Supreme Lord.

"So, we being expansions of the spiritual Lakṣmī, or Rādhārāṇī, our duty is to serve Rādhārāṇī, and through Rādhārāṇī serve Kṛṣṇa. This is Kṛṣṇa consciousness movement. We are missing this point. That instead of learning from Rādhārāṇī how to serve Kṛṣṇa, we are being controlled by the other *prakṛti,* material energy, Durgā, with weapons in her ten hands. This is our position."

Śrīla Prabhupāda possesses a unique ability to link anyone from any walk of life to the common goal of spiritual attainment. His preaching is always perfectly suitable for the time, place and circumstance. To the leaders of this wealthy business community he thus offered a pertinent example.

"In this material world they do not know what is the aim of life. Everyone is very much expert to see his interest. Two businessmen, they are agreeing; but everyone is trying to see his personal interest first. This is called *svārtha-gatim.* That is natural. But Prahlāda Mahārāja says, *na te vidhuḥ svārtha-gatiṁ hi viṣṇum.* Unfortunately, these materialistic persons they do not know what is real interest. The real interest is Viṣṇu, how to serve Viṣṇu."

Prabhupāda came directly to the keynote of his address. "The subject matter was how to become successful in life. Kṛṣṇa comes to instruct this simple truth—that you are being controlled by the material energy. You give up this business, you be controlled by the spiritual energy, and your life is successful. Śrī Caitanya Mahāprabhu has said *jīvera svarūpa haya nitya kṛṣṇa dāsa*. But our disease is, instead of becoming *dāsa* we are trying to become the master of the *prakṛti*. This is called the materialistic way of life. So that will not make us happy at any stage of our life. The success of the human form of life is to understand this: our relationship with God. And we should act in relationship with God. Then our success of life will be achieved. This is the main purpose of Kṛṣṇa consciousness movement."

The Birla family have become equally famous for both their religious interests and business ventures, with Birla temples prominent in most Indian major cities. Śrīla Prabhupāda took the evening's opportunity to invite the family to expand from the merely religious to practicing a full transcendental life. "That is Śrī Caitanya Mahāprabhu's mission," he said. "He wished especially Indians to take this job of preaching the teachings of *Bhagavad-gītā* all over the world. The mission is they must be very, very merciful to all outsiders. That is India's mission. They are in darkness, *tamasi;* bring them in the light: *tamasi mā jyotir gamaḥ*. This attempt has been done by us individually with teeny effort but it is becoming successful. But every one of us should become completely aware of this movement and take this mission."

Śrīla Prabhupāda's speech was direct and frank. "Kṛṣṇa said, 'You just offer a little flower and water to Me.' If you think that, 'We have got money, the money is for my enjoyment, and Kṛṣṇa may be offered a little water and flower,' that is cheating. That is not good. According to your position you must worship. This is wanted. To become very big business man is not ordinary thing; it requires *tapasya,* very great labor, brain, *yat tapasyasi*. But the result, Kṛṣṇa says, *kuruṣva mad-arpaṇam*. He's asking, 'Give it to Me.' So there is no harm to become very big business man, earning money. That is all right. But you give it to Kṛṣṇa. Then in any position you can remain Kṛṣṇa conscious. And if you remain Kṛṣṇa conscious, then you will understand Kṛṣṇa."

Winding up his lecture, Prabhupāda asked for questions several times, but got no response.

Girirāja, whose lawyer father had once offered him a million dollars to give up Kṛṣṇa Consciousness, spoke up. "The process of hearing and then asking questions is the way to clarify our understanding, just like Kṛṣṇa and Arjuna. So actually we must have some questions in our minds, otherwise we would all immediately surrender to Kṛṣṇa."

Prabhupāda agreed, "Yes, either you surrender to Kṛṣṇa, or clear it by question."

Still, there was no response. So the lecture ended, and while other devotees showed a film on the lawn, Śrīla Prabhupāda and a small group of us were invited inside to take *prasādam.*

Aśoka Birla, who had donated three *lakhs* of rupees for construction of the ISKCON Vṛndāvana center, expressed his happiness at the evening's program. Then Mrs. Birla and her brother-in-law, Brijratan Mohta, led us upstairs in the lift to a large and beautifully furnished dining room.

Sitting at the head of a long and highly polished mahogany table, Śrīla Prabhupāda chatted congenially with his hosts, complimenting them on the delicious meal and answering a variety of questions.

After a cordial departure, we finally arrived back at the temple by eleven o'clock. It was a successful preaching engagement, but on the way back Prabhupāda mentioned to Girirāja, "That no questions were asked after the lecture indicated a lack of interest on the part of the guests."

December 18th, 1975

Kīrtanānanda Swami, one of Śrīla Prabhupāda's first disciples and a GBC member, arrived very early this morning from America. He gave a brief report on New Vṛndāvana, our ISKCON farm community in West Virginia. He distributed some delicious *mahā-prasādam* from Śrī Śrī Rādhā-Vṛndāvanacandra.

Prabhupāda asked about Kīrtanānanda's health, and Mahārāja explained that he has been suffering due to paralysis in his left arm. Prabhupāda didn't register much concern, telling him not to worry. He said we should expect the body to give us trouble. We must simply take shelter of the holy names of the Lord.

Kīrtanānanda Mahārāja inquired with some concern how he can improve his ability to remember Sanskrit verses. Prabhupāda almost chided him for asking. He said that because he is a devotee, as long as he speaks the philosophy and chants Hare Kṛṣṇa, these other things are not of such great concern.

Kīrtanānanda Mahārāja has come via New York, and his report on the management of the new temple building there was not encouraging. He said that the project lacked a strong leader and that the financial situation was difficult. Prabhupāda immediately suggested that Madhudviṣa Swami, the GBC for Australia, could go and take charge. Coincidentally, this morning Prabhupāda received a telegram from Madhudviṣa inviting him to the Melbourne *Rathayātrā* on January 10th, 1976.

* * *

During this morning's walk, with Dr. Patel to accompany us, Prabhupāda considerably broadened our perspectives by explaining the real standard of education and its relationship to culture. To describe an educated man he quoted Cāṇakya Paṇḍita, "*Mātṛvat para-dāreṣu:* he sees every woman as mother, except his own wife. And *para-dravyeṣu loṣṭavat:* and other's property, possessions, just like garbage. And *ātma-vat sarva-bhūteṣu:* and feeling for everyone as he himself is feeling the pains and pleasures. If one has attained this stage, then he is considered educated."

Progressing along the soft sands in the pleasant cool of the new dawn, Prabhupāda strongly emphasized that real education is to become *upādhi*-less (free from material designations). With his razor-sharp intelligence, so finely honed on the strap of Vedic knowledge and insight, Prabhupāda exposed the leaders of the world as devoid of true education. He quickly chopped down to size two popular Indian politicians often held in high regard by the masses. "What is education?" he challenged. "*Bhagavad-gītā* says you are not this body. That is the beginning of education. Now education means be nationalist, and drive away and bark. Even in our country, Mahātmā Gandhi was also infected, 'Quit India! Quit India!'"

"He did not mean quit India," Dr. Patel offered. "He meant you quit your matter of ruling. I mean actually—"

But Prabhupāda insisted, "It was his exact word, 'Quit India!' As soon as you think 'You are my enemy, he is my friend,' then there is no education, that's all. This is standard of education: *Sama-darśinaḥ.* Kṛṣṇa says, 'Arjuna, you are rascal. It is not the business of the *paṇḍita* to think like that!' He never thought that the Kauravas were the enemy, no. That is not the fact. It is duty to fight the just cause. That was His instruction."

"Mr. Nehru said Kṛṣṇa was the greatest warmonger," Dr. Patel said.

"And he is a rascal," Prabhupāda retorted.

Dr. Patel laughed. "He was saying so. He thought himself to be a very big man.

"That is asuric position," Prabhupāda said. "'Who is like me?' And *bhakta,* Caitanya Mahāprabhu is teaching: *tṛṇād api sunīcena taror api sahiṣṇunā*—this is education. Therefore Kṛṣṇa has spoken of these people as *mūḍha.* 'No, they have credit, they have passed so many examination.' *Māyāpahṛta-jñāna.* This kind of education has no value because they are forgetting the real point of education."

The conversation went on with Prabhupāda criticizing the *sāṅkhya* philosophers who believe that creation comes about by chance.

Dr. Patel questioned, "But sir, this *sāṅkhya* philosophy also believes in *Vedas.*"

"No, no," Prabhupāda corrected. "*Sāṅkhya* philosophy by the original Kapila. And this later *sāṅkhya* philosophy—"

"Is from another rascal!" Dr. Patel completed.

"Yes! Now you have learned!" Prabhupāda exclaimed.

Everyone laughed loudly, enjoying the education of Dr. Patel. Through Śrīla Prabhupāda's association he is learning the art of good discrimination and giving up his pseudoliberalism. By Prabhupāda's grace he is beginning to understand that not everyone has something worthy to say or hear. A large part of Śrīla Prabhupāda's appeal is his impartiality. His objective statements are irrefutably sensible and logical.

"The real problem," Śrīla Prabhupāda went on to explain, "is that people are not interested in hearing from the *Gītā* and *Bhāgavatam,* although these literatures explain the essence of all knowledge. This subject matter becomes palatable by association, but without the association of devotees no one becomes interested in them. Even though we are giving daily lectures, still it is not palatable for the ordinary man."

Dr. Patel jokingly attributed this to Śrīla Prabhupāda's strong preaching tactics. "You fire them!" he said, laughing his loud, discordant laugh.

Prabhupāda again showed his personal neutrality. If he speaks critically it is not due to passion or prejudice. "How can I say anything which is not spoken by Kṛṣṇa? We have got this test: if anyone has no interest in Kṛṣṇa, he must be with these groups, that's all—*duskṛtina, mūḍha,* or *narādhama.* And Caitanya Mahāprabhu says *yāre dekha tāre kaha kṛṣṇa upadeśa.* So how can I violate? Both ways, I cannot violate. Caitanya Mahāprabhu said that you simply speak what Kṛṣṇa has said. And Kṛṣṇa said that anyone who is not Kṛṣṇa consciousness, he is a rascal, he is a most sinful man, he is the lowest of mankind. So why shall I not say? It is not firing, it is telling the truth."

Then he laughed with Dr.Patel. "But I am not loser. I do not make any compromise. All these, my students, ask. I never made any compromise. But still they understand, and they are with me. In Los Angeles so many scientists used to come. So after talking with them I used to say, 'You are demon! you are rascal!' And they tolerated."

Smiling, Prabhupāda recalled how they had remained afterwards for two hours talking and taking *prasādam.* "They were happy that I found them demons and rascals!"

One devotee suggested that the lack of questions at last night's program was due to the completeness of Prabhupāda's lecture.

"Yes," Dr. Patel said, "it is very difficult to put question to you. You mow the opposition down very badly!"

Everyone laughed in agreement.

When we returned to the temple after the morning walk Prabhupāda looked around the building site. He immediately noticed that a heap of timber brought by lorry from Vṛndāvana was lying unused. Prabhupāda is expert in using everything for Kṛṣṇa; and because he sees everything as Kṛṣṇa's possession he hates to see anything wasted. He questioned Saurabha closely about it, making sure he understood that it must be utilized.

Dr. Patel expressed his satisfaction at how quickly the construction of the temple is progressing, but Prabhupāda thinks it is going too slowly. He personally questions every aspect of the design, labor arrangements, quality, and so on. He is continually advising how everything should be done.

* * *

Another report on book distribution in America arrived today. Mid-morning Hansadūta read out a letter from Tamal Krishna Goswami. Tamal Krishna wrote that the Rādhā-Dāmodara Traveling Saṅkīrtana bus parties (RDTSKP) are now distributing 50,000 hardbound books per month. The book-distribution figures from RDTSKP and the airport distributors amazed Śrīla Prabhupāda.

Tamal Krishna Mahārāja reported that November's sales were 25,000 *Caitanya-caritāmṛtas* and 112,000 *Back To Godheads,* with collections totaling some $120,000. This month they were ordering 50,000 big books, an amount they hope to maintain regularly. One distributor, Pañcatattva, sold 311 books in one day, a new world's record.

Tamal Krishna Goswami said that the party was donating $5,000 per month to the Dallas *gurukula* and another $12,000 per year to the ISKCON Food Relief program. He has also bought two large diesel powered trailers and plans to tour the country, holding *Rathayātrā* festivals. At the end, he requested permission to be Śrīla Prabhupāda's personal secretary for January.

Prabhupāda's response was one of complete satisfaction. He has a high regard for the activities of the all-*brahmacārī* RDTSKP and sent an enthusiastic reply, "Your letter is very, very encouraging to me. I do not know how you are selling so many books. There is no instance in history where religious books were sold with such enthusiasm and success. Is there any such history? The Christians have spread their teachings all over the world, and they have got only one book, so we have got already forty big books published in English. Therefore if we distribute as you are distributing, we cannot even imagine the result. Your program is very nice; please continue more and more. Your idea for holding Jagannātha festivals in the big cities is approved by me, do it. Yes, you come in January."

When Kīrtanānanda Swami had first arrived he reported that sometimes books distributed in America were being ripped up by antagonists.

Prabhupāda took the bright side and compared the distribution to hot sugar-cane juice: too hot to take and too sweet to resist. Whether one admires them or not, his books are potent, which makes them irresistible. Prabhupāda's optimism about the effect of massive book distribution is not unfounded. Almost daily he receives positive evidence of how people's lives are being changed by reading his books.

Stephen Knapp, a *bhakta* from Colorado, sent a long letter thanking Prabhupāda for having saved him from material life. "This letter could be, and no doubt is, the most important that I could ever write to anyone. I have associated with you, Śrīla Prabhupāda, through your books for so long now that you have knocked my material motivation from under me. My mind may still have the desires, but by associating with you I no longer see any sense to struggle with material nature to try to satisfy my mind. I read your *Bhagavad-gītā,* the small edition, four years ago, and since then I've continued to get more and more of your books.

"I have associated with you for so long through your books that you have already answered my questions and now I am indebted to you by service for giving me this spiritual knowledge. But even though I have no talents or value I pray that you will accept my service to you."

He also enclosed a well-written philosophic poem of a dozen verses, glorifying Śrīla Prabhupāda. Prabhupāda listened to a few of them:

"Into this world of darkness where everyone is so confused
with its society of cheaters and the cheated who end up so abused,

in this huge slaughterhouse where everyone is unwillingly forced to die,
and living entities, in all bodies, in their distress do cry,
the spiritual master arrives to give the solution to all our problems
and miseries, this spiritual knowledge is the only way to solve them.
And seeing this, I simply pray,
'My dear Lord, please just give me the company of Your devotees.'"

"In this age when atheists in society become so prominent,
sitting in their temporary and false prestige the fools remain obstinate,
only to be defeated by the laws of nature and suffer the pains of death,
they're engaged in so many activities but are simply dying with each breath.
The spiritual master takes it upon himself to show the fools for what they are,
and teaches us to attain eternal life while still situated right where we are.
And seeing this, I simply pray,
'My dear Lord, please just give me the company of Your devotees.'"

"The materialists who are so engaged in their temporary pleasure
work so hard to enjoy wasting away in their time of leisure.
To work so hard for that which lasts so short of a time,
working under the perishable conceptions of 'I', 'Me' and 'Mine.'
To learn technology so they can more perfectly eat, sleep, and have sex,
like dull-headed animals, they have no concern for any spiritual progress.
And seeing this, I simply pray,
'My dear Lord, please just give me the company of Your devotees.'"

Even with such glorification Prabhupāda doesn't take any personal credit, neither does he take these accomplishments for granted. Letters like these only increase his desire to promote Kṛṣṇa consciousness throughout the world. He is the life and soul of the devotees, always unerringly directing our attention to Kṛṣṇa.

He replied to Steven Knapp, "So to develop attraction for Kṛṣṇa is not difficult. You simply have to hear about Kṛṣṇa, His activities, His name, His form, and His teaching in *Bhagavad-gītā.* Naturally you will develop love for Kṛṣṇa, because we are all part and parcel of Kṛṣṇa. The beginning process is to chant Hare Kṛṣṇa, follow the four regulative principles, and associate with devotees, and eat *prasādam* of Kṛṣṇa. I think you are now living in the temple of Kṛṣṇa, so these things will be very easy for you to practice."

Prabhupāda's books are not only attracting people from non-Vedic cultures; they are also reclaiming those misled by false presentations of it. From Germany an Indian devotee, Tulasī, wrote to thank him for giving real understanding of the *Bhagavad-gītā*. Originally brought up to worship Kṛṣṇa in the Guruvayor temple in Kerala, he later drifted away from spiritual practices. Then he met the devotees in Berlin and read Prabhupāda's books. Now he is living in the Schloss-Rettershof temple near Frankfurt.

He wrote, "As a youngster when I read *Bhagavad-gītā* first time, I was always feeling that Śrī Kṛṣṇa's instructions of devotional service had been purposely covered up by the so-called philosophers and yogis. I felt in those days that probably I am not competent enough to understand *Bhagavad-gītā*. Today I realize Kṛṣṇa's eternal servant (Your Divine Grace) alone has the right to translate and give a purport to that great *Upaniṣad*. My humble obeisances at your lotus feet....

"Guide me so that I can preach the message to the other Indians who go abroad for the sake of foreign qualifications and degrees. How shameful? There is no equivalent knowledge anywhere in the world [other than] what our Ācāryas gave us. And you are the only devotee of Kṛṣṇa who can imbibe this feeling to our millions of people.

"Meanwhile I heard your assessment on Mahātmā Gandhi's life and policy. I must definitely fall at your feet the moment when I see you because you have shown us how dependence on Kṛṣṇa, than surrendering to countrymen and nation, would have made India a *Rāma Rajya*."

Prabhupāda stressed that Kṛṣṇa Consciousness, the gift of Caitanya Mahāprabhu, is particularly the natural birthright of those born in India. The lack of committed response from the intelligent class of men here disappoints Śrīla Prabhupāda. India has become diverted from its real business by what Prabhupāda often calls its "mis-leaders." In pursuit of material advancement they are swiftly leading the populace away from the Vedic culture.

Yet, Prabhupāda hopes to reawaken the natural spiritual

yearning of the Indian people. Then, by their example, the course of the world can be changed. Therefore, it always pleases Śrīla Prabhupāda when an educated Indian takes up the *saṅkīrtana-yajña* of Śrī Caitanya Mahāprabhu.

He gave the boy all encouragement. "I can understand from your letter that you are very intelligent. Generally Indian people are not taking up this Movement, although it is their original culture. They are now in favor of economic and technological advancement, which can never do any good to the people in general. After all, a living being lives by the grace of God. We cannot eat nuts and bolts, however nicely they may be manufactured....

"So if we want to be happy in this life and the next we have to worship Viṣṇu. What Gandhi did to satisfy Viṣṇu? He was trying to satisfy his country, and his country killed him. He manufactured so many things which were never found in *Bhagavad-gītā*.... Kṛṣṇa was personally instructing Arjuna to fight, and Gandhi took *Bhagavad-gītā* and preached non-violence. So what was his understanding? At the end of his life he frankly said, 'I don't believe there was ever such a historical person as Kṛṣṇa.' So what did Gandhi know about *Bhagavad-gītā*?

"My only credit is that I have presented *Bhagavad-gītā* as it is, without any speculation or interpretation. Therefore for the first time in the history of the world people are accepting it and living practically according to the principles of *Bhagavad-gītā*.

"I understand that you are translating *Bhagavad-gītā As It Is* into Malayalam language. Hansadūta has spoken to me about you. Please send me a sample, and we will see about its publication and distribution in India. Maybe in the future you will like to come to India and help preach this message to your countrymen."

December 19th, 1975

Prabhupāda's quarters here are simple, clean, and functional with barely any furniture. The floor is a "crazy-paved" style of either white ceramic tiles or marble chips. Only in his *darśana* room does he have the traditional sheet-covered mattresses to provide seating for guests, and there is a simple *āsana* and a desk and a bookcase.

This morning at about five o'clock I was sitting on the bare floor of the front reception room, trying to chant my *japa*. Prabhupāda came out to brush his teeth in the sink, but I failed to notice because I was nodding asleep as I chanted.

He wasn't angry, but he told me, "Do not sit while you are chanting. Sitting means sleeping."

Being Śrīla Prabhupāda's servant, I sometimes find it difficult to chant good rounds, because I am expected to remain on call in the room adjacent to his throughout the day. I have had to learn to chant almost silently so as not to disturb him, and this makes it harder to be attentive. Previous secretaries and servants have also had trouble chanting properly due to the demands of the engagement.

* * *

Out on the beach in the fresh morning sea air Prabhupāda described how swiftly human beings can descend into animalism when spiritual culture is lost. He recalled that in the concentration camps during World War II people were forced to eat their own stool.

Dr. Patel admitted that as an honorary Colonel for the British he knew that they had a regulation allowing soldiers to drink their urine. "But," he said, "they were not allowed to eat stool."

Prabhupāda shook his head in wonder. "Just see, 'I am making law. You can drink urine.' Just see!" He turned to us with his eyes wide open, while everyone laughed incredulously.

Dr. Patel offered his medical opinion that urine has many properties essential to the body and therefore isn't so bad.

"So you are advising your patients to go and drink?" Prabhupāda asked.

"No, I don't say. But that is not so bad because it convinced the hormones—"

Prabhupāda broke out laughing, and Dr. Patel became annoyed.

"It *does* convince the hormones. I mean, it has been analyzed like that, scientifically. It is not to be joked about!"

Prabhupāda proffered some humorous agreement, "*Ne.* It

is analyzed. And stool is full of hydrophosphates."

The devotees were all laughing by now, and Dr. Patel became a little indignant. "Our Mr. Desai, Morarji, who lost his premiership of India, he is drinking his own urine."

"*Acchā!* Why?" Prabhupāda asked.

Ignoring Prabhupāda's response, Dr. Patel continued, "And look at him! He's so, I mean, so absolutely healthy. I mean it is ... we should not laugh about it, but there is something right in it."

"No, no. I don't laugh; I am surprised!"

Prabhupāda decided to save Dr. Patel from further embarrassment. He moved on, proceeding at a steady pace down the flat sands, changing the subject to speak about the good fortune of taking birth in India.

Dr. Patel, now again at ease, verified the benefits of such a birth by citing the example of his mother who died while gazing at a picture of Lord Kṛṣṇa.

Śrīla Prabhupāda also recalled an incident of an old man in Delhi who requested a picture of Rādhā-Kṛṣṇa a few minutes before his death. He died just as it was placed before him.

Dr. Patel mentioned that his mother had also chanted *Bhaja Govinda* as she died.

Prabhupāda turned to the devotees and remarked appreciatively, "Oh! Just see. Govinda."

Unfortunately, nowadays many Indians are leaving behind their spiritual tradition, in pursuit of modern materialistic advancement. Śravaṇānanda said that one well-known "spiritual mission" in Madras had a slogan above a school playing field entrance that read like an epitaph to Vedic education: "The playing of football will bring one closer to heaven than the study of the *Gītā*."

He said they had refused to rent the field to ISKCON devotees for a program. They were told that the cricket season was coming up soon, and the school did not want the turf to be ruined. Officials frankly said that they did not have time for spiritual training, only physical.

The rapid decline of spiritual culture is especially visible here, where Bombayaites seem particularly intent on imitating

Western culture. Śrīla Prabhupāda commented, "A person born in a Brāhmaṇa family, he is claiming 'I am Brahman.' Similarly, even though born in Aryan family, without any culture they are claiming, 'I am Aryan.'

"Kṛṣṇa observed it in Arjuna, and therefore he chastised him, 'This kind of proposal is *anārya-juṣṭam,* from the non-Aryans. You are forgetting your duty.' That is the beginning of loss of culture. A small beginning, it creates havoc.

"*Yuddha* — everything must be religious. Why *yuddha?* Your ordinary living must be also religious. Otherwise, animal. Animal also lives. But if you don't live religiously, that is animal. If you live like human being, that human being means *dharma.* We cannot expect any *dharma* in the animal society. It is meant for the humans. Cāṇakya Paṇḍita says that a flower without smell and a man without education—the same thing. A flower without smell, similarly, a man without education."

Like an old flower that has lost its fragrance, this city in particular has become a veritable bastion of materialistic consciousness. Evidence of cultural imposition abounds. At the beach, big hotels stand brazenly as crass reminders that modern Indian society is swiftly degenerating, becoming increasingly dedicated to sensuality.

That Śrīla Prabhupāda has had to fight so strenuously with the Bombay municipality simply to build a Kṛṣṇa temple at Juhu is disturbing testimony. Three hundred years of British colonial rule has systematically reeducated the Indian people into thinking that the simple and natural God-conscious way of life they once enjoyed is backward and primitive. Bombay is obviously the one place in India that has achieved graduate status in the school of materialism.

Yet, now Westerners are coming here to study and adopt a culture India is trying so hard to lose. By the strength of Śrīla Prabhupāda's love for Kṛṣṇa and his profound knowledge, he is reversing this trend.

Dr. Patel is one of the few who truly appreciate Śrīla Prabhupāda's contribution. Despite his brash exterior he is always keen to inquire. "Sir, what is the distinction between a culture and an education?"

Prabhupāda answered, "Culture means human being. Just like Cāṇakya Paṇḍita says, *mātṛvat para-dāreṣu para-dravyeṣu loṣṭavat ātmāvat sarva-bhūteṣu yaḥ paśyati sa paṇḍitah.* This is culture. To see every woman as mother. The modern meaning of education is rubbish, to learn ABCDE. This is not education. Without culture, what is the meaning of education?"

"So culture is the background for education?" Dr. Patel asked.

"Yes. Education is required to help culture. Not that you take degrees from the university and remain a dog. That is not education. Here is education: first of all learn how to see every woman as your mother. There the culture begins. And they are, from the very beginning of the college school life, they are learning how to entice one girl. This is education."

Dr. Patel said, "They are following the so-called advanced countries."

But Prabhupāda answered, "Advanced means Freud's philosophy, sex philosophy. This is their education. So how you can expect them to learn? It is not possible. From the very beginning there is no culture, animal culture. Just like dog—as soon as he finds another female dog he wants to have sex. This is education."

"One friend of mine told me that this culture is vulture's culture," Dr. Patel said.

"Yes. Not vultures," Prabhupāda clarified. "It is called hog civilization. The hogs, they eat anything and they have sex with anyone.... Culture means human life; otherwise, dog's life. *Amānitvam,* first of all you have to learn how to become humble. And here all the people, they are educated how to become proud. What is education? And this culture cannot be maintained unless one is God conscious. *Harāv abhaktasya kuto mahad-guṇā,* there cannot be any culture for a godless person, that is not possible. And, *yasyāsti bhaktir bhagavaty akiñcanā.* Just like these European and American boys are offering obeisances to the guru; this is culture. Why he has learned this culture? Because he has become Kṛṣṇa conscious. Therefore, *yasyāsti bhak-*

tir bhagavaty akiñcanā, sarvair guṇais tatra samāsate surāḥ. If you make one devotee of Kṛṣṇa, then all culture will automatically come. One thing. Hare Kṛṣṇa."

* * *

Good news came this morning from South India. Hansadūta brought a letter from Acyutānanda and Yaśodānandana swamis who have been visiting prominent Madhvācārya-*sampradāya maṭhas* throughout Mysore and Mangalore. Their ability to defeat Māyāvādī philosophy so impressed the leaders of the Admar and Pejavara *maṭhas* that they were given letters of recommendation introducing them as bona fide Vaiṣṇavas and praising Śrīla Prabhupāda and his books. As a result, three schools in that area took full sets of Śrīla Prabhupāda's books. They have also enlisted twelve Patron Members.

Now in Mangalore, they intend to join Prabhupāda in Nellore, Andra Pradesh, on January 3rd.

Prabhupāda is extremely encouraged and pleased to see his senior disciples preaching so capably and gaining acceptance for ISKCON by their philosophical knowledge. He wrote to them, "*Saṅkīrtana* will always be appreciated, because it is the special blessings of Lord Caitanya Mahāprabhu on the people of this fallen age of *Kali-yuga.* Śukadeva Gosvāmī says this age is an ocean of faults. But there is one boon: in this age one gets the same result as was achieved in former ages through elaborate temple worship, costly sacrifices, or introspective meditation, simply by chanting the Holy Name of the Lord. It is for this reason only that this Hare Kṛṣṇa Movement has spread so quickly all over the world."

* * *

At the end of a full day Prabhupāda likes to relax. Sometimes he is reflective, making pithy observations about society and the condition of the world. That was his mood tonight.

After I set up the mosquito net over his bed, he lay down. I climbed inside also, sitting cross-legged at his side, gently massaging his hips, legs, and feet.

Prabhupāda talked briefly about Freud. He said that producing such a complicated philosophy and writing volumes of books just to understand sexual attraction, there naturally even in the pigs, is like bringing a cannon to kill a mosquito. "Big philosophy," he said, "is not required for these things."

December 20th, 1975

Prabhupāda is not feeling well; swelling in his legs, feet, and hands trouble him. To see his body puffed with fluid is very disturbing. Nevertheless, he went on his walk, continuing the education of Dr. Patel and the other devotees.

This morning Prabhupāda stressed that one must hear from a bona fide guru if he desires to become knowledgeable in spiritual life. He condemned charlatan gurus who misrepresent the process of yoga and tell people that one can be one's own guru simply by "looking within."

"If there is no need of guru," Prabhupāda said sharply, "why are they writing books to tell people? As soon as you tell someone something, that is guru."

As we walked back to greet Śrī Śrī Rādhā-Rasabihārī, the sound of children's voices singing traditional Hindi songs loudly rang out from the playground of the junior school across the road. This scene reinforced the point that Śrīla Prabhupāda emphasized during the morning walk—everyone must learn from another qualified authority.

Dr. Patel said, "Guru is necessity right from the birth. The first guru is the mother."

Prabhupāda answered, "And these rascals, they preach like that: 'There is no need of guru.'"

"They are rascals, Sir."

"Yes," Prabhupāda agreed. "Simply rascals. *Rascal* means he does not know the thing and he still preaches. That's a rascal. Guru must be there. There are many, they say like that, 'There is no need of guru.'"

When one visitor asked if some effort was required to obtain a guru, Prabhupāda gave his confirmation. "Yes. Therefore Kṛṣṇa says, *tad viddhi praṇipātena. Praṇipāt* means you have to surrender. When you submit somewhere, you must test and then submit. That is *sad-guru.*"

"They say, sir," Dr. Patel said, "that if you are very sincere then the *sad-guru* comes automatically to you ... as you have come to us."

Prabhupāda answered, "Yes. Because Kṛṣṇa is there. If He sees somebody is actually serious to understand Him ... therefore Dhruva Mahārāja, he did not make any guru, but with fervent desire he went, 'Yes, I shall find out Kṛṣṇa.' Mother said, 'Kṛṣṇa can be found in the forest.' He went to the forest and began according to his own way. Then Kṛṣṇa sent Nārada Muni: 'This boy is very serious; go and give him real *mantra.*' That is Caitanya Mahāprabhu, *guru kṛṣṇa kṛpayā pāya bhakti latā bīja.* Two things required, guru and Kṛṣṇa."

* * *

During his massage I pressed gently on Prabhupāda's foot with my thumb to show him the swelling. It left an indentation for several minutes. Prabhupāda said this is due to uremia, a toxic condition caused by waste products in the blood normally eliminated in the urine. It makes it very difficult for him to climb the steps to his apartment when returning from the temple. Yet, he tolerates the inconvenience without complaint and dismissed the sight of the dent with a smile and a shake of his head.

* * *

Despite not feeling well, Prabhupāda went to an outside engagement in the evening. It was held on the twenty-first floor of a block of flats, the home of a wealthy and influential Life Member.

Although it was not well attended and Prabhupāda's lecture was constantly interrupted by noisy children, he spoke strongly for forty-five minutes on *Bhagavad-gītā* (7:1). He emphasized the need to hear from the right source—Kṛṣṇa. As usual in preaching to a mainly Indian audience, Śrīla Prabhupāda kept to the central theme of *dharma*—real religion, what it constitutes, and the duty of those who have the good fortune to understand it.

It was late when we left, and after a long drive home, Prabhupāda revealed that he felt too ill to continue going out

November 26, 1975—
"I immediately ran down the road to number nine. . . ."

December 1, 1975—
"Prabhupāda decided to visit another area of Kurukṣetra called Jyotisar . . . There, we came upon half-life-size deities of Kṛṣṇa and Arjuna, encased in a metal-and-glass house. . . ."

December 17, 1975—"Dr. Patel usually meets Prabhupāda on Juhu beach."

December 22, 1975—"Śrīla Prabhupāda sat on a cushion . . . next to the *vyāsāsana* which bore a small picture of his Guru Mahārāja."

December 22, 1975— "We all stood . . . before the picture of Śrīla Bhaktisiddhānta Sarasvatī . . . and offered flowers."

December 22, 1975—"Afterwards we had a lively *kīrtana* and *guru-pūjā.*"

December 25, 1975— "Prabhupāda sat serene and comfortable . . . and the King of Sanand . . . sat at his side."

December 25, 1975— "A group of costumed dancers . . . performed a stick dance as a greeting."

December 25, 1975—"Śrīla Prabhupāda and the King climbed into the carriage, sitting opposite each other. . . ."

December 25, 1975—"As the procession wound its way through the town, the ladies spontaneously burst into chanting 'Hare Kṛṣṇa, Hare Kṛṣṇa, Kṛṣṇa Kṛṣṇa, Hare Hare. . . ."

January 1, 1976—"Temple presidents Bhāva-bhūti and Śravaṇānanda offered garlands (right), and the devotees danced exhuberantly to the *kīrtana* (above), led by Acyutānanda Swami."

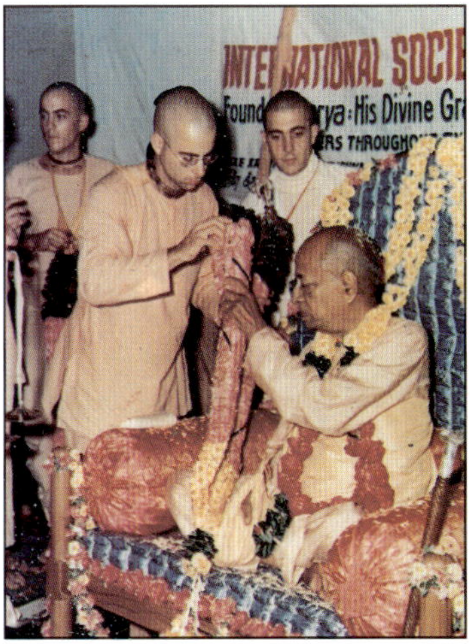

January 3, 1976—"Getting out of the car at the main gate, Prabhupāda was met by the sisters . . . We walked the short distance . . . to the main house."

January 4, 1976—"At 10:30 A.M. Prabhupāda went to the two-acre plot . . . and performed the foundation stone ceremony for the new temple."

January 4, 1976—"Prabhupāda climbed down into a big hole in the ground . . . and laid a few bricks with cement."

January 4, 1976— "With a short speech he unveiled a carved marble commemoration plaque."

January 5, 1976— "After passing through the high arched gateway . . . we entered the walled compound of the temple."

January 5, 1976— "High above Prabhupāda's head the white silken canopy of an eight-foot wide umbrella marked the position . . . of the most important person present."

January 7, 1976—"It felt somehow special and historic to be part of an official photo with Śrīla Prabhupāda."

Back row (left to right): R. L. Reddy, Vommina Subramaniam, G. B. K. Reddy, Y. Venkateswarlu, K. Gopal Reddy, V. Veeraraghava Reddy, J. V. Reddy, P. Narasimhulu. **Front row (left to right):** Yaśodānandana Swami, Acyutānanda Swami, Śrīla Prabhupāda, Tamāl Krishna Goswami, Hari Śauri Dāsa.

January 12, 1976—"He invited Prabhupāda into the cockpit, offering him a seat behind his own."

on so many programs. He said that he wants at least one week of complete rest. He will not even take morning walks. And he wants to eat only fruits, milk, and *kichari*. He looks exhausted and frail, but we are unable to help in any useful way.

Arrangements are being made to go to Australia for the *Rathayātrā* on January 10th, but our plans might have to change due to Prabhupāda's ill health. Moreover, some difficulty has arisen regarding Prabhupāda's visa.

December 21st, 1975

There was no morning walk today. Missing Prabhupāda on the beach, Dr. Patel arrived at his apartment with his son. He took a cardiograph reading and gave Prabhupāda some pills. His diagnosis is high blood pressure.

Prabhupāda rested. He didn't take breakfast, and then ate only a morsel at lunch, complaining of dizziness from the medicine. He remarked that modern drugs are medicines for the demons. Prabhupāda rarely goes to a doctor, although if by some arrangement one comes to him, he doesn't refuse their help. Disease has to be treated, of course, but as far as he is concerned, chanting Hare Kṛṣṇa is the best cure.

In the evening he felt better and ate some guava, three *paraṭhās,* and a *sabji* Harikeśa cooked for him.

As part of his cure Prabhupāda told us that for at least one week he wants to be free of appointments and visitors. Harikeśa is doubtful that we will be able to enforce this rule. Prabhupāda is too enthusiastic to stop preaching and too kind to turn away unexpected visitors.

December 22nd, 1975

Today is Śrīla Bhaktisiddhānta Sarasvatī Ṭhākura's disappearance day. Śrīla Prabhupāda is feeling a little stronger, but the morning walk was again canceled.

He fasted until noon, when there was a huge feast for the devotees. They made many, many preparations, and samples of everything were brought to Prabhupāda. He was pleased and took small tastings of each preparation.

* * *

Shortly after Prabhupāda retired for his morning nap, Dr. Patel came unannounced up to the apartment with two friends. Having heard that Prabhupāda was still not well, he had brought some medicine.

However, I had to refuse him entry to Prabhupāda's bedroom. It is a standing rule that no one may wake Prabhupāda for any reason. Nor is there ever a need, as Prabhupāda never misses any appointments; and he rises at almost exactly the same times every day, as if by his own built-in alarm clock. Unfortunately, the doctor became rather upset and embarrassed in front of his friends at being made to wait. He didn't like being stopped by Prabhupāda's young servant. He even refused my request to wait in the sitting room. When the tactic of raising his voice in protest failed to rouse Śrīla Prabhupāda in the next room, he left the medicine, departing in a huff.

His show of anger doesn't disturb me. I feel secure in the knowledge that I have done the right thing and acted according to Śrīla Prabhupāda's desire.

* * *

As Harikeśa predicted, in the afternoon Prabhupāda decided to receive some visitors, despite his statement yesterday that he wanted a week's complete rest.

One of the visitors was a disciple of a well-known impersonalist. The lady unabashedly glorified her guru and began spouting his philosophy. Perhaps the disappearance day of Śrīla Prabhupāda's own Guru Mahārāja was not the best time for her to have come. Prabhupāda immediately countered nearly every comment she made. Using sharp logic and common sense he did not hesitate to point out the defects of her Svāmī's philosophy. He especially attacked the Svāmī's commentary on the *Gītā.* A typical *māyāvādī,* this guru is well-known for having said that the word *Kṛṣṇa* means "dark." According to him, *dark* means "unknown," and therefore the Absolute is unknowable, that is to say, impersonal.

"If dark is unknown," Prabhupāda said, "or if Kṛṣṇa is unknown, then why does he [her guru] bother to comment on Kṛṣṇa's words in the *Gītā?* Why does he comment on that which he does not know? Therefore only the *bhakta,* only the devotee, can comment on the *Bhagavad-gītā,* not others. Because Kṛṣṇa says, *bhaktyā mām abhijānāti yāvān yaś cāsmi tattvataḥ,* 'to the devotees I am known.'"

After the lady left Prabhupāda told us that her Svāmī is also well-known for having affairs with his secretaries and wealthy widow followers.

* * *

Despite his health, Prabhupāda still received his mail. A very encouraging letter arrived from Hṛdayānanda Goswami. He reported that the devotees in Sao Paulo, Brazil have purchased a bus for $40,000 and are fitting it as a traveling temple. With Śrī Śrī Gaura-Nitāi installed they plan to tour the country.

He also submitted three poems for Prabhupāda's approval. The first two described painful entanglement in material life. The third was a plea for release, and some of its stanzas went:

"Oh, Your Lordship Kṛṣṇa, please hear me!
Your devotee's calling, so sadly.
He forgot Your Lotus feet.
Now he's lost he's met defeat.

O Greatest of Persons, please see me!
Your devotee's falling, so badly.
To enjoy this world, he tried,
Now let it be rectified!

O please, Rādhārāṇī, take pity!
A devotee's trapped in the city!
The nine gates are robbing him,
Take pity! He's near the end."

Prabhupāda heard them appreciatively and replied, "The poem is very nice. However, one should not think of himself as a devotee. Poem three should read:

Your servant's calling so sadly,
Your servant's falling so badly,
A servant's trapped in the city.

"One cannot call himself a devotee, but servant he can call

himself always. Your bus program sounds nice, it is approved by me."

After signing the typed letter, he added in his own hand at the bottom, "Śrī Caitanya Mahāprabhu presented Himself as *patitaṁ kiṅkaraṁ māṁ viṣame bhavāmbudhau. Kiṅkaram* means servant."

Gurudāsa Swami, one of the first devotees in San Francisco and one of the original householders to begin preaching in London, sent an enthusiastic letter from America about his preaching activities and his newfound freedom since recently taking *sannyāsa.*

Prabhupāda was very satisfied to hear that he is wholeheartedly engaged in Kṛṣṇa's service, free from distraction. He wrote back encouraging him to go on and added what he described to us as his new slogan, "I always say, 'Man is good, and woman is also good. But when they combine, then they become bad.' Before there was so much difficulty. But now you are doing well, and Yamunā dāsī is also doing well, and I am very pleased with your work. Please continue like this and keep me informed."

* * *

In the evening Prabhupāda went down to the temple for a special program including *puṣpāñjali,* the offering of flowers to his Guru Mahārāja. The audience was not large—a small core of active Life Members, friends, and well-wishers of ISKCON who have become attracted by Śrīla Prabhupāda and his pure and direct preaching, impressed by the results of Kṛṣṇa consciousness.

Śrīla Prabhupāda sat on a cushion on the floor in front of the Deities and next to the *vyāsāsana,* which bore a small picture of his Guru Mahārāja. He lectured enthusiastically, showing no sign of discomfort from his illness. It was an especially good talk. He humbly presented the eternal message of devotional service as he has received it from his spiritual master.

Having spent the afternoon discussing the Svāmī to whom the *Bhagavad-gītā* and Kṛṣṇa was "unknown", and speaking as the representative of one to whom the Lord most surely is known, he lectured on a verse that gave Lord Kṛṣṇa Himself the final say: *Bhagavad-gītā* Chapter Sixteen, verse seven. "There are two kinds of men," Prabhupāda said, "*asura* and *daiva.* All throughout the whole universe, there are two classes of men. One who knows his relationship with God, he is called *daiva.* And one who does not know, just like animal, they are called *asura.* There is no particular caste or creed, that here is a caste of *asura,* caste of *daiva.* No. Anyone who knows what is God and his relationship with God, *sambandha,* and then works according to that relation and achieves the goal of life, he is called *daiva,* or *devatā.* And one who does not know this, what is the goal of life, what is God, what is my relationship with God, he is *asura.*"

Prabhupāda explained that one is understood to be *asura* or *devatā* according to which path they are following—*pravṛtti* or *nivṛtti.* "*Loke vyavāyāmiṣa-madya sevā nitya hi jantor.* Every living entity has got this tendency. *Vyavāya,* means sex life; *āmiṣa,* meat eating, and *madya,* liquor. Natural tendency. Therefore the country where these things are indulged in without any restriction, that is *asura.* This is especially in the Western countries, and now we have also learned in India. Either Hindus or Musselman, drinking was a sin; now we have got very easily available liquor. Every door there is a shop, and every door there is a meat shop. So India, there was a time that they were all *devatas;* now we are imitating the *asuras.* On the other hand, the boys and girls from the *asuric* countries, they are becoming devotees, *devatā.* So there is no exclusive right for a country to become a *devatā* or a demon. A demon can be turned into the *devatā* and *devatā* can be turned into demon provided he follows this *pravritti* and *nivṛtti*....

"So Kṛṣṇa has described everything in the *Bhagavad-gītā.* And today, this night, we are trying to explain the mission of Kṛṣṇa, because the same mission is being carried out by us beginning from Brahmā. And today is a special day, the disappearance day of my Guru Mahārāja, Bhaktisiddhānta Sarasvatī Gosvāmī. This Kṛṣṇa consciousness movement is so beneficial that He wants to benefit the whole human society, how to stop this process of repetition of birth, death, old age, and disease. My Guru Mahārāja also came for this purpose, and we are also trying to follow his footsteps. And we are teaching our disciples to do the same thing. This is not a new movement, or some invented 'ism.' It is old, at least four or five thousand years, what Kṛṣṇa spoke. The other followers also spoke the same thing, and we are also speaking the same thing. It is up to you to take advantage of it or not. Thank you very much."

After Prabhupāda's lecture, we all stood around the *vyāsāsana*, before the picture of Śrīla Bhaktisiddhānta Sarasvatī. We responsively recited the *praṇāma-mantras* following the lead of Lokanātha Swami and offered flowers. Afterwards we had a lively *kīrtana* and *guru-pūjā* before Prabhupāda returned upstairs.

With great satisfaction he took some *maha-prasādam* that had been offered this evening to his Guru Mahārāja. He also had Harikeśa make some *kachoris.* To see Śrīla Prabhupāda eat heartily is a good sign that his health is improving.

December 23rd, 1975

Śrīla Prabhupāda is feeling stronger, and the swelling in his body has gone down because of the diuretic pills Dr. Patel supplied yesterday. But Prabhupāda didn't take all the pills prescribed. After taking a half tablet, as soon as he got the desired effect, he stopped taking the medication.

He resumed his morning exercise, walking down to Juhu Beach as usual.

Śrīla Prabhupāda asked Saurabha about a dentist interested in opening a clinic in the new temple compound. Saurabha explained that the man had seen the floor plan, which includes a room for medical use, and immediately proposed that he use it to give free treatment to the devotees.

Prabhupāda did not approve. "No, there will be no medical service in the building."

Lokanātha Swami asked if medical facilities should be set up on another part of the land.

Prabhupāda replied, "That we shall do at our convenience. It is not very urgent. When there is spare room, then. Medical service is to cure the material disease, this temporary headache and stomachache. There are so many medical services for these things, but where is the medical service for curing *bhava-roga,* material disease? That is wanted. Medical service does not give any guarantee that there will be no more disease. Our service is to guarantee that there will be no more birth, death, old age, and disease. That is the difference."

Pausing for a moment, he recalled his recent trip to Africa. "In Mauritius I was suffering so much from dental pain. I never went to the dentist; I invented my medicine and it cured."

Everyone smiled in admiration. Prabhupāda seems to know nearly everything. He was referring to his own toothpaste recipe: a combination of ground mustard seed, salt, calcium carbonate, eucalyptus oil, camphor, menthol, and oil of wintergreen. Many devotees are now eagerly making it for themselves, and Prabhupāda asked if they like it.

He grinned when Harikeśa assured him, "Oh yes! The best!" Lokanātha Swami voiced what we all felt, "You are perfect in all respects. You are your own doctor."

Prabhupāda humbly responded, "I am not doctor, but I created many doctors."

We then met up with Dr. Patel, walking in the opposite direction. He stopped to offer his *praṇāmas,* but he said he wouldn't walk on with us. He was still miffed about being turned away yesterday morning. He obviously decided to register his complaint with a boycott. He told Śrīla Prabhupāda how offended he was at being refused admittance.

Although I had given Prabhupāda the medicine, I hadn't informed him about the fuss Dr. Patel made at not being able to see him. Prabhupāda heard his grievance, and without jumping to any conclusions, gently inquired what the reason might be that he was denied admittance. I explained that Dr. Patel had arrived when he was taking his morning rest, so I did not want to disturb him. Prabhupāda indicated his approval of my action. Yet he also discreetly pacified the doctor.

Lokanātha invited the doctor to join us, but he declined.

Although we missed the usual lively debate, without Dr. Patel to monopolize the conversation, the devotees had more opportunity to ask questions.

We had a long discussion about the relationship between Lord Viṣṇu and Lord Śiva. At one point the famous battle between Banasura and Kṛṣṇa was mentioned, where the ultimate weapons of Lord Śiva and Lord Viṣṇu were pitched against each other. The *śiva-jvara* produced intense heat, but the *viṣṇu-jvara,* which generated intense cold, was the victor.

An Indian devotee said that when Prabhupāda was very ill in Vṛndāvana with a high fever he had prayed that the *viṣṇu-jvara* might reduce his fever. "So we were just reading the *Bhāgavatam* when you were sick. Anybody suffering from fever means you read such and such a portion. So it should come down."

It seemed like a nice sentiment, but from Prabhupāda's pure devotional viewpoint it wasn't acceptable. "No, Viṣṇu should not be utilized for curing your fever. That is not *bhakti.* That is business."

Kīrtanānanda Swami asked, "Can a disciple invoke Lord Viṣṇu's help for serving his spiritual master?"

Śrīla Prabhupāda replied more enthusiastically. He also revealed something of his internal mood in his struggle to establish the Bombay temple. "Hm! That is nice. That is for curing Viṣṇu's representative. When we were in danger, there was so much obstruction for constructing the temple, and we prayed to Kṛṣṇa that it should be stopped. We prayed to Kṛṣṇa, 'Please give your protection.' That is for Viṣṇu's purpose."

As we walked along the firm sand near the water's edge we suddenly found ourselves caught in a small cul-de-sac formed by the incoming tide. The flux of the waves revealed a shining object imbedded in the sand, glinting in the sunlight like a valuable gem. Lokanātha ran over to see. It was a piece of broken glass.

Everyone laughed as Prabhupāda declared, "That is called *māyā!* The light is here, but it appears light is there. This is called *māyā.* The real world is the spiritual world and here it is simply reflection, but we are taking this is real world."

* * *

After greeting Their Lordships Śrī Śrī Rādhā-Rasabihārī and receiving *guru-pūjā,* Śrīla Prabhupāda took a tour of the building site. The foundation work has begun, and some of it is already completed. He made a thorough inspection—questioning, advising, and discussing the overall plans with Saurabha.

He seems satisfied with the progress and proud that the building will be unique in this area of Bombay. It was a long, hard struggle to get the land, hold onto it, and finally obtain the permission to build.

Now, with the same determination and strong desire, Śrīla Prabhupāda is pushing on the building effort. This will be the biggest temple and *āśrama* complex in ISKCON to date, and he wants to offer it to Their Lordships Śrī Śrī Rādhā-Rasabihārī.

December 24th, 1975

This is Prabhupāda's final day in Bombay. He is scheduled to go to Gujarat tomorrow.

Dr. Patel joined us again on the beach, his good humor restored. The doctor had previously extolled the value of experimentation in the search for truth, so Prabhupāda took it up as today's theme. He challenged Dr. Patel why the truth should be the subject of experimentation. "If one knows the truth," he said, "there is no question of experiment." As usual, after some debate, Dr. Patel concurred.

Śrīla Prabhupāda emphasized the principle that although the method of searching for the truth may be experimented with, the truth itself is not subject to experimentation.

As we headed back toward the temple, we observed men and women on Juhu Beach going through their daily routines, vigorously swinging their arms and legs, bending and stretching in imitation of the Western mania for exercise. In Bombay especially, Indians are obviously becoming more and more interested in their bodies and less and less interested in their souls.

Lokanātha Swami asked what it is that creates the attraction between men and women, since all bodies are made of the same ingredients.

Prabhupāda gave an elaborate reply. "You want to be attracted. God has made in such a way that both of them are attractive to one another. That's all. You want to be attracted;

therefore woman is made attractive. And the woman wants to be attracted; man is attractive. This is nature's arrangement so that you may be bound up by this attraction. You are already bound up, and by this attraction you will be more tightly bound up. *Puṁsaḥ striyā mithunī-bhāvam etam.* The whole material attraction means a man's attraction for woman and a woman's attraction for man. But when they are seeking, 'Where is woman?' 'Where is woman?' 'Where is woman?' And the woman is seeking, they come here to make this business. And when they are actually attracted or united, then this bondage will become more tight.

"Therefore, the Vedic civilization is how to slacken it, and ultimately by force, separation, *sannyāsa.* Because unless they are separated, there cannot be any spiritual advancement. That is the whole process. Their unity is bondage. I have written a letter, that man is good, woman is good, and when they are united, they are bad!"

Prabhupāda laughed. "Both of them are bad. And the material world is taking this is the best thing. But actually that is not. Man is good, because he is part and parcel of God. And woman is good, part and parcel of God. But when they unite, they become bad."

Lokanātha Mahārāja asked whether *gṛhasthas* could make spiritual advancement.

Prabhupāda's reply was candid, "That advancement is not very solid. But there is advancement, but that is not very solid."

"They say 'We want to come together to serve the Lord.' Is that excuse or is that—?"

Prabhupāda broke into a smile. "Together they go to hell!" He explained that ultimately the spirit of detachment must be there, no matter what the external dress. If a householder is working only for Kṛṣṇa, then he is also a *sannyāsī.*

* * *

Later in the day a telegram arrived from Rādhāballabha, the Los Angeles BBT book production manager. He informed Śrīla Prabhupāda that on the disappearance of Śrīla Bhaktisiddhānta Sarasvatī Ṭhākura they had offered the latest volume of *Śrīmad-Bhāgavatam.*

Prabhupāda telegraphed a reply, "Thank you. Be blessed. My Guru Mahārāja will be very much pleased upon you and all other workers on the holy occasion of his disappearance day."

* * *

I spent the day packing and preparing for tomorrow's trip. Several village programs have been arranged, and Śrīla Prabhupāda is very enthusiastic. He stressed the importance of preaching in the villages, telling Hansadūta, Harikeśa, and me that he had a long-cherished desire to preach from village to village in India. Prior to coming to the West he was unable to do it, but now he is getting the opportunity to fulfill his desire.

CHAPTER FIVE

Sanand, Gujarat; Bombay

December 25th, 1975

At noon Prabhupāda flew due north to Ahmedabad, a short thirty-five minute trip. Jaśomatīnandana and Kārtikeya Mahādevia, one of our more enthusiastic Bombay Life Members, were there to greet him. They drove us in two cars to a small town nearby called Sanand. The car I was in was delayed at a railway crossing, and Śrīla Prabhupāda's car sped ahead.

Reaching the outskirts of Sanand, we found a large group of people in an open field. They clamored excitedly around a small colorful stage erected for Śrīla Prabhupāda's arrival. Śrīla Prabhupāda sat, serene and comfortable on a raised dais, wreathed in about twenty garlands of marigolds and roses. Our host, the portly and venerable king of Sanand, with his long white beard and wearing a large red turban, sat at his side. A *chowkidar* sheltered Prabhupāda from the sun with a large, red-velvet ceremonial umbrella.

Several hundred townspeople gathered in front of the stage. It was quite a sight. A group of costumed dancers, caparisoned in smart, white costumes with unusual pleats and ruffles and wearing bright yellow *pagdis,* headbands with large side frills, performed a stick dance as a greeting ceremony. They then sat in rows at the front, while the townspeople, some dressed in white turbans and others in colorful purple ones, clustered behind to get a glimpse of their revered visitor.

The king's son, Yuvrāj Ṭhākura Sahib, a short, pleasant man in his late forties, gave a brief introductory speech and welcoming address before requesting Śrīla Prabhupāda to speak. Prabhupāda asked for his *karatālas* and then chanted the *mahā-mantra* for a few minutes. He then thanked our hosts and the audience for their warm reception.

The Yuvrāj then invited him to come down off the stage and mount an open horse-drawn carriage that was waiting to take him on a grand reception tour through the town. The carriage had seen better days but was still quite stately. By this time several thousand people had gathered, eager to greet Śrīla Prabhupāda. Their enthusiasm and veneration surcharged the atmosphere.

Hansadūta, Harikeśa, and I were swept up in the excitement. Harikeśa rushed about snapping photos for *Back to Godhead* magazine. Hansadūta went off with a *mṛdaṅga* to join Jaśomatīnandana and Haihaya in *kīrtana* at the front of the procession.

Śrīla Prabhupāda and the king climbed into the carriage, sitting opposite each other, Prabhupāda on the back seat. On Prabhupāda's request I was privileged to ride on the back running board. Taking the colorful umbrella from the *chowkidar's* grasp, I leaned over to provide a shield for His Divine Grace from the sun's rays.

Then we were off on an hour-long ride that took us through the main parts of the town and up the central thoroughfare leading to Sanand Palace. It was wonderful. All along the route excited people clamored to get a glimpse of Śrīla Prabhupāda and his foreign disciples.

A large crowd preceded us, with several hundred women following behind. As the procession wound its way through the town, the ladies spontaneously burst into chanting, "Hare Kṛṣṇa, Hare Kṛṣṇa, Kṛṣṇa Kṛṣṇa, Hare Hare/ Hare Rāma, Hare Rāma, Rāma Rāma, Hare Hare," without any prompting from our devotees. Although I've read in Prabhupāda's books that village people in India are naturally inclined to be devotees, to actually see it practically manifested was a moving experience.

The reception was spontaneous and genuinely heart-warming. There is a piety in India, especially in the villages, that simply doesn't exist anywhere else in the world.

In the main bazaar people came out on their balconies or rooftops and showered flowers or offered *praṇāmas*. The street was hung with mango leaves and colorful strips of paper, fluttering like little flags in the breeze.

As the carriage crept along, people pushed forward and repeatedly stopped it. Sometimes they'd give a garland to Śrīla Prabhupāda. With great respect and devotion others would offer him a brief *pūjā* from small trays equipped with a ghee lamp, a few grains of rice, some *kum kum,* a few *paisa,* a piece of fruit and a few flowers. After waving the tray with the lighted lamp in small circles before him, they leaned forward to dot his forehead with the *kum kum* and then a grain of rice. Śrīla Prabhupāda patiently accepted their offerings with great humility and appreciation, joining his palms together and blessing them with a smile and "Hare Kṛṣṇa!"

When we reached the Palace entrance the carriage came to a halt, turning to face the crowd. Prabhupāda gave a short speech, then the carriage moved through a large arch into the privacy of the royal courtyard.

The reception delighted Prabhupāda. He commented that village people are all devotees because they naturally chant the holy names.

* * *

Sanand Palace sounds much grander than what it actually is: a 450-year-old group of red brick buildings. By local standards it is impressive, but certainly not what we'd call opulent. Prabhupāda is housed in one wing on an upper floor, and I sleep outside his door. Hansadūta and Harikeśa have a room on the roof.

The king's entire family live here: sons, daughters, nephews, nieces, et al. It is a traditional Indian family enclave, and they are all cordial, humble, and helpful.

* * *

Jaśomatīnandana has arranged for a large *pāṇḍāla* tent to be erected, and programs are to be held for the next five days. At 8:30 p.m. Prabhupāda went there to lecture. About 5,000 people turned out, impressive for a town with a population of only 21,000. After a brief *kīrtana* Prabhupāda gave a well-received fifty-minute discourse in Hindi, which Jaśomatīnandana translated into Gujarati.

On the way out of the *pāṇḍāla* area Prabhupāda stopped the car at the entrance and inquired whether all the visitors were being given *prasādam.* He was shown some small white sugar beads which are commonly given out at many temples. He wasn't very impressed, but seemed to think it was better than nothing. We arrived back at the palace by 10:30 p.m.

December 26th, 1975

At about 7:00 a.m. Prabhupāda and his small *yātrā* of devotees took a short morning walk in the countryside. It was a late start by his usual standard, but now that the winter season has set in, the sun is rising later.

Walking down a rough dirt track in the open country we saw that the entire district was flat, fertile, and green. Unfortunately almost every field for miles around was dedicated to growing tobacco.

Prabhupāda expressed his amazement at the foolishness of modern economic systems. He explained that people can easily grow whatever they need in their own district, but instead they grow a product they can't eat. Then they ship it somewhere else at great expense. With the money they receive they buy the very food they could have grown themselves. This system does nothing but make their lives more complicated. And by becoming dependent on just one crop, livelihood is jeopardized because of the fluctuations of world markets which they have no power to influence.

There was also some talk about George Harrison, the former member of the Beatles rock group, who has donated a large country estate just out of London to our Society. Hansadūta has recently come from England, and his mention of Bhaktivedānta Manor naturally made Prabhupāda think of George. Hansadūta reported that George was smoking and drinking again.

Even though the report on George's activities wasn't very encouraging in spiritual terms, Prabhupāda considered only the positive side of his character. "No, no, he is very good boy, George. He showed me in Bombay. He came to see me in

Bombay. He is keeping Jagannātha within his beadbag and chanting."

"Just before I came to India," Hansadūta added, "Mukunda met him for about two hours. He said he was very friendly and said that he would arrange a ninety-nine year lease for us. Give us the right to Bhaktivedānta Manor."

The news pleased Prabhupāda. "No, he's our well-wisher, a good boy."

* * *

After breakfast, Jaśomatīnandana requested Prabhupāda to speak at a morning session of the *pāṇḍāla.* Prabhupāda is not really strong enough to do two lectures a day, but he agreed anyway.

Because most people are at work in the mornings, only about 150-200 people turned up for the lecture. It was disappointing, but Prabhupāda was undaunted. Last night he spoke in Hindi and Jaśomatīnandana translated into Gujarati. But today Prabhupāda announced that he would speak in English. "So they can understand," he said, meaning us, his three servants.

Śrīla Prabhupāda pointed out that because he is presenting Kṛṣṇa as He is, the Supreme Personality of Godhead, he is attracting so many young men and women from the West who are now preaching Kṛṣṇa's message all over the world. "We don't manufacture any concocted things. We simply distribute the message given by the Supreme Personality of Godhead, and this is becoming effective practically. You can see practically these Europeans and Americans, Australians, all over the world. They did not know four or five years ago, or, say, ten years ago, since I have begun this movement, they did not know what is Kṛṣṇa. Although *Bhagavad-gītā* was being presented by so many svāmīs and yogis, not a single man became a devotee of Kṛṣṇa. So our, this presentation, because it is pure without any adulteration, it is acting very nicely."

His recent conversation in Bombay about the *māyāvādī sannyāsī* served to illustrate his point. "One big svāmī, he said that '*Kṛṣṇa* means "black," and *black* means "unknown."' Of course, nobody cares for his speech. Kṛṣṇa is going on, forward.

Everyone is accepting Kṛṣṇa. But this is the most unfortunate thing, that our men go there [to the West] to deprecate Kṛṣṇa."

Finally he stressed Śrī Caitanya Mahāprabhu's order that all Indians should become gurus by understanding *Bhagavad-gītā* as it is. Not considering whether he was speaking to sophisticated residents of Bombay or simple villagers who perhaps had never even ventured beyond Sanand, he urged his audience to preach Kṛṣṇa consciousness all over the world.

"So Bhagavān is not far away from you. He is staying within the core of your heart. If you qualify yourself as devotee, He'll speak with you. But if you commit offenses, thinking Kṛṣṇa as ordinary man, then Kṛṣṇa will never give you instruction. So our request is that you study *Bhagavad-gītā*."

Though devoid of real Vedic qualifications, it was still very satisfying to be used by Śrīla Prabhupāda as examples of the efficacy of Kṛṣṇa consciousness. It always pleases Prabhupāda to be able to point out how the Westerners have eagerly taken up his mission. He gives us credit far beyond what we deserve.

And it is not simply propaganda either. In private he also compliments us for having made the sacrifice of preaching on his behalf. He is always encouraging, correcting, and pushing us on to greater and greater degrees of surrender to Kṛṣṇa.

* * *

In the afternoon the king and many local village leaders came for *darśana*. They discussed the need to educate the people in spiritual values. Prabhupāda again brought up the point that growing cash crops such as tobacco was senseless. He informed them that he was prepared to travel to every village to preach *Bhagavad-gītā*, perform *kīrtana*, and distribute *prasādam*, if they were willing to organize it.

* * *

The evening program began late but was well attended. From 8:00-9:30 thousands of people poured into the grounds and enjoyed *bhajans* until Prabhupāda began his lecture on *Bhagavad-gītā* (16.7): "Those who are demonic do not know what is to be done and what is not to be done. Neither cleanliness nor proper behavior nor truth is found in them."

Once more he spoke in English, his strong, clear voice amplified above the clamor, and Jaśomatīnandana translated into Gujarati. He explained that one's birth or upbringing are inconsequential—Kṛṣṇa consciousness is for anyone who wants to take it. "According to *varṇāśrama-dharma,* the *brāhmaṇas* are called *śuci,* means 'pure.' But this *śuci*—the opposite word is *mucī.* So there is a Bengali Vaiṣṇava poet. He says that '*śuci haya mucī haya yadi kṛṣṇa tyaje, mucī haya śuci haya yadi kṛṣṇa bhaje.*' The purport is that if somebody takes to Kṛṣṇa consciousness, even he is born in the family of *mucī,* then he becomes *śuci.* And if a person is born in the *brāhmaṇa* family or *kṣatriya* family but he does not take to Kṛṣṇa consciousness, then he becomes a *mucī.* This is also confirmed in the *Bhagavad-gītā, māṁ hi pārtha vyapāśritya ye 'pi syuḥ pāpa-yonayaḥ. Pāpa-yoni* means *mucī,* less than the *śūdras.* If he takes to Kṛṣṇa consciousness, *te 'pi yānti parāṁ gatim,* he is also eligible to go back to home, back to Godhead. So even a *mucī* or a *pāpa-yoni* born in the low-grade family, if he takes to Kṛṣṇa consciousness, he becomes a *devatā.* This is also confirmed in the *Śrīmad-Bhāgavatam* [2.4.18] by Śukadeva Gosvāmī,

kirāta-hūṇāndhra-pulinda-pulkaśā
ābhīra-śumbhā yavanāḥ khasādayaḥ
ye 'nye ca pāpā yad-apāśrayāśrayāḥ
śudhyanti tasmai prabhaviṣṇave namaḥ.

"So it doesn't matter where we are born. If we take to Kṛṣṇa consciousness, then he becomes a *śuddha, śuci,* purified, and he is eligible to go back to home, to back to Godhead."

Later in the lecture Prabhupāda again displayed his determination to challenge the atheistic scientists, whom he described as asuric. "Their main proposal is that there is no creator, God. The modern scientists, philosophers, Western people, they don't accept that God is the creator of everything. And their theory of creation is the chemical composition. They think that chemical combination is the cause of life. So the *asuras'* theory of creation is a chance theory, but we don't accept. We are preaching against them, writing books against them. We are challenging this atheistic theory of creation. The

Kṛṣṇa consciousness movement is against the *asuras.* Kṛṣṇa also comes down to kill the *asuras. Paritrāṇāya sādhūnāṁ vināśāya ca duṣkṛtām. Asuras* cannot flourish by their atheistic theory. Unless one comes to Kṛṣṇa consciousness, he has to be put into the different types of *asuric yoni* [lower species] to suffer in this material world."

He summarized by explaining how easy it is to become Kṛṣṇa conscious, urging everyone to adopt the universal panacea given by Śrī Caitanya Mahāprabhu. "To take to this Kṛṣṇa consciousness is made very easy during this *Kali-yuga. Harer nāma harer nāma harer nāmaiva kevalam, kalau nāsty eva nāsty eva nāstya eva gatir anyathā. Kalau,* in this age, if you take to Kṛṣṇa consciousness, simply chant Hare Kṛṣṇa, Hare Kṛṣṇa mantra, then you become *devatā.* This is our program. So our only request is to you, that in whatever position you are—it doesn't require to be changed—simply take to Kṛṣṇa consciousness. Chant Hare Kṛṣṇa *mahā-mantra,* and gradually you'll become *devatā.* That is the recommendation of Śrī Caitanya Mahāprabhu. *Sthāne sthitāḥ śruti-gatāṁ tanu-vāṅ-manobhir.* 'Remain in your place but be Kṛṣṇa conscious.' It is not difficult at all. Thank you very much. Hare Kṛṣṇa."

The crowd was clearly impressed. I doubt anyone had ever spoken so directly and forcefully to them, yet they appreciated it. Even though it was very late, most of the audience stayed after Prabhupāda left to see a film depicting Kṛṣṇa consciousness around the world.

December 27th, 1975

During this morning's walk Prabhupāda again criticized the local farmers for growing tobacco rather than grains, cotton, and other necessities. He said it was a symptom of degradation to grow cash crops instead of food.

"Now eat cash! So cash is also paper. So what is the use of laboring so hard? You eat paper. Paper is available. Growing tea, growing tobacco, growing jute, and no grains. And grain for the animal. So that animal, as soon as it becomes fatty, send it to the slaughterhouse and then finish business. Smoke, eat meat, drink, and be happy! So much land, but it is producing tobacco, which we are prohibiting: no smoking."

The talk of crops also brought up the question of *prasādam* distribution at these programs. Prabhupāda is very keen to see that sumptuous *prasādam* is given out whenever we hold a gathering. He said that otherwise ordinary people will not be attracted.

Although lecturing very strongly every day, he is aware that what he says inevitably will go over the heads of most people. Therefore he told the local devotees, "Then accept this program, distribution of *prasādam*. Then we can go everywhere, whole day program—*kīrtana* and distribution. Simply dry philosophy, what will people understand?"

* * *

Despite our remote location, somehow the mail is still reaching us. The first tally from the annual Christmas book distribution marathon in the West came today via a telegram from Rāmeśvara in Los Angeles. Śrīla Prabhupāda was ecstatic; the distribution is increasing and his response undoubtedly stoked the fire of the devotees' enthusiasm.

"Please accept my blessings. I am in due receipt of your telegram as follows: 'CHRISTMAS WEEK BOOK DISTRIBUTION IN LOS ANGELES DESPITE CLOSED AIRPORT BETTER THAN EVER BY YOUR GRACE 112,000 BTG'S, 8,000 GITAS SOLD STOP ON INVITATION OF GOVERNOR BROWN OF CALIFORNIA 50 DEVOTEES VISITED STATE MENTAL INSTITUTIONS TO HELP IMPROVE CONDITIONS AND MORALE BY GIVING RELIGIOUS MESSAGE. PUBLICITY VERY GOOD, HARE KRSNA.'

"Thank you very much. This is very good. Fight and depend on Kṛṣṇa. That will bring you victory."

The immense distribution of transcendental literature in the West is a sharp contrast to its lack in India. Although India has one of the largest populations in the world, with people naturally receptive to the message of Śrī Caitanya Mahāprabhu's Movement, so little of it is being realized because of a lack of books in the local languages.

So Prabhupāda remains ever vigilant for competent translators. In Vṛndāvana a Gosvāmī and his sons are currently working on translations of his books. Anxious to see how it is progressing, Śrīla Prabhupāda wrote Bhagatjī, for the second time within the last few weeks, asking him to send samples to him. He also requested Bhagatjī to help expedite the opening of a branch of the Punjab National Bank within our temple compound in Vṛndāvana. Negotiations are nearly complete, and Prabhupāda wants it open as soon as possible.

* * *

Prabhupāda is always pointing out the fraudulence of modern scientists. Yesterday he mentioned that in Germany after the first World War they opened a factory to extract fat from stool for eventual human consumption. "How could they even *think* of such a thing?" he said.

He also told us a little about his German Godbrother, a scientifically-minded man. Understanding the limitations of scientific endeavor, he had taken shelter of Śrīla Bhaktisiddhānta Sarasvatī Ṭhākura and received first initiation. He lived with Prabhupāda for some time in Bombay, but could not maintain the strict discipline of spiritual life. Later he returned to Germany.

* * *

Prabhupāda considers Harikeśa's writing assignment important enough that he has given him permission to miss some of the programs to work on it. He is applying himself very seriously to the task, and Prabhupāda frequently calls him to discuss various arguments. Today he even had him come during his massage to discuss it.

Prabhupāda decided to take his massage up on the roof as it was warm and sunny. Being the highest building in the district, it affords a good view for miles all around with a gentle breeze carrying the distinct redolence of the tobacco plants.

Harikeśa came up with the tape recorder. He has recently obtained a small book explaining Leninist philosophy, and using it as a basis, he and Śrīla Prabhupāda engaged in a lengthy discussion.

Prabhupāda brilliantly exposed the defects in communist ideology, showing how to defeat them at their own game of "thesis, antithesis, and synthesis."

"So what is the thesis of life?" Prabhupāda challenged.

Harikeśa answered, "Some people say that life is to be enjoyed. Life is simply there for enjoyment."

Prabhupāda replied, "So the answer is that, whether you are actually enjoying life."

Harikeśa got into the mood. "Well, right now I am not actually enjoying life, so I have to find out ... the means to enjoy and to negate the pain and to make the pleasure more."

"Yes," Prabhupāda agreed. "That's very nice proposal. But whether at the present moment or in the history a man is enjoying life or suffering?"

"Well," Harikeśa replied, "men have actually never really enjoyed because they never understood enough about themselves. They were never able to overcome their difficulties due to ignorance."

"So," Prabhupāda said, "then the next question will be how to enjoy. There may be different theses, so our thesis is that we are trying to enjoy life by covering ourself. The crude example: The contraceptive method was by using one cover, but that was not enjoyable. So then they discovered pills.

"So covered enjoyment is not enjoyment; it is not complete enjoyment. The real enjoyment in this material world is sex. Now, if we want to enjoy sex covered with coats and pants, is that enjoyment pleasing?"

Harikeśa had to admit, "No."

"Therefore actually when they want to enjoy sex in the private room they become naked. So they are seeking enjoyment with this material body, but they are not able to enjoy on account of being covered

"That means covered enjoyment is not enjoyment. It is hampered enjoyment. Therefore we—human beings—we want enjoyment. That's all right, but we are not able to enjoy fully because we are covered by something. This is the thesis. But these rascals, or the ignorant person, they do not know that 'I am covered by something. Therefore my enjoyment is not complete'

"So you answer this. Our enjoyment is not being completed on account of being covered by this material body. This is the thesis."

Before Harikeśa could complete his answer, Prabhupāda went on, "The antithesis will be how to become uncovered. And the synthesis will be that because we are unable to uncover immediately, therefore there must be some synthesis."

Harikeśa had to admit that he had never thought of it that way.

Prabhupāda went on to explain, "This is Kṛṣṇa conscious. The thesis of the covering and the antithesis of the soul should be synthesized by arrangement. And that we are teaching."

"Dialectical spiritualism," Harikeśa offered.

Prabhupāda said, "Yes. Dialectic means spiritualism and materialism. It is dialectic. Two sides there are, the material and the spiritual. These ignorant rascals, cats-and-dogs-like men, they have no information of the thing which is covered. They are simply dealing with the coverings. Therefore their knowledge is imperfect, and they are not successful by so many theses. They do not know the real problem. Who is enjoyer? That they do not know. That enjoyer is covered, and they are talking of the cover.

"In Bengal it is a proverb, saying that *chopra niye tanatani.* The coconut, sweet pulp and water is within, and they are struggling with the fibers above the coconut. Coconut, they have got some information: 'Coconut is enjoyable.' But where is the enjoyable article there? That they do not know. They have simply information, this body. And the coconut's body is covered with fibers, and they are fighting with the fibers.

"None of these so-called capitalists or ... communists, they do not know where the real substance is. Superficially they are fighting on the platform of fiber covering. That's all. *Chopra niye tanatani,* they are fighting just like dogs. Actually they do not know how to become happy, but one dog is barking upon another dog, and they are fighting, attacking, barking—useless.

"The dogs and cats, they do not know what is the value of life. But here is a chance, human being. Therefore dialectic, dialectic materialism. The inside pulp of coconut requires the covering outside; otherwise it would be spoiled. Crude example. But the real substance is inside, not outside. But these rascals, they have no information of the inside substance. They think that, 'Here is coconut. Let us try to find out happiness,' and they are simply struggling to adjust the fibers. Therefore they have been described as *mūḍha,* rascals.

"Therefore, you see despite so many rascal philosophers in the Western country, they simply fight and bomb and cheat and politics, diplomacy—on the surface of the coconut, not inside. So you have to prove that, 'All of you are rascals. You do not know where to get pleasure. You are missing that point.' So we know the thesis, antithesis, and synthesis—that this soul, living entity, is within this body." Prabhupāda concluded by saying, "So in their dialectic process try to bring this thesis that 'Within this body there is the real enjoyer,' and try to convince them in that way. That will be great service."

Harikeśa said, "You've already done it."

Prabhupāda answered, "I have done with few selected men. Now it has to be spread. We have to face bigger field. Then it will be nice. The thesis is the soul, the antithesis is the body, and synthesis is how to adjust the body and soul so that the soul be benefitted from this entanglement."

Śrīla Prabhupāda perfectly analyzed the defective materialistic philosophies, and with only a few choice words defeated the results of lifetimes of speculative thought. The discussion was stimulating and left us feeling full of admiration for him. At a loss for words, we can only admire his genius and offer inadequate homage.

Yet he isn't content to sit back in complacent satisfaction, nor will he allow us to either. Harikeśa suggested that what Prabhupāda had just spoken should be written as a *Back to Godhead* article. So Prabhupāda told him to write it.

Harikeśa said, "You so completely destroy the opposition, it is very hard to say anything more!"

Prabhupāda agreed, but challenged further, "Yes. That you have to prove. You can eulogize your Guru Mahārāja, but you have to learn it and face the public and be strong to defend yourself. That is success, not by praising your Guru Mahārāja. You'll praise your Guru Mahārāja. That is not very difficult. But be victorious to the opposing elements. Then you'll praise your Guru Mahārāja best. At home you can praise your Guru Mahārāja, and Guru Mahārāja be satisfied, 'Oh, my disciples are praising me.' That is good, respectful. That is the qualification. But you have to fight. Then your Guru Mahārāja will be glorified."

These discussions have been going on for weeks, but Prabhupāda continues to prod Harikeśa for further materialistic viewpoints, which he then promptly defeats. He is determined to challenge and destroy every philosophical obstacle to Lord Caitanya's mission. He is always visibly inspired by such debate.

At the same time Prabhupāda is making it clear that he wants to train as many men as possible to take up this task of saving the world. He concluded the discussion by asking Harikeśa to produce a small pamphlet on the subject, urging him to print it even in Russian.

"Oh, in Russian!"

"Hm? They are the greatest atheist."

"A dialectic spiritualism pamphlet in Russian! That's big, Russian."

Prabhupāda's sharp intellect shows in other ways. At the beginning of the massage I had brought out a thin cotton mattress for him to sit on, rather than the usual straw mat. As he spoke with Harikeśa, I knelt in front of him to begin massaging his head. I poured a little of the precious sandalwood oil into my cupped palm, placing the almost full bottle on the lumpy mattress.

Concentrating on being careful not to tip the contents out of my leveled hand, I let go of the bottle and reached up to apply the oil to his head. In a flash Prabhupāda's hand swooped down to catch the uncapped bottle as it toppled on the uneven surface. Not a drop was spilt. Though he was speaking with Harikeśa, he had anticipated my carelessness and saved the expensive oil. His short sharp rebuke, "You rascal!" and critical glare was enough to guarantee that I wouldn't make the same mistake again.

* * *

In the afternoon Kārttikeya drove us five miles to a local village for a program. In the car Prabhupāda talked enthusiastically about village-to-village preaching. He is eager to see this program established and said that mass propaganda of *saṅkīrtana* and *prasādam* distribution will save India. He said that if programs are arranged he will travel in his new car (when it comes), taking a dozen men all around Gujarat to every village.

Upon arrival, he was welcomed grandly and taken to an open area where a thousand or so village people had gathered. The leading men lined up and offered Prabhupāda at least twenty or thirty garlands. Prabhupāda chanted for a few minutes and then began to speak; but it was so noisy, with all the women and children, he stopped.

He chanted again, this time getting the crowd to join in. Again he lectured, this time to a quiet audience. For twenty minutes he gave a simple explanation of spiritual knowledge and impressed on them the need to lead a pure life following God's laws. His main intent was to get them to chant and take *prasādam.*

At the conclusion he returned by car directly to the *paṇḍala* in Sanand for the evening program, which continued to be very well attended. At least 4,000-5,000 people turned out and sat quietly in the cool night air to hear him deliver an enlightening discourse on *Bhagavad-gītā* (7.1) in English, with Jaśomatīnandana translating.

Tonight's topic was about *āsakti,* converting our attachment to Kṛṣṇa. He stressed the role that a pure devotee plays in creating opportunities for the materially attached people to take shelter of Kṛṣṇa.

He repeated, as he continually does, his appeal to the Indian people to take up the mission entrusted to them by Śrī Caitanya Mahāprabhu. "Kṛṣṇa *bhakti,* attachment for Kṛṣṇa, is quite natural. It is already there. Simply it has to be awakened. If you engage yourself to hear about Kṛṣṇa, then your heart will be purified and your original Kṛṣṇa consciousness will be awakened. For this purpose Śrī Caitanya Mahāprabhu also advises, *paraṁ vijāyate śri-kṛṣṇa-saṅkīrtanam,* 'All glories to the *saṅkīrtana* movement,' because simply by chanting the Hare Kṛṣṇa mantra, everything will automatically come. The *saṅkīrtana* movement, Kṛṣṇa consciousness movement, the more you chant Hare Kṛṣṇa *mahā-mantra,* the heart disease, material enjoyment, that will decrease, and then you will understand what is your position, and you will be gradually attracted by Kṛṣṇa. This is the test of *bhakti,* that if you engage yourself twenty-four hours in devotional service, then immediately you become liberated."

He offered them the example of Dhruva Mahārāja to illustrate that even one who is not free from material desire can still be accepted by Kṛṣṇa and go back to Godhead. "Kṛṣṇa is so nice, so liberal, that if you have got a little tinge of aspiration He will fulfill you, and at the same time, you'll go back to home, back to Godhead. Kṛṣṇa is all-powerful, almighty, full with six opulences. So if you have got any material desire, that also Kṛṣṇa can fulfill, but you stick to Kṛṣṇa so that your *āsakti* will be increased. If we want to go back to home, back to Godhead, then we must increase our attachment for Kṛṣṇa, and by that process we can understand Kṛṣṇa, what He is. *Bhaktyā mām abhijānāti.* Then our door to go back to home, back to Godhead is clear."

It was a long lecture and very late when he returned to the palace. He looked strained. He said that he was experiencing heart palpitations because of air in his chest.

So many programs are clearly too much. Only one per day should be the limit, otherwise he is becoming ill.

December 28th, 1975

No morning walk today. After resting until seven-thirty, Prabhupāda felt a little better. Still, Jaśomatīnandana performed the morning program. Prabhupāda told him that he should lead the remaining morning *pāṇḍālas* with help from Hansadūta.

Being Ekādaśī, we observed a half-day fast. Prabhupāda told me that to please Kṛṣṇa, we could fast completely, even from water. The fast was welcome for another reason also—the meals cooked for us by our hosts are swimming in ghee.

* * *

Prabhupāda took his massage on the palace roof again. It was pleasant sitting in the warm sun, looking out over the township and across the green expanse of countryside.

Prabhupāda continued his assault on the material scientists. "They are simply building a big palace on a tiny, shaky foundation. It cannot stand." He compared their inspection of the material nature to analyzing stool. "Some is dry, some is wet, and they are arguing which is best. They are simply fools." He told Harikeśa not to call them directly rascals, though, but to make them realize that they are by explaining the facts nicely.

* * *

In mid-afternoon Kārttikeya Mahādevia drove us in his old American limousine for a program in another nearby town called Bavala (pop. 20,000).

Along the way Prabhupāda incited our enthusiasm for the village preaching programs. He told us that in the 1950s he had made plans to travel all around India, hoping to gather up a force of *brahmacārī* preachers. Somehow it never happened, for he had neither men nor money. And Kṛṣṇa had another plan for him—preaching in the West. He said that now Kṛṣṇa has sent him so many nice young men to help fulfil his long-cherished vision.

Jaśomatīnandana eagerly offered to organize a program in a different village every day, and Kārttikeya even offered his car if Prabhupāda wanted it.

Prabhupāda encouraged Hansadūta take up this engagement, declaring that he would personally travel with the party. It was such an exciting concept, and Prabhupāda was so enthusiastic, the fact that such a program would be almost physically impossible for him wasn't even mentioned. For Prabhupāda, preaching means that there is no consideration other than spreading Kṛṣṇa consciousness, whatever the cost.

In Bavala, like Sanand, thousands of people turned out to greet him. Taken first to a small house and worshiped by local *brāhmaṇas,* he later boarded a camel cart for a procession through the main streets. There were four or five camel carts, many bullock carts, and many, many thousands of people—practically the whole town. Prabhupāda was perched up on a high seat covered with white cloth, and I sat in front of him on the deck. Hansadūta stood directly behind Prabhupāda. This was a little troublesome for Hansadūta because every time the caravan stopped the camel pulling the cart behind us would inch forward so close that he was literally breathing down Hansadūta's neck.

We stopped once at a Svāmī Nārāyaṇa Temple and then went on to a meeting hall. After garlands were given by leading citizens, local children performed a lovely *rāsa-līlā* dance. It was pure and simple, and Prabhupāda enjoyed it. He then led a *kīrtana* and gave a fairly short English lecture on *Bhagavad-gītā* (3.14), about food grains being the result of the performance of sacrifice. About three thousand noisy, but respectful, people packed into an open area to hear Prabhupāda tell them not to grow jute and tobacco but to produce food grains, chant, avoid the four aspects of sinful life, and please Kṛṣṇa by their work. His lecture was brief, but direct and to the point. After explaining that the purpose of life is simply to please Lord Viṣṇu, he outlined the process of work by which this can be achieved. "It is not possible that we can give up sinful activities by our own endeavor, because in this age, *Kali-yuga,* everyone is addicted to some sort of sinful activities. But if we surrender to Kṛṣṇa as He is instructing, fully, without any reservation, He will help us to become free from sinful reactions."

Immediately after the close of the lecture, as the excited townspeople clamored around, he climbed back into the car and returned to Sanand. Upon arrival, he went straight to the *pāṇḍāla* where he gave another lecture, this time in Hindi. It was after ten o'clock when we arrived back at the palace.

December 29th, 1975

No morning walk again today, although Prabhupāda is feeling a little better.

* * *

Rather than take his massage on the roof, Prabhupāda sat on the veranda outside his room overlooking the inner courtyard of the house. He could hear Harikeśa preaching enthusiastically to the king's son and his wife inside a room across the courtyard down on the ground floor. He gave a slight motion of his head and a sidelong glance to indicate it to me. He listened appreciatively for a few moments and said, "He is preaching very nicely!" Smiling, he remarked that Harikeśa is very enthusiastic for preaching, and that that is his greatest asset.

* * *

Our hosts are cooking for us, but Harikeśa still prepares Śrīla Prabhupāda's meals. In this way Prabhupāda can maintain his regular diet suited to his own taste and delicate digestion. He likes to eat alone and rarely allows anyone to remain with him while he honors his *prasādam,* as I found out this afternoon.

Prabhupāda sat down after taking his bath, and I brought in his plate. He began to eat, so I sat obediently in front, eager to serve. I thought myself very privileged to share the intimacy of Śrīla Prabhupāda taking his lunch. Prabhupāda, however, looked up from his plate and raised his eyebrows, questioning why I was there. He clearly felt the intrusion. And, slightly embarrassed, I left. I could understand he likes us to do things with reason and purpose and not simply hang around.

* * *

The only program today was in the evening, the final one in Sanand. After a short half-hour lecture many people came up to the stage and gave garlands to Prabhupāda.

Then the king's son and his wife stood before Prabhupāda, jointly offering a gigantic multitiered lamp of 108 wicks to Prabhupāda. Not only was the lamp heavy, being made of brass, it was also extremely hot. A huge flame shot up from the burning wicks about a foot high, but somehow they held on to the lamp and completed the *pūjā.*

We performed *kīrtana,* and all the family members and prominent citizens sang a traditional *bhajan.* There were some short speeches of thanks, and finally the highly successful pandal series was brought to a close.

December 30th, 1975

Early in the morning Prabhupāda took his leave, graciously thanking the king's entire family for their kindness and hospitality. He was very happy with the programs and talked with the

King's son about organizing the village preaching. Prabhupāda's enthusiasm has clearly rubbed off on the Yuvrāj, and he seemed very eager to help us push forward Śrī Caitanya Mahāprabhu's mission.

Ahmedabad

We drove to one Life Member's house in Ahmedabad. After a brief reception, Prabhupāda boarded a silver carriage drawn by two horses, for a procession through the local district. This time Prabhupāda had me sit directly opposite him, at his feet on the lower front seat.

It was strikingly different from the Sanand and Bavala parades, where Prabhupāda's presence had attracted crowds of thousands. Here only a few hundred people lined up along the route, mainly out of curiosity at the sound of the *kīrtana*. It appeared that the event wasn't well advertised or organized. Yet those who attended the parade were nonetheless respectful and sincere, and Prabhupāda was pleased with their attempts.

We ended up at a small temple of Lord Śiva. After offering respects to the deity, Prabhupāda gave a short lecture in Hindi. Then it was on to a Life Member's house for lunch and a short rest. Jaśomatīnandana then took Prabhupāda to see a house he is thinking of renting for a center. After inspecting it, Prabhupāda sat in the back seat of the car next me, ready to leave for the airport.

Just then a young boy of about ten came up to the window next to me. He peered in and saw the beautiful button I was wearing on my *khaḍi* waistcoat. It was a photo of the Deities of Lord Jagannātha, Balarāma, and Subhadrā in Melbourne. The boy's eyes lit up. Without saying a word he pointed first at the badge and then at himself with his eyebrows going up and down and big smile on his face, as if to say, "Give it to me! Give it to me!" I did my best to ignore him, for I was rather attached to the badge and had worn it for a long time.

When Śrīla Prabhupāda looked over to see what was going on, I half suspected that he might tell me to give it to the boy. I was hoping not. Suddenly Prabhupāda leaned forward with his eyes wide and put up both his hands with his fingers spread. "Ten rupees!" he told the boy with mock seriousness. "Ten rupees!" Our solicitous young visitor was only momentarily taken aback. Shaking his head from side to side he continued to point.

Prabhupāda laughed and sat back. "All right, give him it."

Resigned, I dutifully handed over the badge, and the boy skipped merrily away. His prize was the lotus feet of the Lord of the Universe. Mine was a little more detachment and surrender to the lotus feet of the Lord's servant, Śrīla Prabhupāda.

* * *

We flew back to Bombay at 5 o'clock, and by mid-evening Śrīla Prabhupāda was back in his quarters at Hare Kṛṣṇa Land, Juhu Beach. Upon arrival in his room he again admitted that his heart was getting weaker and that he was not feeling well.

December 31st, 1975

Madhudviṣa Swami, GBC for Australia, contacted us today and requested a confirmation of Śrīla Prabhupāda's intention to attend their fourth annual Melbourne Ratha-yātrā in mid-January.

Australia's seasons are reverse to those in the Northern Hemisphere. So a few years ago Prabhupāda had given his permission to hold the festival during the summer, rather than in the cold of June, in order to attract the greatest number of people.

Although Prabhupāda wanted to attend, after some discussion he finally decided not to go. He reasoned that his legs, feet, and hands were still quite swollen with fluid and he was not feeling well enough to travel such a long distance.

He did go on his walk, though, and otherwise spent a quiet day, meeting a few visitors in the afternoon.

* * *

Hansadūta returned from a day's shopping with a set of small bowls, a *loṭā,* a spoon, and a rimmed plate for Śrīla

Prabhupāda, all made of solid silver. Hansadūta was surprised to discover that Prabhupāda didn't have his own eating utensils, so on his own initiative he purchased a complete set of silverware.

His Divine Grace was very pleased at his thoughtfulness and accepted the gift with humble appreciation. He handed them over to me with the instruction that they should be kept with him as his permanent travel set.

Hansadūta is now thoroughly enlivened with the idea of village-to-village preaching in India. Recent problems in Germany, where he is the GBC, have virtually stopped the preaching there, so he is looking for a new engagement. Prabhupāda is therefore encouraging him to preach in the villages.

Hansadūta spent the entire day inquiring about the price of buses and other equipment, and he talked with Prabhupāda about bringing some men over from Germany to form an all-India traveling *saṅkīrtana* party.

Although Prabhupāda likes the idea, he doesn't want him to abandon his duties in Germany altogether. He told him that even if there are difficulties there, the efforts for the long-term establishment of Kṛṣṇa consciousness have to be maintained.

Since Hansadūta has been instrumental in the development of the German *yātrā,* Śrīla Prabhupāda isn't keen to see him leave, lest everything collapse. But Prabhupāda also has no objection at all to Hansadūta's preaching in India—at least for the time being while the difficulties persist.

Śrīla Prabhupāda likes the idea of having some of his senior preachers active in India. In many ways he is personally carrying the full weight of the Indian preaching. He has few experienced men based here and consequently has to do much of the preaching and management himself. The presence of another one of his trained preachers is therefore welcome to him.

CHAPTER SIX

Madras

January 1st, 1976

Tamal Krishna Goswami arrived from America at 5:00 a.m. this morning to serve as Prabhupāda's secretary for the month of January. Prabhupāda was very happy to see him. He brought with him the newly printed volumes I and II of the *Śrīmad-Bhāgavatam,* Sixth Canto. The books look beautiful with gilt-edged pages and a new full-color painting for the end covers. The painting is of Śukadeva Gosvāmī, surrounded by all the great sages, speaking the *Bhāgavatam* to Mahārāja Parīkṣit on the banks of the Ganges. The front cover and spine are gold stamped, giving an attractive, high-quality appearance. Prabhupāda is very happy to see them.

Prabhupāda also received the first copies of a new pocket-sized book he translated: *Śrī Upadeśāmṛta, The Nectar of Instruction,* by Śrīla Rūpa Gosvāmī. Prabhupāda appeared very satisfied with it and immediately asked how many copies had been printed. When he heard there were only ten thousand, he wanted to know why.

Tamal Krishna Mahārāja explained that the BBT staff thought that the book is meant primarily for devotees, thus the small print run.

But Prabhupāda made it clear that he wants the book for mass distribution as well. He told Tamal to inform Rāmeśvara to print at least 100,000 immediately.

Tamal Krishna Mahārāja then gave the final book distribution figures for the six-day Christmas period. The figures were astounding, and Prabhupāda laughed in clear enjoyment—over 600,000 books distributed! In New York alone they had sold 18,000 *Kṛṣṇa Book* trilogies in just one day! The figures are utterly unprecedented, and Prabhupāda beamed as he heard the scores and some of the stories of how it was done.

* * *

At 8:55 a.m. Śrīla Prabhupāda, Tamal Krishna Mahārāja, Harikeśa, and I flew to Madras. Acyutānanda, Yaśodānandana, Gurukṛpa, and Mahāṁsa mahārājas; Śravaṇānanda and Bhāvabhūti prabhus, the co-temple presidents of ISKCON Madras; members of the Nāma Haṭṭa *saṅkīrtana* party; and a small but very enthusiastic group of life members, all greeted us at the Madras airport. They held a rousing *kīrtana* in the small airport building, bringing everything to a standstill. The life members were swept up by the enthusiasm of the devotees, and at least 30-40 garlands were draped around Śrīla Prabhupāda's neck. Śrīla Prabhupāda was beaming with pleasure at the reception, and after a few minutes we were led out to a waiting Mercedes sedan, loaned for the week by a well-wisher, and driven to a life member's home.

We are staying at the house of Mr. Manical Bhai, an extremely pleasant and respectful Madwari businessman. As a member of the Vallabha *sampradāya* he is a strict vegetarian. It is a large, quiet house, and Prabhupāda has been given a section of the top floor with a porch.

The steep climb was a bit daunting for Śrīla Prabhupāda, as he is still very weak from uremia. Thus we carried him up in a chair. For us, of course, it was a welcome burden, a pleasure to relieve Śrīla Prabhupāda of any strain, but it was definitely not a good sign.

Later in the morning he conducted a well attended press conference. He explained to the reporters that the propagation of the Kṛṣṇa consciousness movement is aimed at educating the foolish modern civilization that indeed there is God, as described in the *Bhagavad-gītā.*

* * *

It was a quiet day with few visitors, and Prabhupāda relaxed. In the evening Mr. Mehra drove him to the Rājeśvarī Kalyāna Maṇḍapam, for the first of two programs arranged by Śravaṇānanda and Bhāvabhūti Prabhus.

The venue is a very popular marriage hall on Cathedral Road, with a seating capacity for about 2,000. The devotees have managed to get a life member to pay for the hire.

The hall is light and airy with two open sides and a recessed ceiling about thirty feet high. At the center back there is a raised platform, with a heavily sculpted gazebolike structure over it, where the weddings are performed.

Opposite this is a modest stage, recessed into the wall. On this the devotees have made simple, but attractive, arrangements for the two days of programs. In the center of the stage they have placed a beautiful *vyāsāsana* for Prabhupāda, a gift from the owner of the Globe Mirror company, another enthusiastic supporter. A large banner across the back wall, prominently featuring the ISKCON lotus flower logo, the name of the Society, and that of Śrīla Prabhupāda, completes the decorations.

When Śrīla Prabhupāda arrived the hall was packed, the mood relaxed and expectant. He mounted the stage and took his place on the *vyāsāsana.* Co-temple presidents Bhāvabhūti and Śravaṇānanda offered garlands and the devotees danced exuberantly to the *kīrtana* led by Acyutānanda Swami.

The devotees had invited the Governor of Tamil Nadu to attend. During the state of emergency he apparently has more authority in the state than the Chief Minister. He gave a short opening speech, praising the work Śrīla Prabhupāda is doing to spread Kṛṣṇa consciousness all over the world. He presented Prabhupāda with a garland, and Prabhupāda in turn gave him one of his personal copies of the Sixth Canto.

Unfortunately the Governor couldn't remain for the entire program because of prior commitments. Prabhupāda didn't seem to mind, though. He was satisfied to have a leading dignitary give support to his mission, especially here in Madras, a city noted for its efforts to smash traditional religious systems.

Śrīla Prabhupāda chanted *jaya rādhā mādhava* and then launched into an excellent fifty-minute lecture on *Bhagavad-gītā* (3.27). He emphasized his theme from the morning's press conference that the purpose of the Kṛṣṇa consciousness movement is to educate the *mūḍhas,* the fools and rascals, who refuse to accept the supremacy of God.

Prabhupāda explained that God is canvassing, 'Here I am,' yet people continue to search for God. The verse itself explained the reason why: *ahaṅkāra-vimūḍhātmā,* simply due to false egotism. "Somehow or other we have now this human form of life," he said. "Kṛṣṇa said that utilize it very nicely so that the problems of life are finished. And that knowledge is very easy. Simply try to understand Kṛṣṇa. That's all. That will solve. And Kṛṣṇa is explaining Himself, what He is. Where is the difficulty? Unless you make some interpretation foolishly, everything is very, very clear. So you can understand Kṛṣṇa.

"And if you understand Kṛṣṇa, then result is *janma karma ca me divyam evaṁ yo vetti tattvataḥ, tyaktvā dehaṁ punar janma naiti mām eti kaunteya.* Where is the difficulty? There is no difficulty.

"Therefore our request is, take to this Kṛṣṇa consciousness. If the foreigners can take to it very seriously, so why not Indians? It is Indians' knowledge. *Bhagavad-gītā* was spoken in India. Why you are neglecting it? Why you are not taking advantage? Why you are falsely proud that you are independent? These are our questions."

Prabhupāda's straightforward approach appealed to his receptive audience who reciprocated by asking some thoughtful questions. The first was about "isms." Someone asked, "Is Kṛṣṇa consciousness Hinduism?"

"It is Kṛṣṇaism," Prabhupāda explained. "Hinduism means a type of faith, or Muslimism is type of faith. But, as it is described in the English dictionary, religion means a kind of faith. It is not that type of religion. It is a compulsory fact. Just like sugar is, compulsorily, must become sweet. If sugar is not sweet, that is not real sugar. Chili is not hot? That is not real chili.

"Similarly, we are part and parcel of Kṛṣṇa. Our duty is to become Kṛṣṇa conscious. There is no question of faith. You may have faith in Hinduism, tomorrow you may have faith in Christianism. Or you may have faith in Christianism, tomorrow in Mohammedan. This kind of faith is not Kṛṣṇa consciousness. Just like laws of the state. It is not that it is meant for the Hindus, or for the Muslims, for the Christian. It is meant for everyone. Similarly, *mamaivāṁśo jīva bhūtaḥ.* We are part and parcel of Kṛṣṇa, so it is compulsory to revive our consciousness that we are part and parcel of Kṛṣṇa. It is not a question of faith. Faith you may accept or do not accept, but here it is a question of 'must.' You must revive your Kṛṣṇa consciousness, otherwise you will suffer."

The second questioner wanted some clarification on the distinction between form and formlessness.

"The personal form and impersonal form, there are two conceptions," Śrīla Prabhupāda replied. "But Kṛṣṇa explains this, that *mayā tatam idaṁ sarvaṁ jagat avyakta-mūrtinā. Avyaktam,* impersonal, that is another form of Kṛṣṇa. So the whole creation is Kṛṣṇa's expansion of energy, just like the sunshine. Sunshine is also the same quality, heat and light, as the sun-globe or the sun-god. But the sunshine is impersonal, and the sun-globe is localized. And within the sun-globe there is sun-god. So that is the main source of everything. *Īśvaraḥ paramaḥ kṛṣṇaḥ sac-cid-ānanda vigrahaḥ. Brahmaṇo hi pratiṣṭhāham.* Kṛṣṇa is the source of *brahmajyoti.* So impersonal or personal, whatever you take, that is Brahman. *Brahmeti paramātmeti bhagavān iti śabdyate* ... whatever you take, that is emanation from Kṛṣṇa. But Kṛṣṇa has said, if you want to approach the Absolute Truth through the impersonal form, then it will be little difficult. Perhaps you may not reach the ultimate goal. You may fall down. There are so many instances.

"We have seen in India so many big, big *sannyāsīs.* They give up this world—*brahma satya jagan mithyā*—but after some days they come down to the *jagat* and engage themselves in politics. Why? They could not stay in the Brahman stage. That is stated in the *Śrīmad-Bhāgavatam.* By concentrating on the impersonal form they think that they have become liberated, but actually *aviśuddha-buddhayaḥ,* impersonal conception is not purified intelligence. *Ye 'nye 'ravindākṣa vimukta-māninas.* You may think that 'I have become liberated.' But it is not. Why? *Āruhya kṛcchreṇa paraṁ padaṁ tataḥ patanty adhah.* After so much trouble and austerity, penances, you may acquire the position in the impersonal Brahman, but there is chance of falling down from there. *Patanty adhah.* Why? *Anādṛta-yuṣmad-aṅghrayaḥ.* 'Because they could not find out how to worship Your lotus feet.' So unless you come to the personal form of the Absolute Truth, there is difficulty and there is chance of falling down."

A third man said that he considered Christianity and Kṛṣṇa consciousness to be the same. He wanted to know what Prabhupāda had to say about that.

Prabhupāda answered, "Everything is Kṛṣṇa consciousness. It is question of degrees. Suppose Kṛṣṇa is there on the top, and it is one hundred steps. So somebody has covered five steps, somebody has covered ten steps, somebody has covered one hundred steps. Like that. So everyone is searching after Kṛṣṇa, but there are degrees of realization of Kṛṣṇa. So either Christian, Mohammedan, or any, they are searching after Kṛṣṇa. That's all right, but it is a question of degrees, how far they have gone forward. The last stage is *sarva-dharmān parityajya mām ekaṁ śaraṇaṁ vraja.* That is the final stage."

Another man asked if the Kṛṣṇa consciousness movement was a development of the Gauḍīya Maṭha.

Prabhupāda answered noncommittally. "No, Kṛṣṇa consciousness is there in the *Bhagavad-gītā.* It is nobody's property. It is Kṛṣṇa's instruction."

The next question caused a stir in the audience. Without being outright offensive a man clearly tried to challenge Śrīla Prabhupāda's own qualifications. "Swamijī, what is the color of Kṛṣṇa? It is blue or black? Not according to *śāstra,* but your experience."

Prabhupāda delighted everyone with his reply. "So, if you kindly advance in Kṛṣṇa consciousness, then you will understand."

Amidst loud applause and laughter he took the next couple of enquiries and then another challenge. A man wanted to know why the Kṛṣṇa consciousness movement was popular in the Western countries, but not in India where Kṛṣṇa appeared.

Challenging the accuracy of his statement, Prabhupāda retorted, "It is very popular here also. Otherwise why you have come here?"

Everyone clapped and laughed at his sharp reply, but the man was insistent. "But it is not *so* popular."

"Kṛṣṇa is popular in India very much. Every house, they observe *Kṛṣṇa-janmāṣṭamī.*"

At the mention of Kṛṣṇa's birthday the crowd clapped loudly, laughing and applauding as Prabhupāda added a punch line and reversed the implied criticism. "Unfortunately, you are forgetting this. That is the misfortune."

Another query came from a man who wanted to know how to meditate on Brahman. "But how do we just meditate and get in touch with that Brahman? Is a thing there, a crucial point? Every one of you knows from—"

Prabhupāda cut in. "Kṛṣṇa does not say that you go everywhere—"

"But how do we just meditate and get in touch with that Brahman? They say that you just have to meditate, transcendental meditation."

"No, what *they* say, I do not know. I know what Kṛṣṇa says, that's all."

"Problem is to know—"

"Our mission is to present before you what Kṛṣṇa says, that's all," Prabhupāda said. "We are not concerned what other says. We are not concerned."

The man's confusion typically illoustrated exactly what Śrila Prabhupāda was always complaining about, that people hear about Kṛṣṇa from any source other than Kṛṣṇa Himself and His bona fide representatives. They therefore simply become confused. Prabhupāda's strong reply stirred the crowd's appreciation of his fixed position and his refusal to be drawn off on a tangent. Many smiled and nodded at his no-nonsense, authoritative approach. It was exactly what they had come to hear.

"All right, we have taken enough. Now no more. Chant Hare Kṛṣṇa. You join with us."

Leaving the devotees to finish with a film show and *kīrtana,* Prabhupāda left via a long arch-covered walkway.

After a short drive back to the house and a chair lift upstairs, he settled comfortably in his room, thoroughly enlivened by the night's preaching. He called in Harikeśa and had him set up the tape recorder so that he could listen to the play-back of his talk.

He grinned and then laughed when it came to the point where he had referred to everyone as *mūḍhas.* "I have spoken very strongly," he said, "but still they did not protest. Rather they appreciated, 'Yes, it is fact.'"

We also appreciated the beauty of Śrīla Prabhupāda's character. He is so pure and free from malice or envy of others that he can speak with utter candor about people's faults and call them fools and rascals without anyone taking the least offense. Moreover, his own innocent wonder at how he is able to do this simply increases his charm many times over.

January 2nd, 1976

Madras appears a pleasant city, not congested and generally clean and well-managed. On the way to Marina Beach for his morning walk Śrīla Prabhupāda commended the well-kept, attractive buildings and wide beach-front road. The shore itself is a clean, wide, long stretch of sand. Along the shoreline fishing boats, catamarans, and nets were beached in clusters. The sea breeze was refreshing, and the lack of commercialization—coconut sellers, *pān* merchants, hotels and the like, and even people—made it a pleasant contrast to Bombay's Juhu Beach. In his usual fashion, Prabhupāda walked up and down the beach for half an hour both ways, engaging us in conversation. He'd stop occasionally to emphasize his points, enjoying the exercise and freshness of sand, sea, and sky. The *sannyāsīs* were all present, as were the local devotees and some Life Members. Prabhupāda continued his expose of modern science, prompting Harikeśa to repeat some of the arguments they have discussed during the past month. Prabhupāda drew the newly arrived Tamal Krishna Mahārāja and other *sannyāsīs* into the debate. The sun had risen and was glinting across the water. Fishermen were repairing their light craft, readying them for another day's work on the unpredictable Bay of Bengal, while our little group discussed the structure of the universe and the eternal soul's ability to live in any condition, even in the fiery globe now so brightly illuminating the entire sky.

After a while Prabhupāda let the subject drop. He walked past a group of mounted police exercising their horses, and then back to the pavement. Various statues of well known personalities and some very handsome buildings lined the beach front. A house with Bengali writing on it came into view, attracting Prabhupāda's attention. It was the former residence of a well known *sādhu*.

Acyutānanda asked if it had belonged to Svāmī Vivekānanda. Prabhupāda confirmed that after coming back from foreign countries Vivekānanda had made his position here in Madras.

Acyutānanda said that a Life Member from Calcutta called Veni Śaṅkara Sharma had written a book titled *An Unknown Chapter of the Life of Svāmī Vivekānanda.* The book claimed that Vivekānanda smoked a *hookah* and ate meat.

To this information, Prabhupāda replied, "Yes, that is known to everyone."

Yaśodānandana knew someone in Hyderabad who used to cook for the Rāma Kṛṣṇa Mission. He told Prabhupāda, "He said they used to cook any kind of meat."

Acyutānanda said that he had once asked that cook, "Did you ever cook human meat?" The cook had told him, "If they told me, I would have done that also." Acyutānanda added, "There was nothing beyond their diet."

The party went on to decipher the Bengali title over the house, identifying it as 'The House of Vivekānanda.'

"They say Svāmī Vivekānanda walked barefoot all over India at some stage of his life. This statue here is his life as a wandering *sādhu,*" Acyutānanda offered.

But Prabhupāda asked, "Who is a *sādhu?* Then the question is, who is a *sādhu?* You cannot say?"

Acyutānanda said, "One who is Kṛṣṇa conscious."

"Unless one is cent-per-cent Kṛṣṇa conscious, he is not a *sādhu,*" Prabhupāda said. "*Sādhu-bhūṣaṇāḥ. Titikṣavaḥ kāruṇikāḥ, suhṛdaḥ sarva-dehinām, ajāta-śatravaḥ śāntāḥ sādhavaḥ sādhu-bhūṣaṇāḥ.* This is *sādhu.*" [The Symptoms of a *sādhu* are that he is tolerant, merciful and friendly to all living entities. He has no enemies, he is peaceful, he abides by the scriptures, and all his characteristics are sublime. S.B. 3.25.21]

As we approached our vehicles Prabhupāda made a wry comment about the monuments erected along the beachfront. "All statues are crying here!"

Amongst them Acyutānanda Swami picked out another figure of recent prominence. This one was not an Indian but a Western woman, Annie Besant, who converted from Christianity to Hinduism. In the days of the British Raj such conversion to Hinduism would almost deify the person in the eyes of the ordinary Indians.

Prabhupāda remarked sardonically, "They come to be *avatāra* here. And she also came from Ireland to become *avatāra* here."

Acyutānanda explained how she had become interested in the *Gītā*. "She was Christian, and her infant died. So she asked the priests whether the child's soul would go to heaven or hell. And why? She felt that the child hadn't done anything. But she was dissatisfied with their answers. Eventually she heard about transmigration of the soul. Then she became interested in the *Gītā* and India."

Prabhupāda asked, "So did she understand?"

Acyutānanda said, "Well, only up to transmigration of the soul."

"She admits," Prabhupāda said.

Acyutānanda said, "Yes."

As we were about to return to our residence, a few Indian gentlemen accompanying us on the walk told Prabhupāda how much they appreciated his practical explanations of spiritual life, although they admitted that sometimes they were difficult to accept. One of them commented candidly, "Two and two will always be four. But we people don't agree so far."

Prabhupāda smiled. "Yes. You want five."

They burst out laughing. "We want five, correct!"

Prabhupāda told them a short story about a grocer's son who was doing business on his father's behalf. He was giving change of four rupees instead of the correct amount, five.

So the customer said, "Why you are giving me four rupees?"

The boy pleaded innocence. "No, I do not know what is the exchange."

So the customer then said, "No, it is six rupees."

To which the boy replied, "No, my father will be angry!"

Amidst loud laughing Prabhupāda explained, "It means he knows perfectly well what is five rupees, but he is innocent when he was giving four rupees. And when the customer wanted six rupees, 'No, my father will be angry!'"

He used the anecdote to illustrate the mentality of men who want to comment on the *Gītā* and other works without accepting the real meaning, adding distortions to suit their own purpose.

"They have created havoc by misinterpreting *Bhagavad-gītā*, all people," he said. "According to their wish, 'Five rupees note means four rupees.' By imagination. They have created havoc all over the world. Otherwise everything is there. If we take Kṛṣṇa's instruction, then whole world becomes immediately happy. But they will not take it. They will manufacture their own: two plus two equal to five or three, not exactly four."

He advised the men to read his books, especially the new *Nectar of Instruction*. When they complained that no books were available at his lecture last night, Prabhupāda was extremely concerned.

Mahāṁsa Swami reassured him there had indeed been a book table present and many books were sold.

The men hadn't seen it, so Śrīla Prabhupāda told the *sannyāsīs*, "Keep the book table in a prominent place so that others can see. And any book which is not in stock, you can note down his order so that you can send him later on. Recently we have published very important book, *Nectar of Instruction*. For the common man it is very nice."

* * *

This morning Mr. Bhai and his wife came upstairs to see Prabhupāda after breakfast and requested him to narrate some stories about Kṛṣṇa's pastimes in Vṛndāvana. They especially wanted to hear about the *rasa-līlā*, Kṛṣṇa's intimate activities with the *gopīs*.

Prabhupāda has, of course, often told us that confidential topics may be discussed only with those qualified to hear. For his hosts he made no exception. He excused himself by saying that personally he wasn't qualified to speak of such things. Despite their persistence, he would not discuss the topic.

* * *

During Śrīla Prabhupāda's massage Gurukṛpa Mahārāja talked with Prabhupāda about some problems he was having in Japan. Gurukṛpa and Yaśodānandana Swamis are in charge of the Nāma Haṭṭa *saṅkīrtana* party, which has been collecting funds in Japan for the development of the Māyāpur project. Trivikrama Swami is also in Japan trying to preach to the local people and establish a permanent temple. Recently the two parties have been engaged in bitter arguments. Although the Nāma Haṭṭa party has raised large amounts of funds for Māyāpur, there has also been some bad publicity, and Trivikrama Swami felt that some of the men were not behaving properly.

Gurukṛpa Mahārāja didn't appreciate Trivikrama's criticism, and he asked Prabhupāda if Trivikrama could be transferred to another preaching field. Prabhupāda will not allow it. He told him he wanted them to work cooperatively and not fight.

Although Prabhupāda was clearly reserved in his attitude, Gurukṛpa stuck to his position, and tried to minimize his own mistakes. Śrīla Prabhupāda dealt with him with care and respect, but held firm to his decision that they must work cooperatively. He wants them to put aside personal differences to advance the cause of Caitanya Mahāprabhu's *saṅkīrtana* movement.

Gurukṛpa Mahārāja left later in the day for Calcutta. He and a few men will return to Japan shortly, to resume collecting for Māyāpur.

* * *

This evening's program was again an extremely successful one. The guest of honor was the Chief Justice of Madras. The Justice gave an introductory speech in which he described how modern materialistic life results in ultimate suffering. He made some good points, but his talk was also riddled with philosophical misunderstanding. Nevertheless, he was polite and respectful.

Prabhupāda didn't correct him directly, but in the course of his lecture redressed his mistaken ideas.

The full house listened attentively as Prabhupāda delivered another lengthy and erudite discourse, from one of his favorite sections of *Śrīmad-Bhāgavatam:* the *bhāgavata-dharma* instructions of Prahlāda Mahārāja to his school friends.

Again he repeatedly stressed the necessity of hearing from authorized sources in order to properly understand what is real *dharma.* He firmly established that *dharma* means three things—to know Kṛṣṇa, to act in relationship to Kṛṣṇa, and finally to achieve the goal of going back to Kṛṣṇa, back to Godhead.

To loud applause Prabhupāda asked for questions, and there was no shortage of enquiries. With Acyutānanda Swami acting as the moderator, he answered them all to everyone's full satisfaction.

Acyutānanda Mahārāja repeated the first question. "This is a world of *śakti,* or energy. There is a worldwide rise in prices of energy resources, like oil, coal, gas, and electricity. This means there is a depletion of these energy resources. Naturally, there will be worldwide destruction of mankind and other living beings and materials in the near future. What are your views?"

Prabhupāda offered a new angle on the subject, and everyone clapped as they appreciated his ability to link everything sensibly and practically to the one central purpose of life.

"Yes," he said, "these material things, they are energies. That is described in the *Bhagavad-gītā: Bhūmir apo 'nalo vāyuḥ khaṁ mano buddhir eva ca, bhinnā prakṛtir aṣṭadhā.* The petrol is also another form of Kṛṣṇa's energy. *Parasya śaktir vividhaiva śruyate.* There are many millions of energies. *Na tasya kāryaṁ kāraṇam ca vidyate.* Kṛṣṇa has nothing to do because everything is being done by His energy. Although He is the ultimate source of everything, He is doing everything by His energy, and it appears that it is being automatically done. It is not automatically done. It is done by Kṛṣṇa's energy. So this material energy is also Kṛṣṇa's energy. It is not a different energy. Petrol is liquid thing, so *āpa.* So it is Kṛṣṇa's energies. Our Vaiṣṇava philosophy is that Kṛṣṇa's energies should be utilized for Kṛṣṇa. This is Kṛṣṇa consciousness. So everything can be utilized for service of Kṛṣṇa. When you use this petrol for spreading Kṛṣṇa consciousness, if we can use 1,000 or 100,000 motor cars using petrol for spreading Kṛṣṇa consciousness, that is the proper utilization of petrol."

Acyutānanda repeated a lady's question. "Kṛṣṇa says to perform your *svadharma.* So how does one know what is his *svadharma?*"

"That is *svadharma* when Kṛṣṇa says, 'You surrender unto Me.' That is your *svadharma.* Because you are part and parcel of Kṛṣṇa, your business is to serve Kṛṣṇa. Just like this finger is part and parcel of my body. So I say, 'Finger, please come here,' he immediately comes. This is the normal condition of the finger. Similarly, if you are really healthy, in normal condition, then you must be ready to serve Kṛṣṇa. That is your *svadharma.*" Prabhupāda's example was simple but lucid, and again the alert audience clapped to show that they understood.

A man, obviously a pantheist, was next. "There are many incarnations, including Kṛṣṇa. So Kṛṣṇa gave *Bhagavad-gītā.* That doesn't mean that the author has not given all the gods, whether including Kṛṣṇa—"

Prabhupāda cut in. "So that I have already explained, that incarnation—whose incarnation? The question will be, *whose* incarnation?"

"God. God."

"God's. So that God is Kṛṣṇa. You do not know that. Now learn it."

"Is not Rāma a God?"

"Yes. Incarnation means *somebody's* incarnation. So who is that somebody? That is Kṛṣṇa. That's all. If you do not know it, you understand now."

Acyutānanda Swami took one last question. "Is it necessary that a person should pass through the three *āśramas —brahmacārī, gṛhastha, vānaprastha*—before coming to *sannyāsa?*"

Prabhupāda answered, "That is the normal rules and regulation, that especially *brāhmaṇa,* he must go through the four *āśramas.* First of all become *brahmacārī,* then *gṛhastha,* then *vānaprastha,* then take *sannyāsa.* This is for the *brāhmaṇas.* And for the *kṣatriyas: brahmacārī, gṛhastha,* and *vānaprastha.* And for the *vaiśyas: brahmacārī, gṛhastha.* And for the *śūdras:* only *gṛhastha.* This is the process. This is normal process. But either one is *brāhmaṇa* or *kṣatriya* or *vaiśya* or *śūdra,* if he takes to Kṛṣṇa consciousness he becomes above these rules and regulations."

Prabhupāda's comments were deeply appreciated because here in Madras, possibly more so than any place in India, the government is making a systematic attempt to dismantle the old caste system. However, in trying to establish a more equitable society their attempts have often resulted in reverse discrimination against the caste *brāhmaṇas.*

Prabhupāda is probably the first person to show them a true platform of equal dealings for all without disturbing the social balance.

As they clapped he continued. "Yes. *Mām ca yo 'vyabhicāreṇa bhakti-yogena sevate, sa guṇān samatītyaitān brahma-bhūyāya kalpate.* So this Kṛṣṇa consciousness movement is that it is giving immediate lift to everyone to come to the transcendental platform, *brahma-bhūyāya kalpate.* But general state is *varṇāśrama-dharma.*

"Therefore Caitanya Mahāprabhu, when He was discussing with Rāmānanda Rāya, He first of all said, 'What is the aim of life?' So Rāmānanda Rāya replied that 'First of all to begin this *varṇāśrama-dharma.*' So Caitanya Mahāprabhu said, 'Yes, this is all right. But this is external. If you know something better, please tell me.'

"So in this way, step by step everything was described by Rāmānanda Rāya, and Caitanya Mahāprabhu did not reject it. He said, 'It is all right, but if you know something better....' Then at last, when Rāmaṇanda said, quoting one verse from *Śrīmad-Bhāgavatam, sthāne sthitāḥ śruti-gatāṁ tanu-vāṅ-manobhiḥ,* that it doesn't matter what you are, you remain in your post. *Sthāne sthitāḥ śruti-gatām.* Through the aural reception if you hear about Kṛṣṇa, then you become perfect. That is the statement.

"So this is required at the present moment, that you remain whatever you are, either *brāhmaṇa, kṣatriya, vaiśya, śūdra,* Englishman, Indian—it doesn't matter. You try to understand Kṛṣṇa, that's all. If you do that, then everything will be perfect.

"That can be very easily done by chanting Hare Kṛṣṇa mantra. Therefore Caitanya Mahāprabhu has given this mantra—it is from *śāstra—harer nāma harer nāma harer nāmaiva kevalam, kalau nāsty eva nāsty eva.* In this age, in *Kali-yuga,* it is very difficult to bring back the fallen population again to the standard of *brāhmaṇa, kṣatriya, vaiśya.* It is practically lost now. The best thing is that all of them combined together, *brāhmaṇa, kṣatriya, vaiśya, śūdra,* or even less than *śūdra, kirāta-hūṇāndhra-pulinda-pulkaśā,* take to this process of chanting and hearing of the Lord's name. Everything will be all right.

"It is confirmed by Caitanya Mahāprabhu when he was discussing with Rāmānanda Rāya. He was a governor of this Madras province under the regime of Mahārāja Pratāparudra of Orissa. And he was politician, but he was a very learned scholar in Kṛṣṇa science. Therefore Caitanya Mahāprabhu was talking with him. He was a *śūdra* by birth, and Caitanya Mahāprabhu was not only very exalted position, *brāhmaṇa* and *sannyāsī;* so Caitanya Mahāprabhu was questioning and he was answering. He felt little hesitation, that 'Sir, You are so exalted. I am a *gṛhastha* and a politician, and how can I...?'

"Immediately Caitanya Mahāprabhu encouraged him, 'No, no, no, don't hesitate! *Kiba śūdra kiba vipra nyāsi kene naya, ye kṛṣṇa tattva vettā sei guru haya.*' He said, 'Don't hesitate!'

"It doesn't matter whether he is a *gṛhastha* or *sannyāsī* or *brāhmaṇa* or *śūdra.* If he knows Kṛṣṇa, he is guru. He is guru. That is wanted. We are teaching that Kṛṣṇa consciousness."

Prabhupāda brought his part of the program to a successful close. It was the final day, and everyone stood out of respect and appreciation as he made his way to the car.

On the way back to Mr. Bhai's house Prabhupāda said he was happy to find the people of Madras eager to hear spiritual instruction. Both the arrangements and the response have pleased him.

CHAPTER SEVEN

Nellore, Andhra Pradesh

January 3rd, 1976

In the early morning Śrīla Prabhupāda, Tamal Krishna Mahārāja, Harikeśa, and I boarded a train heading north to Nellore, a small city in the state of Andhra Pradesh. The local Madras devotees saw us off at the station with a rousing *kīrtana.* The clamor alerted some of the other passengers to Prabhupāda's presence, and several men hovered around the carriage, peering in with great interest. We shut the door and relaxed in the quiet privacy of the first-class compartment.

"First class" is a misnomer, as the compartment was a bit uncomfortable and dirty, with soot from the steam engine speckled throughout. The only advantage was the privacy of the cabin. Still, Prabhupāda said he preferred to travel by train rather than plane; there is more room and a satisfyingly sedate pace.

We carried with us some fruit and other *prasādam* for breakfast. After Prabhupāda ate, we enjoyed the remnants while he took a little rest, stretching out along the seat, which devotees had covered with clean white sheets.

Tamal Krishna Mahārāja went out to wash and swiftly shut the door behind him. When he came back he sidled through the half-open entry and again quickly shut it. "There are three men hanging around in the corridor hoping to see Prabhupāda," he said, answering our quizzical looks. "They'll just come in and ask some nonsense and disturb him, so don't let them in." People in India are often eager to ask for blessings from holy men, but unfortunately they rarely have any serious spiritual intent. There are also many *sādhus* accustomed to offering such meaningless *āśīrbhava,* or blessings.

Śrīla Prabhupāda refers to this kind of *sādhu* as an *āśīrbhava-mahārāja.* Usually they give a wave of the hand, a nod, and exchange a few polite words. There is no spiritual discussion, no transmission of knowledge, and no transformation. Yet both parties are satisfied with this giving and receiving of they know not what—'*āśīrbhavas.*' From our understanding of Prabhupāda's teachings, such intangible exchanges are of no practical value. Naturally, as Prabhupāda's servants, we don't like to see his time wasted with such blessing-seekers.

When Harikeśa and I went out of the compartment, the curious men were still there. On our return, despite our obvious reluctance to let them in, they strained to see past us, knowing that if they caught Prabhupāda's eye, etiquette would oblige him to let them in. Prabhupāda was awake, eye-contact was made, and he instructed us to let them in. The three filed in and sat opposite, smiling and pleased at having evaded the secretaries of someone they knew was a great spiritual leader and holy man.

Thus we all sat: we three somewhat irritated by this polite infringement on Prabhupāda's precious time, they three ignoring us, eager to have his *darśana,* and Śrīla Prabhupāda, as always, a warm and cordial host. Not at all inconvenienced, Prabhupāda received them courteously, asking them a few polite questions: what their names were, where they came from, what they did, and the like. Then he looked directly into their faces and asked, "So, what is it that I can do for you?"

"Swamijī, we just wanted to get your blessings."

"What is that blessing?"

This answer took them by surprise. No one had ever asked them what *kind* of blessings.

Caught off guard, one of them replied, "Well Swamijī, I have this pain in my knee—"

We almost groaned out loud and the man, becoming embarrassed, hastily added, "And for our families also...."

Strike two.

"Ah, and of course we want to do good to others...."

As he trailed off into confused silence, Prabhupāda indicated his three disciples with shaved heads, *śikhās, kurtās, dhotīs,* and *tulasī* beads. He told them, "This is my blessing. These boys have given up everything for Kṛṣṇa's service and to chant Hare Kṛṣṇa. Are you prepared to accept such a blessing?"

At first there was no reply. They were stunned; all kinds of wild thoughts seemed to run through their heads and across their faces. Then, before they could become the beneficiaries of this blessing, they hurriedly stood. One stammered, "Well, actually Swamijī, at the moment we have so many duties with the family and all, this kind of life of a *sannyāsī,* for us it is not possible...." With profuse apologies and many thanks they beat a hasty retreat. We laughed as Prabhupāda sat smiling and shook his head.

"This is the problem. They simply take a *sādhu* as some means for avoiding paying the doctor's bill, that's all. *Āśīrbhava-mahārāja.* They are not serious for spiritual life."

People have no appreciation of a real *mahātmā.*

After a three-and-a-half-hour journey the train pulled into the modest Nellore railway station.

The *sannyāsīs* and devotees from Madras had all traveled ahead on the road. Together with a very large and eager group of local residents, they gave Prabhupāda a tumultuous welcome. The devotees have been preaching in Nellore for several weeks, making Life Members and preparing for Śrīla Prabhupāda's visit; thus many people were anxiously awaiting his arrival.

Prabhupāda got down from the carriage first, followed by Tamal Krishna and Harikeśa. The huge crowd on the platform promptly swallowed him up.

When I finally struggled out of the carriage carrying two suitcases, a shoulder bag, and the bag with the tiffin and cooker, I was amazed to see, through a jam of sweating bodies, Śrīla Prabhupāda just about to disappear under a huge wreath of marigolds. He was patiently standing, hands held together in traditional *praṇāma,* while fifty or sixty people lined up to place garlands around his neck. I dropped the cases and barged through. By the time I reached him the flowers were just beginning to rise above the top of his ears. Harikeśa and Tamal Krishna Mahārāja stood immobilized to the side, looking somewhat overwhelmed by the whole affair.

Stopping the chain of presentation for a moment, I removed all the garlands but two. They were so heavy that I had difficulty lifting them, but Śrīla Prabhupāda had stood very patiently to allow everyone to come forward and drape their offerings around his neck. He was visibly relieved when I removed the garlands. Then as the rest of the crowd moved up one at a time and offered their garlands I immediately removed them, never allowing more than two or three to accumulate at once.

When everyone had made their offering, Prabhupāda walked out to the waiting car, followed by chanting devotees and mobbed by the enthusiastic residents of Nellore.

Harikeśa came up to me and demanded to know where the suitcases were.

"Oh, no! I left them on the platform!" I had forgotten all about them in my rush to aid Śrīla Prabhupāda, and I earned another acerbic rebuke from Harikeśa for my foolishness. Fortunately, when the crowd cleared, the suitcases were still where I had left them. Harikeśa did admit, however, that I had acted correctly and promptly where he had failed regarding Prabhupāda's personal situation.

Prabhupāda was extremely pleased by the whole reception. However, the arrival at our lodgings was a different story.

Turning off into a side road next to the Tirupati-tirumali Deva-stānams Kalyāṇam Maṇḍapam on the southern outskirts just off National Highway 5, we came to the main gates of an enclosed estate. It is owned by our hosts, two sisters, Sujathamma Rebala and Subhaprada Kattamanchi, members of the former royal family of the area. Prabhupāda has been invited to stay with them for the next five days.

The estate is divided into two sections of seven and two acres, all surrounded by a ten-foot-high wall. The sisters are donating both parcels of land to ISKCON. We plan to construct a temple on the smaller plot, and it is to inaugurate this work that Śrīla Prabhupāda has come. Śrīla Prabhupāda is going to install the foundation stone tomorrow.

The two-acre plot is completely undeveloped and rather barren, except for a small house at the back where Acyutānanda and Yaśodānandana Swami's party is staying. The seven-acre plot has a large bungalow for its main residence, separate servants' quarters, a couple of small out-houses, and partially cultivated gardens with some flowers, bottle palm trees, and vegetable patches. This larger acreage will be donated on the demise of the sisters.

Getting out of the car at the main gate Prabhupāda was met by the sisters. Together we all walked the short distance down the drive to the main house. The driveway ended in a small circle with a fountain in the middle at the front of the house. At the side of this, out in the open, we passed a small bust of Kṛṣṇa with a cow. We also noted *tulasī* plants growing here and there along the garden borders.

Because of our plan to establish a temple here, Mahāṁsa Swami said that many people in Nellore have given their support and have become Life Members. The local newspaper has featured an article describing the activities of ISKCON, showing pictures of the devotees performing street *saṅkīrtana* and conducting *pāṇḍāla* programs.

A large pandal has been arranged in the city center for the next few days, with Śrīla Prabhupāda as the center of attraction.

The two sisters' reception of Śrīla Prabhupāda was cordial, but there was a distinct coolness in their temperament, which we all noticed. They gave him a small but pleasant room with a grilled-in veranda. We servants were shown to a room directly above him on the roof. Śrīla Prabhupāda immediately got ready for his massage.

As we sat on the veranda and I began to apply the oil to his head, we heard a familiar clucking noise across the pathway. "What is that?" Prabhupāda asked.

I looked out through the grilled window and saw a hen coop. "It's chickens, Śrīla Prabhupāda."

"Oh. Then that means?"

"Well, it means that at least they are eating eggs," I said, trying to be optimistic.

"Call Harikeśa."

Harikeśa came in, visibly disturbed. "Śrīla Prabhupāda, these people are meat eaters!"

"Oh. Then you must cook separately. You cannot cook in their kitchen. Do not use any of their pots or utensils."

"Śrīla Prabhupāda, there's something wrong here. These people are crazy!" Harikeśa complained.

Prabhupāda bridled, "They are crazy, or you are crazy?"

Being extremely intelligent, on occasion Harikeśa's reactions to a situation tend to be overly intense. On such occasions, Prabhupāda has to help him properly channel his mental energy. Harikeśa is completely dedicated to following Śrīla Prabhupāda's guidance, and a few quick words are usually sufficient to correct him. Yet in this instance he persisted.

"Well, crazy I may be," he conceded, "but there's definitely something strange going on. It's almost as if these people don't want us here. They invited us, but they are almost unfriendly towards us."

Prabhupāda accepted his observation; our reception by the sisters had been decidedly muted, in contrast to the enthusiasm at the railway station. But he gave them the benefit of the doubt. "We are their guests," he said, "so we should deal with them politely. They may not yet be familiar with Kṛṣṇa consciousness, but they are offering the land for the temple, and things should improve when they engage in service to Kṛṣṇa."

In a discussion this afternoon the subject came up again, for we had all noticed the oddly cool attitude of our hosts, as if we were merely necessary inconveniences.

Prabhupāda asked Mahāṁsa Swami for the deed of the gift of land, but it wasn't available. Mahāṁsa thought it was with Gopāla Kṛṣṇa, and Gopāla thought Mahāṁsa had it. Prabhupāda was a little annoyed at their incompetence. He instructed them to bring the deed as soon as possible so that he could check it.

Apart from this, Śrīla Prabhupāda maintained his usual congenial mood and schedule. Tamal Krishna Mahārāja had brought some mail from America with him that he had read out when he first arrived but still needed replying to.

Prabhupāda was enlivened to hear a letter Rāmeśvara wrote two weeks before the Christmas marathon. Rāmeśvara reported that three new airports had been legally opened for book distribution and that our lawyers were working on opening several more, thus giving great facility for increasing book sales.

He also had a question about the system of book distribution Prabhupāda recently approved for the Rādhā-Dāmodara party, by which devotees could hand out big books for nominal sums, provided they covered the costs from other donations. Rāmeśvara wanted to know if the temples could also adopt this method, for previously big books had only been given to people who donated at least three or four dollars. The Rādhā-Dāmodara traveling *saṅkīrtana* party ordered 50,000 books for December alone, and Rāmeśvara thought that distribution would increase tremendously if the temples could also adopt this system.

Finally, he described the enthusiasm for book distribution sweeping the American temples. "This month there is terrific competition between Tamal Krishna Goswami and Jayatīrtha Prabhu [GBC for Los Angeles] to be the outstanding zones for the month. Here in New Dvārakā we are breaking all records and out-distributing everyone in BTG distribution. Just this past weekend (two days) we sold thirty thousand BTGs in Los Angeles alone! Everyone at the BBT including myself is going on book distribution two days per week for the competition, and we are planning to sell 100,000 BTGs in L.A. in just six days between December 19th-24th. In this way book distribution is going on nicely in America, and our warehouse is exhausted to ship so many books out to the SKP parties day and night. Anyway, in Los Angeles, never before in history have so many transcendental literatures been distributed in one city in so short a period of time. Our goal for this month is to sell at least 200,000 BTGs and 12,000 big books all in Los Angeles. By your divine blessings, we would like to be able to increase these figures even more, and become absorbed in book distribution day and night without stopping. Everyone agrees that to distribute your books is the highest pleasure and even the demigods may take birth here just to be able to distribute your books and taste this great pleasure."

He concluded his letter by saying, "I hope you are well and enjoying the book distribution results. I have never seen the devotees in America work so hard to please you as now, by their book selling."

Śrīla Prabhupāda was enlivened to hear the enthusiastic report, especially since he already knew of the success of the marathon. In the past he had deliberately promoted a competition between temples in book distribution, and he teased Tamal Krishna Mahārāja as he dictated his reply to Rāmeśvara.

"Regarding the suggestion for book selling, the point is that the temples must pay the cost of printing. Then they may sell for whatever price they like.

"The transcendental competition is nice. If Jayatīrtha Prabhu defeats Tamal Krishna Mahārāja, then Tamal will have heart failure. Go on selling books. My Guru Mahārāja was very much anxious about selling books and preaching, so you are pleasing him by this bombastic flood of books all over the world. Thank you."

He also added a note of approval and precaution on the new *Bhāgavatam* printing. "The new Sixth Canto *Bhāgavatams* are very nice. Yes, actually they are worshipable Deities. Be careful that our books do not appear like Bible printing. Sometimes the Christians also put gold gilding on their books, but people are adverse to purchasing Bibles. Neither our books should be given free, there must be some remuneration, otherwise it will be like Bible selling."

Unlike most authors, Śrīla Prabhupāda's enthusiasm about the tremendous increase in sales of his books does not derive from personal pride or hope for an increase in his own sense gratification from the income. They are Kṛṣṇa's books, and he is Kṛṣṇa's servant; therefore the profits are also Kṛṣṇa's.

An increase in book distribution means greater numbers of people potentially attracted to Kṛṣṇa consciousness. However, despite the liberality of his mood in contacting as many persons as possible through wide distribution, he wants his books to be properly appreciated, and he knows that something easily obtained is also easily given up.

Along with the mail from America, there were letters from other parts of the world. One man in South India wrote about his interest in God consciousness and his eagerness to read Prabhupāda's books. He had read an article describing Prabhupāda's activities. "Recently I read an article about you—how you were a rich industrialist, how you, to fulfill the wishes of your Guru to preach devotion to Kṛṣṇa in the Western countries, renounced worldly life and how you translated *Śrīmad-Bhāgavatam* into English in waste papers and how you went to America by Scindia ship and how you sat in the New York square and began to sing 'Hare Kṛṣṇa' and lectured the gift of *Śrīmad Bhagavad-gītā* and how the small gathering around you has grown to the present state with 112 centers throughout the world. It seems that God has chosen you to be an instrument in His Divine hands to bring a change for the good in the millions of hearts thirsting for peace and happiness, love and freedom in the spiritual sphere." However, he went on to say he had no money even for postage, so he was requesting the *Bhāgavatam* as a gift.

Prabhupāda tactfully replied, "Thank you for your kind appreciation of our Society's activities and of my humble effort on behalf of Lord Kṛṣṇa.

"Regarding your request for some books, the best thing will be if you ask some able person to buy them for you. Or you may ask for the fare to come to Madras and live with the devotees of our Movement. The address in Madras is 50, Aspiran Gardens, 2nd Street, Kilpauk, Madras-10. If you live with our men following our program then you will also get an opportunity to read all our books."

Trivikrama Swami wrote from Japan concerning his troubled relationship with Gurukṛpa Swami. He also had a question about the supposed American moon landings.

Prabhupāda replied to Trivikrama Mahārāja in the same mood in which he had spoken to Gurukṛpa Swami. He wants the devotees to learn responsible management and cooperation. He is not at all in favor of making immediate changes whenever a problem arises. He advised to refer such questions to the annual GBC meeting in March at Māyāpur.

Prabhupāda also replied to his confusion about the moon landings. "Regarding the 'dust' supposedly brought from the moon, that dust can be gotten anywhere. It has already been openly admitted that the same dust is available on this earth planet. These astronauts and scientists are all bluffing. But Śrīla

Vyāsadeva is the correct authority. Just study *Śrīmad-Bhāgavatam* carefully with full faith in Kṛṣṇa and Guru and all knowledge will be revealed."

* * *

There was no program this evening, so Tamal Krishna Goswami, Harikeśa, and I gathered in Prabhupāda's room and chatted with him for a short while before having a *kīrtana* and a reading from his books.

We talked about book distribution. Tamal Krishna complimented Śrīla Prabhupāda: "I don't think there has ever been a personality who has given such a great gift to the Western world as yourself, Prabhupāda."

Śrīla Prabhupāda modestly acknowledged his tribute. "Yes, actually that is the fact. But let them appreciate, that's all."

"The thing is," Tamal said, "it seems to me, that we are flooding so many books that they must become Kṛṣṇa conscious."

Prabhupāda gave a big grin and chuckled. "Yes, they have no alternative than to read these books!"

Tamal explained that almost every day when our men go out they meet people who already have our books. "Supposing each man meets in a day one thousand or five hundred people—always, without a doubt, at least one or two of the people he meets already have another book, and they are taking a second or third book. Many of them have two or three volumes of *Caitanya-caritāmṛta* or *Bhāgavatam*. And although they may not read it, their children are reading it."

Prabhupāda agreed, "Somebody is reading."

"Oh, yes," Tamal replied. "I made a study. I asked the men in our party when they were all gathered to raise their hand if they had received a book before joining our party. Every single one of them had received a book before joining the movement, without exception. They were attracted through reading a book or a magazine."

When we chanted, several of the house servants sat by the door. The sisters also came, attracted by the *kīrtana*. After about half an hour we stopped. Prabhupāda had Tamal Krishna Mahārāja read from *Śrī Īśopaniṣad*. By the time he had finished reading we were alone again.

January 4th, 1976

Early in the morning Śrīla Prabhupāda called us into his room, wanting to know why the other devotees had not risen by four o'clock for *maṅgala ārati* and *kīrtana*. He was annoyed by our indolence and said, "If our habits are not changed then what is the use of spending so much money?"

Outside, cocks crowed in the dawn, and inside Prabhupāda relaxed after a night of intense concentration and writing, his beads clicking in his hand and his mind keen.

When Harikeśa and I entered the room, eager to share the quiet intimacy of the early morning hours with him, Prabhupāda and Tamal Krishna Mahārāja were already absorbed in a discussion about the foolishness of thinking oneself to be independent.

At Prabhupāda's request Tamal filled us in on the details of their talk. "In no way can anyone say that they're independent," Tamal reiterated. "There is no possibility. At every moment one is dependent. And if anyone says they aren't, they are simply foolish rascals. We have to challenge everyone in the world on this point: 'You cannot be independent.'" He continued, "Politicians like Indira think that they are independent. Prabhupāda was saying that Mujibul Rehman fought so hard for his country's independence, Bangladesh. But when the soldiers came, they killed him and every single family member in one hour, not sparing anyone. He thought he was independent, he thought his country had become independent. But in one hour it was all wiped away."

Prabhupāda entered the discussion in a challenging mood, "So where is your independence? What is the answer? At any moment you have to die. Even Mujibul Rehman or Mussolini or big, big Napoleon. Everyone. He was given horse urine to drink, Napoleon. Such a great hero, but he had to drink horse urine as reaction of his atrocities. Hitler committed suicide and finished himself. Mussolini was forced to be killed, Gandhi was killed. And they are fighting for independence. So where is your independence? If you are thinking independently and doing things independently, then is it not foolishness?

"Suppose within the prison walls, if you want to do things independently, is it possible? You'll be put into further sufferings as soon as you violate the rules and regulation of the jail. Just like they are independently trying to avoid pregnancy, and the same man who has killed his own child, or same mother, he is being killed within the womb. *Prakṛteḥ kriyamāṇāni.* Nature will not tolerate this. In India still these things are not happening because they are not so advanced to use all these contraceptive method. But in Europe, America, it has become a common affair to kill the child within the womb."

Tamal Krishna pointed out that it was starting in India also.

Prabhupāda made a wry face. "Yes, gradually. As soon as you kill, then you must be killed. This law is there, life for life. So where is your independence? Independence means you are inviting more sufferings, that's all. You go on, declare your independence. We are the only sane men. We have accepted that we have no independence. So we have to convince the people. Kṛṣṇa consciousness movement is very scientific. You are foolishly rascal. You are trying to be independent. That is not possible. Kṛṣṇa is asking [you] to surrender. You do that."

Prabhupāda made it clear that the root cause of all suffering is this mood of independence from God. "Discuss all these things amongst yourselves and preach and inform these rascals, so-called civilized scientists and philosophers. That is preaching. We have to present the truth in such a way that they will be convinced."

Changing subjects, Śrīla Prabhupāda gave his appraisal of the mentality of our hosts. Having seen the figurine of Kṛṣṇa in the garden and the surrounding *tulasī* trees, I had thought that perhaps the two sisters did have some genuine interest in Kṛṣṇa, but Prabhupāda saw it differently.

"I have seen in Calcutta one statue of Sir Āśutoṣa Mukherjī. So in the morning, on the day of the birth anniversary, the municipal sweepers with their brush, they will rub it to cleanse the solidly stuck up crow's stool with water. Then in the evening, big, big men will come, gather, and offer him garland one after another, just like they were offering me. In the morning it is brushed with the sweeper's street brush, and in the evening it is offered garland. I have seen it. Here also I see that she has kept Kṛṣṇa's *mūrti* outside. It is *aparādha*."

Tamal Krishna said that he didn't think that the sisters were Kṛṣṇa *bhaktas* at all.

I mentioned that during a short tour of the property I was pleased to see many *tulasī* plants in the garden. But I felt shocked when I came upon a chest-high pedestal holding a *tulasī* plant cut into the shape of a suspiciously familiar bird. "Even that *tulasī* tree around the corner. They have clipped to shape it, cut all the branches," I told him.

"They have no guidance," Prabhupāda said.

Tamal Krishna recalled the previous evening. "Last night when we were reading, they all left. When you mentioned the regulative principles—stressing no meat, crabs, fish, eggs—they all got up and walked out."

Prabhupāda questioned Harikeśa again about the cooking. "You said that the same cooking place will have to do, where they are cooking meat?"

Harikeśa reassured him, "They're not cooking it now."

Living in someone else's house is difficult when the family members are non-Vaiṣṇava. When preaching in India devotees are often obliged to stay in the homes of Life Members, their bad habits tolerated in order to broadcast the message of Kṛṣṇa consciousness. However, Tamal Krishna told Prabhupāda that when Gargamuni Swami returns to India, he doesn't want to do that anymore. He said, "He is determined that he will not eat in anyone's home."

Prabhupāda approved. "That is very good."

"Not only that, but he's not going to sleep in anyone's home either. They want to camp out by the river-sides."

"Very good idea."

"He says that from reading your books it is very clear that Caitanya Mahāprabhu was very careful, strict, to only eat *prasādam* cooked by proper persons."

"No, purchase from Jagannātha temple. People would come to offer Him *prasādam*. So what is the cost of the *prasādam*, that was taken and He purchased. Formerly, the system was there was no hotel, but there were temples. You go and you can purchase very cheap price. I went with my father in my childhood in a place. My father would never take food at anyone's house or in the hotel. He will find out some temple and pay them and take *prasādam.* Still there are many temples. So I was about ten years old at that time, say, seventy years ago. So he paid two *annas* to the *pūjārī,* and he gave us so much. It can be eaten by five, six men. *Kichari,* vegetables, varieties. So much. Two *annas.*"

Tamal Krishna mentioned his experience visiting a temple in Navadvīpa. "They had an arrangement like this. At least a hundred people were taking, respectable people. That temple's very big. Of course, I don't know how bona fide the people who speak at night are, but every night there are speakers with many people coming. I was very impressed by it. Nice rooms for people to stay upstairs, very active, always being cleansed."

Prabhupāda was impressed by Tamal Krishna's description. "That is temple. So we have got so many examples. Introduce this."

* * *

Prabhupāda took a longer walk this morning because there was no temple program to attend. He walked around the grounds, and then to a nearby lake.

Mr. Keśavalal Triveri, who had attended his lectures in Madras, joined us. Pleased to see him, Prabhupāda immediately engaged him in further discussion on the central theme of his Madras lectures and this early morning's conversation—the false spirit of independence.

Mr. Triveri was in full agreement and complimented Śrīla Prabhupāda on his lectures. "For the first time," he said, "I am able to explain to my friends that the true status of the soul is *ātmā,* not *paramātmā; brahman* but not *parabrahman.*"

In the course of the discussion Acyutānanda Swami quoted one of the favorite scriptural references from the *Īśopaniṣad* that the *māyāvādīs* use to declare themselves as God. They say that the words from the Sixteenth Verse, *so'ham asmi,* "I am that", mean that the living being is the same as God.

Prabhupāda refuted his argument with a revealing analogy. "*Asmi* means 'It is my energy.' If I say that I am ISKCON, what is the wrong there? Because I have created this; therefore I say ISKCON means I. I am ISKCON. So what is the wrong there? It is like that. By energy of Kṛṣṇa, everything has come out. Therefore it says, 'I am this, I am this, I am this, I am this.'"

Having the opportunity to closely observe Śrīla Prabhupāda's daily involvement in the affairs of ISKCON has helped me to understand just how apropos this analogy is. He has created ISKCON, he is sustaining it, and, when difficulties arise due to the ineptness of his disciples, he fully supports it.

Mr. Triveri told him about a recent negative incident he had experienced with one *swami.* The *swami* had publicly condemned ISKCON and Śrīla Prabhupāda's preaching activities. The *swami* had read aloud to the public on Janmāṣṭamī day an adverse newspaper article concerning the devotees in Japan. He declared that ISKCON was not a bona fide *sampradāya* and should be avoided.

Prabhupāda strongly defended his ISKCON's world-wide efforts to spread Kṛṣṇa consciousness. He advised Mr. Triveri how to deal with such criticism, "*Doṣam icchanti pāmarāḥ. Makṣikā bhramarā icchanti* ... *Makṣikā,* these ordinary flies, they find out where is sore, and the *bhramarā* [bee], he finds out where is honey. Similarly, *doṣam icchanti pāmarāḥ.* And the Bhaktivedānta Swami is doing preaching all over the world. That has not come to his eyes. He has come to the Japanese incident."

Mr. Triveri said that he had told the man that in a big organization there might be some such incidents.

But Prabhupāda said, "No. Why did you not say, 'You are such a *pāmara* [low minded or sinful] that this thing has come to your notice and not other thing'? Just try to understand what is the mentality of these rascals that 'The good things do not come to your notice.' If something is bad, 'Oh, here is ....' You see. *Pāmarā doṣam icchanti guṇam icchanti paṇḍitāḥ. Saj-jana guṇam icchanti doṣam icchanti pāmarāḥ.* That means they are not even a Vaiṣṇava. You see? Vaiṣṇava means *paramo nirmatsarāṇām.* Even one has got some fault; a Vaiṣṇava does not see that. He takes the good qualities. But they are not even Vaiṣṇava. The mission of Caitanya Mahāprabhu is being preached all over the world—that does not come to their attention. Some Japanese newspaper has written something—it has come immediately. He's a lowest of the mankind. You can say that 'Why this thing has come prominent to your eyes and not the other thing?'"

Mr. Triveri said, "No, I did say in my own way, though I did not quote this, that 'You are a *pāmara*.'"

And Prabhupāda confidently said, "Yes, you can say now that, 'That day I forgot to say that you are a *pāmara*. So I have come to say that you are a *pāmara*. I forgot it. Excuse me, I forgot it. So you are *pāmara*.'"

Mr. Triveri agreed. "As a matter of fact, it is so." And then he added, speaking as the *swami* in question might respond, "And for that, the apology is, 'No, no, I do realize that lot of work is being done about that—'"

Prabhupāda completed the apology: "'But because I am *pāmara*, I am finding out this fault.'"

Mr. Triveri added another anecdote to illustrate the kind of negative response our Society is getting. "One *gosvāmī*, when I said, 'Well, this is a movement which I very much like and like also to join,' then he said that—because I am conducting *Gītā Bhavān* founded by him—he said, 'No, no, no, no. We as a matter of fact we champion that cause. But afterwards, when we realized that it is not *sampradāyic*, we have given it up ... After all, we are qualified. Those *mlecchas* [meat-eaters]....'"

Prabhupāda interjected abruptly. "Nobody cares for you. You are so qualified that nobody cares for you ... If they are *mlecchas*, then you are *nārakī* [resident of hell]. It is said, *vaiṣṇave jati-buddhiḥ nārakī*. Anyone who considers in terms of caste a Vaiṣṇava, he's a *nārakī*. Everyone knows that he is European, he is American, but because he is Vaiṣṇava, one should not see like that, '*mleccha*.' If he sees, then he's *nārakī*."

Yaśodānandana Swami said it proved that they have no faith in the holy name, because the *harināma* purifies everything.

Prabhupāda readily agreed. "This rascal says the *Nāma* has no ... See. We have to meet simply rascals all over. The so-called religionists, so-called *swamis*, so-called yogis, so-called politicians. You see? Simply we have to meet with all rascals."

"This Mahārāja showing that article on Kṛṣṇa-jayantī day,"

Mr. Triveri continued, "reading out to the entire audience. That was a rubbish."

"So what is the wrong there?" Prabhupāda asked. "What was the wrong?"

"He said that, 'This movement has got these black sheep and they have been banned in Japan. Everywhere they will be banned.'"

"But there is something in Japan which is banned," Prabhupāda explained. "But what you have got in Japan?"

"Nothing."

Yaśodānandana added, "First of all, we are not even banned in Japan. The center is still there."

Prabhupāda said, "No, no, that's all right. Banned means we had something. But what proof you have got that you have done something in Japan? So it is better. Just like one man said that 'I have lost fifty thousand this year.' His friend said, 'You are still fortunate because you had fifty thousand. But I have no fifty *paisa* even!'"

Mr. Triveri was encouraged. "So there is something. Here nothing."

"Prabhupāda," Bhāvabhūti said, "they said that if Caitanya Mahāprabhu wanted Kṛṣṇa consciousness in the Western countries, why didn't He go there Himself? That's what they told us."

Prabhupāda answered, "So He left the credit for me!"

The devotees all cheered. "*Jaya! Haribol!*"

"He loves His devotee more than Himself," Prabhupāda said.

Then Harikeśa asked, "Why didn't Kṛṣṇa kill everybody at the Battle of Kurukṣetra?"

"Yes!" Prabhupāda enthusiastically replied, "Kṛṣṇa, by His simple desire He could kill. He said therefore, *bhaviṣyatvān. Pṛthivīte āche yata nagarādi grāma, sarvatra pracāra haibe.* He [Śrī Caitanya] is leaving the task for somebody else."

* * *

When preparing Śrīla Prabhupāda's lunch yesterday, I discovered that the only salt available came in large crystalline lumps that had to be broken and crushed. Because this was somewhat troublesome, I spent half an hour making enough for the following few days, and put the small stone bowl containing the salt on Prabhupāda's *chonki.* I assumed that Prabhupāda would take as much as he wanted from the stock and leave the rest for future use.

During breakfast, however, Prabhupāda dipped pieces of fruit directly into the bowl rather than taking some salt from it onto his plate and leaving the rest. When I cleaned up afterwards I left the salt bowl on the table, thinking it would be all right to use it for other meals.

Though conversing with the other devotees, Prabhupāda, as observant as ever, noticed what I did and immediately rebuked me. Calling me a *yavana* he complained about our Western eating habit of saving remnants of food. "There is no taste, no vitamin, and still they eat."

Harikeśa asked if it would be all right if I kept the salt in the pot, and then put some on the plate when Prabhupāda took his *prasādam.*

"I do not know whether it is all right, but it is not all right that you eat and keep it. This is not all right."

Yaśodānandana explained, "He keeps the salt in a separate bowl. When you require it, he will give you only as much as you require."

Prabhupāda said, "Yes, that is nice."

"That's why the bowl is there," I explained. "That's what I intended to do, but I have to keep it away from the table."

Prabhupāda said, "The principle should be that you should not leave remnants of food. As soon as it is used, it should not be used more. Otherwise it is not possible to give up. *Paraṁ dṛṣṭvā nivartate.* 'I am eating something not very superior, but if I get the chance of eating something superior then I give up this inferior.'"

* * *

At 10:30 a.m. Prabhupāda went to the two-acre plot, where a simple *pāṇḍāla* had been erected in the center. His *vyāsāsana* had been brought from Madras and was nicely decorated with flowers. In front of a small but enthusiastic crowd he performed the foundation-stone ceremony for the new temple.

The guest of honor, Śrī B. Gopāla Reddy, a former governor of Uttar Pradesh and, historically, the second chief minister of Andra Pradesh, presented Prabhupāda with a very large and colorful garland. Mr. Reddy gave a short speech, followed by Mahāṁsa Swami and then Acyutānanda Swami. At last Śrīla Prabhupāda spoke.

After these preliminaries Prabhupāda got off the *vyāsāsana* and climbed down into a big hole in the ground with Acyutānanda. A water pot with a coconut on top was placed at the bottom of the hole along with auspicious items such as *amṛta* and flowers, as well as gold, silver, and copper coins. Then Prabhupāda broke a coconut and poured the water over it all, with the *sannyāsīs* following suit. Prabhupāda climbed back out and with a short speech unveiled a carved marble commemoration plaque. Finally he went back in the hole and laid a few bricks with cement.

With the foundation proceedings over, he happily initiated eleven new Indian disciples from Mahāṁsa's party, distributing chanting beads and new names before returning to the house, leaving the *sannyāsīs* to complete the ceremony with a fire sacrifice.

* * *

Encouraging news of book distribution continues to pour in, to the great pleasure of His Divine Grace.

Hṛdayānanda Goswami reported progress in the Spanish- and Portuguese-language translations. "Everything is going on nicely in my zone. In Caracas some men are now selling one hundred *Śrīmad-Bhāgavatams* daily, and in one weekend the Caracas temple has sold sixteen hundred *Bhāgavatams* and four thousand BTGs. We are now composing the *Bhagavad-gītā Como Ele E* (Portuguese) for distribution in Brazil and Portugal, and it will go to the printer in about two or three months. I think that I am supposed to be your secretary for February, so I hope you will not mind my foolish presence. Actually, I just want to surrender unto You completely; everything is simply causing me pain except surrendering unto You. You are so great that I cannot conceive the extent of your glories. Please let me remain as a dog outside your door...."

Prabhupāda listened carefully smiling at the news, humbly appreciative of his disciple's glorification. He replied, "I am glad to learn that everything is going nicely in your zone. In

South America the people are not so rich nor so enlightened as their North American neighbors, but they are very nice people and somewhat pious and that is their credit. Now just try to deliver Śrī Caitanya Mahāprabhu's message to them. As you are doing, go on publishing books, more and more, in Spanish and Portuguese.

"It is very good that you have concentrated all the production of Spanish and Portuguese literature to Los Angeles. Please thank all of the devotees of the Spanish BBT for the beautiful edition of *Bhagavad-gītā As It Is.* This book publishing was the most important work of my Guru Mahārāja and he ordered me to continue in the Western world. So I am very much indebted to all of you who are helping me to carry out the order of Śrīla Bhaktisiddhānta Sarasvatī Gosvāmī. Please see that all of our books are translated as nicely as this edition of *Bhagavad-gītā As It Is.*

"Jagadīśa prabhu also is thinking to come as my GBC secretary for the month of February. If you come in February I have no objection, I can have three dozen secretaries. If your business will not suffer, you are welcome anytime. I wish to remain with all my disciples together, but we have to do preaching work and therefore have to remain separate. But actually there is no question of separation for one engaged in Lord Kṛṣṇa's service."

Prabhupāda's comment about his desire to be with his disciples was neither flattery nor hyperbole. It has become quite apparent to me that Prabhupāda truly enjoys associating with his disciples. He seems to thrive on it. Indeed, he never seems happier than when he is sitting or walking with his disciples and discussing the philosophy and activities of the Kṛṣṇa consciousness movement. He is such a wonderful and remarkably merciful person that although we are helpless fools, he actually *wants* to be with us. His transcendental nature constantly amazes me.

* * *

For the next few evenings Prabhupāda is to lecture at a *pāṇḍāla* held on the grounds of the Śrī Rebala Lakshminarasa Reddy Public Hall, on Nellore's main street. The hall was a gift to the town by the same family that we are staying with.

At the rear the hall has an open area of about an acre, with a large, brick, stagelike platform built onto a back wall. It is over this that the colorful *pāṇḍāla* has been erected.

The devotees have made adequate preparations with fresh flower garlands, an effective sound system, and a giant painting hanging above the back of the *vyāsāsana* depicting Lord Caitanya dancing and chanting with the animals in the forest of Jhārikhaṇḍa. A large *aśvattha* (ragi) tree overshadows the whole setup with its auspicious presence.

This evening a large crowd of about 6,000 people were gathered, eager to see and hear the *sādhu* who has been converting Westerners into followers of Vedic culture. Over the past few weeks they have seen the devotees perform *kīrtana* on the main streets of their town. Tonight they listened quietly and with full attention as Prabhupāda lectured from the newly received Sixth Canto, Volume One, of the *Śrīmad-Bhāgavatam.* Śrī Kalaprapurna Marupuru Kodandarami Reddy, a local poet and author, sitting respectfully at Śrīla Prabhupāda's feet, translated his English speech into Telegu.

The topic of the lecture was *prāyaścitta,* or atonement for sinful acts. Śrīla Prabhupāda prescribed the chanting of the Hare Kṛṣṇa mantra as the best means to counteract and remove sinful desires.

He related the story of a devotee of Lord Caitanya who after being sprinkled with water by the Nawab Hussein Shah was considered to have been converted into a Muslim. When the devotee asked a local *brāhmaṇa* what atonement he should perform, he was told to drink a kilogram of molten lead, while another *brāhmaṇa* recommended the same amount of hot ghee. Finally the devotee went to Lord Caitanya, who advised him to retire from family life, go to Vṛndāvana and chant Hare Kṛṣṇa.

In his summary Prabhupāda once again indicated his Western disciples as practical evidence of the holy name's efficacy. "So this Kṛṣṇa consciousness movement is the thoroughly wholesale process of cleansing the mind. If we perform this Kṛṣṇa *saṅkīrtana* then immediately the core of the heart, which is filled up with all dirty things, will be cleansed.

"For example, you can see practically all my disciples present here. They are coming from Western countries: Europe, America, or even in India—Parsis and other, Mohammedans, they are coming. But they are now pure, cleansed of the dirty things. In this Movement throughout the whole world there are at least ten to twelve thousand devotees like that, and before this life they were all addicted to all kinds of sinful life. Now they are not committing the four pillars of sinful life. Therefore our request is that you take up this chanting method. It is very easy: Hare Kṛṣṇa, Hare Kṛṣṇa, Kṛṣṇa Kṛṣṇa, Hare Hare/ Hare Rāma, Hare Rāma, Rāma Rāma, Hare Hare."

He also added a caution. "But one thing we must be very careful of, that we should not commit again sinful life. If you chant Hare Kṛṣṇa mantra you become free immediately from all sinful reaction, but if you commit again sinful life, that is your responsibility. Among the ten kinds of offenses one is very grievous. *Nāmno balād yasya hi pāpa-buddhiḥ*—if one thinks that 'I am chanting Hare Kṛṣṇa, therefore whatever sinful acts I am doing, it is becoming counteracted.' Don't commit the mistake of the elephant that takes bath thoroughly and again throw dust on your body."

The audience appeared greatly satisfied with the lecture. Afterward the devotees requested Śrīla Prabhupāda to remain on stage to make a presentation of gifts to various gentlemen who had become Life Members during the day's preaching. As they came forward one-by-one, Acyutānanda Swami announced their names to the crowd, and everyone clapped as each man received a set of books from Śrīla Prabhupāda's own hand.

On the way back to the house Prabhupāda told us that it is very good to tell a story in the middle of a talk. He explained that in *Kali-yuga* people are less intelligent, so the *Bhāgavatam* is ideal for this age because it gives instruction by way of stories.

January 5th, 1976

On their preaching tour in the South, Acyutānanda and Yaśodānandana Swamis have met an assortment of spiritual practitioners who have their own interpretations and twists on traditional Vedic *siddhānta.* Now they are taking full advantage of Prabhupāda's association to get definitive answers to the challenges they regularly face.

On the walk this morning they played the role of impersonalists and challenged Prabhupāda with a barrage of *māyāvādī* arguments. Yet, no matter how hard they tried, they couldn't defeat the Vaiṣṇava exegesis with which Prabhupāda countered all their arguments.

Śrī G. Gopāla Reddy, the president of the local Rotary Club, also accompanied Śrīla Prabhupāda on the morning walk. He is the secretary of a committee that Mahāṁsa Swami has formed for the new temple. The committee has been very active in making new ISKCON life members and obtaining pledges for construction work. Prabhupāda was happy to see him and thanked him for his efforts. Upon noticing a colony of *bhaṅgīs,* or "untouchables," Mr. Reddy mentioned that the government was distributing land to them. He asked whether ISKCON was engaged in any sort of social welfare work, because many people have asked him what our Society did to benefit others.

Prabhupāda replied by asking him what he considered the best social welfare.

When Mr. Reddy said serving the poor and the natives, Prabhupāda told him, "Everyone is poor. Who is rich? First of all find out: Who is rich?" Prabhupāda went on to explain how everyone is poor because each of us must suffer disease, old age, and death. Adjustment of a person's material condition can be done by anyone, but ISKCON was established for a different purpose. "These things are being done by so many other people, and we are doing something which is ultimate. The hospital gives some medicine when there is some disease, but that does not mean there will be no disease. Can they guarantee that, 'I give you this medicine—no more disease?' We are giving that medicine—that no more disease. That is the best social work. As soon as you give up this body—*tyaktvā dehaṁ punar janma naiti*—you'll have no more birth. And if you have no more birth, there will be no more death. And if you have no more birth, then there will be no more disease. This is our prescription. *Tyaktvā dehaṁ punar janma naiti mām eti.* Not that he is finished; he goes back to home, back to Godhead. This is our program."

On the way back to the house one of Mr. Reddy's companions asked Śrīla Prabhupāda how to meditate. Although most people in India are familiar with the concept of meditation, or have even practiced some form of it themselves, the actual purpose of meditation is rarely understood. The man's lack of knowledge became apparent when he explained that he thought the goal of meditation was to make the mind silent.

Prabhupāda immediately corrected him, saying that it is not possible to silence the mind. He recounted a recent *Back to Godhead* article where a woman disciple had analyzed the fallacy of the idea. Prabhupāda had greatly enjoyed the article in which the girl described how she had read in a book that meditation means "to free the mind of all thoughts." So she considered, "How can I be without thoughts? I will think of being 'without thoughts,' and that is a thought." Therefore she concluded it was bogus, and she threw away the meditation book.

Prabhupāda said the point is to think of God. This alone is the real goal of meditation—there is nothing higher. If one is a rascal and has nothing beneficial to say, then it is good if he is silent. Otherwise the *Bhagavad-gītā* never advises silent meditation. Kṛṣṇa says, *satataṁ kīrtayanto mām.* He never said that 'You become silent.' Where is? Can you show me any verse in the *Bhagavad-gītā?* Can you show me any verse where Kṛṣṇa has advised that you become silent? Or the mind is vacant? Where are these things?

"*Man-manā bhava mad-bhakto:* 'The mind should be absorbed in My thought,' *man-manā.* That is recommended. Where does He say that 'Make your mind vacant and think of nonsense'? He never says. And where does He say that you become silent? He never says. *Ya idaṁ paramaṁ guhyaṁ mad-bhakteṣv abhidhāsyati, na ca tasmān manuṣyeṣu kaścin me priya-kṛttamaḥ* [Bg. 18.68]: 'Anyone who speaks about this *Bhagavad-gītā,* he is My dearmost friend,' He said. So why one should be silent? Our ultimate aim is how to become dearmost to Kṛṣṇa, and He never says that 'You become silent.' Rather, He recommends that 'You always be engaged in glorifying Me.' Where is the 'silent'? These are all manufactured by these rascals. Meditation and silence, these are not recommended in the *Bhagavad-gītā.*"

After the morning walk the *sannyāsīs* have been coming into Prabhupāda's room for a few minutes, eager for as much association with him as they can get. As he relaxed behind his desk waiting for breakfast he told them our preaching will go on only if we have spiritual strength. "We may have external strength," he said, "but success will only come if we have spiritual strength. Preaching programs will work only if there is purity." Citing the example of one of his leading Godbrothers in the Gauḍīya Maṭha, he pointed out that he had all kinds of material facility—money, *maṭhas,* etc. But what had he done for spreading Kṛṣṇa consciousness? He explained that simply amassing material wealth will not bring spiritual success, nor does it signify success. He gave the example of milk touched by a serpent: It looks like milk, but it is spoiled.

"How do we keep our spiritual strength?" Prabhupāda asked. We can keep our spiritual strength by being very strict Vaiṣṇavas, he told us: by strictly following the principles and not giving any consideration whatsoever to *māyā's* allurements. *Māyā* is always trying to weaken us, he said, but if we think only of Kṛṣṇa we will have spiritual strength; if we think of something else then we will have no transcendental potency. As always, Śrīla Prabhupāda emphasized that we must remain strictly regulated and chant all our rounds every day.

* * *

All GBC members are required to send in monthly reports to Śrīla Prabhupāda. Satsvarūpa Mahārāja sent his for the month of December from Santa Cruz, California. He is in charge of the Library Party, selling standing orders of Prabhupāda's books to universities in the US and Europe. He and his group have been remarkably successful. They are now trying to approach public libraries, and he outlined his strategy in his letter. He also reported that many extremely favorable book reviews have been received from professors. He wrote, "They are praising your books in language more exalted than any of us disciples can praise!! The reviews from Oxford are from some of the biggest linguistic authorities in the world. All these amazing reviews are certainly one of the most important services of the Library Party."

As well as library canvassing, his party has been preaching in the Santa Cruz area, where many young people reside. In a spirit of cooperation with the West coast GBC, Jayatīrtha, he had allowed one of his party, Cāru, to become president of the Berkeley temple. He hoped to leave another man in Santa Cruz to help with the preaching there. "I think we GBC should try more to help each other in the different zones and not take a sectarian spirit only for 'our zone', especially when the zones are nearby."

He has over 100 preaching engagements alone in Texas colleges during January and February and asked if he could carry small Gaura-Nitāi Deities onto the campuses.

He also wrote about his own growing interest in Prabhupāda's books. "I am becoming more and more drawn to read the many books you have published. Since there are so many books, and since I am, as a *sannyāsī* and a GBC, constantly being called to lecture and answer questions, I take it as a special responsibility. I have therefore, been trying to read <u>at least three hours a day and more</u> whenever possible, although I try not to neglect management duties. In your books and tapes I receive the greatest solace. Is this amount of time spent in reading excessive?"

Finally he mentioned that they are researching the possibility of having favorable scholars make recommendations for Prabhupāda to receive the Nobel prize for literature.

Prabhupāda was happy to hear Satsvarūpa's lengthy report. He was especially pleased with their success in making standing orders and with the idea of placing his books in public libraries, which he said would be a "great victory." He also considered the book reviews very important. In fact, his secretary always carries a file with all the latest reviews, which Prabhupāda shows to visitors at every opportunity.

He also appreciated Satsvarūpa's spirit of cooperation and told him, "Everything should be done cooperatively. 'Our' and 'yours' are material conceptions and have no place in our Kṛṣṇa consciousness movement. If the members of our movement are unable to cooperate, it will be very difficult to spread the mission of Lord Caitanya."

He did not approve of taking Deities into classrooms, lest the students think us fanatics, and recommended instead a large picture of Gaura-Nitāi.

As for Satsvarūpa's reading schedule, Prabhupāda approved wholeheartedly. "Yes, as a *sannyāsī* and GBC your first duty is to read my books. Otherwise how will you preach? In order to remain steadily fixed in Kṛṣṇa consciousness there must be a sound philosophical understanding. Otherwise it will become only sentiment. Whenever you find time please read my books. Shortly we shall be introducing the system of examinations for those students who are ready for second initiation as well as *sannyāsa.* According to the degree, devotees will be expected to read and assimilate our different books.

"Our first business is this book distribution. There is no need of any other business. If this book distribution is managed properly, pushed on with great enthusiasm, and determination and at the same time if our men keep spiritually strong, then the whole world will become Kṛṣṇa conscious."

Rādhāballabha dāsa sent a letter from Los Angeles requesting Prabhupāda's advice about the new printing standard for *Śrīmad-Bhāgavatam.*

Prabhupāda's main concern is practicality. He advised him that the first consideration was cost-effectiveness. He doesn't want the price unnecessarily increased. Scholarly appreciation is important, but more important is Kṛṣṇa consciousness actually being put into practice.

Similarly he sees *The Nectar of Instruction* as a book of great worth because of its practical value. The devotees have been thinking it primarily a book for distribution within ISKCON, thus the small printing. Śrīla Prabhupāda, however, sees it as having a far wider audience.

He expressed the same sentiment to Rādhāballabha that he impressed upon Tamal Krishna Mahārāja a few days earlier. "*The Nectar of Instruction* has come out very nice. It is very important and must be immediately read by all the devotees. In the near future we shall introduce the *Bhakti-śāstrī* examination for second initiation, and this shall be one of the required books of study. Anyone who reads it will immediately understand what Kṛṣṇa consciousness is. Some minister in Bombay recently asked me how to create morality among the students, because the students are all vagabonds. If this book is introduced for study in the schools and colleges it will give a clear idea of what morality actually is. It is a most important book."

Prabhupāda is also closely supervising revisions of his books and has approved of correcting printing and editorial mistakes in earlier editions. Rādhāballabha mentioned that on Harikeśa's advice the BBT has postponed reprinting the First Canto of the *Bhāgavatam* because Prabhupāda was apparently not pleased with the standard of correction.

Prabhupāda confirmed this. "I will have to see personally what are the mistakes in the synonyms and also how you intend to correct them. I was not satisfied with the corrections that were made before. I saw some changes which I did not approve. Nitai may correct whatever mistakes are there, but the corrected material must be sent to me for final approval. So reprinting the volumes will have to wait until the mistakes are corrected and approved by me."

In another package Jadurāṇī dāsī, chief BBT artist, sent some sketches of proposed paintings for an upcoming *Bhāgavatam* production. Śrīla Prabhupāda regularly receives sketches from the artists before allowing them to paint any scenes, but during the recent *Caitanya-caritāmṛta* production marathon he permitted them to paint without prior approval for the sake of expediency. Now that all seventeen volumes are out, the pressure is off, and he confirmed his desire to revert to the previous arrangement.

Being with Prabhupāda is like being at Action Central. It is exciting and educational to observe how he attentively oversees every aspect of ISKCON's development and preaching, especially anything connected with book production and distribution.

* * *

Later in the day Prabhupāda visited the Raṅganātha Temple here in Nellore. This impressive building was founded in

1070 AD on the bank of the River Pennar, sometimes called the Penarkini, by the Śrī Vaiṣṇavas, the followers of Rāmānujācārya. It is home to a very large Deity of Rañganātha, Lord Garbhodakaśayī Viṣṇu.

We entered the temple compound through a massive 110-year-old Gopuram, an edifice similar to a temple dome. It is about 95 feet high and covered with dioramas of hundreds of Viṣṇu *avatāras*. After passing through its high-arched gateway we walked across a small courtyard surrounded by private residences, entering the original walled compound of the temple proper.

Prabhupāda was warmly received by a small crowd of local dignitaries and priests. It was wonderful to see them honor him with pomp and ceremony. After being draped with a newly woven cloth, he was led around the temple precincts preceded by a *shenai* band. The band included a *nadaswaram*, which is a six-foot-long *shenai*. Its exotic wail traditionally announces the presence of an auspicious guest. There was also a *thavil*, a double-headed drum played at one end with a stick and slapped by the player's metal-ringed fingers at the other, producing staccato rhythms.

High above Prabhupāda's head the white silken canopy of an eight-foot-wide ceremonial umbrella offered shade, while simultaneously marking the position to inquisitive bystanders of the most important person present.

Proceeding down the left side of the inner courtyard Prabhupāda was taken first to a small shrine of Rañga-nāyakīdevī, the four-handed seated Deity form of Lakṣmīdevī.

He was led next into a multi-mirrored room used for various festivals. Built in the 1930s, a gazebo structure stood in the center, its four columns covered in mirrors. The gazebo's ceiling had a painting of baby Kṛṣṇa sucking His toe. Beneath it, there was a sitting place for the Deity.

On the gazebo's four corners hung large glass bowls for use as candle holders. The walls of the entire room were mirrored to a height of eight feet, the rest of the walls being decorated with various colorful paintings of Viṣṇu and *Kṛṣṇa-līlā*. The main ceiling was covered with paintings of the *Daśāvatāras*.

Our guides explained that the mirrored room was built to enable people to see the Deity from anywhere in the room.

From there Prabhupāda was led into the main temple, its interior very majestic and imposing. Uneven floors of black stone and colored ceramic tiles accentuated its antiquity. Beams of solid rock running across the tops of about eighty or ninety equally substantial pillars supported the low, stone-slab ceiling. The pillars were spaced so closely together I got the impression of having ventured into a maze.

There was a squat, claustrophobic feel to the nave, and the lack of natural light in the inner chamber made me feel very insignificant indeed.

After a *parikrama* of the Deity room, the *pūjārīs* finally led Prabhupāda into the *sanctum sanctorium.* We walked first through an ancient portal flanked by six-foot-high *mūrtis* of the Vaikuṇṭha guardians Jaya and Vijaya. Then we passed under a small carving of Gaja-Lakṣmī, Lakṣmī flanked by two elephants pouring water on her. We passed thick, heavy doors adorned with at least thirty or forty heavy brass bells hanging from large metal rings. Inside, a final arch of tarnished silver bore the symbols of the *Śrī Vaiṣṇava-sampradāya:* Garuḍa, lotus, *tilaka,* conch, and Hanuman. Ornamental snakes coiled around either side of the arch's underside.

Passing through this archway to the innermost recess we finally came upon a ten-foot-long Deity of Garbhodakaśāyī Viṣṇu, lying resplendent on His back on His couch of Ananta Śeṣa. He wore a high-peaked silver helmet, and His long arms and lotus feet were covered with silver. Lakṣmī sat on a lotus flower on His chest. Overall, His appearance was extremely impressive.

On the back wall, rising from the Lord's navel, Lord Brahmā perched upon his lotus. At Lord Viṣṇu's lotus feet stood Śrī- and Bhū-devis, His eternal consorts. Standing in front of the main Deities were the *utsava mūrtis* (festival Deities) of Raṅganātha Swami. These were flanked by twenty-six-inch-high, beautifully formed Deities of Śrī and Bhū.

As Prabhupāda stepped inside the Deity room we also pressed in close behind, eager to have the opportunity of the Lord's intimate *darśana.* Prabhupāda stood silently as the *pūjārī* made a simple offering to the Lord by waving a plate of burning camphor and coconut before the Deities. The *pūjārī* then distributed the blessings of the Supreme Lord by placing a helmet with miniature shoes of Viṣṇu on the top of it, first on Prabhupāda's head and then on ours.

We left the central temple, crossing to the other side of the compound where Prabhupāda was shown yet another small house divided into two chambers. One room contained various palanquins for the use of the *utsava* Deities. Especially impressive was a golden palanquin built in the shape of Garuḍa. There were others in the shapes of a swan, celestial serpent, an elephant, and a lion. In the inner chamber a shrine housed Deities of seventeen Alwars (personal forms of the paraphernalia of Viṣṇu) beginning with Rāmānujācārya.

After seeing all the Deities, Prabhupāda was given a seat of honor in a covered section of temple enclosure. We were then invited to perform *kīrtana,* and all the locals joyfully joined in. A few minutes later our hosts served us an excellent feast. It was done so quickly and efficiently that Prabhupāda afterward commented that their management had been first-class. He said he wanted us to learn how to manage things as nicely. It was an enjoyable visit, and Prabhupāda was highly pleased.

As we returned in the car, however, Tamal Krishna Mahārāja sounded a bleak note. He mentioned that the temple was now in Government hands, even though the Rāmanujites were looking after it. Every temple in Andhra Pradesh has been taken over by the Government. The takeover scheme was originally meant to usurp the revenue collected by Śrī Bālajī, the famous Deity at Tirupati, who is said to receive at least one *lakh* of rupees per day in donations from pious visitors. Mahārāja said that he thought the long-term strategy was to allow the temples to become gradually run down, and then to close them. Prabhupāda seemed to agree.

* * *

The evening program was very good, and again it was a maximum capacity turn out. Prabhupāda continued his previous night's topic about atonement, with the next two verses from the Sixth Canto.

"Mahārāja Parīkṣit said, 'One may know that sinful activity is injurious for him because he actually sees that a criminal is punished by the government and rebuked by the people in general and because he hears from the scriptures and learned scholars that one is thrown into hellish condition in the next life for committing sinful acts. Nevertheless, in spite of such knowledge one is forced to commit sins again and again, even after performing acts of atonement. Therefore what is the value of such atonement?

"'Sometimes one who is very alert so as not to commit sinful acts is victimized by sinful life again. I therefore consider this process of repeated sinning and atoning to be useless. It is like bathing of an elephant, for an elephant cleanses itself by taking a full bath, but then throws dust over its head and body as soon as it returns to the land.'"

This second śloka describing the bathing of the elephant is a favorite of Śrīla Prabhupāda's. He gave a wonderfully fluent lecture to his spellbound audience explaining how only the process of devotional service can fully eradicate the desires that lead a person to commit sinful acts. To illustrate this point he told the story of Mṛgāri the hunter who had formerly taken great pleasure in half-killing animals but, after meeting the great saint Nārada Muni and becoming a Vaiṣṇava, was reluctant to even step on an ant.

Although he stressed the performance of *tapasya* as a necessity for spiritual advancement he also acknowledged that in this age concessions were required, and given. "*Tapasya* means beginning with *brahmacarya,* celibacy. We have given the meaning of *tapasya:* austerity or voluntary rejection of material enjoyment. 'I do not like to do something because it is not pleasing to me, but for the sake of advancement in spiritual life I must have it.' Now one may say that 'If I give up all these things which I am habituated to, there will be some painful condition.' So therefore *Bhagavad-gītā* has recommended to tolerate, even though it is painful. It is not at all painful, but for those who are trying to practice, in the beginning it may be painful. Bhagavān, Kṛṣṇa, is advising that even it is painful, you must do it and tolerate it. Sometimes to cure our disease, for example a fever, we have to swallow very bitter quinine pills. But Śrī Caitanya Mahāprabhu, considering the people of this age, *Kali-yuga*, He knew that people will not be able to tolerate even such little pain for advancing in spiritual life, so He therefore recommended *harer nāma harer nāma harer nāmaiva kevalam, kalau nāsty eva nāsty eva nāsty eva gatir anyathā*."

The evening ended with another presentation of books to new Life Members. As the devotees showed a film and chanted, Prabhupāda returned by car to the house.

January 6th, 1976

On the morning walk there was some discussion about the Tirupati temple, which houses Bālajī, the richest Deity in India. Prabhupāda suggested that Mahāṁsa Swami approach the managers of the temple for a grant to build our temple here in Nellore. Mahāṁsa explained that in recent years the management of Tirupati, along with that of all the temples in the State, had been taken over by the Government.

This led to a long discussion whether our ISKCON temples could also be taken over. If they could, it would be on the basis of their being "Hindu" temples. So Śrīla Prabhupāda, in order to avoid any government interference, suggested that we register the temples as American property. Apart from that, he said we are not Hindu. The word Hindu isn't in the *Bhagavad-gītā*, and the teachings of *Bhagavad-gītā* are for everyone, not just Hindus. Śrīla Prabhupāda strongly emphasized this point and even said that we could go to court to prove we are not Hindus.

After the morning walk the *sannyāsīs* gathered in Śrīla Prabhupāda's room. Yaśodānandana Mahārāja showed him what he said was a Dvārakā-śilā, a brown-and-white-freckled stone, and asked if it was all right to worship. "It can be used as paper weight," Prabhupāda said, unimpressed.

When Yaśodānandana Swami mentioned that some temples worshipped the Dvārakā-śilā along with the Śālagrāma-śilā, Prabhupāda was dismissive. "That's all right, but we have no such instruction."

Prabhupāda called in Harikeśa, and had everyone sit while Harikeśa read some of his *Dialectic Spiritualism*. Last night he had read to Prabhupāda for forty-five minutes, and Prabhupāda was very pleased. Prabhupāda said that the article should immediately be printed in BTG, as well as be sent to Hansadūta for printing in German and Russian.

Harikeśa used many relevant examples to disprove the theories of Lenin and Engels, most of them given by Prabhupāda over the last few weeks, along with some of his own. He completely disproved their theory of idealistic materialism, showing it to be an illogical, nonsensical notion.

Encouraging further discussion on the subject, Prabhupāda pointed out that there could be no question of a "dialectic" in discussions between materialists, because all parties involved were imperfect. He challenged us that if they are indeed imperfect, what is the value of their discussion? He gave an example to illustrate the point. "If children discuss some serious subject matter, what is the value? They are all children in the cradle of nature, that's all. Therefore *prakṛteḥ kriyamāṇāni.* Just like children, 'Ha! Sit down here.' He has to sit down. Then where is his freedom to discuss? *Prakṛti* says that 'You sit down here. Don't go there!' He has to accept. Then what is the value of discussion?"

Harikeśa continued to read aloud, explaining how food production is dependent on God. Acyutānanda pointed out that in Russia they don't have enough grains, yet the Communists like to accuse the religionists of withholding food to control the population.

Prabhupāda asked why they are having grain shortages, and I recalled that in the papers they had reported insufficient rainfall in the Eastern-bloc countries, forcing them to buy elsewhere.

"Then?" he inquired, and promptly answered his own question. "Then you have to depend on rain, and when we say, *parjanyād anna-sambhavaḥ.* And *yajñād bhavati parjanyaḥ.* That means, rascal, you take one side, *ardha-kukkuti-nyāya.* Cut the chicken in half, and separate the mouth—it is expensive—and keep the rear side. You get eggs." He laughed heartily at the foolishness of trying to grow grains without making the necessary sacrifice. "So this is *ardha-kukkuti-nyāya.* The rascal does not know that if you separate the mouth, there will be no egg."

* * *

Later in the morning Prabhupāda called in Tamal Krishna Mahārāja to formulate a plan he has been discussing over the last couple of days to raise the standards of the *brāhmaṇas* in ISKCON. He expressed concern that many of our men are not familiar with our books. Especially here in India the *smārta-brāhmaṇas* sometimes criticize us for our lack of scriptural understanding. He wants the level of ISKCON education improved and then tested by a system of examinations, recognition being given to those who pass the different exams by the awarding of titles. Prabhupāda said that if a man can't pass at least the *Bhakti-śāstrī* exam, the first level, he must be understood to be low class. The other morning he said that all potential second initiates should be tested to this standard, otherwise they couldn't be awarded the sacred thread.

He is very serious about implementing this system. He instructed Tamal Krishna Mahārāja to immediately send out a letter to all the GBCs so they can discuss how to start this program at the upcoming meeting in Māyāpur.

Later Tamal Krishna read aloud the letter he'd composed, for Prabhupāda's approval.

"To all Governing Body Commissioners

"Re: Examinations for awarding titles of *Bhaktiśāstrī, Bhaktibaibhava, Bhaktivedānta,* and *Bhaktisārvabhauma.* Your response is requested immediately by Śrīla Prabhupāda.

"Dear Prabhus,

"Please accept my most humble obeisances. Śrīla Prabhupāda has requested me to write you in regard to the above examinations which he wishes to institute. Here in India many persons often criticize our *sannyāsīs* and *brāhmaṇas* as being unqualified due to insufficient knowledge of the scriptures. Factually, there are numerous instances when our *sannyāsīs* and *brāhmaṇas* have fallen down often due to insufficient understanding of the philosophy. This should not be a point of criticism nor a reason for fall down, since Śrīla Prabhupāda has mercifully made the most essential scriptures available to us in his books. The problem is that not all the devotees are carefully studying the books, the result being a fall down or at least unsteadiness.

"His Divine Grace therefore wishes to institute examinations to be given to all prospective candidates for *sannyāsa* and *brāhmaṇa* initiation. In addition he wishes that all present *sannyāsīs* and *brāhmaṇas* also pass the examination. Awarding of these titles will be based upon the following books:

Bhaktiśāstrī	—*Bhagavad-gītā, Nectar of Devotion, Nectar of Instruction, Īśopaniṣad, Easy Journey to Other Planets,* and all other small paper backs, as well as *Arcana-paddhati* (a book to be compiled by Nitai prabhu based on *Hari-bhakti-vilāsa* on Deity worship)
Bhaktibaibhava	—All the above plus the first six cantos of *Śrīmad-Bhāgavatam.*
Bhaktivedānta	—All the above plus cantos 7 through 12 of *Śrīmad-Bhāgavatam.*
Bhaktisārvabhouma	—All the above plus the entire *Caitanya-caritāmṛta.*

"Anyone wishing to be initiated as a *brāhmaṇa* will have to pass the *Bhaktiśāstrī* exam, and anyone wishing to take *sannyāsa* will have to pass the Bhaktibaibhava examination as well. This will prevent our Society from degrading to the level of so many other institutions where, in order to maintain the temple, they have accepted all third class men as *brāhmaṇas.* Any *sannyāsīs* or *brāhmaṇas* already initiated who fail to pass the exams will be considered low class or less qualified. Anyone wishing to be second initiated will sit for examination once a year at Māyāpur. Answers will be in essay form and authoritative quotations will be given a bigger score. During the exams books may not be consulted.

"Śrīla Prabhupāda wishes to begin this program at this year's Māyāpur meeting. He requests that you all send your opinions and comments here immediately so that everything may be prepared in time."

Prabhupāda endorsed it with his signature at the bottom and it was duly sent out.

An interesting letter arrived today from Dīna-dayal dāsa, a brahmacārī who has just opened a new center in Pireaus, the port of Athens, Greece. He related how Kṛṣṇa helped him as soon as he arrived in Athens. "The first day I arrived in Athens I went to a small guest house. The owner of the house, an elderly woman of about sixty, happily invited me in and gave me a room without question. Later she said that Lord Kṛṣṇa had sent me to her. I put some *tilaka* on her head and she brought a *mūrti* of Lord Viṣṇu out and we offered some incense to Lord Viṣṇu. A few days later I told her I was leaving and she said I could stay without charge if I wanted, and she invited me to come with her to her metaphysics group of about forty people. The teacher of the group asked me to speak and I told them about you, Lord Caitanya, and Lord Kṛṣṇa. Everyone chanted Hare Kṛṣṇa, Hare Kṛṣṇa, Kṛṣṇa Kṛṣṇa, Hare Hare/ Hare Rāma, Hare Rāma, Rāma Rāma, Hare Hare, and they were interested in your books and *Back to Godhead.*"

Dīna-dayal also enclosed a Greek newspaper article describing his activities. He pointed out that it included Kṛṣṇa's name four times, as well as Śrīla Prabhupāda's. He was attracting guests by offering free English lessons, which he conducted using *Kṛṣṇa Book* as the basic text. The article also mentioned a program of free food distribution for the poor.

Prabhupāda was pleased to hear of Dīna-dayal's pioneering activities and sent him a letter, commending him and encouraging him further. "Lord Caitanya Mahāprabhu desires that in every city, town, and village Kṛṣṇa consciousness should be preached. Therefore I left Vṛndāvana to come to your country. And now you have left your country also on behalf of Śrī Caitanya Mahāprabhu, therefore your life is glorious. May Kṛṣṇa bless you that your preaching attempt becomes successful. As soon as a devotee endeavors to serve Kṛṣṇa, Kṛṣṇa immediately wants to help that devotee. Kṛṣṇa will certainly protect and maintain you. You are an intelligent, sincere boy, so try to introduce this movement to the people of Greece. Everyone in the world is suffering. Despite so many attempts on the part of the governments and planning commissions of the world, still the suffering continues. People are thinking that by more education, hospitals, food, and so many other things they will become happy. But we actually have the ingredient which alone can make them satisfied—Kṛṣṇa consciousness. So please deliver Kṛṣṇa to everyone you meet; instruct them in the philosophy of *Bhagavad-gītā As It Is.* If it is possible to get our books translated into Greek that will be very helpful for your preaching. In the meantime as you are preaching to intelligent persons such as the lawyer you met, they will be able to read English, so you can give them our English books."

Prabhupāda approved of his idea to introduce Kṛṣṇa consciousness through the medium of teaching English based on the Kṛṣṇa book, coupled with chanting and *prasādam* distribution. At the end of the letter Prabhupāda emphasized the actual requirement for successful preaching. "The important thing is that you behave nicely, chant all your rounds and follow strictly the regulative principles. Example is better than precept. These spiritual practices are our actual strength."

Akṣayānanda Swami sent some information regarding his recent preaching in Kanpur, where the Vṛndāvana devotees have been holding a series of *pāṇḍāla* programs. He reported good attendance and publicity. Their presence had also inspired some local men to help us acquire land for a center. "I beg to inform you," he wrote, "that Śrī R.N. Bhārgava, of Nath Opticians, 18/53, The Mall, Kanpur, our Life Patron Member, is offering us fifteen acres of land in Kanpur at a place called Katri Corner."

He gave a detailed description of the land and its location. Although the site is a little remote and undeveloped, it was offered for ISKCON's unconditional usage. He also described another piece of land that might be available for lease near the Kailash Temple in Kanpur. However, the conditions on this property are not clear because of litigation between the brothers that own it. Finally, he reported that several devotees have arrived in Vṛndāvana from the West to help with the Deity cooking and *pūjārī* work at Kṛṣṇa Balarāma Mandira.

In India it is not uncommon to receive gifts of land, but the intentions behind such offerings are not always completely genuine. Prabhupāda appreciated Mr. Bhārgava's offer because there were no strings attached. "Regarding the land of Śrī R.N. Bhārgava," he wrote, "since he is offering it to us for our unconditional use, why not take it? If there is possibility of developing the land, then we can take it." Nevertheless he showed more interest in the centrally located property, even though it could only be leased. He wrote, "That land would be the most ideal for establishing our center in Kanpur."

And as always, he expressed his concern about the land we already had. "I am glad to know that new men are coming to help with the activities in Vṛndāvana temple. The kitchen department should be very clean and things should not be wasted. This is the first consideration. Yesterday we have visited a very old and famous Raṅganātha Temple here in Nellore. Everything is being managed very nicely, and there are very nice arrangements for those who come for *darśana.* So similarly our temple in Vṛndāvana must be managed expertly that everyone who comes is given *caraṇāmṛta* and *prasādam* of the Deity."

* * *

In the early evening Prabhupāda held *darśana* about half an hour for some guests. They wanted to know why no intelligent, well-educated Indians are coming forward to join ISKCON and why only the Westerners are taking it up when it isn't even their culture.

Prabhupāda told them the Indians are too attached to family life, and he cited the example of M. K. Gandhi. This greatly surprised the guests, as Gandhi is generally revered throughout India as a great renunciate. How could he be an example of an attached person?

Prabhupāda skillfully broadened their perspective by explaining that Gandhi had been so attached to the concept of being Indian that he had to die before giving it up. He explained that this is the *gṛhamedhī* concept—identification with and attachment to one's own body, the immediate expansions of the body, and the greater expansion, one's nation. Whether the attachment is immediate or extended, the mentality of bodily identification is the same.

The guests nodded appreciatively as they began to perceive that only Kṛṣṇa consciousness can give real detachment. They could understand that it is not the property of India, but a universal principle that has nothing to do with nationality.

Prabhupāda went on to say that the one advantage Westerners have is that they are generally not as attached to their families as Indians. But lacking a positive alternative, they end up as hippies. "Now," he said, "I am offering something positive, and so many men are coming."

* * *

Prabhupāda continued his evening *pāṇḍāla* lecture series from the Sixth Canto.

Kecit kevalayā bhaktyā vāsudeva-parāyaṇāḥ
aghaṁ dhunvanti kārtsnyena nīhāram iva bhāskaraḥ.

"Only a rare person who has adopted complete, unalloyed devotional service to Kṛṣṇa can uproot the weeds of sinful actions with no possibility that they will revive. He can do this simply by discharging devotional service, just as the sun can immediately dissipate fog by its rays."

He stressed that *kecit* means "somebody," not just anybody. It does not refer to the *karmīs, jñānīs,* and yogis but to those situated on the platform of *anyābhilāṣitā-śūnyaṁ,* the mood of pure devotional service to Kṛṣṇa. He told the packed audience that they should begin devotional service in the recommended way, by hearing from an authorized source. This in turn will enable them to perform *kīrtana* and preach. And by hearing and speaking about the Supreme, Lord Kṛṣṇa can be conquered.

He ended his long lecture with the same message of encouragement that seems to characterize his Indian preaching tours. "Our miserable condition of life is due to our material attraction or *pāpa,* impious activities. Here it is confirmed that *kevalayā bhaktyā, aghaṁ dhunvanti kārtsnyena:* totally you can kill all reaction of sinful activities. And a very good example is given here—*nīhāram iva bhāskaraḥ. Nīhāra* means fog. In the fog you cannot see what is there in your front. But as soon as there is sunrise, immediately fog is dissipated. If you come to Kṛṣṇa consciousness, the light is there. Therefore the darkness of life is dissipated.

"So this movement is giving the chance to everyone. It doesn't mean for any particular nation, particular country, or particular person. For everyone. Caitanya Mahāprabhu said, 'All over the world, in every village and every town, this message will be spread,' and that is being done now. So it is a great movement. I request you all to join wholeheartedly. Thank you very much. Hare Kṛṣṇa."

Each night there is an increasing number of gentlemen coming on stage to receive books from Prabhupāda. The devotees go out preaching during the day, and Prabhupāda's presence has greatly enhanced the Life Membership enrollments. There is a great deal of enthusiasm on the part of the local people, so the future looks promising for preaching in Nellore.

January 7th, 1976

On the walk this morning Acyutānanda Swami made Prabhupāda laugh when he humorously described his meetings with a few well-known swamis and *sādhus.*

As they walked, the conversation sobered when Prabhupāda condemned the modern mentality of exploiting nature for personal sense gratification. "Prahlāda Mahārāja said *tat prayāsaṁ na kartavyam:* 'This kind of endeavor you should not do, exploitation,' unnecessarily trying for developing economic condition. The modern civilization is: 'Exploit nature and materially be opulent.'"

Yaśodānandana said, "It has been seen everywhere we travel that there is plenty of rice everywhere, there is plenty of food growing everywhere, but the government is advertising that there is scarcity of food. Yet there is plenty growing everywhere."

"And reduce population, kill it," Prabhupāda added. "Hiraṇyakaśipu was doing that."

"Birth control?" Acyutānanda wondered.

"Yes," Prabhupāda said. "Prajāpati. He stopped Prajāpatis to beget children."

As the walk progressed the devotees questioned him on a variety of topics. In India the multiplicity of religious thought and ritual sometimes puzzles inexperienced devotees. Having Śrīla Prabhupāda personally present is a good opportunity to clear up any confusion.

One devotee asked Prabhupāda about a particular type of Durgā worship he had come across in South India. He said that a Life Member in Bangalore told him that worship of Śānti Durgā was in the mode of goodness. He wanted some clarification.

Acyutānanda offered his understanding that *sattva-guṇa* is also *māyā.*

Prabhupāda said, "From *Brahma-saṁhitā* we understand, *sṛṣṭi-sthiti-pralaya.* The *pralaya* [destruction] is *amaṅgala,* and *sṛṣṭi* [creation] is *maṅgala. Sthiti* [maintenance] is also *maṅgala.* So *Gaurī* has got three functions, Durgā."

Ānandamoya, a French devotee stationed in Hyderabad, wanted to clarify what seemed an apparent contradiction concerning the fall-down of devotees and the eternal nature of devotional service. He asked, "A devotee who has tasted the nectar of the lotus feet of the Lord can never forget it. Does it mean that his journey in the material world is about to finish?"

Prabhupāda didn't answer himself. Instead he said, "Answer, somebody."

Mahāṁsa replied, "He falls down due to certain offenses, but afterwards, by the mercy of a pure devotee, he comes back. Because he has tasted the nectar of devotional service, he may try to enjoy the material world for some time. But afterwards, he will be fed up again and come back."

"There's a statement in the *Bhagavad-gītā* that if one is engaged in the service of the Lord, even if he falls down, he is to be considered saintly," Tamal Krishna said.

Prabhupāda agreed. "Yes, if it is accidental. If it is purposefully, then he is not saintly; then he is offender."

Another devotee wasn't certain what accidentally actually meant. Prabhupāda elaborated. "Accident. He had former habit and unknowingly he has done something wrong. That is accident. That is explained by Bhaktivinoda Ṭhākura. Not purposefully doing wrong. That is *aparādha. Nāmno balād yasya hi pāpa-buddhiḥ.*"

Acyutānanda also asked about two sets of Deities, one within ISKCON and another elsewhere. At our New Delhi center the Deities are called Śrī Śrī Rādhā-Pārtha-sārathī. Since *Pārtha-sārathī* means 'the chariot driver of Arjuna (Partha)' he wanted to know how Rādhārāṇī, who is only present in Vṛndāvana-*līlā,* could be included when Kṛṣṇa is in that role.

Prabhupāda answered, "When Kṛṣṇa is Pārtha-sārathī, Rādhā is out of Him? Does it mean? *Rādhā-kṛṣṇa-praṇaya-vikṛtir hlādinī śaktir.* When He is fighting, the *hlādinī śakti* is there. It is not manifest."

The other set of Deities Acyutānanda Swami had seen were of Rādhā, Rukmiṇī, and Kṛṣṇa together. "So won't Kṛṣṇa feel embarrassed to stand between Rādhā and Rukmiṇī at the same time?"

Prabhupāda laughed. "Why? Why embarrassed? Two sides? One side, Rādhā..."

"Yes. One side Rādhā, one side Rukmiṇī." Acyutānanda said.

Tamal Krishna asked, "Is that bona fide, Prabhupāda?"

"Yes," Prabhupāda said. "I don't find any fault."

Acyutānanda wanted to be certain. "It's not *rasābhāsa?*"

So Prabhupāda went on to say, "Not *rasābhāsa.* But it is not mentioned in anywhere. This is mental concoction ... they should not have done like that."

Acyutānanda also asked about the clay which devotees use to anoint themselves with *tilaka.* "The *gopī-candana* comes from the lake where they say the *gopīs* drowned themselves, and that it is near Dvārakā. Is that a true story?"

Prabhupāda was noncommittal. "Maybe they might have gone."

In his room after the walk Prabhupāda continued talking about the *māyāvādīs,* especially one in South India who has attracted many followers by displaying magic.

At one point Acyutānanda Swami said he heard one of his followers criticize us, saying that we were bookworms.

Prabhupāda immediately responded, making us all laugh, "And he is stool worm! He will become this in his next life for cheating so many people!"

* * *

Just after breakfast some reporters from the local press came for an interview. The conversation soon came to the subject of Gandhi's nonviolent movement, which he tried to establish on the basis of the *Bhagavad-gītā.*

Again, there were surprised looks and new-found realizations when Prabhupāda deftly revealed how Gandhi had spoiled the *Gītā* by trying to derive the philosophy of non-violence from it. He explained how in practical terms Gandhi could not establish nonviolence because he himself was shot dead. Therefore his whole movement was a failure. He went on to argue that apart from that how could a politician be nonviolent. In the *Bhagavad-gītā* Arjuna was explicitly instructed by Kṛṣṇa to be violent. He told him to fight and to arm himself with the weapon of knowledge. So how could Gandhi construe a message of non-violence from the *Gītā?* Śrīla Prabhupāda concluded that Gandhi unfortunately had no knowledge.

The pressmen, won over by Śrīla Prabhupāda's charming demeanor and brilliant responses, left well satisfied and impressed by their meeting.

* * *

Even in remote Nellore the mail is being delivered, and Prabhupāda continues to provide resolutions to problems general and personal, great and small, throughout ISKCON.

One letter came from Brahmānanda Swami in Nairobi. He was formerly Prabhupāda's permanent secretary, but since he was also the GBC for Africa, Prabhupāda sent him back there in November to deal with some disturbances.

Brahmānanda reported that some irresponsible devotees had caused difficulties, damaging our reputation among the Indians, especially in Mombasa. This caused a great strain because we depend on the Indians for financial support. As such, the temple has fallen into debt.

Although Prabhupāda had inquired when Brahmānanda would be able to take up his secretarial duties again, Brahmānanda asked to remain in Africa. "I think that we should return to our decision at Māyāpur last year, that every month a different GBC secretary remains with Your Divine Grace to handle the correspondence and to be in your association. Śyāmasundara was your secretary and out of his zone for so long, and his zone deteriorated. So I do not think that any GBC, including myself, can remain away from his zone for any lengthy period and expect things to just go on, especially in regards to the spiritual standards. So I request that I will remain here until the Māyāpur festival time." Tamal Krishna Mahārāja also confirmed to Prabhupāda that the situation in Africa is not at all good. The devotees are living on donations of rice because no money is coming in from the Life Membership Program. Prabhupāda declared that the irresponsible men who have caused the difficulty should not be given responsible positions again. He described them as "simply loafer class."

He also blamed Brahmānanda Mahārāja for not keeping a check on his zone. "This is the business of GBC," he said, "to see that things go on nicely and to check bad influences." But he gladly noted Brahmānanda's sense of responsibility, and he shared a little news of his current preaching. "As you report that things have deteriorated in Africa, you can stay there if necessary The first business is that the GBC must see to the management of their zones. Still, I require a permanent secretary. In addition, one GBC man may come and go. Here we have been given a nice piece of land measuring nine acres. The local people are very enthusiastic, and the plan is to construct a Rādhā-Kṛṣṇa Temple complex."

Several letters came in from the South Seas area. Upendra wrote from Hawaii explaining that after having left us in New Delhi filled with enthusiasm to preach, he was refused entry into Fiji because of insufficient funds. He was put back on board the very same aircraft and immediately flown back to Hawaii. Now he wanted to know how and where to proceed.

Apart from this, he also posed some philosophical questions that clearly illustrate what Śrīla Prabhupāda commented on yesterday: the need to elevate the standard of the devotees' knowledge by systematic study of his publications. "There are times when I take all my relationships within ISKCON and the pleasures and difficulties as something like a dream only. I am reminded of the time you explained to me that there is no reality in this world save and except the Divine Name and service to Him. In the *Śrīmad-Bhāgavatam* I have also read that all this having to do with past, present, and future is a dream only. I am understanding 'Yes, even these relations as my wife, my children or my friends or close Godbrothers in Kṛṣṇa consciousness, ISKCON, are as like sticks meeting in a stream, to be separated in time but with the same end of Kṛṣṇa *bhakti*, back to Home or the Ocean.' That they are still part of these past, present, and future of the measuring temperament, though the devotional service and sentiments therein are eternally developing or lasting. It was raised that 'No, our relationships formed here in ISKCON with one another are eternal in themselves in addition to the service. That ISKCON and we members as we are known now shall be known there. All this I was unable to support scripturally and lest I make an offense and direct error I place this before you.

"This previous question is no doubt the result of my unexercised mind in Kṛṣṇa consciousness, which brings me to: So long these years as your weak disciple I kept the anchor of sense gratification not pulled up and so my 'rowing' was strenuous and appears to have gotten me nowhere with little result. Now again preaching I find myself heavily unstudied in your books and feel incompetent. After so long with bad habits and many fall-downs I know that the renewed attempt will be more difficult. Kindly advise me specifically in this connection. After having committed so many offenses and spending years not studying your books what is my position and what is the hope for me?"

Prabhupāda replied clearly to dispel his confusion, and as always was full of encouragement for pushing forward the preaching mission. "As to your question concerning whether relationships between devotees are eternal, the answer is 'yes.' This is confirmed by Śrī Narottama dāsa Ṭhākura: '*cakhudāna dilo yei, janme janme prabhu sei*', he is my lord *birth after birth.* In this way you have to understand, by studying carefully the philosophy. We have got so many books now and I want all of my disciples to read them carefully. Soon we shall be instituting *Bhaktiśāstrī* examinations and all *brāhmaṇas* will have to pass. So utilize whatever time you find to make a thorough study of my books. Then all your questions will be answered."

Madhudviṣa Swami also wrote from Fiji, explaining some managerial problems confronting him. The Society in Fiji is being organized mainly by Mr. Deoji Punja and his family, and gradually others are becoming involved. In legally registering ISKCON Madhudviṣa wants to make sure that all trustees are conforming to Prabhupāda's standards, following the regulative principles and chanting sixteen rounds daily. Mr. Punja is adhering to the principles, but one or two of the other present trustees are not, although they are very favorable and have given large donations. He requested Prabhupāda to ask them personally to stand down in favor of Deoji's brother, Karṣanjī.

Prabhupāda knows it is a sensitive issue. The impetus for the establishment of ISKCON Fiji arose originally from Deoji's and his brother's enthusiasm to invite Prabhupāda there. Prabhupāda does not want to act in a way that might strike people as arbitrary. Thus he advised Madhudviṣa to arrange everything locally, with a consensus of agreement. "If any of the trustees are to be dropped, this has to be discussed between the trustees themselves. These are all important men and we should be careful lest they become offended. If I say something it will not look well. If some of the trustees are not abiding by the principles or not chanting sixteen rounds, then they should be induced by the other trustees who are following, to step down. I think you can follow what I mean."

From New Zealand a new devotee named Ralph requested Prabhupāda to clarify whether it is proper to attend lectures and *kīrtanas* held by the two renegade *sannyāsīs* Siddha Swarūpānanda Goswami and Tuṣṭa Kṛṣṇa Swami. He has heard conflicting reports but is personally attached to their association, while at the same time regularly attending the ISKCON temple's morning program. Since the possibility of initiation is approaching for him and several devotees in New Zealand, he wanted Prabhupāda to clarify finally what the proper attitude should be.

Śrīla Prabhupāda obliged. "There is no reason why you cannot associate with any of my disciples, providing that they adhere to our principles. As long as Siddha Swarūpā Mahārāja and Tuṣṭa Kṛṣṇa Mahārāja act as *sannyāsīs,* i.e., dress in *dhotī,* keep shave headed with *śikhā,* follow strictly the rules and regulations, and preach from my books, I have no objection. Sometimes there will be a little misunderstanding between Godbrothers, that is even going on amongst liberated souls. What is important is that everyone must engage in Kṛṣṇa's service under the direction of the spiritual master."

Happily, not every letter reported problems. Briṣākapi, the president of ISKCON Washington, D.C., sent a cheerful narrative, along with photos, about a new fifteen acre property they've purchased, "in the wealthiest county in America, in the wealthiest city in the county, Potomac, Maryland. It seems to be Kṛṣṇa's desire that we have this property, for without His special mercy we would have never been able to afford it. "The total purchase price is $657,000, financed $30,000 down and 30 to pay at 9% interest. Payments for the first ten years with no interest at $3,000 per month. At ten years we will owe $297,000. This balance will be financed over 20 years at 9% interest for $2,300 per month."

Smiling, Prabhupāda raised his eyebrows at the figures mentioned. Such news indicates ISKCON's increasing prosperity, and the bestowal of Lord Śrī Kṛṣṇa's special mercy.

Briṣākapi made two specific requests. "We are located only forty minutes by airplane flight from New York City, and because this is the capital of America, we pray you will bless this city with your presence. When you come we will try to make arrangements for you to meet with the President of America, senators, congressmen, and other important people.

"As you know, we have installed here already 40" Gaura-Nitāi Deities and a 25" Rādhā-Kṛṣṇa. We have not yet installed Lord Jagannātha, Lady Subhadrā, and Lord Balarāma Deities. I was reading in the newsletter that you would be installing Sītā Rāma, Lakṣman, and Hanumanjī Deities at the new temple in Bombay, and we were wondering if we should install Sītā Rāma, Lakṣman, and Hanuman in Washington D.C. the capital of America, since Lord Rāmacandra is the perfect king."

Moreover, he reported a boom in book distribution, the D.C. temple selling over 300 big books and 2,000 BTGs daily on the streets and in the airports. He also enclosed a list of devotees for initiation and a declaration of their love and commitment.

Prabhupāda was very happy to hear such news and pleased to oblige his requests. "I am very pleased that we have now got such a wonderful property in the nation's capital, Washington D.C. The photos show that there is good opportunity to develop it into a very important center. And since you say that it is in a most aristocratic location, it is certainly Kṛṣṇa's mercy. If you can make arrangements for me to meet the President, I shall surely go.

"As far as your desire to have Sītā Rāma Deities, it is a good idea, but you should wait for some time. First see that you have sufficient *brāhmaṇas* who are very well trained and qualified, then you can consider to install Sītā, Rāma, Lakṣman, and Hanuman. They are the ideal King and it will be very suitable that they reign over the capital of America. Now you have got Gaura-Nitāi Deities, so you can go ahead and get Prabhupāda and Bhaktisiddhānta Deities immediately. Guru and Gaurāṅga worship is standard for all our temples."

In accepting his new disciples, especially the *brāhmaṇas*, his concern over raising the standards again showed. "Enclosed are the sacred threads for the *brāhmaṇas*. They should be allowed to hear the Gāyatrī mantra through the right ear from the tape recording. *Brāhmaṇa* means to be very clean—inside by chanting the Lord's glories and outside by regular bathing. Teach everyone by your personal example. Also you must see that the *brāhmaṇas* are given sufficient time to read the books. Soon we shall be introducing the *Bhaktiśāstrī* examination, which all *brāhmaṇas* will be expected to pass. It will be based on *Bhagavad-gītā*, *N.O.D.*, *Nectar of Instruction*, *Īśopaniṣad*, and the small paperback books like *Easy Journey*. A *brāhmaṇa* should be a *paṇḍita*."

* * *

After much delay and frequent requests, now nearly at the end of Prabhupāda's stay in Nellore, the deed of gift for the two parcels of land has finally been produced. But it is a "gift" with many conditions. Scrutiny of the fine print revealed several dubious clauses. Prabhupāda sat at his desk as Gopāla Kṛṣṇa and Mahāṁsa Swami read out the details. One clause insisted that on the two-acre plot, a temple, a comparative religious studies library, and a meditation hall be built.

Prabhupāda shook his head. He indicated that as far as we are concerned, we have no use for such things. A temple with the Deities of Rādhā-Kṛṣṇa is sufficient because They are the only objects of our meditation. Moreover, the *Vedic* knowledge is complete, so what is the need for comparison?

Other conditions were more explicit. They declared that if the project is not completed within three years, then the land

and whatever stands on it will be turned over to another charitable organization, such as a certain mission based in Calcutta.

As for the seven-acre plot of land on which the house and gardens stand, the document stated that if ISKCON did not take possession and utilize it fully within one year of the death of the sisters, then it will also be turned over to "some suitable charitable organization." The same mission in Calcutta was named.

Everyone agreed. It seemed clear there was some kind of plan to have ISKCON begin development of the land. Then by some ploy its timely completion will be prevented, thus giving reason to have it seized and handed over to this Calcutta mission. It would not be difficult to thwart any building project by somehow or another cutting off the supply of cement, which the government controls and rations.

With this information many pieces of the puzzle now fell into place. This Calcutta mission is also well known as the *murgi* (chicken) mission because its members keep large chicken farms and are known meat eaters. These two sisters raise chickens and eat meat. This mission also has a consistent formula for the layout of their *āśramas*—a temple, a comparative studies library, and a meditation hall.

Even the planting of the *tulasī* bushes, which we had taken as a sign of devotion to Kṛṣṇa, took on a new meaning considering these revelations. There are two kinds of *tulasī* trees, one with green leaves, and one with blue leaves; the green being named after Lord Rāma, and the blue after Lord Kṛṣṇa. Inspecting the garden on our first day here, I had noticed many *tulasī* bushes planted in an alternating sequence—green, blue, green, blue—Rāma Kṛṣṇa, Rāma Kṛṣṇa. I also recalled the *tulasī* bush in the pot that had been trimmed into the shape of a large bird—no doubt now that it is a chicken.

There was the *mūrti* of Gopāla Kṛṣṇa placed outside, exposed to the elements. And the strange, withdrawn reception we received upon arrival. Now it is obvious to us all that our hosts are definitely not devotees of Kṛṣṇa.

Analyzing their ulterior motives, Prabhupāda pointed out

that ISKCON is one of the only organizations in India with the manpower and money to initiate large projects like the one proposed here. People are steadily losing interest in other missions, and this particular Calcutta mission is reportedly experiencing considerable difficulty with dwindling membership and income. It seems clear, therefore, that ISKCON is being set up to give a strong start to the project, only to be removed later by what now has shown itself to be a deceptive legal manoeuvre. Who the villains of this piece of trickery are is not clear, but Prabhupāda did say that, being widows, the sisters would have been easy targets for unscrupulous so-called spiritualists with no interest in regulated spiritual practice. Still, he wasn't blaming anyone, but some action must be taken to protect our interest.

Prabhupāda decided our course of action. Mahāṁsa Swami is to meet with the sisters and explain to them that a gift is something given unconditionally. That the donation of land should be in the spirit of *Bhagavad-gītā* 17:20: "That gift which is given out of duty, at the proper time and place, to a worthy person, and without expectation of return, is considered to be charity in the mode of goodness."

He said that if they refuse to give it unconditionally, then we should politely back out and withdraw from the project.

* * *

Late in the afternoon Śrīla Prabhupāda went to the local Rotary Club, where a special meeting was convened in his honor. Mr. G. Gopāla Reddy, the gentleman who accompanied Śrīla Prabhupāda on morning walks, and the current president of the club, received him warmly, lauding his worldwide preaching efforts.

Then, to a small but attentive audience he delivered a well-rounded lecture on the general philosophy of Kṛṣṇa consciousness. Describing his Kṛṣṇa consciousness movement as "a tiny little attempt" to convince people about God, he asked them all to heed the advice of Śrī Caitanya Mahāprabhu. "Therefore Caitanya Mahāprabhu says that His mission is especially to the Indians, those who are born in India. *Āmāra ājñāya guru hañā tāra ei deśa.* This instruction was given when Caitanya

Mahāprabhu was traveling in South India. 'If you want to help Me, then you become a guru under My instruction. You become a guru.'

"'Sir, I have no education. I am not a *brāhmaṇa.* I am this, I am that. How can I become guru?'

"So Caitanya Mahāprabhu says, *āmāra ajñāya guru hañā tāra ei deśa.* 'Where you are living, you just try to deliver them. But you become a guru.'

"'How I shall become?'

"*Yāre dekha tāre kaha kṛṣṇa upadeśa:* 'Simply you instruct what Kṛṣṇa has said, that's all. Then you become guru. You don't require any other qualification.'"

Alluding to the spread of the British Empire, he contrasted the motives of its representatives with that of Śrī Caitanya's. "India's mission is not that we colonize in another country and exploit them and bring money and become a 'Lord.' No. India's mission is how to revive Kṛṣṇa consciousness throughout the whole world. That is India's mission. Revive your Kṛṣṇa consciousness, be fixed up in Kṛṣṇa, and then distribute this knowledge. This is Indian mission."

He finished to polite applause. He was invited afterward to pose for a photograph, the leading members of the Rotary club lining up in back, and Prabhupāda, the *sannyāsīs* from our camp and myself all sitting in front. It felt somehow special and historic to be part of an official photo with Śrīla Prabhupāda.

* * *

This evening's pandal lecture was the last because tomorrow Prabhupāda returns to Madras and then goes on to Bombay.

The open courtyard was once again filled to capacity with thousands of attentive men and women sitting quietly and absorbed, as Prabhupāda concluded his series on the Sixth Canto of the *Śrīmad-Bhāgavatam.* He then made his presentations to new Members in what has become a nightly ritual.

Prabhupāda is very happy and satisfied with the trip—apart from the peculiarities of the land offer.

January 8th, 1976

Before leaving to catch the train to Madras, the two sisters came to see Prabhupāda in his room. He thanked them for their hospitality. Without directly bringing up the strange conditions put upon the deed of gift, he preached to them very positively that they should try to become real devotees of Kṛṣṇa.

He had me read to them the *Gītā* verse concerning charity in the mode of goodness. He emphasized that one should not expect any reward or gain; this was the criterion for activity in Kṛṣṇa consciousness. He encouraged them to try to rise to this standard. Even though the sisters appeared to be involved in a surreptitious scheme to take advantage of him, Prabhupāda still tried to uplift them and give them his mercy. They had invited him to their home, and therefore he wanted to do some good for them. They listened, but what he said drew very little response from them, apart from obligatory acceptance of his thanks for the stay. Everyone in our party was glad to leave. It was unpleasant living in such close proximity with people who made us feel unwelcome and who ate meat.

* * *

The train ride to Madras was pleasant. This Nellore trip has given me my first opportunity to journey with Śrīla Prabhupāda on a train, and we were all happy to see him enjoy the trip. It was without strain and much more comfortable than flying, which he tends to dislike.

Śravaṇānanda and Bhāvabhūti were waiting at the station to pick us up. They arranged a shenai band to greet him at the station and with great fanfare escorted him to a waiting car. This time they arranged for Prabhupāda to stay in our own center in Aspiran Gardens, a nice house in a pleasant suburb.

Prabhupāda liked it. He had a quick tour, and when Śravaṇānanda and Bhāvabhūti mentioned that they were thinking of getting another place, he told them to stay where they are. He noted some small bushes with curry leaves growing, as well as some drumsticks, a long, thin beanlike vegetable that

Prabhupāda likes very much. He requested Harikeśa to use them in his lunch.

* * *

I shaved Śrīla Prabhupāda's head for him as we sat out on the small ground-floor front veranda, and then he took his mail. Tamal Krishna Mahārāja informed him that the telegram sent to Australia from Bombay stating that Prabhupāda was unable to attend Ratha-yātrā had been returned undelivered. Prabhupāda considered what to do. He said that he would go to Australia if Madhudviṣa Mahārāja had already made arrangements. Since they may have advertised that Prabhupāda would be present, he didn't want to spoil the event. Yet, this will certainly pose a big difficulty, because Prabhupāda is still not well enough to endure such a long plane ride.

Another travel quandary arose when Tamal Krishna Mahārāja discovered that our plane to Bombay was to depart in mid-evening. Prabhupāda never travels on Thursday afternoons, especially between 4:30 and 7:30, for he considers these hours inauspicious for travel. On a previous visit to Australia to open the new Melbourne temple in May 1975, Śrīla Prabhupāda delayed his departure from Perth to Melbourne for one day to avoid traveling on a Thursday afternoon. He was prepared to do the same today. But after some discussion he finally decided to take the late flight, thus avoiding the most inauspicious hours while still keeping his schedule.

We left in the Mercedes in mid-evening, Prabhupāda observing all the little roadside shacks selling bananas and varieties of fruits and vegetables. He told us that in south India people are still pious, still mainly vegetarian. He also recalled Śrī Caitanya Mahāprabhu's preaching in the south and indicated that he was well pleased with the programs the devotees had arranged for him and the reception he received.

As a final touch, Śravaṇānanda had arranged through a Life Member to have the car drive right onto the airport tarmac, right up to the plane. Thus at about nine o'clock we flew out, arriving in Bombay late at night.

CHAPTER EIGHT

Bombay and Calcutta

January 9th, 1976

Hare Kṛṣṇa Land
Juhu Beach, Bombay

Madhudviṣa Swami phoned early today, and Tamal Krishna Mahārāja informed him that Prabhupāda is not feeling well enough to travel the long distance to Melbourne. Although extremely disappointed, Madhudviṣa withdrew his request for Prabhupāda to attend. Despite his weak health, Prabhupāda is still willing to go if their Ratha-yātrā arrangements are dependent on his personal presence.

Only after receiving Madhudviṣa's assurance that the festival could go on without him did he finally decide not to go. Prabhupāda was more concerned that their preaching carry on unhampered than about his own comfort.

He spent a quiet day, foregoing even his morning walk.

* * *

In answering his mail, Prabhupāda reiterated to Nitai in Vṛndāvana that he wants all his students to take *Bhaktiśāstrī* examinations. He requested Nitai to prepare a guide to Deity worship called *Arcana-paddhati* based on the *Hari-bhakti-vilāsa* by Sanātana Gosvāmī. He asked him to have it ready by the Gaura Pūrṇimā festival.

Nitai reported that the plans for the new *gurukula* are being drawn up and will be submitted soon, and that already some highly qualified men have applied for the position of principal. Prabhupāda said that he would consider who to appoint later, when the school is actually built.

There was also a long letter from Tuṣṭa Kṛṣṇa Swami in New Zealand. He and his men are preaching vigorously and have launched several new projects as well as developing their farm. He has opened a vegetarian restaurant with money that a boy inherited from his family's beef farm. They had good publicity from the press and on television, and he also has plans to start a Vedic University as part of his development of a *varṇāśrama* community. In one short paragraph he also affirmed his desire to distribute Prabhupāda's books, although he mentioned some devotees were "hesitant due to previous pressure put on them to collect certain quotas each day." (A main point of contention between Tuṣṭa's faction and the body of devotees is that they dislike the major emphasis that ISKCON leaders and devotees place on the importance of book distribution, and the pressure sometimes applied to encourage devotees to distribute the books.)

Pleased with their preaching efforts, Prabhupāda sent a long letter in reply, dealing with the report point by point. He especially stressed the importance of book distribution. "So far the devotees being hesitant to distribute books on account of pressure, sometimes pressure is required, especially when one is not so advanced. Of course it has to be applied properly, otherwise there may be some bad taste. But spontaneous service can only be expected from advanced devotees. It is *vaidhi-bhakti*—*vaidhi* means 'must.' Sometimes devotees are promised a plate of *mahā-prasādam* for the biggest distributor. There is no harm. Actually one should try to serve Kṛṣṇa to his or her full capacity without thought of reward—service is itself the reward. But this takes time to actually realize, and until that platform is achieved some pressure or inducement is required."

He was pleased about the opening of the restaurant but cautioned him that it should not be seen simply as a place for promoting vegetarianism. "We should not waste time encouraging vegetarianism as opposed to meat eating. We want to encourage *prasādam* taking, and that is automatically vegetarian."

Happy about the proposal to start a Vedic University, Prabhupāda outlined to Tuṣṭa his recent plans for instituting examinations within the Society and explained that anyone who wants to become *brāhmaṇa* will have to sit for an examination once a year at Māyāpur.

At the same time he also pointed out that, "In our Vedic Universities we will not encourage anyone to become merely a bookworm. There must be life—rising early in the morning, attending *maṅgala ārati,* taking *prasādam* etc. The man who is studying will be *brāhmaṇa,* the farmer will be *vaiśya.* In this way there will be divisions, but they are all one in the service to Kṛṣṇa."

January 10th, 1976

Prabhupāda felt a little better this morning. He took his walk following the usual route along the beach and enjoyed a long and interesting talk with a local movie director. Bombay is the center of India's film industry, the third biggest in the world. Many people connected with the movie trade are now becoming interested in the activities of ISKCON. This particular man was polite and receptive but had many philosophical misconceptions about spiritual matters, which he allowed Śrīla Prabhupāda to correct.

* * *

During the massage Tamal Krishna Goswami went over the day's mail. He read out a letter from Yamunā dāsī. She and Dīnatāriṇī dāsī have a small farm in Oregon. On Śrīla Bhaktisiddhānta Sarasvatī's disappearance day Jayatīrtha installed Deities of Śrī Śrī Rādhā-Vanabihārī there.

They are hoping to start an *āśrama* for senior women, and they requested financial assistance from the BBT to buy a place. Their idea is to have about twelve women and gradually begin a preaching program. Yamunā, however, did express some apprehension, admitting, "Generally women are mad after sense gratification, to dip and gossip, so thus we feel to proceed with careful attention." In a separate letter Jayatīrtha also inquired whether a BBT loan could be given for the ladies' project. He said the property they are looking at costs $100,000, requiring a down payment of $25,000. He wanted to know what priority Prabhupāda gives to this kind of project, suggesting that he might help oversee managerial and financial matters. He also suggested that Yamunā and other *āśrama* members could earn some income and help support themselves by sewing Deity clothes for the *sannyāsīs*' traveling parties.

Prabhupāda's personal opinion is that women should not live independently. "Why don't they go to L.A.?" he asked Tamal Krishna. Nevertheless, since they are eager to begin the project, he encouraged them. "You can attract the fair sex community. Most of them are frustrated being without any home or husband. If you can organize all these girls they will get transcendental engagement and may not be allured to the frustration of life. Your engagement should be chanting and worship of the Deity."

He also tactfully laid down strict guidelines for the ladies to follow, stressing that as single women they should live very humbly and not "dress nicely to attract men" nor attempt to start any large program. "In *bhakti* there is no grotesque program. A humble program is better. We are doing all these grotesque programs to allure the masses. My Guru Mahārāja used to say that no one hears from a person coming from a humble, simple life. You remain always very humble."

To Jayatīrtha, however, Prabhupāda spoke more candidly, describing their desire to be independent as a "defect." He further elaborated on this by saying that according to Vedic culture a woman cannot live independently. He decided that if they wanted this badly enough, he would allow it. But they must function managerially and financially independent of ISKCON, although he conceded that Jayatīrtha could check on them now and then to see if they were chanting and following the rules of the Society. He also made it clear there could be no connection whatsoever with *sannyāsīs.*

Viśvakarmā dāsa, the Toronto president, sent a report detailing the successful purchase of a large church on a main street in the heart of Toronto. Last year Śrīla Prabhupāda told them to try to purchase it, and despite great opposition from the clergy they completed the deal by having some enthusiastic Indian members conduct the negotiations. It cost $400,000 in total, and although the temple only provided $80,000 deposit, they were able to secure the rest as mortgages. Now they plan to reinstall Śrī Śrī Rādhā-Kṣīra-corā Gopīnatha in mid-January.

Śrīla Prabhupāda was delighted, and considered the purchase of the church a great victory, "a topmost triumph." "Christianity is now declining," he wrote, "therefore they are having to sell all their churches to us. Because they have no clear idea of God, people are not satisfied with them. But we can explain what God is, so people are appreciating more and more our movement. Now by Kṛṣṇa's grace you have a beautiful temple, use it to preach very vigorously. If you all strictly follow the principles and chant sixteen rounds, your spiritual strength will be insured, and our movement will become increasingly prominent."

On hearing that over 200,000 cars per day pass by the church, Prabhupāda recommended that they immediately erect a neon sign with the flashing words of the full *mahā-mantra* on it. He said it will be a great achievement if they can accomplish this.

Prabhupāda also acknowledged receipt of a five-page report from Viśvakarma describing the activities of Svāmī Bon, Prabhupāda's Godbrother. Apparently Bon Mahārāja visited some of the universities in North America, openly criticizing Śrīla Prabhupāda and his books. He also advised professors not to use the books. Prabhupāda told Viśvakarma that in the future we should completely avoid him and have no further connection with him.

Jaśomatīnandana also sent an update on his attempts to secure a suitable center in Ahmedabad. The building he had taken Śrīla Prabhupāda to see had several defects, and since then he has located a much better place in the city center, but it is only available initially for a three month period.

The owners are thinking of using it for some charitable cause, so Prabhupāda encouraged him to accept it despite the time limit. "Even if you can stay only three months, what is the loss? You can always look for another place. Now people are seeing how genuine our movement is, they are coming forward to offer us so many places. We simply have to maintain our strict principles, keeping ourselves pure. Otherwise, there are so many bogus institutions doing business in the name of God and simply cheating the people. We have to be careful not to degenerate like these others. Our strength depends upon regularly chanting the required sixteen rounds and rigidly adhering to the regulated principles."

Prabhupāda recently received some material, via Bhagatjī in Vṛndāvana, translated into Hindi by Nṛsiṁha Vallabha Gosvāmī. Bhagatjī also reported that the negotiations for establishing a bank branch in our temple are now in the last stage. The head office has agreed, and they are simply waiting for approval from the Reserve Bank. Satisfied with the progress on the bank, Prabhupāda wrote Bhagatjī to settle terms with the Gosvāmī regarding his books.

* * *

Harikeśa has completed his article "Spiritual Dialecticism." Prabhupāda is so pleased with it that he had it sent to Rāmeśvara in Los Angeles today, with a request that it be printed in *Back To Godhead* magazine. He also suggested that if they receive a good response from the article, it can be released as a small book.

* * *

In the early evening Prabhupāda called me to give him a dry, full-body massage. He is not feeling well, and took rest at eight o'clock. I felt frustrated that I was unable to help him in any way. Then, amazingly, at 9:30 p.m. he got up and continued his translation work throughout the entire night!

January 11th, 1976

Prabhupāda obviously felt better this morning. The movie producer came down to the beach again and engaged Prabhupāda in a lively debate. He wasn't shy to express his thoughts and opinions, but he listened with great respect and attention to Prabhupāda's responses. Prabhupāda was so enlivened by the man's questions and challenges that the walk took much longer than usual. We recorded two full sides of tape on the reel-to-reel Uher recorder. Prabhupāda showed no signs of illness and at the end of the walk he seemed stronger than ever.

* * *

A letter arrived today from Bahūdaka, Vancouver temple president, giving a positive report of university preaching and increased *saṅkīrtana* activity. Despite some initial reluctance from the school faculty to have them, they have given many classes to the students and were received so favorably that many teachers invited them back.

For the last year Bahūdaka has been overseeing the development of their new farm, but he recently returned to the city center in order to encourage book distribution, which has seriously dwindled. He is personally going out to distribute books two days per week and expressed the sentiment that all ISKCON leaders should do this, both as an example to others and for their own enlivenment.

Prabhupāda liked his report. He recalled the struggles of his other Canadian center in Toronto in getting the church property. Then he pinpointed the reason for the opposition. "Our movement is authorized. Our books are based on the statements of the most exalted devotees. And if we follow strictly the guidelines for devotional service as they are given in *The Nectar of Devotion* and *The Nectar of Instruction,* then no one can touch us. All the groups are declining, including the Christians. We are being harassed by the authorities and they are all Christians. Because they are losing ground, and we are increasing, they are trying to stop us. There is always a battle between the demons and the devotees; but the devotees always win because they are protected by Kṛṣṇa."

Prabhupāda also accepted some new candidates for initiation. As he has been repeatedly doing in many letters recently, he stressed the importance of becoming fixed up in the philosophy by regular study. He also mentioned the upcoming *śāstra* examinations. In response to Bahūdaka's question regarding the use of the harmonium, Prabhupāda asserted that the harmonium is only to be used for chanting in *bhajana* provided it is played melodiously. He said it is not to be played for *kīrtana* or *ārati.*

* * *

During the day he relaxed, taking advantage of the absence of visitors to read, chant, and conserve his energy. In the evening he gave the Sunday Feast lecture in Hindi.

January 12th, 1976

Dr. Patel joined us on the walk this morning. In his usual boisterous manner he often interrupted Prabhupāda before Prabhupāda could finish what he was saying. Sometimes he was so eager to speak that he couldn't get his words out at all. His overly-familiar manner with Śrīla Prabhupāda sometimes annoys us disciples and leads to a little friction between him and us. But Prabhupāda has infinite tolerance, born from his eagerness to help others advance in their spiritual lives. He sees only the good in others, and this morning his liberal and friendly dealing was clearly manifest.

Dr. Patel had been energetically defending the position of medical science and its practitioners against Śrīla Prabhupāda's criticisms. He insisted that they do not claim to be able to save life, nor is that even their goal. His opinion was that they are simply trying to help people live the limited life they have in a better way. He felt that Prabhupāda's impression of atheistic scientists was a thing of the past. He compared them favorably to previous impersonalist Vedic philosophers, declaring that nowadays most scientists accept there is a God or some superior force.

Prabhupāda countered that impersonalism is also atheism.

One of the doctor's companions objected. The man held the typical impersonalist view that *jñāna,* the cultivation of knowledge, is superior to *bhakti,* devotion to the Personality of Godhead.

After taking Prabhupāda's permission, Dr. Patel explained to the man that the Vaiṣṇava concept that God is ultimately realized as the Supreme Person is correct. He described the progression of realization from *brahman* and *paramātmā* to *bhagavān.* Then he declared that as little as two years ago he had been inclined to the impersonal school of thought. But by very carefully studying various Vaiṣṇava works, and especially Śrīla Prabhupāda's books, he was now convinced that devotion to the Supreme Lord, Kṛṣṇa, is the highest understanding.

The devotees all cheered at his pronouncement, and Śrīla Prabhupāda was also very pleased. It is clear that despite Dr.

Patel's habit of challenging, albeit good naturedly, and his tendency to carry his own opinion, he has actually become Śrīla Prabhupāda's follower. Prabhupāda recalled that his teacher at school used to say that if a boy is slow to understand he will also be slow to forget; and a boy who is quick to understand, will be quick to forget. He declared that Dr. Patel had been slow in learning but now he will not forget.

They also talked briefly about the present Government of India and Prime Minister Mrs. Gandhi's declaration of a state of emergency. People are unhappy with her, but with thousands of her political opponents jailed, everyone is afraid to speak.

Dr. Patel criticized her dictatorial attitude, but Prabhupāda, who often refers to democracy as "demon-crazy," said that if sinful people vote in a sinful government, why complain?

Apart from that, he explained that having a dictator is not bad if the dictator is actually religious. Then there is no need of elections.

Dr. Patel sarcastically noted that Mrs. Gandhi went to the temples.

But liberal-minded Prabhupāda chose to see the good in her, as he did with Dr. Patel. "No, no. She has got the tendency of spiritual life, and she requires improvement, that's all. She has spoken in Chandigarh that 'Now we require spiritualism.'"

* * *

Since we were due to leave for Calcutta on the early afternoon flight, Prabhupāda took his massage at 9:30 a.m. and his lunch at 11:45 a.m.

Tamal Krishna Mahārāja came in with the mail, holding two letters from Rāmeśvara. One was a BBT report and the other a letter written on behalf of the Los Angeles community.

Written on December 18th, the BBT report included details of the previous day's book distribution from the Atlanta airport: astounding figures establishing a new one day record. Tripurāri Swami and his party sold 2,900 hardbound books, with Cārudeṣṇa topping the list with 303 books sold. Fifteen other men sold over 100 each.

Rāmeśvara also enclosed a few copies of a new publication, *The Kṛṣṇa Consciousness Movement is Authorized.* The pamphlet explains the basic concepts of the movement, quoting favorable statements from many prominent scholars and book reviews garnered by Satsvarūpa Mahārāja's Library Party.

The Los Angeles report dated December 25th gave a detailed description of their Christmas marathon activities and the results, which were truly amazing. Devotees worked day and night with virtually no rest for the entire six days, staying out until one or two o'clock in the morning and going back out again a few hours later at six or seven. Over 100 men and women participated in the marathon, which Tulasī dāsa and Hāsyapriya dāsa expertly organized. They sold 6,523 big books (*Bhagavad-gītā* and *Śrīmad-Bhāgavatam,* etc.) 419 *Kṛṣṇa* trilogies and 93,031 copies of *Back to Godhead* magazine. Collections totalled over $60,000. Gopavṛndāpāla sold 529 big books, and four women—Jadurāṇī, Mūlaprakṛti, Dīkṣāvatī, and Gaurī—all sold over 300 each. Mahātmā sold over 2,000 BTGs.

Needless to say, Śrīla Prabhupāda deeply appreciates the efforts of his disciples to sell his books. He said there is nothing mundane about the great efforts his disciples are making to spread Kṛṣṇa consciousness on his behalf.

He sent back an enthusiastic reply. "The book distribution in Los Angeles during the six day period is transcendental *samādhi.* They are working in trance, not on the material platform. No common man can work so hard, it is not possible. Working without sleep means no death. Sleeping is dead condition. Your book distribution is really intoxication."

Prabhupāda welcomed the printing of the new pamphlet *The Kṛṣṇa Consciousness Movement is Authorized.* He said it is very important for establishing the authenticity of his movement, especially among the educated and influential classes of man.

Prabhupāda is eager to see our Kṛṣṇa consciousness movement accepted by every sector of society, and the best way to start is from the top. He wrote back with some suggestions how to distribute the pamphlet. "You can send it to important members of the government, businessmen, entertainers, sportsmen, etc. Another device is that you can address it to 'Any Respectable Gentleman, Post Office, City, State'. The postman will then deliver it to some respectable gentleman. Everyone who gets it will think, 'I am a most respectable gentleman because he has given it to me.' The best thing is to find out the customers list to some big magazine like *Time* or *Life*, and post it to them."

* * *

We left on time, flying out to Calcutta at 2 p.m. At the outset of the journey Prabhupāda entrusted his soft red attache case to my care. The case holds all his important documents, and either he or his secretary generally carries it. Since the secretary is now changing every month and I am a regular member of the traveling party, Prabhupāda added its guardianship to my duties. I felt privileged to be entrusted with this responsibility, and I sat next to him on the plane with the case carefully tucked under the seat in front of me.

After some time Prabhupāda got up to go to the bathroom. I rose to escort him down the aisle and picked up the case, not wanting to leave it unattended. Prabhupāda shook his head with slightly amused disbelief. Obviously no thief could make off with the bag while we were flying thirty thousand feet in the air. Apart from that, Tamal Krishna Mahārāja was in the opposite aisle seat. Prabhupāda chuckled, while I blushed and replaced the bag under the seat.

In mid-flight the captain came back to visit Prabhupāda and sat next to him while they talked. He was very polite and respectful, expressing his admiration for Prabhupāda's preaching work. He invited Prabhupāda into the cockpit, offering him a seat behind his own. Somehow Tamal Krishna and Harikeśa also managed to squeeze in, and all three remained in the cabin as the plane landed at Dum Dum airport. They came out smiling.

Prabhupāda enjoyed the experience. He said that in principle flying a plane is like typing—a mechanical skill. Once you knew the procedures and which dials to look at, it became easy to master.

Sudāmā, Jayapatākā, and Śrīdhara Swamis and other devotees met us at the airport.

Rather than going straight to the temple, Prabhupāda first went to inspect a flat he is thinking of purchasing for his former family members. Then he traveled to the temple in our own bus.

ISKCON Śrī Śrī Rādhā-Govinda Mandir
3A Albert Road, Calcutta 17

ISKCON Calcutta is situated in a large, old, two-story semi-detached building built during the time of the British Raj in what was once the European quarter. Although at one time rather impressive architecturally, with an arched entrance and an upper veranda adorned with large, capped columns, it has become quite dilapidated over the years. ISKCON occupies only the top floor on one side.

The temple overlooks some gardens and a lake bordering Albert Road. At times the devotees have to bathe in the lake because there often is no water.

Prabhupāda climbed the wide interior stairway and, removing his shoes, entered the only large room in the place, now converted into a temple room. He offered his obeisances to the presiding Deities Śrī Śrī Rādhā-Govinda and Their Lordships Jagannātha, Balarāma, and Subhadrā.

Then, without giving an arrival speech, he went out along the wide front veranda to his room at the end. This room is kept exclusively for his use, but the devotees use the small adjoining bathroom when he is away.

Overall, the building is not very impressive, but Prabhupāda wants to keep it because it is close to the central business district.

I looked through the back rooms for somewhere to stay, without success. There are only a few cramped rooms, allocated for Deity paraphernalia, the *brahmacārīs,* some storage facilities for books, and an access to the roof.

I noticed that the cooking is done on coal-fired buckets on a small porch in the rear, which accounts for the soot and grime covering everything in the area. There is so little extra space that Tamal Krishna Mahārāja decided to set up an office right outside Śrīla Prabhupāda's door on the veranda. I moved into the Life Membership room at the opposite end.

Prabhupāda is not at all pleased with the current state of affairs, for the standard of the temple management has deteriorated. Reports have been submitted that many Life Members are upset with the state of things and their dealings with the temple president, Bhagavat. He has only recently replaced the long standing president, Gargamuni Swami, but is unable to cope very well with the service. Śrīdhara Swami from Bombay is here now and has been requested to take over the responsibility; but he also is not keen on management.

Prabhupāda settled in quickly, immediately engaging Jayapatākā and Sudāmā swamis in conversation about our Māyāpur center. It sounds as if everything is developing nicely there. Plans are being drawn up for a temple some 350 feet in height, and Prabhupāda instructed Jayapatākā to buy more land. The devotees have purchased an ocean-going boat capable of sailing to Orissa and intend to install Gaura-Nitai Deities on board.

Jayapatākā reported that a small Bengali book titled *Gītār-gāna*, which Śrīla Prabhupāda had written before going to the West in 1965, is now in print and selling many copies. Containing all the *Gītā* verses in Bengali prose, it was written in such a way that no one could misinterpret the meaning. Prabhupāda was very pleased to hear that all the Māyāpur *gurukula* children are studying it and learning to chant the verses. Smiling, he recalled how his Godbrothers used to call him *kavi,* "poet," and that even at school he would write English verse.

Halfway through the conversation Prabhupāda sent Sudāmā Swami to the kitchen to cook some *samosas.* He also told him how to make a quick chutney from chopped tomatoes, green chili, and lemon juice. Sudāmā did it all very expertly.

Sudāmā Mahārāja has only recently returned after falling away from his spiritual practices for some time. When he left the room, Prabhupāda, obviously pleased with his eagerness to serve, said that he was "a nice boy" who had been misled. He was exceedingly happy to see him back and enthusiastically engaging in devotional service.

January 13th, 1976

Today was Ekādaśī, and Śrīla Prabhupāda took his morning walk along the Gaṅgā. Hundreds of pilgrims were taking a dawn bath there, having come for the Gaṅgā-Sāgara *melā.*

Prabhupāda explained that *sāgara* is the sea, so the *melā* is a spiritual gathering on an island in the Gaṅgā's estuary.

Evidently eager pilgrims had traveled from as far away as Rajasthan in the northwest. They camped simply along the banks of Mother Gaṅgā, washing their few possessions, as well as themselves, in the holy waters, unmindful of the boats and other river traffic passing by. They sat contentedly on the pathways cooking breakfast and drying out their clothing.

Noting the shining *loṭā* one man carried, Prabhupāda remarked that if even the *loṭā* is so clean, we can understand how clean he must personally be.

Prabhupāda also recalled how he and his mother had bathed in the same spot when he was a child.

* * *

Because it was Ekādaśī we skipped breakfast and fasted until noon. But at lunchtime the devotees inadvertently broke the Ekādaśī vow because the cook accidentally put peas into the vegetables. No one noticed until too late. Fortunately I arrived late for lunch because I had been massaging Śrīla Prabhupāda. Just as I was about to eat, Jayapatākā Mahārāja shouted for me to stop. Although initially annoyed at being told not to eat, I was relieved when he pointed out the peas.

Shamefaced, Tamal Krishna Mahārāja went to Prabhupāda to report what had happened and to find out what should be done.

Śrīla Prabhupāda told us we were all nonsense. He angrily rebuked us, "Now you have to fast for three days!" This shocked everyone. "Yes, that is the procedure," he confirmed. Seeing the stunned look on our faces he relented but said that we should observe Ekādaśī for the rest of the day and then again tomorrow on Dvādaśī.

* * *

During the morning Śrīla Prabhupāda noticed I was limping because of a boil forming on my leg. Later, while talking with Jayapatākā Mahārāja, he called me in and told me to show him the boil. Prabhupāda was so thoughtful that he asked Jayapatākā to go out and buy some medicine to heal the boil. I was somewhat embarrassed that a *sannyāsī* should be running an errand on my behalf, but Prabhupāda was more concerned to see that it was cured. Like a loving father, he always takes time to see that we are properly looked after, especially concerning our health.

* * *

In the evening Prabhupāda spoke in Hindi and Bengali to the large crowd that packed the temple room. The *darśana* seemed especially sweet and enjoyable because Śrīla Prabhupāda is the local Calcutta success story. Although Prabhupāda always remains wholly transcendental in consciousness, he is fully familiar with the surroundings and cultural idiosyncrasies of Bengal. There thus seemed a special rapport between him and the audience as he preached on the necessity of becoming Kṛṣṇa conscious.

January 14th, 1976

Prabhupāda took his walk along the Gaṅgā again. Although it was early morning, hundreds of people lined the river bank bathing, doing *pūjā,* and washing their clothes.

Śrīla Prabhupāda commented on the simplicity of village life and the importance of the Ganges. Many people have come to the *melā* for spiritual purification, carrying only a few simple possessions. Everywhere *dhotīs* and *sarīs* hung on fences or were spread out on the ground to dry, their owners sitting or squatting nearby, patiently waiting.

Prabhupāda remarked that even if they only have one piece of cloth, they will not fail to wash it every day. That is Vedic culture.

* * *

After breakfast *prasādam* Prabhupāda and I went to see an apartment at Park Circus. He is thinking of purchasing it for his son and daughter, who met us there. Prabhupāda didn't say much to them, and after a few minutes we returned to the temple.

* * *

About 12:30 p.m. during his massage, which he took sitting

on a mat in a little patch of sunlight on the bathroom floor, Tamal Krishna Goswami came to report on a visit he and Jayapatākā Swami had just made to the Śrī Caitanya Maṭha.

They had talked with Mādhava Mahārāja, Prabhupāda's Godbrother, showing him Prabhupāda's translation of *Śrī Caitanya-caritāmṛta.* They asked if Prabhupāda's books could be displayed there during a current five-day festival the Maṭha was holding. But Mādhava Mahārāja only gave them excuses why it was not possible. As they were leaving the Maṭha, Tamal Krishna and Jayapatākā stopped to talk with the secretary. He appeared interested and friendly, and he inquired about the books. The secretary said that he felt they should follow our example in preaching but were tied up too much in routine temple maintenance work.

Looking at their advertising brochure, Prabhupāda noted that the invited speakers included no *sannyāsīs* or spiritual personalities, simply government ministers and the like.

Whereas for us, Śrīla Prabhupāda's books are the main feature of our preaching work, he noted that after forty years the Gauḍīya Maṭha is still selling Śrīla Bhaktisiddhānta Sarasvatī's books. He was critical that they have not been able to produce any literature of their own. He said that many of his Godbrothers were envious of his success. He specifically named three of them.

Prabhupāda's comments show that he has learned not to expect anything from them. He told us we should avoid dealing with them. He said that rather than help, they will simply attempt to spoil our own work.

* * *

Madhudviṣa Swami arrived from Australia in the afternoon. He is taking a break from management and intends to stay with Śrīla Prabhupāda for a few weeks to bathe in the nectar of his association. He reported that the Rathayātrā in Melbourne was very successfully executed, although the devotees were disappointed that Śrīla Prabhupāda could not attend. He showed some favorable press reports, and told Prabhupāda that the devotees in Australia are enthusiastically pushing forward the movement there. He also gave a large donation of $10,000 guru-*dakṣiṇa* for Śrīla Prabhupāda.

* * *

Mrs. Lalitā Bose, an influential woman and good friend to Prime Minister Indira Gandhi, visited Prabhupāda in mid-evening. She is the niece of "Netajī" Subhas Chandra Bose, an old school friend of Śrīla Prabhupāda's who became a national hero (especially in Bengal) during the agitation for Indian independence in the 1930s and '40s. He had advocated the use of force as a means to drive out the British, organizing an independent Indian army in Singapore during the Second World War with the intention of marching to India to liberate her. Mysteriously, he was killed in an air crash at the end of the war.

Prabhupāda said the real reason the British decided to quit India was because of the increasing violent opposition to British rule, not because of Gandhi's non-violence movement. When they understood that the police and army were no longer co-operative, they knew they could no longer rule.

Mrs. Bose was talkative and loud, but respectful and willing to help where she could. She laughingly told Prabhupāda that Netajī had organized an army to conquer India, and now Prabhupāda had organized an army of Vaiṣṇavas to conquer the world.

Prabhupāda requested her to assist with the on-going visa problems his American disciples are having preventing them from staying in India for extended periods.

During their conversation she also remarked that Mrs. Gandhi had said she thought Śrīla Prabhupāda was a very pure saint.

After she left, Prabhupāda called in Madhudviṣa and Tamal Krishna mahārājas. He asked them to organize a bus program throughout India for *saṅkīrtana* propagation and *prasādam* distribution. Mrs. Bose's comment about Mrs. Gandhi had encouraged him. He told them that if this is her true sentiment, then we should immediately take advantage of the favorable climate.

Despite the current state of national emergency and paranoia that ISKCON is a front for the CIA, Prabhupāda is certain that the Kṛṣṇa consciousness movement can change the face of the country if ISKCON's leading devotees can establish large-scale programs in India for at least one year. He is intent on beginning this program and talked animatedly about how it should be organized.

Tamal Krishna expressed some doubt about his own involvement because of his responsibilities in America. Madhudviṣa Swami, however, was excited about the scheme and promised to research the cost of vehicles.

As the conversation became more relaxed and moved into other topics, Tamal Krishna Mahārāja recalled how Prabhupāda had personally obtained the London Deities, Śrī Śrī Rādhā-Londonīśvara. Prabhupāda had been invited to London to officially open the temple, but the Deities that had been ordered had not arrived on time. Only a few days before the proposed installation date the devotees spotted some Rādhā-Kṛṣṇa *mūrtis* in a shop window. Prabhupāda immediately went to the shop and personally persuaded the owner, an Indian man, to let him have Them. Even as he and the man spoke, Prabhupāda ordered the devotees to carry Their Lordships into a waiting van, despite the man's hesitation. Later Prabhupāda settled everything very amicably with him.

These reflections on his past struggles to establish ISKCON revealed just a hint of his inner, intimate—and to us, hidden—relationship with Their Lordships. Prabhupāda's smiles and laughter at Tamal Krishna Mahārāja's recollections made me wonder what kind of special *līlā* he has with Śrī Śrī Rādhā-Londonīśvara. Prabhupāda said that They are the best in the Society; the first large Deities to be installed.

January 15th, 1976

For a change Śrīla Prabhupāda took his walk around the grounds of Calcutta's famous Victoria Memorial. Many people were out exercising and walking. Rather than speak, Prabhupāda had us perform a gentle *kīrtana* the entire time.

* * *

Later in the morning Prabhupāda went to see another flat. And then just before massage time he sent me to show two friends of his the place we saw yesterday.

Tamal Krishna Mahārāja gave Prabhupāda his massage. It was a surprise to me that it was the first time for him. When I returned he was still massaging Śrīla Prabhupāda. Prabhupāda told Tamal Krishna to stop, insisting that I complete the massage, even though only his right leg remained to be done. Tamāl had a luncheon appointment, and Prabhupāda didn't want him to miss it.

Madhudviṣa Swami, keen about Śrīla Prabhupāda's suggestion last night to preach in India, spent a good part of the day finding out about obtaining a bus. Śrīla Prabhupāda also spoke with Madhudviṣa about the new building in New York. He asked him if he wanted to manage it. Madhudviṣa Swami liked the idea. He has been the GBC in charge of Australia and New Zealand since mid-1972, and he seems ready for a change.

* * *

Later in the day I came before Prabhupāda wearing a new raw silk *dhotī,* which he immediately noticed. He asked me whether it was silk and how much it cost. Remembering that in Vṛndāvana he had complimented me for getting a good *dhotī* for only fourteen rupees, I thought he might not be happy that I had spent 175 on this one. However, he was quite pleased and remarked that silk is very nice.

January 16th, 1976

We walked in Victoria Gardens again, but without an accompanying *kīrtana.* Prabhupāda said little, and we all chanted *japa* as we walked around the huge, empty, marble edifice.

On the way out to the memorial grounds, we passed the police barracks just as an officer cantered out riding a magnificent thoroughbred. It must have been fully seventeen hands high and beautifully groomed. As we admired the elegant creature Śrīla Prabhupāda commented, "The horse is the most beautiful animal."

In surprise Tamal Krishna Mahārāja asked, "Not the cow, Śrīla Prabhupāda?"

"Cow is not beautiful," Prabhupāda replied, matter-of-factly, as if we should have known.

Harikeśa laughed. For him it was *deja-vu.* He told us that last year Prabhupāda went out for his walk, saw a horse, and made the same comment. His secretary had asked the same question about the cow and received the same reply—except it was Brahmānanda Swami and not Tamal.

* * *

This morning's newspaper carried a feature story on our Māyāpur Candrodaya Mandir. After breakfast *prasādam* Jayapatākā Swami read the whole article to Śrīla Prabhupāda, noting a certain amount of cynicism on the part of the writer. The man had noticed the *pūjārī* offering *bhoga* to Śrī Śrī Rādhā-Mādhava in a Deity room warmed by a heater. The author questioned who the heater was for, since he had been told that everything we did was for God's pleasure and not our own. What would God want with a heater? He concluded that it must have been for the devotee's comfort.

Prabhupāda said that this is the atheistic mentality. He is compelled to question who it is for; whereas a devotee knows that it is for the Lord. If the Deities can enjoy *bhoga,* why not heat? This inability to understand that God has senses is impersonalism. In their experience personality means "having limited senses." Therefore God must be impersonal in order to be unlimited.

"Actually," he said, "unlimited means you can eat six *rasagullās,* but Kṛṣṇa can eat unlimited coconuts. Kṛṣṇa has senses, and He appreciates the heater."

* * *

Prabhupāda told us today how to make *baḍa* by grinding up rice and *urad dahl* after first soaking them, making a paste, spicing it with chopped green chili, salt, and pepper, and then deep-frying small balls of it in hot ghee. An accompanying chutney can be made from the soft, white flesh of a young coconut mixed with green chili, salt, and lemon juice. He took a few *baḍas* made by Harikeśa in the evening to gain strength for his night's translation work.

CHAPTER NINE

Sri Dhama Mayapur

January 17th, 1976

After a walk in a nearby park, Śrīla Prabhupāda set off for Māyāpur at 7:30 a.m. Prabhupāda, Madhudviṣa Swami, Tamal Krishna Goswāmī, and Jayapatākā Swami were in the lead car; Śrīdhara Swami, Harikeśa, Caitya-guru, who has come from Bombay to associate with Śrīla Prabhupāda, and I followed in another car.

Two hours later and seven kilometers beyond the town of Rānaghāṭa our party stopped to take breakfast in a large grove of several hundred mango trees. The grove has become a regular resting point for Śrīla Prabhupāda whenever he goes to Māyāpur. Seated on a folded *chadar* on the leaf-strewn grass, with the spreading arms of the huge trees forming a pleasant canopy above, Prabhupāda seemed completely at ease in the natural setting. We had brought various fruits, *baḍa,* fried cashew nuts, and sweets. The *sannyāsīs* sat in a row alongside His Divine Grace, while Caitya-guru and I served the *prasādam* out on leaf plates. After a relaxed half an hour, hands and mouths washed, we proceeded to our destination, the birthplace of Śrī Caitanya Mahāprabhu.

A large gathering of ISKCON Māyāpur devotees, led by Bhavānanda Goswāmī and Sudāmā Mahārāja, were eagerly waiting to greet Śrīla Prabhupāda when we arrived around eleven o'clock. As we approached we saw that the construction of a beautiful and impressive gate-house had been completed at the entrance to our property. The gate-house is fifteen feet thick, with three archways. The center archway is wide and high enough for a truck to pass under, while the two side ones are for pedestrians. Above the archways sit five domes, the large central one capped with an ornate, brass spire reaching some fifty feet or so into the air. There are several small rooms in the domes on either side. The entire structure is attractively painted, the domes in saffron and maroon with yellow on the facing wall. Large footprints of Lord Caitanya adorned with a *tulasī* leaf sprig and surrounded by lotus flowers are emblazoned on the front, with the words SRI MAYAPUR CANDRODAYA MANDIR below them.

Prabhupāda got out of the car on the main front road. As everyone looked on in great delight, he stepped forward and cut a large ribbon, officially opening the gateway. The formal ceremony over, the metal gates were opened, and he happily walked through the arch and entered the temple compound, followed by a stream of devotees. He moved steadily along the road, past the original thatched hut where he first stayed when he got the land, past flower beds and crops, toward the main building.

All the while he was surrounded by a dancing, chanting party of about twenty or thirty young Bengali *brahmacārīs,* all Vaiṣṇavas, heads shaven and decorated with *tilaka,* loudly chanting Hare Kṛṣṇa. These are all privileged residents of Lord Caitanya's holy *dhāma,* whose greatest joy in life is clearly the presence of the Lord's pure devotee.

Entering the ground-floor temple room Śrīla Prabhupāda greeted the beautiful brass forms of Śrī Śrī Rādhā-Mādhava. Śrī Śālagrāma-śilā is also present, Māyāpur being one of the few ISKCON temples in which Prabhupāda has so far sanctioned His worship.

After a lively *guru-pūjā* Prabhupāda gave a short talk, describing the benefits of life in the holy *dhāma.* "It was Bhaktivinoda Ṭhākura's aspiration that the Europeans, Americans, and Indians all together dance jubilantly and chant 'Gaura Hari.' So this temple, Māyāpur Candrodaya temple, is meant for transcendental United Nations. What the United Nations has failed, that will be achieved here by the process recommended by Śrī Caitanya Mahāprabhu, *pṛthivīte āche yata nagarādi grāma, sarvatra pracāra haibe mora nāma.* So you have come from all parts of the world and are living together in this temple.

"So train these small boys. I am very glad, especially to see that the small children from all other countries, and Indian, Bengalis, all together, forgetting their bodily consciousness. That is the greatest achievement in this movement, that everyone forgets the bodily conception of life. Nobody thinks themselves here as European, American, Indian, Hindu, Muslim, Christian. They forget all these designations, and simply they are ecstatic in chanting the Hare Kṛṣṇa mantra. So kindly what you have begun do not break it. Continue it very jubilantly. And Caitanya Mahāprabhu, the master of Māyāpur, He will be very much pleased upon you. And ultimately you will go back to home, back to Godhead. Thank you very much." To the cheers of the devotees he went upstairs to his rooms on the second floor.

Prabhupāda is obviously extremely happy to be in Māyāpur. The entire project is well-managed and progressing wonderfully. Built to Śrīla Prabhupāda's own specifications, the central guest house building has good facilities. He especially likes the wide verandas encircling the three upper stories, giving the guest house a spacious, palatial effect. On each of the two upper floors there are eight rooms, each measuring twenty-two by fourteen feet and twelve feet in height, split into groups of four by a central stairway. Most are equipped with two ornate, wood-frame beds, a table, and a chair. At either end of the floor are large bathrooms with four shower stalls, toilets, and sinks.

Śrīla Prabhupāda's own quarters have two interconnected rooms, one for working and giving *darśana,* one for sleeping. The rooms are very simply furnished. His sitting room has only a raised wooden *āsana* and a low desk, and the floors are covered with white-sheeted cotton mattresses and bolsters. In the bedroom there is an *almirah,* a small table with a very beautiful Deity of Lord Caitanya on it, and Śrīla Prabhupāda's bed, exactly the same type as in the guest rooms. He also has the bathroom at the end of his floor reserved for his exclusive use.

Next door to Prabhupāda, Caitya-guru and I am sharing the servant's room. The first thing I did after setting up Śrīla Prabhupāda's dictaphone was install the summoning bell, the lead of which is long enough to reach from his desk right to my bedside. Śrīla Prabhupāda has only to push a button to instantly alert me that he needs something.

As we unpacked, Prabhupāda chatted with the *sannyāsīs* for a few minutes. He expressed his satisfaction with the enthusiasm of the devotees, the beautiful grounds, and the spiritually vibrant atmosphere.

He glanced around his room. His eyes rested for a moment on an intricately carved, three-dimensional, wooden plaque on the far wall. It depicts Śrī Śrī Rādhā and Kṛṣṇa and was a gift from an admirer in Indonesia. On the wall beside him hung a large canvas oil painting depicting the Māyāpur foundation-stone-laying ceremony. It shows him sitting with some of his Godbrothers while disciples and admirers stand around. Above and behind him, dioramas of the Pañca-tattva perched on a shelf. In such a perfect setting I was struck by how the simplicity and deep spirituality of his surroundings seem to perfectly complement Śrīla Prabhupāda's own transcendental nature.

Later, giving Prabhupāda his massage, I surveyed the beautiful gardens and the wide-open expanse of fields from the veranda's vantage point. All around I could see rice fields in various stages of development: hues of emerald green maturing to yellow-gold. Clumps of *dahl,* strips of vegetables, nearly ripened wheat, and small green forests dotted the distant skyline. In the clear sky kingfishers flashed brilliant blue, green parrots flitted here and there in pairs, and cranes stalked the flooded paddies. It was beautiful. Following the line of the road toward the Gaṅgā and Jalangi Rivers were the *maṭhas,* temples established by the followers of Śrīla Bhaktisiddhānta Sarasvatī. Their spires and domes reach to the sky, sentinels and reminders of real progress in human life. The melodious *kīrtana* of the Bengali devotees floated out from the temple below us, pervading the entire atmosphere.

In this environment Prabhupāda is clearly more relaxed and happy than I have seen him so far, like someone who has returned home from afar. Māyāpur struck me as idyllic, and as I rubbed the mustard oil into his lotus feet, I suggested that it would be a fine place for Prabhupāda's retirement. He mused for a moment and then replied, "Either Vṛndāvana or Māyāpur. No other place, that is for sure."

* * *

Early in the evening Harikeśa came in to see Prabhupāda, looking very glum. He admitted that he had left the *almirah* in Prabhupāda's Calcutta room open. Śrīla Prabhupāda was very angry with him. He could not understand how he had been so careless.

Prabhupāda keeps many important items locked up in his rooms—in cupboards or *almirahs*— especially in main centers where he has permanent rooms like Bombay, Vṛndāvana, Calcutta, or Māyāpur. Because Harikeśa has been traveling with Prabhupāda for quite some time, Prabhupāda entrusts him with keeping records of the banking as well as other transactions, but he said that now this carelessness meant he cannot be trusted.

Harikeśa felt he should immediately ring Calcutta. But Prabhupāda made it clear: the only solution was for Harikeśa immediately to leave for Calcutta to personally lock up the *almirah.* That was the only way to be certain. Harikeśa immediately made the arrangements and left soon after.

Apart from this incident, the evening was very pleasant. Prabhupāda sat relaxed and happy in his room. Both doors were left open on either side of him, allowing a gentle breeze to flow through, while the sounds of an ecstatic *sandhyā-ārati kīrtana* led by Sudāmā Mahārāja reverberated in the night air.

There were no visitors. After a hot cup of milk from our own cows, Prabhupāda took rest at ten o'clock before starting his night's translation work.

January 18th, 1976

First thing this morning Śrīla Prabhupāda went on a tour of all the buildings on our property. He inspected the entire grounds, beginning at the new *pukkur,* a small reservoir near the main gate dug out over the last year and now partially landscaped. He said fruit trees should be planted on the high banks surrounding it and a path made all around.

While walking Prabhupāda discussed accommodations for

the devotees who would be visiting during the festival. Jayapatākā Mahārāja wanted to build temporary grass cottages on the open land, but Prabhupāda objected. He said it was better to spend money on something permanent. Prabhupāda told him instead to build rooms along the entire length of the northern boundary wall and to have them ready for the festival—a whole new guest house building. With the festival only six weeks away, Jayapatākā expressed doubts how it could be completed in time. Prabhupāda told him if they engage at least one hundred men it could be done. Then Bhavānanda Mahārāja raised the objection that there was no money. Prabhupāda told him that if that was the only problem, he would give him the money. But he said they must start immediately. Jayapatākā, however, was still apprehensive. He said there was a shortage of bricks. Nevertheless Prabhupāda pushed him to begin construction. He told them that they should do whatever they can, but the work must begin immediately.

Leaving the *pukkur* we hesitated to go down the steep incline of the embankment. Jayapatākā, however, had no problem running down, even in his wooden shoes. Prabhupāda laughed. "Victorious flag—Jaya-patākā," he called out, appreciating his disciple's dexterity.

Walking south along the inner road Prabhupāda inspected the boundary-wall rooms. Some were being used for living quarters, and some were being used for storage.

At the dispensary Prabhupāda said that he would give some herbal formulas for minor ailments. He also suggested that the devotees keep a stock of general medicines for curing common complaints without the need for a doctor.

At least five or six rooms were being used for weaving. Looking in at the looms, Prabhupāda revealed a little of his vision of a spiritual society in Māyāpur. He said, "Some envious persons might criticize, 'Oh, this is temple and they are weaving. They are not worshiping?' And yet others may accuse us as religionists—parasites. But in the *Bhagavad-gītā* Kṛṣṇa says *svakarmaṇā tam abhyarcya siddhiṁ vindati mānavaḥ*. Whatever a person knows, he can work in that way and get perfection, provided he is Kṛṣṇa conscious. Because they are preparing the cloth for the devotees and not for business, they are therefore serving Kṛṣṇa."

Prabhupāda suggested that some of the rooms be turned into shops where cloth, books, *prasādam, mṛdaṅga* drums, and *karatālas* could be sold.

Then he turned back to inspect the *gurukula* on the northern side of the main gate. Prabhupāda was disturbed to see clay dioramas from last year's festival now lying broken and neglected in some of the rooms. He wanted to know why other temples could keep their dolls for years, but ours have been destroyed within one year. When Jayapatākā Mahārāja offered "vandalism" as the excuse, Prabhupāda strongly criticized him for allowing vandals to come in. "You are so careful—that is the defect!" Prabhupāda told him sarcastically. "We have so many enemies, and you do not take care of it." He repeated this several times as he continued his tour. With mild sarcasm he called his disciple "the most foolish person in the whole world" for not securing them properly.

Walking out the main gate and down to the far south-westerly corner of our property, Prabhupāda inspected the outside of the boundary wall. Its surface is being plastered and sculpted into a series of decorative panels. They will then be painted by our artists with advertisements for Prabhupāda's books.

At the end of the wall we arrived at the new *prasādam* hall where our free-food program regularly serves *prasādam* to many thousands of local people. At its side a large, metal turnstile has been specially installed. This is an invention borrowed from the New York subways, but new in these parts. Its purpose is to prevent the villagers from crushing in all at once when coming to take *prasādam.* The hall itself is big enough to hold 1,200 people at once. Prabhupāda was impressed. Looking at its cavernous interior and very high, corrugated-iron ceiling, he laughingly said it resembled the Bombay railway station.

Nothing escaped his sharp eyes. Outside, he saw a broken-down three-wheeled vehicle. He wanted to know why it was occupying valuable space. When told it was a donation from someone who had joined our *āśrama* he quoted an old Bengali saying. "'A blind cow given in charity to a *brāhmaṇa.*' When something is useless—all right, charity!" He ordered it to be removed, right then and there, from our land. "We do not require such charity," he said.

From there he inspected the kitchen area, a separate building with accommodations for householders on the upper floor. He was not pleased to see dirt on the steps. He said they looked as if they had not been cleaned "for three hundred years," and he demanded to know why. When told the place was cleaned every night, he retorted, "What is the use of such cleaning, if it is dirty the next morning?"

One of the managers said it was difficult to get the devotees to clean in the early morning because they all wanted to complete their *japa.* Prabhupāda, however, said cleaning must come first, and the chanting of *japa* another time. He stressed that unless they are prepared to work, no one should be allowed to join us. "*Śrī-vigrahārādhana-nitya-nānā-śṛṇgāra-tan-mandira-mārjanādau.* This is all temple. This is not ordinary hotel, free hotel. If they cannot take care as temple, they must go away. Simply eating, sleeping, that's all, not working. See that they do not make it a free hotel for eating and sleeping. Don't allow this. It should be clean. Why in the evening? Every morning it should be cleaned and washed and mopped. They must give up *japa;* first of all clean. In the name of *japa* they are dozing, and everything is unclean. This nonsense should not be allowed. Ask them, 'Stop *japa-ing.* First of all clean. Then make *japa.*'

"Under a plea of *japa* they are simply dozing," he said. "You should not give shelter to persons who, in the name of so-called *japa,* take advantage of free boarding and lodging. You should be very careful. Everyone should be, according to his capacity, engaged to some work. Don't allow this stupidity."

His inspection was thorough and penetrating, delving into every aspect of management, from the buildings to the crops. He was pleased to hear that the devotees are growing sugar cane and making *gur* from it. With humor and practical intelligence he encouraged the devotees to continue working hard for Kṛṣṇa, for the development of both Māyāpur and their own spiritual lives.

On his return to the temple he greeted the Deities, received *guru-pūjā,* and circumambulated Śrī Śrī Rādhā-Mādhava three times before returning to his room.

Morning *prasādam* for the devotees was date juice and puffed rice, the main meal being served at 11:00 a.m. For his breakfast Prabhupāda took only a small amount of fruit and *baḍa.* Jayapatākā Mahārāja brought him the season's first jug of date *rasa,* the clear, sweet sap from the date palm. He drank a small amount from his cup, appearing to enjoy it.

Prabhupāda called me at 9:30 a.m. to begin his massage. He wanted to have it early because the sun was shining on the veranda outside his room. Whenever possible and if not too hot, he enjoys having his massage while exposed to the health-giving rays of the sun. It was finished by 11:00 a.m., and after bathing, he sat on his *āsana* in his room. With his eyes closed he remained in an upright position for about forty-five minutes. Occasionally his lips moved as he silently chanted or said something. He appeared completely absorbed—I wondered, perhaps, in Goloka Vṛndāvana?

Māyāpur is definitely not the material world. There is a transcendental aspect, tangible even to a neophyte like me. After months of arduous travel on behalf of Lord Caitanya, Prabhupāda has come here to recuperate and relax. Always completely immersed in thoughts of Kṛṣṇa, who knows what he actually sees and hears?

* * *

A letter came from Sweden written by Dwarakeśa dāsa. In it he explained that he was a Hungarian who had escaped from Hungary several years ago, later becoming a devotee. Now the Hungarian government was allowing illegal emigrants back, although once returning, it would be difficult to get out again. He felt he should go back and attempt to deliver Kṛṣṇa consciousness to his countrymen. The devotees in Sweden already had contacts with a yoga club there, and he was enthusiastic to preach.

Prabhupāda encouraged him. After so many recent conversations and discussions on Communism it seemed like Kṛṣṇa responding to Śrīla Prabhupāda's desire to spread Kṛṣṇa consciousness in the Communist countries. "If there is possibility to preach amongst the Communists," he wrote, "you must do it immediately. The intelligent Communist people will very easily understand our philosophy. We can convince them on the basis of *samaḥ sarveṣu bhūteṣu,* a Kṛṣṇa conscious person is equally disposed to every living entity (B.G. 18:54)."

He explained that communism is no better than capitalism because both exploit the animals and other living beings. Prabhupāda told Dwarakeśa he should make the present imperfect idea of communism perfect by following the description of perfect communism given in *Śrīmad-Bhāgavatam.* "It is stated that you feel for the poor animals as well as the human beings. *Śrīmad-Bhāgavatam* instructs that even if there is a snake or a lizard in the house, it is the duty of the householder to see that they are also eating, not starving. So you have to begin your preaching with such broader idea of communism

"So far as coming out of Hungary once you enter, if you can preach, what is the need of coming out?"

Mahāṁsa Swami wrote. He is having difficulty persuading the two sisters in Nellore to relax the conditions on the deed of gift of land.

Prabhupāda responded, "We are not at all interested to be dictated by them." He told him that because we have already installed the foundation stone, "We do not wish to go back." To this end he stated his willingness even to purchase the land and still allow the two ladies to carry on living in one portion of the building, as devotees. Prabhupāda was adamant, though, that we shall not concede to any special conditions.

* * *

In the early evening, just on dusk, a few of the senior devotees and myself were sitting with Śrīla Prabhupāda in his room, conversing. From a distance, gradually drawing nearer, we heard the loud trumpeting of a conch shell accompanied by bell ringing and the chanting of mantras. Bhavānanda Mahārāja laughed and told Prabhupāda it was Anantarāma Śāstrī, an Indian devotee in his mid-twenties who had joined us last year with three other *śāstrīs.* Unfortunately the others left, but he has stayed on. As his name implies, he is very knowledgeable in the scriptures and well-versed in the performance of various types of *pūjā*. He can also quote practically any Sanskrit verse from memory.

Bhavānanda explained that each evening as the sun goes down, he tours the building, floor by floor, with his conch, bell, and a large, clay incense burner, chanting various mantras to keep away ghosts and other subtle beings.

The sound grew louder, and Prabhupāda smiled in welcome as Śāstrī entered his room in a cloud of frankincense, the reverberations of the conch temporarily drowning out our conversation. It was an impressive ritual, made more so by Śāstrī's ability to both blow air through his mouth and suck it in through his nose at the same time, thus keeping the conch blowing uninterruptedly for several minutes. He walked around both rooms, waving a bamboo fan over his clay bowl to disperse the fragrant smoke. It also acts as an effective mosquito repellent. After a couple of minutes he respectfully backed out the door and continued his nightly round.

The *pūjā* triggered Prabhupāda's remembrance of his time in Allahabad in 1945. He told us he was paying only two hundred rupees for a whole house then. But the place was famous as a ghostly haunted house. Nobody would rent it, but Prabhupāda took it. "I don't care for ghosts," he said, smiling. "Actually there was a ghost, and all the servants, they were met. But I was chanting."

Later Madhudviṣa Swami and I sat with Prabhupāda as he talked about how the British knew the art of ruling. By giving Indians control as supervisors they were able to rule a large, populous continent with only a few thousand men. In general the Indians appreciated them. But after innocent people were shot at an anti-British rally in Amritsar, Gandhi's movement was able to gain momentum, and the British lost their respectability.

Speaking about governments in general, Prabhupāda said that even bad or demonic governments are allowed by Kṛṣṇa in order to punish people for sinful activity. He explained that Kṛṣṇa is behind everything. He emphasized this point by playing back to us on his dictaphone some of his latest translation work from the Seventh Canto, in which he was making the same point.

Madhudviṣa Mahārāja also asked a few managerial questions regarding ISKCON Fiji. Deoji Punja, who was instrumental in establishing ISKCON there, is chanting the *mahā-mantra* and following the regulative principles. He is channeling money from his supermarket and other shops into building a Kṛṣṇa temple, but meanwhile he is still selling meat and liquor in the stores. Madhudviṣa expressed uncertainty about whether to tell him to cease such sales or not.

Prabhupāda said that he should be allowed to continue, and not forced to give it up. He quoted *Bhagavad-gītā* (18.48): "Every endeavor is covered by some sort of fault, just as fire is covered by smoke. Therefore one should not give up the work which is born of his nature, O son of Kuntī, even if such work is full of fault." Prabhupāda expressed confidence that if he is chanting Hare Kṛṣṇa, these things will soon be properly adjusted.

January 19th, 1976

Jayapatākā Mahārāja has been busy initiating the work on the new building for the northern boundary. As Prabhupāda walked down the road to nearby Hoola Ghat, Jayapatākā reported that they could get up to 250,000 bricks within a month. So the work on the new building is to begin immediately.

Arriving at the *ghāṭa* Prabhupāda made a quick inspection of our newly acquired boat. He went on board and carefully inspected the interior, as Sudāmā Mahārāja explained the setup. Prabhupāda was pleased and agreed to install the Deities of Śrī Śrī Gaura-Nitai in a few days' time when preparations are complete.

From there he visited the *gośālā,* where he inspected the cows and calves. Pippalai, a devotee from Mexico, is nicely managing everything.

Crossing the fields to return to the temple, Prabhupāda questioned Jayapatāka Swami how each field is being utilized, stressing that every bit of land must be used. They discussed purchasing new land. Prabhupāda told him that about seventeen-hundred rupees per *bigha* (one third acre) is a reasonable price, not the four or five thousand that some farmers are demanding.

* * *

For breakfast Prabhupāda again had some of the season's first produce, some sugar-cane juice from our own fields. He is very happy to see our men using the land to grow foodstuff. The *dahl* we drink daily is home-grown, and the *chapatis* are made from our own wheat.

* * *

During the day Bhavānanda Mahārāja came in to ask for advice about how to deal with the married couples and children in the *āśrama.* The girls especially have become a problem because in the villages they are generally married by the time they reach puberty, but in our *āśrama* there are not enough young devotee men available. Prabhupāda said that the young girls in Māyāpur can be married to local men, and that we will give a dowry of five hundred rupees. These men can then be invited to live with us, but our *brahmacārīs* should be kept single.

Prabhupāda agreed that finding suitable husbands for the single women is a problem throughout our ISKCON society. We are training boys to remain celibate *brahmacārīs.* Since women in *Kali-yuga* form the majority of the population, who, then, will marry them? Prabhupāda suggested that a man could have more than one wife. He laughed, "The idea is he is already spoiled, so he may as well take more!" However, he feels that public reaction would not be good, so it is doubtful whether this idea can ever be implemented.

* * *

As evening *ārati* went on downstairs Prabhupāda talked in his room to his Godbrother Dāmodara Mahārāja, Harikeśa, and a few visitors about the difficulties of preaching. Dāmodara Mahārāja is a rather simple person, younger than Prabhupāda's eighty years. And he is reported to spend his time flitting from one Gauḍīya Maṭha to another without any particular preaching goal. He has a reputation for indulging in gossip and is apparently not taken very seriously by his Godbrothers. But Śrīla Prabhupāda treats him with respect.

Speaking sometimes in Bengali and sometimes in English, they discussed how there are so many envious men who want to impede the spread of Kṛṣṇa consciousness. It is a fact that even Prabhupāda's own Godbrothers display jealousy at his apparent sudden success. Especially here in Māyāpur, there have been many instances of obstacles being deliberately created to hinder the development of Śrī Māyāpur Candrodaya Mandir.

Prabhupāda showed no surprise, only perhaps some disappointment. Taking a philosophical perspective, he told us that the whole material world is full of jealousy, even in the higher planetary systems. For that reason Lord Caitanya has said one must be very humble. Jealousy will always be present, so one should learn to tolerate. He said that is the best way to deal with it.

Dāmodara Mahārāja recalled that their spiritual master, Śrīla Bhaktisiddhānta Sarasvatī Prabhupāda, was also criticized.

"So if they can talk against Prabhupāda, then what to speak of me," Prabhupāda told him. "I am nothing to Prabhupāda."

Dāmodara Mahārāja tried to see the bright side of things. "That will happen to a preacher. Those who are really preaching, there will be something negative, something positive. There should be light and darkness, both things should be there. Otherwise how we can differentiate good from bad? There should be anti-party, otherwise how we can realize your glories? Maybe one day they will realize it."

Śrīla Prabhupāda was humble, but frank. "Whether they realize it or not does not matter to me. Whatever my mission, I will continue. I am not going to wait for their realization. I shall continue service to my Gurudeva."

"I mean to say, many of them have already realized it," Dāmodara Mahārāja hastened to add. "Those who have realized, they have admitted that it is a noble service; it is a pleasure to us."

"It is written clearly in *Caitanya-caritāmṛta: kṛṣṇa śakti vinā nahe kṛṣṇa nāma pracāraṇa.* Even if they have no common sense, what can be done?" Prabhupāda said.

Dāmodara Mahārāja agreed. "We have to admit this. That *kṛṣṇa śakti* is there."

Prabhupāda shrugged. "This is something new in the history of the world, and still they are jealous. What can you do? They are just finding faults. In Vṛndāvana Nṛsiṁha-vallabha Gosvāmī came to me. He said, 'So many people are jealous about you.' I said, 'First of all you create something like this, then you become jealous.' They do not have that power."

Dāmodara Mahārāja said that he had inquired from his Godbrothers, and their feelings were changing. They were becoming more favorable.

Prabhupāda responded evenly. "Whether they change their feelings or not does not matter to me. Sometimes I was amazed at their feelings."

Prabhupāda felt the problems were due to a lack of understanding of proper Vaiṣṇava dealings. "What bothers me is their dictating mood. Why they should dictate? First of all let them become like me. Equality brings friendship. Whoever is older, he will dictate; and whoever is younger, he will respect the superior. This is the rule. Neither they are equal nor senior, then why they should dictate? Who is superior, he will dictate; and who is equal, he should live like friend; and who is junior, they should follow and obey. This is the Vaiṣṇava rule. Those who are neither equal nor higher, now they can dictate? That is a mistake. Either, first of all become higher then him, then dictate; or become equal with him, then you suggest. You are lower, and you want to dictate. What is this nonsense?"

One of the visitors explained that he had met a local political official who was suspicious and critical of our Society. The guest explained how he had tried to defend ISKCON. "Those who are born in luxury and comforts have left everything for the holy name. And Prabhupāda is the person who had preached this holy name in the Western world and convinced them about spiritual life. It is really a wonderful service. There is something to know and something to realize from this wonderful service. Unfortunately," he said, "the politician did not listen." In truth, there are many who ascribe Prabhupāda's success in bringing so many Westerners to India as nothing more than a CIA plot.

The man's observation pleased Prabhupāda. It is a fact. "All these boys and girls have come all the way from America. I did not bribe them to take up Kṛṣṇa consciousness and to come here. They have come on their own. People call us CIA. Being a devotee by giving up all intoxication, giving up all kinds of desires and smoking, by dancing and chanting in the street, yet they will have the investigation on CIA. What a less common sense these people have! They have not got any common sense."

When the guests left, Prabhupāda relaxed in his room, reminiscing with Madhudviṣa Mahārāja and me about the years before he came to the West, telling us something of the sequence of the major events of his preaching life.

1950	Left home.
1952	Lived in Jhansi.
1955	Went to Mathurā. Gave his Deity of Lord Caitanya to Keśava Mahārāja's temple in Mathurā.
1956	Moved to Vṛndāvana.
1958	Wrote *Easy Journey to Other Planets.*
1959	Took *sannyāsa.*
1960	Started *Śrīmad-Bhāgavatam* translation.
1962	Finished and published Part I, *Bhāgavatam* First Canto.
1963	Finished and published Part II, *Bhāgavatam* First Canto.
1964	Finished and published Part III, *Bhāgavatam* First Canto.
1965	Left Calcutta for U.S.A.

These evening conversations are always sublime. Just being able to sit with Śrīla Prabhupāda and hear him speak is so remarkably satisfying, especially when he recalls his young childhood experiences, the British rule in India, and his efforts to spread Kṛṣṇa consciousness.

As it often does, the electricity went off and we lit the oil lamps, adding to the intimacy of the atmosphere. Sitting in the soft glow of the lanterns, his mood was gentle and at ease, as if he was with the best of friends. At such times, in such an air of informality, we try not to become so familiar lest we forget our position. Nevertheless Prabhupāda makes himself completely accessible, a genuine helper and guide in our struggle for transcendental life. I am realizing more and more that association with a pure devotee is really the essence of spiritual life.

January 20th, 1976

Prabhupāda took his morning walk in the fields to the east of the building, examining the proposed site of the big future temple. Saurabha, our ISKCON architect, is drawing up plans for a structure at least 350 feet square.

* * *

Prabhupāda's concern for the future development of his *gurukula* system is growing as more correspondence comes in from the West. The latest arrived from Jayatīrtha, explaining the difficulties they are facing in complying with government regulations in Dallas. Several proposals for relocation of the school have been touted, but nothing definite has been decided.

Śrīla Prabhupāda wrote him a long letter thoroughly outlining his desires for educating the Society's children. He condemned modern educational systems, saying they meted the greatest violence upon the young by training them as sense gratifiers. He said that the *karmī* system was producing "cats and dogs who feel quite at home in a society of sense gratification." Therefore they could not appreciate the *gurukula* system based on *vairāgya vidyā*, knowledge based on renunciation.

He wrote, "They will never accept that one must undergo austerities to break the influence of the modes of material nature upon the living entity in order that he may experience the transcendental bliss on the platform of pure goodness. Therefore they see our school as a threat and a cruel punishment to the children. Complying with the authorities' requests would mean a gradual watering down of our standards," he said, "until it becomes unrecognizable and useless."

His solution was to send the young boys to the newly developing Vṛndāvana *gurukula*. "To live in Vṛndāvana and to grow up there is the greatest fortune. To spend even one fortnight in Mathurā-*maṇḍala* guarantees liberation." He described Kṛṣṇa-Balarāma Mandir as "the finest in the world." He said that by living there the boys will be able to follow all the practices of *brahmacārī* life and become very blissful. There are many other advantages also. The fact that living in India is much cheaper would ease the burden on the parents. "Therefore in all ways it is obvious that the best place to have this *gurukula* is in Vṛndāvana. This should be done before the US Government starts to cause a disturbance which will harm us, and before we have to waste large sums of money on a risky endeavor, which may turn out to be a complete failure."

* * *

In the evening His Divine Grace told us more about his life before establishing ISKCON. He explained that when he began publishing *Back to Godhead* many people appreciated it, including his Godbrother Bon Mahārāja and others.

One librarian friend asked him, "Why not write books? Paper is thrown away, but a book is kept."

So in 1958 he wrote *Easy Journey to Other Planets.* In 1960 he began the First Canto of the *Śrīmad-Bhāgavatam,* publishing the first part in 1962. In 1963 came Part Two, and by the end of 1964 Part Three. Each printing was eleven hundred copies, the cost donated by a wealthy business magnate.

In 1965 he came to Māyāpur to pay respects to his departed Guru Mahārāja. The next day he returned to Calcutta and sailed for the U.S.A. It took twenty-seven days via the Suez Canal and the Straits of Gibraltar. For two days at sea Prabhupāda had severe chest pains and thought he might die at any time. Later in New York he became ill with the same complaint, and doctors told him that it was a heart attack. He understood this was the same as the trouble aboard ship, but at that time he did not know what it was. He said that in New York the chanting of the devotees had saved him.

Before leaving India, the American embassy in Delhi had bought nineteen copies of each volume of his *Śrīmad-Bhāgavatam* and given a standing order for all the future volumes. They then sent them to different universities and libraries in America. After Prabhupāda arrived in Americia he went to one library and offered his books, but they already had them. Then he went to a university in Philadelphia and it also had obtained them.

One teacher paid Prabhupāda's fare from Butler, Pennsylvāṇīa to the main bus terminal in Philadelphia. Prabhupāda went from there to New York, where he rented a small room. At that time he had an idea to get a small temple, so he wrote to a rich man in Bombay asking him for money. The man agreed, but the government disallowed it, although Prabhupāda got special permission to collect funds from resident Indians. Then he went to the Salvation Army asking for help, but they refused.

He wrote to his Godbrother Tīrtha Mahārāja asking for men and *mṛdaṅga* drums, but he also refused to help. Prabhupāda had originally asked him for funds for going to the West and publishing his books, but Tīrtha refused. Instead, he had indirectly hinted that Prabhupāda should go as his representative. In this way Tīrtha Mahārāja would get the credit if the mission was successful. "I understood his mind," Prabhupāda told us, "and carefully avoided him after that."

While on board the ship the captain's wife, who was a palmist, told Prabhupāda that if he survived his seventieth year he would live to be one hundred years old. Seeing us smile at this he added, "So, somehow or other the heart attacks were not fatal, so now let us see."

Madhudviṣa Swami said that he had told Mr. Punja in Fiji that Prabhupāda was getting old and couldn't travel there. Mr. Punja, who hadn't heard about the prediction, replied, "Oh, don't worry, Prabhupāda will live to be one hundred!" Madhudviṣa Swami asked him how he knew. He said that he had given Prabhupāda's birth details and signature, as well as a recording of his voice, to a fortune teller in Fiji who predicted Prabhupāda would live to be one hundred.

"So let us see," Prabhupāda repeated with a noncommittal grin.

He recalled how he had gone to a very prominent astrologer in Calcutta when he was a *gṛhastha* and asked what his future would be. The man laughed and said only, "Oh, this will be your last birth here!"

Prabhupāda also talked about the position of women in Indian society. Formerly a respectable woman would not be seen in public, but remained secluded, traveling only in sedan-chairs and closed carriages. Kṛṣṇa's wives played tennis on the roofs of the palaces; and Advaita Ācārya's wife, Sītā-devi, traveled in a veiled chair. Prabhupāda said that his own mother and his wife did the same. Only prostitutes would be seen publicly.

Formerly a woman's status could be understood by her dress: a married woman kept her head covered, an unmarried woman under her father's protection had an uncovered head, a widow wore a white sari with no border, and a prostitute parted her hair on the side, not in the middle. In this way Vedic society was so nicely arranged that one could easily understand another's status.

Prabhupāda seems to know practically everything. No matter how seemingly ordinary the subject matter, he can always offer a completely spiritual perspective. He is like a cornucopia of knowledge, overflowing with truth and wisdom. The friendliness and warmth of his personality makes each exchange a completely fulfilling experience. We are indeed extremely fortunate to have his personal association.

January 21st, 1976

As we walked this morning, Prabhupāda discussed plans for the new temple and the proposed exhibitions it's to house. It will be a cultural center as well as temple.

His idea is to have displays depicting various levels of material existence. The exhibition is to begin on the lower levels by depicting hellish regions and lower planetary systems. As the visitor ascends the interior of the dome by an escalator, various levels of material existence will be revealed, gradually rising to the abodes of the demigods, then Satyaloka, and the Vaikuṇṭha planets. At the very top will be a dazzling display of Kṛṣṇa's own transcendental planet, Goloka Vṛndāvana.

Tamal Krishna Mahārāja suggested that by charging a rupee per person for the escalator rides alone, most of the maintenance costs could be covered.

Prabhupāda also heard some amusing stories from Tamal Krishna and Sudāmā mahārājas. They explained that when new devotees joined the Rādhā-Dāmodara TSKP they often donated all their belongings, sometimes to the great chagrin of their friends or relatives.

One boy, a musician, was convinced to join. He returned to his apartment just as the members of his band were about to depart for an engagement. Since the equipment was his, he took it all, sold it, and donated the proceeds for preaching work. Needless to say, his friends were quite unhappy at the unexpected dissolution of their group. But as Tamal Krishna pointed out, it was the loss of the equipment that upset them, not the loss of their friend.

After greeting the Deities and *guru-pūjā*, Prabhupāda went straight up to his room without giving a class.

* * *

In mid-morning Jayapatākā Swami brought in a Life Member who had come for the day from Calcutta to visit Māyāpur and meet Śrīla Prabhupāda. Prabhupāda welcomed him and asked what his business was.

The man told him he owned a glass manufacturing factory. When Prabhupāda asked what the glass was made from, he replied, "From silicon, Swamijī, from sand."

"And who owns the sand?" Prabhupāda asked.

"Bhagavān, God, owns the sand."

"Oh, you are stealing from Bhagavān?" Prabhupāda challenged.

The man laughed. He was slightly embarrassed but obviously appreciated Prabhupāda's swift expose and lesson in proprietorship. He thought for a minute, and then, as if to offset the implied criticism, ventured that he gave a lot in charity.

Prabhupāda got him a second time. "Oh, then you are just a little thief," he said teasingly.

Everyone laughed and the man was happy to be further enlightened as to his real position as subordinate to God.

Prabhupāda's point was that no one can manufacture anything. We are simply taking ingredients supplied by God and transforming them into another form, yet we think of ourselves as the owners.

This is the mistake of the materialists. Prabhupāda explained that real honesty is to use everything in the service of Kṛṣṇa.

* * *

Prabhupāda gave Madhudviṣa Mahārāja a signed letter, sending him to New York as the *ad hoc* temple president until the Māyāpur GBC meeting. After their conversation in Calcutta about the difficulties in New York, the need for a strong leader, and Prabhupāda's suggestion that Madhudviṣa take it up, Madhudviṣa Mahārāja told Prabhupāda he was willing to go there.

Rūpānuga, the current GBC for New York, will be offered Madhudviṣa's present position in Australia, and Madhudviṣa will take over affairs on America's East Coast. No devotees in

Australia have yet been informed that he is going to New York.

There was some discussion about other possible changes of zones for GBC personnel. Śrīla Prabhupāda said that the GBC members themselves should hold discussions about exchanging zones and then propose a formal resolution at the meetings. On the whole he thought it a good idea for GBC men to swap zones every three or four years. He explained that a change will be refreshing and encourage detachment. It would discourage the tendency for the leaders to think of a particular area as their "own" zone.

* * *

Later in the evening, together with Tamal Krishna Goswāmī, Prabhupāda discussed the position of women in our Society. Recently this has become somewhat of a contentious issue in America, provoking conflict between the *gṛhasthas* and the celibate *sannyāsīs* and *brahmacārīs.*

Tamal Krishna has found himself at the center of the dispute because, along with Viṣṇujana Swami, he is in charge of the Rādhā-Dāmodara traveling *saṅkīrtana* party. Their bus parties, composed almost entirely of *brahmacārīs* and *sannyāsīs,* regularly visit many temples around America. The temples, in contrast, are generally run by married men.

Tamal Krishna's idea is to arrange that no women live in the ISKCON temples. He feels their presence creates distractions for those pursuing a renounced way of life, the essence of Lord Caitanya's movement. He feels that many temples are not serious about sustaining the standards of *vairāgya* and are becoming mere extensions of household affairs, much to the detriment of the welfare of the *brahmacārīs,* who are the real backbone of the movement.

Prabhupāda overcame all his arguments. Although sympathetic to Tamāl's concerns, he said that it is neither desirable nor possible to keep women from coming to join us, nor would it be practical to house them separately. His conclusion is that if we simply preach, then all difficulties will be resolved naturally in due course of time.

* * *

In the evening Saurabha showed Prabhupāda the preliminary plans for the new temple. He estimates the cost will come to at least eighty crores of rupees (eighty million dollars). Saurabha's drawings revealed magnificent plans for an entire city, centered around a huge temple structure. It will be surrounded by satellite temples, bathing *ghāṭas,* a commercial area, a *gurukula* campus, and other facilities. The whole area will be protected from flooding by a latticework of canals. The main feature is to be a gigantic planetarium within the dome of the main temple.

Śrīla Prabhupāda was extremely enthusiastic about the plans. He wants the planetarium to demonstrate the Vedic alternative to modern scientific cosmological propaganda, illustrating the structure of the universe as described in the *Śrīmad-Bhāgavatam.* Impressed with Saurabha's work, Prabhupāda suggested that the plans be presented to the state government with an application for official acquisition of the land we require. Prabhupāda always thinks big; he even suggested that we try to get them to relocate Calcutta's Dum Dum airport nearby. For Prabhupāda no vision is impossible, because it is for Kṛṣṇa.

January 22nd, 1976

This morning's walk took Prabhupāda north down the main road toward the Gaṅgā. He looked over the new building site, which Caitya-guru is going to supervise. Already some laborers are beginning work on the foundation. Prabhupāda instructed Saurabha to make up the site plans for the new residences.

Reiterating the point he made to the sand manufacturer yesterday, Prabhupāda explained that it is the sense that everything belongs to God that makes the difference between a *karmī* and a devotee. The ordinary men are constructing big houses to live in, and so are we. The materials, the bricks, wood, cement, and iron, are all supplied by God. But those who do it for their own benefit are "simply eating their sinful activities." Our construction, however, is for Kṛṣṇa's purpose; it is not for our own use.

As he strode down the road Prabhupāda noted storm clouds forming in the distance. He told us that rain at this time of year is good for the food grains. He quoted a verse from a book called *Khānara Vacana: Yadi varṣe māghera śeṣa, daṇḍa rājā puṇya deśa.*" This is the month of Māgha. So at the end of Māgha if there is a little rain, then it is to be understood that the king of that country is very pious and blessed. This time a little rain is required."

On the way back to the temple for the morning program, Prabhupāda saw that several men were standing around an almost-mature wheat crop. They were banging empty tins in an effort to drive away the birds, lest they eat the entire crop. Prabhupāda disagreed with their strategy. He said that every living being has a right to eat, so the solution is simply to grow more. Then there will be enough to go around. This is the Vedic conception.

Prabhupāda's ability to relate even the most seemingly ordinary event to *śāstra* always amazes everyone. Tamal Krishna Mahārāja expressed his appreciation of the scientific nature of the *Vedas,* and Prabhupāda agreed. "Therefore, we say, 'perfect.' *Śruti-pramāṇam.*"

* * *

Satsvarūpa Mahārāja sent a lengthy zonal report for December and the early part of this month. His Library Party is doing especially well. Many professors are taking orders for their own personal libraries, and teachers are placing orders for the abridged paperback *Bhagavad-gītā* for use in their courses. Altogether, the party has sold over 700 standing orders and is still going strong.

As well as this, many important book reviews are coming in as a result of their efforts. And Satsvarūpa Mahārāja himself is very actively preaching; he has at least one college engagement every day until the end of February, and on some days as many as five.

He also reported increased book distribution in several temples under his direction, notably Gainesville, Miami and Houston.

Previously the Denver temple had been trying to develop a

jewelry business with the hope of making large profits. But Prabhupāda has recently written, telling them that book distribution should be our only business because other types of business will simply create a bad atmosphere. Kuruśreṣṭha, the president, closed down the business, taking his men out on book distribution. Kuruśreṣṭha admitted that doing business was putting him in mundane consciousness, and the promises of huge amounts of profit coming to the temple never actually came about.

Satsvarūpa summed this situation up perfectly by saying, "The business world is such *māyā* that it entangles one with hopes of tremendous profits that are never finally realized."

Prabhupāda was happy to hear his thorough report, and he replied emphasizing the book distribution. "Even the proposal to open a new temple in Houston is secondary," he said. "Book distribution is our first business." Prabhupāda feels that the work of the Library Party is most important, as also is the college preaching. So Prabhupāda encouraged him, "Go on vigorously expanding this preaching. You are proceeding in the right way."

Jayatīrtha's November report for the West Coast zone also arrived. His was the top zone for book distribution for that month, remitting $116,000 to the BBT, a new record. However, he admitted that Tamal Krishna Mahārāja's RDTSKP topped them by $4,000. Yet, he expressed confidence that December would be a different story. They planned to hand in $200,000 and were aiming for a yearly total of $750,000 to the Book Fund.

His letter also included a section describing some newly-formed devotee businesses; but he had a different angle of vision than Kuruśreṣṭha. He pointed out that all business affairs are conducted outside of the temple precincts so as not to affect the spiritual atmosphere and that no temple president is allowed to become directly involved. He felt it is important for the temple presidents to concentrate solely on spreading Kṛṣṇa consciousness.

Jayatīrtha enumerated various reasons why he thought the devotees should be allowed to continue doing business. "I understand from several recent letters from Your Divine Grace to

Satsvarūpa Mahārāja that you are not very anxious to see businesses going on in the Society, except for book distribution business. I understand your objections, but I would like to make a few points in relationship to the businesses currently going on in the zone The businesses are handled by *gṛhasthas* who would generally not be engaged in *saṅkīrtana* activities otherwise. If they make a request to stop doing business and engage in direct preaching work, we move to facilitate this. The businesses make substantial contributions to the temples, and in this way allow the temples to distribute more books. I have seen that in temples that are depending completely on *saṅkīrtana* for all expenditures, that there are usually debts, and, at the same time, the preachers are forced to concentrate on collecting money rather than distributing books Another advantage is that it provides opportunity to engage *gṛhasthas* in activities that are beneficial to the Movement, rather than simply living off the temples. At the same time they are able to associate with other devotees, thus making it easier for them to maintain their Kṛṣṇa consciousness than it would be if they had to work at *karmī* jobs."

Finally he ended his report with another suggestion for relocation of the Dallas *gurukula,* this time to a large property in Santa Cruz. It will cost a large amount of money to continue to maintain the Dallas operation and start the new *gurukula,* and a BBT loan would be required to cover the costs. So he wanted to know what Śrīla Prabhupāda desired in this respect.

Śrīla Prabhupāda had already sent a lengthy outline to him about the *gurukula* a few days ago, which Jayatīrtha obviously hadn't received when he wrote this letter. Nevertheless, Prabhupāda answered his questions, presenting a perfect solution to several dilemmas.

He cleverly linked up the business aspirations of the *gṛhasthas* with their proclivity to have children, who then require education. "You have suggested that some men are best engaged in doing business. I agree. All *gṛhasthas* who are interested in doing business should do so in full swing. *Yat karoṣi yad aśnāsi yaj juhoṣi dadāsi yat/ yat tapasyasi kaunteya tat kuruṣva mad-arpaṇam.* Let this be the guiding principle. So let all the *gṛhasthas* who wish to, execute business full fledgedly in the

USA, and in this way support *gurukula*. Business must be done by the *gṛhasthas*, not by the *sannyāsīs* or *brahmacārīs*. Neither the *sannyāsīs* or *brahmacārīs* can be expected to support *gurukula*. The parents must take responsibility for their children, otherwise they should not have children. It is the duty of the individual parents. I am not in favor of taxing the temples. The parents must pay for the maintenance of their children. Neither can the BBT be expected to give any loans. Now the BBT 50% for construction is pledged to the projects in India—Bombay, Kurukṣetra, Māyāpur. The profits from the businesses should first go to support *gurukula* and balance may be given for the local temple's maintenance. *Gṛhasthas* can do business. It is best if the Temple Presidents are either *sannyāsīs* or *brahmacārīs*. If the *gṛhasthas* want to do book distribution, they should be given a commission of 5 to 10%, of which part must go to the *gurukula*."

Prabhupāda told him that important temple personnel can be maintained by the temple. He also suggested that by farming and selling the produce, *gṛhasthas* can make a living. "I can give good suggestions," he said, "but it is up to the GBC to practically execute them."

A third report also arrived, from Jagadīśa, who dwelt mainly on the situation of the *gurukula* in Dallas. They are drawing up plans for extensive renovation and expansion of the present facilities to bring it in line with government requirements. They are expecting their funds to increase through the new tax imposed on the North American temples. Apparently the school has suffered due to great inadequacies in the previous administration, but Jagadīśa just spent the last four months in Dallas trying to bring things to a higher standard. His letter was optimistic about the future developments. "I am convinced we are making good progress. And what is that progress? That you will be pleased with what we are doing. That is more important by millions of times than any other measure of success."

Since he had just written a long letter to Jayatīrtha covering these same topics, Prabhupāda did not reiterate his feelings, but referred Jagadīśa to Jayatīrtha's letter.

However, he did pick up on the theme of finance, particularly the proposed taxing of the temples, as well as a previous request for a BBT loan. "Actually it is the responsibility of the parents to maintain *gurukula.* By taxing the temples or taking loan from the BBT the parents are being allowed to avoid their responsibility. Before having a child the parents should see whether they shall be able to pay for their child's education. The GBC should make an injunction that if they beget children, then whatever the expenses are for supporting *gurukula* they must pay it."

He requested Jagadīśa to discuss everything with Jayatīrtha. He is clearly attempting a major restructuring of the *gurukula,* and wants his GBC to take the burden as much as possible.

* * *

In the early afternoon, immediately after lunch, Tamal Krishna Mahārāja and I sat with Śrīla Prabhupāda on the sunlit veranda. He sat on a chair and we at his feet, simply relishing his divine presence and the transcendental atmosphere of the holy *dhāma.*

Prabhupāda looked out through the arched porticos, over his ISKCON compound, and beyond the front gate. In the distance glistening slivers of light danced on the tranquil surface of Mother Ganges as she flowed down to Navadvīpa town and then beyond, on her long pilgrimage from the Himālayas to the Bay of Bengal. It was wonderfully gratifying to see him so perfectly and naturally situated—in his own environment so to speak—and hear him talk about various aspects of the movement as he shared his philosophical insights into the world and life in general.

He seems very much at ease in Māyāpur. He loves sitting and looking out over the flat and fertile land, its open fields stretching into the distance, the verdant landscape dotted with small, green trees and occasional temple spires.

A seemingly limitless expanse of rice paddies in every stage of development shows the results of the simple, honest labor of local villagers. Other fields yield carefully cultivated bounties of *dahl,* sugar-cane, vegetables, and other necessities of life. Men and beasts amble slowly up and down the road and along the rutted tracks.

It seems the perfect place to meet one's basic requirements of maintaining body and soul together. And in the midst of this natural opulence we are here; grateful recipients of the generosity of His Divine Grace, who is so expertly revealing the true spiritual nature of ourselves, the *dhāma,* and the all-merciful Lord, Śrī Caitanya Mahāprabhu.

* * *

In the evening a devotee brought the prototype of a new *mṛdaṅga* to show Śrīla Prabhupāda. Instead of a clay shell it had one of fiberglass, but was still fitted with leather straps and heads. Devotees in the West are working to produce a completely synthetic drum to replace the clay ones, which break very easily. Prabhupāda felt the shell was a little too thick and heavy, otherwise he liked it. He even played a little on it himself, although he said he was out of practice.

January 23rd, 1976

Śrīla Prabhupāda took his walk across the fields to the proposed temple site. He discussed with Jayapatākā Swami the possibility of convincing the government to give us the land we need for building the temple.

In pursuance of this idea, he later dictated a letter for Jayapatākā Mahārāja to hand-deliver to his New Delhi airport acquaintance, Mr. Chaudhuri, who works at the Department of Development and Planning in Calcutta. Prabhupāda viewed that meeting as Kṛṣṇa's arrangement. He wants the government to acquire the land for us, and fortuitously Mr. Chaudhuri works in the very department that decides such matters.

After briefly describing to Mr. Chaudhuri the Māyāpur project and his hopes of building an international city based on the Vedic culture, he requested him to visit Māyāpur for further discussion.

* * *

Every day Prabhupāda gives an abundance of practical guidance, ranging from advice on purchasing land, setting a daily monetary rate for the painting of the front wall, advising on what goods to sell from the rooms near the front gate, to deciding the conditions of employment for the building construction workers.

Jayapatākā Mahārāja has employed a huge number of men for the new building work, but today Prabhupāda told him that if he can't get it finished by the festival (which is in six weeks), then he should reduce the number of men to only fifty.

Jayapatākā Swami said he thought everything but the plumbing could be done. Prabhupāda said plumbing and electricity are not important, as long as the place is habitable. He told Jayapatākā to get a guarantee from the contractor that the basic construction would definitely be finished on time.

As he walked, he turned his attention to the situation in Nellore. He confirmed to Gopāla Kṛṣṇa that the foundation stone should be taken to Madras, which, he said, was a better place for a temple anyway. He also cautioned him that if we accept charity from such fallen women then we will have to share in their sinful activity. "But our Kṛṣṇa can eat even fire," he added. "If there is forest fire, Kṛṣṇa can eat. Unless He is able to eat other's sinful reactions how can He say *ahaṁ tvāṁ sarva-pāpebhyo mokṣayiṣyāmi.* He is capable, otherwise how can He say like that?"

* * *

The rest of the day Prabhupāda spent quietly in his room. He isn't lecturing in the mornings here, although he enjoys discussing a wide range of topics with his disciples and a few visitors in his room.

* * *

At lunch Prabhupāda requested that I learn how to cook from Harikeśa.

January 24th, 1976

Each morning at *guru-pūjā* Prabhupāda is personally giving out sweets to all the children here. He sits on the *vyāsāsana* as each child comes forward to receive his *prasādam.*

There is a small, two-year-old boy from Australia called Dāmodara, who persistently remains in front of the *vyāsāsana* each morning with his hand held out. Śrīla Prabhupāda gives him half a sweet, which Dāmodara pushes into his mouth. Then he moves his hand over the back of his head, wipes his open palm on his *śikhā,* and again holds it out.

Again Prabhupāda gives him another piece of sweet, and again Dāmodara repeats the ritual. There are no words exchanged, simply the boy's chubby palm going out for the sweet, up to his mouth, over his head, and back again for more. This exchange with Dāmodara has gone on for several mornings now, and Prabhupāda laughs to see him wipe his hand in such a fashion. "Who has taught him this?" he asked.

While this is going on the other children leap and dance and chant. Adoration for Prabhupāda and excitement to be in his presence shine in their eyes. It is obvious the young children are spontaneously attracted to Śrīla Prabhupāda because they instinctively understand that he is their best friend.

As he has done each morning, at the end of the program Prabhupāda circumambulated the Deities, accompanied by all the devotees and a *saṅkīrtana* party. He stopped to vigorously ring the bells hanging from the ceiling on either side of the small temple room, causing everyone to loudly chant and jump in ecstasy.

* * *

Mail continues to flow in steadily from around the world. One letter came from Puṣṭa Kṛṣṇa Swami in South Africa about the Mercedes car that he had promised to purchase for Prabhupāda. He said that although he intends to pay for it himself, for now he has taken money from Prabhupāda's book fund to finance the purchase. His intention is to repay it later.

Hearing this, Prabhupāda shook his head. Smiling, he told us the story of the disciple who invited his guru to his home and gave him a grand reception with nice decorations, elaborate *prasādam,* and all. The guru was delighted and amazed at such expenditure.

"Oh, it is all coming from you, O Spiritual Master. It is all your mercy," said the disciple.

The guru was pleased at this, until he returned home to discover that it really *was* coming from him. For when he looked in his bank book his balance was now zero!

January 25th, 1976

Prabhupāda decided to take his walk on the roof of the temple building. On the way up he inspected the top floor, where all the *brahmacārīs* stay. He did not like what he saw—everything was dirty and poorly maintained. Walking around the end of the veranda he saw thick wire strung to the wall as a crude washing line, gouging grooves in the plaster. He was very displeased.

He soon got everyone into action, cleaning and rearranging everything. He ordered the *brahmacārīs* to move immediately to the front-wall dwellings, saying that the rooms in the temple building were to be used only for guests. He commented that *brahmacārīs* means it will be dirty.

Jayapatākā Swami has decorated the roof-top area with potted *tulasī* plants and various flowers and shrubs. There are two rooms, one on either side of the central stairwell, where he and Bhavānanda Mahārāja stay. The flat roof offers ample space for walking, in addition to a panoramic view. From it one can observe not only our whole compound, but miles of open country.

As we walked around, Anantarāma Śāstrī joined us. Prabhupāda expressed his satisfaction that such an educated man has joined our movement, and he instructed Bhavānanda Mahārāja to make sure he is well looked after so that he may not go away.

Although a somewhat self-conscious individual, Śāstrījī was eager to recite a poem he had composed for Śrīla Prabhupāda's pleasure. As we walked, and without asking first, he broke out into melodious verse, singing the praises of Bhagavān Śrī Gopāla—or at least it seemed so. His chanting was impressive to my untrained ear; but Prabhupāda was alert. When Śāstrī sang *nāciye nāciye aile gopāla,* "My dear Gopāla, please come to me dancing," Prabhupāda stopped him.

"Don't manufacture knowledge. Take knowledge from Bhagavān. Don't order Bhagavān. Just follow Bhagavān. That is not wanted. don't write concocted poetries. That is not beneficial. Simply follow." Prabhupāda told him that his singing was sense gratification because he was giving instruction to Gopāla, "please come to me, *nāciye* dancing." He stressed that our process is to take instruction. "It is all nonsense. Why should you ask Gopāla to come to you? You cannot order. You must follow. We are to carry out the order of God, not to order God to carry out my order. That is mistake."

Prabhupāda went on for some time, condemning the attitude with which people generally approach God. He explained that in India they sing a traditional *ārati* song which repeats the words *sab ko sampatti de bhagavān. De bhagavān* means "give me." And in the West, he explained, the Christians also have the same idea. "The whole world," Prabhupāda observed, "they have accepted God as the order supplier: I order, You supply. The Christian church also, 'God, give us our daily bread.'"

"And if God doesn't give, then God is dead," Tamal Krishna Mahārāja added.

"Dead. This is going on. And our prayer is, 'I don't want anything. Simply engage me in Your service.' This is the real prayer, which is taught by Caitanya Mahāprabhu."

* * *

Jayapatākā Swami returned later in the day from Calcutta with a favorable report. Mr. Chaudhuri and his family will come to visit Śrīla Prabhupāda on Sunday, February 1st. The man was very happy to see Jayapatākā Mahārāja and enthusiastic to help.

* * *

Harikeśa is becoming increasingly ill. He looks weak and emaciated and has no strength. It is all he can do just to cook Śrīla Prabhupāda's lunch.

Prabhupāda observed him going to the toilet just after eating breakfast. He shook his head and quoted a Bengali proverb, "He who cannot sleep immediately upon resting and he who passes stool immediately after eating will very soon be called by Yamarāja. On the other hand, he who passes stool before eating and urine after, the physician cannot make a living from!"

* * *

In the evening I came into Prabhupāda's room just in time to catch the tail end of an hour-long conversation between Harikeśa and Śrīla Prabhupāda.

Harikeśa was posing questions about the description of Vedic cosmology in the newly published Fifth Canto of *Śrīmad-*

Bhāgavatam. Many confusing diagrams and captions have been included by the editors, and Prabhupāda said it will have to be revised because the editors have made mistakes.

Harikeśa was trying to clarify his own understanding of the position of the sun and moon, the general structure of the universe, and the exact length of one *yojana.*

I listened intently as Prabhupāda described how the planets move within the universal shell. He pointed to the chandelier hanging from the ceiling and compared the situation of the lights with that of the planets. He explained that all the planets move in unison around the Pole Star, and within that structure the sun has its own orbit.

Harikeśa asked many questions, until our ability to understand his explanations was stretched to its limits, and Prabhupāda finally stopped. Prabhupāda's knowledge appears fathomless.

I sat and watched as he got up from his seat and moved toward the door, smiling all the while. He seemed to have a deep serenity, to be carrying within himself a vast, limitless wellspring of knowledge and understanding and to possess a beautiful sobriety of the soul that attracted my mind more than ever before. I became absorbed in the natural flow of his movements, the gentility of his demeanor, and the soft expressiveness of his features.

Everything within the periphery of my vision, except Śrīla Prabhupāda, began to recede and fade as he seemed to emanate an increasingly bright effulgence, filling the whole room and beyond. It wasn't an ordinary light, nothing that could be *seen* like the beams from a torch or bulb. But it was there, more subtle than sunlight, expanding and shining through my mind and intelligence, pervading my consciousness, touching my soul. I became overwhelmed with appreciation of Prabhupāda's purity and grace. The feeling of wanting absolutely nothing whatever in life, other than to simply serve his lotus feet without any other concern, welled up in my heart.

I have never experienced a satisfaction greater than this. I felt it intensely. For perhaps the first time, I experienced what I can only describe as feelings of unconditional surrender, an unequivocal love, fully devoid of any material distraction or selfish interest. His very being shone and radiated, pervading everything, and I was his eternal servant.

It's hard to describe. It didn't seem that Śrīla Prabhupāda was doing anything more than he ever does. He is himself. But somehow, for once, my own consciousness suddenly opened and became receptive enough to perceive him more clearly than ever before.

And then he disappeared through the door and down the corridor— leaving me once again wondering just who he really is.

January 26th, 1976

Before Prabhupāda took his walk he sat in his room and listened while Bhavānanda Mahārāja read aloud a newly released pamphlet. It was from the neighboring Caitanya Gauḍīya Maṭha, which is led by one of his prominent Godbrothers, Tīrtha Mahārāja. This propaganda piece, written in somewhat convoluted prose, declared the glories of Tīrtha Mahārāja, making several outrageous claims. The tract described him as Śrīla Bhaktisiddhānta Sarasvatī's most confidential disciple, "almost a counterpart." It also stated that his preaching had attracted people from all over the world, that his *maṭha* stretched for over a mile (which would include ISKCON's temple), and that twenty-four hour *kīrtana* is going on there (only *our* men are doing this). Obviously he was trying to claim a status for himself that he does not deserve.

Prabhupāda's reaction was very cool. He queried that if he is such a great personality, why does he have to advertise it. "Why is he trying to explain?," he said. "What is the use of explanation? If a great personality is unknown, and he has to be known by explanatory notes, then how is he a great personality?" Displeased with the false propaganda, Prabhupāda told us, "If he is reciting such false things how he can be a Vaiṣṇava? He is simply a pounds-and-shillings man. He was never very dear to Guru Mahārāja, who feared that if he sent him away he would cause much trouble. Therefore he let him stay as manager, even though so many complaints were there against him." He shook his head with distaste.

"Whereas others trained their sons to be *brahmacārīs* and *sannyāsīs,*" Prabhupāda continued, "he trained his to be a lawyer. They sent their sons to the temple and *gurukula,* but he sent his to the office because he always intended to go to court to take over the Gauḍīya Maṭha proprietorship. His past is very black. I do not wish to discuss it!"

Prabhupāda told Tamal Krishna Mahārāja to keep the paper, "because these rascals they may create some trouble."

Bhavānanda Mahārāja told a story indicating that they were already creating "trouble" for us. Recently, Bhavānanda was detained and brought to court on kidnapping charges after a Bengali village woman and her son had joined our *āśrama* against the wishes of her husband. In court, our lawyer, reputedly the best in Nadia, asked Bhavānanda who was behind it all. The lawyer said the husband was a simple village laborer who would not have had the intelligence nor the money to bring such a case. The lawyer was convinced that the man had been put up to it by one of the Gauḍīya Maṭha members attempting to harass us.

Recently members from the Caitanya Maṭha proposed that we link with them. But despite Śrīla Prabhupāda having gone there several times, Tīrtha Mahārāja will not visit Māyāpur Candrodaya Mandir. Prabhupāda reasoned that he only wants the connection in order to capitalize on Prabhupāda's preaching success, to claim it for himself. If Western devotees go to his Maṭha, it will increase his prestige. Obviously disagreeing with the idea that he is a senior preacher to himself, Prabhupāda named two other prominent godbrothers in Navadvīpa district who have a similar frame of mind. Prabhupāda told us, "That was the policy ... that, 'Although Bhaktivedānta Swami is propagating throughout, he is subordinate to us, under our instruction.'"

He rose and went up onto the roof for his walk. As we walked around the perimeter he talked extensively about Vedic culture, giving some fascinating insights into its psychology.

Prabhupāda recalled that formerly, at least before Indian independence, people were still very honorable. He remem-

January 17, 1976—
"Our party stopped to take breakfast in a large grove of several hundred mango trees."

January 17, 1976—
"Prabhupāda stepped forward and cut a large ribbon, officially opening the gateway."

January 17, 1976—
"The metal gates were opened and he happily walked through the arch. . . ."

January 17, 1976—
"He moved steadily along the road, past the original thatched hut where he first stayed when he got the land. . . ."

January 28, 1976—"Śrīla Prabhupāda is enjoying his walks in the mornings . . . and he enjoys the company of the young *gurukula* students."

February 5, 1976—"The head *pūjārī,* Janānivāsa, assisted by . . . Jagadīśa, performed the *abhiśeka* ceremony of Śrī Śrī Gaura Nitāi."

February 7, 1976—"Brightly painted in green, yellow and red, the 'Nitai Pada Kamala' was gaily decorated . . . with strings of orange marigolds."

February 7, 1976— "Tamal Krishna Mahārāja helped Śrīla Prabhupāda on board over the rickety bamboo ramp."

February 16, 1976—"More and more visitors are coming for *darśana* in the evenings. . . ."

February 20, 1976— "Prabhupāda gave a wonderful lecture requesting the devotees to do two things: help develop Māyāpur and distribute many books."

March 6, 1976—"With his senior *sannyāsīs*, Prabhupāda went to the Caitanya Gaudiya Math at 6:30 A.M. to meet Govinda Maharaja."

March 7, 1976— "As he descended the staircase I walked immediately in front of him, keeping always just two or three steps ahead, with my eye on his feet."

March 10, 1976—"Many of the new arrivals are being housed in the new building . . . in temporary shelters made from split bamboo and tarpaulins erected on the bare concrete."

March 11, 1976—"'If you fall down, then punishment is you make suicide . . . Then next life we shall see.' Viṣṇujana Mahārāja withdrew to the back as the other *sannyāsīs* sought clarification."

March 12, 1976—"Everyone gathered around for a close inspection before it suddenly rose in the air and headed off across the fields."

March 12, 1976—"He also visited the newly erected public exhibition and saw some of the displays."

March 15, 1976—
"Sridhar Swami and Prabhupāda took *prasādam* together on the veranda. . . ."

March 16, 1976—
"At a grand initiation ceremony . . . he awarded *sannyāsa* to seven men. . . ."

March 17, 1976—
"Prabhupāda took his morning walk on the roof with an entourage of GBCs and new *sannyāsīs*."

March 17, 1976—
"Prabhupāda laughingly depicted the intransigence of the scientists with a funny story about 'scissor philosophy.'"

March 17, 1976—
"His hand emerged from beneath the surface with two fingers moving like a pair of scissors. 'No, it is scissor! It is scissor!'"

March 18, 1976—
"All the devotees gathered on the lawn for a group photo, forming a huge 'U' with Śrīla Prabhupāda in the center."

bered one lawyer whose father had died insolvent, owing many *lakhs* of rupees. When he became a wealthy barrister he then called all his father's creditors and repaid them.

He explained that this is the law of Manu. If a son inherits all the assets of his father, he must also inherit all his debts. However, a father leaving his son large debts means he is an enemy. One would never expect to find an enemy within his own family, but according to Caṇakya Paṇḍit there are four enemies in the family: the father who dies a debtor, a son who is a rascal, a mother who marries again, and a beautiful wife.

"Now everyone is hankering after very beautiful wife. And Caṇakya Paṇḍit said, 'Then you are bringing one enemy.' Just see what is the type of civilization. Because if you become too much attached to wife, then you'll never be able to go out of home and take *sannyāsa.* Of course," he added laughing, "everyone's wife is very attractive."

"Even if ugly!" Tamal Krishna Mahārāja chimed in.

"Yes. It is in one's eye that she is very beautiful. It does not require others' recommendation. It doesn't matter whether she is low caste or high caste; if she is attractive, then it is all right. Therefore, *rūpavatī bhāryā śatruḥ.* Caṇakya Paṇḍit's instructions are very, very nice."

Prabhupāda laughed as he recounted how his father had saved him from this material entanglement. "You know my story? My father's instruction?" he asked us. We smiled eagerly and crowded in a little more to hear. "Yes. My wife was never beautiful to my sight, so I wanted to marry again, and my father advised, 'Don't do it. She is your friend, that you don't like her.' Just see."

"But still, Prabhupāda, you said that your school work was a little impeded," Tamal Krishna said.

"Hm? No, that is natural. In young time, when there is young girl. That is also said, *yauvane kukkarī sundarī.* When a woman is in full youth, even she is like dog, she is beautiful."

Everyone laughed loudly, and Tamal Krishna asked whose statement that was.

"I do not know, but this is going on," Prabhupāda grinned. As usual, he gave the philosophical underpinning, "It is by nature's arrangement the woman is given one chance at the time of youthfulness. Otherwise how she will be given protection by a man? They require protection. If somebody is not attracted, then how she gets protection? This is natural."

He revealed the psychology of arranged marriages, still prevalent in India. In the West this practice is considered objectionable, and no one understands its true purpose. But a spiritually based society is different. "The social system in India is that a boy, say twenty or twenty-five years, and a girl, twelve to sixteen years, they must be married. Must be married. And before marriage the girl should not see any boy, and the boy should not see any woman. Then life is all right. Nowadays it has been practice that the boy goes to see the girl, but formerly it was not so. He should see the girl when the marriage actually takes place, not before that. The psychology is that when they require a man or girl, so whatever she is or he is, they accept and remain chaste. So there is no separation."

He strongly denounced the defective, cultureless modern civilization, comparing it to a society of pigs, because the pig has no discrimination in the matter of eating and having sex. They eat anything and have sex even with their immediate relatives.

He declared that, overall, people are acting on the level of animals. He quoted the *Bhāgavatam's* description of democracy—people who are like hogs, dogs, camels, and asses glorify and vote in as their leaders other big animals. "Just study whether it is not the civilization of asses and pigs. You have to understand first of all. Is it not?" He gave a succinct one-sentence appraisal of modern life: "They are working hard like an ass just to become an ideal pig! Is it not this civilization? Yes. How *śāstra* has picked up the example, just see. *Nāyaṁ deho deha-bhājāṁ nṛloke kaṣṭān kāmān arhate viḍ-bhujāṁ ye.* This is not civilization. "*This* is civilization, *tapasya:* no meat-eating, no this, no this, that, and become perfect. Ideal *brāhmaṇa* life. This is civilization. *Athāto brahma-jijñāsā.* Unless you become civilized like this, there is no opportunity of *brahma-jijñāsa.* And so long you do not inquire about Brahman, that you remain, that pigs and hogs and asses. Whole day and night eat stool, and as soon as you get another opposite party, have sex. Doesn't matter whether it is daughter or mother or sister. That's all.

"Take Freud's philosophy and become highly advanced in civilization! Now Freud's philosophy is being translated in Hindi and so many other languages. We are advancing in civilization, Indians. They are translating this Freud's philosophy, pig civilization." He laughed. "People therefore do not come to us. They avoid us because 'They [the devotees] are not pigs.'"

* * *

A telegram arrived from Mahāṁsa Swami in the South: "NELLORE LADY REFUSED RELAXING CONDITIONS. PLEASE ADVISE."

It seems Mahāṁsa hadn't yet received Prabhupāda's letter written on the eighteenth, so Prabhupāda reiterated his clear and simple instructions. There should be no relaxing of conditions on our part. We can either purchase or accept charity, but we cannot accept any of their conditions. When he signed the letter later in the day he added in his own handwriting, "If they decline, then try to acquire the land through Government because we have already installed the Foundation Stone."

* * *

Sometimes during his evening massage Prabhupāda chats a little before sleeping. This evening as he lay on his bed in the quiet semidarkness, with me perched cross-legged alongside him, he asked if there were any mosquitos inside his net. "It is such a cruel animal," he said.

I asked if the living entity obtained that sort of body because it desired to harm others.

Prabhupāda said, "Yes, it wants to drink the blood of others, so it is given facility. But only a very small body so it can only take less than a drop. It has one pipe, and in less than a second it can immediately penetrate the skin, so wonderful is its creation." But he added that, still, nature has an arrangement whereby before biting, the mosquito buzzes in the ear just to warn its victim: "'I am here.' The scientists cannot make even one such mosquito, yet they claim God does not exist," he said.

Every night when Śrīla Prabhupāda takes rest, Ānakadundubhi comes into Prabhupāda's work room to set up a very large, square net over his desk and *āsana* so that he can translate in the night without botheration. The net is almost like a small tent, and sometimes mosquitos get trapped inside it during its erection. Therefore I have developed the habit of checking it after finishing Prabhupāda's massage in the bedroom. I sit inside it for a minute or so and capture and remove any that may have been trapped.

Last evening I was attempting to remove a couple of the unfriendly insects when, to my surprise, Śrīla Prabhupāda also entered under the protective canopy to begin his night's work. He was sitting behind his desk unperturbed as I, on my hands and knees on the other side, tracked down one last mosquito. I had his woollen cap in my hand, using it as a swatter. Seeing my prey settled high in one corner of the net, I swung. "Whap!" The tiny body fell to the ground, apparently dead. I wasn't too happy at having killed it, but what could be done? If it wasn't removed, it would bite Śrīla Prabhupāda all night, disturb his translation work, and maybe even give him malaria.

I picked up the corpse and tossed it out from under the net. It landed a few inches away on the clean white sheets. Prabhupāda silently watched the whole procedure. Suddenly, as we both looked on, it stirred, shook its wings and flew off. It wasn't dead after all. Śrīla Prabhupāda gave a happy exclaim, "Ah! Hare Kṛṣṇa!" He was very pleased to see that I had only stunned my quarry.

I was also happy and became more so when he narrated a similar history of his own. "I also did this. One insect was buzzing; it was very annoying, and I gave it a slap and it fell down." His face softened with compassion and regret. "Then I was very sorry, 'Oh! I have killed this poor creature.' But suddenly it got up and flew off. Oh! Then I was very glad!"

His remembrance gave me another revealing glimpse of Śrīla Prabhupāda's kindness and concern for every living being, even those that might be aggressors. I felt happy to have escaped an offense to the mosquito and privileged to have shared a moment of intimate confession with Śrīla Prabhupāda.

January 27th, 1976

This morning Mahāmāyā dāsī, one of the Western ladies serving here in Māyāpur, gave me a polite note requesting me to ask Śrīla Prabhupāda a question for her. She wanted to know whether women could be allowed into the temple room during menstruation. "If so," she asked, "should they wear silken garments?" The reason she asked was because ladies in India generally do not enter the temple during this time.

I broached the subject with His Divine Grace after his morning nap. He immediately became disturbed, and without replying to my question, sent me to get Tamal Krishna Mahārāja. When Tamāl came in, Prabhupāda asked him, "What is this? He is *brahmacārī*, and he is being approached by this woman?"

I explained to Tamal Krishna what the inquiry was, and showed him the note. He then assured Śrīla Prabhupāda that things were not what they seemed. He described the letter as very discreet and polite, having been signed 'The *mātājīs* of Māyāpur.' "Apart from that," Tamal Krishna said, "Hari-śauri is actually a householder." Although I wear white cloth, because I have never once made any reference to my wife, Śrīla Prabhupāda assumed that I was a *brahmacārī*.

Prabhupāda gave a diffident smile. "Oh, I thought he was *brahmacārī*, and he is being approached by some woman for this. Now I can understand it is all right." So he gave his permission for the ladies to attend the temple functions and approved the wearing of silk. Later they were duly informed.

Prabhupāda's reaction was all the more endearing not just because of the vigilance he demonstrated in protecting his disciple's spiritual life, but also because he was completely free from any false ego in the matter. He did not become at all defensive when he saw that things were not quite what he had first thought. Rather, he showed his purity and absence of false ego by his humble and objective response.

* * *

Every day I try to give Prabhupāda a really good workout during his massage. For at least one-and-a-half hours I rub, squeeze, and knead his body while he sits meditatively.

Tamal Krishna Mahārāja mentioned to me that on the day he had given Prabhupāda his massage in Calcutta, he had noticed that when no one else was present, Prabhupāda's body was very soft and supple, but as soon as a visitor entered he became alert and his body tensed up. It is a fact. Here in Māyāpur, with no visitors to speak of, he sits so relaxed and quiet that he practically seems unaware that I am massaging him at all. Several times he has inquired, when I have completed my work, whether I was finished or not. It is almost like someone taking their car into a garage for a service, going off for an hour or so, and then returning to inquire whether everything is done.

January 28th, 1976

Śrīla Prabhupāda is enjoying his walks in the mornings. He mentioned today that he finds it especially pleasing that he can take his full exercise without leaving our property. Because it is still a little brisk before the sun rises he is wearing a saffron colored cape to prevent catching a chill. And he enjoys the company of the young *gurukula* students as they join him on the road to enter the temple for the Deity greeting and *guru-pūjā.* He derives a great deal of satisfaction from their enthusiastic participation in the dancing and chanting. They share a natural rapport and he returns their affection with smiles and words of encouragement.

* * *

After lunch this afternoon Śrīla Prabhupāda sat at the end of the veranda, enjoying the view of the Gaṅgā. Suddenly loud shouting and the slam of a door broke his tranquillity. He sent me to investigate.

I found Tamal Krishna Mahārāja sitting in his room before a plate of *prasādam,* clearly upset. He had just had an argument with Harikeśa over who should get the remnants of Śrīla Prabhupāda's *prasādam.* As I stood, Harikeśa came back in and began berating him again.

Several days ago Tamal Krishna had asked Prabhupāda if he could eat the extra that was cooked for him because he found the kind of rice the devotees eat here in Māyāpur too coarse for his digestion. Prabhupāda had approved.

However, Harikeśa had previously received instructions from Śrīla Prabhupāda while we were in Vṛndāvana that all his remnants could not be monopolized by his immediate servants, but should be distributed to other devotees. As cook, Harikeśa resented Tamal Krishna's acquisition of all the leftovers; while Tamal Krishna argued that he was only taking what was left in the pots and not what was left on Prabhupāda's plate. Thus the dispute. Tamal Krishna also complained that he should not have been interrupted while he was honoring *prasādam.*

Prabhupāda called them both onto the veranda. After hearing their arguments, he managed to resolve the issue to everyone's satisfaction. Prabhupāda said that Harikeśa should not have interrupted Tamal Krishna while he was eating. Respecting *prasādam* is a very important function, and there should be no disturbance. He said that otherwise one's appetite is lost and indigestion results.

He gave his permission for Tamal Krishna to eat what was left in the pots, but also confirmed his desire that his *prasādam* be distributed.

He told us there is absolutely no difference between what is on the plate and what is in the pot. Whether cooked for guru or Kṛṣṇa it is all *prasādam* and all just as spiritually potent. When I mentioned that in the *Caitanya-caritāmṛta* there was a distinction made between *mahā-prasādam,* the remnants of the Deity offering, and *mahā-mahā prasādam,* which is the spiritual master's remnants, Prabhupāda said the distinction was made for reference only. It is all *prasādam.*

Then he went on to explain that the Vaiṣṇava attitude in dealing with one another is one of humility. He gave the example of the pilgrims that come here to Māyāpur. As one man comes along the road, another tries to touch his feet. The former shies away from being so honored because he is thinking, "I am not a Vaiṣṇava, I am just an ordinary man. I am simply trying my best to become a Vaiṣṇava." On the other hand the person who is touching his feet is thinking that unless he gets the dust of a Vaiṣṇava on his head he will not be able to advance.

"Actually," Prabhupāda said, "this is a fact. One has to be blessed by a devotee to become a devotee. And he who is the servant of the servant of the servant—one hundred times removed—is not worse than he who is directly serving the guru. If one thinks, 'Because I am direct servant, I am better than others,' then he is not a Vaiṣṇava. To offer respects to Guru and not to his disciples, this is wrong. This is not Vaiṣṇava. One has to be humble and try to serve all Vaiṣṇavas—not some and not others."

January 29th, 1976

Prabhupāda is taking his morning walk on the roof every day now and following the same daily routine: massage at 10:00 a.m. on the veranda and answering letters; lunch at 1:30 p.m., a rest, and return downstairs by 4:00 p.m.

* * *

A short report arrived from Hansadūta, who is now back in Germany. He stated that relations with the government are getting worse. They are harassing the devotees and threatening more raids on the temple. Although after months of investigation and persecution the only offense they can attribute to us is a very minor one of collecting money without permission, on this basis they are freezing our bank accounts and withholding 700,000 DM. The German devotees are becoming discouraged but are still struggling to distribute books.

In the meantime, since he left our party, Hansadūta has been busily purchasing vehicles for the formation of an all-India village-to-village traveling *saṅkīrtana* party. Two forty-five-seater Mercedes buses and a van will be driven overland to India to arrive by the festival. He has also decided to introduce the program in Germany, and another two buses have been purchased for touring there.

Hansadūta expressed his devotional sentiments in his final paragraph. "I feel helpless in this matter, and pray to Kṛṣṇa to give me intelligence to combat these rascals. I know that Kṛṣṇa can reverse the situation in a minute and if He likes I may go on struggling a whole lifetime to convince them of the value of your message without success; still I am thankful that by your mercy that I have been awakened to devotional service which is the ultimate goal of life. I shall try to spread your teachings under all circumstances to everyone."

Prabhupāda sent a short reply of encouragement comparing his struggle there with the fight between Hiraṇyakaśipu and Prahlāda Mahārāja and to Kaṁsa's fight with Kṛṣṇa. "Prahlāda must come out triumphant," he told him. So similarly, in this case Kṛṣṇa will come out triumphant without a doubt. Prabhupāda also approved his plan for village preaching.

* * *

For the past few days I have been going down to the kitchen, with Prabhupāda's approval, to learn how to cook from Harikeśa. We are using Śrīla Prabhupāda's three-tiered cooker.

Previously Harikeśa used to time it so that Prabhupāda's *prasādam* was ready for him immediately after he had bathed and dressed. But because he is taking his massage early now, Prabhupāda has agreed to a fixed time of 1:30 p.m. for lunch.

Because of his illness, Harikeśa was late beginning today. By the time Prabhupāda was back in his room and *prasādam* was due, we were still cooking. Foolishly, I did not go up and inform Śrīla Prabhupāda the reason for the delay, although I thought of doing it. I grew increasingly uneasy as the clock ticked on to 1:35, 1:40. Instead I kept thinking, "Another few minutes. Another few minutes and he'll be finished."

Suddenly Ānakadundubhi, the extremely lanky English devotee who sometimes stands guard at Prabhupāda's floor, burst into the kitchen. "Hari-śauri! Hari-śauri! Prabhupāda has been ringing the bell for the last ten minutes, and no one is answering. I think you had better go up!"

I zipped up the stairs full of anxiety and opened the door to Śrīla Prabhupāda's room. I got down to offer my obeisances, but froze halfway as the blast of Prabhupāda's anger hit me. I have never seen him so furious. He sat with his back stiff and straight. His face was flushed and his top lip quivered as he shouted at me for being negligent. "I have been ringing for ten minutes! You didn't hear? Where have you been? Where is *prasādam?*"

I tried to explain why we were late, that I was just waiting until his *prasādam* was ready. But the more I tried to pacify him the more agitated he became as he rammed home his point.

"I don't want your *prasādam!* Don't bring it! You rascal! Now you sit in your room and don't go anywhere unless I call you!"

His anger had the right effect. Due to dullness I had neglected my duty, which was to serve him and keep him informed about what is happening. His sharp words crashed through the cloud of ignorance covering my brain as I realized that my inattentiveness was simply *māyā.* I hung my head and stopped trying to defend my position. Finally he relented a little. "Now bring whatever is done. It doesn't matter, just bring whatever is there." I ran down and brought up whatever was ready. He accepted it without further comment and with no sign of any agitation whatsoever. As easily as it had arisen, his anger had abated.

After clearing his plate and wiping the desk down, I retired to my room and did not stir from there for the rest of the day.

There was no personal motive in his chastisement. Whether displaying anger or a soft and gentle humor Prabhupāda is always on the transcendental platform. The effect of his instructions are always the same, no matter how they are delivered. One always ends up more Kṛṣṇa conscious.

Prabhupāda is mercifully showing me the proper service attitude. In the spiritual world everyone is fully and completely aware of their duty to Kṛṣṇa, at all times, without even a moment's diversion. Prabhupāda is trying to train us to the highest standard. My false ego has taken a battering. And I am left humbled and relieved, with a deeper understanding of what real spiritual awareness is all about.

January 30th, 1976

Gopāla Kṛṣṇa arrived today with news from Nellore. It turns out that the two sisters will not change the conditions on their "gift" of land under any circumstance.

Prabhupāda decided on a radical solution to the dispute. He told him to remove the foundation stone from the property in Nellore and send it to Madras. He then sent a letter to Śravaṇānanda and Bhāvabhūti instructing them to find some land immediately, buy it, and begin collecting for a temple.

Gopāla Kṛṣṇa also reported that contracts for the completion of the work in Bombay are now finalized, the work set to go ahead without delay.

In discussing the India projects Tamal Krishna Goswāmī suggested to Prabhupāda that his Rādhā-Dāmodara party could send all their profits above cost, possibly US$50,000 monthly, directly for the projects in Purī, Māyāpur, Bombay, and Kurukṣetra, rather than through the Los Angeles BBT. Tamāl thought that his men would be all the more enlivened if they knew specifically where their collection money was going.

Prabhupāda was agreeable and sent a letter to Rāmeśvara to confirm these arrangements. He also informed him that the BBT should immediately send US$100,000 to India right away and seven lakhs of rupees each month thereafter to Bombay as part of the EEC contract fulfillment.

Caitya-guru has been put in charge of organizing the project of building more rooms along the northern side of the property here in Māyāpur. The work is now going on vigorously. The plans have been drawn up, and already 150 men are digging the foundation. The new building will run the full length of the land from east to west. It'll be some 1,000 feet long, half the width of the existing guest house, with the same style of arches and eaves.

Looking out across to the building site from his balcony, Prabhupāda tried to instill some sense of urgency into Caitya-guru by stressing that he wants this all to be done by the festival. "It can only be done by your mercy, Śrīla Prabhupāda," Caitya-guru told him.

Prabhupāda laughed and replied, "And if it is not done, that means I have no mercy?"

January 31st, 1976

For many months a thief named Agarwal has been masquerading as Acyutānanda Swami in several states. He's been making Life Members and keeping their fees. Our men only heard about him when the new "Members" came to claim their benefits. He was eventually apprehended with stolen Life Membership forms, rubber stamps, and other paraphernalia. Before being handed over to the police he made a plea for mercy. Thus he was brought here to Māyāpur to see Śrīla Prabhupāda. He admitted to fraudulently using ISKCON's name to extort funds; but he claimed that he was truly interested in becoming a devotee.

After speaking to him Prabhupāda showed great mercy. Rather than involve the police he decided to give him a chance to reform himself. The man was to stay here in Māyāpur, chant Hare Kṛṣṇa, and render some service.

Agarwal seemed to be serious. He has even accompanied Prabhupāda on some of his walks. Prabhupāda therefore made no further reference to his nefarious activities. However, early this morning he was intercepted at the front gate. He was on his way out with his bags packed.

Jayapatākā Mahārāja asked Śrīla Prabhupāda what should be done with him. Prabhupāda said we should turn him over to the police. Later in the morning Agarwal was taken to the Navadvīpa lock-up and formally charged.

It is an excellent example of the term "unfortunate." Although an outright criminal, Agarwal had somehow or other received the special mercy of a pure devotee of the Lord. But because of his nature he could not take advantage of it, so he is now suffering the results of his mischievous deeds.

* * *

Prabhupāda has invited Gaura Govinda Mahārāja, at present in Orissa, to come to Māyāpur and translate his books. Since there are some delays in occupying the newly donated land in Bhuvanesvar, Mahārāja is there alone without men or money. So Prabhupāda felt it best that Gaura Govinda come here, at least until the festival.

* * *

Prabhupāda continues to follow his usual daily routine. The days are quiet, with no visitors to speak of. It is satisfying to see him getting the well-deserved rest and replenishment he needs.

Harikeśa however, is getting sicker each day. This morning

as I massaged Prabhupāda on the veranda, he watched Harikeśa slowly emerge from his room. Harikeśa was pale. He hunched over as he shuffled along the veranda to the bathroom before going downstairs to begin cooking. Though it was 11:00 a.m. he had just got out of bed. Prabhupāda asked me what he plans to do.

I told Śrīla Prabhupāda that Harikeśa thinks his condition is colitis. And he feels that if he stays in India, it will only get worse. He feels that only a return to the West will enable him to get well. But while he feels this way, Harikeśa just doesn't want to leave Prabhupāda's service. But Prabhupāda told me that one's health is primary.

February 1st, 1976

As I laid out the straw mat on the sunlit veranda to prepare for his massage, Śrīla Prabhupāda drew my attention to some sparrows making a nest. They had chosen a hole in the wall behind the electrical circuit box just outside Prabhupāda's sitting-room window. He said their chirping disturbed him at night while translating his books. So before they could build a complete nest and settle in, I removed the bits of straw they had gathered.

But as I began the massage one of the birds returned and started to rebuild the nest, flying back and forth with small pieces of straw. I crumpled some paper and stuffed it into the hole to block it.

So when the sparrow came back and found its access barred, it pecked, undaunted, at the paper for almost half an hour, trying to open up the hole to continue its home-making. When the bird found this too difficult, it flew off and returned with its mate. Together they worked hard to remove the paper, eventually succeeding. By pecking and tugging in unison, they removed the paper and began to build again. All the while Śrīla Prabhupāda watched without comment.

When the birds flew away to get more straw, I again filled the hole with the paper, this time forcing it in tight so that the sparrows couldn't remove it. Again the sparrows spent a long time trying to regain access, but this time were unsuccessful. Eventually they accepted defeat, gave up, and left.

Prabhupāda then drew an interesting parallel. He told me that even though the birds had eyes, they could not see. Although they were trying so hard to build their house, they couldn't see that the person who had prevented them stood nearby watching. So they continued on in ignorance, trying to make adjustments and struggling against the superior arrangement.

He explained how, in the same way, materialistic persons, though having eyes, cannot see how *māyā,* the material energy, is supervising all their efforts. They simply struggle on, making adjustments, hoping to improve their lives and secure their place in the material world, not understanding that *māyā* is watching their every move and defeating them at every step.

* * *

As promised, Mr. Chaudhuri and family arrived. Śrīla Prabhupāda happily received him, like a father receiving his son. Mr. Chaudhuri clearly has the highest regard for Śrīla Prabhupāda and is impressed with the Māyāpur project. With Jayapatākā Swami he looked over the entire compound. Prabhupāda showed him the plans for the Vedic city and the land that he wants the government to acquire for the project.

Mr. Chaudhuri promised to help Jayapatākā Mahārāja in every way possible to get the application approved. His wife was even more enthusiastic and challenged her husband that if he is truly a Hindu then he must help Śrīla Prabhupāda.

Mr. and Mrs. Chaudhuri took lunch on the balcony. As we served them sumptuous *prasādam,* Prabhupāda sat to the side in his chair, hosting them graciously. While they ate, he kept the conversation light and jolly, thus allowing them to eat without distraction.

* * *

Harikeśa spent considerable time in Śrīla Prabhupāda's room this evening trying to persuade Prabhupāda to give him *sannyāsa.* His chief rationale was that unless one is a *sannyāsī* it is difficult to get the facility to preach in our Society. He said he has visited many temples but is rarely asked to give a class. Yet he feels that if he was a *sannyāsī* he would always be offered the opportunity to preach.

Śrīla Prabhupāda, however, did not agree with his viewpoint. He also brought up other practical considerations, such as who would do his service of transcribing his nightly dictations, the cooking, and so forth? Prabhupāda thoroughly defeated all Harikeśa's arguments. Then he sent him out.

I was out on the veranda as Harikeśa emerged into the night air, with his ego somewhat shattered, but quite blissful. He was satisfied to have been put in his place by the mercy of Śrīla Prabhupāda.

February 2nd, 1976

In the early morning before *maṅgala ārati* Prabhupāda sent me to get Tamal Krishna Goswami. He told him that after serious consideration, he had decided that Harikeśa may take *sannyāsa.* He suggested that Harikeśa travel and preach with the Rādhā-Dāmodara party. He should be trained to eventually take charge of one of the buses.

This was clearly a surprise to Tamal Krishna Mahārāja, who has successfully headed up the RDTSKP for the last three years. During this time he has expanded the party's operation from one bus doing small festivals in colleges to more than a dozen vehicles with nearly one hundred men selling tens of thousands of books each month all over America.

He was a little wary because he and Harikeśa do not always enjoy a smooth relationship; they are a somewhat volatile mix. Nevertheless, Tamal agreed to the proposal because Prabhupāda wants it. He admitted that Harikeśa certainly has the intelligence and qualification to do the job.

As for his personal services, Prabhupāda thought of a good solution: Dayānanda and his wife, Nandarāṇī. Dayānanda is here in Māyāpur hoping to learn Sanskrit. So Prabhupāda said that if he became his secretary, he could personally teach him Sanskrit. Dayānanda could then assist him with his translation work. Nandarāṇī could transcribe his nightly work as well as cook. I was sent to inform Harikeśa of Prabhupāda's decision.

The unexpected news immediately sent Harikeśa in a mental spin, simultaneously elated and distressed. He had happily accepted his defeat last night and was looking forward to staying with Śrīla Prabhupāda as his menial *brahmacārī* servant indefinitely. Now, although he is happy about being awarded *sannyāsa*, it means he will have to leave the party. He lamented to me, "Once you leave Prabhupāda's personal party, everyone knows, you never come back!" The *yajña* is to be held in three days.

* * *

In another discussion later in the day with Bhavānanda Mahārāja, Prabhupāda decided that the Deities for the proposed new temple in Māyāpur should be life-size, like the Hyderabad Deities. He wants to install Pañca-tattva, Lord Caitanya, and His personal associates, with at least five predecessor gurus, Rādhā-Kṛṣṇa, and the eight principal *gopīs*.

February 3rd, 1976

Prabhupāda walked on the roof this morning. Sudāmā Mahārāja told him that many students in the West are now beginning to appreciate his extraordinary feat of spreading Kṛṣṇa consciousness all around the world. He said even some yogis and swamis hold him in high esteem for what he has done.

Bhavānanda Mahārāja complimented Prabhupāda as the only true resident of Bhāratavarṣa. He explained that is because Prabhupāda is the only one to actually fulfill Lord Caitanya's instructions. Prabhupāda gracefully conceded. He acknowledged that it is now a matter of history. Then Prabhupāda mused for a moment, thinking of the difficulties he has had with some of his Godbrothers. He explained they are unable to recognize his achievements because of envy. But he said that this was not a new thing. Even during the time of his Guru Mahārāja, although they knew Śrīla Bhaktisiddhānta liked him very much, they would refer to him as *kaca-gṛhastha*, "a rotten *gṛhastha*." And he said that even now they are thinking, "What is this? This *gṛhastha* has come out more than us?"

Yet, Prabhupāda said that not all of the Gauḍīya-maṭha

men felt like that. Previously his Godbrother Śrīdhar Swami had rented rooms from him in Calcutta when he was still a family man. He recalled how Govinda, Śrīdhar Mahārāja's chief disciple, had appreciated him even then. "He always used to say to Śrīdhar Mahārāja that 'Mahārāja, you are seeing Abhay Babu as *gṛhastha,* but he is more than many yogis.'"

Continuing his walk down on the ground he went to the front of our land. He wanted to inspect the progress on the new building. There he questioned Jayapatākā Swami about the Śrī Caitanya Gauḍīya Maṭha. They have erected a new building at the gateway to their property, meant to house a Deity of Śrīla Bhaktivinoda Ṭhākura, the father of Śrīla Prabhupāda's spiritual master. Prabhupāda wasn't at all happy about it. He felt they were going over the head of Śrīla Bhaktisiddhānta Ṭhākura. Śrīla Bhaktisiddhānta had lived there for many years but had never contemplated such a thing.

Prabhupāda told Jayapatākā he should have challenged them that "He [Bhaktisiddhānta] could not understand where Bhaktivinoda Ṭhākura should be placed. You have understood. You are so intelligent. Over intelligent! That means rascals. Over intelligent means rascal. Bhaktisiddhānta Sarasvatī Ṭhākura, he remained so many years, and he could not understand. You have understood to make Bhaktivinoda Ṭhākura a gatekeeper. You tell him next time when you go that 'You are over intelligent.'"

* * *

Hṛdayānanda Goswami arrived from South America to be Prabhupāda's secretary for the month. Tamal Krishna Mahārāja will return to America and then come back to Māyāpur with his men for the Gaura Pūrṇimā festival.

Two *brahmacārīs,* Mahāvīra and Viraha, also came with Hṛdayānanda. Both of them hope to take *sannyāsa* initiation. Boyish and eager, Mahāvīra is from North America but has been successfully preaching in Brazil. Viraha is a somber Venezuelan with little knowledge of English. Both are in their mid-twenties, and Hṛdayānanda Mahārāja highly recommends them for *sannyāsa.* He has a huge zone, the whole of Latin America, and is in dire need of *sannyāsī* assistants to help guide the booming projects.

After settling in, Hṛdayānanda Mahārāja came to Prabhupāda's room to give him an update on his preaching activities. He read him a book review written by an Indian professor in Mexico, Dr. Vajpeye. The review stated that Prabhupāda's books are important because "they expose the terrible cheating of bogus swamis."

Prabhupāda was so pleased to hear this assertion he started in his seat. He was both excited and happy that such a learned man was able to perceive how true Vedic knowledge is being spoiled by misrepresentation. "This is required," he said. He requested that 100,000 copies of the book review should be made. He wants them distributed throughout India, especially Bombay and Madras where there is so much propaganda from these bogus gurus and yogis. "This is my intention," he said, "to stop the so-called swamis and yogis from cheating the public."

He feels this can be done by distributing his books. Such charlatans are ruining India's culture by concocting their own methods of spiritual practice. But now, by reading his books, important men are beginning to realize what is going on.

During mail time Prabhupāda heard from Svarūpa and Raṇadhīr prabhus, who manage the BBT Mail Order Department in Los Angeles. They reported a successful year, with collections of $20,000 for 1975.

In response Prabhupāda requested them to send the pamphlet *Kṛṣṇa Consciousness Is Authorized* out to their members along with a book catalog so that they may purchase our books. He also told them that we are going to print many copies of Dr. Vajpeye's review and distribute it widely throughout India. "He has got practical experience of how they are cheating the innocent people in foreign countries, and he has written, 'The authorized edition of *Bhagavad-gītā* will help to stop the terrible cheating of "gurus" and "yogis" who are false and unauthorized.'"

They also reported that the BBT is preparing some blowups of the book reviews to be displayed here in Māyāpur during the upcoming festival. Prabhupāda added a postscript to his letter, emphasizing that these blow-ups are "most important."

Prabhupāda considers these favorable book reviews to be very important. He keeps the most recent ones on file and regularly shows them to his visitors. He is also pleased with the new booklet *Kṛṣṇa Consciousness Is Authorized* because it presents the favorable endorsements of many respected professors.

Another letter arrived today from Madras that confirmed Prabhupāda's feelings. It stated that after Prabhupāda's visit, Svami Chinmāyānanda had gone there and given a ten-day discourse on the *Bhagavad-gītā.* Afterward one man told our devotees, "What Prabhupāda achieved in two days, Svāmī Chinmāyānanda failed to do in ten!" Needless to say, Śrīla Prabhupāda is delighted when he hears such accounts.

Prabhupāda is acutely aware of the power of the printed word. Our entire movement is based on his books, and he carefully supervises every aspect of their production and distribution. In a letter to Rādhāballabha in Los Angeles, he approved a new kind of water-resistant cloth cover and gold stamping on the bindings, "if it will increase the appeal."

He even personally checks and approves the paintings for the books. Before proceeding with their paintings the artists regularly send him their preliminary sketches for him to review.

He answered Rādhāballabha's questions on illustrations for *Śrīmad-Bhāgavatam,* Seventh Canto, dealing with Prahlāda Mahārāja. Prabhupāda gave the kind of insightful instruction that was possible from only him.

"There should be no effulgence around Prahlāda. Hiraṇyakaśipu should not be shown with a pipe. He was a non-smoker."

"Kṛṣṇa killing Śiśupāla took place inside, not outside."

"Yes, you can show dead bones, skulls, and snakes in the dungeon. Prahlāda was not actually attacked with the tridents, just threatened."

It seems that Prabhupāda's idea of instituting examinations on *śāstra* has drawn an enthusiastic response from the GBC men, but also some consternation.

Satsvarūpa Mahārāja wrote to ask whether the devotees

should be allotted more time to study. This would mean less time on *saṅkīrtana* and other engagements, like cooking, building, managing, and so forth.

Satsvarūpa suggested that we establish a more structured college-curriculum style approach to the morning and evening classes held in the temples. "My question," he asked, "is whether the one-verse per class format which you have established could be changed in order to cover more material in a regular outlined way, in preparation for the examinations. I would like to try such an outlined presentation myself, and even suggest it to the GBC for introduction to the whole society, but I am in doubt whether it is your desire and whether I may have the wrong idea on this."

Prabhupāda told him that the exams are for those who want some academic qualification. "Just like a *brāhmaṇa* with *śāstric* knowledge and a *brāhmaṇa* without. It is optional; one who wants may take. The real purpose is that our men should not be neglectful of the philosophy."

Since the exams are not to be held until next year on Gaura Pūrṇimā, Prabhupāda sees no need for the devotees to give up their normal engagements to do more study. And as far as his idea for teaching classes, he wrote, "This should be discussed at the GBC meeting. If it does not hamper our normal procedure then it is welcome."

February 4th, 1976

In the early morning Prabhupāda took up the topic of cheating gurus again. He told us some of the nefarious activities of a few so-called gurus. One well know swami had been found in bed with his secretary. So his disciples sued him.

He also told us about a Sikh guru in America who enjoys his disciples' wives. And they consider this a "blessing."

In Bombay there is a deviant line of Vaiṣṇavas who follow a similar procedure. When a couple gets married the girl spends her wedding night with the guru, so that she becomes "guru *prasādam*"!

In the course of the conversation, Hṛdayānanda Mahārāja

revealed that he'd drafted the review from Mexico. Dr. Vajpeye only signed it. But Prabhupāda was not disappointed. The fact that he signed showed that he agreed with the statements. Again, Prabhupāda stressed that exposing bogus gurus is an important part of our preaching work. But he said that it can only be done if we are spiritually strong ourselves.

Prabhupāda regretted that sometimes his own men, though knowing the proper standards, don't always live up to them. In that connection, Hṛdayānanda also brought news of Paramahaṁsa Swami, Prabhupāda's former secretary, who hasn't been heard of for several months. He has left ISKCON and is now a gas station attendant in Oregon.

Apparently he and another *sannyāsī* spent a month in Bangkok where they broke all the regulative principles. Paramahaṁsa returned to the USA., and the other *sannyāsī* came to South India where he spent a few days with Śrīla Prabhupāda before going back to Bangkok. This devotee is also reported to have been going to see movies in Japan.

On hearing this Prabhupāda simply commented, "Yes, I could understand it from seeing his face."

Śrīla Prabhupāda also mentioned another wayward disciple named Audalomi dāsa who had been told by doctors that he would die within a few months. He asked to be given *bābājī* initiation. Prabhupāda had reluctantly agreed, and thus Audalomi Mahārāja came to spend his last days in Māyāpur chanting Hare Kṛṣṇa. But when another doctor informed him he would not die so soon, he returned to his wife in the U.S.A., gave up his devotional service, and became like a *karmī* again. He was last seen surfing on the West Coast.

Added to this, another disturbing report was related about one of our *sannyāsīs* who is currently preaching here in India.

Prabhupāda shook his head regretfully. He said that he is doing his best to push forward this movement with whatever men Kṛṣṇa sends him, although he is aware that some of his men are deviating from the principles he has laid down for us. Despite this, as long as a person is willing to keep trying, he is willing to engage them in Kṛṣṇa's service, with the hope that they will eventually become purified and attain success on the spiritual path. In the meantime, they can do something useful for pushing on the movement.

* * *

The acceptance of *sannyāsa* has become so popular recently that even some of the ladies are asking about it. Aditya dasi sent an enquiry from Bombay. "I am writing this letter on behalf of myself, as well as the other women in our Society. Sometimes the question has come up, but no one seems to know the real answer, about *sannyāsinīs*. I know that *sannyāsa* is the highest order of spiritual life, therefore is it not possible that we can be eligible? Myself, I do not feel like a woman, although I am in this body."

Prabhupāda's reply was concise and clear. Quoting from *Bhagavad-gītā,* he told her the soul is neither man nor woman, and for those engaged in Kṛṣṇa's service, there is no distinction between man and woman. "Anyone acting for Kṛṣṇa, he is a *sannyāsī* or *sannyāsinī*. Spiritually everyone is equal. But materially a woman cannot be given *sannyāsa*. But you should not be bothered, because you are serving on the spiritual platform."

Prabhupāda complained to his secretaries that he is constantly being bombarded by requests for *sannyāsa* from devotees who are not fit to accept such an exalted position. It has become such a problem that he has approved a suggestion by Tamal Krishna Mahārāja. From now on any request for taking *sannyāsa* must be accompanied by a recommendation from another *sannyāsī* or GBC. The candidate's request will then be considered at the annual GBC meeting in Māyāpur. If accepted, the man will be put on a one-year waiting list and then initiated the following year. It is hoped this will shield Śrīla Prabhupāda from being unnecessarily disturbed and help to further qualify the candidates.

Prabhupāda also told us that he wants the number of GBCs increased to twenty men. More and more he is referring new plans for preaching, managerial arrangements, and so forth to the GBC for discussion, taking a less-active part himself. He wants them to become fully responsible for the management of the Society.

* * *

There was a big storm in the evening. The lights went out as huge gusts of wind blew sudden and furious. We had to run to bolt down all the windows and doors.

Prabhupāda sat happy and undisturbed in the darkness of his room. The distant heavens meanwhile lit up as multiple forks of bluish-yellow lightning streaked across the sky, making an awesome display of the power of material nature. Prabhupāda repeated that rainfall at this time of year is considered auspicious and very welcome.

February 5th, 1976

The discussions of the morning walks are getting very lively now with Hṛdayānanda, Tamal Krishna, and Harikeśa all debating with Śrīla Prabhupāda on the latest scientific theories. They, of course, get soundly defeated.

Hṛdayānanda Mahārāja presented the theory that although God originally created everything, once things were set in motion, there was nothing else for Him to do. Therefore He is now inactive; God has become dormant.

Prabhupāda replied that being dormant doesn't mean being out of the picture. Prabhupāda demonstrated this by using himself as an example. "I am walking now, but if I choose not to walk for half an hour, that doesn't mean I am not active. The capacity to act remains. One simply has to understand how God is acting."

Prabhupāda explained that when he was a child he wondered how the gramophone was working. He thought there must be a man inside the box, otherwise, how could it work?

Although his perception was childish, still he knew there must be some person behind it. Similarly, nature is working, and this indicates an active God behind it. "Just like there was cloud and rain. Now it is not raining," he pointed out. "So there is activity already. It is being managed. So you cannot say God is dormant. He is acting because his creation is acting. And God says, 'Under My direction the nature is working.' How can you say He is dormant?"

Hṛdayānanda threw in another point of contention. "The main argument among the atheistic philosophers is that, 'God could not exist, because if He existed, if God were good, then why would we be suffering? God would stop our suffering.'"

Prabhupāda's swift retort exposed the faulty logic. "Because you are criminal. There are so many persons in the state. Not all of them are suffering in the prison-house. Only the criminals. So that is the proof you are criminal." He concluded by saying that whether we enjoy or suffer is simply a question of the use of our God-given free will.

* * *

After *guru-pūjā,* Śrīla Prabhupāda presided over a combined Deity installation and *sannyāsa* initiation ceremony.

The head *pūjārī,* Jananivāsa, assisted by the newly arrived GBC of the American mid-west, Jagadīśa, performed the *abhiṣeka* of Śrī Śrī Gaura-Nitāi. The beautiful, twenty-inch, neem-wood Deities were installed as the proprietors of the boat "Nitāi Pada Kamala." Sudāmā Mahārāja plans to sail up and down the Ganges with Their Lordships and other Māyāpur devotees, preaching from village to village.

After the Deities were installed, Harikeśa and Viraha were awarded *sannyāsa.* Mahāvīra will wait until Gaura Pūrṇimā.

Prabhupāda had the mantra and purport from *Caitanya-caritāmṛta Madhya-līlā* 3.6 read aloud. "[As a *brāhmaṇa* from *Avanti-deśa* said] I shall cross over the insurmountable ocean of nescience by being firmly fixed in the service of the lotus feet of Kṛṣṇa. This was approved by the previous *ācāryas,* who were fixed in firm devotion to the Lord, Paramātmā, the Supreme Personality of Godhead."

Prabhupāda gave a short talk explaining that *sannyāsa* is simply a facility to preach and spread Kṛṣṇa consciousness. He awarded the men their new cloth and *tridaṇḍas,* the traditional monk's staffs. Then he told Harikeśa to "simply add Swami" to his name. He renamed Viraha, Viraha Prakāśā Swami. Then he returned to his room while the devotees conducted the fire ceremony.

As soon as he settled in his room Prabhupāda asked Hṛdayānanda Mahārāja how the two new *sannyāsīs* would be engaged. He was informed that Viraha Prakāśā Swami plans to stay in Māyāpur for a few weeks to get Prabhupāda's association before returning to South America. But Prabhupāda said that was not good. He should immediately go out and preach.

Hṛdayānanda Mahārāja explained that Viraha Prakāśā only speaks Spanish, so it would be difficult for him to preach in India. But Prabhupāda promptly called for the two new *sannyāsīs* and told them, "Leave immediately for somewhere—anywhere—and preach. When there is a fire, if you don't know the language, somehow you communicate and the message gets through. Even if you cannot speak the language properly it doesn't matter. Preaching must be done." He said that the best use of intelligence is to accept *sannyāsa* and go preach. It is also the best way to associate with the guru. Personal association is not so important, but to associate with the teachings of the guru is essential. Prabhupāda said that he had not seen his Guru Mahārāja for more than ten or fifteen days in fourteen years. Thus his words were of personal encouragement and comfort to Harikeśa as well, since he is now leaving Prabhupāda's personal service.

February 6th, 1976

The two new swamis left for Calcutta this morning. Harikeśa Mahārāja will eventually go to the U.S.A. via London. I gave him my quilted cotton jacket, a *bagalbundi* from Vṛndāvana, because he had no clothes for colder climates.

Before he left he gave me a three-page handwritten list of instructions on how to cook for Śrīla Prabhupāda.

HOW TO COOK FOR SRILA PRABHUPADA

1. Take bottom section of cooker and put perhaps 3 or 4 heaping tablespoons of yellow split *mung* or *toor-dahl* which has been well washed and immediately let it boil so that you can regulate the temperature to a small rolling boil. Water level should be 5/8 full. Add turmeric (till nice deep colour) and salt.

In 2nd section put 4-6 oz rice (nice basmati) and clean and wash 1 or 2 times (not too much) then add twice as much water or slightly less.

In 3rd section whatever vegetables you want to steam should be placed here and do not cover the holes.

Cover with lid and wait 45 minutes.

Vegetables (typical steaming schedule)
Cauliflower
potato
zucchini
loki
eggplant
tomato
(beans or peas)
portals etc.

Dahl should be completely merged, not solid, not liquid, chaunched with chili, cumin, asafoetida, either *methi* or *dhanya* but never at the same time, sometimes ginger in *chaunch* is nice.

Paneer cheese

Boil milk, curdle with yogurt, take out and put in cloth. Press under cloth with heavy weight by forcing out all water. Cut cheese into chunks and deep fry brown. Meantime make *masalā* (as you like) put in water and tomato—then cheese and boil till cheese is very soft.

Wet veg.

Masalā, add water, turmeric, salt, sometimes yoghurt, then steamed veg—heat and serve.

Dry veg.

masalā, add steamed veg, turmeric, salt, fry for short while.

Some *masalās*—

cumin	cumin	ginger
anise	anise	cumin
chili	*methi*	anise
(*hing*)	chili	*hingmethi*
	(mustard)	anise
	(*hing*)	*hing*

Coriander powder, turmeric, salt, sweet *neem* (curry leaves) are also used.

As you change the ratios of one spice to another in the *masalās* you get an infinite variety of tastes.

Recipe for *Suktā*

Wok on very low heat with sufficient ghee to fry the vegetables first. Use whatever you like of the below list but *kerala* (bitter melon) is absolutely essential:

kerala, radish, potato, green banana (*plantain*), pepper, green tomato, carrots, beets, beans (string beans), *mooli.*

When little soft add salt-spice by pushing aside vegetables and in the middle cooking cumin, anise, green chili, *methi,* not very dark, continue frying. When finished add water and boil down. Add turmeric. Mash poppy seeds (white) to paste-add-dry fry *methi,* anise, cumin, chili and grind-add to top after putting off the heat, serve liquid.

Sak-

Masalā with *methi,* chili, cumin, anise and add spinach leaves, cover and cook. In the meantime deep fry to brown, *badi,* and break up into prep with salt-finished (do not add extra water).

Rice cooks automatically in the cooker-just keep it hot.

He went in to take a final leave of Śrīla Prabhupāda and then he was gone.

Dayānanda and Nandarāṇī Prabhus, who are both excited at the unexpected turn of events, were familiarized with their new duties. They began immediately.

* * *

It rained again early this morning, delaying the construction work on the new building. But later the thick mist and clouds cleared away as the warm sunshine evaporated the haze.

Prabhupāda was out on the balcony just after breakfast. He paused to look out over the rail and smiled as the sun's rays filtered through. "*Nīhāram iva bhāskaraḥ!*" he quoted from the Sixth Canto. It is a verse that describes how the appearance of the holy name destroys sinful life just as the sun dissipates fog. Everything he sees reminds him of Kṛṣṇa.

* * *

Prabhupāda has been invited to do a program in Dacca in Bangladesh, where he will also accept a gift of some land and a temple. Jayapatākā Swami has been negotiating with some Gauḍīya Maṭha members there. Apparently they are willing to hand over their small preaching center to ISKCON.

Hṛdayānanda Mahārāja will go there next week to prepare for the program.

* * *

Just after lunch *prasādam*, Prabhupāda sat on a chair out on the veranda. Tamal Krishna Mahārāja and I sat at his feet, eager as ever to share some quiet moments with His Divine Grace. Prabhupāda volunteered to us that he had a dream last night in which he saw a planet where pious Mohammedans go.

We smiled. I asked if such a place actually exists.

Prabhupāda tilted his head from side to side. "Oh yes," he said smiling.

* * *

Jagadīśa and Nitai have come to Māyāpur to discuss with Śrīla Prabhupāda their proposals for the formation of the Vṛndāvana *gurukula*.

Nitai has been writing regularly with suggestions about curriculum and registration of the school. He feels that our gurukula should be affiliated with other centers of learning, such as Agra University. This will help the students and other devotees to easily get student visas. Thus they will be able to stay in India without difficulty.

Prabhupāda called for the other senior men to discuss their ideas for the school's curriculum. The two of them gave an elaborate outline of a comprehensive course of study, beginning from first-level grammar school up to Master's level in graduate studies.

After hearing their proposals Prabhupāda indicated that he considered many of their ideas to be impractical. Nitai's scheme seemed too academic and grandiose, attempting to cram in too much in too short a time.

Prabhupāda emphasized that he wants the children to become devotees, not simply scholars. He is also not keen on the idea of affiliation with other schools, because then we will be required to conform to certain government standards that he doesn't feel are necessary.

Overall, Prabhupāda's response to their proposals was not very favorable. So they will reconsider and modify them.

February 7th, 1976

Today is Śrī Advaita Ācārya's appearance day, a half-day fast, and the day chosen for the launch of the boat.

In the early morning Prabhupāda was driven in a jeep to Hoola Ghat on the Jalāṅgī River, where he inspected the "Nitāi Pada Kamala." Its renovations are complete, and the Deities have been installed below deck. The small wooden forms of Śrī Śrī Gaura-Nitāi will be taken on procession through villages whenever the boat lands.

It is a good facility, a twelve-ton "Jali" class boat, about forty feet long and fifteen feet wide. It has a shallow draft and was previously used to transport hay, although the maritime authorities have licensed it to carry up to fifty-six passengers. The devotees have added a cabin above deck along most of its length. Brightly painted in green, yellow, and red, the boat was gaily decorated for today's occasion with strings of orange marigolds. The high mast is painted in yellow and red strips like a barber's pole. Inside the cabin the main support beams are yellow with bright-red lotus-flower motifs.

Tamal Krishna Mahārāja helped Śrīla Prabhupāda on board over the rickety bamboo ramp. Prabhupāda carefully inspected every corner of the boat. Then he sat for a few minutes on a straw mat, while the devotees held *kīrtana*. Prabhupāda likes the idea of preaching on the boat, and he encouraged Sudāmā Mahārāja to make it a success.

Later in the morning Sudāmā Mahārāja sailed away down the *Gaṅgā* with seventeen men, including four of the older boys from the *gurukula*, on their maiden voyage. It was a very magnificent sight. Many local villagers lined the shore, eager to witness their departure.

* * *

During his massage Prabhupāda heard a letter from Balavanta dāsa, the temple president in Atlanta, in which he learned that the devotees were making a tea from *tulasī* leaves. "Immediately stop it!" he exclaimed. He was very disturbed by this news and said that such "tea" should not be made even for Lord Jagannātha during His yearly convalescence.

Balavanta also questioned whether the devotees on traveling *saṅkīrtana* could eat bread made by *karmīs.*

Prabhupāda replied that they may not, unless it is an emergency situation. In any event he indicated that such food cannot be offered to the Deities. As a substitute he suggested they eat farina fried in a little ghee with sugar added. Or *puris* because these would last for three or four days.

* * *

Recently I have been trying to improve my standard of cleanliness because Prabhupāda frequently refers to me as a *mleccha.* Still, I continue to make mistakes.

Today, as usual, after *prasādam* Prabhupāda sat out on the veranda in his chair. As Tamal Krishna Mahārāja and I sat at his feet, he admired the vista of Śrī Māyāpur *dhāma,* occasionally making short comments.

Prabhupāda asked me for a drink of water, and I reached out for his silver cup. In my eagerness to serve I moved too quickly, caught the top edge with my palm and almost knocked it over. In the act of recovery I poked the tip of my finger into the water. I was caught in a dilemma. Should I inconvenience Śrīla Prabhupāda by making him wait while I empty the cup and get fresh water? Or should I offer him the cup even though my finger had touched its contents?

I offered him the glass. A wrong decision. Prabhupāda shook his head and gave me a sour look. Then he laughed and quoted from *Bhagavad-gītā,* "*Pravṛttiṁ ca nivṛttiṁ ca janā na vidur āsurāḥ!* You are simply *mleccha!*"

In an attempt to rectify my bad habits I have begun to take three baths daily: one upon rising, one just before massage, and one in the late afternoon. Still, it seems very difficult to know what a fitting standard of cleanliness is, although due to Śrīla Prabhupāda's association I am gradually learning.

The other evening I told Prabhupāda that sometimes I wonder if I will ever be able to live up to the correct standard. *Brahminical* cleanliness just doesn't seem to come naturally. I explained that at home, before becoming a devotee, I had been practiced to bathe not more than once a week.

Prabhupāda assured me I will learn gradually. But he also laughingly agreed that for a Westerner to be clean is somehow a very artificial condition.

* * *

Immediately after lunch Prabhupāda went upstairs and took his afternoon nap in one of the roof-top rooms on the roof. He enjoyed the fresh open-air. The setting was so peaceful and quiet that he has decided to stay up there every day from 10:00 a.m. until 4:00 p.m., taking his massage, bath, and lunch all there.

February 8th, 1976

For the first time since we arrived, Prabhupāda gave a class after *guru-pūjā,* speaking in English on the *Śrīmad-Bhāgavatam* Seventh Canto 9.1. The subject was Prahlāda Mahārāja's prayers to Lord Nṛsiṁhadeva.

After a brief, fifteen-minute discourse, he surprised everyone by requesting a Bengali devotee, Subhāga, to come forward and repeat what he had said in Bengali for the benefit of the local devotees.

Subhāga, a gentle, nervous type of fellow, became a little flustered at the thought of speaking before Śrīla Prabhupāda. He was unable to get out more than a couple of sentences. In his nervousness his mind had gone blank and he couldn't remember anything Prabhupāda had said. Prabhupāda requested Nitaichand dāsa, a young man born here in Māyāpur, to speak instead. He was more successful.

It has put all the bilingual devotees on their toes. They're all wondering if they will be called upon in future classes.

* * *

The room on the roof facing east has been cleared out and prepared for Prabhupāda. He went up just after taking his morning nap and stayed there until mid-afternoon.

During massage Dayānanda read the English translation and word-for-word transliteration of the two prayers Prabhupāda wrote while on board the *Jaladūta* when he first sailed to America. The prayers were sent to him by a devotee in Los Angeles, Jayaśacīnandana, who had translated them into English from Bengali.

Prabhupāda was pleased with the translations and suggested they be published in the new printing of the song book for all the devotees to learn and sing. One of them was already named *Markine Bhāgavata-dharma.* Prabhupāda named the other *Prayer to the Lotus Feet of Kṛṣṇa.*

Yaśodānandana and Acyutānanda Swamis will be arriving here around February 25th. Since Prabhupāda's visit to Nellore they have been preaching throughout eastern Andhra Pradesh with good success. They reported that Gurukṛpa Mahārāja has sent money for a new traveling *saṅkīrtana* bus which they are having specially constructed in Bombay. The bus will be ready in time to take them on a tour of Karnataka in April.

* * *

Because his digestion is poor and he is suffering from excess mucus, Prabhupāda has been adjusting his diet. His liver is not functioning properly, and his digestion is not good. He has stopped taking evening *prasādam.* For breakfast he is eating only fruits, and for lunch he has a variety of vegetable preparations, but no dahl or rice.

Today he decided to take his evening milk in the form of milk sweets like *rasagullās* or *sandeśa* made with *gur,* a local form of brown sugar made from boiled-down cane juice. He reasoned that the sugar would be good for his liver and the solid milk would give him strength to work on his books throughout the night. (As a liquid, milk is too difficult for him to digest.)

He called in his new cook, Nandarāṇī, and explained how to make *rasagullās.* The curd has to be thoroughly kneaded. Then when rolled, a small piece of rock candy can be placed in the middle. The whole thing has to be cooked until sticky.

February 9th, 1976

On his morning walk Prabhupāda explained that the *varṇāśrama* system is not necessary for our ISKCON society; it is a material arrangement. When one chants the holy name and performs devotional service one immediately rises above that platform, like using a lift instead of stairs. However, as long as some bodily concept is present, *varṇāśrama* is useful and it can be utilized.

He talked about various aspects of the Vedic social system and told us that his mother was married at age eight. He gave a few examples of others who were married while as young as five years. In such child marriages the couples would live separately until the girl reached puberty. Then they lived together at the boy's parents house. Prabhupāda's own wife was eleven at the time of their marriage. At the age of thirteen she moved in with his family, and at fourteen she gave birth.

He said the social system for getting girls married was so strict that in one *śāstra* it says if a girl is not married by the first menstrual period then the father has to eat the menstrual liquid! Everyone winced at the thought. Prabhupāda explained that of course that is not to be taken literally. But it was meant to stress the importance of properly protecting the girls. By marrying the girls before puberty they would naturally become attached to their husbands and remain faithful throughout their lives. Thus their chastity was preserved, and there was no disturbance in society.

Prabhupāda said that in our ISKCON Society, however, getting married is not so important. That's because life becomes perfect by serving Kṛṣṇa. He is the real husband.

* * *

It is very pleasant to give Prabhupāda his massage out on the roof. He has me place his sitting mat on a large, wooden table about the size and height of a bed. This provides me just enough room to manoeuvre around, while Prabhupāda sits contentedly in the warm rays of the sun.

On completion of the massage, he bathes outside in his *gamsha,* sitting on a *chonki,* washing off the oil with warm water from a brass bucket. Then he retires inside the room to dress, eat lunch, and rest.

* * *

Dayānanda came up with the day's mail. A letter from Brahmānanda Swami was included. It was a long, rather depressing missive.

In it Brahmānanda described the struggles that he, Navayogendra, and Nanda Kumāra swamis are having in trying to restore good relationships with our Members. He wrote how collections have become so bad in Nairobi that they could not even buy any fruit or milk, nor post letters, during one five-day period. Furthermore, he explained how some Mombasa devotees had previously visited local prostitutes, later leaving the temple. However, he reported that relations with the local Hindu community are gradually improving. And despite all the problems, he had still managed to send $800 to the BBT.

Chayavana Swami, who had been in charge of the African *yatra* in Brahmānanda's absence, had left and gone to live with his father in Florida. From there he sent a letter to the White House telling them how our movement could stop the spread of Communism in Africa if they gave us backing.

Prabhupāda didn't comment at length, but he did compliment Brahmānanda for paying his debts to the BBT.

As far as Chayavana's letter was concerned, he wasn't impressed. "That was a foolish letter sent by Chayavana," he wrote. "He was crazy. These things should not be done without first asking." We have heard that Chayavana is now in India and on his way here to see Śrīla Prabhupāda. So Prabhupāda is hoping that he can be rectified by spending some time in Māyāpur with himself and in the company of other *sannyāsīs.*

* * *

In the afternoon we had a visit from the federal home minister, Śrī Tarun Kanti Ghosh. A tall, good-humored man, with an impressive mien and an aura of extravagance, he seemed surprisingly young to have such a high-ranking political position. He is from a Vaiṣṇava family who worships a Deity of Lord Caitanya in their home. And he deeply admires Śrīla Prabhupāda and his disciples.

Although he has been here before, he was taken on a tour. He greatly appreciated the transcendental atmosphere of Māyāpur. Afterward he relished *prasādam,* then Prabhupāda entertained him very nicely in his room for an hour, conversing on various topics. He left paying high tribute to Śrīla Prabhupāda for the great work he is doing in spreading the movement of Lord Caitanya far and wide.

February 10th, 1976

Prabhupāda is constantly meditating on the development of ISKCON. He regularly discusses managerial concerns as well as spiritual standards in order to assure that everything in the Society is running efficiently. He is constantly on the watch for signs of mismanagement. It is common for him to call in his GBC men at all hours to garner information and give direction. We are all untrained, both materially and spiritually, and Prabhupāda has to educate us in both realms in order to create a Society with a solid framework for advancement.

Early this morning, before his walk, he sent me to get Tamal Krishna Mahārāja. After some discussion he authorized him to send out the following letter to all the temples and GBCs: "This morning Śrīla Prabhupāda called me into his room. He was concerned over the appropriation of money for use in travelling and communicating between centers by the devotees. More and more His Divine Grace is noticing the frequency of plane flights and trunk calls, both of which are very costly. He has therefore ordered that henceforward no one should take plane flights. If anyone has to go to another temple, he should book a train reservation, but he can not take a plane. With regards to trunk calls, His Divine Grace does not want any more trunk calls booked, except in case of dire emergency. Everything should be done by mail. Telegrams should be utilized only when absolutely necessary. If you consider this desire of Śrīla Prabhupāda carefully, I think you will see that the result will be a huge savings of money and much more cool headed management."

Prabhupāda told us that one of our Western diseases is that we are so wasteful, especially in regard to spending money. He himself is mindful of every single rupee spent, not out of miserliness, but because he understands perfectly how everything belongs to Kṛṣṇa and how to utilize it in His service.

* * *

While walking on the roof Prabhupāda told us about "ten hands and two hands." Because Kṛṣṇa is everywhere, in all the ten directions, He is therefore said to have ten hands. In comparison, we limited beings have only two hands. "So my father used to say, 'When Kṛṣṇa takes your money or possessions in ten hands, how you can protect it with two hands? And when He gives you in ten hands, how much can you take in two hands?'"

He laughed. "So in my case it has become practical. Everything He has taken in ten hands, and now He is giving in ten hands. I am practically experiencing. My Guru Mahārāja ordered me, 'You do this.' I was trying to save my business, my family, with two hands, and Kṛṣṇa took it in ten hands. And now, after making me a beggar, He is giving me, ten hands: 'You take as much as you like.'"

He paused for a moment and reflected aloud on the sagacious advice he had received. Affectionately remembering his father, Prabhupāda recalled how he used to invite saintly persons to his home to solicit their blessings. But his only prayer was that his pet son, Abhay, would be blessed to become a devotee of Rādhārāṇī.

Now we can appreciate that his desire was gloriously fulfilled. His readiness to share the intimacies of his past made us eager to solicit more details. We took advantage of the opportunity to find out more about his early days and relationships.

Hṛdayānanda Mahārāja remembered Prabhupāda saying that he was not much impressed with the saintly persons who came to his house.

Prabhupāda agreed. "Yes. Not all of them were real

Vaiṣṇavas. That was my discrimination from the very beginning of my life. I never liked these bogus swamis and yogis." But he said that his father did not discriminate too much about the standards of behavior of his visitors. He even sometimes gave *gañja* to a *sādhu* he was friendly with.

When Tamal Krishna questioned his reasoning, Prabhupāda explained that the general Indian public didn't make too many judgements about those who appeared to be *sādhus. Gañja* smoking was not considered by them to be such a bad thing for a *sādhu.* Although it was not done by the higher-class spiritualist, it was for the "bogus swamis and yogis."

Prabhupāda said that the Western hippies had picked up the habit of smoking *gañja* from people like Allen Ginsberg, who had learned it from these so-called *sādhus* in India. Prabhupāda said that it was Śrīla Bhaktisiddhānta Sarasvatī who had taught him that any kind of intoxication was bad. "Śrīla Bhaktisiddhānta was very strict," he said with a chuckle. He stopped for a moment, and with a reserved laugh he revealed that as a lifelong celibate, Bhaktisiddhānta was so strict that sometimes he would criticize his father, Bhaktivinoda Ṭhākura, for having married twice. If there was some fight between them, he would tell Bhaktivinoda, "*Strī-saṅgī!* You are attached to women!"

Of course this was a transcendental relationship, and Prabhupāda explained it in such a way that we could not misinterpret it. He told us that they had a special relationship, so we should not take it as an ordinary thing. Nor should we advertise it, but he mentioned this to illustrate how strict a *brahmacārī* Bhaktisiddhānta was.

Bhaktisiddhānta Sarasvatī Ṭhākura was very outspoken against so-called *sādhus*—so much so that everyone in the Navadvīpa area feared him. At one point, the Navadvīpa *gosvāmīs* conspired against him and devised a wicked scheme. They raised a 25,000-rupee bribe, a huge sum of money in those days, and requested the police to kill him. But the police refused to cooperate, informing Śrīla Bhaktisiddhānta Sarasvatī instead. The police admitted that they did that kind of thing, but not to a *sādhu.*

Prabhupāda then told us a little about his own relationship with his Guru Mahārāja. He explained that he had gone to Mathurā in 1933 to see Śrīla Bhaktisiddhānta Sarasvatī during the Gauḍīya Maṭha's annual *parikrama* tour of the Vṛndāvana area.

At that time, Prabhupāda had taken a seat on the same couch as Śrīla Bhaktisiddhānta Sarasvatī. He was thinking that "he is a respectable gentleman, and I am also a respectable gentleman." So Prabhupāda could not understand that there would be anything wrong if he sat on the same seat. When he noticed everyone else was sitting on the ground, however, he understood and got down.

But Śrīla Bhaktisiddhānta never cautioned him for sitting on the couch, and he simply preached to him about Kṛṣṇa consciousness. It was during that tour that Śrīla Bhaktisiddhānta noted Prabhupāda's eagerness to hear. A short time later Prabhupāda was formally initiated, in Allahabad.

The conversation was fascinating and, at least for me, a privileged insight into Śrīla Prabhupāda's past. It was one of those especially relishable opportunities that comes along with being in his personal service.

* * *

In class, speaking from *Śrīmad-Bhāgavatam* 7.9.3, Prabhupāda explained that although Prahlāda was an inexperienced young boy, nevertheless the demigods, being unable to pacify Lord Nṛsiṁha, asked him to go forward to speak. Even Lakṣmīdevi, the Lord's eternal consort, could not approach Him, what to speak of pacify Him. Prabhupāda explained that it was something like putting a small boy in the cage of a lion. But Prahlāda felt no difficulty. He sat at the feet of the Lord, feeling completely protected.

Prabhupāda stressed the necessity of becoming humble if we want to make advancement in Kṛṣṇa consciousness. If a person is proud, Kṛṣṇa consciousness is not possible. "Those who are very much proud, they do not take Kṛṣṇa consciousness very seriously. They think, 'These poor fellows, who had no money, no foodstuff, they have come in the name of Kṛṣṇa for begging. So it is for them. It is not for us. I am very rich. I am very opulent. I am very educated. I am very aristocratic. So for me there is no need of.'

"The Indians say like that in your country. 'Now we have known this Kṛṣṇa, Hare Kṛṣṇa. Now it is not needed. Now it is technology.' So these puffed-up persons cannot understand Kṛṣṇa. One has to become very humble."

He cautioned us that a devotee must always feel insignificant before guru and Kṛṣṇa. "If somebody thinks that 'I have become more than my guru, more than Kṛṣṇa,' then he is finished. So never we should think that 'I have become very big personality.' That was the instruction of my Guru Mahārāja, that *baḍa Vaiṣṇava:* 'I am very big Vaiṣṇava. Everyone should come and obey my orders.' This is condemned position. The real position is one should be very humble and meek."

He also commented about the constant requests he has been receiving for *sannyāsa.* "It doesn't require to change. There are so many questions sometimes: Whether it is necessary to take *sannyāsa?* By the routine work, it is necessary. But if one is serious, so for him it is not necessary—*ahaituky apratihatā*—because for a serious student of devotion, Kṛṣṇa is in his hand."

Class was short. And afterward the devotees accompanied him with a lively *kīrtana* as he circumambulated the Deities in what has now become a regular feature of his morning program. Walking around the Deity room three times Prabhupāda vigorously rang the bells hanging on either side of the temple room. The more he rang them, the more energetic the chanting became. As he came before the Deities he spun clockwise on the spot before moving on around. The *kīrtana* party accompanied him, in front and behind, and by the end, every one was jumping up and down and singing ecstatically, as Prabhupāda's face beamed with satisfaction.

* * *

Bhavānanda Mahārāja came in to see Prabhupāda later this morning, requesting permission to join the boat party. He said he was feeling strained from the burden of constant management and felt it would enliven him to go out and preach in the villages.

Prabhupāda pointed out that he could not speak Bengali, so how would he preach? Bhavānanda Mahārāja said he had a white body, so if he danced and chanted that would attract many people.

Prabhupāda raised his eyebrows. "Yes!" He agreed it was a good idea. Bhavānanda left immediately.

February 11th, 1976

The observance of Ekādaśī today is coupled with a half-day fast for Lord Varāhadeva's appearance, although the Lord's appearance is actually tomorrow.

As Prabhupāda took his morning walk, he had Jayapatākā Mahārāja confirm the observance procedure by reading out from the *Gauḍīya Pañjikā,* a yearly Vaiṣṇava almanac the Gauḍīya Maṭha produces. Since the auspicious appearance of Lord Varāha falls on Dvādaśī, which is the day for breaking the Ekādaśī fast, the two are combined.

Prabhupāda said that it would suffice to celebrate Lord Varāha's appearance by singing the appropriate verse describing him from the song of the ten *avatāras.*

Śrīla Prabhupāda also verbally listed the proper fasting periods to observe for other auspicious days: Lord Nityānanda's, Śrī Advaita's, Lord Balarāma's, and Śrīmatī Rādhārāṇī's appearances are all half-day fasts. Lord Nṛsiṁhadeva and Lord Rāmacandra's appearances are full-day fasts until sunset, while Gaura Pūrṇimā is a fast until moonrise.

Tamal Krishna Mahārāja inquired about observing the appearance and disappearance days of great Vaiṣṇavas. He described how we observe a half-day fast for our immediate predecessor *ācāryas.* He wanted to know if we should also do the same for personalities like Śrīla Narottama dāsa and others like him. Prabhupāda said yes, if it is possible. But he added that if devotees are engaged in preaching work, they may not. He said that the main thing is to sing some songs of praise and perform *kīrtana.*

Tamal Krishna also asked about chanting while observing Ekādaśī. "We should always chant twenty-five rounds on Ekādaśī if initiated?"

"Initiated? Everyone. Why initiated?"

"So that should be standard for our movement on Ekādaśī day?" Tamal asked.

"Standard is sixteen. But if one can chant more, then he is welcome," Prabhupāda replied.

Tamal Krishna pressed to know if twenty-five was mandatory or not. When Jayapatākā Mahārāja suggested it was "recommended," Prabhupāda seemed to disagree.

"No. Ekādaśī means that, fasting and chanting." However, when Tamal Krishna Mahārāja referred to his men going out on book distribution, Prabhupāda was quick to clarify. "No, no. That is also preaching work. For that purpose you can stop this. But generally, one who has no preaching work, he can chant extra."

* * *

Vrindavana Chandra De, Prabhupāda's second son, arrived today. Prabhupāda is trying to engage him in Kṛṣṇa's service. Prabhupāda is purchasing a flat in Calcutta for his former family, where they will live as guests. In return, Prabhupāda wants Vrindavana Chandra to sell his books. Vrindavana owns a company called *Vrinda Books* and has already sold a complete set of the *Śrī Caitanya-caritāmṛta* to Calcutta University. Prabhupāda encouraged him to distribute them throughout West Bengal.

In turn, Vrindavana Chandra wanted Prabhupāda to get them a bigger flat. But Prabhupāda refused. As a *sannyāsī* he is not obligated in any way; it is simply out of his mercy that he has arranged adequate accommodation for them.

* * *

Chayavana Swami has finally written. He has gone to Vṛndāvana "to rest," he said. "I have been very ill and travelling too much. So now I am helping to take care of the Deities here."

Prabhupāda was pleased to hear his message. But being aware of Chayavana's disturbed state of mind, he mercifully offered him a chance for rectification. "I think it will be good if you will live with me and assist me in so many ways. Here there are other GBC and *sannyāsīs* like Jayapatākā Mahārāja, Bhavānanda Mahārāja, Tamal Krishna Goswami, etc. It will be nice if you stay with experienced men. I hope you will be benefitted this way."

Svarūpa Dāmodara also sent a letter from America. He is unable to leave there for at least six months due to a pending immigrant visa application. So he will not be able to attend the programs planned for early April in Manipur, his home state. Svarūpa Dāmodara is busy setting up the Bhaktivedānta Institute to aid preaching in the scientific field in colleges and universities. He, Rūpānuga, Mādhava, Sadāpūta, Ravīndra Svarūpa, and Śubhānanda prabhus are the core members. He wanted to know if he could start up a *saṅkīrtana* party to fund a proposed college lecture program in the fall.

Prabhupāda discussed the idea with Tamal Krishna Mahārāja, who suggested that since his Rādhā-Dāmodara TSKP is already collecting and has a very solid university program, the Institute members could travel on their buses. This would solve their funding problems and guarantee many opportunities for the type of preaching they want to do.

Prabhupāda liked the idea. He wrote back suggesting Svarūpa Dāmodara accept the offer.

Svarūpa Dāmodara also suggested that the candidates for the titles of "Bhaktivedānta" and "Bhaktisārvabhauma" could submit a thesis on a Vaiṣṇava topic. Some of these scholarly essays could then be published into small books.

Prabhupāda liked the idea and told him, "Regarding publishing books, these books can be published by you and men in your rank. Ordinary men cannot write such books. So therefore if a book is written by one man with 'Bhaktivedānta' or 'Bhaktisārvabhauma' and it is of high quality, then it may be considered by me for publishing."

February 12th, 1976

Today is the appearance day of Lord Varāha. There is no fast.

During his massage Prabhupāda talked about his Godbrothers. He is of the opinion that one day the Caitanya Maṭha and others will want to amalgamate with us because they are not able to maintain all their buildings and programs properly.

He suggested that either we could jointly manage or we would manage and they would run the *maṭha*. Or perhaps we would simply supply their financial necessities and jointly preach. Prabhupāda said it would be ideal if their Indian devotees and our Western devotees went village to village to preach together.

Prabhupāda recalled that when he visited his Guru Mahārāja at Rādhā-kuṇḍa in 1935, Śrīla Bhaktisiddhānta told him of a "blazing fire" that would occur in the Gauḍīya Maṭha and how he wanted to rip up the marble in the Bhag Bazaar temple and use it to sell books. Prabhupāda said that this was when he understood how his Guru Mahārāja could be pleased. He explained that the fight for control of the *maṭhas* that occurred immediately after Śrīla Bhaktisiddhānta's disappearance was the first *aparādha.* It was *guror avajñā,* disobeying the orders of the spiritual master. Since then many more offenses have been committed.

He remarked his Godbrothers are now useless, because instead of combining together to preach vigorously and defeat Tīrtha Mahārāja's cunning, they were all simply scheming how to become the next *ācārya.* Thus they could not unite successfully. They all had the same disease that infected Tīrtha Mahārāja. Śrīla Bhaktisiddhānta never said that one man would be the next *ācārya.* Otherwise, why did he not directly nominate one? Śrīla Prabhupāda said that some of his Godbrothers claimed that Bhaktisiddhānta indirectly indicated Tīrtha Mahārāja should be the next guru.

But Prabhupāda said this was just like the impersonalists, who cull indirect meanings from straightforward instructions. What Bhaktisiddhānta Sarasvatī did order was that a twelve-man Governing Body Commission be formed in his absence. But they ignored him.

Prabhupāda's comments were candid and revealing. It is apparent that among his Godbrothers, Prabhupāda stands out as the one who truly desired to please his Guru Mahārāja by vigorously spreading Lord Caitanya's movement all over the world. As Śrīla Prabhupāda himself often says, *phalena paricīyate,* the value of something is judged by the fruit it produces.

* * *

Gaura Govinda Swami sent a letter from Bhubaneswar requesting to be excused from coming to Māyāpur as Prabhupāda had suggested in his last letter. He has just managed to construct a small brick-and-thatched cottage on our land there and is getting some help to establish ISKCON from some of the local people. Now he has to submit plans to the municipality before he can begin temple construction.

Prabhupāda excused him from attending the festival and offered his full blessings for his project. He told him if he works sincerely, he will certainly be successful. He suggested that he support himself by translating and publishing our books into Oriyan, the local language.

Prabhupāda also sent a letter to Saurabha in Bombay, requesting him to provide Gaura Govinda with suitable plans for the proposed temple complex.

February 13th, 1976

Today is Lord Nityānanda's appearance, a half-day fast. Nityānanda Prabhu liked *urad dahl,* so this was one obvious preparation that was made for His feast.

* * *

Pṛthu Putra Swami reported by mail from Kanpur that he is having good success with his preaching work. He is regularly holding programs in the homes of prominent citizens.

He suggested that Śrīla Prabhupāda attend the upcoming Kumbha Melā festival to be held at Allahabad in February 1977. He mentioned that many people still remember Prabhupāda's attendance at the Māgh Melā five years ago. He also offered some mellifluous prayers to Śrīla Prabhupāda, comparing him to Śrī Kṛṣṇa's flute because it is through him that we receive the words of Lord Kṛṣṇa.

Prabhupāda appreciated his sentiments. He asked Pṛthu Putra to go ahead and book a suitable berth at the Kumbha Melā.

* * *

This evening we were very happy to hear Prabhupāda say that he has been feeling well for the last two days.

Nandarāṇī regularly makes fresh batches of *rasagullās*, which Śrīla Prabhupāda keeps in a jar next to his desk. He has been taking a little milk with rock candy along with a half, or sometimes a whole, *rasagullā* and also a little *sandeśa*. His strategy of taking his milk in solid form seems to be working, as his strength is increasing.

In the evening, I came in with a cloth to wipe his desk top after he had eaten some *rasagullā*. There was a small pool of sugar water on the glass top, and many tiny ants had surrounded it.

As I carefully flicked the ants away with the cloth in order to wipe up without harming them, Śrīla Prabhupāda sat and watched. He looked first at me, then at the ants, then back again at me. "Formerly you would have killed them," he said, smiling. His comment was as revealing as it was true. My mind flashed back to the days as a young boy when I had delighted in pouring scalding hot water down the nests of ants. I blushed with embarrassment as Prabhupāda's observation reminded me of this dark episode in my past.

Prabhupāda saw my flushed face, and his smile broadened. Seeing Prabhupāda's pleasure at my reformed character, I reflected how it must be the same as the happiness that Nārada Muni must have felt when transforming the hunter Mṛgāri. A sense of deep gratitude surged through me as I contemplated my good fortune at having also met such a wonderful spiritual master.

February 14th, 1976

The roof is a very convenient place for Śrīla Prabhupāda to take his morning walk. Its sizable 45-foot width by 150-foot-long expanse is large enough for him to get sufficient exercise without having to leave the building. It also limits the number of devotees who accompany him to just a few senior men. The panorama from the roof is magnificent. From that single vantage point, Prabhupāda can view what is going on within our entire compound. The perimeter of the roof is profusely decorated with potted plants and *tulasī* trees, creating a pleasurable, natural ambience.

A peculiar event has been occurring each morning. Just after Prabhupāda arrives on the roof, a very large black bee appears. It flies around Prabhupāda and his party a few times, as if in circumambulation. Then it comes to rest atop a small concrete spire marking the spot where the Deities stand in the temple room, four floors below. Tamal Krishna Mahārāja remarked that it appears to be just like one of the black bees described in the *Kṛṣṇa Book*, which constantly fly around Kṛṣṇa in glorification of His Supreme Personality. He said that now it seems that this particular bee is also coming to offer his respects to Śrīla Prabhupāda.

Prabhupāda appreciated his sentiments. He even stopped to inspect the bee for a minute today before it flew off.

* * *

Prabhupāda called in Hṛdayānanda Mahārāja to discuss the Māyāpur temple management with him. He is becoming increasingly concerned that things are not being managed properly, especially since Bhavānanda Mahārāja left to join the boat party. Hṛdayānanda Mahārāja volunteered the services of Mahāvīra, the American *sannyāsa* candidate residing in Brazil. He explained that Mahāvīra had considerable managerial experience and doesn't have any pressing engagement at present.

Mahāvīra was called. After a brief discussion Prabhupāda agreed that he could begin helping immediately.

* * *

Bhagavān sent a very encouraging letter from France. He reported that they are opening a new center in Belgium in order to facilitate book distribution. He also stated that the Dutch *Bhagavad-gītā* is being composed, and many, many books are being sold throughout his zone in southern Europe.

He related some amazing *saṅkīrtana* stories from France, where they sell books mainly door-to-door. "One devotee went into a hospital and the nurses dressed him up in a white surgeon's outfit, and he distributed *Gītās* to the doctors. One nurse even took some *Gītās* from him, and while he went to the other floors she sold four big *Gītās* to the patients.

"Another devotee went to a factory and the foreman took orders from all the workers. Later, when the devotee returned to the factory, the foreman had distributed twelve big *Gītās* for him!"

Bhagavān also suggested some innovations in the presentation of the forthcoming French edition of *Śrīmad-Bhāgavatam* Canto One, which will go into production shortly. He plans to remove the painting depicting the creation from the front cover and put it inside on the end papers. He wants to put a painting of Kṛṣṇa and Balarāma on the cover, which he thinks will help increase the door-to-door sales.

Prabhupāda was all smiles hearing his report. Nothing pleases him more than news of his books being sold or news of how the people of the world are appreciating them. He approved the idea for a new cover and told Bhagavān his ideas were very good. He said that Bhagavān should sell books in huge quantity and then print again.

However, not every GBC man is experiencing such success. Brahmānanda Swami sent yet another disheartening report.

Although he is working hard, fulfilling many roles as GBC, Nairobi temple president, Life Membership director, correspondence secretary, and so on, he seems to have become despondent in his attempt to preach in Africa. He has major problems to deal with and very few devotees to help him. Nanda Kumāra Swami is there, but he is untrained and cannot cope with more than just the *pūjārī* work and cooking.

Because of his vast responsibilities in Africa and all the problems he has to face there, he expressed his inability to attend the festival in Māyāpur this year. Out of the seventeen devotees in Africa, only five have missionary visas. The rest will have to leave due to a change in immigration laws. Most of the local men that had joined have now left, stealing practically everything of value as they went.

"So the question comes to mind," he wrote, "Why are we here? At least I have little hope that the Africans will ever take seriously to Kṛṣṇa consciousness." Brahmānanda explained that their primary field for preaching is among the Indian community, but they are also being forced to leave by the government.

He gave a very bleak overview of the potential for preaching in the entire continent. "This is really a disturbed part of the world and offers very little opportunity to spread our Movement. Americans cannot travel to the Congo or Uganda. We are already banned in Zambia. Tanzania has refused our attempt to register there, and I have been arrested twice there. Ethiopia, from where I have just returned in December, is very tense and going Communist very rapidly. Mozambique just had a revolution, there is open war in Angola. Our men just returned from Sudan which is incredibly poor and destitute, as so is Chad, Central Africa Republic, etc. Only Nigeria seems to offer any opportunity of establishing a center. All the other GBC's have civilized areas of the world that are developed, to spread this Movement."

There were two bright spots though. He has paid off $1,860 from his BBT debt of $12,000. And in Mauritius a small band of *brahmacārīs* are being well received and preaching enthusiastically all around the island.

Prabhupāda was sympathetic, but purposeful. In his reply he encouraged Brahmānanda to work vigorously and continue with his efforts to preach. He also suggested he base himself in Mauritius, which Prabhupāda described as "a nice place by the sea." As for whether he should remain in Africa or not, Prabhupāda said that will have to be discussed by the GBC.

February 15th, 1976

In this morning's class Śrīla Prabhupāda described his ambitious plans for showing the higher regions of the universe in the Vedic Planetarium he's proposed for Māyāpur.

"There is a Siddhaloka. We shall show how this planet works, Siddhaloka. The description of the Siddhaloka is there in the *Śrīmad-Bhāgavatam.* The Siddhaloka persons, they can go from one planet to another without any machine, or airplane.
"Like the yogis, those who are perfect yogis, they can go from one place to another without any vehicle. There are many yogis still existing. They take bath in four *dhāmas*—in Hardwar, in Jagannātha Purī, in Rāmeśvaram. And similarly ... yogis can do that. They attain *aṣṭa-siddhi,* eight kinds of perfection. So the

Siddhaloka means they are born *siddhas*. They haven't got to practice this mystic yoga system."

To illustrate this point he gave the simple but effective example of *siddhas* that live within our immediate experience. He pointed out how birds and insects can fly automatically, but we cannot. We have to create so many big machines.

Prabhupāda's idea in having a planetarium is to show that the statements made in the Vedic scriptures are authentic and based on scientific fact, not simply mythology, as commonly misunderstood. "So there is no question of disbelieving," he said. "It is not to be rejected, 'Ah, there cannot be any ... This is unbelievable.' We have got this information from the *śāstras*. We are staunch believer: 'Yes there are *siddhas*.' That is called theism. One who believes in the statements of *śāstra*.

"Very highly intelligent persons, thoughtful persons, philosophers, scientists, mathematicians—they are called also *muni*. They came also to satisfy the Lord. Not these ordinary *munis*, but very exalted *munis* and *siddhas* from Siddhaloka.

"There are many *lokas*, Caraṇaloka, others. They are all described. So if there is chance, we shall present these *lokas*, how they are situated, where they are situated, how they are moving, how the sun is moving around them.

"The sun is not fixed up; sun is moving. So all these things, we have got such dream to show. If there is opportunity, we shall do. The modern scientists or astronomers, they say, 'Sun is fixed up. The earth is moving.' So we don't say that. It has got its orbit. So there are so many things to be known still from Vedic literature, it is not yet unfolded, but we are trying."

* * *

During his massage, Śrīla Prabhupāda heard a letter from Jaśomatīnandana in Ahmedabad. He is preaching steadily, has a rented house for the next three months, and is beginning to make Life Members.

However, his main focus is on publishing transcendental literature. He has plans to print the *Bhagavad-gītā* in three parts, and he is beginning to collect subscriptions to a monthly Gujarati edition of *Bhāgavata Darśana*, the Indian equivalent of

Back To Godhead magazine. He described a fairly elaborate idea for raising thousands of subscriptions, even before the magazine comes out.

Prabhupāda was extremely pleased to hear about his preaching efforts. "I am very pleased with your monthly *Bhāgavata Darśana.* That is a solid program. Please continue it steadily.

"Yes, I approve your distribution ideas, namely subscriber agents, news agents. The subscription drive is a solid program. And if you regularly publish and get registered, you can get a one or two paisa charges postal concession. Also in the future there are many cities such as Bombay, Surat, and Calcutta with large numbers of Gujaratis, you may arrange for getting subscriptions there."

A letter from Mike Darby, a high school student in West Virginia, bore ample testimony to the efficacy of reading Śrīla Prabhupāda's books. He has written a term paper for one of his high school classes based on the teachings contained in *Caitanya-caritāmṛta.* In order to continue his work, he requested a personal interview with Śrīla Prabhupāda next time he is in America. He warmly expressed his appreciation. "I have read most of your books on transcendental science and have enjoyed them very much. No, I have not just enjoyed, but tried to base my life on their teachings. What you have written is so perfect because this knowledge has been passed down from the Supreme Lord Śrī Kṛṣṇa."

Prabhupāda is always happy to hear from grateful recipients of his books. He works literally day and night, tirelessly, only for this. If someone reads his books and understands that Kṛṣṇa is God and everyone is meant to serve Him, then, as he often says, his mission is a success.

He told Mike to come see him later this year when he next tours America.

* * *

Hṛdayānanda Goswami and Subhāga Prabhu left for Bangladesh today to examine the property being offered to us there. Prabhupāda does not plan to go there personally, but he said if the offer is suitable to our needs we could send some men there to develop the place.

Sudāmā Mahārāja came back from his travels on the Nitāi Pada Kamala boat. Gurukṛpa Swami, who arrived early in the morning, went to join it for a few days after hearing how successfully they are faring.

The devotees on the boat program have been received enthusiastically wherever they go. After docking at a village, they take Śrī Śrī Gaura-Nitāi ashore and go on a procession through the village, door to door. All the villagers give a rupee and some foodstuffs, and in return they receive a *Gītār-gāna.* In this way hundreds of books and large amounts of *prasādam* are being distributed. Everyone traveling on the boat is very enlivened, especially the *gurukula* boys.

Śrīla Prabhupāda sent Jayapatākā Swami to Calcutta to meet Mr. Chaudhuri. He will help Jayapatākā approach government officials with our request for acquiring land in Māyāpur for our proposed Vedic City.

February 16th, 1976

Last night Prabhupāda had *rasagullā* and *nimkies,* tasty home-made biscuits, which are offered to the Deities each evening. He spilled some *rasagullā* juice on the mat; immediately hundreds of ants came to enjoy. This has happened a few times. Each time as I clean up, Prabhupāda stops to watch me and makes some pertinent philosophical remark.

Prabhupāda often likes to use such simple real-life examples to illustrate philosophical points in his classes. I felt honored when this morning he mentioned me and the ant episode to convey a point he was making in his lecture.

In the verse Prahlāda Mahārāja clearly stated that the Lord is not impressed by any of our material qualifications. He can be satisfied only by devotional service, which even Gajendra the elephant could offer.

Prabhupāda described how modern men think themselves very intelligent by building atom bombs or by gaining wealth.

However real intelligence is going back home, back to Godhead. "To get some money by hook and crook. That is not intelligence. That intelligence I see, I was telling Hari-śauri, I was explaining that, that even a small ant, as soon as there is a drop of sugar juice, immediately, within a second, hundreds of ants will come: 'Here is a drop of sugar juice.' This is nature's study. This kind of *buddhi,* intelligence—how to eat, how to sleep, how to have sex, and how to defend—even in the ant is there. That is not *buddhi-yoga.*

"The real *buddhi-yoga* is how to be engaged in devotional service of the Lord. How to become first-class devotee of Kṛṣṇa, that is called *buddhi-yoga.* How to go back to home, back to Godhead. That is *buddhi.*

"Everyone has got intelligence. Even the ant has got intelligence. We study sometimes. The sparrow, he has got intelligence. But the perfect intelligence is there when one is searching after the Absolute Truth."

In conclusion, Prabhupāda explained that material achievement and opulence are not needed in order to approach God. Only the favor of guru and Kṛṣṇa is required.

And with Śrīla Prabhupāda as our guru, clearly we are well favored.

"So don't be disappointed," Śrīla Prabhupāda said, "that 'Because I am poor, I cannot become devotee.' Everyone can become devotee, even the children. Just see how the children, they are dancing. They are chanting. They are offering obeisances. That is *bhakti-yoga.* Everyone can become devotee, provided he is properly guided. That is required.

"Kṛṣṇa says, 'I'll give you intelligence.' If one is working under the direction of the spiritual master with love and faith, then Kṛṣṇa, from within as *caitya-guru,* the guru within the heart, He'll help you. And He'll send you bona fide guru to help you externally. So both ways, you'll be helped, and you'll become like Prahlāda Mahārāja. Thank you very much. Hare Kṛṣṇa."

* * *

Prabhupāda strongly reprimanded the temple managers

this morning. There was no running water in the building again for the third consecutive morning.

The bathroom water system is gravity fed from holding tanks on the roof. The pumps that fill the tanks have to be turned on by hand. As the festival approaches, more and more devotees are arriving, putting a greater demand on the system. But no one seems to be paying attention.

Prabhupāda also corrected Mahāvīra for telling everyone that he is now the temple president and manager of Māyāpur. Mahāvīra has set himself up in an office. Several devotees already are complaining that he is asserting himself as the supervisor of the entire project, demanding that they follow his instructions, although he knows very little about how the Māyāpur management operates.

"First become expert in all departments before becoming manager," Prabhupāda told him. "You have to be servant of everyone before you can manage. One cannot demand respect."

* * *

More and more visitors are coming for *darśana* in the evening, and Prabhupāda has worked out a new system to facilitate them. Most of the guests are simple villagers. They come and sit in his room and simply stare.

So Prabhupāda told us to stand at the door and give out sweets. The guests should not be asked directly to come in, but they also should not be refused entry. If they wish to enter his room they can be escorted to the balcony. There they will be given a seat and *prasādam,* and then asked to fill in a form giving their name and business. Then Prabhupāda will call them. This, he said, is "screening without a screen."

Those who simply wish to look can come to the door, offer their *praṇāmas,* and receive some *prasādam.* They will then go away happy. Those who have something specific to discuss will gladly wait.

It is actually a botheration for Prabhupāda to give *darśana* to so many people, but he cannot refuse them. So he has decided on this procedure. It will satisfy the people and save him from criticism.

Prabhupāda mentioned one well known yogi who, for the same reason, used to see the public only once a year. Prabhupāda said that he could not do that, but this new system would suffice as a good compromise.

* * *

Hansadūta has really taken Śrīla Prabhupāda's desire for village-to-village preaching seriously, and not just in India. A letter from him arrived today telling Prabhupāda that he has managed to purchase four Mercedes buses. Two of them are for use in India. The other two will be used in Germany, despite the current governmental difficulties in preaching there. Hansadūta expects the buses, which are carrying thirty devotees each, to arrive in Vṛndāvana by April 1st.

With his letter Hansadūta enclosed a flier advertising the impending traveling *saṅkīrtana* program. The flier is intended to persuade devotees to join their party. It has a picture of the four buses across the top and begins with the following heading.

PRABHUPADA'S WORLD SANKIRTANA PARTY

"Entangled in temple life? Burned out on *saṅkīrtana?* Then this new program is for you. Simply chanting and dancing and distributing Kṛṣṇa *prasādam.*"

To further entice the devotees, it mentions that Prabhupāda has promised to travel with the party. An attractive description of the recent tour of Gujarat is also given. His intention is to establish a regular overland bus route between Germany and India so that at all times of the year devotees will have the opportunity to participate in village-to-village preaching. The flier also mentions that a separate party under Gargamuni Swami is also now on its way to India with six Mercedes vans and thousands of dollars of preaching equipment.

Śrīla Prabhupāda was very happy to see the eagerness and enthusiasm with which Hansadūta has applied himself to establish this preaching program. In his reply Prabhupāda confirmed his intention to participate. "Yes, with great pleasure I will accompany and we shall go village to village. I have seen the pictures, and the buses look very nice. They appear costly."

Śatadhanya dāsa is in Tokyo. He sent a report explaining how he is working along with Trivikrama Swami to rectify the problems that have arisen there due to Gurukṛpa Mahārāja's traveling party. Although the Nama Haṭṭa *saṅkīrtana* party is enthusiastically collecting funds for the development of Māyāpur, their questionable collecting techniques have caused a barrage of bad publicity. Śatadhanya expressed his feelings that some professional public relations efforts will be required in order to restore our good standing with the Japanese immigration department.

Śatadhanya also mentioned that he and Trivikrama would like to open a temple in the city center. Until now, no real attempt has been made to establish a permanent center and recruit Japanese devotees. At present we have only one Japanese *brahmacārī*; but meanwhile Christian groups report very good results in recruiting local people.

Prabhupāda wrote back encouraging him to try to rectify our position. He said that Trivikrama Swami is "well expert" in Japanese dealings, and if Gurukṛpa Swami is not needed there, he may be sent to Bangladesh.

February 17th, 1976

Instead of going to the roof for his morning walk, Prabhupāda decided to inspect the construction site of the new building.

Work is going on at full speed, with hundreds of workers digging, carting, shoring, and stacking. It is an impressive sight. The foundation stretches about 1,000 feet—the entire length of the northern boundary of our property. It will be an extremely long building, two stories high, and built in the same style as the main Guest House with a veranda and decorative arches. They are building the two floors upon a high plinth, so if the Ganges floods, the rooms will not be affected.

When Prabhupāda asked what would be done with the plinth, Jayapatākā Mahārāja said it will be filled with dirt.

Prabhupāda considered this a waste of valuable space; he instructed them to make it into a basement instead. That way there will be extra rooms for storage.

Prabhupāda appeared satisfied with the progress of the work, and is hopeful that it will be habitable in time for the festival.

* * *

For class each morning Dayānanda is reading aloud from the unedited transcripts of the prayers of Prahlāda Mahārāja. While not grammatically correct, the Indian-English style of Prabhupāda's translations have a unique charm and flavor of their own.

Today he read Text Ten of Chapter Nine: "Prahlāda Mahārāja continued to think that a *brāhmaṇa* who has qualified himself with all the *brahminical* qualities, twelve in number, as they are stated in the book known as *Sanat-sujāta,* such a *brāhmaṇa,* if he is not a devotee and to the lotus feet of the Lord, he is especially lower than a devotee who is a dog-eater even. But his mind, words, activities, wealth, and life—everything—is dedicated to the Supreme Lord. Such a low person is better than a *brāhmaṇa* as above mentioned because such lowborn person can purify his whole family; whereas a so-called *brāhmaṇa* falsely in prestigious position cannot purify himself."

Prabhupāda gave a long talk. At one stage he pointed out that in the Vedic civilization one's position in human society is determined by what he eats. Generally meat-eaters, especially pig- and dog-eaters, are considered the lowest, untouchable. But worst of all are those who feast on the cow.

"In India still, generally those who are meat-eaters, they take meat of such animals like goats, lambs, like that. And they never take cow's flesh, because cow is protected, *go-rakṣya.* So in the *Bhagavad-gītā,* even if you are meat-eater, don't eat cow. You can eat other animals: pigs, goats. But don't eat cows' flesh. That is very sinful.

"Why it is sinful? Because it's a very, very important animal in the human society, very important animal. You get milk and milk products. Then your brain becomes very nice, memory sharpened. That is therefore important. Don't eat." But

Prabhupāda said that in Kṛṣṇa consciousness it doesn't matter what one's background is, provided one has adopted the process of Kṛṣṇa consciousness.

"So here it is proof that dog-eaters, or pig-eaters, or any low-grade man is not prohibited to become a devotee. That is our Kṛṣṇa consciousness movement.

"They say that without becoming a Hindu or born in India, nobody can become *brāhmaṇa,* nobody can become *sannyāsī.* But here is the proof. In the *śāstra* the dog-eater is also highly praised. When? When he sacrifices everything, his body, his mind, his words, only for Kṛṣṇa. This is called *tridaṇḍa-sannyāsa.*"

* * *

Gurukṛpa and Hṛdayānanda Swamis arrived back from Calcutta. Hṛdayānanda Mahārāja has to wait for his visa to go to Bangladesh. Gurukṛpa Mahārāja paid only a quick visit to the boat before deciding to return to Māyāpur to take advantage of Śrīla Prabhupāda's association.

* * *

During the massage today, Prabhupāda received a letter and article entitled "Matter Comes from Life," written by Mādhava dāsa, another of our Ph.D. scientists. The article, which is to be published in *Back To Godhead* magazine, established scientifically that matter comes from life. Mādhava is confident that this point can be proven to the scientists by utilizing newfound experimental evidence, documentation, and many logical arguments.

He also submitted a list of four questions that he hoped Śrīla Prabhupāda would answer because, as he put it, "You are *sat, cit, ānanda* and are thus full of transcendental knowledge."

The first question was, "Jung has said that matter is just a symbol (or name) that we apply to Reality, but we may as well call it spirit or consciousness or any other name. Is this view consistent with our philosophy?"

Prabhupāda replied, "Matter originally is spirit. And when spirit is not distinctly understood, that is matter. Just like a tree is also a manifestation of spirit soul, but the consciousness is covered. When the tree is cut, it does not protest. But the moving entity has stronger consciousness than the tree. There is consciousness in the tree though. Also consciousness in a dormant state is matter; consciousness in a completely developed state is spirit. Matter is the symbol of undeveloped consciousness."

His second question was in regard to the function of the mind. "Does thinking occur in words, pictures, or what?"

"Thinking is a subtle form of matter," Prabhupāda answered. "Just like it says in *Bhagavad-gītā: bhūmir āpo'nalo vāyuḥ* ..." Like the ether is subtle, the mind is more subtle—subtle form of matter."

The third question concerned the external world, which we perceive only through our senses, and thus the mind, and, ultimately, the consciousness. "What does this say about where things are actually happening? Is it in the mind, out there in the world, or in the spiritual world?"

Śrīla Prabhupāda wrote, "Everything is in the spiritual world. Kṛṣṇa is the sum total of spirit, and everything is coming from Him. Matter, spirit, everything comes from Him. He is the Supreme Life, the origin of spirit and life. Therefore matter emanates from life. *Nityo nityānām* ... He is the Supreme Consciousness of all other consciousnesses."

Finally Mādhava asked for direction on how to prove that the moon is farther away than the sun.

"The moon is situated 1,600,000 miles above the sun," Prabhupāda replied. "You may refer to the Fifth Canto and read carefully."

Prabhupāda is extremely eager for this scientific preaching to be developed. He told Mādhava that it must be recognized that we are not just a religious sect.

Recently, Mādhava taught a course at the prestigious MIT, in Boston, entitled "Truth Beyond Relativity." The course was based on understanding the three aspects of the Absolute, and it was so well received that eight scientists took copies of *Bhagavad-gītā.* This is the kind of news that delights Śrīla Prabhupāda, and he ended his reply by telling him, "I am very much pleased with your program. Thank you very much."

Prabhupāda also stated that he wants ISKCON scientists to publish their research articles in *karmī* science magazines as well. "If they don't accept what we say, we will go on explaining. If they do accept, then that is their benefit and our victory."

Regarding his answer to Mādhava's question about how to distinguish between spirit and matter, I questioned Śrīla Prabhupāda further on it in mid-afternoon.

He told me, "Yes, everything is Kṛṣṇa's energy. Kṛṣṇa is the Supreme Spirit, and everything is coming from Him. Kṛṣṇa is everything, *sarva-bhūta-stham ātmānam.* Just like skin and fingernail—both grow from the same source. Yet in one there is feeling and in the other there is none. One can be cut and the other cannot. But it is the same energy, coming from the same source. Matter comes from light, and that light is the *brahmajyoti,* which is Kṛṣṇa's bodily effulgence."

As the massage continued, Prabhupāda listened to a compilation of the best reviews of his books, including ones from Oxford and Harvard Universities.

Hearing these reviews, he became very enlivened. He enthusiastically told Dayānanda and Hṛdayānanda Mahārāja that he is eager to publicize his books here in India. He wants a special office set up exclusively for this purpose. He said that he will give personal direction if a good man would take up the engagement. Dayānanda was so inspired, he immediately volunteered himself. And Prabhupāda accepted.

* * *

Acyutānanda and Yaśodānandana swamis arrived in the evening from South India. They gave an encouraging account of their successful preaching activities in many cities. The leaders of the Rāmānuja and Mādhva *sampradāyas* received them well. They even got letters of appreciation from them commending the work that Śrīla Prabhupāda is doing and clearly stating their acceptance of his disciples as genuine Vaiṣṇavas.

* * *

Prabhupāda told us today that everyone should shave up every *pūrṇimā,* or full moon.

February 18th, 1976

With so many *sannyāsīs* around I am constantly being asked to run here and there on errands. This distracts me from my service to Śrīla Prabhupāda, but it is difficult to refuse their requests. Therefore I asked Śrīla Prabhupāda during his walk what I should do. His simple quote made things very clear. "Everybody's servant is no one's servant." That settled my mind. I decided to tend to him alone, and the *sannyāsīs* will have to make their own arrangements.

There is concern among the *sannyāsīs* that some of the *sannyāsa* candidates are not actually qualified for the renounced order. One candidate in particular, Mahāvīra prabhu, is under question.

Without naming any names, Jayapatākā Mahārāja brought up his doubt to Śrīla Prabhupāda. "*Brahmacaris* don't like to take instructions from the elder devotees. And then they want to take *sannyāsa,* so they think they can be independent and give orders themself and not listen."

Prabhupāda replied that therefore *sannyāsa* should not be given all of a sudden. The problem is that they want to become *sevya* instead of *sevaka;* served instead of servant.

With a few brief words Prabhupāda exposed the fundamental problem. With a mixture of humor and irony he said, "Yes. And, ultimately, God. When everything failure, then to become God. Everyone, if he wants to become a master, that is materialism."

* * *

A striking analogy was given in the *Śrīmad-Bhāgavatam* verse this morning explaining the relationship between Kṛṣṇa and his devotee. If a face is nicely decorated, so its reflection in a mirror will also be. Prabhupāda explained that therefore if Kṛṣṇa is satisfied, the devotee, as his reflection or reliant part and parcel, is also automatically satisfied. Since Kṛṣṇa is complete in Himself, whatever service we do to please Him is actually for our own benefit.

Prabhupāda used our attempts to build a big temple here in Māyāpur as a practical example to illustrate his point, giving us deeper realizations of the nature of our work. "Everything belongs to Kṛṣṇa. Just like we are constructing this temple. We are feeling that 'I am constructing. We are constructing.' But actually it is Kṛṣṇa's.

"The bricks, the iron, or the cement, or anything that we are collecting, that is Kṛṣṇa's property. The brick is not your property. The earth is not your property. You are taking Kṛṣṇa's earth, and you are making it a brick. Still, it is Kṛṣṇa's property. But the endeavor, the energy, which you are giving to Kṛṣṇa, that is taken into account. 'Oh, he is working for Me. He wants to give Me something.' That Kṛṣṇa consciousness is important.

"Otherwise by His will He can construct 16,000 palaces for His queens. What this tiny temple will satisfy Him? But still, He's satisfied. 'Oh, you have done so much? Very good.' Recognized. Kṛṣṇa has created the whole universe. He doesn't require any endeavor. Simply by His breathing, many millions of Brahmas are coming out. And each Brahmā is creating a universe.

"So to create a temple, He doesn't require our help. He can create millions of temples by His will. There are already. So we should always remember this, that Kṛṣṇa does not require our service. But if we give some service to Kṛṣṇa, that is our benefit. This is the formula."

* * *

Gopāla Kṛṣṇa sent a letter enclosing samples of the new *Śrīmad-Bhāgavatam* printed in India on government concessional paper. Prabhupāda was extremely pleased with him for finally getting his books into print here in India. Many other Hindi and English books are to be printed in Delhi at a cost of only ten rupees each for the best quality paper. Bhārgava is production manager, and Amogha will help with university sales.

In response to Gopāla Kṛṣṇa's requests, Prabhupāda asked Dayānanda to contact Rāmeśvara in Los Angeles. He wants Rāmeśvara to send to India, via the devotees coming for the festival, numerous color separations, the booklet *Kṛṣṇa Consciousness Is Authorized,* reviews by professors, and a complete list of universities and colleges that have standing orders for his books.

Śrīla Prabhupāda countersigned Dayānanda's letter, thus clearly declaring his strong desire for this new phase of preaching in India. "Śrīla Prabhupāda's scheme is to push these books on a gigantic scale here in India. He is personally organizing and motivating the project. We have especially experienced here that His Divine Grace smiles and is very pleased to hear the comments by the professors. These books are especially Prabhupāda's glory, and those comments prove that Prabhupāda's glory and the philosophy of Kṛṣṇa consciousness is being appreciated by the intelligent men of the West.

"Prabhupāda recently said, 'I know those that are sane, they will accept. No one is distributing so much quantity of religious books. Therefore I challenge all these fools and rascals. After eighty years no one can expect to live long. My life is almost ended ... it is ended. So you have to carry on. And these books will do everything Simply by bluffing words, these bogus gurus and yogis are nothing. But when the people read our books, then they will get good opinion. Everywhere (India esp.) the book demonstrations and opinions (Professor's comments) must be widely spread.'

Devotee: 'Now we are going to flood India with your books just like they have done in America!"

Prabhupāda: 'Thank you, that I want, then you will be first-class. Organize book distribution here, and I shall be very much obliged.'"

* * *

Jayapatākā Mahārāja returned from Calcutta and reported that his meeting with the government ministers, arranged through Mr. Chaudhuri, was very successful. The land acquisition should be no problem and can be done quickly.

He explained that land acquisition works in this way: if the government is convinced that a major project is important or beneficial enough for the district, then an average price for a parcel of land for the last ten years is calculated. The land owners of the plots required must sell at that price. This prevents artificial inflation of land values, which is to no one's benefit. Initially, we are asking for only twenty-three acres, and we will ask for more later.

February 19th, 1976

The morning walk was on the roof again, but it has become too hot for Prabhupāda to have his massage in the sun, even when a breeze is blowing. It is, however, still very pleasant to be on the roof during the morning hours, and Prabhupāda seems to enjoy the simple facilities. Because of the heat, he sits in the shade atop the wide, wooden bench in the lee of the room to receive his massage. But for bathing he sits in his *gamsha* on a *chonki* in the sunshine and washes off the oils from a bucket of solar-heated water.

He still takes his meals in the sparsely furnished room. He has a couple of hours entirely to himself, while I stay close by in the adjoining room. Then he goes back down to his quarters at about four o'clock to greet guests and meet with devotees.

* * *

Because the weather has become quite hot, some visiting devotees are buying flavored ice on sticks from the stalls in front of the temple. Jayapatākā Swami asked Prabhupāda if we can make our own iced sherbet drink for the Gaura Pūrṇimā festival. He's afraid that the devotees will become ill because the local confection is generally made from bad water.

Prabhupāda was disturbed to hear that devotees are eating outside. He quite emphatically said, "No one may buy anything from the market. If they eat these things they will fall down! No one should eat anything not offered to the Deity."

* * *

Prabhupāda's son, Vrindavana Chandra, and also his sister, known affectionately to the devotees as Pisimā, Bengali for 'Aunty,' arrived in the afternoon. She plans to stay for the whole festival.

February 20th, 1976

Today was the appearance day of Śrīla Bhaktisiddhānta Sarasvatī Gosvāmī Prabhupāda, which we all observed with a half-day fast.

The Gauḍīya Maṭha down the road has invited the Governor of Pondicherri to speak at its function, which is being held at the *samādhi-mandir* of Śrīla Bhaktisiddhānta. Jayapatākā Swami was supposed to ask the governor to visit our temple later, but somehow he failed to do so. The only way it could be arranged at this late date would be for Jayapatākā Mahārāja to go to the Caitanya Maṭha this morning and ask the governor's aide-de-camp.

Prabhupāda decided against this because, as he jokingly put it, "the hosts are host-ile!" The Gauḍīya Maṭha didn't invite Prabhupāda, and we have not invited them. "Anyway," he said, "one book distributed in America is more important than the visit of any governor. In America we have never approached any politicians for support."

* * *

Prabhupāda kept his usual schedule today with a walk, greeting the Deities, and giving class, on *Śrīmad-Bhāgavatam* 7.9.13.

He clearly defined the nature of our movement. "If we want to adjust this chaotic condition, then we require the incarnation of God. That is already there. *Nāma rūpe kali kāle kṛṣṇa avatāra.* This Hare Kṛṣṇa movement is the incarnation of Kṛṣṇa in the form of name.

"The *saṅkīrtana* movement which was inaugurated by Śrī Caitanya Mahāprabhu, and Śrī Caitanya Mahāprabhu is Kṛṣṇa Himself. So this Hare Kṛṣṇa movement is not different from Kṛṣṇa or Caitanya Mahāprabhu. So if we take shelter of this holy name of the Lord, Hare Kṛṣṇa, then we shall be saved."

He revealed also how the name of the temple here is a beautiful metaphor. It's based on the statements of Prabodhānanda Sarasvatī, one of the great devotees of Lord Caitanya, describing the temple's purpose of saving the fallen souls. In Prabhodānanda's *Śrī Caitanya-Candrāmṛta* Lord Caitanya is compared to the full moon. He said, "The ultimate benefit of life is compared with the moon. So spreading Kṛṣṇa consciousness means spreading the moonlight. Therefore we have named this temple Śrī Māyāpur Candrodaya [The Rising Moon of Śrī Māyāpur]. Śrī Caitanya Mahāprabhu is Gaura-Hari, and Prabodhānanda Sarasvatī said, *sādhavaḥ sakalam eva vihāya dūrāt caitanya-candra-carane kurutānurāgam.*"

* * *

Śrīla Prabhupāda sent me down to the temple at 9:00 a.m. to see whether many visitors had gathered for the coming program in honor of his Guru Mahārāja. To my surprise, the temple was empty.

Prabhupāda then called for Hṛdayānanda Goswami to discuss why there were no visitors yet on such an important day. Hṛdayānanda Mahārāja said that it was probably due to the fact that the general public are not aware of the occasion. The festival had obviously not been well-advertised, because at Gaura Pūrṇimā tens of thousands of people come here during the festival week. Prabhupāda wasn't very satisfied. He thought more should have been done to attract the public.

After an early massage Prabhupāda went down to the temple room at 11:10 a.m. He offered his obeisances to the large painting of Śrīla Bhaktisiddhānta Sarasvatī Ṭhākura that had been placed on the *vyāsāsana.* He seemed very satisfied to see the beautiful decorations. There were long, multicolored drapes hung along the back wall, as well as strands of marigolds draped around the *vyāsāsana,* and banana trees and leaves were placed all around.

Moving to the front of the *vyāsāsana* area, he sat comfortably on an *āsana* on the floor, with his back to the *jali*-work fence.

Acyutānanda Swami sang songs glorifying Śrīla Bhaktisiddhānta, notably *Ohe Vaiṣṇava Ṭhākura.*

Afterward Prabhupāda gave a wonderful lecture requesting the devotees to do two things: help develop Māyāpur and distribute many books. He said this was his Guru Mahārāja's desire. His Guru Mahārāja's father, Śrīla Bhaktivinoda Ṭhākura, had rediscovered the birth site of Lord Caitanya, and it was his attempt to develop it. Then Śrīla Bhaktisiddhānta Sarasvatī Ṭhākura continued the effort. And now he and his Godbrothers were also doing what they could. "We have got great ambition to develop this place nicely and gloriously, and fortunately we are now connected with foreign countries, especially with the Americans. Bhaktivinoda Ṭhākura's great desire was that the Americans would come here and develop this place and they would chant and dance along with the Indians.

"So from this place Śrī Caitanya Mahāprabhu started this movement, and He desired that 'As many towns and villages are there, this Kṛṣṇa consciousness movement should be spread.' So this Kṛṣṇa consciousness movement is now in your hand. Bhaktisiddhānta Sarasvatī Ṭhākura, he wanted me to do something in this connection. He wanted from all his disciples. Especially he stressed many times that 'You do this. Whatever you have learned, you try to expand in English language.'"

Prabhupāda told us how in 1935 he had gone from Bombay to visit his Guru Mahārāja in Rādhā-kuṇḍa. At that time he had received some frank and revealing advice from his spiritual master which formed the basis of all his future endeavors.

"When he was in Rādhā-kuṇḍa, I was at that time in Bombay in connection with my business life. So I came to see him, and one friend wanted to give some land in Bombay for starting Bombay Gauḍīya Maṭha. He's my friend. So that's a long story. But I wish to narrate this, the Bhaktisiddhānta Sarasvatī Gosvāmī's mission.

"Bhaktisiddhānta Sarasvatī Ṭhākura Prabhupāda immediately took up the land. He continued that 'There is no need of establishing many temples. Better we publish some books.' He said like that.

"He said that 'We started our this Gauḍīya Maṭha in Ultadanga. The rent was very small, and if we could gather two to two-hundred-fifty rupees, it was very nice, going on. But since this J. V. Datta has given us this stone, marble stone *Thakurbari*, our competition between the disciples has increased. So I don't like any more. Rather, I would prefer to take out the marble stone and sell it and publish some books.'

"So I took that point, and he also especially advised me, 'If you get money, you try to publish books.' So by his blessing it has become very successful by your cooperation. Now our books are being sold all over the world, and it is very satisfactory sale. So on this particular day of Bhaktisiddhānta Sarasvatī Ṭhākura's advent, try to remember his words. That he wanted many books should be published about our philosophy, and it should be given to the English-knowing public especially, because English language is now world language. We are touring all over the world. So anywhere we speak English, it is understood, except in some places.

"So on this day, particularly on the advent of Bhaktisiddhānta Sarasvatī Ṭhākura, I'd especially request my disciples who are cooperating with me that you try to publish books as many as possible and distribute throughout the whole world. That will satisfy Śrī Caitanya Mahāprabhu as well as Bhaktisiddhānta Sarasvatī Ṭhākura. Thank you very much."

After his speech we gathered in front of the *vyāsāsana* and performed the *puṣpañjali-pūjā,* an offering of flowers. Prabhupāda had Acyutānanda Swami chant the four *praṇāma* prayers to Śrīla Bhaktisiddhānta. Then, following Śrīla Prabhupāda's lead, we offered a flower to Bhaktisiddhānta's picture on the *vyāsāsana.* This procedure was repeated three times.

Prabhupāda then called Bhānu dāsa, a Japanese-Canadian *brahmacārī* from the Nama Haṭṭa party, to offer the *ārati.* The special feast cooked in Śrīla Bhaktisiddhānta's honor was brought in and set out on low tables directly in front of the *vyāsāsana.* Śrīla Prabhupāda stood in front and played his *karatālas,* while Acyutānanda Mahārāja lead an ecstatic *kīrtana,* which had us all jumping high in the air.

During the *kīrtana* Prabhupāda asked me to gather a sample of every preparation onto his plate and take it upstairs. He wanted to check what the devotees had cooked to glorify his Guru Mahārāja. He also wanted to offer his own respects by taking Bhaktisiddhānta's remnants.

After the program finished, Prabhupāda returned upstairs and ate the feast. He was happy with all the arrangements, but he again appeared disappointed that only about 100 guests had come. In fact, during his massage, he had criticized the management for erecting such a large building and not inviting anyone to come—only local people, no one from Calcutta.

"Only the Deity program is going nicely," he remarked. Referring to the two English identical-twin brothers who are the head *pūjārīs,* Prabhupāda declared, "The two brothers Paṅkajāṅghri and Jananivāsa—there is no comparison. Everyone should know, there is no complaint."

* * *

In the afternoon two *sannyāsīs* from the neighboring Gosvāmī Maṭha came to invite Prabhupāda to visit their temple tomorrow.

Earlier in the day, toward the end of the massage, a *brahmacārī* from his Godbrother Śrīdhar Swami's *maṭha* had also visited. He had a short discussion with Prabhupāda about Śrīdhar Swami's coming here to visit. The *brahmacārī* returned with a few others in the afternoon and held further discussions.

February 21st, 1976

Early in the morning Prabhupāda called for Acyutānanda and Hṛdayānanda swamis and requested them to go to the Gosvāmī Maṭha to speak on his behalf. He told them to invite their devotees to come with us and preach from village to village. Since we have the finances and they know the language, it could be a very successful combination. Such a united preaching effort would benefit everyone—ISKCON, the Gauḍīya Maṭha, and the general public. He said to tell them that if there is a problem with the management of their temple, we shall provide all the finance necessary. They have only to come preach with us.

He observed that none of them are preaching, rather they are simply begging for money to support their temples. They have no preaching potency, and their forces are dwindling, so why should they not join us?

On his walk he discussed the idea further, stressing that money is no problem. They simply have to come and preach with us. Hṛdayānanda Mahārāja mentioned that before Prabhupāda went to the West, Indians were not interested in his message. But now that he has money, they are willing to listen. Prabhupāda agreed. "Money is the strength all over the world. America is prestigious. Why? They have got money. So I have got American disciples. Why shall I not have money? If a guru of the Americans remains poor, it is contradictory."

His emissaries returned later in the day without any immediate response from the Gauḍīya Maṭha members. But in the evening a few men from the *maṭha* came to discuss his offer. Lately, Prabhupāda has been sitting out on the large lawn at the side of the temple in the early evening, and he received them there. Several of the men were favorable, provided something could be worked out about looking after their *maṭha*. It would be a wonderful step toward a unified preaching effort if they agree to do it. It may indicate the beginning of a full merger with all the *maṭhas* over the next few years.

* * *

The verse for today's class described how Prahlāda Mahārāja was not disturbed by Lord Nṛsiṁhadeva's killing of his father, just as a saintly person is not disturbed by the killing of a snake or a scorpion. Śrīla Prabhupāda retold an incident from his early involvement with the Gauḍīya Maṭha, which directly related to this verse. "A *sādhu* does not want to kill even an ant. But in the case of *vṛścika-sarpa-hatyā,* they are happy. *Vṛścika,* scorpion, and *sarpa*....

"So long, long ago, sometime in the year 1933 in this Caitanya Maṭha, there was a big snake came out in my front. I was taking bath. Everyone was looking what to do. So Guru Mahārāja was on the upstairs. He immediately ordered, 'Kill him.' So it was killed.

"At that time, 1933, I was newcomer. So I thought, 'How is that? Guru Mahārāja ordered this snake to be killed.' I was little surprised. But later on, when I saw this verse, I was very glad. *Modeta sādhur api vṛścika-sarpa-hatyā.* It remained a doubt, 'How Guru Mahārāja ordered a snake to be killed?' But when I read this verse I was very much pleased, that these creatures, or creatures like the snake, they should not be shown any mercy, no."

Naturally one might question why saintly persons become glad to see a snake killed, and he explained that snakes are so envious that they will bite an innocent victim, even without provocation; they are so cruel.

Similarly, Caṇakya Paṇḍit compared an envious man to a snake. "Caṇakya Paṇḍita says, *sarpaḥ krūraḥ-khalaḥ krūraḥ sarpāt krūrataraḥ khalaḥ.* Such person is called *khala,* envious, jealous.

So there are two living creatures. One is snake, and one is jealous or envious person.

"This man, envious man, is more dangerous than the snake. Why? He's a human being. Yes, because he's human being and he has got developed consciousness and he has practiced to use the developed consciousness for becoming jealous, he's more dangerous than the snake. So therefore Caṇakya Paṇḍit concludes, *mantrauṣadhi-vaśaḥ sarpaḥ khalaḥ kena nivāryate.* The snake, although by nature he is so ..., still, he can be controlled by mantra and some herbs. In India they still do that. But this *khalaḥ,* the jealous person, he cannot be pacified, any means. Therefore he's more dangerous than the snake. He cannot be controlled either by mantra or by bribe or this or that, no.

"So Prahlāda Mahārāja said, 'My Lord, nobody is unhappy, even the saintly person [over the killing of my father Hiraṇyakaśipu]. Saintly person, we common man, we may be unhappy, 'Oh, my father is killed.' Or my mother may be unhappy that 'My husband is killed.' But be sure, my father was a *khalaḥ.*"

* * *

During his massage Prabhupāda heard two reports sent by Rūpānuga. Rūpānuga had enclosed a newspaper article describing a major victory in our attempts to preach in the universities. Gabhīra dāsa, in Washington, D.C., after a battle with the university authorities, has now been accepted as an authorized chaplain. He has now been given an office on campus for counseling the students.

Śrīla Prabhupāda was very, very happy to read the article, and he sent a letter to Gabhira to congratulate him for his efforts. Prabhupāda sees this as an important breakthrough in our preaching work. He asked Rūpānuga to continue to do the same in other universities.

Rūpānuga also informed Prabhupāda that Ravīndra Svarūpa from Philadelphia had just successfully completed his oral examination for a Ph.D. in religion. Prabhupāda was pleased to hear this, and told him that we need many Ph.D.s for the new Bhaktivedānta Institute.

As far as the temples in Rūpānuga's zone are concerned, they all seem to be going well, with significant increases in book distribution.

Even within the courts in Atlanta, the devotees have won respect for their preaching activities. He told Prabhupāda that a federal court judge there had remarked that he had never, during his history on the bench, seen such religious fervor. The judge said that it was a new phenomenon in America, and he did not know exactly how to deal with it. "We have had preachers," the judge said, "but these people are at it twelve hours per day, 365 days a year. I've never seen anything like it."

At one point in the court proceedings the judge asked the city attorney whether he was willing to argue that Kṛṣṇa consciousness was not a genuine religion. "Oh no," came the reply, "I am not at all willing to argue that point."

The Atlanta temple has a new farm project in Tennessee, which provides them with milk. Prabhupāda was pleased to hear this. He commented that all our temples should have an auxiliary farm to provide them with milk, vegetables, flowers, and fruits.

And in the northeast USA, a new preaching center has been established in an important college town called Amherst. One of the five main universities there is now providing sufficient funding for them to hold four programs a week. There is great interest in cooking courses, with up to half the students in one dormitory being vegetarian.

In Washington the temple president recently received an inheritance. Apparently his idea is to use it to provide security for his wife and family, freeing himself for preaching. Prabhupāda didn't think much of the idea. "I think Bṛṣākapi should follow the example of Rūpa Gosvāmī. Rūpa Gosvāmī took *sannyāsa* and gave 50% in charity, 25% for family use, and he kept 25% for emergency. Kṛṣṇa wants to see that the life is sacrificed. But also accumulation, money, should be given to Kṛṣṇa. Life to Kṛṣṇa, and money to wife, is not a good decision."

The only problem Rūpānuga reported was with the New York temple. He said that the new twelve-story building is practically a zone in itself and requires full-time attention from a qualified man. Rūpānuga was hoping to be freed of that responsibility now that now Madhudviṣa Swami is there. Since Prabhupāda has already decided that Madhudviṣa Mahārāja should take charge of New York he was happy to hear that Rūpānuga was in agreement.

Another letter arrived from Yamunā dasi, indicating that she would like to develop a cow-protection program. The impression given was that they wanted to run their women's *āśrama* along the lines of a big temple.

Prabhupāda explained in his reply that it is too difficult for women to engage in large-scale cow protection. He recommended that they keep the program small and manageable, with just a few cows for offering milk and sweets to the Deities. He explained that expansion means they will have to take help from men. Therefore he reiterated the instructions he had given previously, "Simply keep yourself aloof from men—chanting, many more times as possible, read books, worship the Deity A widow is forbidden to use ornaments, nice *sari,* decoration, combing the hair nicely. These are forbidden for the woman who is not with husband."

* * *

Because Prabhupāda has been stressing the great importance of book distribution in India, Acyutānanda and Yaśodānandana swamis are eager to get some books printed in South India for mass distribution. It seems that book distribution is the next major project for ISKCON India.

Prabhupāda said that once his books have been sold extensively throughout India, we will be able to defeat all the bogus yogis and impersonalists. As well as this, the books will greatly boost the Life Membership program.

"Not that we are beggars," he said, "but we must give the public some return. Therefore I have started up this Life Membership program so the people will feel some gain for their contribution and will be encouraged when they see us spread and increase."

February 22nd, 1976

Before his walk Prabhupāda suggested that Dayānanda and I write to the devotees in London and New Zealand to find out whether we can sell Indian clothes and brassware there. He said that he has some capital in Lloyds Bank, and if we start exporting Indian cloth and other items, the government will think well of us. At the same time we shall make a useful profit. Actually from Māyāpur the devotees are already supplying many ISKCON temples with cloth that has been made on our own hand-looms.

* * *

Sudāmā Vipra Swami arrived from the Philippines in the early morning. He is another *sannyāsī* who has joined forces with Siddha-svarūpānanda Goswami's group, although reports are that he does not follow the principles very strictly any more. Yet Śrīla Prabhupāda was happy to see him and greeted him very warmly.

* * *

Śrīla Prabhupāda is developing a heavy cold. Sometimes the mornings are very damp and foggy. Such weather has caused his chest to become full of mucus, making his voice sound thick and muzzled. Still, he is walking in the morning and giving class, although today he didn't say much.

In this morning's verse, Dayānanda read out Prabhupāda's translation of a beautiful detailed description by Prahlāda Mahārāja of the fierce appearance of Lord Nṛsiṁhadeva. "My Lord who is never conquered by anyone, certainly I am not at all afraid of Your very ferocious mouth, tongue, bright eyes like the sunshine, movement of Your eyebrows, very pinching sharp set of teeth, garland of intestines, hands soaked with blood, fixed up high ears, Your tumultuous sound which causes the elephants to go away to a distant place and Your nails which are meant for killing Your enemies. Undoubtedly I am not afraid of them."

For a devotee like Prahlāda, the Lord is never to be feared, even when He is in an angry mood. Yet, Prabhupāda said, devotees are afraid of living in the material world. This is the essential difference between the devotees and the demons.

"Prahlāda Mahārāja will say that 'This fierceful attitude of Your Lordship is not at all fearful to me, as it is fearful to me, this material existence.' This material world is very, very fierceful to the devotees. They are very, very much afraid of.

"This is the difference. Materialistic persons, they are thinking, 'This world is very pleasing. We are enjoying. Eat, drink, be merry, and enjoy.' But the devotees, they think, 'It is very, very fierceful. How soon we shall get out of it?' My Guru Mahārāja used to say that 'This material world is not fit for living for any gentlemen.' He used to say, 'No gentleman can live here.' So these things are not understood by the nondevotees, how much pinching this material world is. Unless one becomes detestful of this material world, it is to be understood that he has not yet entered in the spiritual understanding.

"This is the test of *bhakti*. If one has entered the domain of devotional service, this material world will be not at all tasteful for him. Jagāi and Mādhāi were too much materialistic, woman-hunters, drunkards, meat-eaters ... So these things have become now common affairs. But it is very, very fearful for the devotees.

"Therefore we say, 'No intoxication. No illicit sex. No meat-eating.' It is very, very fearful. But they do not know it. They indulge in. The whole world is going on on this platform. He does not know that he is creating a very, very fierceful situation by indulging in these sinful activities."

* * *

During his massage a newly arrived *brahmacārī* named Ṛkṣarāja asked Prabhupāda if he could take *sannyāsa*. He mentioned he had worked with Chayavana Swami in Africa.

Prabhupāda abruptly retorted, "You know he has gone to hell? That is not recommendation; that is disqualification!" But he told him that anyway, if he was recommended by a GBC member, he could take the vow. Although he added that for preaching in the West *sannyāsa* is not recommended, because people there have no respect for a *sādhu*. But he added that here in India, it is effective for preaching.

Hearing this, Ṛkṣarāja said he would be willing to remain in India to preach if he was given *sannyāsa.*

* * *

Relaxing in his room in the early evening, Prabhupāda enjoyed hearing Yaśodānandana Swami narrate some stories of his party's travels in the South. Mahārāja described one place where they saw *mūrtis* of Lord Nṛsiṁhadeva high up in the hillsides. One of them had eight arms and a garland of intestines, with the demon Hiraṇyakaśipu lying ripped open across His lap. Nearby, there was another Deity with a large mouth full of fearsome teeth.

Prabhupāda listened with interest. He enjoyed Yaśodānandana Swami's descriptions of their successes in the south.

* * *

Jayapatākā Mahārāja reported that the boat program was going well. One day they sold 250 *Gītār-gānas,* and many people are requesting them to do programs in their villages. They also have three new devotees shaved up and chanting. Upon hearing of their success, Prabhupāda's eyes grew big and bright. A smile of innocent surprise lit up his face, as if it were something very great and unexpected. His genuine response, almost a childlike wonder, was completely endearing.

Although he is the transcendental overseer of a large international movement, operating with thousands of men, millions of dollars, and selling tens of millions of books every year, he is still so humble and unassuming; the perfect *ācārya* and pure devotee.

February 23rd, 1976

During class this morning Prabhupāda described the important role the temple plays in helping people to advance in spiritual life by *ajñāta-sukṛti,* unknown pious activity. "*Sukṛti* means the way by which one can approach the Supreme Personality of Godhead. That is called *sukṛti. Ajñāta-sukṛti.* This temple means to give chance to the people in general, *ajñāta-sukṛti.* Anyone who will come to this temple where the Deity is there, and even by imitating others, if one offers obeisances to the Lord, that is taken into account. That is not useless, because this is Kṛṣṇa's desire. He gives the four principles, that 'Always think of Me,' and 'become My devotee,' 'worship Me,' and 'just offer little obeisances.' These four principles will deliver you from this bondage of material existence, and 'without any doubt, you'll come back to Me.'

"So, so simple thing. It is not at all difficult. This child, he can do this. Old man can do this. Learned man can do this, without any knowledge. Even an animal can do it. Very simple. *Bhakti-yoga* is very simple."

He stressed that any person can advance, even unknowingly, simply by gaining the association of devotees, and our temples offer that opportunity. "Therefore, somehow or other, if somebody comes into the temple, and even by imitating one offers obeisances.... We have seen so many people. Our devotees are offering obeisances. They also think that 'It is the etiquette. Let me do that,' by association.

"Therefore it is recommended, *sādhu-saṅga.* Simply by association, one can be delivered. It is so nice thing. Unfortunately they'll not associate with *sādhu.*"

* * *

A telegram came from Los Angeles, saying that *Śrīmad-Bhāgavatam,* Sixth Canto, Volume Three has been completed and would be offered to Śrīla Bhaktisiddhānta on his appearance day. Prabhupāda was extremely pleased. "Yes, keep this on file," he told Dayānanda. "It is a very important telegram!"

* * *

From Vṛndāvana, the manager of the Punjab National Bank informed Prabhupāda that the final approval for our new subbranch has been made. The bank is eager to open straight away. He requested Śrīla Prabhupāda to open the branch with an initial deposit of five *lakhs* of rupees.

Prabhupāda approved, although his suggestion to the manager was that he could have an opening ceremony and personally make the deposit when he goes there in late March, if they so desired.

* * *

Yaśodānandana, Gurukṛpa, and Acyutānanda and Sudāmā swamis all left for Calcutta to visit the Nitai Pada Kamala.

Gopāla Kṛṣṇa arrived. He informed Prabhupāda that all the planned book printing is now underway. Gopāla Kṛṣṇa has ambitions to distribute books to almost 10,000 libraries throughout India. One book agency that supplies every library has agreed to take the books on a six-months trial basis. Gopāla Kṛṣṇa, however, prefers that our own men visit all the Indian universities. He wants to establish an Indian library party along the same lines as the existing Library Party, which has met with so much success in the West.

Śrīla Prabhupāda was very enlivened by his efforts and encouraged him to continue. He said that Gopāla Kṛṣṇa was now fulfilling his strong desire to see all his books printed in Hindi and then widely distributed.

* * *

The construction of the new building here is moving along quite quickly. The foundation and basement level work has been completed, and shuttering work has begun on the first floor. But it is apparent that the building will not be ready for use by the beginning of the festival.

* * *

A government man named Mr. Ganguli arrived in the evening to stay overnight. He is a senior officer from the same department as Mr. Chaudhuri and came to personally see the Māyāpur project and discuss the land acquisition proposal. Prabhupāda talked with him for a few hours, discussing in detail all the plans and requirements for the land.

February 24th, 1976

Because of his cold, Prabhupāda didn't talk much this morning on his walk.

There was one interesting bit of information. Gopāla Kṛṣṇa, who is trying to develop contacts in Eastern Europe, especially in the Soviet Union, told Prabhupāda he had heard that Harikeśa Swami is trying to go to Hungary, but Gopāla couldn't elaborate.

* * *

Class was short. It continued with Prahlāda Mahārāja's theme that the material world is simply a place of suffering. Prabhupāda explained why the soul continues to try to enjoy it, even after having come to the Kṛṣṇa consciousness movement. "The illusory energy is so strong, even one gets the body of a pig, he thinks, 'It is very nice.' This is called *prakṣepātmika-śakti. Māyā* has got especially two energies: *avaraṇātmika* and *prakṣepātmika.* Generally *māyā* keeps us covered with illusion, and if one is little enlightened, wants to get out of the clutches of *māyā,* there is another potency of *māyā, prakṣepātmika.*

"Suppose one thinks, 'Now I shall become Kṛṣṇa conscious. This ordinary material consciousness is so disturbing. Let me become Kṛṣṇa conscious.' So *māyā* will say, 'What you will do with this? Better remain in material consciousness.' This is called *prakṣepātmika-śakti.* Therefore sometimes some man comes in our Society. After staying for a few days, he goes away. This is *prakṣepata,* thrown away. Unless he's very sincere, he cannot stay with us; he'll be thrown away."

* * *

Mr. Ganguli left in the morning after seeing the general plans for the development of the land, and he seemed very favorable. He told Prabhupāda that we should ask for all the land we need at one time rather than a few acres at a time. So they finally decided to ask for 270 acres.

This is the entire area from the back road in the east up to the Gaṅgā and from the Jalāṅgī in the south to the present temple-boundary wall. The city will cover one hundred acres. The rest will be used for agriculture and cow protection.

* * *

Tonight Prabhupāda told Dayānanda that he wants the latest reviews of his books published in a new section of BTG, as well as in the Hyderabad-based newspaper *Hare Kṛṣṇa Explosion.* He is very enlivened by the work of the Library Party and the response of the scholars. He wants to take full advantage of the favorable reviews in order to increase the distribution of his books.

* * *

Gopāla Kṛṣṇa gave the finalized dates for the second half of the festival after Gaura Pūrṇimā. There will be a *paṇḍala* in New Delhi from 26-31 March, one day in Modinagar, and then on to Vṛndāvana.

February 25th, 1976

Today is Ekādaśī. More and more devotees are arriving for the festival.

* * *

This morning, before going out for his walk, Śrīla Prabhupāda called Sudāmā Vipra Swami into his room. Sudāmā Vipra, a gangly, loud, and capricious fellow, has a questionable reputation among the devotees. Prabhupāda is aware of this.

But Sudāmā Vipra professes to have faith in Śrīla Prabhupāda. So Prabhupāda did not directly reprove him, merely tactfully hinting at Sudāmā Vipra's shaky position while encouraging him to do better. As Prabhupāda sat at his desk applying *tilaka,* he quoted one of his favorite sayings: "Big, big monkey, big, big belly; Ceylon jumping—melancholy!" He told him, "So don't become like big, big monkey. In the beginning you were so enthusiastic for *sannyāsa,* now you must do something."

Sudāmā Vipra promised he would try.

When Prabhupāda walked out of his room, he was joined by other senior devotees. As they all climbed the stairs and emerged onto the roof, Prabhupāda continued to emphasize the actual qualification for a *sannyāsa.* He said that if one has any thought that a woman is beautiful, that material wealth and comfort are desirable, or if he has any desire to enjoy material life, he cannot take *sannyāsa.* If one takes *sannyāsa* simply as a means to beg and fill his belly, he will only cheat himself; others will not be fooled.

Hṛdayānanda Mahārāja said that outside India such a *sannyāsī* would starve.

Prabhupāda laughed. He inquired from us, "So I do not know why our disciples are so anxious to take *sannyāsa.* Everyone comes, 'Give me *sannyāsa.*' What is the idea?"

Though he was in good humor, it was clearly a complaint, one he has voiced quite frequently over the last couple of months. Nearly every week he receives requests for *sannyāsa.*

Jayapatākā Swami replied that a *brahmacārī* who gets tired of taking instructions asks for *sannyāsa* so he can become independent. Prabhupāda said that this is not good. *Sannyāsa* is designed for rendering service to everyone. It is not, "I am *sannyāsa,* you are my servants!"

Jayapatākā Swami asked Prabhupāda if one must be fixed up to take *sannyāsa,* or does one take *sannyāsa* to become fixed up?

Prabhupāda replied that the four *āśramas* are meant to fix one up gradually so that ultimately he becomes free of material desires and actually becomes *sannyāsa.* If one has material desires he must become a *gṛhastha* and accept *sannyāsa* later in life.

The conversation turned to Sharma dāsa, an American devotee who came here after serving in Africa. Disturbed by the misbehavior and poor standards there, he came to Vṛndāvana to see Śrīla Prabhupāda late last year, saying he only wanted to chant Hare Kṛṣṇa. Prabhupāda allowed him to come here to Māyāpur.

At present he is living at the *gośālā,* chanting one hundred and fifty rounds a day and eating only the remnants of foodstuffs left by the devotees.

Recently he came to see Śrīla Prabhupāda to get permission to build a tree hut to live in, so that he could avoid seeing anyone. He complained that he was being disturbed because devotees coming to see him interrupted his chanting. But Prabhupāda condemned his idea, which he said was "living like a monkey." He said that Sharma's so-called renunciation was actually another form of sense gratification. It was also based on selfish interest, even if it was only a small display of it.

Prabhupāda gave the example of two thieves, one who stole a diamond and the other who stole a cucumber. Prabhupāda explained that simply because one steals in a small way, it does not mean that he is not a thief.

Jayapatākā Swami asked if *gṛhastha* life was meant for the

one who steals cucumbers. Prabhupāda laughed. "Yes. Kṛṣṇa is giving allowance for stealing cucumber."

Prabhupāda conceded that Sharma at least wasn't doing anything bad. But he said that active service is better. Prabhupāda was not displeased with him, as something is better than nothing. He allowed him to stay here because if he leaves he may end up going elsewhere to practice something other than Kṛṣṇa consciousness.

Some of the senior men also felt that Mahāvīra was not mature enough to take *sannyāsa.* As Prabhupāda circumambulated on the roof, he turned and smiled at Mahāvīra, whose name is another name for Hanuman. "So, Mahāvīra prabhu," he asked, "do you still want to take *sannyāsa?* But don't be like this big, big monkey!"

"I will try to jump, Śrīla Prabhupāda."

"Don't try. Do it! *Sannyāsa* means one *must* turn out successful."

Later, just before entering the temple for the morning program, Prabhupāda saw some light cane-work construction lying at the side of the road. He asked what it was. Sudāmā Vipra explained that he was building a hut from split bamboo. He has arranged to rent some land on our banana plantation for $2,000 per year. He wants to stay in Māyāpur, yet in a little seclusion, apart from the main body of devotees. Prabhupāda didn't comment much, he was simply pleased that Sudāmā Vipra Mahārāja is here in the *dhāma.*

* * *

In the mail today was an update from Dīna Dayal on his preaching in Greece. He has acquired an apartment in a good area of Athens, just near the British embassy. Bhaktijana and Rohiṇī Kumāra have joined him. They held a grand opening in an auditorium. They obtained police permission to hang a poster with Prabhupāda's picture on it all around the city to advertise the opening. Over 150 people attended. Dīna Dayal has begun translating prayers and articles from *Back To Godhead* into Greek. He asked which book Prabhupāda wanted translated first.

Prabhupāda was satisfied with his attempts to preach. He advised him to maintain his efforts, increasing only gradually. He asked him to translate *Bhagavad-gītā As It Is* first.

Nitai also wrote to inform Śrīla Prabhupāda about his attempts to gain affiliation for our *gurukula* with two Sanskrit colleges, one in Delhi and one in Benares. His idea was to adapt their curriculums to our needs.

Prabhupāda wasn't too concerned from the academic standpoint, but he wrote back approving his idea because it may help our students get visas.

* * *

Bilvamaṅgala dāsa brought the finished plans for the Māyāpur temple from Saurabha in Bombay. The total area required has again been revised; now we will apply for 320 acres.

February 26th, 1976

During the morning walk, Jayapatākā Mahārāja commented that it seemed easier to preach and make devotees in Bengal than other places in India.

Prabhupāda agreed, telling us that Bengali culture is much adored all over India. The guru of Mahātmā Gandhi had even said, "Whatever Bengal does today, other provinces will think tomorrow." He explained that many leading figures in recent Indian history were actually Bengalis, then he named a few: Surendranath Bannerji, who started the Congress party in 1887, Vivekananda, Ravīndranath Tagore, and Aurobindo Ghosh.

Prabhupāda said that Aurobindo was actually born in England, but later he turned against the British. At one time Aurobindo seriously practiced yoga. However, later he had some connection with a French woman and became quite fat. Prabhupāda said that meant that from a yogi he became a *bhogī,* or a sense enjoyer. He said that the next stage is *rogī,* diseased. So yogi, *bhogī,* and *rogī.*

That reminded me of something amusing I had been told when I first joined the Sydney temple in 1972. I brought it up to see if Prabhupāda would confirm it. "A yogi passes stool once a day, a *bhogī* twice, and a *rogī* more."

Prabhupāda stopped and smiled. He raised his eyebrows quizzically. "Who told you?"

Jayapatākā laughed. He said that some devotees deliberately held their stool until the next day in order to be a yogi. Even though it gave them stomachache. Everyone laughed, Prabhupāda as well, but with a little surprise. "Acchā?"

As usual, and much to everyone's delight, he had a phrase and a story to enlighten us further on the foolishness of imitation. "That is called *makṣi manda kanāni.* A clerk was making a 'fair book' [good copy] from the 'rough book.' So he went to the toilet room and he was ... like this." At this point he made grabbing motions in the air. "So all of a sudden his boss came. 'What are you doing here?'

"'Sir, I am trying to capture one fly.'

"'And why?'

"'No, I am making the fair copy of the book. But in the original book, there is a fly smashed. So I have to paste one fly.'"

We all laughed heartily as Prabhupāda chuckled and added, "There are such fools. *Makṣi manda kanāni.* There is a fly pasted. So in the fair copy there must be a fly, paste."

* * *

Śrīla Prabhupāda often quotes the teachings of Prahlāda Mahārāja in his conversations and letters, and he seems to derive great inspiration from his prayers.

In this morning's *Śrīmad-Bhāgavatam* verse, Prahlāda Mahārāja declared that only Kṛṣṇa can give us permanent protection. Loving parents cannot save a child, a physician cannot save a patient, and a boat cannot save a drowning man. Prabhupāda gave many appropriate analogies to elaborate upon Prahlāda's statements.

"The human life means if somebody is being killed, so he should be immediately taking warning, 'Oh, my turn is coming. Let me go away.' There is one story in this connection. Not story, these are facts. A hunter spread his net. So some little birds, they fell down in the net and they are crying. So the father, mother when they came, they saw that their children are in danger. 'It is caught by the net of the hunter.' So mother immediately jumped over it to save the children, and she was also captured. Then the father saw. 'If I go to save them, I'll be captured. Let me go away. Let me take *sannyāsa.* That's all.'"

We all laughed.

"That is intelligence. You cannot give protection to your family, to your society, to your.... No, you cannot give. That is not possible. They must die. They must be captured by the network of *māyā.* You cannot save them. If you want to save them, then make them Kṛṣṇa conscious. That is the only remedy."

Prabhupāda emphasized his point by describing practical examples from his disciples' preaching and from his own life. "And *udanvati majjato nauḥ.* Everyone is drowned, either you take figuratively or really. In the sea, ocean, there are always waves. So your tiny boat or big ship, that is not safe side.

"We have got experience. When I was going to New York on ship, I had no money to go by plane. So in the deep sea ocean, especially in the Atlantic Ocean, it was nothing, like a small ball, tottering like this. At any moment it can be capsized. Although very big ship with very big load, but it is nothing in the sea. So that is not sure. There is no surety that because you are in a big ship you'll be saved—no.

"In your country, it happened, say, fifty, sixty years, the Titanic. In the first voyage, everyone was drowned, all big, big men. So nature's freak is so strong, that you cannot say that 'Because I have got a nice ship, I'll be saved.' No, that is not possible. Without Kṛṣṇa's protection, all these counteracting measures will be all useless. Therefore teach people how to take shelter of Kṛṣṇa."

* * *

There was a very amusing incident in mid-morning, when Prabhupāda had a visit from a *yoginī,* Yogashakti Ma. She came smiling into Prabhupāda's room, her long hair streaming over saffron clothing, accompanied by three male followers. She wanted to invite Prabhupāda to a World Yoga and Peace Conference they plan to hold. The address they gave was an apartment in Calcutta.

She expressed her hope that leaders of various yoga and peace groups could get together and exchange their different experiences to everyone's benefit, so that the world could be a better place to live, where everyone could become happy. Of course, she would be at the center of it, as the organizer.

To this end she had issued a leaflet. One of her men read it out. It proclaimed "Health, Harmony, Happiness" through *jñāna, dhyāna, bhakti, karma,* and so on. In other words, a hodgepodge of ideas with no real focus. She finished by saying that their goal was to serve God and humanity.

Hearing the bit about serving God, Prabhupāda called her bluff. "Who is God?" he asked her.

But neither she nor any of her followers could answer. One of them mumbled, "Hari Om." Another said something about the Creator and "love of us all."

Prabhupāda continued in his simple, direct, and matter-of-fact manner. "If there is a toilet, and you go there and throw some scent, does that make it a nice place? Trying to make the toilet a nice place is less intelligent. Kṛṣṇa says *duḥkhālayam aśāśvatam.* This material world is temporary and full of suffering, so trying to be happy here is simply a waste of time."

He was going to continue but couldn't. His analogy visibly shocked them. She had conjured up an image of attaining bliss on earth, and Prabhupāda frankly and abruptly shattered her sentimental vision.

They all took it like a slap in the face. One of the men became visibly disturbed. Speechless, he began to shake. Agitated and disturbed in mind, he wouldn't stay a moment longer. He simply offered his respects, uttered "Hari Om," and got up and left. Yogashakti Ma and the others followed.

Prabhupāda continued to sit at his desk, a smile gracing his face. He wasn't concerned that his words had disturbed their idealistic notions. They were typical *māyāvādīs*—in *māyā.* He had spoken the truth as revealed by God Himself, Lord Śrī Kṛṣṇa. If they couldn't take it, it was no fault of his. He laughed. "By their *yoga-śakti,*" he told me, "they have one flat in Calcutta. We have no such *śakti,* and we have a hundred centers like this [Māyāpur]!"

Prabhupāda is simply wonderful. Others may or may not appreciate, but he cannot compromise the truth for anyone.

His only interest is in serving Kṛṣṇa and Kṛṣṇa's mission—nothing else. By Kṛṣṇa's grace he is enjoying worldwide success. He has neither the need nor desire to have his name associated with anything that deviates from the strict principles of *bhāgavata dharma.*

* * *

Kirtiraja just arrived from Europe. He had traveled overland in the convoy of Mercedes vans with Gargamuni Swami. He has been preaching in Poland. A few people there have shown genuine interest in our movement. He explained that the Polish people live very austere lives, as no luxury items are available. But they are avid readers. Therefore Kirtiraja planned to print and distribute as many books as possible.

Prabhupāda was so eager to see this program started that he offered to give him a loan to begin printing books in Polish and Russian.

As for preaching in Europe, a letter from Mukunda and Bhaja Hari in London conveyed some interesting news. They confirmed that Harikeśa Swami has gone to Hungary on a two-week tour of yoga schools and clubs. Hansadūta spoke to him shortly after his arrival in London, and the next day he was off. The British devotees want him to remain in England and Europe to preach in the universities and colleges.

Prabhupāda approved. He expressed confidence in Harikeśa's speaking and said that he could stay there. He also said that Harikeśa could read more books and preach now that he is a *sannyāsī.*

Their letter also mentioned several recent meetings with ex-Beatle George Harrison, who has allowed us the use of his large country estate, Bhaktivedānta Manor, at Letchmore Heath. Mukunda was one of the first devotees to meet with him, in the late sixties. The devotees are eager to arrange a more permanent arrangement with him.

George's business manager advised him not to donate the property for tax reasons. So our men proposed he give us a ninety-nine year lease at one pound per year. George was agreeable to the idea but perhaps favored a shorter period.

Prabhupāda requested that they send him the lease agreement for approval.

* * *

As Śrīla Prabhupāda relaxed on the balcony, Hṛdayānanda Mahārāja came out to see him. This is his first extended visit to India. He's beginning to understand the significance and magnitude of the projects Prabhupāda has begun here.

He expressed his newfound enthusiasm and realization to Śrīla Prabhupāda. "Your American disciples are beginning to appreciate the importance of India, Śrīla Prabhupāda. When we first arrived we could not understand why you were so busy here, but now we can see that it is the most important place on the planet!"

Prabhupāda looked at him very gravely, raised his eyebrows, and replied decisively, "It is the most important place in the universe!"

Prabhupāda has also instructed Hṛdayānanda Mahārāja to begin plans for the planetarium, based on the descriptions given in the Fifth Canto of *Śrīmad-Bhāgavatam*.

Although the title "Temple of Understanding" has been bandied about as a name for the new temple, Prabhupāda rejected it as soon as Saurabha first delivered the plans. This morning, on his walk, he gave a proper title, revealing as well a little of his vision of its importance. He said it will be called the "Temple of the Vedic Planetarium."

"We shall show the Vedic conception of planetary systems within this material world and above the material world," he said. "We are going to exhibit the Vedic culture throughout the whole world, and they will come here."

In Bombay he had discussed with Dr. Patel the importance of combining culture and education. This is clearly why he has decided to establish the Vedic planetarium along with the temple here in Māyāpur, the world headquarters of his Kṛṣṇa consciousness movement. The temple and surrounding city will show people the Vedic culture, and the planetarium will educate them as to the scientific basis of the culture.

He explained, "Just like they come to see the Taj Mahal.

They'll come to see the civilization and the culture—the philosophical culture, the religious culture—by practical demonstration with dolls and other things."

Jayapatākā Mahārāja suggested that every temple in the world could have a model of the proposed city to advertise the project.

Prabhupāda was enthusiastic. "Yes, actually, it will be a unique thing in the world. There is no such thing all over the world. That we shall do. And not only simply showing museum, but educating people to that idea. With factual knowledge, books; not fictitious."

* * *

Tatpur dāsa, an Indian devotee stationed in Hyderabad, arrived to take *sannyāsa.* Previously he wrote, requesting it. Prabhupāda had sent him an enthusiastic reply, inviting him to come to Māyāpur for the festival. He said he could then take *sannyāsa* and preach in Bengal. Prabhupāda is always eager to see his Indian disciples step forward and take up the responsibility of preaching here.

Meanwhile, Mahāvīra prabhu has had second thoughts, both on taking *sannyāsa* and staying in Māyāpur. He came to see Śrīla Prabhupāda on the roof during massage to ask permission to return to Brazil. He obviously felt a little awkward, or perhaps embarrassed, that he now wants to leave Māyāpur after having caused so much agitation as a manager.

Timidly he approached Prabhupāda and began, "Prabhupāda, I know that it is the duty of the disciple to satisfy the desire of the spiritual master—"

Prabhupāda immediately enjoined, "Yes, and it is my desire that you help manage Māyāpur."

Mahāvīra's discontent with his new assignment troubled his mind enough that he continued. "But Śrīla Prabhupāda, I think they need me in Brazil. I want to satisfy your desire, but I think I am better suited to Brazil."

Prabhupāda still indicated that he wanted him here in Māyāpur. But finally, seeing Mahāvīra's anxiety, he kindly consented to his return to South America. "All right, whether a *gopī* or a cow, both are serving Kṛṣṇa. Go to Brazil. You may serve there."

February 27th, 1976

Prabhupāda is not feeling well, yet he continues to receive visitors and take his walks. On top of a bad cold, he now has uremia again, so he is not taking rice.

His sister, who is still staying here, insists on cooking for him. But he complains that she uses too much chili and ghee, or sometimes heavy doses of mustard oil, which cause some digestive problems.

* * *

He didn't talk much on his walk, but he nonetheless delivered a straight-to-the-point class. The verse described how every living being is acting under the influence of the modes of nature, which comprise Kṛṣṇa's material energy, *durgā.*

"*Durgā* means "fort." We are packed up within this fort. You see the round sky. It is just like a football, and within, we are packed up. *Duḥ* means "difficult," and *gā* means "going." *Durgā.* So just like in the fort, in the jail, if you are put, it is *dur-gā,* very difficult to come out; very, very difficult. *Duḥ* means it is not so easy. You cannot enter in the fort or in the jail. Big, big walls, you cannot enter there without permission, and you cannot come out without permission.

"So this *durgā-śakti,* material energy, is very, very powerful. You cannot come out from this fort of material existence without superior permission. That is Kṛṣṇa's permission."

Prabhupāda explained that knowing everything to be Kṛṣṇa's means we should offer it all for His use. Just like the devotees who bathe in the Gaṅgā; they scoop some water up and offer it back to the Gaṅgā. Similarly, Kṛṣṇa doesn't need our offering, it is already His. But by our doing so, He becomes pleased with us, and thus we are released. If we don't do this then we are "fool number one."

* * *

Jagat Guru dāsa, another candidate for *sannyāsa* at the upcoming festival, arrived today from Africa via the Middle East. He came to the roof during massage to tell Prabhupāda about his recent preaching activities.

While in Dubai Jagat Guru met two brothers who were followers of the Vallabhācārya *sampradāya.* They were impressed with Prabhupāda's work, especially his books. As a result they had donated $12,000. But they requested their donation be given personally to Śrīla Prabhupāda.

Handing the money to Śrīla Prabhupāda, Jagat Guru questioned whether he should inform the Los Angeles BBT to credit the $12,000 to the African book bill. Since Brahmānanda Mahārāja had sent Jagat Guru through the Middle East specifically to collect money to pay off the BBT debts of the African yatra, Jagat Guru assumed the donation would be used for that purpose. Prabhupāda, however, said no. The money was a donation, and therefore separate from other collections. It could not be used to pay off book debts.

Jagat Guru was a little surprised. Because of Prabhupāda's quick response, he could hardly believe that Śrīla Prabhupāda had fully comprehended his statement and request. Shortly after Jagat Guru repeated himself. But Prabhupāda remained firm. The money was a donation to his book fund, and Śrīla Prabhupāda had accepted it.

As far as the debt in Africa was concerned, he good humoredly said of Brahmānanda Swami, "We will not hang him, but he will have to work to pay off his debt."

Prabhupāda said that his Guru Mahārāja had continually started big projects and kept the whole Gauḍīya Maṭha in debt in order to keep his men active and busy. The disciple is always indebted to the spiritual master. He said that, anyway, to be in debt is not such a bad thing, because then the men will not become lazy.

* * *

Devotees in Hyderabad have been publishing an English newspaper called the *Hare Kṛṣṇa Explosion.* Generally a few advance copies of each issue are sent to His Divine Grace.

Some *sannyāsīs* have complained about a small article appeared in the latest edition, Volume 21. The article was titled, "Hindus Converted to Muslims." It explained how Muslims would sometimes convert Hindus simply by sprinkling them with water. Being bound by a very strict caste system, such persons were immediately ostracized from the Hindu community and forced to become Muslims. The article, which was simply a quote from the *Caitanya-caritāmṛta,* had no explanation, nor was it related to anything else in the paper. Acyutānanda Swami felt it inflammatory, especially in view of the community tensions in Hyderabad.

Prabhupāda agreed. The article was pointless, and he was upset about it. He immediately wrote a letter to Mahāṁsa Swami ordering him to stop production. "You must stop circulation of this paper immediately. It is not being properly managed. Who is this rascal who is writing such articles? See to this immediately."

He also criticized a children's quiz that was included in the magazine, which offered prizes for participants. Prabhupāda said it was gambling.

February 28th, 1976

Prabhupāda sat at his desk as he put on his *tilaka* this morning. He told us he was the very same man now as he was before. Previously he had been unable to do anything in India because he had no money. But now with his intelligence and our cooperation, he said that he could do something.

Moving from his room, Prabhupāda climbed up the stairs out onto the roof, picking up a small entourage on the way. As he walked around, glancing over to the new building site, he explained that our concern about money was not ordinary. He expanded his point with a very nice metaphor. He explained that his mission was to reunite Lakṣmī, the Goddess of Fortune, with Nārāyaṇa. In other words, the demoniac want to enjoy the property of God without God, or Sītā without Rāma. Just as Hanuman had worked to release Sītā from Rāvaṇa's hands, Prabhupāda said that he was also working for the same purpose.

"We are not satisfied that Rāma should remain alone and Sītā should be under the custody of Rāvaṇa. I don't want," he said. "Sītā must be released from the custody of Rāvaṇa. With opulence it means we are bringing Sītā nearer, nearer, nearer. That is wanted. Otherwise, for a *sannyāsī,* what is the use of these big buildings? No. We want these big buildings for service of Rāma."

Kirtiraja's presence stimulated Prabhupāda's thoughts about Communism once again. Prabhupāda analyzed the Communists' attempts to wrest money from the capitalists. Although they claim they want to redistribute the world's wealth to the poor class, in fact it is simply one Rāvaṇa taking from another Rāvaṇa. He said that there can be no benefit. He added that Communism has already failed. Kirtiraja agreed. The poor were no better off. In Poland fresh food was scarce and expensive.

Prabhupāda also recalled that on his trip to Moscow in 1971 the only fruit available was strawberries. He concluded that they were being punished by Nature, but because they are rascals they cannot see it.

* * *

Down in the temple room, sitting before an increasing number of Western devotees, Prabhupāda described the futility of trying to create unity in the world by mundane methods. Citing the United Nations as an example, he asked, "Where is the unity?"

He explained how previously there had been the League of Nations, then there was war. They made big plans again, but every twenty years or so there is another conflagration, especially in Europe. He said that they are simply demons, and our mission is to save them. "They have to give up the demonic activities. They have to take to Kṛṣṇa consciousness. Then they will be saved. So we are just trying to introduce the real civilization.

"Actually there is no civilization at the present moment. They are simply cats and dogs and fighting one another. There is no civilization. Atheists, demons, they are predominating.

"And because they have got big, big skyscraper building and many motor cars, India has become victimized. 'Oh, without this motor car and without this skyscraper building, we are condemned.' They are trying to imitate. They have forgotten their own culture, the best culture, Vedic culture. "This is the first time that we are trying to conquer over the demonic culture with this Vedic culture. This is the first time. So it is very pleasing that you have joined this movement.

"If you want to make the human society happy, give them this culture of Kṛṣṇa consciousness. That is being described by

Prahlāda Mahārāja, that *saṁsāra-cakra.* If you become involved in this demonic culture, then the *saṁsāra-cakra,* the wheel of repetition of birth and death, will go on. You cannot stop it. It is not possible. But if you take to Kṛṣṇa consciousness, then there is possibility. This is the purport of this verse. Thank you very much. Hare Kṛṣṇa."

* * *

More news on Chayavana Mahārāja arrived today. It appears that he left ISKCON's Kṛṣṇa Balarāma Mandir to reside in Rādhā-kuṇḍa. There he was behaving very erratically, smoking *bidis,* clearly not in control of his senses. Finally, due to some immigration problems, he has now been arrested by the police.

During his massage Prabhupāda heard a letter sent by Chayavana from Rādhā-kuṇḍa, written just before he was arrested. He is clearly a very troubled soul. Commenting on his arrest, Prabhupāda said that he *should* be punished because he has committed so many sins. He said that punishment would correct him. If he is not punished in this lifetime he will have to suffer in the future, so it is better that it happens now.

He explained how it is like a surgeon having to cut out a boil: it may be painful, but if dealt with immediately then one becomes cleansed. If left untreated, it will only give more trouble. He said that for a devotee if there is an accidental fall-down Kṛṣṇa will excuse. But if the devotee persistently sins, then Kṛṣṇa will allow some punishment for his correction.

* * *

Around mid-day Śrīla Prabhupāda was sitting quietly in his room. A large, heavily built young man ran screaming along the veranda right past Śrīla Prabhupāda's window. A half-dozen other devotees, led by Gurukṛpa Swami, followed him.

Prabhupāda's eyebrows raised in surprise. "What is that?"

I looked out the door and recognized the fugitive as a young American devotee who has been the subject of a discussion over the last few days. Over six feet tall and about 250 pounds, he seems a little mentally slow, with a heavy overhanging brow and deep-set eyes that move evasively when he speaks. Although shaven headed and dressed as a *brahmacārī,* he claims to be a paid-up Life Member. Therefore, he considers himself exempt from doing any service in the *āśrama.* He has a room in the Guest House, and his persistent refusal to do anything other than read Prabhupāda's books has created some resentment among the other devotees.

Prabhupāda sent me out to find out what was going on. It was quite a scene. The men had him hemmed into one corner of the balcony. He was fending them off and yelling at the top of his lungs, "He-e-elllp!" I saw Gurukṛpa kick him and several others tussling with him.

My presence made them aware that Prabhupāda was being disturbed by the commotion. So things quieted down, and Gurukṛpa came before His Divine Grace to explain what was going on.

The boy had gotten into a violent argument after refusing to do any service. The devotees were trying to forcibly remove him from the building. To avoid them, he tried to take refuge on Prabhupāda's floor.

Prabhupāda considered the situation and presented his conclusion. He said that if visiting devotees wanted to read and chant exclusively, there was nothing wrong in it, at least here in Māyāpur. That is provided they were actually reading and not just using this as an excuse to sleep. However, he condemned the notion of giving money to the temple and then asking for Life Membership status. He remarked that this was simply business and not a proper devotional attitude.

Life Membership is for uninitiated devotees. If someone actually joins the movement, then he should surrender everything—his money, his intelligence, his life. That is real Life Membership. For the business of the devotee is to give everything to the spiritual master and thus become his menial servant.

He said the boy should be allowed to stay and not be disturbed. Everyone filed out of his room. With a wry smile Prabhupāda shook his head. "These boys are too sophisticated," he concluded, referring to the "Life Member" *brahmacārī.*

* * *

A letter from an organizer of the Manipur Gītā Mandal

came via Calcutta. They were requesting the names of all those planning to accompany Śrīla Prabhupāda on his forthcoming trip to Imphal. Any foreigner requires a special "inner line permit" in order to enter Manipur.

After discussing with Śrīla Prabhupāda, Dayānanda sent our names and that of his wife, along with a suggested date of departure from Delhi of April 10th 1976.

* * *

When he spoke with Kīrtirāja the other day, Prabhupāda had approved certain plans for preaching in Poland. But upon hearing that Hansadūta had already formulated another strategy, he canceled his own suggestions. He told Kīrtirāja simply to follow the GBC's instructions.

This policy of referring things for GBC approval, both individually and collectively, is something he is doing more and more. Prabhupāda often says that he wants to be relieved from management as soon as possible, not when he leaves the planet but long before, so that he can retire and write his books.

* * *

An increasing number of devotees are discovering the sweetness of evening *darśanas* in Prabhupāda's room. The devotees rarely have an opportunity to associate with Śrīla Prabhupāda in such an informal and intimate setting.

Prabhupāda has been responding to their eagerness with some blissful recollections of his early days in America in 1965–66, including the difficulties he went through. This evening he told us that when he came to America he had not expected to remain long, as his original visa was valid for only two months. But for a year he continued to extend his stay: two months, two months, two months, each time thinking to remain a little longer and give things a try. He would go to the shipping agency and inquire when the next ship back to India was, but he would never go.

Eventually the clerk, a friendly Indian man, inquired, "Swamijī, you are asking, but actually, when you will go?"

Prabhupāda would laugh and tell him, "No. Actually I don't want. But sometimes when I am a little disappointed, I think about it."

Then as preaching opportunities started to unfold, he began paying a lawyer $150 a month to get his visa extended. Eventually he took a man's advice and went to Montreal to apply for residence. Three months later he reentered the country with his Green Card via Santa Fe, New Mexico, where Subala had begun a center.

He went on to tell about his life on New York's Second Avenue. He would stroll along the river bank, unaware that the area was notoriously dangerous. Eventually someone informed him that sometimes snipers shot pedestrians there at random. "I was innocent," he said. "I didn't know they were killing people there."

It was fascinating to listen to His Divine Grace reminisce about the early days of his mission.

Never self-laudatory, and always humble about his success, Śrīla Prabhupāda captivates his audience with his unique and remarkable character. He has a combination of youthful simplicity coupled with an astonishingly deep perceptiveness of human nature and life in general. He attributes everything to Lord Kṛṣṇa's special mercy rather than to any expertise of his own. This selfless quality makes him irresistibly attractive, an ideal teacher, and our most trustworthy friend.

February 29th, 1976

In his lecture this morning Prabhupāda vividly described how the covering power of *māyā* influences a person's sense of enjoyment. He explained that in Burma they have a drink called *naphi.* People keep special pots into which they place dead bodies of animals, which are then left to decompose. Later, after some years, the fluids are drained and bottled to be drunk at festivals.

When Śrīla Bhaktisiddhānta's men opened a center in Rangoon, they cooked *puris* in ghee. The neighboring people actually complained about the "horrible smell."

* * *

After having spent some time in America and Europe gathering funds, men, and equipment, Gargamuni Swami arrived with his TSKP in a grand style. Their large, blue-and-white Mercedes vans came driving down Bhaktisiddhānta road one after another, with mounted loudspeakers blaring out the *mahā-mantra.*

When they entered the front gate, Śrīla Prabhupāda came out on the veranda to see the spectacle, and all the devotees eagerly gathered around to greet them.

Gargamuni Swami rushed up to Śrīla Prabhupāda's rooms, where he enthusiastically described his future preaching plans. He showed Prabhupāda a wonderful new preaching aid he had bought in America—a portable eight-millimeter film display. It resembled a briefcase but it had a screen inside the lid, which was slotted for cassette films. The machine cost $250 and each cassette the same amount.

Each of his preaching parties is equipped with one. In this way they will be able to walk into any businessman's office, show him a film about Kṛṣṇa consciousness, and then sign him as a Life Member. Gargamuni's plan is to launch a bold new membership drive.

Needless to say, His Divine Grace was very enthusiastic. Fully enlivened, he called all the *sannyāsīs* to his room and told them to plan a tour route from village to village between the 15th and 26th of March. He said he would also participate.

* * *

Prabhupāda refused to allow Pisimā to cook for him any more, because after eating her lunch yesterday he became ill and had to take rest at 8:00 p.m.

He called her in and told her to return to Calcutta. She argued with him. Then Prabhupāda shouted at her in Bengali, and she became upset and started to cry. He was telling her to go, and she refused. Finally she got up in tears and left the room.

They have a very special, transcendental relationship. Apart from being Śrīla Prabhupāda's sister (she even looks like him), Pisimā is also an initiated disciple of Śrīla Bhaktisiddhānta Sarasvatī and a great devotee of Lord Kṛṣṇa.

As he relaxed on his *āsana* afterward, he told me she should stay in Calcutta and look after their childhood Deities.

He shook his head and laughed. "She has some idea of traveling with me. She thinks I am her brother. This is the problem. Therefore Caitanya Mahāprabhu took *sannyāsa.* Not because it changed Him as a person, but to get away from the family. Generally family members don't take instruction. I was the same person before taking *sannyāsa* as after. I took *sannyāsa* for this reason. Otherwise, I could have done the same things without it."

March 1st, 1976

There was lively discussion on the walk this morning about modern scientific theories.

Prabhupāda enjoys instigating debates. This way he not only exposes the flaws of the prevalent world view that everything is simply a chance combination of matter, but he also convinces us of the superior nature of Kṛṣṇa consciousness.

This morning Hṛdayānanda Mahārāja brought up a popular concept, commonly referred to as the atomic theory. He explained that this theory states that everything is constituted of different atoms; the ultimate truth is the atomic particle. By different combinations of these particles, different material manifestations are produced. According to this, there is no other cause except this endless combining of atomic particles.

Śrīla Prabhupāda questioned, "Where from the atom comes?" Then he went on to explain that the atomic theory is there in Vedic conception. It is called *paramāṇuvāda.* "This material, matter, everything, is a combination of atomic particles. Either you take earth or take water or air or fire, everything is a combination of atoms. That's a fact. But we know that these atoms are coming out as the energy of Kṛṣṇa. *Bhinnā. Bhinnā* means the quality of different—not the same quality. *Apareyam.* 'This is inferior quality, but there is another, superior quality, *jīva bhūta,* and that is the living entity.'

"So two kinds of atoms are coming from Kṛṣṇa: one is the spiritual atom, and the other is the material atom. So spiritual atoms, they are many, many times greater than the material atoms. And these material atoms are this universal, innumerable universes. Some of the spiritual atoms, when they want to enjoy independently, they are given the chance of enjoying this material atom. So in the material world it is combination of material and spiritual atoms. In the spiritual world, there is no material atom—everything is spirit."

Prabhupāda said that the physicists have not been able to find out the spiritual atom. They are therefore puzzled, and their scientific research is incomplete. Although *Bhagavad-gītā* gives them information, unfortunately they will not take it.

Acyutānanda Swami said that because they are so sinful, they cannot see. He compared them to Duryodhana, in that Duryodhana was so sinful that even Kṛṣṇa personally could not convince him. He had no reservoir of pious activities to draw on.

Prabhupāda liked his comparison. He agreed, "The Duryodhana party, and we are Pāṇḍu's party. So there must be war always, fighting. And they'll be smashed." He quoted *Bhagavad-gītā* (1.19). "*Hṛdayāni vyadārayat.* You know that? 'Breaking the heart of Dhṛtarāṣṭra.' So we have to make preaching in such a way to break the heart of this Dhṛtarāṣṭra company. Then it will be preaching."

Śrīla Prabhupāda mentioned that a description of the atom is given in the *Śrīmad-Bhāgavatam.* There it describes that six *aṇus* make one *paramāṇu.* It is this *paramāṇu* that the scientists are detecting. Prabhupāda concluded, therefore, that no scientist has a proper understanding of the atom.

Acyutānanda Mahārāja asked how they were able to make an atomic bomb if they didn't know what the atom is.

Prabhupāda's simple reply effectively removed his doubt. "Suppose if you can make a nice vegetable preparation, that does not mean you know everything of the vegetable. You are still rascal." He pointed over to the new building gradually being made manifest by the hired workers. "Just like this mason worker. They know how to set up the bricks and do nice work. But that does not mean they know where from the brick has come."

* * *

In the verse for *Śrīmad-Bhāgavatam* class this morning, Prahlāda Mahārāja explained the futility of striving for a better material situation. People in general aspire to heavenly life, to live longer and enjoy greater standards of material happiness. But even the demigods became afraid merely by the movement of Hiraṇyakaśipu's eyebrow. Yet Hiraṇyakaśipu was destroyed within a moment by Lord Nṛsiṁhadeva.

Prabhupāda told us therefore that we should avoid getting entangled in the pursuit of material enjoyment. Sex life is its pinnacle, but its result is simply troublesome.

There is an ever-increasing number of devotees attending class, many of them *brahmacārīs.* So when Prabhupāda told us it is better to avoid sex life altogether and remain *brahmacārī,* there was a collective response of "Jaya! Jaya Prabhupāda!"

"Either illicit sex or legal sex," he said, "there are many, many sufferings. But those who are miser—miser means one who cannot use the benefit he has got, this human form of life—they know there are so many after-effects; they are not satisfied. "So the whole Kṛṣṇa consciousness movement is how to become *dhīraḥ,* selfless. Then life is successful. And anyway, don't be involved, entangled, with these material things.

"This morning we were calculating that there are ... as many atoms, so many living entities are also there, and there is struggle here. So in this human life the chance is how to get out of this material atomic combination and go back to home, back to Godhead. This is the chance."

* * *

Hansadūta prabhu arrived in Māyāpur today with Pṛthu Putra Swami. He had stopped off in Vṛndāvana for a few days on his way from Europe by air. Meanwhile his *saṅkīrtana* buses are being driven overland through Turkey, Iran, and Pakistan.

Now that the village-to-village *saṅkīrtana* program is about to commence, Prabhupāda is becoming more and more enthusiastic. Very keen "to do something wonderful in India," he again called a meeting of all the senior men to make plans for traveling *saṅkīrtana.*

* * *

Jayapatākā Mahārāja purchased a concrete mixer for seventeen-thousand rupees to help speed up construction of the new building. The work is now so far behind that Prabhupāda has ordered a double shift to begin immediately. Prabhupāda wants it to be ready for the festival, at least as sleeping accommodation, but it doesn't appear possible at the present rate of progress.

* * *

I have contracted a heavy cold, the skin on my heels is deeply cracked, and I have a cut on my hand. Moreover, my left thumb joint is bruised, and my knees have become swollen and sore, with sacks of fluid on them, making it painful to kneel. I therefore have to use a pillow to cushion my knees when I massage Prabhupāda's head. The physical discomfort is making it hard for me to focus my mind on my service. I must be more attentive to avoid offenses at Prabhupāda's lotus feet. The evening massage is also becoming difficult to perform. It has been getting increasingly longer each night.

Every evening after the *pūjārīs* fumigate Prabhupāda's bedroom with incense to drive out the mosquitos, Ānakadundubhi dāsa and I drape a large net around the bed. When Prabhupāda lies down to take rest at about 10:00 p.m., the lights go out. I slip under the net and perch cross-legged at his side to massage up and down his legs and feet as he softly slumbers.

Previously the massage lasted between a half an hour and forty-five minutes. But here in Māyāpur the sessions have been going on for an hour, or longer. Tonight it went on for over two hours, the longest ever. I left Prabhupāda's room just after midnight.

I find it very difficult to sit in the dark, sweating under the mosquito net, breathing air thick with incense smoke with no breeze for relief, and with not a sound save Śrīla Prabhupāda's soft snoring. It is difficult to stay awake on the job. Occasionally I do drift off, only to snap suddenly back to consciousness without knowing how long I have been out.

But tonight, by Kṛṣṇa's grace, I was able stay awake by chanting *ślokas* within my mind. I remembered that in the *Gītā,* Kṛṣṇa called Arjuna Guḍākeśa, the "conqueror of sleep." My little experience is giving me a glimpse of what a high degree of sense control is required to earn the title of Guḍākeśa.

Serving Śrīla Prabhupāda personally is sometimes very demanding; but it is extremely rewarding and always fully satisfying to the heart.

March 2nd, 1976

The *sannyāsī-gṛhastha* controversy continues to simmer, although in Śrīla Prabhupāda's presence the criticism's are muted. Even among the *sannyāsīs* there is no clear consensus.

When Prabhupāda brought it up for discussion on his walk this morning, Hṛdayānanda Mahārāja said he doesn't think the *gṛhasthas* are such a burden on the Society. But Gurukṛpa, Yaśodānandana, and Gargamuni swamis disagreed and were quite pushy. They feel that the presence of many women and children in the temples creates an atmosphere of laziness.

Prabhupāda agreed that the women and children could live on farms. There the children could be brought up as devotees and the women engaged in small cottage industry. The city centers could then be used simply for preaching.

Gurukṛpa doubted the *gṛhasthas* would agree to such a proposal.

Prabhupāda's response was quick and straight to the point. "Then don't allow. Don't allow that. Unless they follow the rules and regulations, what is the use?" He was concerned that all the devotees be conscientious about their service and spiritual practices, and he was satisfied to hear from Gargamuni that in general, most devotees do attend all the programs in the temple.

Prabhupāda's main point was that all devotees must be fully engaged in service. He doesn't want any laziness.

He brought up the same point again at the end of his *Śrīmad-Bhāgavatam* lecture. He told us that the disease of everyone in the material world is the desire to be a master. Whether a person has charge of one or two family members or the entire universe like Lord Brahmā, the disease is the same. So when people come to our Kṛṣṇa conscious Society, the leaders have to be alert to see to the treatment of this disease.

"Prahlāda Mahārāja has understood this so-called false prestigious position of becoming a master. He says that 'I am quite aware of this false thing. Kindly engage me ... *Nija-bhṛtya-pārśvam,* means just like apprentice. One apprentice is engaged to one expert man. By and by, the apprentice learns how to do the things. Therefore he says, *nija-bhṛtya-pārśvam.* 'Not that immediately I become very expert servant, but let me....'

"Our institution is for that purpose. If somebody comes here, he must learn how to serve. Those who are serving, one should learn from him how he's serving twenty-four hours. Then our joining this institution will be successful. And if we take it that 'Here is an institution where we can have free hotel, free living, and free sense gratification,' then the whole institution will be spoiled. Be careful. All the GBCs, they should be careful that this mentality may not increase. Everyone should be very eager to serve, to learn how to serve. Then life will be successful."

* * *

About 10:30 a.m. he heard some disconcerting reports about the Vṛndāvana temple from Hansadūta and Pṛthu Putra Swami. They said the devotees in Vṛndāvana are eating three large meals a day and even owe money for food supplies. Akṣayānanda Mahārāja is spending all his time in management at the temple. Consequently there is no preaching program going on.

Prabhupāda wasn't happy to hear about this. He told Gurukṛpa Swami to go there immediately. He gave him instructions to reorganize everything and to send Akṣayānanda Swami out preaching to raise funds through Life Membership.

* * *

In the evening Prabhupāda called all the *sannyāsīs,* and whatever GBC men were present, to discuss the position of women in our Society. He is concerned that a major conflict seems to be looming between the *sannyāsīs* and *gṛhastha* temple presidents. They appear to be at odds on many issues.

There are reports that *sannyāsīs* are not allowed to preach in certain temples in America because they are speaking out against marriage and almost exclusively supporting *brahmacārī* life. There are also allegations that large buildings are being purchased, simply for use as residences. Thus difficult monetary obligations are being incurred, and it is the *brahmacārī saṅkīrtana* members who end up paying for them. Preaching programs have begun to suffer as a result.

And some *sannyāsīs* are objecting that *brahmacārīs* are being told to get married if they feel some sexual agitation, rather than being encouraged to strive for higher principles of austerity and celibacy. They argued that the presidents prefer to get them married off in order to keep them in their temples for fund-raising rather than let them travel and preach with *sannyāsīs.*

Prabhupāda heard the complaints but said that all things must be decided by the GBC and no one can go against their decision. He declined to make any final statement one way or the other, but he again suggested the women and children could live on ISKCON farms and help develop small-scale cottage industries. He said that our whole preaching program is detachment from material enjoyment: stopping sex life altogether. *Gṛhastha* life is a concession to those unable to give up sex immediately. But he added that in actuality, marriage is not at all required. It is simply burdensome. Licit or illicit, the after-effects of sex simply mean difficulty.

March 3rd, 1976

In the morning Prabhupāda met two of his Godbrothers, Govinda Mahārāja and one other, who came from the Caitanya Gauḍīya Maṭha to see him. Prabhupāda referred to Govinda Mahārāja as an old friend. After Tīrtha Mahārāja, who is now apparently crippled, he is second in command at the Caitanya Maṭha. Prabhupāda gave him a copy of his translation and commentary on the *Caitanya-caritāmṛta, Ādi Līlā* One. He also discussed his book production and distribution with Govinda Mahārāja. Their meeting was short but pleasant. It seems Prabhupāda will reciprocate with a visit to their *maṭha.*

* * *

Evening brought disturbing news that Jagadīśa, who is now back in America, has sent all the Dallas *gurukula* children and teachers home without consulting anyone. It so disturbed Prabhupāda that he immediately called all the *sannyāsīs* and GBCs into his room for discussion. Jagadīśa was here in Māyāpur just a short while ago, but he had not mentioned that he was contemplating such radical action.

Prabhupāda was incredulous. He said that the *gurukula* must be continued at all costs. He knew of the difficulties in conforming to government regulations and of the devotees' attempts to find another place, but he never anticipated Jagadīśa's drastic decision. He was very perturbed and feared that everything there would be finished. So after consulting with his GBC men and *sannyāsīs,* he ordered Dayānanda prabhu, who was formerly the headmaster there in Dallas, to return tomorrow. He gave him instructions to take charge and keep the school open.

Even when I reminded Prabhupāda that Jagadīśa will be arriving here in a few days for the GBC meetings, he remained insistent that Dayānanda leave at the earliest opportunity and do all he can to prevent the closing. After much discussion he finally sent everyone out.

I returned about 9:00 p.m. to find him sitting on the carpet in his bedroom, before his small Deity of Lord Caitanya, deep in contemplation. He looked very strained.

Kneeling before him, I asked how we could avoid bad management. Should we simply pray to Kṛṣṇa to reveal the faults, or what?

With resignation in his voice, Prabhupāda replied. "We cannot hire outsiders. Everything must be done by our own men. Unless a man is Kṛṣṇa conscious, he cannot manage nicely. A bad man cannot do good management. The only way we can be sure of our leaders is if they follow the instructions of the spiritual master."

* * *

On a happier note, Puṣṭa Kṛṣṇa Swami arrived very late in the evening with Prabhupāda's new Mercedes limousine, which he had driven from Germany. He was immediately appointed Śrīla Prabhupāda's new secretary. Before packing his own bags Dayānanda gave him a quick briefing.

Siddha Svarūpānanda Goswami also arrived. He went to the banana plantation we have near the Jalāṅgī river to stay with Sudāmā Vipra Mahārāja.

March 4th, 1976

Dayānanda prabhu left at daybreak, bound for Dallas. He was armed with two letters from Śrīla Prabhupāda: one addressed to the parents of the students asking them to return their children to the school, with an additional request that they be prompt in paying tuition fees; and one to the devotees involved with the running of the school, asking them to cooperate with Dayānanda to keep it open.

* * *

Instead of walking on the roof, Prabhupāda took a twenty-minute ride in his new, maroon Mercedes. Gargamuni Swami's van rode in front, playing *kīrtana* over the loudspeakers. As we drove through the surrounding villages the inhabitants stood wide-eyed looking at the procession.

The car is classy and comfortable, and Prabhupāda is very pleased. He is happy to have it because previously devotees have had to beg various Life Members for the use of their cars whenever he arrived at their temples. Prabhupāda felt that this created a bad image for the Society.

There is a complication to keeping it in India though, because import tariffs are two to three times the value of the car. Puṣṭa Kṛṣṇa Mahārāja has obtained a six-month *carnet,* after which the car must be taken out of the country. He hopes to make an arrangement to send it to Nepal, renew the *carnet,* and then bring it back in.

Once back inside the temple compound's front gate, Prabhupāda got out of the car and decided to walk down toward the *prasādam* hall. At the end of the line of the boundary wall, opposite the southern gate, he stopped to inspect the circular-shaped toilet block. It is meant to provide basic amenities for the families occupying the rooms on the front wall.

He was repulsed by what he saw. Human faeces lay strewn on the outer pathway. Poking several of the doors open with his cane, he saw that each and every toilet was completely blocked with stool and overflowing. Śrīla Prabhupāda was shocked. He could not believe it possible that the maintenance of the block was so neglected. He demanded to know who was responsible.

One devotee explained that the newer Bengali devotees are simple village people and not accustomed to using flush toilets. He said the Western devotees never used this block.

Prabhupāda rejected the excuse. He was disgusted. "I could understand if they [the Bengali villagers] do not react to this, because they are used to passing stool in the fields. But you Westerners, you are not trained in such a way."

He asked, "How our Western men can allow this situation without doing anything about it?" He called the managers and told them to immediately have the toilets fixed and cleaned.

After entering the temple, greeting the Deities, and receiving *guru-pūjā,* he gave *Śrīmad-Bhāgavatam* class. The verse expressed Prahlāda Mahārāja's feelings of humility as he described himself as born in a family infected with the hellish qualities of passion and ignorance. It was a wonder to Prahlāda that Lord Nṛsiṁhadeva had touched him personally on his head, even though that favor had never been extended to great personalities like Lord Brahmā, Lord Śiva and even Lakṣmī, the Lord's eternal consort.

The toilet incident was obviously still on Prabhupāda's mind. He often draws upon real-life incidents and presents them in a more-refined philosophical way in class. But today, without any delay, he directly complained about what he had seen. He spelled out the serious implications very clearly. Prabhupāda took full advantage of the description in this verse to express his disapproval of our inaction in the face of a gross display of ignorance.

"This is the position. Prahlāda Mahārāja, humbly submitting, because he is Vaiṣṇava, that 'What is my position? My position is that I am born of *rajas-tamo-guṇa.*' This birth takes place according to quality we acquire. Just like I was rebuking that toilet. This is so nasty, *tamo-guṇa,* and if I have no response to such *tamo-guṇa* place, that means I am also of that quality.

"Just like between fire and fire, there is no reaction; but fire and water there is reaction. Similarly, *sattva-guṇa* and *sattva-guṇa,* there is no reaction. *Tamo-guṇa-tamo-guṇa,* there is no reaction. In English it is called incompatible, when different qualities [mix]. Acid and acid, you mix; there is no reaction. But acid and alkaline, if you mix, there will be effervescence immediately.

"So if one is developing *tamo-guṇa,* then, if he becomes a pig next life there is no reaction. He'll be very glad that 'I am pig,' 'I am dog.' There is no reaction. But if one is *sattva-guṇa,* then he cannot tolerate. Immediately obnoxious: 'Oh, such a nasty condition.'

"So I am very sorry there was no reaction in such a nasty toilet room. And you are getting sacred thread, the quality of *brāhmaṇa, sattva-guṇa.* It is very regrettable. Nobody reacted. This is the position, that unless we curb down these *raja-guṇa, tamo-guṇa,* there is no improvement. If a person in Kṛṣṇa consciousness is found to have no reaction in *raja-guṇa, tamo-guṇa,* then he's a dull stone. It is not improving. It is simply show bottle. So show bottle will not help.

"This prescription is there. If one develops Kṛṣṇa consciousness, then it is to be understood that he has surpassed *sattva-guṇa,* the *brahminical* qualification. Why we offer sacred thread to a person who is coming from very, very low family? Because it is to be understood by chanting Hare Kṛṣṇa mantra, by following the regulative principle, he has already come to the platform of *sattva-guṇa.* But if it is a false thing, there is no need of second initiation.

"Our process is 'Don't do this. Do this: Chant Hare Kṛṣṇa mantra, sixteen rounds; and don't do this—no illicit sex, no meat-eating.' That means he's becoming purified from the rotten condition of *rajo-guṇa* and *tamo-guṇa.* But if he does not, then there should be no second initiation. This should be the rule."

Prabhupāda's criticism had its effect. By mid-morning the whole block was thoroughly cleansed and disinfected. The managers vowed to keep it that way.

* * *

The work on the new building is going on enthusiastically even though it is clear it will not be habitable for the festival. The several-hundred hired workers usually arrive around 7:00 a.m. Within a half hour everything is in full swing. Sometimes a great clamor and loud shouts can be heard from them as they respond to the urging of our devotee supervisors to work faster and harder. Even though they are being pushed, they are in good spirits, full of smiles. They often chant "Hare Kṛṣṇa!" and "Jaya!" due to their association with the devotees.

Some of our Western men are also helping with the construction. They balance mortar, bricks, and mud in the wok-shaped *karai* on their heads, much to the delight of the laborers. The new cement mixer is a boon, but its loud clatter has been creating a distracting background racket during Śrīla Prabhupāda's morning *Śrīmad-Bhāgavatam* discourse. So now it is shut down while he speaks.

* * *

During his massage, which he took downstairs on his veranda, Prabhupāda glanced across the fields toward the *gośālā*. "So our Siddha Svarūpa and Sudāmā Vipra like to stay at the banana plantation?" he asked.

I took his enquiry as a prompt to ask some questions of my own. I wanted to hear Prabhupāda's response to some specific points of contention between Siddha Svarūpa's followers and our ISKCON devotees. "Śrīla Prabhupāda, when Siddha Svarūpa first surrendered—"

Prabhupāda cut me off. "He never surrendered!" Then he chuckled. Seeing my surprised look, he explained that they had come and made some offering of men and assets. Therefore he was trying to engage them in devotional service.

I asked whether our devotees should read Siddha Svarūpa's books, because ISKCON devotees have been told that they are not bona fide.

Prabhupāda laughed and replied good humoredly. "We don't take notice of what they say. We just take their money!"

Although between his disciples there seem to be major differences preventing cooperative action, Prabhupāda smilingly gave his own perspective on the two camps. "Of course I have affection for them. I don't send them away, and they are coming to see me. Just like there may be so many animals; some are a little fiercer than others." He also pointed out that they are coming to us, not us to them. Prabhupāda always refers to ISKCON as "us." He said that there are differences, just as there are between him and his own Godbrothers, but that we share a common platform of chanting Hare Kṛṣṇa and taking *prasādam.*

I mentioned that in New Zealand our men discouraged Siddha Svarūpa's people from visiting the temple. But Prabhupāda said, "Why? They can come. Our centers are only for this purpose—to chant Hare Kṛṣṇa and take *prasādam.* Gradually they will come to sense."

* * *

Śrīla Prabhupāda sent Śatadhanya with a message to his Godbrother, Śrīdhara Swami, inviting him to come to see him here in Māyāpur. He offered to send his car.

* * *

During the evening, as the temple room reverberated with a thunderous *sandhyā ārati kīrtana,* Acyutānanda Swami, Puṣṭa Kṛṣṇa Swami, and I had a debate on the balcony about whether or not everything in the material creation is actually spirit.

Acyutānanda Swami, a witty, brilliant speaker, argued that everything is not spirit, at least not in the sense that spiritual means everything is conscious. Thinking that everything made of matter is conscious, he said, could lead to madness. You might walk around on tiptoes not wishing to hurt the floor, or you might hesitate to close the door, not wishing to hurt the door. In this way he spoke quite convincingly that matter is not spirit. Later I went in to see Śrīla Prabhupāda to get a proper understanding. When I put the question to him, he immediately cited *Śrīmad-Bhāgavatam* 1.5.20. He had me read it aloud: "The Supreme Personality of Godhead is Himself this cosmos, and still He is aloof from it. From Him only has this cosmic manifestation emanated, in Him it rests, and unto Him it enters after annihilation. Your good self knows all about this. I have given only a synopsis."

He then explained that everything is spirit, and thus everything is conscious. The material energy is conscious, but undeveloped. It can develop consciousness by Kṛṣṇa's will. *Prasādam* is matter but changes into spirit, and it is therefore conscious.

He gave me an example he used a few days ago, how the body produces skin and nails: one is sensitive and the other insensitive. Cut one and you feel pain, cut the other and you feel nothing. Yet the body as a whole is conscious.

The universe is Kṛṣṇa's body and thus is conscious. *Jīvas,* the individual souls, are very minute consciousness, but there is also "mass consciousness." If you touch a stone it is conscious, yet unconscious, or undeveloped. The term "matter" simply indicates the state of one of Kṛṣṇa's eternal spiritual potencies.

I left his room happy in mind and gratified in heart. This is one of the advantages of being with him personally—all doubts can be immediately resolved. As disciples, we may read Prabhupāda's books yet still end up speculating. But a few direct words from His Divine Grace and everything becomes clear. He always refers to a scriptural verse when asked a question and has the purport read out. Invariably it explains the point perfectly. He is intimately familiar with everything in each of his books, and his deep realizations enable him to answer every question to one's complete satisfaction.

March 5th, 1976

Prabhupāda is a reservoir of information on all topics. He has quotes and meaningful comments to make on all varieties of topics, and with just a few words he can enlighten his eager listeners on any subject. He has a clear vision of what constitutes the best qualities and attributes required by man for peaceful and successful human life. His observations on culture and education are especially penetrating. He likes to quote the great sage Caṇakya, whose writings offer penetrating observations on the psychology of human living.

During his walk he told us how, according to Caṇakya, true beauty can be understood. "Man with education is compared with the *kokila.* The bird, *kokila,* is very black, but his sound, sweet, so sweet, everyone likes. *Kokilānāṁ svaro rūpām vidyā-rūpām kurūpāṇām, nārī-rūpāṁ pati-vrataḥ.* A woman's beauty is how she is chaste and devoted to the husband. That is beauty, not personal beauty. Education is the beauty for the brain. And those who are saintly person, they should be simply forgiving. That is their beauty."

Though simple points, when understood in the greater context of Śrīla Prabhupāda's mission, each small aspect fits like a clear note into the harmonic melody of Kṛṣṇa conscious life. And Prabhupāda is the expert conductor, in knowledge of all the available elements, masterfully blending them together to produce a beautiful symphony on a universal scale. Every moment with him is an opportunity to learn and to advance another step toward Kṛṣṇa, the ultimate goal of life.

* * *

In class Prabhupāda described the relationship of the living being with Kṛṣṇa as "responsive cooperation." People sometimes ask, if God does not discriminate, then why are there rich and poor people in the world? The answer is that because of responsive cooperation, how ever much we surrender to Kṛṣṇa, that much He returns to us.

He explained how there are many men, who after making *lakhs* and *crores* of rupees, retire to Vṛndāvana. They leave all their money to their wives and families, requesting them to send two hundred rupees a month "for serving God." But this is not a good policy. If we give two hundred to God, then Kṛṣṇa will give us two hundred in return. He does not discriminate. Rather we discriminate, and Kṛṣṇa reciprocates.

Prabhupāda offered himself as an example: "Just see practically. Our Kṛṣṇa consciousness movement was started with forty rupees. Now that forty rupees added with Kṛṣṇa, it has become forty *crores*. You see practically. When I started for your country, I came to Māyāpur. I offered my obeisances to my spiritual master. Then I went. At that time I had no money even to purchase the ticket. And after that, I have come with forty *crores*. This is the secret. *Ye yathā māṁ prapadyante.* If you fully surrender to Kṛṣṇa, then Kṛṣṇa is there."

* * *

Bhavānanda Goswami returned from the boat program, enthusiastic and full of wonderful stories about the response they have been receiving. Śrīla Prabhupāda relished hearing about the daily programs in the villages and big receptions they got wherever they went.

Bhavānanda described how they simply dock the boat, perform *kīrtana,* and then walk in procession with Śrī Śrī Gaura-Nitai. The villagers become very eager to have the party visit their homes. The devotees make it a point to sell everyone a *Gītār-gāna,* which they daily distribute by the hundreds.

Prabhupāda was excited at the news of the book sales. He made it clear this was the success of the party. He praised Bhavānanda that he had begun book distribution in India. He now wants 100,000 *Gītār-gānas* printed immediately.

* * *

Atreya Ṛṣi dāsa, the GBC for the Middle East, arrived from Iran. He came up to see Prabhupāda just as he began his lunch. Rather than ask him to come back later, Prabhupāda had me set a plate for Atreya by his side. He personally filled Atreya Ṛṣi's plate with *prasādam* from his own plate, as he heard about his efforts to preach in Iran. He was very happy with Atreya and promised him all the men he needs to get things going in the Middle East.

* * *

In the evening, on the lawn adjacent to the guest house, dozens of local villagers came and put on a whirling, exuberant display of flame throwing and stick fighting, especially for Prabhupāda's pleasure. While some danced around in a huge circle, twirling their hard bamboo *lāṭhis* over their heads, behind their backs, and between their legs, others put on mock fights, clashing and banging their sticks together. Still others blew huge clouds of flames high into the air and lit up the night sky. Prabhupāda came out onto the balcony and watched it all for fifteen minutes, enjoying it very much.

Afterward all the villagers were fed sumptuous *prasādam.*

March 6th, 1976

About 6:30 a.m. Prabhupāda went with his senior *sannyāsīs* to the Caitanya Gauḍīya Maṭha to visit Govinda Mahārāja. He was received cordially in the *darśana maṇḍapa,* or viewing area, at the *samādhi* tomb of Śrīla Bhaktisiddhānta Sarasvatī Ṭhākura. After offering his obeisances to his Guru Mahārāja, he sat on the spacious marble floor as many members of the *āśrama* gathered around. As Govinda Mahārāja and Prabhupāda talked, delicious *gulabjamuns* were passed around to the visitors.

After about twenty-five minutes, Śrīla Prabhupāda returned to Māyāpur Candrodaya Mandir. He was in time to greet the Deities and give his lecture on *Śrīmad-Bhāgavatam* 7.9.28.

In the lecture he stressed the need to hear about Kṛṣṇa consciousness from the guru, who must be a pure devotee, rather than try to approach Kṛṣṇa directly. Even Prahlāda, though a *śaktyāveśa-avātara,* an especially empowered representative of the Lord, felt his first duty was to serve his spiritual master. Prabhupāda said we should therefore be very careful not to mix with the *sahajiyās,* the professional men, or *Vaiṣṇavas* who are not well behaved.

* * *

Large numbers of devotees are flowing in for the festival now. The rest of the GBC members arrived in one party at 9:30 this morning. They were Tamal Krishna Goswami, Madhudviṣa Mahārāja, Satsvarūpa Mahārāja, and Jayatīrtha, Rūpānuga, Jagadīśa, and Bhagavān prabhus. Only Kīrtanānanda and Brahmānanda swamis are missing. Prabhupāda called them all in to his room and immediately raised the *sannyāsī-gṛhastha* controversy. He preached that we must become attached to Kṛṣṇa's family, not the material, bodily-based concept—the "stool family" or "pig family," as he put it. *Sannyāsa* means to reject such conceptions. He said that this is wanted. Household life is a concession only. However, since our Kṛṣṇa conscious Society is based on this principle of renunciation, all Kṛṣṇa conscious persons are actually *sannyāsīs*; the outer dress doesn't matter. Still, he said, if our householders can rise to the level of formal *sannyāsa* that should be encouraged. His delivery was a perfect synthesis.

Having the tone set by Prabhupāda, the GBCs began their annual meetings in the afternoon.

March 7th, 1976

With all the GBC here and so many *sannyāsīs,* it is getting too crowded on the roof for Prabhupāda's walk. So he came down and exercised around the grounds this morning.

As he descended the staircase I walked immediately in front of him, keeping always just two or three steps ahead, with my eye on his feet. It's a precautionary habit I have developed since we have been here in Māyāpur. Similarly, whenever he goes up, I follow immediately behind him. This way, should he trip or slip, I can prevent him from tumbling down.

He went out to inspect the front wall on which Pāṇḍu dāsa is now painting pictures of Prabhupāda's books. Jayapatākā Mahārāja told Prabhupāda each panel will take about five days to complete, but Prabhupāda said he isn't concerned how long it takes, as long as it is done nicely.

* * *

Now there are several hundred devotees attending the morning program, and a really festive air pervades our whole compound. As many *sannyāsīs* and GBCs as possible crowd into the fenced-off area around Śrīla Prabhupāda's *vyāsāsana,* and the *kīrtanas* are increasingly ecstatic.

Although everyone is here to celebrate Lord Caitanya's birthday, Śrīla Prabhupāda is the main attraction at the festival.

In class, he revealed a little more of the devotional psychology of Prahlāda Mahārāja. Prior to Lord Nṛsiṁhadeva's appearance, Prahlāda always referred to Hiraṇyakaśipu as "the best of the demons." He would never call him "father." Prabhupāda explained that after Hiraṇyakaśipu was killed personally by the Lord, he was therefore liberated, and thus Prahlāda's mood changed. He therefore began to refer to him as "my father."

Devotees listen intently to his lectures and afterward dance and chant with tremendous energy and enthusiasm as Prabhupāda circumambulates the Deity room, vigorously ringing the bells that hang at each side of the temple room.

* * *

Śrīla Prabhupāda surprised me when I entered his room at about 11 a.m. this morning to prepare for his massage. For almost half an hour he preached to me, explaining that he wants all his disciples to become gurus. Each of us is to make thousands of disciples just as he has and in this way spread Kṛṣṇa consciousness all over the world.

He didn't seem to be speaking in general terms either but directly to me. He seemed very enlivened at the prospect of spreading Kṛṣṇa consciousness in this way.

In the evening, when the GBC men filed into his room to make their report about their day's meeting, he brought up the same topic, before discussing their resolutions. He asked me to explain to everyone what he had said earlier. But when I hesitated, he did it himself, repeating in brief this principle of becoming guru.

He told them that just as he had made thousands of disciples he wants each one of them to make ten thousand each. He encouraged them to become increasingly more qualified and rise to the position of being spiritual masters. He stressed that this can be done only if they maintain spiritual strength by strictly following the four regulative principles and chanting the prescribed number of rounds.

It is all dependent on enthusiasm, he told us. At seventy years he had left Vṛndāvana with no money, men, or any facility. He did everything only on this principle of enthusiasm. Without directly saying it, Śrīla Prabhupāda made it clear that all internal arguments and disputes can be resolved by turning our attention to the higher ideal of preaching Kṛṣṇa consciousness to the world.

He then heard the report of the day's meeting. He had previously instructed them to officially elect a chairman and secretary to conduct their meetings and that these posts are to be retained for one year. Tamal Krishna Goswami was chosen as the first GBC chairman and Satsvarūpa Mahārāja as the secretary.

Their day's discussion focused on redefining ISKCON zones. India now has two, Europe two, America and Canada six, and South America two. In addition, there are North and South Africa, the South Seas, the Middle East, eastern Asia, and the Rādhā Dāmodara TSKP.

The GBC agreed to rotate some members. Hansadūta and Gopāla Kṛṣṇa prabhus will oversee India; Madhudviṣa Swami was confirmed as GBC for the East Coast of America. Jayatīrtha will shift from Los Angeles to Germany and England, Bhagavān dāsa will remain in France and the Mediterranean, and Brahmānanda Swami will remain in Africa. Rūpānuga dāsa replaces Madhudviṣa in the South Seas, Gurukṛpa Swami will go to the Northwest Coast of America and to Japan, Jagadīśa prabhu, mid-west America and Canada, Satsvarūpa and Kīrtanānanda swamis will retain the same zones. Hṛdayānanda Mahārāja is joined in South America by newly elected Pañca Draviḍa Swami as provisional GBC; and another new member, Balavanta, got the American southeast. Atreya Ṛṣi is the GBC for the Middle East. Rāmeśvara, who has not yet arrived, will become GBC for southern California. This was Śrīla Prabhupāda's personal request that he be added to the body.

New BBT Trustees were nominated, and various other business matters were completed.

* * *

A letter came today from Harikeśa Swami. It was a long, detailed, and ecstatic report of his recent and unexpected preaching trip in Hungary. He explained that when passing through London, he had met Alanatha dāsa, who was just preparing to go to Hungary in response to an invitation from a yoga school. Alanatha invited Harikeśa along, and he gladly accepted.

Taking books, pamphlets, posters, and instruments, the two of them met with great success. Although they were highly restricted in what they could say, the Hungarian reception to *kīrtana* and *prasādam* was extraordinary. "I simply engaged them in *kīrtana* and made them all kinds of nice *prasādam* which they went wild over," he wrote. "The Hungarians like to eat a lot and they are so poor and have not much selection of foods, that they never had anything so nice. Milk and grains and milk products are very cheap and this is the basis of our *prasādam,* so I made very much and very opulently *halavā* and *puris* and a drink made from whey and sometimes Simply Wonderfuls [a milk sweet], and they loved it. They could not believe how anything could taste so good. From the point of view of *prasādam* they became completely convinced.

"And what to speak of *kīrtana.* After a short while as they learned how to chant the mantra and play *karatālas,* we started having *kīrtanas* which to me seemed as good as any *kīrtana* in any temple in the movement. They chanted and danced like real mad men and they would go on as long as I could; every night very raging hour *kīrtanas* where at the end everyone collapsed on the floor in ecstasy and then we gave them *prasādam* while I chanted *bhajans,* which they fell over each other to record....

"It even occurred in public that although I had to always cover up the philosophy out of fear of being stopped and thrown out of the country, these people became so enlightened due to the ecstatic *kīrtana* that they actually forced me to speak about Kṛṣṇa although they didn't have any idea what was the force behind the chanting. I started speaking about the soul very reluctantly and I was refusing to do it, but all of a sudden out of my control, a sanskrit verse *nityam śāśvato 'yām purāṇaḥ* etc. came out of my mouth, and they all jumped on me as if half crazed, demanding to know what was that; and I had to surrender and pray to Kṛṣṇa for protection, and I started to explain everything to them. The translator became so excited that her face lighted up like a Christmas tree and she became so excited that she could no longer speak properly. It seems that this is what they have been waiting for because their lives are so very empty. But they were all afraid for us at the end because what I had said was very revolutionary."

Despite the restrictions for speaking, Dely Karoly, the yoga instructor who had organized the programs, will organize outdoor *kīrtanas* and wants the devotees to return as often as possible. Included in his letter were photos of men and women dancing with upraised arms and japa beads around their necks. There is such a demand that he hopes to return frequently and visit Bulgaria, Romania, and East Germany in the summer.

He asked if he should make a recording of the chanting because, he predicted, along with *prasādam*, it would sweep the country. Harikeśa Mahārāja described his experience as the "most wonderful of my whole life." He also asked if he should continue on to join the Rādhā Dāmodara party in America or remain to preach in Europe.

Prabhupāda was delighted with his report. He told me, "This is needed—to travel and preach and make new devotees."

After so many months of getting trained by Prabhupāda how to defeat Marxist philosophy, it seems Kṛṣṇa has now given Harikeśa the opportunity to use it.

Prabhupāda replied, encouraging him to take the newly found opportunity to preach to the Communists. He approved his plans for mass *kīrtana* and *prasādam* distribution but advised him to preach very tactfully in such places. He said that printing our books can wait. "First let their hearts be cleansed by chanting Hare Kṛṣṇa and taking Kṛṣṇa *prasādam.* To take birth in such place is due to impious past, so it is not easy for them to immediately accept our philosophy."

He ended by advising him to work with Kīrtirāja prabhu to introduce Lord Caitanya's *saṅkīrtana* movement to Eastern Europe.

* * *

During the evening massage, I related to Prabhupāda a story my mother had told me when I was fourteen. When I was still in the womb, an elderly relative had advised her to have an abortion. She had even given her some knitting needles with which to do it. My mother refused, burying the needles in the back yard. Another relative, however, had actually accepted a similar proposal, and they had buried the child in their back yard.

Śrīla Prabhupāda was shocked. He shook his head in amazement. "Now I can understand the advantage of a birth in India. People here could not even *dream* of such a thing." Then he added, "Kṛṣṇa saved you because He knew you were a devotee." He lamented over the unfortunate position of women in the West, who he said are encouraged by their parents to behave like prostitutes in order to capture some rich man while still youthful. He pointed out the risks they are prepared to take to become murderesses simply out of sexual urge.

March 8th, 1976

In the early morning Prabhupāda called Tamal Krishna Goswami into his room. He told him that Madhudviṣa Swami should be made GBC Vice Chairman for the year and that Gargamuni Swami should be given GBC responsibility.

Tamal Krishna Mahārāja replied that the GBC had already considered Gargamuni Mahārāja, but they had decided not to appoint him because he does not regularly chant his rounds. Some of Gargamuni's men have left him, complaining that his devotional standard is not strict.

Prabhupāda said that despite this he should become a GBC member, the reason being that Gargamuni has "creative energy" that should be used constructively. Otherwise he may become frustrated and misapply it.

Prabhupāda also told Tamal Krishna that he should become a BBT trustee because of the tremendous work his party is doing in book distribution. He suggested that Gopāla Kṛṣṇa be tried out for one year here in India, not as a full trustee but as a BBT manager, to see how he does. The BBT Trustees will then be: Śrīla Prabhupāda as the head, Rāmeśvara, Bhagavān, Hansadūta, Hṛdayānanda, and Tamal Krishna, all for Europe and America; and for India, Gopāla Kṛṣṇa, Girirāja, and Jaśomatīnandana prabhus.

* * *

As the sun arose, Śrīla Prabhupāda toured the temple grounds. He took the opportunity to ask Siddha Svarūpānanda Goswami and some our ISKCON authorities about their dispute. He wanted to hear all the points of contention in order to try to settle the long-simmering quarrel.

Madhudviṣa Swami spoke up first. His South Seas zone was the most seriously affected when Siddha Svarūpa and his followers left ISKCON. One temple was closed and several others were severely depleted in manpower. Siddha's group is most active in New Zealand and Australia, sometimes causing friction with anti-ISKCON propaganda.

Madhudviṣa itemized several points of contention, especially the tendency of Siddha Svarūpa's followers to focus their allegiance on him rather than Śrīla Prabhupāda. He also complained that they prefer to distribute books written by Siddha Svarūpa rather than Śrīla Prabhupāda's literature.

Siddha Svarūpa vigorously denied the allegations.

Prabhupāda himself said he didn't think Siddha's having a following was a serious thing. On the whole, he seemed to minimize the complaints against Siddha Svarūpa. He hoped to heal their rift, and told them in a good humoredly fashion, "Whatever is done is done. Now let us make some adjustment and work combinedly. That is my proposal."

Siddha Svarūpa, however, didn't think he could comply

with this request. "Śrīla Prabhupāda, the problem is that to work combinedly, they think that that means that I surrender to them and I do everything as they say; otherwise I am not surrendering. So as far as I am concerned, I cannot work with them." The discussion became a little acrimonious as Siddha Svarūpa became increasingly defensive. He eventually revealed his underlying mentality when he adamantly proclaimed that he would never accept control by anyone, especially the GBC.

Śrīla Prabhupāda offered to make him a GBC member, but he refused even to consider this alternative. This seemed to be the real crux of the issue. He doesn't want to work with his Godbrothers on any level.

Another of Madhudviṣa Mahārāja's complaints was that those who have left ISKCON to join Siddha Svarūpa now lack the discipline they had formerly.

This seemed to strike a chord with Śrīla Prabhupāda. He clearly explained that unless there is discipline, there is no question of "disciple."

Siddha Svarūpa didn't have any disagreement with that but said he considered that the person being disciplined must voluntarily put himself under someone's discipline.

Prabhupāda agreed with his point. "Accepting a spiritual master means voluntarily accepting somebody to rule him. There is no question ... I have no power to rule over you unless you voluntarily surrender."

When Gurukṛpa Swami mentioned that *vaidhi-bhakti* means sometimes doing things that one does not like to do, Prabhupāda also agreed. To illustrate the point he told a story of a famous lawyer during the days of British rule, C. R. Das, who was earning a huge amount of money. He was also a supporter of the Congress party, but in a meeting it was decided that party members should not cooperate with the British court system. He fought the proposal, offering to use his earnings to promote the party, but the resolution was passed. This meant he lost everything, but because the majority decided, he had to do it.

Prabhupāda said that of course we are not interested in democracy; we follow the instructions of the spiritual master. But the point is that we have to work in a cooperative and systematic way to spread Kṛṣṇa consciousness all over the world so that people may be highly benefited. He said that whatever misunderstandings are there should be adjusted, and we should work wholeheartedly together to relieve the suffering of the people.

Ultimately, in Prabhupāda's summation, he said there seemed to be a disagreement not in philosophy but in the matter of process. "You are thinking this way, he is thinking that way. That is the difference. Otherwise he [Siddha Svarūpa] is also eager to push on Kṛṣṇa consciousness; you are also."

Tamal Krishna Mahārāja suggested the problem was that both parties believe Prabhupāda was thinking their way.

So Prabhupāda brought the discussion to an end by declaring that he will give his personal verdict and they should all accept that. "Not your way, not his way. Let me understand what is the way you are trying to follow, what is the way he is trying to follow. Now I shall give my verdict, that 'This is the right way.'" Turning to Siddha Svarūpa he asked him, "Are you agreeable to this?"

"Yes."

"Then thank you, no more talk now. We shall talk later."

* * *

About mid-day, as Prabhupāda took his massage on the roof, Siddha Svarūpa came to see him with a nice poem he had written. He was upset and crying as he read it out by way of apology for his defensive manner during the earlier conversation.

After talking sympathetically with him for a few minutes, Prabhupāda had me find Madhudviṣa Swami. As the two sat before him, they discussed the dispute, now in a much more relaxed mood.

Prabhupāda urged them to settle their differences. He gave them indications of what he did and did not approve of.

Siddha Svarūpa and his followers are not inclined to worship Deities in a large temple setting, yet some of them have recently asked for *brahminical* initiation in order to worship Deities in their own homes.

Śrīla Prabhupāda told Siddha Svarūpa that Deity worship is

not to be introduced in private homes until his men have been trained up to the proper standard found in ISKCON temples. However, he gave full endorsement for their *kīrtana* and *prasādam*-distribution programs.

Siddha Svarūpa Mahārāja has been criticized for not strictly adhering to the fundamental practices like attending *maṅgala ārati*, worshiping the Deity, and wearing the attire of a *sannyāsī*, so Prabhupāda requested him to travel with him for a while so as to become more fixed up in the regulations of *sannyāsa* life. However, Siddha Svarūpa was not keen on this idea and declined Śrīla Prabhupāda's offer. He said that he preferred to preach on his own, "As I know how."

Prabhupāda didn't push the point, and he said that as long as the *Bhagavad-gītā* is distributed there is no fault. But he did ask him to shave his head.

When matters appeared settled, Prabhupāda asked each of them how old he was. Madhudviṣa Swami was the elder by one year. Turning to Siddha Svarūpa, Prabhupāda said, "So Madhudviṣa Mahārāja is senior to you both in age and in *sannyāsa.* So you work cooperatively together and take good instruction from him."

Outside Prabhupāda's room they offered their obeisances to each other and embraced. So to some extent, relations were improved by the medication of Śrīla Prabhupāda's touch, and he seems to be healing the rift.

After they had gone, I questioned Śrīla Prabhupāda again on the criticism that Siddha Svarūpa's men are more attached to him than to Prabhupāda.

Prabhupāda shrugged it off, saying it is all right, it is not harmful. He said that each of us has to become a guru and accept many disciples. But as a matter of etiquette, one should wait until his own spiritual master has departed before doing so.

After lunch, I questioned him further. He told me that having a following is not such a serious offense. But if someone thinks that he is qualified, and accepts disciples in the presence of his own spiritual master, that in itself would be his disqualification. Replying to my question whether one has to be a pure devotee to make disciples, he said that one has to be strictly following the principles. That is the requirement. Then he can be considered to be on a pure platform.

* * *

Not much mail is coming in now, since most leaders are here for the festival. But today Puṣṭa Kṛṣṇa Swami read out a very pleasing letter from Robert Veiga, a science student in Dallas. He is studying physics and math, but he comes regularly to the temple and chants sixteen rounds. He began by glorifying Śrīla Prabhupāda.

"You are the only person that I have approached that claims (with logical argument) to be relaying the undaunted truth. Every scientist that I have ever approached for truth reprimanded me quickly by stating that absolutes are not part of the 'real world,' and therefore only relative truths can exist. Although some scientists are Deists, they do not have a place for God in everyday activities. I therefore submit to you as my authority."

His idea is to attempt to prove to the scientists, using their own weapons of "mathematical trickery, logic, deductive and inductive instruments," that they are wrong in their conclusions. He wrote that once this is done, "the knowledge in the *Śrīmad-Bhāgavatam* can be presented and verified to the best extent possible."

However, he has received conflicting advice from the devotees on whether he should continue with his studies and what his service should be. Therefore he requested Śrīla Prabhupāda's guidance.

Prabhupāda was very glad to receive such a letter—once again a confirmation that his books are having the effect he desires. Although, as he often says, he is "a layman" in the science field, his arguments are convincing many men of science of the fallibility of their theories and the superiority of the Vedic version.

His reply encouraged Robert to continue with his studies. "There is a Bengali proverb: *tor shil tor noda, tor bhangi dater goda.* 'I take your mortar and pestle and I break your teeth.' This means we use the scientists' own weapons and with them we defeat their atheistic philosophy.

"There is another example. A hatchet is sitting before a tree. The tree asks, 'What are you doing here?'

The hatchet replies, 'I have come here to cut you down.'

The tree then said, 'You cannot cut me down alone, but with the help of my descendants you can do it.' The idea is that the ax-handle is made of wood, and so without the assistance of the wooden tree, the hatchet is useless. Similarly, we can use our materialistic knowledge to defeat the atheistic philosophy of the scientists.

"So you can continue your studies and learn what is *shil* and *noda* (mortar and pestle) so you can break their *dater goda* (break their teeth)."

* * *

Sharma dāsa came over from his hideaway at the *gośālā* at 4:00 p.m. to see Śrīla Prabhupāda with a request to leave Māyāpur. He wanted to go to chant at Rādhā Kuṇḍa. With so many devotees here now for the festival, he complained that he is again being disturbed in his chanting.

Prabhupāda told him that this indicated that his mind was restless. Previously he had asked to live in a tree, and now Rādhā Kuṇḍa. "You are not fit for *nirjana-bhajana*," Prabhupāda told him. "This is for *mahā-bhāgavatas* like Haridāsa Ṭhākura, who are completely undisturbed. Haridāsa Ṭhākura lived in a cave with a large snake but was not perturbed." He added that if one's mind is even a little disturbed, *nirjana-bhajana* will not be possible.

After this meeting, Sharma prabhu later told Puṣṭa Kṛṣṇa Swami that he had decided to return to Africa and preach. Prabhupāda was pleased to hear this.

* * *

In the evening Prabhupāda told Puṣṭa Kṛṣṇa Mahārāja and myself that he likes the idea of having one servant, along with a *sannyāsī* as his secretary. Puṣṭa Kṛṣṇa Mahārāja is very competent, and apart from the regular secretarial duties, is also transcribing Śrīla Prabhupāda's translations and commentaries. Prabhupāda said that I should become trained up in cooking. Then if we three travel, it will be convenient and inexpensive.

* * *

There are 150 western devotees here now.

Hearing that some Australian devotees have been purchasing fruit from the market, and also remembering Prabhupāda's previous comment that no one should eat anything without first offering it to the Deities, I asked him if they should stop.

Prabhupāda wasn't disturbed. He replied, "Fruit may be offered within the mind."

* * *

Today I presented Śrīla Prabhupāda with some new neck beads, strung and cleaned up by Rasajñā dāsa, a young Australian devotee working with the Nama Hatta party in Japan. The tiny beads on his existing strand were beginning to split off. So he accepted the new set and, to my great delight, gave me the old ones, some of which I presented to Rasajñā prabhu.

March 9th, 1976

During the walk Śrīla Prabhupāda again criticized some of his Godbrothers for making false claims. He said that in sixty years they have not been able to attract any foreign students, nor have they published any books. Still they are envious and proudly claim to have all the blessings of Śrīla Bhaktisiddhānta.

As we walked, the discussion turned to how to combat the flooding of the Ganges in our future city here in Māyāpur. He told us to make a system of canals to drain the land. He also suggested that we could use the need for flood avoidance as a reason to get our land acquisition application through on an emergency basis.

Prabhupāda urged us to use our abilities as Europeans and Americans to make our plans. He joked that even though he is an Indian, "I have no Indian plans. My plans are all American." He told us that generally when Indians think of emigrating, they head for London. But, in the days when he was planning to go the West, he only thought about going to America. He was even dreaming sometimes that he had come to New York.

Now the movement has a good reputation with the Indian government, although having so many American followers can also be a problem. Indira Gandhi has such high regard for him that she received him even in the midst of the National Emergency. She had expressed great appreciation and faith in him for what he has done, but she admitted she is afraid of the Americans.

Toward the end of the walk, Madhudviṣa brought up a question about the role of *sannyāsī, brahmacārī,* and *gṛhastha* in ISKCON. "In one of your purports you say that a *sannyāsī* should never discourage a young man from getting married. But on the other hand, we have understood that a *sannyāsī* should encourage young men to remain *brahmacārī.* So it seems to me like there's some kind of a—"

Prabhupāda replied, "According to time, circumstances. Just like Kṛṣṇa says, *niyataṁ kuru karma tvam*: 'Always be engaged in your prescribed work.' And, at last, He says *sarva-dharmān parityajya mām ekaṁ śaraṇaṁ vraja.* Now we have to adjust. That is not contradiction. That is suitable to the time and circumstance. *Karma-kāṇḍa* is also recommended in the Vedas. There are three divisions: *karma-kāṇḍa, jñāna-kāṇḍa* and *upāsana-kāṇḍa* You have to become the eternal servant of Kṛṣṇa. Either you go through *karma* or *jñāna* or yoga, it doesn't matter. The ultimate aim is how to reach Kṛṣṇa. That is wanted."

* * *

The GBCs came to see Prabhupāda at the end of their meeting. Again they gathered in Prabhupāda's room, and one by one the results of their day's deliberations were read out.

They have been debating the *gṛhastha-sannyāsa* issue and wanted Prabhupāda's confirmation on new guidelines on how those in the *gṛhastha āśrama* should be handled. They made a series of strictures aimed at preventing householders, including Temple Presidents, from being financially dependent on the Society. Their idea was that the Society should not become overburdened and thus have its resources diverted from the preaching effort. The proposals were very restrictive, and not even all the GBC *sannyāsīs* were in agreement as to how far they should go in implementing them.

Tamal Krishna Mahārāja, with one or two other *sannyāsīs,* is the main driving force behind the new reforms. As the GBC

Chairman, he spoke logically on each point as it came up for Prabhupāda's approval, philosophically establishing its necessity, strictly distinguishing the interests of the Society, and promoting it over that of individual concerns.

After hearing all their arguments and resolutions, Śrīla Prabhupāda accepted most of them. But he requested the removal of one designed to prevent single women with children from joining a temple. And he dismissed another that required a man to remain financially responsible for his wife and family for his whole life up to the point of taking *sannyāsa.* Prabhupāda emphasized that our principle is to give facility to help *everyone* become detached from sex life and to become Kṛṣṇa conscious.

He said that *gṛhasthas* must live physically apart from the temple if husband and wife wish to associate together, but after two or three children, he said, what is the need to continue living together? If they want to improve their Kṛṣṇa consciousness, he said, they may separate. The man can move to a different temple and dedicate himself to preaching, although he said that the *vānaprastha āśrama* may not be accepted before one is fifty years old. The women and children can be supported by the temples, and nurseries can be established. If a man wishes to separate from his family when his children are young, he must still send money for their support. Śrīla Prabhupāda said that we can give them facility to become detached, but they cannot be irresponsible. When the children reach eight years old, they may be sent to a *gurukula* in India, and ISKCON will take full responsibility for them.

On other business, the *sannyāsa* initiation issue was finalized. The GBC confirmed the new system, whereby nominations can be made only by GBC men who are *sannyāsīs.* The nominee must then work at least one year with that GBC member before being given his *tridaṇḍa.*

* * *

Sixty-five devotees arrived from the USA today.

March 10th, 1976

News of yesterday's GBC resolutions has traveled fast. Among the householders there is considerable resistance and resentment. Most temple presidents are householders and, according to the new directives, they will all have to go out and establish outside sources of income while still continuing to run their temples. Many feel that certain *sannyāsīs* are questioning their sincerity in being fully dedicated devotees, as if being married is at odds with the spiritual principles.

Some of the GBC are already having doubts about whether their decisions were either practical or fair. Madhudviṣa Swami spoke for several others in voicing his concern during Prabhupāda's walk.

In response, Śrīla Prabhupāda suggested the *gṛhasthas* form a small committee to have further discussions.

There was some discussion back and forth, and Tamal Krishna Mahārāja, as the champion of the GBC reforms, repeatedly reminded everyone that the resolutions were not meant to govern the way the *gṛhasthas* conduct their personal affairs. He agreed that a committee for that purpose was a good idea. But he said it is for the GBC only to decide what support the Society gives them.

Śrīla Prabhupāda stressed that the important thing is that we do not develop factions within our Society. Unity is possible only when *harer nāma* is there constantly.

Puṣṭa Kṛṣṇa Mahārāja brought the discussion closer to the root of the differences between *gṛhastha* and *sannyāsa.* "What about the distinction between the enjoying spirit and the renouncing spirit? For example, between the *brahmacārīs* and the *gṛhasthas* ... The *brahmacārīs* have this tendency; at least, this is the attitude—towards renunciation. And so far we can see, a *brahmacārī* who gives up his *brahmacārī* life means he's more inclined towards the enjoying spirit, at least to some extent. So how do we deal with this situation?"

"If you want to enjoy," Prabhupāda asked, "who can stop you?"

Tamal Krishna Mahārāja again made his point. "But we cannot support it. We cannot support his enjoyment. That he should take on his own self to do."

Prabhupāda explained that according to different positions and attitudes, the four *āśramas* are existing. Therefore everyone is not on an equal platform. But the whole idea, he said, is how to give up the propensity of enjoyment. That is wanted.

On the other hand, Puṣṭa Kṛṣṇa presented a criticism that the householders have of the renunciates. "Sometimes the *brahmacārīs* and *sannyāsīs* may have a very strong aversion towards association with women and/or householder life, things of this nature. And sometimes the *gṛhasthas* will criticize the *sannyāsīs* and *brahmacārīs* that 'This is fanaticism,' or it's, to the other end, 'It's just as bad as the enjoying spirit, because you're meditating on the same thing, but only you're averse to it.'

It was like a seesaw, one party accusing the other. And the last thing Prabhupāda wanted was the formation of different factions. He said that the whole world is full of different *isms,* one party against another. We should not bring that attitude into our Society. He said that the accusations of one side against the other are all fanaticism. He gave the solution. "Real unity is in advancing Kṛṣṇa consciousness. In *Kali-yuga,* you cannot strictly follow; neither I can strictly follow. If I criticize you, if you criticize me, then we go far away from our real life of Kṛṣṇa consciousness.

"You should always remember that either *gṛhastha* or *brahmacārī* or *sannyāsī,* nobody can strictly follow all the rules and regulations of them. In the *Kali-yuga* it is not possible. So if I find simply fault with you, and if you find fault with me, then it will be factional, and our real business will be hampered. Therefore Caitanya Mahāprabhu has recommended that *harer nāma,* chanting Hare Kṛṣṇa mantra, should be very rigidly performed, which is common for everyone—*gṛhastha, vānaprastha,* or *sannyāsī.* They should always chant Hare Kṛṣṇa mantra. Then everything will be adjusted. Otherwise it is impossible to advance. We shall be complicated with the details only."

On the whole, throughout the discussions, Prabhupāda has naturally lent his support to the more renounced position. Yet he obviously wants everyone to have the opportunity to develop their Kṛṣṇa consciousness.

He said that we should neither neglect the regulations nor pursue them so fanatically that we miss the point of actual spiritual advancement. He repeated the real formula for success. "If we advance in Kṛṣṇa consciousness, simple method, chanting twenty-four hours, *kīrtanīyaḥ sadā hariḥ,* then things will be automatically adjusted. You cannot find in *Kali-yuga* everything is being done very correctly, to the point. That is very difficult."

He recalled with amusement his own experiences in establishing his movement in the early days in New York. "Just like our poet, Allen Ginsberg. He was always accusing me, 'Swamijī, you are very conservative and strict.'

"Actually, I told him that 'I am never strict, neither I am conservative. If I become conservative, then I cannot live here for a moment. So I'm not at all conservative.'" We all laughed as Prabhupāda described what he had to tolerate. "I was cooking, and I saw in refrigerator of Yeargen [a young man he was staying with], he kept some pieces of meat for his cat. So still, I kept my things in that refrigerator. What can be done? I had no place at that time."

* * *

As if to help us keep a proper perspective on our tiny lives, the *Śrīmad-Bhāgavatam* verse described the position of the Lord in His form as Kāraṇodakaśāyī Viṣṇu, the creator of the material worlds. His existence is *turīya,* in the fourth dimension. Prabhupāda compared how He lies in slumber on the Causal Ocean with an expert swimmer who lies for hours with eyes closed on the surface of the water.

As Viṣṇu exhales, the material universes come out, and when He inhales, everything is again retracted into His body. All this happens within a few seconds by His measurement. Yet that interim period between His breathing out and breathing in is, for us, an incalculable number of billions of years.

Therefore, Prabhupāda told us that by studying Kṛṣṇa, one becomes liberated. "So these verses should be studied very carefully, understanding each word very carefully. Then you'll understand Kṛṣṇa. Don't be lazy in understanding Kṛṣṇa, because if you try to understand then you'll not take Him as ordinary human being, as foolish persons are taking. Rascals, they think Kṛṣṇa as one of us. Then you'll not be a *mūḍha.* You'll be intelligent. Of course, we cannot know Kṛṣṇa perfectly. He's so big and we are so small that it is impossible. But you can understand Kṛṣṇa as much as He explains Himself in the *Bhagavad-gītā.* That much will help you.

"You cannot understand Kṛṣṇa. It is not possible. Kṛṣṇa cannot understand Himself. Therefore He came as Caitanya, to understand Himself. Caitanya Mahāprabhu has recommended human life is meant for understanding Kṛṣṇa. There is no other business. If you simply stick to this business, your life is successful.

"Our Kṛṣṇa consciousness movement is meant for that purpose. We are opening so many centers so that the people of the world may take advantage of this opportunity and understand Kṛṣṇa and make his life successful. Thank you very much."

* * *

Around mid-day, eight coaches arrived carrying about three-hundred-and-fifty devotees from North America. Several *sannyāsīs*—Tripurāri, Viṣṇujana, Gurudāsa, Revatīnandana, and Parivrājakācārya—were among them.

Many of the new arrivals are being housed in the new building, where construction work has now stopped. The first floor level has been cast, and Jayapatākā Mahārāja has arranged for temporary shelters made from split bamboo and tarpaulins to be erected on top of the bare concrete. The facilities are woefully inadequate. The devotees have to bathe from hand pumps, and the toilets are simply holes in the ground, but they don't seem to mind. They are happy just to be here in the holy *dhāma* with Śrīla Prabhupāda.

Rāmeśvara, Rādhāballabha, and the BBT staff were also among the group of newly arrived devotees. They brought with them two-hundred-and-fifty-five photographic enlargements of our temples and Deities from around the world, *Śrīmad-Bhāgavatam* illustrations, and book reviews. They are all mounted and encased in protective perspex sheets, destined to be placed in a gigantic public display here in Māyāpur. Prabhupāda looked through at least fifty of them. He was in ecstasy. Rāmeśvara also brought with him the newly printed Seventh Canto, Part One.

Surprisingly, Dayānanda also returned today. He had flown to Dallas and found himself unable to do anything with the *gurukula.*

Shortly after he left here, Jagadīśa prabhu arrived for the GBC meetings. After meeting with him, Śrīla Prabhupāda accepted his reasons for what actually turns out to be only a temporary closure of the Dallas *gurukula.* Prabhupāda took Jagadīśa's assurance that the issue would be carefully studied in the meetings, and a solution has been found in line with Śrīla Prabhupāda's desire. The GBC recommended a series of smaller regional schools, rather than a single, centralized one. By keeping the number of students down and having several in different states, the hope is to minimize governmental attention and so avoid restrictive codes and regulations. At the same time emphasis will be given to the development of the Vṛndāvana school, and parents will be encouraged to send their children there.

With Śrīla Prabhupāda's approval, Jagadīśa and Hṛdayānanda Mahārāja had rung Dayānanda in Dallas to inform him to leave things as they are. Dayānanda then persuaded Rāmeśvara to buy him a ticket back to Māyāpur, apparently hoping to be reinstated as Śrīla Prabhupāda's secretary. Thus his unexpected arrival today.

Prabhupāda was not very happy to see him. He seemed to have expected he would stay there, and he was irritated Dayānanda has spent so much money going and coming and achieving nothing. Rather than restore him as his secretary, he called in Atreya Ṛṣi prabhu and offered him Dayānanda's services in Iran.

* * *

Evening *kīrtana,* which has been getting bigger and wilder every night, was extraordinary to say the least. There were at least six hundred exuberant devotees, chanting and dancing with Madhudviṣa and Gurukṛpa swamis in the middle, leading them.

* * *

Prabhupāda has been receiving many gifts of sweets, dried fruit, honey, money, and other things from visiting devotees.

* * *

As Gaura Pūrṇimā nears, the electrical power has been going off for longer and longer periods. Today it was off almost all day, but it came on again in the evening, in time for Prabhupāda to view a new ISKCON movie in his room. It was shown on Gargamuni Swami's Fairchild projector. The movie was about the production of his books and was called *Brilliant as the Sun*. Prabhupāda loved it. He ate potato *sabji* and *puris,* as he watched, finishing with a *rasagullā.*

March 11th, 1976

Prabhupāda took his walk on the roof with the GBC members and *sannyāsīs.*

Jaśomatīnandana dāsa from Gujarat had visited one of Prabhupāda's leading Godbrothers in a neighboring *maṭha* here in Māyāpur. He reported back that, on hearing of Prabhupāda's achievements, the Godbrother had commented, "Your Guru Mahārāja was previously a businessman, and we are, from our childhood, we are Vaiṣṇava. So therefore he is doing business and getting money." For those who have worked here in Māyāpur over the last few years, such attitudes and comments are not new. But the lack of propriety in speaking such things to Prabhupāda's own disciples is still surprising.

It was an insult, but Prabhupāda turned it to his advantage. From the roof he looked across the expanse of open fields he plans to build a transcendental city on, toward the few buildings clustered around a small temple that comprise the Godbrother's headquarters.

"Business means four things," he chuckled. "Yes, we are businessman. I was student of economics. I know how to do business, and the business principle means you require four things: land, labor, capital, organization. So, ordinary man cannot do that. Otherwise, everyone would have done some business and become millionaires. But it requires these four things: land, labor, organization, and capital.

"So where you have got these? You have neither land, neither capital, neither place. So how you can do business? I am doing business because I have got all these things. I went to America—land. Then I worked—labor. Then I earned some capital, and I have got brain how to do it."

We see on a daily basis that Prabhupāda knows precisely how to use each of these in devotional service. Therefore, by Kṛṣṇa's grace every facility is being supplied. It is regrettable that his Godbrothers choose not to see his success as purely spiritual.

As he walked around the roof, Prabhupāda nodded approvingly as he heard the auspicious tones of a *shenai* and drum reverberating through the compound. Jayapatākā Mahārāja has installed the players in the small rooms in the main gate to help create a festive atmosphere. All the devotees are appreciating their music. Tamal Krishna Mahārāja recalled the excellent reception given to Śrīla Prabhupāda during our visit to the Nellore Raṅganātha temple two months ago when Prabhupāda was honored with a *shenai* band and the large ceremonial umbrella.

Jayapatākā Swami asked whether such an arrangement could be made here in Māyāpur to honor His Divine Grace.

Prabhupāda approved, saying that such liturgy is not a pompous display or self-aggrandizement. It is *ācāryopāsana*, worship of Kṛṣṇa's representative, and is therefore needed, because that is the way of spiritual advancement. Only with full faith in the guru can one understand spiritual truth.

Pañca Draviḍa Mahārāja wanted to know how a person can attain perfection simply from one *lava*, one eleventh of a second's association with a pure devotee.

Prabhupāda stopped and turned to him as we all gathered around. He said that it is like dry wood, which can be ignited immediately. Similarly, if one is sincere, then he immediately becomes spiritually ignited. And if he is still "moist" from material contact, it may take hundreds of years or lifetimes. The pure devotee is like a match, and the recipient the wood. If both are good then there is fire. "When you go to the fire, you become dry. But willfully we put again water. This nonsense business makes us wet. This process is already there, how to become dry. But instead of taking the process, we put water. Then how it will be ignited? The rules and regulations are the drying process. But without following the rules and regulation, if you again become victimized by *māyā,* then there is water and again dry it. So this is going on, watering and drying, watering and drying. Difficulty is that we dry and again water."

Viṣṇujana Mahārāja, the tall, charismatic coleader of Rādhā Dāmodara TSKP, who was listening in the background, spoke up for the first time. "Śrīla Prabhupāda, how did Choṭa Haridāsa achieve perfection by killing himself after apparently pouring water on his devotional creeper by talking to a woman?"

He was referring to the close associate of Śrī Caitanya Mahāprabhu who drowned himself in the Gaṅgā after being rejected by the Lord.

Prabhupāda's reply was very grave. "His instance was that even an associate of Caitanya Mahāprabhu can fall down. And if one falls down, his punishment is that, suicide. There is no other punishment. He must commit suicide. This is Caitanya Mahāprabhu's instruction. Otherwise he is Caitanya Mahāprabhu's personal servant. He cannot fall down. But Caitanya Mahāprabhu showed this instance that 'Even one is My personal servant, he can fall down.' And if anyone by any cause he falls down, his punishment is he must commit suicide. This is instruction." Everyone's eyes widened as they took in the statement.

Prabhupāda elaborated. "This falldown, there is possibility in any moment because we are very small. We can be captivated by *māyā* at any moment. Therefore we shall be very, very careful. And if you fall down, then punishment is you make suicide. That's all. Then next life we shall see."

Viṣṇujana Mahārāja withdrew to the back, as the other *sannyāsīs* sought clarification. Satsvarūpa mentioned that in *The Nectar of Devotion* it says devotional service is so pure that there is no *prāyaścitta,* or atonement, necessary if one falls down. Just again engage in your service.

Prabhupāda agreed, but said that Choṭa Haridāsa's case was not typical. His was exemplary punishment that was enacted between him and the Lord. Caitanya Mahāprabhu was *vajrād api kaṭhora,* harder than the thunderbolt and softer than the rose.

"But, Prabhupāda," asked Tamal Krishna, "if you were as strict as—"

"No, I am not Caitanya Prabhu. I am not ... Why you are comparing me? I am an ordinary man."

Gurukṛpa Mahārāja brought the exchange to its point, asking the question that was undoubtedly on everyone's mind. "So in ISKCON, if someone falls down, it means that he should commit suicide?"

Prabhupāda's monosyllabic answer couldn't be clearer. "No."

Gurudāsa Mahārāja laughed. "We wouldn't have much of a movement, then."

Prabhupāda clarified, "No, no, if he falls down, that is automatically suicide. If he falls down, that means it is suicide. He got the chance. If he falls down, that is suicide. Spiritual suicide. If one gets the chance of becoming eligible for going back to home, back to Godhead, and if he commits mistake and it is stopped, is it not suicide?"

His conclusion was that we should be very strong-minded and continue our devotional service with determination.

* * *

This is the official beginning of the festival. Just before class started, Prabhupāda gave the hundreds of assembled devotees his personal welcome. His simple, heartfelt message expressing his appreciation for their attendance here in Māyāpur was greeted with large smiles and cheers. "First of all, we must welcome all the devotees. There may be so many inconveniences. Please do not mind it. This is Caitanya Mahāprabhu's place. Be joyful always. Thank you."

His thoughtfulness immeasurably deepened everyone's affection and gratitude to him. Without Śrīla Prabhupāda none of us would be here, none of us would have even heard of Māyāpur, or Kṛṣṇa consciousness, or tasted the happiness of spiritual life. So his humble concern about the lack of amenities was all the more endearing.

As he had told us earlier on the walk, it was out of his concern for the devotees that he built a Guest House first, even before a temple. Some locals have criticized him for it, but he told us that wherever there are devotees, then God will come. Kṛṣṇa is not a dull stone; He is drawn by the affection of His devotees. Therefore making a place for God, without facility for His devotees, is merely idol worship.

* * *

About thirty Australian devotees arrived at 8:30 a.m.

Parikramas have begun with a visit over the Jalāṅgī river to Śrīla Bhaktivinoda's house at nearby Godruma-dvīpa.

* * *

After having heard and approved the last of the new GBC resolutions, Prabhupāda added another of his own: that no decision is to be changed for one year, except by him personally.

* * *

Prabhupāda was given $600 in donations, and Jayatīrtha brought one boy in with a donation of $5,000, to be used for building a house for him here in Māyāpur. Plans are already underway for it, and Śrīla Prabhupāda has chosen a site near the *pukkur.*

* * *

Jagannātha Suta dāsa, the production manager of *Back to Godhead,* taped a lengthy interview with Śrīla Prabhupāda. It's for a special article on the upcoming bicentennial anniversary of the American Declaration of Independence.

The conversation naturally centered on whether the living being is actually independent or not. Prabhupāda is scheduled to be in the capital, Washington, D.C., this coming July 4th. BTG will carry the article in that month's issue.

March 12th, 1976

Hundreds of devotees from around the world are packed into rooms all around the temple compound. The atmosphere is very festive.

The *shenai* band sits up in the compartments on the main gate, and at dawn the wail of the pipe and the melodic rhythms of the drum create an almost mystical atmosphere. The exotic sounds enliven the mind and drift across the fields to call the faithful to the holy *dhāma* to pay their homage to the Supreme Personality of Godhead, Śrī Caitanya Mahāprabhu, on the coming anniversary of His Divine Appearance.

During the walk, which Prabhupāda took on the roof, the black bee we had seen in February reappeared after a few weeks' absence. Repeating its past behavior, it flew around Śrīla Prabhupāda and his entourage several times. Then, as it had done previously, it landed on the spire of the small dome.

Everyone gathered around for a close inspection before it suddenly rose in the air and headed off across the fields. Prabhupāda said it was very beautiful.

Accompanied by at least twenty men, Prabhupāda went down and walked around the grounds. He checked the management and gave advice, even expressing concern over plants that had not been watered.

He told Jayapatākā Mahārāja how to systematize the removal and collection of visitor's shoes at the temple entrance by using tickets. Yaśodānandana Mahārāja suggested that instead of charging for the shoe service, people could be requested to give a donation to the Deities.

Prabhupāda rejected the idea. People should simply come and see the Deities. That is our main concern, he said. The Deity is not a beggar but the Bestower. His Guru Mahārāja had said it was better to be a street sweeper and earn an honest living than to make a living by showing the Deity. "It is a question of heart, that a man should come and visit the temple—he must give something. Why he is to be asked? Voluntarily he should give."

"But encouraging is not recommended?" Lokanātha Mahārāja asked.

"Encouraging means your behavior should be so nice that he voluntarily gives," Prabhupāda said. "That is encouraging, not that begging and 'Put something here. My belly is empty.'" We all laughed.

He said that asking someone to contribute to the institution by some payment was another thing. "But why should you earn by showing the Deity? You work so nicely they will become voluntarily member, contributing. That is nice. But not that 'Now we have got Deity. He's starving. Please give me something.' No. That is not good practice."

He also briefly recollected his early days in New York in 1965–66, telling us that part of his daily routine was to go "loitering" along Fifth Avenue. He said that his purpose was to study the Americans, how they were walking, how they were shopping.

Satsvarūpa Mahārāja remembered that Prabhupāda had once said those were happier days, when he had only himself to maintain, rather than thousands of disciples.

Prabhupāda laughed. "Yes," he agreed. "There was no chance of finding fault. Now I have to find fault."

He also visited the newly erected public exhibition and saw some of the displays. The presentation of so many international projects was impressive. Prabhupāda suggested that a book be published showing all the temples and Deities around the world, with a short explanation of each. He said this would be good for preaching work.

However, the structure that houses the exhibit is terrible. It is constructed along the banks of the *pukkur* from bamboo, dirty old tarpaulin sheets, and crudely woven, split-bamboo fencing. Access is poor, up a slippery mud slope. It compelled Prabhupāda to again complain about the management.

* * *

During class he explained to his hundreds of eager followers the benefits of Deity worship. He compared it to the process of yogic meditation by which one tries to see the Lord within the heart.

"You may practice this *haṭha-yoga,* or gymnastic yoga, for many, many births—you cannot see Kṛṣṇa. Kṛṣṇa can be seen when you smear with love ointment in your eyes. And that is possible through *bhakti.* So therefore why not practice *bhakti-yoga* from the beginning if you want to see Kṛṣṇa?

"Kṛṣṇa says, 'He's first-class yogi who is always trying to see Kṛṣṇa within the heart.' So it is very difficult task? In our *bhakti-yoga* we can teach this art of seeing Kṛṣṇa within the core of the heart in one minute. It is so simple. "You are seeing Kṛṣṇa here.

You must have impression; and try to keep that impression within your heart always. Then you become first-class yogi. Why so much gymnastic and pressing the nose? No. Take directly.

"If you are engaged twenty-four hours in the service of the Deity, you cannot see except the Deity. This *bhakti-yoga* practice is so simple. Therefore *kaniṣṭha adhikārī,* those who are neophyte, they must take to Deity worship. By Deity worship he is elevated to the position of seeing the Lord within the heart. This is very important thing.

"You can see, He is there, but you have no knowledge, or even if you have knowledge, you are not competent to see Him. But if you practice Deity worship.... Therefore it is the duty of guru to engage the neophyte devotee always in Deity worship."

* * *

Devotees crowd into Śrīla Prabhupāda's room in the early evenings, eager to get as much association with His Divine Grace as possible. Many of them have worked hard all year round, selling books and doing other temple duties, and their visit to the holy *dhāma,* and especially the opportunity to see Śrīla Prabhupāda, makes it all worthwhile.

This evening was no exception. The atmosphere couldn't have been more congenial. Śrīla Prabhupāda was very relaxed and enjoyed the company of his faithful disciples. He is always aware and deeply appreciative of the sacrifices they are making on his behalf. Although he is our spiritual master, our instructor in every aspect of life, his dealings with us are full of respect and compassion. A few minutes with Śrīla Prabhupāda can change anyone's life.

Someone brought in some sweets to be handed out, so I put them to one side. Prabhupāda glanced over, concerned as ever that his guests receive a little *prasādam.* "Oh, you are not distributing?"

"Well, there are so many devotees, I thought I would give the sweets out when every one leaves."

"They will never leave!" Prabhupāda said, laughing.

All the devotees cheered, "Jaya, Śrīla Prabhupāda!" Even a few simple words from him are enough to completely capture everyone's heart.

March 13th, 1976

Mahāṁsa Swami is here, and on this morning's walk he gave Śrīla Prabhupāda an update on some land in Hyderabad being donated to ISKCON. Mr. Hari Prasād Badruka, the current owner, wants to create a joint trust and have ISKCON develop the land, but legal complications have caused a delay. We may get only 250 acres, rather than the 600 originally promised. Mahāṁsa expects the case to clear through the courts within a month or so.

After walking around the roof, Prabhupāda came down to the front of the property. He wanted to take another look at the displays in the exhibition area, which is now complete. He particularly enjoyed seeing the favorable reviews written by some of the most important scholars in the fields of linguistics, Asian studies, Sanskrit studies, psychology, and philosophy. The reviewers' enthusiasm for his books, and their personal appreciation for him as an author and spiritual leader, had all the devotees cheering as Prabhupāda himself read one out loud.

It was a review by Dr. Geddes MacGregor, Emeritus Distinguished Professor of Philosophy from the University of Southern California. "No work in all Indian literature is more quoted. Because none is better loved in the West than the *Bhagavad-gītā.* Translation of such work demands not only knowledge of Sanskrit but an inward sympathy with the theme and a verbal artistry. But the poem is a symphony in which God is seen in all things. His Divine Grace A. C. Bhaktivedanta Swami Prabhupāda is, of course, profoundly sympathetic to the theme. He brings to it a special interpretative insight. Here we have a powerful and persuasive presentation in the *bhakti* tradition of this dearly beloved poem. The Swami's introduction makes clear at once where he stands as a leading exponent of Kṛṣṇa consciousness."

The acceptance of his works by the scholarly community in the most important universities in America and Europe is a source of deep satisfaction to Śrīla Prabhupāda. The clarity and power of his translations and purports has enabled the professors to appreciate the authenticity of Kṛṣṇa consciousness and, more importantly, distinguish it from the impersonal hodgepodge usually associated with the Hindu spiritual outlook.

Satsvarūpa Mahārāja, the leader of the Library Distribution Party responsible for garnering the reviews, read out several more. Each one drew more and more applause from the devotees and bigger and brighter smiles from Śrīla Prabhupāda.

"Ever since 1893, when Swami Vivekananda proclaimed monism and tolerance to the World's Parliament of Religions at Chicago, nonspecialists in America have pictured Hinduism as an easy-going phantasmagoria of smiling faces disappearing like dewdrops into the shining sea. *The Nectar of Devotion* should bring them up sharp."

Midst lots of laughter, he went on. "His Divine Grace A. C. Bhaktivedanta Swami Prabhupāda, whose shorn, orange-clad disciples have brought the inseparable twins of *bhajan* and *baksish* to the streets of America, has no doubt that such impersonalism is nothing less than rascaldom."

"Jaya!" all the devotees exclaimed.

"With all the books on *Vedānta* and bland neo-transcendentalism that are at present available to the English-speaking public, it is good to have on the popular market such an uncompromising statement of an opposing view from the pen of one who is as firmly rooted in a disciplic tradition, *guru-paramparā,* as Bhaktivedanta Swami."

At this the devotees were ecstatic. "Haribol!!" they shouted, as Prabhupāda, a huge grin stretching right across his face, moved further down the exhibits.

Ghanaśyāma dāsa, a leading Library Party member, pointed out another review, written by Dr. Daniel H. H. Ingalls, Chairman of Harvard University's Department of Sanskrit and Indian Studies. He apparently rarely, if ever, gives reviews, but for Śrīla Prabhupāda he agreed. "I am most happy to have these handsomely printed volumes which embody the work of so learned and sincere a believer in the message of the *Caritāmṛta.* I thank you."

Another was written by the current representative of

Hinduism to the World Council of Churches. Mahābuddhi, another active Library Party member, added that the man ordered not one, but two, standing orders for the library.

"*Śrīmad-Bhāgavatam,* the Indian classic par excellence on *bhakti-yoga,* attributed to Vyāsa, is one of the most important and influential religio-philosophical works within the Vedic tradition. Thanks to the devoted and scholarly endeavors of Śrī A. C. Bhaktivedanta Swami Prabhupāda, the entire work of twelve cantos will be available in a superb English edition for the benefit of the English-reading peoples.... This monumental work is immensely valuable alike to historians of religion, linguistic scholars, cultural anthropologists, pious devotees, as well as to the general reader interested in spiritual matters. I recommend it highly to every student of Indian philosophy, culture, and religion."

Each review offered glowing testimonial of such high appreciation they could hardly have been better if the devotees themselves had written them. As Dr. Garry Gelade, a psychologist at Oxford University, wrote: "It is a work to be treasured. The opportunity to receive the profound teachings of the *Śrīmad-Bhāgavatam* in the West has been made possible by the devoted labor of Śrīla Prabhupāda. The clarity and precision of his commentaries on the text have rarely been equaled. No one of whatever faith or philosophical persuasion who reads this book with an open mind can fail to be both moved and impressed. The spirit of its message shines brightly from the pages."

Ghanaśyāma pointed out another one from Dr. R. E. Asher, the chairman of the Department of Linguistics at Edinburgh, one of the biggest linguistic schools in the world. He is known all over the world for his studies in different kinds of languages. "It is axiomatic that no book can be expected entirely to satisfy all its potential readers. Here is one, *Śrīmad-Bhāgavatam,* however, which can be said to come remarkably close to that ideal.... We have here the ideal of what an edition of a Sanskrit text for a Western audience should be."

Prabhupāda stopped at the review written by Professor

Kailash Vajpeye, who had been invited to the University of Mexico to take charge of Oriental studies, specifically Hinduism. Satsvarūpa read it out. His statement amounted to a verbal broadside against the so-called swamis and yogis, and it drew the most enthusiastic response from the devotees and Śrīla Prabhupāda as well. "As a native of India now living in the West, it has given me much grief to see so many of my fellow countrymen coming to the West in the role of gurus and spiritual leaders. Just as any ordinary man in the West becomes conscious of Christian culture from his very birth, any ordinary man in India becomes familiar with the principles of meditation and yoga from his very birth. Unfortunately, many unscrupulous persons come from India, exhibit their imperfect and ordinary knowledge of yoga, cheat the people with their wares consisting of mantras, and present themselves as incarnations of God. So many of these cheaters have come, convincing their foolish followers to accept them as God, that those who are actually well versed and learned in Indian culture have become very concerned and troubled. For this reason I am very excited—"

At this, Śrīla Prabhupāda suddenly interrupted the reading. "Send this copy to Indira Gandhi," he told his GBC men, "and request her to stop giving passports to all these nonsense. Do this. Yes."

Satsvarūpa continued his recitation of Professor Vajpeye's eulogy. "For this reason I am very excited to see the publication of *Bhagavad-gītā As It Is,* by Śrī A. C. Bhaktivedanta Swami Prabhupāda. Śrīla Prabhupāda, from his very birth, was trained in the strict practice of *bhakti-yoga,* and he appears in a succession of gurus that traces back to the original speaking of *Bhagavad-gītā* by Śrī Kṛṣṇa. His knowledge of Sanskrit is impeccable. His penetration into the inner meaning of the text is befitting only a fully realized soul who has indeed perfectly understood the meaning of *Bhagavad-gītā.* Personally, I intend to use this book in the courses which I am directing by invitation of the Mexican government on the language, culture, and philosophy of India. This authorized edition of the *Gītā* will serve a double purpose in Spanish-speaking countries. One, it will help to stop the terrible cheating of false and unauthorized gurus and yogis; and two, it will give an opportunity to Spanish-speaking people to understand the actual meaning of Oriental culture."

Prabhupāda was extremely pleased with the display and said a building should be erected as a permanent exhibition. He also enthusiastically approved Madhudviṣa Swami's idea that every temple have a display of his books along with the reviews. The whole display, he said, was "very enlivening, encouraging, very good."

* * *

Many devotees, led by Jayapatākā Swami, went out on *parikrama* very early in the morning to avoid the heat of the day. But they ended up returning after the start of Śrīla Prabhupāda's lecture, and he was not at all pleased with this. He said that the morning program of hearing *Śrīmad-Bhāgavatam* is more important, and so there should be no more early *parikramas.*

* * *

The Australian devotees had a special *darśana* with Śrīla Prabhupāda. They presented him with $1,350 dollars guru-*dakṣiṇā* and sixty-nine kilos of their famous Australian ghee. The meeting was short but sweet, and Prabhupāda encouraged them all to continue distributing his books in ever-increasing quantities.

In the late evening he called Gargamuni Mahārāja, the newly appointed Māyāpur GBC, and sold the ghee to him for use here for twenty-five rupees per kilo.

* * *

Prabhupāda also viewed plans for the palace the devotees in New Vṛndāvana, West Virginia are building for him. He was extremely pleased with it and accepted an invitation to visit there this summer.

* * *

Arundhatī dāsī, the wife of an early disciple, Pradyumna dāsa, came for *darśana.* Prabhupāda immediately greeted her, inquiring about her husband's whereabouts. Arundhatī explained that Pradyumna was in Udupi in South India, studying Sanskrit.

Prabhupāda requested that he come see him. He didn't

seem very satisfied that Pradyumna was simply studying and not doing any active service.

* * *

Thirteen members of Prabhupāda's former family came to see him. They will stay for Gaura Pūrṇimā. Prabhupāda met with them all briefly, making sure they were comfortably situated. After some light conversation they went out. Prabhupāda was warm and cordial, but he didn't give them any special attention beyond that which he extends to all his visitors. He clearly has no sense of bodily identification and deals with everyone equitably. He has truly realized that every living being is spirit soul, part of Kṛṣṇa. His dealings at every moment reflect his sense of all existence as a homogenous whole.

March 14th, 1976

During the morning walk on the roof, Rāmeśvara prabhu raised a common doubt: If Kṛṣṇa knows everything, past, present, and future, then He must know that a soul is going to fall into the material world, yet He allows it. Therefore He must be cruel.

This set off a long and lively discussion about the individual soul's fall-down from the spiritual realm. Prabhupāda explained that ultimately the soul always has a choice to serve Kṛṣṇa or not. Otherwise we would simply be like dead stones. Therefore Kṛṣṇa cannot be blamed for allowing the soul his independence. Despite this little independence though, the soul requires assistance from the guru, Kṛṣṇa's representative, in order to regain his position as Kṛṣṇa's servant. And who gets that assistance is decided by Kṛṣṇa.

Revatīnandana and Pañca Draviḍa swamis wanted to know what it is that decides why one man and not another gets the good fortune of having a good spiritual master.

Prabhupāda said that it is due to *ajñāta-sukṛti,* past pious activities unknowingly performed.

Then it seems like chance, Revatīnandana said.

"Not chance," Prabhupāda told him. "Just like a sinful man. Some saintly person comes to him and he gives some money to him. He does not know that 'I am doing very pious activity,' but because he has given, he becomes pious."

Revatīnandana's mind jumped to the next logical point. "If not even a blade of grass moves unless Kṛṣṇa sanctions it, then why does someone have the opportunity to perform such *ajñāta-sukṛti,* and another person not?"

Prabhupāda explained it in terms of a dual intervention from both guru externally and Kṛṣṇa within the heart. "Suppose a saintly person comes to a very sinful man. He needs some money. Immediately Kṛṣṇa says, 'Give him some money. He requires.'

"So he says, 'All right, sir, take it.' So Kṛṣṇa desires—he gives. Unless Kṛṣṇa dictates from within, how he can give?"

If that is the case, I asked, where is the question of the free will of the individual?

Again Prabhupāda had the answer. "Free will under Kṛṣṇa. You can become free will and become a big man immediately. Your free will sanctioned by Kṛṣṇa. You are not so free that whatever you like, you can do."

"So even if I want to perform some *ajñāta-sukṛti,*" Madhudviṣa asked, "it is only by Kṛṣṇa's mercy that I will do it?"

"Yes. That is stated by Caitanya Mahāprabhu. *Ei rūpe brahmāṇḍa bhramite kono bhāgyavān jīva, guru-kṛṣṇa-kṛpaya pāya bhakti-latā-bīja:* As soon as he gives to a saintly person, *bhakta,* he immediately acquires some asset of future development. Immediately."

I still had a remaining doubt. The world is full of sinful people, and not all get contact with devotees, or if they do, not all give. Therefore I asked, if Kṛṣṇa is giving dictation to sinful people to give to the saintly persons, does He give dictation to every sinful person? It seems that there is some discrimination.

Prabhupāda's answer cleared my doubts. He said that it isn't just a question of our free will; Kṛṣṇa has His also, and that is supreme. "You cannot bind Kṛṣṇa to dictate in a similar way. If He likes, He can ask a sinful man, "Do this." If He doesn't like, He may not act. That is Kṛṣṇa."

"So, ultimately it is simply by the mercy of Kṛṣṇa that a living entity comes back to Kṛṣṇa," Revatīnandana Mahārāja concluded.

"Yes. So it is Kṛṣṇa's business where to show mercy, where not to show. You cannot oblige Him that 'You show mercy everywhere.' No. *Nāhaṁ prakāśaḥ sarvasya yoga-māyā-samāvṛtaḥ.* You cannot oblige Kṛṣṇa, 'You do this.' That is not Kṛṣṇa. If one is obliged to act to your dictation, then he is not Kṛṣṇa. Therefore whatever Kṛṣṇa likes, He'll do. Ordinary people, they think *karma-mīmāṁsā,* 'If I do good work, Kṛṣṇa will be obliged to give me good effect. Why shall I care for Kṛṣṇa?' They say like that. But we say, even if you do good work, if Kṛṣṇa does not want it, then it will not produce good result. That is Kṛṣṇa. Everyone has got the mercy, but that mercy is not obligatory. If He likes, He can give you mercy; if He does not like, He may not."

Pañca Draviḍa Mahārāja was curious, why then, if it is a question of *ajñāta-sukṛti,* the Indian people, who from their birth water the Tulasī tree, chant Hare Kṛṣṇa, and do so many pious activities, don't seem to be taking to the Kṛṣṇa consciousness movement. Meanwhile, so many Westerners are becoming Prabhupāda's followers.

Prabhupāda used a metaphor to explain the position of the Indian people. It was perhaps a revelation as to why he is putting so much personal effort into his Indian preaching, despite the seemingly poor response. "That is temporary," he said. "They may come again. It will never go in vain. Just like this cloud. Cloud is meant for raining. Now it is not raining, but when there is sufficient cloud, it will rain. You cannot say there is no rain. There is, but it is not sufficiently collected. When it is sufficiently collected, then...."

Even without sufficient cloud it sometimes rains, he said. "That is superior direction. It is not your direction."

Revatīnandana asked about Kṛṣṇa's appearance in the material world. It seems that He comes whenever there are certain conditions.

Prabhupāda disagreed. Kṛṣṇa comes when He wants, not according to conditions. Looking at his watch he made a sudden declaration, emphasizing his point, finishing the debate, and making us all laugh. "Now it is 6:30. Generally I go down. If I like, I don't go!"

* * *

Down in the temple room during his *Śrīmad-Bhāgavatam* discourse, Śrīla Prabhupāda told us about *bhāva,* ecstasy. "At the present moment," he said, "we have got a *bhāva:* 'I am this. I am that. I belong to this family. I belong to this nation.' *Bhāva* is ecstasy, and everyone is overwhelmed with such kind of ecstasy. The politicians, they think that we are simply wasting time in chanting and dancing. 'They have no sense how to improve the position of the country.' They do not like because they are in different *bhāva.*

"But we are trying to change that *bhāva.* The *bhāva* must be there. The whole Kṛṣṇa consciousness movement is to purify the *bhāva.* That is stated here. *Pariśuddha-bhāvaḥ.* We are not negating everything. We are simply changing from material *bhāva* to spiritual *bhāva.* That's all.

"Here is a big building, but there are many other hundreds and thousands of big buildings in this district or in this country. But here the *bhāva* is changed. In your country there are many big, big skyscraper buildings. In comparison to those buildings, this is nothing. But still you have come, spending thousands of dollars, here, to change the *bhāva.* That is required. Otherwise you American boys and girls, you have no business to come here to see this big building, no. To change the *bhāva.* That is required. That is very important thing."

Getting down from the *vyāsāsana,* the devotees crowding around, Prabhupāda embarked on his daily circuit of the temple room. Pṛthu Putra Swami struck up a loud *kīrtana,* and Prabhupāda began to exhibit his own *bhāva,* dancing up and down the whole time. The devotees were wild with delight as he rang the bells hanging down on either side of the temple room, strongly pulling on the ropes for prolonged spells, encouraging the devotees to chant and dance with increasing enthusiasm, and smiling all the while.

After his third circuit he came before their Lordships and began to dance. Hundreds of devotees converged around him, leaping with excitement as he put first one hand in the air and then, handing his cane to Madhudviṣa Swami, raised the other. With both arms extended and a huge smile on his face, he urged the ecstatic crowd to greater and greater heights of spiritual abandon as he himself jumped up and down enthusiastically.

It was a personal demonstration of what Lord Caitanya's festival is really all about—purification through association. Visiting the *dhāma* is wonderful, but seeing and being with Śrīla Prabhupāda is the concentrated essence.

* * *

During his massage, Prabhupāda replied to a couple of letters, one from Ambarīṣa prabhu and one from his former personal servant, Śruti Kīrti. Both of them reported having some difficulties, Ambarīṣa with his parents and Śruti Kīrti with the local temple president in Hawaii.

Ambarīṣa has moved to Boston and is attending university there, to satisfy his parents. He said that he is helping the local temple there, and he suggested that a restaurant serving Kṛṣṇa *prasādam* would be very successful among the huge student community. He also reaffirmed his commitment to fund the Kurukṣetra project.

Śruti Kīrti reported the successful reestablishment of the Govinda's restaurant near the University of Hawaii. It is becoming popular among the 25,000 students there. He is disturbed, however, because of some misunderstandings with the local temple management. Thus he asked for a new engagement.

Prabhupāda put the two together. He wrote Ambarīṣa, approving his move to satisfy his parents, "although they do not know that someone who is a devotee is best educated." He told him that Śruti Kīrti will come to Boston to help him start a restaurant.

To Śruti Kīrti he sent Ambarīṣa's address and advised him to join Ambarīṣa in Boston immediately, "for there are many, many young people, and a Hare Kṛṣṇa Restaurant where we serve delicious Kṛṣṇa *prasādam* will be appreciated there."

* * *

Right after dealing with the mail, Puṣṭa Kṛṣṇa Mahārāja allowed some devotees from the Los Angeles BBT—Rāmeśvara, Rādhāballabha, and Jagannātha Suta—to come onto the veranda. Prabhupāda approved specific criteria for the *Śrīmad-Bhāga-*

vatam covers. The artists had drawn a new color scheme, a different one for each of the twelve Cantos. Although Prabhupāda said that originally he had planned to use the illustration of the spiritual sky that presently adorns the First Canto for all the volumes, he accepted their idea but told them very clearly that after this there could be no more changes.

Jayatīrtha prabhu also showed up. He asked that Rāmeśvara be awarded *sannyāsa*. Prabhupāda immediately and happily granted the request. Jayatīrtha told Prabhupāda that Rāmeśvara is a *naiṣṭhiki-brahmacārī,* having never had sex in this lifetime.

Gradually more GBC members arrived on the balcony. Pañca Draviḍa Swami brought up the *sannyāsa/gṛhastha* conflict again. Tamal Krishna Goswami, Gargamuni Swami, and Bhagavān dāsa eventually joined the discussion, which went on until 1:30 p.m.

The topic came up again because many devotees feel that the resolutions passed are too drastic. The resolution calling for all householders to earn a living outside of the temple financial structure includes temple presidents. Śrīla Prabhupāda was told that such regulations were meant to protect ISKCON from becoming financially overburdened.

Prabhupāda gave his approval in principle, but there is considerable discontent among the temple presidents. Most of them are married and feel that they are simply being discriminated against by the *sannyāsīs*. They are very apprehensive about how the new resolutions will be practically applied.

They also resent what they perceive to be inferences that as married men they are less useful than the *brahmacārīs* and *sannyāsīs* and perhaps even burdensome to the preaching mission.-

Many GBC members, including some of the *sannyāsīs,* are now also having doubts about whether the resolutions passed are actually fair.

Thus the debate was resumed, and Prabhupāda listened as various devotees expressed their views.

Tamal Krishna Goswami was apparently not prepared to concede any ground on the issue, even though nearly everyone else's complaint is against him and his marked pro-*sannyāsa/brahmacārī* inclination.

It got late, and Śrīla Prabhupāda sent everyone for lunch without coming to any real conclusions.

When everyone had gone, Tamal Krishna Mahārāja remained behind for a minute with Śrīla Prabhupāda. It appeared he wanted to gain Prabhupāda's affirmation on his feeling that it is better to be strict. He told Prabhupāda that as a *sannyāsī* he is personally uncompromising in dealings with women, to the point that he doesn't speak to any women whatsoever, even when preaching. He feels that unless the Society is conscientious on this matter, there will be a loss of purity and determination to preach.

Prabhupāda agreed, Tamal Krishna then left, and Prabhupāda took his bath.

When Prabhupāda returned to his room I asked him whether Mahārāja's attitude of avoiding women in his preaching is a material consideration.

"Yes, it is," he said. However, noting my critical tone of voice, he corrected me, "But does that mean he is not a devotee?" As he sat down at his desk putting on his *tilaka,* he noticed a beautifully decorated bookmark that I had just placed there. Picking it up he asked me where it came from. I told him it was a gift from Kṛṣṇa Rūpa dāsī, an Australian *brahmacārīni* living here in Māyāpur. He exclaimed very appreciatively, "Such nice service, how can it be refused? I have never stopped them from rendering service simply because they are women."

After *prasādam* he went for his usual nap, but arose early, within fifteen minutes. I answered the ring of the bell and found him sitting on his bed, looking deeply troubled. He was unable to rest because of the controversy. He had a headache. "This is a very serious thing, this difference of *sannyāsī* and *gṛhastha,*" he said with a frown. "Everything will be spoiled."

I recalled his comments that the Gauḍīya Maṭha fell into difficult times because Śrīla Bhaktisiddhānta Sarasvatī had ordered his disciples to form a GBC to conjointly manage, and they had simply argued and made their own plans. "We made a GBC Śrīla Prabhupāda," I said, "but still there is splitting."

Prabhupāda's reply was brusque and revealing. "Personal ambition!" Then he went to sit in his *darśana* room again.

In the evening the entire Governing Board Commission came in to see Prabhupāda. Things had come to a head. After some discussion, Jayadvaita dāsa, a *brahmacārī,* was invited in to speak as the representative of all the temple presidents. They had held meetings to discuss the implications of the new resolutions, and he presented the results. It seemed that much of the basis of the conflict stemmed from the activities of the Rādhā Dāmodara *saṅkīrtana* party. They have gained some notoriety for taking unmarried men from temples without asking, thereby undermining temple authorities.

Brahmacārīs were being told that if they remained in the temples they would end up married, entangled in family affairs, and therefore useless. On the other hand, they could accept the alternative of a carefree life, traveling and preaching with the RDTSKP buses.

It was claimed that the effect on the temples was to put them in great difficulty because they were losing the *saṅkīrtana* men, their most valuable assets.

Tamal Krishna Mahārāja was still adamant, defending his party and their record-breaking book distribution. He proclaimed the accusations as outright lies. However, he seemed alone. Most GBC men, although highly appreciative of the RDTSKP's book distribution and sympathetic to the principle of *vairāgya* as being the foundation for a spiritually strong society, were now backing away from their earlier stance.

After hearing both sides, Prabhupāda spoke. He broke the deadlock. He finally settled the issue by wonderfully preaching to everyone that it does not matter what one is, one can do anything and go anywhere for Kṛṣṇa. We are not to discriminate against anyone on the basis of external dress. One is to be judged on the basis of one's advancement in Kṛṣṇa consciousness.

Quoting the verse *yei kṛṣṇa-tattva-vettā sei 'guru' haya,* he told them, "We cannot say simply, because one is *gṛhastha* then he must go away." Everyone is entitled to the same facility to preach," he said. Śrīla Bhaktivinoda was a *gṛhastha,* and his son a life-long celibate and *sannyāsī,* but both of them were gurus. There was no difference. He said that the tendency to form factions was not good and he wanted it to stop immediately. He stressed there must be cooperation between the temples and the traveling parties, and that no one fixed principle applied to everyone.

Living in the temple is preaching also—cleaning, cooking and doing Deity worship. A *brahmacārī* may be allowed to go with the *sannyāsīs,* but not if he is holding a responsible position in the temple.

He stated the proper etiquette for a man to join a traveling party; he should do so only with the permission of the temple president. Ideally, he said, it is better that the *gṛhasthas* manage the temples and the *sannyāsīs* go out and preach. This example was set by the Six Gosvāmīs, who turned over the management of their temples to their married disciples. As for the *brahmacārīs,* Prabhupāda said they may do either—travel and preach, or remain in the temple.

As Prabhupāda gave his verdict, the room became increasingly packed with devotees eager to understand the solution to the conflict.

Finally Prabhupāda concluded that this competitive spirit and attitude of "puffed-up prestige" was not good. Everyone should remain as a humble servant. Thus he made it quite clear that he disapproved of the resolutions and ordered the GBC to meet and strike out the controversial ones.

Everyone left happy and relieved that the conflict that had grown over a period of a year or so was finally resolved.

Only Tamal Krishna Goswami remained in Prabhupāda's room, requesting me also to leave so that he could spend a few minutes alone with Śrīla Prabhupāda. I later heard from Mahārāja what he discussed with Śrīla Prabhupāda. Seeking solace and feeling defeated, he began to lament to Prabhupāda that now he felt discouraged, like an enemy in the camp. He said that he didn't want to be an obstacle to the progress of Śrīla Prabhupāda's movement, so perhaps he should not even preach in America any more. Maybe he should go preach where he would not be a disturbance to anyone, like China or somewhere else.

After twenty minutes of commiseration, he got up and left. I was out on the balcony, and I watched him make a lonely walk down the veranda and disappear up the stairs.

I entered Prabhupāda's room and found him clearly relieved at having resolved the matter. He smiled at me and said, "Of all the GBC, he," indicating Tamal Krishna Mahārāja with a tip of his head, "is the most intelligent. But the problem is, those with intelligence want to control everything. And he wants to control the whole Society. He wants to be the supreme controller."

March 15th, 1976

Right before *maṅgala ārati* Prabhupāda buzzed me. He called for Tamal Krishna Goswami and Trivikrama Swami, but I could only find Trivikrama, since Tamal Krishna had already entered the temple. Prabhupāda told Trivikrama Mahārāja that he wanted him to go immediately to China with Tamal. He had been meditating on it all night, he said, and decided that we should definitely do something in the Communist countries.

He also called for Gopāla Kṛṣṇa prabhu and told him to leave for Russia as soon as possible. Prabhupāda said that there are opportunities there for book distribution to libraries, and as an Indian businessman, Gopāla Kṛṣṇa would be well received.

Both Trivikrama and Gopāla were excited by the prospect of opening up vast new preaching fields. They both happily agreed.

Word was sent out to Tamal Krishna Mahārāja, but by the time he arrived in Śrīla Prabhupāda's room, His Divine Grace had gone to the bathroom to freshen up for his morning walk.

Tamal Krishna was clearly shocked at the idea of going to China. As we waited, he began to pace the room, voicing all the reasons why he could not possibly go. Madhudviṣa and Gurukṛpa swamis accompanied him to give some support. Prabhupāda had altered a decision many times previously upon further discussion of an issue. They felt that Tamal had good, strong arguments that might change Prabhupāda's mind upon his hearing them.

After a few minutes Śrīla Prabhupāda returned and sat behind his low desk to apply his *tilaka.* Tamal Krishna Mahārāja sat before him and presented all the reasonable arguments why he should not go to China.

He hadn't expected that Prabhupāda would take what he had said last night literally. He explained how, after leaving Prabhupāda's room, he had met with his entire Rādhā Dāmodara party, and they had discussed their plans for the coming year. They were all enthusiastic and determined to make it the biggest year ever in book distribution. If he were to leave the *saṅkīrtana* party now everything might collapse; the preaching was only going on by his personal presence. There was no one else who could organise it.

Gurukṛpa Mahārāja spoke up in support, volunteering to go instead so that Tamal could stay in America and continue the book distribution. It was a very strong argument. Book distribution is Śrīla Prabhupāda's greatest joy and not something he will jeopardize.

Nevertheless, Prabhupāda rejected the offer. "No! He must go!" Visibly irritated, Prabhupāda asserted, "The Rādhā Dāmodara party is going on by Kṛṣṇa's energy, not Tamal Krishna Goswami's! You said it [China], and I thought about it all night. I wanted to do something there, and I took it as Kṛṣṇa speaking through you."

It quickly became clear to everyone that Prabhupāda was very serious. Madhudviṣa and Gurukṛpa backed away, their silence leaving Tamal Krishna isolated.

His position rapidly weakening, but still resistant, Tamal Krishna Mahārāja tried again. He said that he had indeed mentioned going to China but he might just as easily have said he wanted to go to the moon and preach. He wasn't being serious; it was a joke.

Now Prabhupāda became angry. "Vaiṣṇavas do not joke! You said it, and I took it that this was Kṛṣṇa's indication. I thought about it all night. We have no men there, and I took it as a good opportunity to do something there."

Tamal Krishna was sinking fast, but he tried one last argument. He said that he could understand that His Divine Grace wanted something to be done there but any *sannyāsī* could do it. It shouldn't be a GBC member, who has so many other important responsibilities.

Prabhupāda's face was flushed. His back straightened, and his upper lip twitched on the left side. His anger was barely restrained. His hands shook as he held his *tilaka* mirror and applied the sacred clay to his forehead.

"Why not GBC? All your resolutions are finished. First resolution, then revolution, then dissolution—no solution! I have to manage everything myself! I give you a little power, and you create havoc! GBC is for solving situations, not for creating situations." He was determined and fixed in his decision. He forced his disciple to surrender, making it quite clear there was no option. "I want it, but you do not want. It is my very strong desire. Now I take everything from you. You can either go to China, or you simply sit here in Māyāpur and chant!"

Tamal Krishna Mahārāja bowed his head and conceded. He finally understood there was no alternative and surrendered, agreeing to do whatever his spiritual master required. Despite the prospect of foregoing everything that he had worked several years to build up—the most successful preaching party in the Society—Prabhupāda's desire was paramount. It was a fruitless glory if he didn't please Śrīla Prabhupāda.

Tamal asked only one concession, that Dhṛṣṭadyumna dāsa, a leading *brahmacārī* from RDTSKP and a *sannyāsa* candidate, accompany him, not Trivikrama Swami.

Prabhupāda, now wreathed in smiles, happily agreed. Obviously pleased by the submission of his leading *sannyāsī* disciple, he strode out to take his morning walk, much of which he spent happily discussing how the new preaching assignment would be fulfilled.

* * *

Whether Śrīla Prabhupāda was thinking specifically of the morning's incident or not during class is hard to say. But what he said must have given considerable encouragement and reassurance to his newly East-bound disciples. "If you want to remain in *sattva-guṇa,* in purity, then Kṛṣṇa will help. Just like here, as soon as Brahmā was disturbed by the demons full of *rajo-guṇa* and *tamo-guṇa,* immediately the Lord came in Hayagrīva-*mūrti* incarnation. Kṛṣṇa is also very much anxious to give us protection. If you remain a pure devotee, always surrendered to Kṛṣṇa, you should know it very well that Kṛṣṇa will give you protection in any calamity. Don't be worried. Simply we must have the faith. That is surrender.

"Surrender means *avaśya rakṣibe kṛṣṇa, viśvāsa-pālana.* You must be faithful that 'I am engaged in Kṛṣṇa's service. I may go to hell or heaven. It doesn't matter. I am going to serve Him. It is sure that Kṛṣṇa will give me protection.' So There should be no hesitation. If somebody is ordered, 'Go to hell and preach Kṛṣṇa consciousness,' he should remain faithful to Kṛṣṇa, and Kṛṣṇa will give all protection. This is the principle."

* * *

Śrīla Prabhupāda's godbrother B. R. Śrīdhara Swami came in Prabhupāda's car from his *maṭha* in Navadvīpa. He stayed for most of the afternoon. He and Prabhupāda took *prasādam* together on the veranda. Śrīla Prabhupāda had him stay in the room right next to his own, and after a light rest, they talked for most of the afternoon.

During their conversations they exchanged reports on each other's preaching activities. Prabhupāda told me afterward that Śrīdhara Mahārāja had said that he regarded him as the real *ācārya.* Śrīdhara Mahārāja told him that Lord Caitanya had given His prediction that the chanting of the holy name would go to *every* town and village, but he and his Godbrothers had not taken this statement literally. Now by Śrīla Prabhupāda's efforts he said he could understand its real meaning.

* * *

The GBC met later in the day to redefine zones and to strike out the 'revolutionary' resolutions.

Madhudviṣa Swami was placed in charge of the Rādhā Dāmodara TSKP, as well as New York, Montreal, Toronto, and Ottawa. Rūpānuga prabhu got himself reassigned the southern part of America's East Coast; Gurukṛpa Swami will now manage Australia, New Zealand, Hawaii, Japan, and Fiji; and Jagadīśa prabhu will go to the U.S. Northwest.

By evening they reported that the temple presidents were all now satisfied. Prabhupāda approved a new system for the annual meetings, whereby an initial GBC meeting will be followed by an official temple presidents, meeting, which will consider the resolutions of the GBC and make recommendations as they feel necessary. The GBC will then meet a final time to respond and make any adjustments they feel warranted. In this way the presidents are to be given a voice and the opportunity for controversy possibly avoided.

Prabhupāda made it clear however, that the GBC decision must be accepted as final. The presidents' meeting will be advisory only.

* * *

Tamal Krishna Mahārāja gave a report on his project for China. He has fully accepted his new assignment and has begun to apply himself to the task. Dhṛṣṭadyumna's father is the chairman of Seagram's international division, with links in Hongkong. They intend to consult with him to see how to enter China as businessmen.

Prabhupāda said that he wants something permanent done there—slowly but surely. Tamal Krishna is taking the task very seriously, and Prabhupāda is clearly pleased.

* * *

In a casual moment, while he and I were alone in his room, Prabhupāda suddenly, without prompting, volunteered some interesting information about himself. He told me that once an astrologer informed him that in his previous life he had not committed a single sin. He had been a physician, and just one time, in the course of his work, he had killed a poisonous snake in order to extract the venom for medicine. But this was not considered sinful.

My mind immediately raced with speculation as to who he might have been. I thought of Murāri Gupta, the great devotee and physician in *Caitanya-līlā,* but I was hesitant to ask. If the spiritual master reveals something about himself out of his own accord, all well and good, but I didn't feel it my place to intrude directly into his persona. Still, it seemed an opportunity too good to miss, so I discreetly tried to draw Śrīla Prabhupāda into revealing more. "Um, when would that birth have been, Śrīla Prabhupāda?"

His reply was very nonchalant and noncommittal, "Oh, one

birth is, say, utmost one hundred years. So you simply calculate from 1896 previously," and then changed the discussion.

Opportunity lost.

March 16th, 1976

GAURA PURNIMA. The Appearance day of Śrī Caitanya Mahāprabhu. Everyone fasted until moon rise and then took an Ekādaśī feast, although Prabhupāda said this was not compulsory.

* * *

Prabhupāda kept to his regular schedule, walking first up on the roof and then coming down to walk around the grounds.

Prabhupāda's attentiveness to every detail is nothing short of amazing. As soon as he came out into the cool morning air on the rooftop, he noted a *loṭā* that was standing next to the freshly watered *tulasī* plants. None of us thought anything of it, but vexation immediately crossed Prabhupāda's face. He asked one of the devotees to check if there was a *loṭā* in the toilet room.

"No, Śrīla Prabhupāda," was the reply.

Prabhupāda shook his head. He recognized it as the one he has been using. "See how *aparādhī,* offender. They have used that *loṭā* for watering. Great offender. This is going on, *mlecchas* and *yavanas.*" The thought of using a contaminated receptacle to water Śrīmatī Tulasī Devi was abominable to him, and he warned us to see that it does not happen again in the future. "One who has used that, he has no sense how to water the *tulasī* plant. He should be instructed, 'You never use that toilet *loṭā.*'"

It was yet another indication of our lack of Kṛṣṇa consciousness. Obviously some of us still think of Tulasī Devi as a mere plant, but Prabhupāda is fully conscious of her exalted position.

During the walk Prabhupāda spoke continuously, engaging everyone in debate, challenging and exposing the defects in the philosophy of the Communists and scientists, and training his men how to present Kṛṣṇa consciousness as the topmost system.

He seemed more enlivened than usual, obviously invigorated by the presence of his leading preachers. He talked the whole walk, particularly on the point of leadership in human society. If change is required, or continuous revolution, as the Communists say, then that means imperfection in the leaders. But we have had the same leader, Kṛṣṇa, for millions of years without any need of change.

Then in another incident he demonstrated his ever-watchful concern for our spiritual lives. Surrounded by his *sannyāsīs* and GBCs, he descended the central staircase to the first floor. He caught sight of a woman waiting to go up to the second floor. He stopped and asked what she was doing.

She said she had to go to see Hṛdayānanda Goswami.

Prabhupāda became very concerned, and sent for Hṛdayānanda Mahārāja.

When he came, Prabhupāda demanded to know why he was having a woman visit him in his room. As everyone stood around, Prabhupāda chastised him, saying a *sannyāsī* should not even talk to a woman. Hṛdayānanda explained that it was a misunderstanding. She was actually coming with her husband to discuss her initiation.

"That may be," Prabhupāda said, "but I have to respond as I understand it."

It was a salutary lesson in how careful one must be to protect one's spiritual life.

* * *

Somehow, as if by divine arrangement, the verse from *Śrīmad-Bhāgavatam* 7.9.38 was an exact reference to the appearance of Lord Caitanya. It wasn't planned, as Prabhupāda has been lecturing on the verses in order since mid-February. Yet it was exactly appropriate. Puṣṭa Kṛṣṇa Mahārāja loudly read out the translation to the packed assembly. "In this way, my Lord, You have appeared in different incarnations, as human beings, as animals, as a great saintly person, as demigods and as a fish and a tortoise. In this way You maintain the whole creation in different planetary systems and kill the demoniac principles in every age. My Lord, you therefore protect the principles of religion. In the age of *Kali* You do not assert Yourself as the Supreme Personality of Godhead. Therefore You are known as

Tri-yuga, or the Lord who appears in three *yugas.*"

Śrīla Prabhupāda gave a long lecture, revealing the purpose of Lord Caitanya's descent here in Śrī Māyāpur Dhāma, 490 years ago. He explained that the Lord's mysterious advent can be understood only by the mercy of great devotees like Śrīla Rūpa Gosvāmī. "Caitanya Mahāprabhu is described here as *channaḥ kalau.* In the *Kali-yuga* He's not appearing as other incarnations, not like Nṛsiṁhadeva or Vāmanadeva, or Lord Rāmacandra. He is appearing as a devotee. Why?

"Now, this is the most magnanimous *avatāra.* People are so foolish, they could not understand Kṛṣṇa. When Kṛṣṇa said, *sarva-dharmān parityajya māṁ ekaṁ śaraṇam* [give up everything and surrender to Me], they took it: 'Who is this person ordering like that, *sarva-dharmān parityajya*? What right?'

"That is our material disease. If somebody is ordered to do something, he protests, 'Who are you to order me?' This is the position. God Himself, Kṛṣṇa, what can He say? He orders, the Supreme Person, Supreme Being. He must order. He's the Supreme Controller. That is God. But we are so foolish that when God orders that 'You do this,' we take it otherwise: 'Oh, who is this man? He's ordering like that. Why shall I give Him?' 'I have created so many *dharmas,* 'isms.' I shall give it up? Why shall I give it up?' Therefore the same Lord came again as Caitanya Mahāprabhu.

"Today is Caitanya Mahāprabhu's appearance day, so we must discuss this very thoroughly, [the way] that Rūpa Gosvāmī understood it. Therefore we have to go through guru. Rūpa Gosvāmī is our guru. Narottama dāsa Ṭhākura said, *rūpa-raghunātha-pade, hoibe ākuti, kabe hāma bujhabo, se yugala-pirīti.* If we want to understand the transcendental position of the Supreme Personality of Godhead, then we have to go through *guru-paramparā* system. Otherwise it is not possible.

"So this is *channaḥ-avatāra.* He's Kṛṣṇa, He has come to give you Kṛṣṇa-*prema* [love of God] but He's acting like a Kṛṣṇa devotee. This is covered. He is not commanding now, 'You do this'—yes, He's commanding, 'Do this,' but in different way.

"Because people misunderstood, 'Oh, who is this person commanding?' Even some so-called rascal scholar, he has said, 'It's too much to demand.' They have remarked like that. Yes, sophisticated persons, they are thinking like that. But our process is to submit. Unless we submit, there is no hope of advancing in Kṛṣṇa consciousness. That is Caitanya Mahāprabhu's teaching.

tṛṇād api sunīcena taror api sahiṣṇunā
amāninā mānadena kīrtanīyaḥ sadā hariḥ

"If you want to chant Hare Kṛṣṇa mantra, then you have to take this principle, *tṛṇād api sunīcena.* You have to become humbler than the grass. Grass, it is lying on the street. Everyone is trampling down. Never protests.

"*Taror api sahiṣṇunā.* And more tolerant than the tree. The tree is giving us so much help. It is giving us fruit, flower, leaves, and when there is scorching heat, shelter also. Sit down underneath. So beneficial—still, we cut. As soon as I like, I cut it down. But there is no protest. The tree does not say, 'I have given you so much help, and you are cutting me?' No. Tolerant, yes. Therefore Caitanya Mahāprabhu has selected.

"And *amāninā mānadena.* For oneself one should not expect any respectful position, but he, the devotee, should offer all respect to anyone. *āmāninā mānadena kīrtanīyaḥ sadā hariḥ.* If we acquire this qualification, then we can chant Hare Kṛṣṇa *mahā-mantra* without any disturbance. This is the qualification. So Caitanya Mahāprabhu came to teach these principles."

* * *

In mid-morning Prabhupāda spoke again, this time at a grand initiation ceremony and fire *yajña.* He awarded *sannyāsa* to seven men, *brāhmaṇa* to fifteen devotees, and *hari-nāma* initiation to twenty five.

The devotees had beautifully decorated the entire temple room with flags, festoons, and banana trees. Prabhupāda's *vyāsāsana* had an abundant array of flowers hanging from its umbrella.

A central aisle was left clear, from Prabhupāda to the Deity room at the other end of the temple. On either side the new initiates sat before him, each with a leaf plate containing some grains and a banana for offering into the fire. Behind them, over five hundred devotees crammed in, eager to watch the ceremony.

Śrīla Prabhupāda described *brāhmaṇa* initiation as the means of elevating one to the highest position in society. It is not dependent on birth, but qualification, and it culminates in *sannyāsa.* "Caitanya Mahāprabhu also wanted to introduce this system. *Kibā śūdra, kibā vipra, nyāsī kene naya, yei kṛṣṇa-tattva-vettā sei 'guru' haya.* He never accepted this, that by birth ... no. Either he is a *brāhmaṇa* or he is a *śūdra,* by caste or by birth; either he's a *gṛhastha* or a *sannyāsī,* it doesn't matter. He can become a guru. How? *Yei kṛṣṇa tattva vettā.* One who knows the principles of Kṛṣṇa consciousness, one who understands Kṛṣṇa, he can become a guru.

"So guru is the post given to the *sannyāsīs,* to the *brāhmaṇas.* Without becoming a *brāhmaṇa,* nobody can become a *sannyāsī,* and *sannyāsī* is supposed to be the guru of both all the *āśramas* and all the *varṇas.*

"So the preaching work ... We require so many *sannyāsīs.* People are suffering all over the world for want of Kṛṣṇa consciousness. My Guru Mahārāja used to say that there is no scarcity. This is false propaganda. The only scarcity is that there is no Kṛṣṇa consciousness. That is the difficulty. Actually that is the fact.

"Anyone who knows the science of Kṛṣṇa, he can spread this Kṛṣṇa consciousness movement. And there is great necessity, great necessity. And the preaching work is meant for the *sannyāsīs.* So we have got some *sannyāsīs* who are doing very nicely, so today we shall make a number of *sannyāsīs* more to spread Kṛṣṇa consciousness all over the world. And those who are going to take *sannyāsa,* they should remember how much responsibility they have got. Live like a very strict *sannyāsī.*"

Noting the youthfulness of the *sannyāsa* candidates (all except Hansadūta are in their mid-twenties) and the fact that all are from the West (Prabhupāda decided not to award it to Tatpur dāsa this year after several doubts were raised by others on his maturity), Prabhupāda encouraged them to push on the movement. "Caitanya Mahāprabhu took Himself *sannyāsa* at the age of twenty-four years. So it is not that in old age one has to take *sannyāsa.* That is not in the *śāstra.* From *brahmacārī āśrama* one can enter into the *gṛhastha āśrama* or *vānaprastha āśrama* or *sannyāsa āśrama,* as he thinks fit. There are no such rules and regulations that only the old man without any energy, he'll take *sannyāsa.* No. Rather, the young men ... Just like Caitanya Mahāprabhu did personally. He had beautiful wife, young wife, sixteen years old. At home, very, very affectionate mother, and His position was very great. As a young man He could collect hundreds of thousands of men by His order only, to make civil disobedience movement upon the Kazi, in this land. So the civil disobedience movement was started by Caitanya Mahāprabhu for a good cause.

"So there are so many things. I especially appeal to the natives of this land to take part in this movement of Caitanya Mahāprabhu for the benefit of the world. And we are trying to construct a very attractive temple here. Let them cooperate. It doesn't matter whether he is Hindu, Muslim. Caitanya Mahāprabhu is for everyone."

Hansadūta, Rāmeśvara, Ādi Keśava, Dhṛṣṭadyumna, Pramāṇa, Śatadhanya, and Jagat Guru were effulgent in their new saffron *lungi* and *uttarīya.* One by one they prostrated themselves before Śrīla Prabhupāda and received from the hand of His Divine Grace the *tridaṇḍa* that will now symbolize their total commitment to a life of renunciation. Then each first initiate came forward to receive his new spiritual name and a set of beads. Finally, the sacred fire was lit and mantras chanted, bringing the ceremony to a highly successful completion.

* * *

Attendance at our temple for the Gaura Pūrṇimā day was phenomenal. Estimates of the number of visiting pilgrims entering the front gate ranged between 9,000–25,000 per hour, depending on the time of day. The flow continued for well over seven hours.

Most of the visitors saw the picture exhibit as well as the temple. The road was so packed it became nearly impossible to walk. The local police reported that people were coming from all over Bengal simply to see our ISKCON temple.

Many devotees sold copies of the *Gītār-gāna,* and mass distribution of *halavā prasādam* went on throughout the day.

Prabhupāda was extremely pleased with the turnout. Before our ISKCON temple was established here, only a few hundred people would venture to this side of the river from Navadvīpa on Gaura Pūrṇimā day. None would come after dark.

Now, within a mere three years, the Śrī Māyāpur Candrodaya Mandir has become the chief attraction, not just in the local district but in the whole of Bengal. This has drawn the attention of hundreds of thousands to the sacred birthsite and activities of Lord Caitanya.

* * *

In the early afternoon Tamal Krishna Mahārāja brought the Rādhā Dāmodara party for a special *darśana* with Śrīla Prabhupāda. Rādhā Dāmodara TSKP has over one hundred men working out of six Greyhound-style buses, twenty-five men under Tripurāri Swami working in six airports, and another ten men presently converting two more buses.

Over seventy eager young men, most in their early twenties, packed the room and crowded the doorways. They gave Prabhupāda a large donation of travelers checks, and he encouraged them to continue their work of book distribution and fund raising.

He complimented their efforts, and showed them the plans for future Māyāpur development. Encouraging them to collect more and more funds for Māyāpur's construction, he told them, "So you are the pillars of this construction work. We are doing all our construction work on your contribution. So go on preaching and distributing books."

Prabhupāda was in the best of humor, and deeply appreciative of the work his disciples are doing to establish Kṛṣṇa consciousness in the world. Typically, he wanted to know whether they were all comfortably situated. Tamal Krishna informed him they were occupying an entire wing of the building on the floor above.

Prabhupāda shook his head in mild wonder. He said that when this first building was completed, he was thinking, "Such a big building! How will it be filled?" Now it is packed and overflowing. He likened it to the appearance of *Matsya-avatāra*, the fish incarnation. When He first appeared He was tiny, and a *muni* kept Him in his water pot. Yet He continued to grow and grow, and each time He was put into a bigger container. Finally He was put into the ocean, and still that was not big enough.

Glancing affectionately at the bright youthful faces, Prabhupāda declared, "Caitanya Mahāprabhu's soldiers to fight with *māyā!*"

They cheered back, "*Jaya,* Prabhupāda!"

Prabhupāda went on to explain that cooperation is the essence of the movement. Quoting a line from *Ohe Vaiṣṇava Ṭhākura* he told them, "The purport of the verse is that even Lord Caitanya Mahāprabhu—He is God himself, Kṛṣṇa Himself—He felt, alone, unable to do this task. So this is the position. You are cooperating; therefore I am getting the credit. Otherwise alone what could I do?

Ekakī āmāra nāhi pāya bol. Caitanya Mahāprabhu Himself wanted our cooperation. He is God, Kṛṣṇa. And therefore cooperation is very important thing. Nobody should think that 'I have got so great ability. I can do.' No. It is simply by cooperation we can do very big thing. 'United we stand; divided we fall.' So be strong in pushing on Kṛṣṇa consciousness, and Kṛṣṇa will help. He is the strongest.

"Still, we must be combined together. *Saṅkīrtana* means many men combined together chanting. That is *saṅkīrtana.* Otherwise *kīrtana. Bahubhir militvā kīrtayeti saṅkīrtana. Bahu* means many; many combined together. That is Caitanya Mahāprabhu's mission—combined together. All nations, all persons, they should combine together. There is hope in our society, combination. There are Hindus; there are Muslims; there are Christians; there are black, white. Combine them. That looks very beautiful, just like combination of many flowers."

Bringing the *darśana* to a close, Prabhupāda glorified them with a final few words of praise. "Hare Kṛṣṇa. All glories to the *saṅkīrtana* party, Rādhā Dāmodara!"

* * *

Nanda Kumāra Swami has arrived from Africa and gave a depressing report on ISKCON's Africa mission. Brahmānanda Swami is struggling very hard but meeting with little success.

* * *

Hansadūta Swami's two Mercedes buses finally came in from Germany, via Vṛndāvana, to considerable fanfare and interest from the devotees. Akṣayānanda Swami accompanied them.

The bullock cart party from Hyderabad has also arrived, successfully completing a journey of some fifteen hundred kilometers.

* * *

The beautiful moon rose at 6:20 p.m. Brilliant and full in the sky, it bathed the countryside in its cooling luminescent rays, symbolizing the transcendental appearance of the Lord and the fulfillment of His mission.

Prabhupāda broke his fast, taking his *prasādam* at 7:45 p.m.

The grounds and temple were mobbed with pilgrims. It was virtually impossible to go down into the temple room, and the narrow road to the front gate was jammed with tens of thousands of *Vaiṣṇavas.*

At one point Prabhupāda sent me out to see how many visitors had come, and he was very, very happy to hear of the large crowds. Typically, he wanted assurance that *prasādam* was being distributed to all.

March 17th, 1976

During his morning walk on the roof, Prabhupāda heard a brief report of yesterday's festival. He was extremely pleased. Crowd estimates ranged up to 200,000 visitors. Prabhupāda said that's why he had originally planned four buildings as well as a temple.

Turning to Jayapatākā Mahārāja he told his entourage of GBCs and new *sannyāsīs,* "All this credit goes to Jayapatākā Mahārāja. Yes. He is struggling from the very beginning. Others who were in the beginning, they have all gone away."

He also heartened Tamal Krishna Mahārāja by declaring, "Next year the Chinese men must come!"

As he strolled around the perimeter of the roof, Prabhupāda switched to his favorite topic, science and the theory of chance. He said that the scientists cling to their various theories, even though they lack proofs and are constantly defeated by the superior power of God.

Yaśodānandana Swami offered the French philosopher Voltaire as a prime example of stubbornness. He was an atheist. When a Catholic priest came to him and asked, "Why don't you accept God?", he refused. But at the end of his life he became crazy, driven to consuming his own stool and urine.

Prabhupāda laughingly depicted the intransigence of the scientists with a funny story about "scissor philosophy." One man declared that a piece of paper had been cut with a knife. A second said no, it was done with scissors. An argument ensued, and the first man, being stronger, took the other to a river. There he told him, "Now, if you don't agree that it was a knife I shall throw you into this water!"

The other continued to insist, "It was scissors!"

So he was tossed into the river and began to drown. Still he would not concede. As he disappeared, his hand emerged from beneath the surface with two fingers moving together like a pair of scissors. "No, it is scissor! It is scissor!"

To loud laughter, Prabhupāda thrust his hand into the air and wiggled his fingers in imitation, both charming and entertaining us as he told us this was the definition of a rascal—even thought he is losing his life, still he obstinately refuses to accept the superior force of God. This is the typical materialistic scientific mentality.

* * *

In the late afternoon, two letters from Siddha Svarūpa and Sudāmā Vipra swamis were delivered to Śrīla Prabhupāda's room. They both departed abruptly on the eve of Gaura Pūrṇimā after a violent, unprovoked incident in which Sudāmā Vipra punched Caru dāsa in the stomach as he descended the stairs, knocking him to the floor.

Sudāmā Vipra's letter claimed that Caru is involved in a plot, led by Madhudviṣa and Gargamuni Swamis, to kill Siddha Svarūpa. If anything were to happen to Siddha Svarūpa, Sudāmā Vipra threatened, there would be what he called a "fratricidal war," and Madhudviṣa would be killed.

Prabhupāda shook his head in disgust. He didn't believe the accusation, and he said Sudāmā Vipra was crazy. Calling him a first class *guṇḍā,* or thug, he instructed Puṣṭa Kṛṣṇa Mahārāja to keep the letter on file as a precaution.

Siddha Svarūpa's letter was apologetic, but agreed in principle with Sudāmā Vipra's. Under the circumstances, he wrote, he found it impossible to remain in Māyāpur.

March 18th, 1976

Prabhupāda followed his usual program.

He had us discuss the position of the sun and moon during his walk, contrasting what the scientists say with the statements of the *Śrīmad-Bhāgavatam.*

As a simple example of how the planets move in relationship to each other, he pointed to a tree. He explained that all the planets are like the branches in relation to the trunk. Their positions are fixed and the whole structure is moving, rotating around the Pole star. And the sun is moving on its own course around the whole thing. He confirmed that the *Śrīmad-Bhāgavatam* describes the moon as a self-luminous planet covered with a cooling atmosphere, not a reflective one. Because it is further away than the sun, it is not as bright.

Śrīla Prabhupāda presents himself as a layman, and of course, we are not experts in science either, but still, it is clear that the modern theories cannot match up to Prabhupāda's exegesis of the Vedic literatures. It is apparent that most things taught in the schools and colleges on these subjects are bogus.

Tamal Krishna Mahārāja had a sudden realization of the revolutionary nature and importance of Śrīla Prabhupāda's future plans for Māyāpur. "The scientists are getting smashed to bits by your statements, Śrīla Prabhupāda. This destroys their whole theory ... I think that this Māyāpur building, we must build a big planetarium in it."

"Yes. That I am going to do, Vedic planetarium."

"Oh, boy. You're going to bring a lot of ... A lot of scientists will come here just to dispute this."

"Yes," Prabhupāda agreed. "World people will come to see the way the planetary systems."

"We should advertise it very widely that this is the actual, factual explanation of the universe."

"This will be automatically advertised," Prabhupāda told us. "As soon as the temple is finished, people will come like anything." Then he started laughing. He summed up his approach to the scientists. "The thing is, on principle, we shall only go against them. On principle. Whatever they say 'Yes,' we say 'No.'"

We all laughed in appreciation. Prabhupāda is a genuine revolutionary. He has a clarity of vision that is unlimited in scope. He is challenging the whole of the world's scientific community without any fear or doubt.

And there are no doubts in our minds about him. Prabhupāda is out to change the world, and there is nowhere where we'd rather be than right here with him.

* * *

The day was peaceful, and the devotees were happily content to see Śrīla Prabhupāda during class and for *darśana.*

Immediately after class all the devotees gathered on the lawn at the side of the temple for a group photo, forming a huge U, with Śrīla Prabhupāda in the center.

* * *

Some devotees are now beginning to leave for Vṛndāvana for the second leg of the festival.

March 19th, 1976

Prabhupāda had a lot to say this morning on his walk about the poor standards of today's education and civilization. One of the devotees began to object, "But they will say—"

Prabhupāda quickly replied, "They say anything because they are rascals. *Pagale ki na bale chagale kiba na khaya*: 'A madman, what he does not say? And a goat, what he does not eat?'"

He went out onto the front road to inspect the new paintings being done on the wall. On the whole, he liked the style, but he said Pāṇḍu should use brighter colors. The present ones are too dark. "It is India," he said, smiling. "It is not London, always foggy!"

* * *

Prabhupāda reminded his new initiates, and all of us, in class about the good opportunity he has given us through initiation to cross over to the other side of the river of death.

Prabhupāda especially stressed that we should not fall back. "We finish all the resultant action of contamination of this material life, provided we remain without being fallen again. Therefore there is *daśa-vidha-nāmāparādha.* You know the ten kinds of offenses.

"So if you chant Hare Kṛṣṇa mantra, being careful not to commit the ten kinds of offenses, then you are immediately liberated. The most dangerous offense is if we think that 'I am so fortunate. I have got this *hari-nāma* and it can vanquish all kinds of sinful reaction, so very good instrument. So I go on committing all kinds of sinful activities and chant Hare Kṛṣṇa. Then it will be neutralized.' This is the most dangerous offense. *Nāmno balād yasya hi pāpa-buddhiḥ.* Because I know that by chanting Hare Kṛṣṇa I shall be free from all resultant action of sinful life, let me go on, and throughout whole day I shall commit all kinds of sinful activities and in the evening I shall chant Hare Kṛṣṇa. Then everything will be finished. This rascaldom is very, very dangerous.

"We must be very careful. Don't take Hare Kṛṣṇa mantra as an instrument to neutralize your sinful activities. It is a fact that as soon as you are initiated with Hare Kṛṣṇa mantra, you become free, but don't commit it again."

* * *

Māyāpur is again peaceful. Most pilgrims have returned home, many of our devotees have left, and work has recommenced on the new building.

Prabhupāda was sitting quietly in his room, relishing the blissful atmosphere created by the melodic Bengali *kīrtana* floating out from the temple room below. He told us the chanting is the only solace; it is nothing material. He even suggested that five hundred men at a time could come here to Māyāpur simply to chant.

March 20th, 1976

Before the festival a man named Prabhu Svarūpa came to Māyāpur to see Prabhupāda. He requested ISKCON's involvement at a place called Haridāspur, just on the border with Bangladesh. Śrīla Prabhupāda agreed to visit there with his foreign disciples, and so today he left by car in the early morning, a drive which took three hours.

Haridāspur is named after Śrīla Haridāsa Ṭhākura, the great *ācārya* of the holy name, to commemorate his stay there.

The man's *āśrama* turned out to be a very small cottage situated on six *bighas* (two acres) of land, on the outskirts of the village, with a small, run-down shrine to Ṭhākura Haridāsa.

Prabhupāda spent four hours in a derelict, single-room, brick building with only gaping holes for a roof, door, and windows and an uneven, overgrown, earthen floor. We had to hang our *chadars* over the openings to give him some privacy while he took his breakfast, massage, bath, and lunch, all in the same place.

Other devotees also came in several buses and were entertained by Gurudāsa Mahārāja, who told them stories of Haridāsa Ṭhākura and Lord Caitanya.

After his lunch, Prabhupāda gave a brief, fifteen-minute speech to the small crowd, comprised mainly of our own devotees. Then he left.

After Śrīla Prabhupāda's speech, *prasādam* was served. It was cooked locally in mustard oil, and later in the day many devotees were reported to be suffering diarrhoea from it.

Despite the inconvenience, the poor reception, and the long drive, Śrīla Prabhupāda had no complaints. He was merciful and kind to Prabhu Svarūpa and asked him to work with Jayapatākā Swami to let us gradually help to develop the place.

* * *

Prabhupāda decided when he got back that he will not go on TSKP with Hansadūta Swami because the strain of traveling by road is too much for him. But he encouraged Hansadūta to continue on with his plans to tour and preach throughout India.

We were back in Māyāpur by late afternoon. Prabhupāda had a brief rest and then allowed the devotees to come for *darśana.* He was relaxed and peaceful, appreciative that so many young Westerners have come so far and done so much for spreading Kṛṣṇa consciousness. Yet he hardly acknowledged his own great sacrifices.

His presence alone generates a pleasing atmosphere of transparence and sobriety. The devotees crowd his room just to be there with him, regardless of what he says. But he always has something valuable to say, a lesson to teach, another insight to offer. A year's hard work is fulfilled simply by being with him for a few minutes. And to be with him here in Māyāpur, the spiritual world, is an added bonus.

Today he talked about the present generation and why so many have become hippies, rejecting all the so-called comforts offered by their parents. He said that the fact that the young people are adopting lower standards is an indication that such a so-called civilization actually stems from irreligion. Lacking guidance, women have become uncontrolled and have fallen prey to lusty men, with *varṇa-saṅkara,* or unwanted, irresponsible children the direct result.

March 21st, 1976

Today was Śrīla Prabhupāda's final day in Māyāpur.

Jayapatākā Mahārāja was instructed during the walk to arrange a meeting with Śrīla Lalitā Prasāda Ṭhākura, the only remaining brother of Śrīla Prabhupāda's Guru Mahārāja, Śrīla Bhaktisiddhānta Sarasvatī. Prabhupāda wants to meet with him on his way into Calcutta tomorrow.

Apparently Śrīla Bhaktisiddhānta had some difference of opinion with Lalitā Prasāda. Lalitā Prasāda is a *bābājī,* a member of a class of reclusive devotees who remain aloof from the general population and simply chant the *mahā-mantra.* His brother, on the other hand, was a *sannyāsī,* an active preacher who created a large movement and attracted much opposition in the process. Apparently Lalitā Prasāda considers himself more confidentially situated in his relationship with the previous *ācāryas* and Kṛṣṇa.

Despite this, Prabhupāda has been negotiating to get either a lease or ownership of the birthsite of Śrīla Bhaktivinoda Ṭhākura, the father of Bhaktisiddhānta and Lalitā Prasāda, and our spiritual great-great grandfather. He wants to renovate the place and maintain a preaching center there. Prabhupāda has met with Lalitā Prasāda previously, who said he was willing to cooperate with us. He has not been able to develop the birthsite, but still some of his men are hesitating. He has a committee to manage his affairs, and now it appears they want another meeting.

Without raking up the controversial points, Śrīla Prabhupāda made a few observations by which we could understand the actual symptoms of confidential service. "So what is the use of such men? Why he's keeping these men? They cannot do anything. He gets some pension, and he spends that money. But they are not doing anything. So what is the meaning of this committee?"

Jayapatākā Mahārāja told Prabhupāda that the Ṭhākura has admitted that many times he has told some of his men to leave their family life and take up some preaching, but they don't do it.

"How they'll do it?" Prabhupāda rejoined. "They do not know how to preach. Neither they are trained up. That means it is his disqualification. He could not train them how to preach. Even Caitanya Mahāprabhu, He was training Haridāsa Ṭhākura, Nityānanda, 'Go there. Preach there. Do that.' My Guru Mahārāja was doing that. But he [Lalitā Prasāda] has no power. He cannot do it. He simply talks that he is a very confidential devotee. That's all. He cannot preach. Otherwise Prabhupāda developed this Māyāpur, and he could not do anything. That means he has no such power."

"He should have developed that place," Jayapatākā Swami ventured.

"Yes. He simply talks of big, big work. In the beginning, Prabhupāda had no committee, nothing of the sort. That he'll not admit, that he has no power to do so. He simply thinks that he's very confidential son of Bhaktivinoda Ṭhākura."

Going down to the front gate, Prabhupāda went to inspect the painting of the front wall.

The *gurukula* children were gleefully yelling "Jaya Prabhupāda! Haribolo!" all the way down the road. Prabhupāda reciprocated with smiles and "Hare Kṛṣṇa!" He has a ingenuous rapport with them, innocents entrusted to him to send back to home, back to Godhead. And they love him without reservation, putting in him their full trust, as guileless young children do.

As he made his way out the gate, he emphasized why he has had such success in his preaching mission. "You must be always convinced that if we simply take up the knowledge given by Kṛṣṇa, then you are perfect. That's all. A little success is there for me, [more] than other swamis and yogis. It is due to my conviction on this point. I never compromised with anything which is not spoken by Kṛṣṇa. Did you mark it or not?"

All the devotees replied in unison. "Yes."

One of the devotees recalled a previous instruction Prabhupāda had given. "One time you told us, Śrīla Prabhupāda, to meet every man at his door and ask him to give up everything he knows and chant Hare Kṛṣṇa."

"Yes. That is simple. 'You rascal, you give up whatever you have learned to chant Hare Kṛṣṇa.'" He smiled at us. "Don't say rascal, but indirectly. 'Whatever you have learned, it is all nonsense. You give up everything, kicked out, and simply become adherent to Caitanya.' This is our preaching. And what Caitanya Mahāprabhu said, *yāre dekhe, tāre kaha 'kṛṣṇa'-upadeśa.* That's all."

Pañca Draviḍa Mahārāja asked him to repeat the reason for his success.

Prabhupāda obliged. "Because I stick to Kṛṣṇa's word! I go to present *Bhagavad-gītā as* it is. We don't make any amendment. Therefore we decry eulogizing Gandhi, Dr. Rādhākrishna, Aurobindo, this, that ... all rascals! Because they tried to amend it."

Prabhupāda recalled a recent review of his *Bhagavad-gītā As It Is* by Francois Chenique, Professor of Religious Sciences at the Institute of Political Studies in Paris. This man has written very appreciatively. "Śrīla Prabhupāda's edition thus fills a sensitive gap in France, where many hope to become familiar with traditional Indian thought, beyond the commercial East-West hodgepodge that has arisen since the time the Europeans first penetrated India. Whether the reader be an adept of Indian spiritualism or not, a reading of the *Bhagavad-gītā As It Is* will be extremely profitable. For many this will be the first contact with the true India, the ancient India, the eternal India."

"That is admitted by the French professor," Prabhupāda said. "That they have all tried to make it modernized. But I have not done that. 'Here is a spiritual master in disciplic succession, so we are indebted to him, to understand the original traditional knowledge.' Everyone who is after truth will accept. And if you are bogus, want to be cheated and cheat others, then he'll not. Ninety-nine percent are cheaters and cheated. This is the position. All these cheaters they are cheating and they accept to be cheated.

"If I am very clever but I don't go to be cheated, nobody can cheat me. But these rascals, they *want* to be cheated. If you say, 'What is the wrong in illicit sex?' that means you want to be cheated. And if we say, and the press will go, 'Oh this swami is very conservative.' This is the position. We want cheap things because we want to be cheated. And here are so many cheaters, they will take advantage and cheat you. This is going on."

Pañca Draviḍa mentioned again that Allen Ginsberg had said that Prabhupāda was very conservative.

"Yes. Because he wants to be cheated. And he cheats others. Some followers, he is cheating."

Pañca Draviḍa Mahārāja repeated a slogan the Rāma Kṛṣṇa mission uses to summarize its philosophy. It means 'Whatever path one follows, you get the same result.' It well represents the kind of mentality Prabhupāda was describing.

Prabhupāda agreed with his observation. "*Yato mat tato pat.* Yes, this is going on. This business is to ruin the innocent persons, who are being cheated. And we don't want to cheat them. Whatever Kṛṣṇa says—our business is very simple."

* * *

A letter from Raṇadhir dāsa, who runs the BBT Mail Order department in Los Angeles, informed Śrīla Prabhupāda of the mailing of 200,000 copies of *The Kṛṣṇa Consciousness Movement Is Authorized* to the "leading citizens of the United States." As well as this they are compiling a list of over twenty-five-hundred professors who have ordered one or more of Prabhupāda's books. In addition, Raṇadhir enclosed a list of all the libraries and professors who have taken a standing order of the full set.

Prabhupāda was very pleased to receive the material. He asked Puṣṭa Kṛṣṇa Mahārāja to keep the lists in his standing file. (Prabhupāda's secretary carries two files. One is for correspondence and is cleared out every few months. The other is a standing file containing important documents, newsclips, etc. that Prabhupāda uses in his preaching). In his reply he asked Raṇadhir to "please continue with this important work."

There was also a letter from a devotee in Nairobi, Mahāvirya dāsa. Writing his letter on the appearance day of Śrīla Jagannātha dāsa Bābājī, he described rather dramatic reasons why he now wants to permission to take *bābājī* initiation. "Recently while here in Nairobi ISKCON center, the temple was attacked, and I was practically sliced to death by thieves and murderers. I was unconscious for two days, hospitalized for twenty-eight, and now I presently have the use of only one hand and arm. I consider this the Lord's mercy. I am suffering still, conditional, fallen and the greatest fool, so I beg you to please give me permission to chant daily ninety rounds."

Even with that heartfelt plea, Śrīla Prabhupāda was cautious. Mahāvīrya is still only twenty-seven years old. So Prabhupāda wrote back, deferring his decision until next time he goes to Nairobi. As he told him, "I gave *bābājī* initiation to one other devotee but now he is off somewhere restless."

* * *

Tamal Krishna Mahārāja reported to Śrīla Prabhupāda that Viṣṇujana Swami has disappeared. He has failed to appear since he asked Śrīla Prabhupāda his questions about Choṭa Haridāsa up on the roof. One of the devotees saw him the day after, on the morning of March 12th, on the train to Calcutta, and no one has seen him since.

Prabhupāda didn't seem to take it too seriously. He appeared unperturbed. He doesn't think there has been any mishap, he thinks he simply doesn't want to serve.

* * *

With Prabhupāda's permission I took my one and only bath in the Ganges before we left. She was flowing swiftly, and swimming was difficult.

Prabhupāda has decided to bring along Anantarāma Śāstrī as part of his party, to assist with the Sanskrit grammar checking in his books.

* * *

In the afternoon devotees gathered in Prabhupāda's room for a last *darśana.* On behalf of the temple in Philadelphia, Ravīndra Svarūpa prabhu gave him an eighteen-carat gold ring made by Gopīnātha dāsa. Prabhupāda held it for a moment, puzzled as to what the design was. "It is a crown?" he asked.

Ravīndra Svarūpa reached forward and turned it up the other way. That revealed the words "Hare Kṛṣṇa," with three small diamonds forming the diacritic dots under "Kṛṣṇa."

Prabhupāda smiled with pleasure and appreciation, and he slipped it on the little finger of his right hand. Then, opening the drawer in his desk, he pulled out another ring, a large, decorative, golden one with a big, black stone, which he handed to Bhavānanda Mahārāja. Very gratefully, Bhavānanda immediately put it on, and it fit perfectly.

CHAPTER TEN

Calcutta, New Delhi, Modinagar and Aligarh

March 22nd, 1976

At 5:30 a.m. Śrīla Prabhupāda descended the stairs amid a loud *kīrtana* and excited shouts from the devotees. He stepped into the back seat of the car, and we sped off for Calcutta, accompanied by an escort of six vans and one of Hansadūta Swami's buses. Puṣṭa Kṛṣṇa Mahārāja drove our car, Tamal Krishna Mahārāja sat in front, and I sat in the back next to Prabhupāda.

It wasn't long before I began to nod off to sleep. Despite Prabhupāda's objecting several times, and my own best effort, I just could not keep alert. Prabhupāda became so annoyed that he had Puṣṭa Kṛṣṇa stop the car and made me change places with Tamal Krishna so that I sat in the front. After that embarrassment I stayed awake for the rest of the journey.

All along the route, as we passed through the small villages, young children came running out to see the procession. They laughed and danced and waved as we went past, attracted by the loud *kīrtana,* broadcast from Gargamuni Swami's vans.

We stopped off at the *āśrama* of Śrīla Lalitā Prasāda, the brother of Śrīla Bhaktisiddhānta Sarasvatī Ṭhākura. As the last remaining son of Śrīla Bhaktivinoda Ṭhākura, he is very old. His *āśrama* consists of a small temple and a few red-brick dwellings, none of which are well maintained. Prabhupāda talked for some time with him and some of his management committee. They discussed the plans he had for development of Śrīla Bhaktivinoda's birth site. Nothing conclusive was arrived at with regard to their giving some land or even a lease on the property.

We all took *prasādam* before leaving, Prabhupāda with Lalitā Prasāda and we disciples with the local devotees of the *āśrama,* up on the open roof. Jayapatākā Swami, eager as ever to preach and advertise ISKCON's world-wide missionary efforts, told a group of our hosts about our preaching in the West. They were all eager to hear, and Mahārāja tried to impress upon them the great need for Kṛṣṇa consciousness in all the countries of the world. He told them of a law recently passed in Sweden, which makes it no longer illegal for members of the same family to have sex with each other. They are becoming increasingly degraded, he said, and only Lord Caitanya's movement can save them. The simple Bengali Vaiṣṇavas were all shocked to hear such things. They were very appreciative of Śrīla Prabhupāda's preaching and his Western disciples.

After an hour or so, we departed, nothing being positively decided.

Śrī Śrī Rādhā-Govinda Mandir
3A Albert Rd., Calcutta 17

Śrīla Prabhupāda gave a short, but very pointed talk upon his arrival at the packed Calcutta temple. He first congratulated the *pūjārīs* for looking after the Deities so nicely. Then he went on to explain that these same Personalities, referring to Them by Their names in Māyāpur, Śrī Śrī Rādhā-Mādhava, are combined in the form of Lord Caitanya.

Having just come from the birthplace of Lord Caitanya, Prabhupāda told his attentive, and mainly non-Indian audience that it was Lord Caitanya's desire that the inhabitants of *Bhārata-bhūmi* spread Kṛṣṇa consciousness all over the globe. Although it is the duty of the Indians, he said, *Bhārata-bhūmi* can be understood in a broader sense as well. "In one sense *Bhāratavarṣa* means this planet. Formerly there was one flag, *Bhāratavarṣa,* and the capital was Hastinapura. Gradually the control of the Pāṇḍavas declined. Up to Mahārāja Parīkṣit, the whole world was *Bhāratavarṣa.* Now it has become a tiny land, peninsula. So in that sense anyone who has taken birth on this planet, it is the duty of him to spread Kṛṣṇa consciousness. So by the grace of Kṛṣṇa, you European boys and girls, you have taken very seriously, and Kṛṣṇa will be very much pleased upon you."

Prabhupāda expressed his regret that the Indian people are not taking the Kṛṣṇa consciousness movement seriously. He noted that even our immediate neighbors show no interest. Although they live in the same building, their only interest is making money, and dealings with them have sometimes been acrimonious.

Prabhupāda said that even the villages of Bengal are in "pitiable" condition. He condemned the attempt of modern leaders to convince the villagers that their conditions will improve by industrialization. So they have given up their Kṛṣṇa conscious culture, and the only result is misfortune.

Of course, being from Bengal, Śrīla Prabhupāda has watched the degradation of their culture over the decades, especially since independence. He ascribes this to their pursuit of Western materialistic ideals, and he made a plea to the room full of Westerners now before him to help reverse the trend.

"Anyway, Calcutta is my birthplace, so you have kindly come here and are conducting this temple. I am very much obliged to you. I cannot remain here. I have to go here and there. Try to raise the standard of Kṛṣṇa consciousness, even there are so many inconveniences. I know. You are coming from a country where material conveniences are greater. But Caitanya Mahāprabhu has advised, *tṛṇād api sunīcena taror api sahiṣṇunā, amāninā mānadena kīrtanīyaḥ sadā hariḥ.*

"So some of you, you have come with your big, big buses and vans to preach in India. You take Caitanya Mahāprabhu's blessings and try to enlighten these people. The *Bhāratavarṣī,* the inhabitants of *Bhāratavarṣa,* naturally they are already inclined. Just like in the villages, when we were passing, the boys and children, they were also dancing. That is natural.

"Some way or other, this India is in a very precarious condition. So you have come, taking so much trouble. And take little trouble—there is no trouble; by the grace of Kṛṣṇa and Caitanya Mahāprabhu there will be no trouble. You'll be happy. Try to preach this Kṛṣṇa consciousness movement in India at least for some time and help them to rise to their standard of Kṛṣṇa consciousness. Thank you very much."

* * *

Calcutta temple is packed with devotees, and there is no running water. This is a continual problem, now exacerbated by the crowd of visiting devotees. In the best of times the water only comes on for a few hours each day.

We have to haul water to Prabhupāda's bathroom and store it in a small tank. Most devotees are bathing in the lake across the road. So Prabhupāda called for the new temple president, Abhirām dāsa, a tall American previously in charge of our Miami center. He told him to immediately install a new holding tank.

March 23rd, 1976

Prabhupāda took his walk around the lake opposite the temple and inspected a large house on the corner of it that may be up for sale soon. Although it is run down, Prabhupāda was interested in buying it because of the lakeside location. A price of fourteen lakhs of rupees was mentioned.

He asked Abhirām to make the necessary applications to gain responsibility for beautification of the lake and its gardens and gradually try to get permission to build a magnificent temple in the center of it. Since it is one of Calcutta's most prestigious locations, a gorgeous temple on the lake would attract tens of thousands of people, he said. Prabhupāda has ever-increasing plans for spreading Kṛṣṇa consciousness. Especially in India he is keen to do something wonderful with the combination of Western money and Indian culture.

* * *

There was only one letter to reply to today, from Kīrtanānanda Swami, who reported to Prabhupāda his reason for not being able to attend the festival. The West Virginia state health authorities had placed a quarantine order on New Vṛndāvana because some devotees had become sick with jaundice. Kīrtanānanda Mahārāja said that some inimical state authorities overreacted to the situation. Now he thinks their community will be obliged to accept some regulation by the state. His mood has been to keep things as simple as possible, but, as he admitted, "either due to [the authorities'] lack of vision, or our lack of expertise, simplicity has been taken for dirtiness."

In his reply, Prabhupāda told him if it is necessary to make alterations he may do so. Yet, he clearly stated his opinion of the modern so-called sanitary arrangements in the West. "If the water supply is sufficient, there is no question of insanitation. Disease comes when there are dirty conditions. Concerning the [existing] outhouses, if they are not approved then you can have a septic tank, or pass stool in the open field. I was doing that. I never liked to go to the nonsense toilet so I was going in the field."

* * *

In the early evening Prabhupāda went to the Mullik's house on Harrison Road, now Jatindra Mohan Avenue, in the area where he lived as a child. He was greeted enthusiastically by Kashinath Mullik, along with other family members and friends.

Prabhupāda was very, very happy to see Śrī Śrī Rādhā-Govinda, the original Deities that had provided his spiritual inspiration as a small child. Although the area has changed considerably from his childhood days, and the little courtyard and shrine are quite run down, the Deities are obviously still well-looked after and offered daily *pūjā.*

The Mulliks and the other friends were delighted to see him, although Prabhupāda told us that most of his contemporary friends were now dead. Only one or two of those present were actually people he had played with in his childhood. He told us the Deities have been worshiped by the Mulliks for over two hundred years. At one time They owned the whole area. Even now the government building across the street is the property of Rādhā-Govinda.

In a short speech Śrīla Prabhupāda recalled his childhood history. His family lived just down the street behind a building called Govinda Bhavan, and as a three- or four-year-old he would come every day to see the Deities. "And that is the inspiration of my devotional life. Then I asked my father that 'Give me Rādhā-Govinda Deity; I shall worship.' So my father was also

Vaiṣṇava. He gave me small Rādhā-Govinda Deity. I was worshiping in my house. Whatever I was eating, I was offering, and I was following the ceremonies of this Rādhā-Govinda with my small Deity. That Deity is still existing. I have given to my sister.

"So then I introduced *Rathayātrā*. My *Rathayātrā* was being performed very gloriously. My father used to spend money. In those days ten rupees, twenty rupees was sufficient. I hired one *kīrtana* party and all small friends, and there was another De family here, so we performed this *Rathayātrā* ceremony. According to our children's imagination, it was very gorgeous.

"Gopīśvara Mullik was my father's friend. So he was criticizing my father that 'You are performing *Rathayātrā* ceremony and you are not inviting us.' So my father said, 'That is children's play. What shall I invite you? You are very big man.' 'Oh, so you are avoiding! In the name of children you are avoiding us.'

"On the whole, this *Rathayātrā* festival was very gorgeously performed. Then imitating me, the others, my brother, he also introduced *Rathayātrā.* And all of them introduced *Rathayātrā,* and the destination was this Thakurbari, from there.

"So practically what I am doing now, the same thing, Rādhā-Kṛṣṇa worship and introduction of *Rathayātrā.* I am not doing anything else. You know very well. We are now performing *Rathayātrā* ceremony practically in all big cities of the world, in San Francisco, in Philadelphia, London, Melbourne, Paris .... So the same thing, the same Rādhā-Kṛṣṇa worship and same *Rathayātrā,* in a bigger scale. But the same thing was begun as play from this quarter, this Thakurbari.

"So this Thakurbari, Rādhā-Govindajī, is my life. That is the beginning of my spiritual life. And after so many years, still Rādhā-Govindajī has dragged me [here]. It is His kindness."

Prabhupāda humbly suggested that his good fortune was due to his previous activities. He quoted *Bhagavad-gītā* 6.41, which states that the unsuccessful yogi takes birth in the family of the pious and prosperous. The De family, he said, was practically the same as the wealthy Mulliks, and his own father was a very pure Vaiṣṇava. With these opportunities provided by birth, he said, he was simply developing them on a wider scale by Kṛṣṇa's arrangement.

Looking lovingly at Śrī Śrī Rādhā-Govinda he ended his little speech. "So about this movement it may be said this Rādhā-Govinda Deity is the inspiration. You are all fortunate that you have come here. So let us offer our obeisances." Prabhupāda humbly bowed down, touching his head to the floor. And then, amid much affection from his old friends, he climbed back in the car to return to his own recently established Rādhā-Govinda Mandir.

Driving back in the car we crept through the heavy evening traffic, with cars constantly honking and overcrowded, dilapidated buses blasting black sooty emissions into the atmosphere. Seeing the congested streets teeming with tens of thousands of people made me reflect upon how different it must have been in the first decade of the century when Prabhupāda and his young friends roamed these precincts. At that time the transport would have been by horse and buggy or horse-drawn trams, and the population was much smaller. It must have been a vastly different Calcutta from the present.

Prabhupāda pointed out to Abhirām, Puṣṭa Kṛṣṇa Mahārāja, and myself some of the places of his childhood activities. He showed us his old school, attended before going to Scottish Churches college, and the field where as a boy he used to play soccer.

We came into what was formerly the old Muslim sector, and Prabhupāda told us that in 1911 there was a massive riot there, in which he was almost killed.

It was an exciting evening, made especially sweet by the opportunity to listen as Śrīla Prabhupāda mercifully shared his reminiscences of his younger days.

March 24th, 1976

New Delhi

Prabhupāda took the first flight to Delhi, where he was met by a small band of devotees led by Gurudāsa and Lokanātha swamis. Among them, surprisingly, was Chayavana, the errant *sannyāsī* from the African *yātrā*, now free again after his arrest in Rādhā Kuṇḍa.

Our host for the next few days is Mr. Laxman S. Agarwal, a short, balding man and the owner of one of India's biggest businesses, Sylvania Light Company. Prabhupāda has stayed with him several times. Previously he helped to arrange for Śrīla Prabhupāda to meet with prominent government officials over the continuing visa problems of our American devotees.

He greeted Prabhupāda with a garland made of marigolds and rupee notes, then led us out to his Mercedes, which he is allowing us to use for the next few days until Prabhupāda's car arrives from Calcutta.

His modern two story semidetached house is located in the prestigious diplomatic enclave of Caṇakya Purī, and is similar to what one would expect to find in a well-off Western suburb. Situated in a clean, neat cul-de-sac, it has marble floors throughout and a small high-walled backyard with a lawn. Right outside the front yard, the devotees have erected a small colorful *pāṇḍāla* on the road's central grassy reserve.

Śrīla Prabhupāda's room is on the ground floor, about sixteen feet square. It's quite comfortable, with an attached bathroom, wood paneling throughout, and French windows opening onto the back lawn. It is furnished simply with a small wooden bed, a low desk, and an *āsana.*

The Agarwals are devotees of Kṛṣṇa and have a beautiful set of thirty-inch marble Rādhā-Kṛṣṇa Deities. They keep the Deities on the first floor of their home and worship Them daily in a simple fashion.

March 25th, 1976

For his morning exercise Prabhupāda took an easy walk up and down the grass reserve of the front street. He answered questions from his small band of listeners—Gurudāsa Swami, Atreya Ṛṣi, Chayavana, Puṣṭa Kṛṣṇa, Gopāla Kṛṣṇa, Yadubara, and myself.

Yadubara queried why devotees get sick if sickness is a punishment for those who violate God's laws.

Prabhupāda's answer was frank. "Devotees—to become a devotee is not so cheap thing. You don't think that because you have got *tilaka* you have become devotee. Why do you think like that? "Bhaktivinoda Ṭhākura sang, *ei ta eka kalir chelā, nāke tilaka, galayā mālā:* 'Here is another follower of *Kali.* He has got *tilaka* and *mālā.*' *Sahaj bhajan kacen mamu, saṅga laiyā parer wala, ei ta eka kalir chelā:* 'He is worshiping, *bhajan,* and taking another's wife. Here is a servant of *Kali.* Simply he has changed his dress with *tilaka* and *mālā.*' Bhaktivinoda Ṭhākura says.

"If you take *tilaka* and *mālā* and do all nonsense things, then you are not a devotee. You are *Kali-chelā.* To become a devotee is not so easy thing."

"Devotee means perfect," Atreya Ṛṣi added.

"Oh yes, certainly," Prabhupāda said. "Devotee means he is above these material laws. That is devotee. *Brahma-bhūyāya kalpate.* He is in the *Brahman* stage. That is devotee. That means *sahajiyā*—'Because I have got a *tilaka* and *mālā,* I have become devotee.' This kind of cheating will not do."

Chayavana seemed especially interested in the topic. Prabhupāda directly told him that if you do something that is forbidden, then you suffer; that is the law of *karma.* He said that a devotee follows Kṛṣṇa's instructions. Kṛṣṇa is giving the real truth, and if one takes it he is a devotee; if one does not, he is a nondevotee.

Then what is the role of mercy, Puṣṭa Kṛṣṇa Swami asked, for those who take and those who don't?

Prabhupāda replied that mercy means, if either unknowingly or by some bad habit, one does some wrong, that will be excused. But he warned that deliberate transgressions are not forgiven.

Gurudāsa Mahārāja asked what "unknowingly" means.

Prabhupāda explained. "Unknowingly means, suppose you are a smoker. So now you have given up everything. But in the association of some smoker you incline, 'All right, let me smoke.' Then you regret, 'Oh, I have done this.' It can happen. So that is excused. "But if you think, 'Now I am a devotee of Kṛṣṇa. I can smoke like anything, and everything will be excused,' then you are a rascal."

He said that the mercy of Kṛṣṇa is that He wants us to come back to Godhead even though we have no desire. If we take even one step forward, Kṛṣṇa will take ten steps toward us.

Then why is there punishment and suffering, another devotee asked. If God is all-loving, why does He make us suffer?

Prabhupāda told him Kṛṣṇa loves us, but if we don't do what He says, then we must naturally suffer as the child is burnt by the fire when ignoring the advice of his father. Yet, he said, that suffering is also mercy because through such experience the soul will be purified and give up his enviousness of Kṛṣṇa. "So this question of freedom of *jīva* and control of Kṛṣṇa," Atreya asked, "that there is freedom, but at the same time there is no freedom, is a very fine line between the two that sometimes we do not understand."

"But why don't you understand?" Prabhupāda rejoined. "Just like you belong to a free nation, America. Does it mean you are free to do anything and everything? When you say, 'I belong to this free nation,' then yes, you are free. But that does not mean that you can do anything and everything."

It was a topic that devotees often debate: just how much independence does the individual soul have? Puṣṭa Kṛṣṇa Mahārāja pursued the point. If a person is habituated to smoking, is he free in that activity or has he surrendered his freedom?

It is like the person who smokes despite the government printing a warning on the box, Prabhupāda explained. One is free to do it, but not free from the results. Therefore, the living entity has minute, but not absolute, independence—like a child who is free to play, but as soon as he does something wrong, his father is there to correct him.

Puṣṭa Kṛṣṇa again took it further, wanting more clarification. "This idea of freedom and independence. Is it possible for anyone theoretically to surrender to Kṛṣṇa at any time?"

"Yes."

"So, let's say someone is in a very degraded condition of life, modes of ignorance and passion: his mind always disturbed. In surrendering to Kṛṣṇa, is it possible that he can be independent even of the mind?"

"You are independent of the mind always. It is *your* mind. You are not the mind. Then you are independent of the mind always."

"So even a person merged in the mode of ignorance can by some good fortune surrender to Kṛṣṇa?"

"Not good fortune," Prabhupāda told us. "God, Kṛṣṇa, says, 'You do it. Here! Immediately you become fortunate.' There is no question of waiting for becoming fortunate. You become fortunate immediately. Suppose if I say, 'Take this bag, $100,000.' You can take it. Immediately you become rich man. Why don't you take it?"

Understanding Prabhupāda's point that even good fortune is dependant on the mercy of the Lord, Gurudāsa Mahārāja asked how *kṛpā-siddhi* works.

Prabhupāda's reaction took us all by surprise. "*Kṛpa-siddhi* means that you are not willing to take this bag of money. I say, 'Take it! Take it! Take it!'" He suddenly turned and very vigorously pushed Gurudāsa in the stomach, as if he were trying to give him the imaginary bag.

Everyone broke out laughing, and Gurudāsa was simultaneously astonished and delighted at the sudden abrogation of the formal guru-disciple relationship. Śrīla Prabhupāda continued the mimicry and the pushing. He feigned resistance—"No!"—and then began pushing again. "That is *kṛpā-siddhi.* Even you are unwilling, I give you in your pocket, push it. That is *kṛpā-siddhi.*"

There is nothing dry in Śrīla Prabhupāda's expression of philosophy. He makes the philosophy come alive because he lives it himself. In so doing he attracts us to use our little independence to surrender to his lotus feet.

Gurudāsa mentioned that since we see everyone in the world as potential devotees, we should also serve them so they can become devotees.

But Prabhupāda clarified the distinction between showing mercy and serving others. "That is not service. That is mercy." He explained that although a devotee has a mood of service, Vaiṣṇava philosophy is that we serve the higher devotees and show mercy to the lower ones. He said the popular *māyāvādī* idea that one should serve everyone is wrong.

This puzzled me because it says in the *śāstras* that the most advanced devotee sees himself as the lowest of all. So I asked if that is so, then where is the question of the advanced devotee showing mercy to someone whom he sees as "lower"?

Prabhupāda replied that the advanced devotee does not see anyone as lower than himself, but his mood is one of sympathy, "Oh, here is a person, he can be a devotee. Let me raise him to the standard." He concluded, "It is duty. It does not mean he is thinking 'I am higher.' No."

"In other words," Puṣṭa Kṛṣṇa Mahārāja added, "He doesn't consider that he is advanced and that therefore he is showing mercy to lower."

"Yes," Prabhupāda affirmed. "He is always thinking, I am lower than the worm, but Lord Kṛṣṇa wants it, so let me do some service. That's all." It is simply a question of offering assistance to help another advance.

Prabhupāda illustrated his point through another comical exchange with Gurudāsa. "Therefore we say *prabhu*. *Prabhu* means 'You are my master. Please order me. What can I do for you?' That should be the attitude. Not, 'Gurudāsa *Prabhu,*' [Prabhupāda said *prabhu* in an exaggerated fashion, with a bite of sarcasm in it] please come here and brush my shoes!'"

We all laughed again, perhaps recognizing something of ourselves in the parody, as he continued. "What kind of *prabhu!?* He should say, 'Gurudāsa Prabhu, can I brush your shoes?' That is real Vaiṣṇava."

* * *

There was no *Śrīmad-Bhāgavatam* class, since most of the devotees are staying across town, either at the temple or in hotels.

* * *

An unexpected visitor turned up in the afternoon: Mr. Alan Kallman from New York. He produced Prabhupāda's first Hare Kṛṣṇa record in 1966. He arrived with a lady friend, and at long last gave Prabhupāda his royalties from the record's sales. They amounted to about 170,000 rupees, to which he added a personal donation of $2,000. Although he is not a devotee, it was obvious that he has great admiration and respect for Śrīla Prabhupāda.

And Śrīla Prabhupāda, in turn, was very happy to see him, greeting him as an old friend. He had his guests sit while we fed them sumptuous *prasādam*. As they ate, Prabhupāda chatted

March 23, 1976—"He suggested we gain responsibility for the beautification of the lake . . . and build a magnificent temple in the center of it."

March 24, 1976—"Mr. Agarwal greeted Prabhupāda with a garland of marigolds and rupee notes, then led us to his Mercedes. . . ."

March 25, 1976— "Many important people from New Delhi's social elite . . . gathered to hear his powerful lecture. . . ."

March 27, 1976— "Mr. Agarwal proposed to transform an adjoining 100 acres . . . into a 'Krishna Jayanti Park.'"

March 27, 1976—"After breakfast Prabhupāda held an excellent press conference. . . ."

March 28, 1976—"Mr. Agarwal hosted a program in front of his house, which was well attended by his neighbours. . . ."

March 28, 1976—"We were able to perform *guru-pūjā* and offer flowers personally to Śrīla Prabhupāda. . . ."

March 29, 1976— "Prabhupāda was met in front of the temple by . . . Mrs. Modi and a large crowd of our devotees."

March 29, 1976—"After . . . taking a tour of the marble complex, he gave a short talk in a back room before going to the Modi mansion. . . ."

March 29, 1976— "The *vyāsāsana* . . . looked almost like a silver spaceship. . . ."

April 3, 1976—"Gurudāsa Mahārāja has been locating various gardens . . . in big *āśramas* behind high stone walls. . . ."

April 4, 1976— "Prabhupāda presided over the second big *yajña* of the festival in the courtyard of the temple."

April 5, 1976— "Prabhupāda stopped and immediately began to bargain with him."

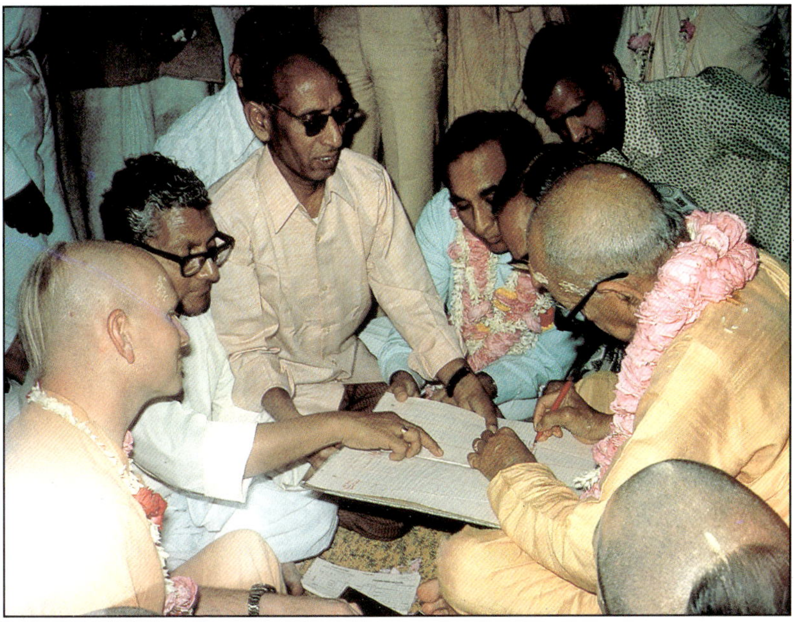

April 5, 1976—"In mid-morning he attended the opening of a new branch of the Punjab National Bank. . . ."

April 5, 1976— "He . . . and the bank manager amused the devotees by exchanging jokes and telling humorous stories."

April 9, 1976—"He drove to Mathurā to speak at a *paṇḍāl* at . . . the birth site of Lord Śrī Kṛṣṇa. . . ."

very amicably with them and would not let them go until they had eaten everything. He smiled brightly all the while, clearly delighting his guests. He is expert at entertaining and encouraging people to increase their devotional service to the Supreme Lord.

* * *

In the evening Prabhupāda was invited to speak to the New Delhi Rotary Club at the Imperial Hotel. The meeting was held in a large, stately room where devotees had set up a small stage covered with a white cloth for Prabhupāda to sit on. Many important people from New Delhi's social elite, as well as a half-dozen GBC members, gathered to hear his powerful lecture from *Bhagavad-gītā* 2.11.

First he explained the difference between Darwin's idea of evolution and the Vedic concept. He then extensively described the difference between the body, the soul, and Kṛṣṇa. His presentation was well received, and a couple of thoughtful questions were raised at the end. "Swamijī, in our ancient books Kṛṣṇa has also been projected as a person who has lived for a certain period of history and who was associated with number of friends and relatives for a temporary time. Our books of literature also projected the Supreme Being as the Perfect One. How do you reconcile the two things? Your teachings are based on the assumption that that person who lived for that period of time is the Perfect Person. But how do you fundamentally assure that what He has said is correct? How do you reconcile the two points?"

Prabhupāda's reply was lucid and thorough. "That I have already explained, that one has to understand Kṛṣṇa. I have already explained that if that person, Kṛṣṇa, whom you think that He lived for a certain period with friends and relatives just like ordinary man, if you simply study what is this person, then you'll be confident. *Janma karma ca me divyam yo jānāti tattavataḥ.*

"To understand Him in fact, it is not so easy. That is also explained in the *Bhagavad-gītā.* Out of many millions of persons, one becomes *siddha,* perfect. So that perfection is not complete perfection. That perfection means *ahaṁ brahmāsmi.* 'I am not this material body; I am spirit soul.'

"So one who understands this position of oneself is calculated as perfect, but in that perfect stage if one endeavors to understand Kṛṣṇa, out of many such millions of persons who are trying to understand Kṛṣṇa in perfection, one may understand. So it is not so easy. That factual understanding is possible.

"How it is possible? *Bhaktyā mām abhijānāti yāvān yaś cāsmi tattvataḥ*; only through devotion you can understand. So these problems will be solved when you become a devotee. Then Kṛṣṇa will reveal. You cannot understand Kṛṣṇa or His name, His form, His pastimes, His activities by your imperfect senses. But when you are engaged in His service, then He reveals Himself, 'Here I am.' So this is the process. If you want to understand that person, Kṛṣṇa, who is accepted as the Supreme Personality of Godhead, then you have to take shelter of *bhakti-yoga* and associate with *bhaktas*. Then it is possible. Otherwise not."

A second man had a question about Hitler and Gandhi's philosophy of nonviolence. He said that at the time of the Second World War, Gandhi, who was also a great admirer of the *Gītā*, a great scholar and a great commentator on it, wanted not to fight Hitler, but to try to bring about a change of heart in him. He asked if that wouldn't have been more effective than punishment? In other words, he implied that Gandhi felt punishment was a fault. The man had detected what he thought was a paradox because Kṛṣṇa instructs Arjuna to fight his enemies in the *Gītā* and Gandhi was for nonviolence.

Prabhupāda explained that Kṛṣṇa does not directly punish anyone, but everyone in the material world is subject to the punishment of *māyā*, the material energy. This is unsurmountable; no one is excused. In other words, whether Gandhi wanted to fight or not, Hitler would still receive the *karmic* reactions for his activities. However, if one surrenders to Kṛṣṇa then one may avoid punishment. Otherwise there is no other solution.

That concluded the evening's proceedings, and after the Rotary members expressed their appreciation, Prabhupāda returned to Mr. Agarwal's house.

* * *

Due to the hot weather, Prabhupāda had his bed and net set up in the back yard, where he took his rest in the cool night air. Mr. Agarwal took the opportunity for his association and also had a bed and net set up along side him. They chatted for a while before going to sleep.

March 26th, 1976

Today is Ekādaśī.

During his walk out on the front road, Puṣṭa Kṛṣṇa Swami asked Śrīla Prabhupāda what would bring him the greatest pleasure. Without any hesitation, Prabhupāda replied, "You all become fully Kṛṣṇa conscious, cent percent Kṛṣṇa conscious. People are suffering for want of Kṛṣṇa consciousness. Let them have this Kṛṣṇa consciousness and become happy. That's all."

Puṣṭa Kṛṣṇa also asked about Lord Caitanya's prediction that the holy name will be spread to every town and village. He wondered to what extent that will come true. Does it mean a temple will be established in every town or just that preachers will travel there and tick it off as another place visited?

Prabhupāda told him that travel is essential, and if possible there should be centers. He asked, why just village to village? We should go door to door.

Then Prabhupāda gave a short class to the few devotees present. In the verse Prahlāda Mahārāja expressed the mood that Śrīla Prabhupāda himself epitomizes. "My dear Lord Nṛsiṁhadeva, I see there are many saintly persons indeed, but they are simply interested for their own deliverance, and thus, without caring for big, big cities and towns, they go to the Himālayan forest for meditating, taking *mauna-vrata,* the vow of silence. They are not interested to deliver others. So far I am concerned, I do not wish to be liberated alone and leave aside all these poor fools and rascals. I know that without Kṛṣṇa consciousness, without taking shelter of Your lotus feet, nobody can be happy, and therefore I wish to bring them to You, to the shelter of Your lotus feet."

Prabhupāda said this is the mood of one who is perfectly convinced of the efficacy of the Kṛṣṇa consciousness movement. Those who are preaching must be convinced that without accepting Kṛṣṇa consciousness no one can be released from the stringent laws of material nature. Unfortunately the ordinary man is a *kṛpaṇa,* a miser, because he fails to use his human form for anything but sex indulgence, eating, and sleeping. So a preacher has to be merciful.

"By the grace of Kṛṣṇa you have to adopt such means that they may be interested a little about Kṛṣṇa consciousness. Otherwise they are so dull and miserly, they do not understand that the Kṛṣṇa consciousness movement is very, very important for them. They have no sense even to understand. But the preacher who is Kṛṣṇa conscious, he knows that without Kṛṣṇa consciousness these people are condemned. They cannot be happy. They cannot be liberated. They will simply remain within this material world, accepting one body after another. And whichever material body we accept, it is meant for suffering. It is not meant for any happiness."

Śrīla Prabhupāda stressed the need for preaching and distributing Lord Caitanya's mercy to everyone. "So only the Kṛṣṇa conscious devotee, he can deliver them. He goes from town to town, village to village, house to house, to bring this message of Kṛṣṇa and deliver him.

"Prahlāda Mahārāja is promising, 'I do not wish to go alone. Give me some strength so that I can deliver some of them. It is not possible to deliver all of them.' This is a very important engagement for a Vaiṣṇava. Bhaktivinoda Ṭhākura has written in his *Caitanya-śikṣāmṛta,* we can understand a Vaiṣṇava very nicely when we see that he has converted so many conditioned souls into Vaiṣṇava life. That is the estimation of a Vaiṣṇava. If I simply try for myself—I may be very advanced devotee—that is not very much appreciated by Kṛṣṇa."

Prabhupāda recalled that Śrīla Bhaktisiddhānta Sarasvatī would become very pleased if one of his *brahmacārīs* went into Navadvīpa and sold a few copies of his daily newspaper. "Therefore we become very much engladdened when we see that some of our books and literatures are sold. They will read and be benefitted. So this is the mission of the high-class Vaiṣṇava, how to preach Kṛṣṇa consciousness among the suffering humanity, and this is the purport of this verse said by Prahlāda Mahārāja, and we are following the footprints of Prahlāda Mahārāja.

"Never mind, even it is imperfectly done, we must execute the orders of Caitanya Mahāprabhu. I may not be so very expert in delivering the message of Kṛṣṇa, but my duty is to try to my best capacity how to distribute this knowledge to the suffering humanity."

It is a fact that Śrīla Prabhupāda is absorbed twenty-four hours a day simply in this mood of trying to liberate as many conditioned souls as possible. His mind never deviates from it. Because of his determination, we are now here, engaged in the practice of Kṛṣṇa consciousness. And he constantly urges us to pursue this mood of being merciful to others, as our means to perfection.

* * *

Dhanañjaya prabhu, formerly the president of ISKCON Vṛndāvana, came to report on a new business he has set up in Vṛndāvana. With Śrīla Prabhupāda's financial backing and encouragement he is now overseeing the making of crowns and dresses for the Deities. He said the business is going well. Śrīla Prabhupāda was happy with his efforts and immediately asked him to repay the 20,000 rupees loan he gave him.

* * *

This was the first day of our *pāṇḍāla* at the Rām Līlā festival grounds. It was very well attended by nearly 4,000 people, a very receptive crowd that asked many questions after Prabhupāda's lecture. Prabhupāda stayed to see a play by the devotees, and he was greatly pleased by the whole affair.

March 27th, 1976

Prabhupāda was driven to the Buddha Jayanti commemorative Park for his walk this morning. It is a spacious park with natural rocky outcrops cleverly integrated with carefully cultivated patches of bright purple shrubs and groves of frangipani, neem, and banyan trees. Spacious lawns are divided by manmade waterways and connected by small bridges and dams.

Walking down the red, sandstone pathways that wind in and out of clumps of bamboo, bougainvillaea groves, and various types of shrubs, Śrīla Prabhupāda discussed an idea with

Mr. Agarwal to transform an adjoining 100 acres of undeveloped land into a 'Kṛṣṇa Jayanti Park.' Mr. Agarwal reasoned that Śrī Kṛṣṇa was a far more important and enduring figure in the history of India than Lord Buddha, so why not a park in His honor? Prabhupāda liked his idea and encouraged him to do it.

* * *

After breakfast Prabhupāda held an excellent press conference wherein he spoke very strongly to reporters about the necessity of accepting the *Bhagavad-gītā.* He emphasized how unfortunate the people of India have become. Although they have access to a wonderful spiritual culture, they are avoiding Śrī Kṛṣṇa's instructions, seeking material enjoyment instead. This is due to the influence of bad leaders, which they themselves have selected.

One reporter asked if Prabhupāda had been to see some other "spiritual leaders."

Prabhupāda demanded to know why he should. When Kṛṣṇa's words are there in the *Gītā,* why should he pander to rascals and cheaters?

It was a lively interview, with Prabhupāda pointing to the lack of interest in the *Bhagavad-gītā* as the primary cause of India's difficulties.

The reporters asked intelligent, philosophical questions and appreciated his forthright answers and analysis. One of them asked if a disciple had ever disagreed with him on a spiritual matter. Laughing, Prabhupāda replied, "Not unless he is a fool, a damn fool!"

* * *

During his massage he answered an interesting inquiry from Prāṇada dāsa, a devotee in St. Louis. He wanted to know what the Vaiṣṇava perspective was on the Tantra *śāstras.* "Sometimes you cite these *śāstras* as reference in your books, yet the conclusion of Tantric philosophy and its practices appear to be quite different than Vaiṣṇava philosophy and practices. Are they in any sense correct or authoritative, and if so, what is the explanation of worshipping God as Mother (Divine) and their engaging in disciplinary activities which promote realization through sexual interplay and other prohibitions which we observe in our Kṛṣṇa Society? Are these *śāstras* considered 'in pursuance of the Vedic version (ref. Nectar of Devotion).' What is their status?"

Prabhupāda replied simply but conclusively. "The Vaiṣṇava *tantras* are bona fide *śāstras,* just like the *Nārada-pañcarātra.* But not the atheistic *tantra* which have nothing to do with the Vedic literature. The point is that Kṛṣṇa is the Supreme Personality of Godhead, and He is always *puruṣa* (male) not female (*prakṛti*). Worship of the Mother as *prakṛti,* is not recommended by Kṛṣṇa for the intelligent class of men."

* * *

In the afternoon, Mr. Surendra Kumar Saigal, the owner of the Tiger Lock Company, paid a visit. He requested Prabhupāda to come to Aligarh to do a program. Prabhupāda immediately agreed, setting the date for March 30th. From there he will drive to Vṛndāvana.

Puṣṭa Kṛṣṇa Swami has also made arrangements with Balarāma dāsa in Melbourne for Prabhupāda to go to Australia on April 18th. From Australia he will visit Fiji, Hawaii, Los Angeles, Detroit, Toronto, New Vṛndāvana, Washington, D.C., New York, and then London, Paris, Tehran, and then return to India. Thus, most of Śrīla Prabhupāda's summer itinerary is now finalized.

* * *

Ṛddha dāsa, from South Africa, finally arrived with Prabhupāda's car after driving it cross-country from Calcutta. This evening he reported that his passport and some money was missing. Chayavana Swami has been seen hanging about in the front yard acting rather mysteriously. It is known he has no money, and circumstantially it seemed he might be the culprit.

Puṣṭa Kṛṣṇa Swami confronted him straight away with his suspicions, but he calmly denied any knowledge of it.

Chayavana has spoken already to Prabhupāda about his engagement. Prabhupāda told him to simply chant and associate with devotees. Chayavana appears to be very disturbed.

* * *

Gopāla Kṛṣṇa took Śrīla Prabhupāda out to see a property he is considering purchasing for a new temple. The present facility at Bengali Market, which in any event is woefully inadequate, has run out of lease and has to be vacated. Gopāla took him to a big house in a prestigious location. Some men showed him around and made various proposals, but later they turned out to be mere schemers trying to make some money as unofficial intermediaries. The site is actually owned by the American Embassy, and purchase of it can be negotiated only by a written bid directly to the State Department. Prabhupāda told Gopāla to go ahead and try for it.

* * *

The program at Rāma Līlā grounds had to be canceled today after a huge wind blew the *pāṇḍāla* down. It was so badly flattened that it could not be erected again in time. It was a great disappointment, but nothing could be done.

* * *

In the evening there was another calamity. Because there was no program, Śrīla Prabhupāda stayed back in his room. He gave *darśana* to a few visitors. Then at about 9:00 p.m., after everyone had left, he rose from behind his low desk to go to the bathroom. As he stepped down the few inches from the *āsana,* the carpet suddenly slipped out from under him. He fell with a crash on the wooden edge of the seat, ending up in a sitting position on the floor. It happened in a second. And although I was seated directly in front of the desk, there was nothing that I could do. Helpless and shocked, I simply looked on as Śrīla Prabhupāda sat where he had fallen and rubbed his hip.

Amazingly, he uttered not a sound, neither when the carpet slipped, nor after the fall. He simply sat with his eyes closed for about ten or twenty seconds tolerating the pain he surely felt. Then with my help he rose to his feet. His foot was also injured, but without comment he walked to the bathroom. When he came out, he advised me that the carpet should be properly adjusted. But apart from this he made no reference to the incident again.

March 28th, 1976

Mr. Agarwal hosted a program in the *pāṇḍāla* in front of his house, which was well attended by his neighbors because it was Sunday morning. Prabhupāda enjoyed it, and so did the devotees. We were able to perform *guru-pūjā* and offer flowers personally to Śrīla Prabhupāda as he sat regally on the small stage upon a nicely carved and opulently upholstered wooden seat, provided for the occasion by Mr. Agarwal.

* * *

Ṛddha's passport was found discarded under a car in the driveway, but five-hundred rupees was missing. Citsukhānanda revealed that he too had lost five-hundred dollars at about the same time.

Circumstances seemed to indicate Chayavana as the possible culprit. So Puṣṭa Kṛṣṇa Swami searched his belongings. He found a savings book from a Seattle bank with a deposit entry of $23,000 in it. He showed it to Prabhupāda, who said that the matter should be handled discreetly.

Considering the delicacy of the situation, Prabhupāda called Chayavana in. Not wanting to directly accuse him of any wrongdoing without proof, he began by preaching to him about helping to spread the Kṛṣṇa consciousness movement. He then suggested that if he had any money, he might like to help with the purchase of a house here in Delhi. Chayavana said he would be glad to help, but he had no funds.

Prabhupāda then called for the passbook and showed it to him. When Chayavana saw it he laughed and explained that it was all false. He faked it in order to show customs officials in Africa that he had sufficient means to support himself while in their country. Prabhupāda turned to Puṣṭa Kṛṣṇa Swami, who agreed that it could very well be. So Prabhupāda laughed and said, "You made it to cheat the karmis, and now you are cheating us." He therefore let the matter drop, and Chayavana left.

Because of economic hardship everywhere in India, the incidence of thievery by low-class persons is fairly common, and even in our temples it is fairly frequent. Even though condemnable, it is somehow understandable. But later, Prabhupāda made a telling comment. "I thought it was just the Indians, but now the Westerners are stealing as well."

He is disgusted with the behavior of his wayward disciple, Chayavana. He told me very frankly, "This is why my godbrothers criticize. These men come and insist, 'Give me *sannyāsa*, give me *sannyāsa*.' Why? What is the attraction? Then when they have it, they again fall down. One becomes a first-class thief and woman hunter, another goes back to his wife. What is the use of such *sannyāsa*? Chayavana is intelligent and was doing nicely in Africa, now he is a third-class thief. Ṛṣi Kumāra was such a nice *brahmacārī* and *sannyāsī*. I was expecting him to do something wonderful—now he is a demon."

* * *

The Rām Līlā grounds *pāṇḍāla* resumed this evening and was a big success. After an excellent lecture by Śrīla Prabhupāda, over 8,000 rupees worth of books were sold. The audience sat entranced as the devotees staged a drama called "The Entrance of Kali." Prabhupāda stayed to watch the play and truly enjoyed it.

* * *

A newspaper printed an excellent article today, the result of yesterday's interview. Prabhupāda was happy with it because the reporter had accurately noted his main theme. The headline read, "Kṛṣṇa Forgotten in Land of His Birth."

March 29th, 1976

Modinagar

Early in the morning Śrīla Prabhupāda went by car to Modinagar, a small industrial town founded by the Modi family. They are well-known throughout India for cloth and other manufactured goods. It has six colleges and a huge factory complex. A notable feature is a grand Lakṣmī-Nārāyaṇa temple compound, built from red sandstone with three large, steeplelike towers, set back from the road across a broad, open courtyard.

Prabhupāda was met in front of the temple by the widowed Mrs. Modi and a large crowd of our devotees. After paying his respects to the Deities and taking a tour of the marble complex, he gave a short talk in a back room before going to the Modi mansion, where we will reside until tomorrow.

The mansion is situated on several acres of land and enclosed by a high wall. The house is quite dark and seems to lack personal warmth, but the reception was quite cordial.

In the evening Prabhupāda returned to the temple lecture hall and gave a long discourse to a crowd of some 2,500, the majority being women and children. After an exuberant *kīrtana,* he spoke for about an hour.

The *vyāsāsana* was one of the most spectacular we've seen yet. In shape it looked almost like a silver space ship, and it was detailed with flowered patterns and bright colors.

On his return to the house, Mrs. Modi gave Śrīla Prabhupāda a thousand rupees as *dakṣiṇā.*

March 30th, 1976

Śrīla Prabhupāda took a brief walk around the Modi estate before his departure. During the walk he noted some large bottle palms, similar to the ones we had seen at the sisters' estate in Nellore. He suggested they would be suitable trees for decorating the grounds of our Māyāpur complex.

Śrīla Prabhupāda then took his leave and we headed off for our next program.

* * *

Aligarh

Aligarh is a city with a population of about 300,000. A very old center of learning, it is also notable as the place where the Muslim League was founded in the fight to gain Indian independence from the British. It's university is also of national importance. Because Aligarh is very near to Vṛndāvana, most of the people speak *Brajbhāṣā,* the dialect of Hindi peculiar to this area.

We are staying at Surendra Kumar Saigal's home on Marris Road, the main residential area for the wealthy populace. The house, which was erected around 1918, is a large, single-story colonial-style building, with very high ceilings, dark rooms, and a cool interior. It stands behind a high front wall on three acres of spacious lawns and landscaped gardens. Two large *ashok* trees dominate a central circular lawn. Frangipani, mango, and eucalyptus trees are scattered here and there, with bottle palms standing like tall sentinels along the pathways.

Prabhupāda is staying in an unusual seven-sided room at the end of the front veranda. We servants are staying in a room at the opposite end. A few other devotees are also residing here for the program.

As soon as Prabhupāda arrived, Surender Kumar's wife invited him to see a beautiful Deity of Kṛṣṇa. Stepping inside a small room off the back veranda, Mrs. Saigal revealed her worshipable Lord. He is three feet high and carved from white marble, complete with crown, *chadar, dhotī,* and a brass flute. Her worship of the Lord is not very elaborate, with offerings consisting primarily of incense and flowers, but Prabhupāda encouraged her devotion and immediately suggested that she obtain a Deity of Rādhārāṇī. "Why keep Kṛṣṇa alone?" he said.

* * *

Prabhupāda held an afternoon *darśana* in a central room packed with devotees and visitors. He began by emphasizing to Mr. Saigal and his family the necessity of offering everything to Kṛṣṇa so that it becomes *prasādam.* We should offer whatever we consume, he told them.

One of the devotees suggested that perhaps *bhakti-yoga* is not much of an intellectual process.

Prabhupāda immediately corrected him by quoting the *Gītā* verse *na me bhaktaḥ praṇaśyati,* "I am never lost nor is he ever lost to Me." How can one who knows Kṛṣṇa be ignorant? he asked. If Kṛṣṇa is merciful to him, how can he remain a fool?

A visitor asked a question relating to the Arya Samaja, an organization that claims religiosity but rejects the idea that God can appear in the form of the Deity. Its followers uphold the impersonal concept of the Absolute.

Prabhupāda replied that to worship *nirguṇa-brahman,* the formless aspect of God, is all right, but Śrī Kṛṣṇa Himself *is* the Deity; He is not stone or wood. He mercifully appears in this form to enable us to render personal service to Him.

Surendra Kumar also introduced Dr. V. N. Sukla from Aligarh University, who holds a doctorate in *Bhāgavata* philosophy and is a recognized Vaiṣṇava and a Sanskrit scholar. He is a very learned and amiable man in his late forties and is clearly quite impressed with Śrīla Prabhupāda. They chatted for some time and Prabhupāda asked him to translate *The Nectar of Instruction* into Hindi.

* * *

In the evening a large *pāṇḍāla* program was held on the Government of India Press Colony grounds, just off Marris road. The crowd numbered some 7,000—an excellent turnout.

The devotees had already been chanting for half an hour when Prabhupāda arrived, and the audience was eager to hear him. Clearly it was a special event for them to see so many Westerners chanting and dancing and to meet the personality who has inspired them to do so.

Prabhupāda was given a vote of thanks by the head of the nearby Rāma Tīrtha Mission, who had helped organize the *pāṇḍāla* on just a few days notice.

Prabhupāda was noticeably pleased with the program and gave a splendid lecture about the value of chanting Hare Kṛṣṇa. He quoted a statement from *śāstra* that there was no amount of sin that could not be eradicated by the chanting of the holy name of Kṛṣṇa.

Prabhupāda stayed to see a film that was shown at the end. All-in-all, it was a well organized program, and Prabhupāda was very satisfied with all the arrangements.

March 31st, 1976

Before leaving Aligarh, Prabhupāda was presented with three books about the life and teachings of Rāma Tīrtha, by the head of that mission. Although cordially received, he paid them scant attention, being already familiar with their contents.

I peeked inside. They were full of *māyāvāda* speculation. Some of the recorded lectures began with, "Myself, in the form of ladies and gentlemen."

Prabhupāda left the books behind. Taking leave of his hosts he boarded his car for the hour-long drive to Śrī Vṛndāvana *dhāma.*

CHAPTER ELEVEN

Sri Vrndavana Dhama

March 31st, 1976

Śrīla Prabhupāda arrived in Vṛndāvana to an enthusiastic greeting from the devotees, most of whom have traveled from Māyāpur. We arrived in time to greet the Deities, and Prabhupāda gave a short class on the nine processes of devotional service. Perhaps half the devotees have returned to their home temples, but there was still a large crowd, and the temple was packed to capacity.

He then returned to the quarters he had left just over three months ago. He spent the day relaxing and recuperating from the hectic travels and demands of the last few days.

April 1st, 1976

For his morning walk, rather than take the usual route along Chatikara road, Prabhupāda drove out to the local municipal park. Another car, filled with *sannyāsīs,* followed him. He didn't speak much during the walk, save to comment that the park was very poorly maintained.

* * *

In class Prabhupāda read from *Śrīmad-Bhāgavatam* 7.9.46, wherein Prahlāda Mahārāja speaks about *mauna,* or the vow of silence. In India even today, people sometimes practice *mauna,* although generally it is not done for spiritual purposes. Neither is it strictly followed, as the practitioner often communicates with a small blackboard and chalk, or a pencil and paper.

Therefore, Prabhupāda said, there is no question of not talking; one must talk. But that talk should only be about Kṛṣṇa. If all we talk about is mundane activities, then we should practice *mauna.* But for one who is preaching Kṛṣṇa consciousness, there is never enough to be said. "Śrīla Rūpa Gosvāmī says that 'I have got only one tongue and two ears. So how can I enjoy or serve Hare Kṛṣṇa only with one tongue and two ears? If I had millions of ears and trillions of tongues, then it would have been possible.' He is feeling like that. So he is expecting so many ears and so many tongues to chant Hare Kṛṣṇa *mantra.*"

Then he added, with perhaps a touch of irony, a comment relating to our present state of affairs. "And so far we are concerned, conditioned soul, even sixteen rounds becomes very, very difficult job for us because we are practiced to talk nonsense. We cannot find out little time, say for two hours, for chanting Hare Kṛṣṇa, but we can find twenty-four hours for talking nonsense. Therefore one who cannot chant Hare Kṛṣṇa *mantra,* he should stop his talking. That is called *mauna.* Don't talk any more. Better remain silent. This is recommendation by Prahlāda Mahārāja."

He concluded by saying that nowadays no one can follow the strict practices mentioned in the scriptures. Therefore, we should simply rely on the mercy of Lord Caitanya and chant the Hare Kṛṣṇa *mahā-mantra.*

* * *

Śrīla Prabhupāda went out in mid-morning to inspect some land directly opposite the Kṛṣṇa Balarāma Hasanan Gośālā Bhūmi Trust, on Mathurā road. The property is for sale, and Prabhupāda was thinking of purchasing it to use as a *gośālā.* He took with him Akṣayānanda Swami, Bhagatjī, and one or two other devotees.

Upon returning, he discussed it with Bhagatjī, who was not in favor of buying it. He said the land was full of stones. When Śrīla Prabhupāda asked him how he knew, Bhagatjī laughed and pointed to Prabhupāda's books. "You know what is within the verses of these books; and similarly, I am a farmer's son, and I know what is within the earth!" Prabhupāda laughed and decided not to buy the land.

The rest of the day was quiet and restful. Prabhupāda gave a short *darśana* in the late afternoon.

* * *

Gurudāsa Swami is taking the devotees out on *parikrama* each day. He used to live here in the early days of ISKCON Vṛndāvana, and thus he knows many wonderful stories and histories about the different places of Kṛṣṇa's pastimes.

April 2nd, 1976

During his morning walk Prabhupāda visited one of his Godbrother's *maṭhas* on the road out to Mathurā. We found the gates closed when we arrived and no sign of life within, what to speak of any kind of program going on. After loitering around for a minute or two without contacting anyone, we returned to our temple.

Later, Prabhupāda commented, as he started class, that when we chant the Sanskrit *ślokas* at the beginning of the discourse over the microphone, it is very attractive and pleasing to outsiders. His mood is clearly different than that of his godbrothers.

Anantarām Śāstrī led the chanting of the Sanskrit, Puṣṭa Kṛṣṇa Swami read out the English translation, and then Śrīla Prabhupāda delivered his lecture.

In commenting on the verse forty-seven, Prabhupāda gave his disciples, many of whom are engaged in book distribution in the West, extra impetus to execute their service with renewed vigor and enthusiasm. He explained the purpose of the Kṛṣṇa consciousness movement. "It is not active like a sword. But it is *astra.* It is killing the demons, but in a different way. The demonic habits are being killed by this Hare Kṛṣṇa movement. This is *astra,* but it is being used in a different way, because in this age people are so fallen, this real *astra* weapon cannot be used upon them. They are already dead.

"So therefore another type of *astra*—to awaken them to life. That is Hare Kṛṣṇa, *mahā-mantra astra.* Otherwise they are already dead. 'Beating the dead horse.' A horse is dead; what you will get by beating with whips?

"So there are big, big demons. Hiraṇyakaśipu, he was required to be killed by the nails of the Lord, Who appeared as a ferocious lion. But here, the tiny demons, there is no need of nails or any sword. They are to be awakened simply by Kṛṣṇa consciousness, chanting Hare Kṛṣṇa."

Since it is so difficult to comprehend spiritual topics in this age, he stressed that as neophyte devotees we must be actively engaged in Kṛṣṇa conscious activities. Recalling his recent meetings with Sharma dāsa in Māyāpur, he told us that to imitate Haridāsa Ṭhākura by trying to chant in a secluded place is simply cheating. For those whose minds are still disturbed, they should be actively engaged, especially in book distribution. "Suppose you are going to distribute books," he said, "but what is the idea? 'It is Kṛṣṇa's books; it must be distributed.' So Kṛṣṇa is remembered there. At the same time, because it is Kṛṣṇa's book, if somebody purchases, if he pays something, he'll look at it—something—that 'What this nonsense has written? Let me see.' Then he will get some idea. And if he reads one line, he comes hundred times forward to Kṛṣṇa consciousness. This is the idea."

* * *

Quite a bit of mail had piled up and needed to be answered. Puṣṭa Kṛṣṇa Mahārāja brought it to Prabhupāda's attention during his massage, which he took in the back bedroom today. It is too hot now to sit for a full session in the sun.

It seems Upendra prabhu has finally made it to Fiji all right. He and Deoji Punja sent telegrams seeking confirmation of Śrīla Prabhupāda's participation in a foundation-stone-laying ceremony in Lautoka in late April. They're building a new Kāliya Mardana temple.

Prabhupāda replied that he intends to arrive in Fiji around the 24th of this month. But that will depend upon whether a proposed meeting with the Chief Minister of Punjab, concerning a donation of land in Kurukṣetra, happens or not. If it does, Śrīla Prabhupāda may have to attend a conference in Kurukṣetra on April 29th.

A man from London wrote suggesting we open a new center in Ceylon. Prabhupāda sent his letter on to Pradyumna, who is staying in South India at the Śrī Pejavāra Maṭha in Udupi. He advised Pradyumna to help the man start something in Colombo.

Citsukhānanda, the American we saw in Delhi, wrote requesting approval to start a new farm project in northern California. Prabhupāda gladly gave his sanction, telling him that "constructing temples, protecting cows, gathering milk, making ghee, and then opening Hare Kṛṣṇa restaurants are all good programs for *gṛhasthas.*"

Nirañjana dāsa, a young Indian student from Glasgow, Scotland, sent a long letter informing Prabhupāda, among other things, that he has completed the Hindi translation of the first section of *Bhakti-rasāmṛta-sindhu.* This was welcome news, as Śrīla Prabhupāda has put a great amount of time and effort into seeing that his books get translated into the local languages. He told Nirañjana to send whatever translations he has completed thus far and encouraged him to continue with other small books, then send them to Bombay as they are completed.

Yaśodānandana Swami is back in South India, where they held some successful programs from March 25th-28th in Kakinada. In a letter to Puṣṭa Kṛṣṇa Swami, he requested confirmation of Prabhupāda's attendance at a program in Bangalore at the end of May. He also related an interesting story about Prahlāda Mahārāja and a Deity of Varāha Narasiṁha that he saw in Simhachalam, a place about 250 miles south of Jagannātha Purī. "The story of this temple is related in the Vishnu Purana. Briefly it is as follows: After Hiranya Kasipu attempted many times to kill his son, he finally devised a very sinister plan.

"He sent his servants to throw Prahlada off a hill into the ocean and instructed them to throw a hill on top of him so that he would die. The servants carried Prahlada on top of Simha Giri and threw him into the ocean. As soon as they were ready to throw the hill over the devotee Prahlada, Narasimha came and rescued Prahlāda out of the ocean.

"Prahlada, out of devotion for his Lord, requested the Lord to kindly manifest Himself on top of the Simha Giri (the hill where Narasimha saved Prahlada) and asked Him to please show Himself in the form of Varaha. He also requested to show him the form in which he would later kill Hiraṇya Kasipu.

"So the Lord manifested Himself as Varaha Narasimha. And Prahlada worshiped that Deity there on top of the hill. It's fabulous. It's unique."

Prabhupāda replied to the letter informing Yaśodānandana Mahārāja that if he is required to attend the proposed Kurukṣetra conference, he will stay in India. Otherwise, he will go to the West. He also said that if the story of Prahlāda is in the *Purāṇas* then it is all right.

Hansadūta Swami wrote two letters from Calcutta. Although during the GBC meetings he was appointed co-GBC with Gopāla Kṛṣṇa for Vṛndāvana, he and his men have remained in Calcutta rather than come for this part of the festival because they want to get properly organized for their upcoming village-to-village *saṅkīrtana* programs.

He has twenty-five men, but all of them are new to India, and none of them speak the local languages. Therefore he asked Śrīla Prabhupāda if Lokanātha Mahārāja from Bombay could join them. Another reason he is reluctant to come to Vṛndāvana is because his former wife, Himāvatī dāsī, is here.

His second letter informed Prabhupāda that Bhavānanda Goswami is on his way to Vṛndāvana to speak with Śrīla Prabhupāda about a manpower shortage in Māyāpur. Apparently they have only ten men there now. Hansadūta feels that men should be sent to the Indian Yātrā from the Western temples, to strengthen the preaching here. He has personally brought men from Germany and England, so he wondered why other GBC men couldn't do the same.

Prabhupāda told him that Lokanātha Mahārāja may join his traveling party and that he has arranged for some devotees to return to Māyāpur to help out there rather than return to the West.

As far as Himāvatī is concerned, Prabhupāda told him not to worry about coming here just yet. He may manage Vṛndāvana conjointly by correspondence. He informed him that Himāvatī is now engaged in organizing a nursery for young children here in Vṛndāvana.

April 3rd, 1976

This morning Gurudāsa Mahārāja once again located another nice garden for Prabhupāda to take his morning walk. This one was in a big *āśrama*, behind high, stone walls. A casual visitor would never suspect that such a place of serenity and beauty existed.

A few *sannyāsīs* accompanied Prabhupāda. He seems to be enjoying the outings. On the whole, he is relaxed and very much at home here in Vṛndāvana.

* * *

Each morning Śrīla Prabhupāda displays great devotion and love, affectionately looking upon the Deities' divine forms at *darśana* time. He stands, surrounded by his devotees, as the Govindam prayers boom over the sound system. The curtains open and he looks intently for a few seconds. Then he gets down and fully prostrates himself in obeisance to Their Lordships Gaura-Nitai. Then he pushes himself back up to his knees, again touches his head to the floor, and then stands erect. He then repeats this procedure at the altar of Kṛṣṇa-Balarāma. Then finally, again before Rādhā-Śyāmasundara, Who must be the most beautiful Deities in all of Vṛndāvana. After sipping a little *caraṇāmṛta* he turns to walk back across the temple-room floor to the *vyāsāsana*. As he crosses in front of each altar, he does a clockwise, 360-degree pirouette.

In today's *Śrīmad-Bhāgavatam* verse Prahlāda Mahārāja explained that Kṛṣṇa is everything: the air, fire, sky, earth, water, everything subtle or gross including the mind, consciousness, and false ego, as well as whatever is expressed by words or the mind. Prabhupāda vividly explained why we worship the Deities and how the same mood of devotion should be applied to everything we do.

He recalled a recent challenge by a man in Delhi. The man had asked that if God is everywhere, what is the use of going to the temple? Prabhupāda reversed the logic. If God is everywhere, why *not* go to the temple? He is certainly there also.

He told us that it is like electricity. Electrical energy is everywhere, but wiring and the switch enable us to utilize it. "Similarly," he said, "Kṛṣṇa is everywhere, and you can worship Kṛṣṇa from anything. Everyone knows that this Deity is made of stone. The floor, the marble stone, is black and white, and the Deity is also black and white. Everyone knows. But why you see the black-and-white Deity in this temple and gather together and offer prayer? Is it the same marble of the ground, black and white? That means you are seeing in a different position. That is love, love of Kṛṣṇa.

"Those who haven't got the love, they are seeing that 'The same stone on the floor and same stone in the Deity. What these foolish men are worshiping?' They say that 'I can worship this stone also.' "No. No. Kṛṣṇa says, 'Yes, the stone on the floor, that I am, but I am not present there.' This is called *acintya-bhedābheda.* They think that 'If Kṛṣṇa has spread Himself in everything, then He has lost Himself. So He has no more form.' This is called material calculation. These foolish persons, they do not know.

"I have several times given you the example. You take a big piece of paper and make it small pieces and you throw it in the air. The big sheet of paper is no longer existing. It is finished. So their calculation is like that, that 'If Kṛṣṇa is all-pervasive, then where is His form? His form is finished.' But that is nonsense.

"This is Kṛṣṇa—*māyā tatam idaṁ sarvam:* 'I am spread everywhere, all-pervasive. But in My person I am not there.' But a devotee should understand that Kṛṣṇa is on the throne and Kṛṣṇa is on the floor. Therefore we should be very careful to take care of the floor, to take care of the throne, to take care of the flower, to take care of the dishes. Everything you should worship like Kṛṣṇa. You cannot neglect anything. *Śrī-vigrahārādhana-nitya-nānā-śṛṅgāra-tan-mandira-mārjanādau.* Everything is one. You cannot say, 'Kṛṣṇa is here, sitting. I can neglect this floor.' That is foolishness. You should take as much care to worship the Deity, to decorate the Deity, as to keep the temple very, very clean. That is Kṛṣṇa conscious. You cannot say that 'He is working on the garden; therefore he is inferior. I am working directly on the Kṛṣṇa altar.' No. The person who is working in the garden, Kṛṣṇa's garden, he should be as careful as the man who is worshiping the Deity in the temple. That is wanted."

He concluded by saying that we should be very careful to keep this understanding. Just like the devotee who takes the dust of Vṛndāvana on his head. This is the proper mood, because Vṛndāvana dust *is* Kṛṣṇa. If we remember that every atom is Kṛṣṇa, then our Kṛṣṇa consciousness will be very, very strong and firmly established. Likewise the great sky is also Kṛṣṇa. So Kṛṣṇa can be everywhere in His all-pervasive form, or He can appear in the small form of the Deity just to accept our service. Of course, this is the vision of the very advanced devotee, he told us, and we should not imitate, but this is the ideal platform to aim for.

April 4th, 1976

This morning's walk took us past a small temple of Katyayanī, the goddess Durgā. Prabhupāda explained that one can worship her in order to gain admittance to Kṛṣṇa. It's for this reason that her deity is prevalent in Vṛndāvana. He offered her his respects by quoting out loud *Brahma-saṁhitā* verse 5.44, describing Durgā as the shadow potency of Rādhārāṇī.

* * *

Prabhupāda presided over the second big *yajña* of the festival today. Wearing fragrant rose garlands, he sat serenely in the temple courtyard on the semicircular side steps, seated on one of the *āsanas* from his *prasādam* room. Puṣṭa Kṛṣṇa Swami sat next to him, holding an armful of new *japa* beads. I stood on the other side holding a decorative ceremonial umbrella, to shield him from the direct rays of the hot sun.

He initiated thirty-five candidates into *harināma* and created another thirty-three *brāhmaṇas.* Among them was a boy from Iran, and Prabhupāda particularly noted him in his talk. "We manufacture devotees from any part of the world. Just immediately we initiated a devotee, Bhṛgu Muni dāsa. He is from Iran. So Caitanya Mahāprabhu's mission is this, that *pṛthivīte āche yata nagarādi grāma, sarvatra pracāra haibe mora nāma.* Caitanya Mahāprabhu wanted that in every village and every town on the surface of the globe they should at least hear Hare Kṛṣṇa *mahā-mantra.*"

After handing out the *japa* beads he gave a short talk explaining the meaning of initiation, which he summarized as "the beginning of receiving transcendental knowledge."

* * *

Puṣṭa Kṛṣṇa Swami, who was officially appointed Prabhupāda's permanent secretary at the GBC meeting, was also made the new GBC for South Africa. He arranged a special *darśana* with Prabhupāda for Jagat Guru Swami and several other men who are about to leave for Africa. Two are from South Africa, and the others are Canadian, British, and American.

Prabhupāda told them about the enthusiastic reception he had received in South Africa last year. He particularly recalled that the whites eagerly purchased his books, despite the fact that Indians are not well liked there.

Jagat Guru Mahārāja told him they intend to travel on a bus and go to other countries as well, like Rhodesia, Malawi, and Mozambique.

As they talked, Prabhupāda began to consider going to Australia via Africa because the trip to Australia is very long. He thought that a direct flight from South Africa to Australia might be quicker than going straight from India. But after Puṣṭa Kṛṣṇa said going via South Africa would be just as long, he dropped the idea.

He also encouraged the men to preach in Mauritius and to hold *Ratha-yātrā* in Durban, where there are many Indians.

As they left, Puṣṭa Kṛṣṇa Swami noted how enthusiastic they all were to preach. Prabhupāda smiled. "Yes. That is life. One who is enthusiastic to preach, he is living. Others are dead."

April 5th, 1976

For his walk Prabhupāda went to look at some vacant land in Rāman Reṭi that he wants to purchase. He suggested that our householders build their own houses there and "colonize it" like our Los Angeles community.

As we walked about, a local farmer passed, carrying a large basket of green beans on his head. Prabhupāda spotted him and immediately began to bargain with him. After a lengthy exchange, he purchased the whole basket. The man went off happily, having done his whole day's business within a few minutes.

Gurudāsa Mahārāja complimented Prabhupāda on getting a good bargain. Prabhupāda laughed, telling us it was something he had learned in his childhood. "My father used to do that. He'd go to a vegetable vendor. He has got a big basket, and he'll say, 'What do you want for all, the whole basket.' So he is ready because he'll sit down so long [to sell in the market], so at very cheap rate he'll give it. And it was not required in the family so much. My mother became very angry, that 'You are bringing so much vegetable, it is being spoiled.' But he would purchase like that. If you give him in those days fifty rupees to go to the market, he will spend all the money and bring at home. Hare Kṛṣṇa."

* * *

In mid-morning he attended the opening of a new branch of the Punjab National Bank here in our guest house. Prabhupāda was in a jovial mood, and he and the bank manager amused the devotees by exchanging jokes and telling a few humorous stories. As the devotees eagerly crowded into the room to listen, Prabhupāda explained how Kuvera, the treasurer of the demigods, had offered Dhruva Mahārāja any benediction he wanted. Dhruva Mahārāja simply asked Kuvera to bless him with continual devotion to Lord Kṛṣṇa. To the cheers of the devotees, he explained that in the same way he now has a bank that can give him any amount, but he simply requested the bank's blessings that he remain Kṛṣṇa's servant.

The bank manager also told a similar story, but requesting Prabhupāda's blessings. He then told a joke about a man who was due for a heart transplant. He could choose to use a general's heart, a businessman's, or a banker's. When he chose the banker's he was asked why. "Oh, because I am quite sure it has never been used!"

Prabhupāda laughed heartily and ended the meeting with a joke of his own. "The story is that one poor man was informed by his friend that 'money draws money.' That's a fact. If you have got money, you can draw [attract] money. So he went to the bank, and the cashier was counting a huge amount of money and he threw his coin on the cash." Prabhupāda started laughing even before he finished. "And he was waiting, 'When the whole money will come to me?'

"Then the cashier saw this man is standing, 'What is that? Why you are standing?'

"'Sir, I heard that money draws money, so I had one coin. I have dropped with your money. I am waiting when it will come to me.'

"So he said, 'No, no. The fact is that, money draws money. Now my money has drawn your money!'"

Prabhupāda laughed so much his belly and shoulders shook. All the devotees, who rarely see him so relaxed and open, laughed and cheered along with his jubilation.

* * *

Anantarām Śāstrī is staying with me in the servant's room. He is doing some Sanskrit work on Śrīla Prabhupāda's translations. He chants the Sanskrit verse at the beginning of class, and sometimes, when Śrīla Prabhupāda can't immediately quote a verse, he is able to supply the necessary *śloka.*

Today he showed me several verses he has written in Sanskrit, glorifying Śrīla Prabhupāda. In them he poetically describes Prabhupāda's achievements in preaching and lauds his pure, devotional qualities.

bhaktisiddhānta-śiṣyaya
bhaktivedānta-nāmine
prasannāya praśāntāya
tasmai śrī-gurave namaḥ

"Let me offer my obeisances to my Guru Mahārāja, who is a disciple of Śrīla Bhaktisiddhānta, who is always calm and joyful, and bears the name of Bhaktivedānta."

kṛṣṇaika-ceta mada-moha-vināśa-kārin
mad-dṛṣṭi-gocara prabho prabhupāda-svāmin

doṣābhivṛtti-paradūṣita-manda-buddheḥ
sañcintayāmi caraṇau tava bhakti-hetoḥ

"O Lord, O Prabhupāda. May you always be the object of my vision. Only the name of Kṛṣṇa can destroy my pride and illusion. Although my mind and intelligence are contaminated by wicked inclinations, I meditate upon your lotus feet in causeless devotion."

vṛndāvane ramaṇa-reṭi-prasiddha-bhūmau
tatrāpi kṛṣṇa-balarāma-supāda-mūle
jñānam paraṁ parama-kṛṣṇa-sudharmīty uktaṁ
dantas tu deva prabhupāda namo namas te

"In the most holy land of Vṛndāvana, in Rāman Reṭi, at the lotus feet of Śrī Kṛṣṇa Balarāma, you are preaching the topmost knowledge of the Supreme Personality, Lord Kṛṣṇa, Who is the fountainhead of religion. O master of the senses, O my lord Śrīla Prabhupāda, let me offer my obeisances to you."

As he explained their meanings to me, tears began to stream down his face. Although I didn't say anything, it put me off. I appreciated his devotional sentiments, but his display of emotion made me uncomfortable. It seemed more an attempt to impress me with his own level of devotion than actual loving feelings for Śrīla Prabhupāda.

April 6th, 1976

During his walk at the Raṅga Gardens today Prabhupāda answered questions about the tendency of devotees to wear extra paraphernalia like Rādhā Kuṇḍa clay beads, *tulasī* beads interspaced with silver or gold beads, and items like the used sacred threads from the Deities, which they wrap around their wrists.

Śrīla Prabhupāda said that the Deity threads should not be worn. It is becoming a fad throughout the Society, and the practice should be stopped. He quoted another of his very apt Bengali sayings: "A crow eats stool; but young crows eat more stool!" He said there is always a tendency, at the slightest opportunity, to revert back to being like "hippies." We should not allow it, he said. If that happens, whatever prestige we have so far will all be finished.

* * *

There was a bit of mail today. One long letter came from Puru dāsa in Los Angeles. It had actually been sent to Hṛdayānanda Mahārāja in early February, when he was still the visiting secretary, but somehow wasn't acknowledged until now.

Puru was concerned about the temple purchasing sour cream that was known to have rennet, an extract from the stomach lining of a calf, in it and another batch, that had gelatin in it. The rationale used was that almost everything in *Kali-yuga* is contaminated. And Śrīla Prabhupāda had previously allowed the use of white sugar, which is bleached over animal bones. He had also allowed the purchase of milk that had fish-liver oil added.

A further motivation was the very cheap purchase price of five cents per pound. Therefore the GBC, Jayatīrtha, had consented to the purchase of the sour cream because the amount of rennet was very small—about 1 cc per 150 gallons or 1/50,000 of an ounce per pint.

Still, despite the seemingly insignificant quantity, some devotees were disturbed by its use, and thus Puru requested a direct statement from Śrīla Prabhupāda to settle the matter. "It seems to me, though I am a fallen, fault-finding rascal, that only Śrīla Prabhupāda can say whether or not this sour cream is offerable to the Deity, and can be used. I certainly do not know. There are valid arguments on both sides, but the only real point is whether or not Kṛṣṇa is pleased with such offerings, and only His pure devotee can tell us that."

He added as a postscript that the temple has over four-hundred pounds of it in the refrigerator, and some had reasoned that Śrīla Prabhupāda would not want to see the sour cream wasted. He wanted to know if they should use it up, never buy it again, dump it, or continue to use it and not be agitated over its contents.

Prabhupāda's reply was short and clear. "Concerning the use of sour cream in the temple, it should be stopped immediately. Nothing should be offered to the Deities which is purchased in the stores. Things produced by the karmis should not be offered to Rādhā Kṛṣṇa. Ice-cream, if you can prepare it, is OK, but not otherwise. Now, you have such a big stock of this sour cream, so sell the stock at any cost. Who is the rascal who has purchased without permission?"

Another letter was from Kṛṣṇa Kānti dāsa in Los Angeles informing His Divine Grace about a professional recording studio called "Golden Avatar" he has just established. His aim is to produce first-class Kṛṣṇa conscious recordings. He enclosed a stereo cassette with the first record album to be recorded entirely within the studio in its first ten days of operation.

He also offered to record Śrīla Prabhupāda when he visits Los Angeles this summer. He especially wants to make a recording of Prabhupāda chanting the Hare Kṛṣṇa mantra, since the only other record of him doing this is still owned by Alan Kallman.

Prabhupāda listened with great satisfaction to the tape, called "Hare Kṛṣṇa Festival," which has a new marching-band version of the *mahā-mantra.*

He wrote back encouraging Kṛṣṇa Kānti in his work. "I very much liked the chanting on this tape. It is very excellent and should be popularized and it will be a great success. Introduce this into every home and that will help them, and if they read our books, then finished—no more material life. Yes, when I come also I can make a tape of chanting Hare Kṛṣṇa but the chanting of Hare Kṛṣṇa by the other boys on this tape is very nice. Thank you."

* * *

Rāmeśvara Swami came in about 11:00 a.m. to discuss some BBT business. He told Śrīla Prabhupāda of their desire to print a large full 20" x 24" poster-size picture of Śrīla Prabhupāda for people to frame. He asked Prabhupāda if there was any particular picture that he preferred. Without any hesitation, Prabhupāda told him to look on the outside cover of *Caitanya-caritāmṛta Ādi Līlā* Volume 3. Rāmeśvara eagerly took down the book from the wall shelf and held up a picture of a radiant Śrīla Prabhupāda sitting on a cushion on the lawn at Bhaktivedānta Manor in England. He had a mild smile on his lips and a light, silk chaddar draped over his shoulders.

Prabhupāda nodded his approval, then again reaffirmed it, even though Rāmeśvara pointed out that he wasn't wearing a flower garland in the photo.

* * *

Today was the first of a three-day program in the back area of the temple, just inside the main entrance. It was held from 5:00-7:30 p.m. Many distinguished guests in the area came to offer their appreciation of Prabhupāda's work.

April 7th, 1976

This morning we drove out well beyond the outskirts of the Vṛndāvana village. At one point Prabhupāda stopped the car and climbed out. He then began walking across the fields.

As we meandered across the uneven fields, a local farmer, the owner of the land, came over to see us. Very respectfully he offered his *praṇāmas* and told Śrīla Prabhupāda in Hindi that he considered it a great honor for him and his family to have Prabhupāda walk on his land.

Prabhupāda was very touched by the man's sentiment and mentioned the incident several times later on. He noted that in the West if you tread without permission on someone else's land, they become angry and may even shoot you. How nice, he said, is a culture where the owner approaches and thanks you, considering himself to be blessed.

* * *

Today's *Śrīmad-Bhāgavatam* class was on 7.9.52. Prahlāda Mahārāja's prayers are now completed, and Lord Nṛsiṁhadeva addressed him. The Lord called him *bhadra,* which Śrīla Prabhupāda translated as "perfect gentleman" and also *asurottama,* best of the *asuras,* or demons. Because of His great satisfaction with his behavior, the Lord offered Prahlāda any benediction he wanted.

Prabhupāda said that therefore if we require anything at all, we simply have to please Kṛṣṇa. It is not necessary to work hard for money and other material gains, because Kṛṣṇa is *bhagavān*, the possessor of every opulence. By pleasing Him, whatever we need will be supplied. We simply have to become perfect gentlemen. That, he said, is only possible if one becomes a devotee. He gave some good examples to illustrate how only a genuine devotee is actually a perfect gentleman; others are not. "A devotee is perfect gentleman. Why? Now, because he has developed all good qualities. That is *bhadra.* A devotee cannot be *abhadra.* Therefore a devotee is never rude to anyone.

"When Rūpa Gosvāmī was here, some very learned scholar came to talk with him on *śāstra.* So when he approached Rūpa Gosvāmī, he asked, 'I want to talk with you about *śāstra.*'

"And he said, 'I am not a very learned man. How can I talk with you? You are so learned man.'

"So the man said, 'If you think that you are not learned, then you give me in writing that: 'I am not learned.'

"So he immediately gave him: 'All right, take it. I am not learned.'"

Prabhupāda laughed. "So when he was going away, that cheat, he was thinking, 'I am the most learned scholar, and Rūpa Gosvāmī's defeated.'

"Then Jīva Gosvāmī was standing outside. He said, 'What is that paper?'

"'No, your uncle has written frankly that he is not learned. I am learned.'

"'All right, talk with me.' Then Jīva defeated him.

"So sometimes devotees are so gentle. If such foolish person comes to talk, unnecessarily waste of time, 'All right, you take in writing that I am not a learned. Go away.' You see? This is *bhadra.* Instead of wasting time with a rascal, better give him a paper: 'Go away, sir.'"

Then as a contrast he described the *abhadra* from his own practical experience. "I have seen with my own eyes in Calcutta. One hotel man was cutting the throat of a chicken, and it was half-cut, and the half-dead chicken was jumping like this, and the man was laughing. His little son, he was crying. I have seen it. He was crying. Because he's innocent child, he could not tolerate. And the father was saying, 'Why you are crying? It is very nice.' Just see! So without being devotee a man will become cruel, cruel, cruel, cruel, cruel. In this way go to hell. And a devotee cannot tolerate.

"We have studied in the life of Lord Jesus Christ. When he saw that in the Jewish synagogue the birds were being killed, he became shocked. He therefore left. He inaugurated the Christian religion. Perhaps you know. He was shocked by this animal-killing. And therefore his first commandment is 'Thou shall not kill.' But the foolish Christians, instead of following his instruction, they are opening daily slaughterhouse. So unless one becomes a perfect devotee, he cannot become *bhadra,* a gentleman. That is not possible."

He concluded with an apt and encouraging parallel between Prahlāda, the *asurottama,* best of the demons, and ourselves, also sons and daughters of the demons. "Prahlāda was born of a father, Hiraṇyakaśipu, and the most ferocious *asura,* so he cannot escape the relationship with his father. 'How can I say that I am not son of *asura*?' But he is *uttama.* He surpassed that platform. How it is possible? Now, because Kṛṣṇa is pleased upon him. *Prīto' ham.* Although he is born in an *asura* family, low-grade family, but because Kṛṣṇa is pleased upon him, he becomes immediately *bhadra.* This is the facility.

"So those who speak that these Europeans and Americans cannot become Vaiṣṇava, they are mistaken. If Kṛṣṇa is pleased upon them, immediately they become the best of the *brāhmaṇas.* Here it is said, 'Never mind you are born in the family of *asura,* but because I am pleased, you are all-purified. You don't be disappointed.' It is only that we require to please Kṛṣṇa. Then everything is all right."

* * *

During the evening program, the leading visitors all spoke in Hindi. Śrīla Prabhupāda reciprocated by having some of his *sannyāsīs* speak. Acyutānanda Swami made all the visitors laugh by his witty remarks and his combination of Hindi, Bengali, and

English. Akṣayānanda Mahārāja has been learning Hindi, so he spoke as well.

Then Śrīla Prabhupāda spoke, especially emphasizing the remarks made by our god-cousin, Bhakti-dīpa Mahārāja, who is the disciple of one of Śrīla Prabhupāda's senior godbrothers. He used to live with Prabhupāda before His Divine Grace came to the West.

For our benefit, Prabhupāda spoke in English, but he addressed much of his remarks to his visitors, as a way of urging them to accept his foreign disciples as genuine Vaiṣṇavas.

He told them about the successful acceptance of Lord Caitanya's Movement, even in the most remote parts of the globe. He specifically mentioned Australia, where last year he established a temple of Lord Caitanya in Melbourne. He told them that for the first time in the history of the world, the Vedic culture is being spread in its true form. All this, he said, is in fulfillment of Lord Caitanya's prediction. And, in initiating so many foreigners into the chanting of the holy name, he is simply acting as Kṛṣṇa's and Lord Caitanya's representative.

"Kṛṣṇa consciousness means to follow what Kṛṣṇa says. That is Caitanya Mahāprabhu's mission. Caitanya Mahāprabhu has said, *āmāra ajñāya guru haña tāra ei deśa.* Wherever you are, it doesn't matter. Either you are in India or in America or France or anywhere, any *deśa,* or any country, just try to deliver them. Because guru's business is to deliver the fallen souls. Guru's business is not to exploit the *śiṣya.* It is his business how to deliver them.

"So who can deliver? He who is actually guru in the *paramparā* system. We have to take the authority of becoming guru from Śrī Caitanya Mahāprabhu. Within 500 years His order is that *āmāra ajñāya guru haña* ...'You cannot become guru all of a sudden. You must take order from Me.' He is *jagad-guru.* So Caitanya Mahāprabhu says you, all of you, to become guru and deliver. Because there are so many innumerable fallen souls in this age we require hundreds and thousands of gurus. But not cheaters. This is the time when it requires hundreds and thousands of gurus."

Certainly it would be hard for anyone to find fault in Śrīla Prabhupāda's personal qualifications, and in fact, Prabhupāda mentioned that many people have complimented him as having performed a miracle. But he strove to impress upon his guests the qualifications of his disciples also.

"They give me so much credit that 'You have done wonderful miracle.' I do not know how to play any miracle. Our Dīpa Mahārāja knows me from the very beginning. I do not know how to play magic. But only magic is that I don't adulterate. That's all. Kṛṣṇa says, 'Always think of Me.' So I am teaching them, 'Chant Hare Kṛṣṇa. You'll think of Him.'

"So who can chant Hare Kṛṣṇa unless he is a devotee? Ordinary man cannot chant. He has no taste. But these boys, they are taking my word very seriously. I have asked them to refrain from four kinds of sinful activities: illicit sex, intoxication, meat-eating, and gambling. They are seriously following. They have no illicit sex.

"Caitanya Mahāprabhu was questioned by a *gṛhastha* devotee, 'How we can understand a Vaiṣṇava?'

"So He summarily replied *asat saṅga tyāga ei vaiṣṇava ācāra.* This is the first principle—don't associate with *asat.* So next line He described who is *asat. Asat eka strī saṅgi, kṛṣṇa abhakta āra*—finished. In two lines we can understand who is a Vaiṣṇava.

"These people, European and American, they are ordinarily very much accustomed to these habits: illicit sex, gambling, meat-eating. But upon my word they have given up everything. And other things? They are reading the Vaiṣṇava literature very nicely, and they are pushing the Vaiṣṇava literature all over the world. By their personal efforts they are giving service. We have about sixty-five volumes, books, each book four-hundred pages. And they are introducing in the universities, colleges, libraries. Even sometimes they are beaten. In this way, these boys, they are helping this movement. So this movement has captured the spiritual ideas of the Western people, by the grace of Śrī Caitanya Mahāprabhu."

Finally he expressed his main point of frustration. "Unfortunately in India they are not received very well. The government is thinking they are CIA. A CIA has become Vaiṣṇava dancing in Vṛndāvana!?" The audience laughed.

"Just see their intelligence!" Then he continued, "And Purī also, they are not allowed to enter in the Jagannātha temple. These things are going on. So this is very regrettable, and our Śrīman Bhakti-dīpa Mahārāja has strongly protested against this idea. Therefore I thank him very much. Hare Kṛṣṇa."

His speech was well received, and his guests seemed impressed with the devotees, the majestic ISKCON temple, and most of all the vibrant spiritual atmosphere created by Śrīla Prabhupāda. It was a very successful program.

April 8th, 1976

A couple of interesting questions came up during the walk this morning. Pañca Draviḍa Mahārāja asked Śrīla Prabhupāda what he was thinking when he first went to the West. What idea for a program did he have?

Prabhupāda replied with a laugh. "This idea: I shall speak to don't eat meat, and they'll immediately kick me out!" Everyone laughed.

"That was my program. I was going to say 'Don't eat meat. No illicit sex,' and immediately they will kick me out! 'All right.' I never thought that you would accept it. That is the idea of my poetry [written on the boat when he first arrived]. I was asking Kṛṣṇa, 'I do not know why You have brought me here. As soon as I will say these things, they will kick me out. What is Your program, I do not know.'" Prabhupāda chuckled to himself.

Lokanātha Swami offered, "You are so expert. For one year you did not mention those rules and regulations, I heard."

"No, I simply said, 'Come and join and chant.'"

"And when they developed higher taste, then you said, 'Now no more meat-eating.'"

Lokanātha Mahārāja also had a question about the local people here in Vṛndāvana. "Śrīla Prabhupāda, what is the position of the *brijvāsīs,* those who are living in Vṛndāvana now? What happens to them next life?"

"Simply by living, if they do not commit anything sinful, they'll go back to home. Simply by living, without committing any sinful activities. Always remember Kṛṣṇa, this is Kṛṣṇa's land; that will deliver them."

"They don't need a spiritual master?" Madhudviṣa asked.

"Yes," Prabhupāda replied. "Spiritual master is always needed. Without abiding by the orders of spiritual master and serving him, nobody can be ... Otherwise rascal."

I began to say, "So all these local *vrajavāsīs,* they all accept—"

Prabhupāda immediately thought of the farmer the other morning who offered his respects because he'd walked on his land. "No, *vrajavāsīs,* they are generally, naturally, they are Kṛṣṇa conscious. Otherwise how is this illiterate farmer, he is offering? This is natural."

Pañca Draviḍa asked, "But he has no spiritual master?"

"No, no, he has a spiritual master. And even without spiritual master they have already elevated to Kṛṣṇa consciousness."

"So they will go back home?"

"Oh, yes," Prabhupāda assured him, "because spiritual master is within, *caitya-guru.*"

From what he told us about the position of the *vrajavāsīs,* it may seem that it is an easy way to go back to home, back to Godhead. But, of course, getting a birth in Vṛndāvana is not easy.

* * *

In class Prabhupāda explained what is required of us if we want to please Kṛṣṇa and get His blessings. "We have to surrender. That will please Kṛṣṇa. And without pleasing Him? You cannot see Kṛṣṇa. You may have your eyes, big, big eyes, but you cannot see Kṛṣṇa. You have to please Him. That pleasing activity is *bhakti.*

"Without that *bhakti,* it means sitting down silently ...'No, no, I am chanting. I do not want to go out. I am busy.' This means excuse. What you will chant? You will think of money and woman, that's all. Just work. Go to sell books and work hard. That is wanted. Therefore we do not give that opportunity. My Guru Mahārāja did not give this opportunity, and we are following the same principle. No opportunity of sitting idle. No, you must work. That will rectify. Yes."

* * *

I have been learning how to make *chapatis* from Bhagatjī, who Prabhupāda said makes the best. They are thick but well cooked, and each one puffs up perfectly and tastes sweet. Each day he comes to cook them for Prabhupāda's lunch, stopping briefly to ask Śrīla Prabhupāda what he would like to eat, before entering the kitchen at the bottom of the garden. Prabhupāda is encouraging me to learn in preparation for the next few months on the road. He said he would personally show me how to use his three-tiered cooker.

* * *

In the early afternoon some Gauḍīya Maṭha men came and took a big feast here. Then in the evening they returned and, along with the High Commissioner and District Magistrate from Mathurā, attended our program. They spoke on Kṛṣṇa consciousness and gave their recognition of Śrīla Prabhupāda's efforts to glorify the holy *dhāma* all over the world.

April 9th, 1976

Today is *Rāma-navamī,* the appearance day of Lord Rāmacandra, and everyone fasted until 4:00 p.m.

Prabhupāda walked through a nearby forest for his daily exercise. We drove out along Chatikara road a couple of miles and when he saw the wooded area he decided to get out. As we walked, he noticed a newly constructed roadway and enquired why it was there. I suggested that there might be a village on the other side of the woods. But Prabhupāda said that, no, the government would not build such a nice road simply for villagers. He concluded they were planning some industrial development and criticized them for following the West, leading India away from its spiritual goals.

Prabhupāda laughed about his own approach to Western civilization, which he described as *ajagara-vṛtti.* The python allows the mouse to dig a hole, then he eats the mouse and moves in. The Americans have worked hard to build their cities, Prabhupāda said, and he is now going there, taking their money, and bringing it back to India.

Another approach, he said, is *madhukara-vṛtti,* the way of the bee, which flits from flower to flower collecting a little here and a little there. But because the bee stocks its honey, there is the danger of its being taken away. For this reason he said that we should follow this policy: spend all funds on book publication or temple construction, and not keep any money in the bank.

* * *

In the *Śrīmad-Bhāgavatam* Lord Nṛsiṁhadeva described *śreyas-kāma,* the person who desires the best possible thing in life, as one who strives to please the Lord, because it is only God who can award the fulfillment of one's desires.

Śrīla Prabhupāda stressed that we should never think ourselves to be independent, as every aspect of our being is controlled, even our breathing. "Some demigod is controlling. Breathing, there is control. You can breathe for so many years, and live. And when the breathing is finished, then you are not in control. The great scientists, they are giving oxygen gas, injection. Can you increase the period of breathing for a moment? No. Controlled. So the yogis, they try to save the breathing. That is yogic process. They practice breathing control so that they can increase their life. Suppose I shall live for eighty or a hundred years. There is breathing period. If I can save breathing, then I can live more. Just like your bank balance. If you don't spend it, your balance is all right. But you spend it; then the balance will be zero some day. Similarly, the yogic process is to control the breathing. And the breathing is lost in large quantities when there is sex life."

At this point he began to breath rapidly and loudly into the microphone, making everyone laugh. "Finished! So to control the breathing, it requires celibacy, no sex life. That is called yoga; not showing some gymnastics and smoking and "yoga system." This is going on. Your country is cheated by so many rascals, yogis. You know it very well."

Prabhupāda told us that therefore in order to become advanced, or *dhīra,* very sober, we require the guidance of a genuine guru.

* * *

At mid-day *ārati* some devotees were singing over the microphone a mantra glorifying Sītā Rāma: "*Raghupati rāghava rāja rāma, patita pāvana sītā rāma.*" They were also chanting some other mantras.

Śrīla Prabhupāda sent me into the temple with the message that they stop. He wanted them to simply chant the Hare Kṛṣṇa *mahā-mantra,* since this automatically includes Lord Rāma. He said that the other mantras were not necessary.

* * *

At 6:30 p.m. Prabhupāda drove to Mathurā to speak at a *paṇḍala* held at *Kṛṣṇa-janma-bhūmi,* the birthplace of Lord Śrī Kṛṣṇa. Prabhupāda spoke in Hindi to a very noisy crowd of about five thousand people. Although it is Kṛṣṇa's own *dhāma,* we were disappointed to see some of the younger people being unruly and downright disrespectful to the devotees. But apart from that, it was a well-attended and successful program.

On the way back to Vṛndāvana some other residents of the *dhāma* created a minor stir. As we drove by some small roadside shops, a large hog suddenly shot out from between a couple of rickshas, frantically running from a snarling dog. There was a loud clang. It had run head first into the rear wheel of our car. Then it disappeared into the night, the dog in hot pursuit.

* * *

Prabhupāda's itinerary has been finalized for the next few weeks. He'll be leaving here for Bombay on April 11th, Melbourne on April 18th, New Zealand on the 26th, Fiji on the 29th, and then to Hawaii on May 5th for about a month.

He is translating more these days, being increasingly encouraged because the BBT in Los Angeles has at last caught up with the backlog. When Rāmeśvara was here he had assured him that as soon as he finishes a section it can be immediately put into production. Thus he had pleaded with Śrīla Prabhupāda that he should stay a while in Hawaii, where it is hoped he will be able to rest and translate more.

He has an invitation to go to Bangalore on May 11th, but it is very doubtful whether he will go. Mahāṁsa Swami has also invited him to Hyderabad on Janmāṣṭamī for the new temple opening. But at the moment the building is still under construction.

* * *

Prabhupāda was telling me some of the psychology of family life as I gave him his evening massage. He explained that a child usually puts food directly into its own mouth, but when older, he may distribute it among his family. It's the same selfishness, only extended. On the other hand, he also told me that the reason why Westerners squander money so much is because they have no family affection, so therefore they are not careful how they spend it.

April 10th, 1976

As we walked in the same forest again this morning, Yaśodānandana Swami, who returned from the South yesterday, asked Prabhupāda to confirm Ahobalam in South India as the actual place of Lord Nṛsiṁhadeva's pastimes. He had taken photos that he wanted to publish in *Back To Godhead.* However, Jayādvaita and others doubted the claim.

Prabhupāda said if there is some controversy, it should be avoided. "You know the *taka-taliya-nyāya*? There was a tree, *tal* tree. So one crow was there, and the *tal* fruit fell down. Two paṇḍits, they began to argue, 'Because the crow sat down on it, therefore the *tal* fruit fell down.'

The other said, 'No, the *tal* fruit was falling down, and the crow could not sit on it.' And they began to fight: 'No, this.' 'No this.' 'No this,' and so on."

He said that the main point is that Lord Nṛsiṁha is our worshipful Deity, no matter where He is. Then he quoted from the *Brahma-saṁhitā.* He is situated everywhere, why just this place or that place?

He then noted that Yaśodānandana Mahārāja was barefoot in the forest. Yaśodānandana shrugged it off, saying it was all right. But Prabhupāda got a little annoyed with him. He said it was not all right. It was a risk in the forest. Then he told him to go sit down. Then, out of consideration for his disciple, he said we should walk on the road.

* * *

For his last class this morning (tomorrow we go to Bombay), the verse was the last one in the chapter, "Prahlāda Pacifies the Lord with Prayers."

The narrator of the story, Nārada Muni, said: "Prahlāda Mahārāja was the best person in the family of demons. Demons always aspire for material happiness, yet even though Prahlāda was somewhat allured when the Supreme Personality of Godhead offered him benedictions for material happiness, because of his unalloyed Kṛṣṇa consciousness he did not want to take any material benefit for sense enjoyment."

Śrīla Prabhupāda gave an excellent discourse, thoroughly explaining the mood of selfless service in the devotee and the reciprocal feelings of the Lord. He told us how the Lord once approached a devotee of Lord Caitanya, Īśāna, desiring to give him a benediction. Īśāna's roof was full of holes, allowing the rain in, and Lord Caitanya offered to repair it.

Īśāna rejected the offer, though. He said the birds were simply living in the trees with no roof at all. So why should he bother the Lord simply for this?

Similarly, there was also an exchange between Rūpa and Sanātana gosvāmīs, with which Prabhupāda further beautifully illustrated the real devotional sentiment. "There is another narration of Sanātana Gosvāmī and Rūpa Gosvāmī. They were living in this forest of Vṛndāvana. Sanātana Gosvāmī was elder brother, and Rūpa Gosvāmī was younger brother. So they were living underneath a tree. So they had no means. Rūpa Gosvāmī thought that 'If I could get some articles, I could prepare something and invite my guru, Sanātana Gosvāmī.'

"So just after a few minutes one very nice young girl came with so much presentation of rice, *dahl,* ghee, and so many other things. So she came and offered to the Gosvāmī. 'Baba, please take this presentation. We have got some ceremony at our home, so my mother has sent. You take it.'

"So he was very glad: 'Oh, I was thinking if I could get some nice things, I could prepare and invite Sanātana Gosvāmī.' So he was very glad to receive those articles and invited Sanātana Gosvāmī and prepared so many nice foodstuffs and offered them to the Deity, and Sanātana Gosvāmī was given the *prasādam.* Sanātana Gosvāmī was very pleased, and he inquired, 'Rūpa Gosvāmī, where you got these nice things? You are living in this ... How you could receive all these things?'

"'Yes, my dear brother, I was just thinking in the morning. In the meantime a very nice young girl came and offered so many things, so I could—'

"'What is that? Who is that young girl in this forest? How was she looking?'

"'Oh, she was very, very beautiful.'

"'Oh, Rādhārāṇī. Oh.' So he was very sorry. 'You have taken service from Rādhārāṇī? Oh, you have done very wrong. We are trying to serve Rādhārāṇī, and you have taken service from Rādhārāṇī?' He rebuked him.

"This is pure service. They are avoiding to take service from Kṛṣṇa or Rādhārāṇī. And Kṛṣṇa Rādhārāṇī was finding out the opportunity how to serve the devotee. This is the competition between Kṛṣṇa and His devotee."

Then a bit later in the lecture he told an amusing anecdote to express the principle of being prepared to do and use anything in Kṛṣṇa's service. "A *sannyāsī* is supposed to walk. But if somebody criticizes, 'Sir, why you are flying on airplane?' no, that is our not principle. The Jain *sannyāsīs,* they never use cars. Now they have begun. Because I am traveling all over the world, now the Jains, they are also." Everyone laughed at that comment.

"But our philosophy is different. We are preaching Kṛṣṇa consciousness. Suppose I have to preach Kṛṣṇa consciousness in Europe or America. So because a *sannyāsī* has to walk, therefore I shall walk throughout the whole life to go to America? This is foolishness. If I can go to America within fifteen hours for preaching facility, why shall I not use the airplane? It is called *niyamāgraha,* to follow the regulative principles without any profit.

"No. If we get opportunity, preaching facilities for going on car, on airplane, using typewriter, dictaphone, microphone, we must use it. Because this is Kṛṣṇa's property, it must be used for Kṛṣṇa. This is our philosophy."

* * *

The devotees are visibly surcharged from their association with Śrīla Prabhupāda during the last few weeks. Now they will all be returning to their respective temples to push on the *saṅkīrtana* movement.

As Śrīla Prabhupāda has stated many times, his idea is to bring as many devotees as possible to the Māyāpur/Vṛndāvana

Gaura Pūrṇimā festival. He knows that they will become purified by contact with the *dhāmas* and thus return fully enthused with spiritual potency to preach for another year.

Of course, it is Śrīla Prabhupāda's association that is the chief motivating principle. We may not know Kṛṣṇa, but Śrīla Prabhupāda is in our midst, and it is due to the strong reciprocal loving relationship with him that all the devotees are working so hard year after year.

* * *

We have completed packing for the upcoming tour. We will be traveling overseas until mid-August, apart from a brief stay in Bombay.

Śrīla Prabhupāda instructed Śāstrījī to remain in Vṛndāvana. He wants him to work with the *gurukula,* rather than add to the travel expenses by coming along. So the party will be just Puṣṭa Kṛṣṇa Swami and myself.

April 11th, 1976

Ekādaśī-brata. Prabhupāda, Puṣṭa Kṛṣṇa Swami, Caitya-guru dāsa and I left the Kṛṣṇa Balarāma *mandir* at exactly 4:30 a.m., bound for Delhi—and near disaster.

After an hour and a half of uneventful motoring we entered the divided road in Faridabad district, an industrial complex on the outskirts of Delhi. Puṣṭa Kṛṣṇa Swami was at the wheel. He was explaining to Caitya-guru the finer points of driving the Mercedes, showing him the various switches and dials, because the car will be garaged here in Delhi while we are traveling overseas. Caitya-guru has been charged with its upkeep.

His attention diverted, Puṣṭa Kṛṣṇa failed to notice up ahead an oxcart overtaking a camel cart, moving into the center of the road. By the time he looked up it was too late. He was traveling too fast to stop.

Trying desperately to brake, he locked the wheels. The car began to skid; we were right on top of the oxcart. He tried to squeeze between the oxcart and the high curb of the central divider. The axle of the cart gouged into the rear passenger door next to Śrīla Prabhupāda. The impact ripped the entire wheel off the cart and sent the occupants tumbling down into a heap of straw. Our car cannoned through the gap and kept going.

Puṣṭa, badly shaken, put his foot down and kept going, not daring to stop. In India riots can quickly flare over such incidents, and drivers have been killed by angry onlookers.

The car door was slightly sprung, and you could see daylight through the top edge; but miraculously, no glass was broken and no one was hurt. I was shocked and looked to Śrīla Prabhupāda to make sure he was all right. He was unharmed. But he was so angry, he said to Puṣṭa Kṛṣṇa, "You are going so fast—!" and then bit his lip. He maintained a formidable, stony silence for the rest of the trip.

On arrival in Delhi Śrīla Prabhupāda had to climb out of the opposite door, the one on his side being so badly damaged it could not be opened. It had a huge rip in it. Prabhupāda said very little.

Puṣṭa Kṛṣṇa was acutely embarrassed and apologized.

This was a feature of Śrīla Prabhupāda's anger that I have not seen before. For a minor mistake or offense he can respond with either a mild or sharp rebuke or sarcasm, and that is sufficient correction. A major act of stupidity and carelessness, however, invokes demonstrative ire. His back straightens, his top lip quivers on the left side, and the blast of his anger can knock all the nonsense out of you. Only full surrender and rectification in these cases will ease his anger.

But his silence is the strongest response, reserved for a *mahā-aparādha,* an offense so great it is beyond comment. In this case I had the feeling that Puṣṭa Kṛṣṇa's apology was not enough.

* * *

Before we flew to Bombay Prabhupāda inspected another house that was still under construction. He was considering it as a possible new temple for ISKCON New Delhi but rejected it as too expensive.

Then he went to see the Deities, Śrī Śrī Rādhā-Pārtha Sarathī. They are now in the flat where he previously stayed at 9, Todar Mal Lane, because the lease on number 19 has run out. The situation is difficult, but They are being well looked after.

CHAPTER TWELVE

Bombay

April 11th, 1976

We landed in Bombay at 10:30 a.m. to a big airport reception from the devotees.

The ISKCON Bombay devotees honored Śrīla Prabhupāda with a lavish foot-bathing ceremony and *guru-pūjā* on his arrival at Hare Kṛṣṇa Land. They do this every time he visits.

The landscape is changing rapidly, what with the construction steadily progressing. Śrīla Prabhupāda was pleased to see that contractor, E.E.C., has already begun work. They've started the actual temple structure and will begin precasting of the domes soon.

This evening Prabhupāda gave a long *darśana* that lasted until 8:30 p.m.

April 12th, 1976

Prabhupāda made a careful inspection of the entire building site before taking his walk on the beach. All the ground-floor construction for the temple, the auditorium, and the twin-towered guest house is finished.

As usual, Dr. Patel joined us. Their discussion was lively. Śrīla Prabhupāda told him about our recent application for 350 acres of land in Māyāpur. He also informed him of his plan to build a Vedic Planetarium to exhibit the different planetary systems.

Dr. Patel said he had recently read a news article wherein Russian scientists were prepared to accept that there are other planets in the cosmos that have human life. He thought that the Russian interest in Vedic culture would eventually bring about an end to the purely materialistic philosophy of Marx, replacing it with the idea of spiritual communism. He declared that in another twenty years, Communism would be as watered down in Russia as it presently is in India.

When Gurudāsa Mahārāja said absenteeism from work is the biggest problem in Russia, Śrīla Prabhupāda joined in with a short story to illustrate the problem of centralization. "There is a story in Bengal. A woman had seven sons. The mother requested her first son, 'My dear boy, now I am going to die. Take me to the Ganges side.'

"He said, 'Why? You have got so many other sons, why you are requesting me?'

"And then second son, third ... Everyone said like that, and she died without Gaṅga. So this [Communism is like that] ... Everyone has to work. And he thinks that 'Why I shall work? Let him work. No work today.'"

Dr. Patel conjectured that it is therefore important for individuals to have a sense of possession. Even with all of our philosophical understanding that we are not the body, we still have the sense that we possess a body. This is a concept difficult even for aspiring devotees to give up, what to speak of the Russians.

Prabhupāda, however, pointed out that spiritually there is a higher sense of possession. Everything is possessed by God; that is perfection.

* * *

Class was on the verse *brahmacārī gurukule vasan danto guror hitam,* from *Śrīmad Bhāgavatam* 7.12.1.

In the simple setting of Śrī Śrī Rādhā-Rasabihārī's temporary, open-sided, tin-roofed temple, now looking more inadequate than ever as the very large complex rises by its side, Śrīla Prabhupāda delivered a strong lecture. He emphasized the need for *tapasya,* or austerity, in human life.

He said that Vedic culture means to control the senses, especially the sex urge, because sex is the highest material pleasure. One should therefore learn *brahmacārī* life, celibacy, from the guru. However, if one becomes a devotee, his taste for material life automatically diminishes. Therefore there is no need to practice *brahmacārya* as a discipline separate from devotional service.

Yet even advanced devotees are sometimes victimized by sex desire. Thus he warned us that although mixing between men and women is inevitable, we must be very cautious. "Therefore you should be very, very careful. Very, very careful. Just like in our Society, compulsorily we have to mix with women, not only women, very beautiful young girls. But if one is not agitated even in this association of beautiful women and girls, then he is to be considered *paramahaṁsa,* he is very advanced. *Paramahaṁsa* means he's above all these material qualities. So we cannot avoid in our Kṛṣṇa consciousness movement.

"That was the problem from the very beginning. In India there is restriction between men and women, free intermingling, but in your country there is no such restriction. Therefore I got my disciples married. They criticize me that I have become a marriage-maker. Anyway, I wanted at least to regulate. That is required."

Prabhupāda explained that if a man gets married and sticks to one wife, and if he takes permission from his spiritual master before having sex, observing the *garbhādhāna-saṁskāra,* or purificatory rites, then he is also considered a *brahmacārī.*

He said that the ability to observe the *brahmacārī* standards depends on the relationship between the guru and disciple. "This can be possible when one is very thickly related with the guru. Otherwise ordinary relationship will not do. One who is convinced that 'If I can please my guru, then Kṛṣṇa will be pleased...' This is called *sudṛḍha,* full faith. 'And if I displease my guru, then I have no place.'

"Of course, guru cannot be a false guru. False guru has no such thing. If guru is genuine and the disciple is genuine, then both of them are benefited, and they go back to home, back to Godhead. Thank you very much."

* * *

Gurudāsa Mahārāja told Prabhupāda that Mr Kanailal Taparia, a Bombay Life Member, has offered the use of some land and buildings near Fogal Āśrama in Vṛndāvana. It's about a seven-minute walk from our temple, just off the *parikrama* path. The property has a few buildings on it but is mostly undeveloped. Prabhupāda is eager to get it because we need a place for our householders to live. The women and children currently occupy rooms in the guest house, and Prabhupāda is not happy at the disturbance they cause for our guests.

* * *

As in Vṛndāvana, Prabhupāda also wants a *gurukula* here in Bombay. There may be a side benefit from this as well: there is a law that we can rightfully evict any existing tenants if we claim use of the buildings for a school.

April 13th, 1976

On the walk along the sands of Juhu beach, Dr. Patel suggested to Śrīla Prabhupāda that he have a Sanskrit school in the new temple complex. Prabhupāda said that he has no objection, but it is not essential since he has already translated so many Sanskrit texts into English, which any educated person can read.

Dr. Patel still seemed to think that there was an advantage to reading the original language, but Śrīla Prabhupāda said that even so-called Sanskrit *paṇḍitas* cannot read it properly. Apart from that, it isn't just a question of understanding the language, it requires hearing attentively. The message of the *Vedas* is learned by hearing, not by studying. The message is to become Kṛṣṇa conscious.

He quoted a song by Narottama dāsa Ṭhākura that states that if one does not take to Kṛṣṇa consciousness he is knowingly committing suicide. Being absorbed in material affairs is exactly the same as drinking poison.

Kṛṣṇa consciousness means always thinking of Kṛṣṇa, but generally people do some meditation for fifteen minutes and think of something else for twenty-four hours. Prabhupāda described a personal experience he'd had with Mohandas K. Gandhi. "I have seen Gandhi's prayer meeting; I attended. Utmost, five minutes reading *Bhagavad-gītā,* then again politics, immediately. Immediately politics. I was in Delhi. I attended the meeting when *Nawa Khalia* prayers ... This was his prayer. I have seen. And as a result of this, in that prayer meeting he was killed. He could not chant the holy name."

Regarding the Doctor's suggestion for learning Sanskrit, Prabhupāda concluded that if a student is serious he can learn simply from reading his books, because in them he has given the word meanings. After studying a few sentences one can understand the verb, the subject, object, and so forth. Prabhupāda told Dr. Patel that if he would have had more time he would have made a Sanskrit grammar based on *Bhagavad-gītā,* but now he is too busy. He suggested Dr. Patel do it, since he knows both Sanskrit and English. "You can do that. People will read it, *Bhagavad-gītā* grammar. On the *Bhagavad-gītā* teach them grammar. Just like Jīva Gosvāmī compiled *Hari-nāmāmṛta-vyākaraṇa,* similarly, you write. You have the knowledge of Sanskrit, and through English, [teach it using] *Bhagavad-gītā* grammar. People will take it."

* * *

In today's class we continued on with *Śrīmad-Bhāgavatam* 7.12.2, hearing a description of the activities to be performed by the *brahmacārī* student.

Śrīla Prabhupāda stressed that development of character is the first stage of training, because without good character everything else is useless. He told the story called *punar mūṣika bhava:* Again You Become a Mouse.

A mouse was being chased by cats, so by the grace of a great sage, he was transformed into a cat. Then he had trouble with dogs, and again the sage transformed him, this time into a dog. In this way, eventually he was changed into a powerful tiger. But then he looked hungrily at the same sage who had elevated him. Instantly, the sage turned him back into a mouse.

The idea is that by the grace of a higher power one may be elevated to a higher position in life, but if one abuses the privilege, then again the opportunity may be withdrawn. Scorning the material scientists, Prabhupāda told us not to misuse our human form of life. "So our civilization is like that, that in the gradual process of evolution we have come to the platform of human being. This human being is meant for understanding God, but they are forgetting God. Therefore the next stage is *punar mūṣika bhava,* again become monkey. That is waiting us. The nature's law is like that, that from monkey we have become human being, and in the human being we are dancing like monkey. So nature will say, 'All right, again you become monkey.'"

He told us that a devotee also has the potential to return to his origins. Kṛṣṇa says in *Bhagavad-gītā* that if one prepares himself correctly, one can go to the heavenly planets, to the abode of the demigods, or even beyond, to the spiritual realm.

"This Kṛṣṇa consciousness movement is simply a very scientific movement that will help the human society not to be degraded again; to be elevated. Kṛṣṇa says 'If you prepare yourself to come to Me, back to home, back to God, you can do that.' So what should be our aim of life? We shall go to the higher planetary system or back to home, back to Godhead? 'Back' we say, because we have come from God.

"Just like one man is put in the prison house. He has come from his free home. By his work he is criminal; therefore he is put into the prison house. Similarly, we are all part and parcel of God. Our real home is *vaikuṇṭha.* But we have come here. How we have come, that is a very mysterious thing, but we are part and parcel. Bhaktivinoda Ṭhākura has sung, *anādi karama phale, pori bhavārṇava jale.* Somehow or other we have fallen; therefore the real aim of life, how to get out of this *bhavārṇava,* nescience, that is the aim of life."

The verse mentioned the importance of worshiping the guru, and Śrīla Prabhupāda stressed this as the most important aspect of human life. He also explained who is a real guru. "If you have got real guru, and if you follow him, then your life is successful. There is no doubt. But if you have a so-called, bogus guru without any knowledge of the *śāstra,* then your life will be spoiled. Especially the *māyāvādī* guru, Caitanya Mahāprabhu has warned. *Māyāvādī* guru means one who thinks that everyone is God—if you approach such guru, then your life is spoiled. *Māyāvādī bhāṣya śunile haya sarva nāśa.* Finished. Your spiritual progress finished."

He concluded that training should begin at a young age and be centered on character development. Afterward, further academic studies can be introduced. He quoted a Bengali phrase, "When the bamboo is green, you can bend it, but when it is yellow, dried, it will crack."

* * *

Pradyumna, tall, bespectacled, thin, and somewhat eccentric, arrived from South India today. He has a reputation among the devotees as a Sanskrit scholar. Some of them, even Prabhupāda sometimes, call him Paṇḍitjī.

His wife, Arundhatī dasi, had spoken with Prabhupāda in Māyāpur, and he had requested that Pradyumna come to see him. Prabhupāda wants him to join his party as his Sanskrit editor. Rather than translating all the Sanskrit himself, he wants Pradyumna to do it. This strategy will save a lot of time and effort and speed up the publication of the *Bhāgavatam*, because it will free Prabhupāda to concentrate on writing his purports.

After some discussion it was decided that Pradyumna prabhu will join us in Hawaii in May.

* * *

Punjabi Premananda, a local student, sent a letter to Prabhupāda after attending the walk this morning. He asked a number of questions, seeking clarification from Śrīla Prabhupāda on his comments that knowing Sanskrit and studying are not as important as simply hearing the *śāstras*. He is currently reading a Sanskrit work by Rāmānujācārya, the *Vedānta-sāra*, with Sanskrit commentary by two other *ācāryas*. He asked whether he should stop this and simply hear.

He also mentioned that a number of politicians were going village to village on *pādayātrā*, traveling by foot, and in this way getting many donations of land. He suggested that Śrīla Prabhupāda might do the same.

In his letter he typed in capitals for emphasis. "IF YOU STARTED PADAYATRA or at least if YOU WENT TO VILLAGES IN CAR FOR THE TIME (FOR A FEW MONTHS) then naturally many people will give land which can be used for KRISHNA'S SERVICE. AND SO MANY PEOPLE WILL BE BENEFITTED BY HAVING YOUR DARSHAN (VISION). I am not at all commanding you, just an idea that struck my mind regarding the above said content of the PADAYATRA."

Finally, on the comment Prabhupāda had made that Gandhi was simply reading the *Gītā* for five minutes and then discussing politics, he added his agreement that it is very difficult to think of Kṛṣṇa and work in an office. He is studying for his

BA in philosophy and psychology, and he wanted to know how he could keep his mind fixed on Kṛṣṇa consciousness.

He added a telling comment, a confirmation of Śrīla Prabhupāda's many remarks about the unfortunate condition of the youth of India. "I find so much opposition, when I just mention about Krishna, or try to tell them about Krishna consciousness to my college friends. They simply criticize and say, 'Oh, you are a bore, you always bore us, why do you speak about other-worldly?'"

Prabhupāda answered all his points, first of all explaining that reading *Bhagavad-gītā* is all right, but if one does it independently there is a chance of being misled. Therefore one should hear from an authorized source, i.e., a self-realized person, a bonafide guru.

"Mental speculation will not help. Hearing is the main point. In the *Bhagavad-gītā* it is written, *dharmakṣetre kurukṣetre* ... When you hear from a realized soul, a person who knows things, he explains that Kurukṣetra is a place where religious ritualistic ceremonies are performed from time immemorial. But if you read the books of some cunning politician, he'll mislead you, and you'll learn that Kurukṣetra means this body, which is not actually the fact."

Concerning his suggestion for *pādayātrā*, Prabhupāda welcomed it. With the same enthusiasm he has recently injected into Hansadūta Mahārāja, Prabhupāda encouraged the boy to participate. "If Indian young men join me, I am immediately ready for this travelling touring from village to village, town to town. However, my foreign disciples have the language defect, they can't speak the village language, otherwise I would have started this program long ago. If some young men like you would join me then along with some foreign disciples, I can immediately take up this program. If you are very eager, please get hold of at least half a dozen young men like you, then with another half dozen foreign disciples, I can immediately take up this program and tour village to village and town to town. It will be very, very effective, I know that."

On the boy's last point Prabhupāda gave him the simple straightforward method for remembering Kṛṣṇa: simply chant.

"Your associates are harassing you for your interest in spiritual culture; yes, that is due to India's great misfortune. They're impressed with so-called politicians and scholars of the modern age. The example is given in this connection that when a man is ghostly haunted, he speaks all nonsense. At the present moment they're all ghostly haunted and in this delirious condition, the only cure is chanting the Hare Kṛṣṇa *mahā-mantra.*"

* * *

Prabhupāda showed us how to prepare lunch with his three-tiered cooker today. Before his massage was finished, he got up and we went to the kitchen. He loaded the cooker, putting *dahl* in the bottom tier, rice in the middle, and vegetables on top. He set the cooker on a low flame and had Pradyumna make some *chapati* dough. Thirty-five minutes later he came back to the kitchen and chaunched the *dahl,* spiced the vegetables, made *chapatis,* and then ate. It was a simple, wholesome meal, expertly prepared with a minimum of fuss.

We were fortunate to share his remnants, which to me tasted far better than usual, having been cooked with his own hands.

* * *

Prabhupāda has had me collect the bitter leaves of the neem tree and dry them in the sun on the roof. Today, after crushing the dried leaves, I filled a bag with the fine powder, to take with us on the coming tour for use in cooking, to stimulate and improve his appetite.

A few other items which have also been left on the roof to be exposed to the sun's powerful rays are some of the many books Prabhupāda uses for translation work. These books have been stored in his *almirah,* and when Pradyumna sorted through them he discovered that many had become infested with book worms. Thus Prabhupāda prescribed a prolonged dose of sunshine to remedy the problem.

April 14th, 1976

Today is Hanuman Jayantī and Balarāma Rāsayātrā. The devotees celebrated with a big festival.

* * *

Prabhupāda talked a lot on his walk, especially focusing on the topic of the *gurukula*. He told Girirāja, the temple president, that a large *gurukula* should be constructed on our land here in Bombay. He said that twice a day the boys can come to the beach and sport and swim. In this way they will grow healthy, get a good education, and become men of good character. They will learn to control their senses, and this will save them from becoming "nonsense."

Prabhupāda said there are many wealthy persons in Bombay who would want to put their children in such a school, because they are not concerned whether their children become expert technologists or not. When you have wealth, you can hire others to do such work.

He told of a man he knew in Allahabad who was a PhD, yet he could not get a job. The man was manufacturing soap bars at home and going by cycle every day to sell them in the market. Although he had a PhD, he was living like a coolie.

Prabhupāda emphasized that therefore one should not make much endeavor for economic advancement, because whatever one is due, either success or failure, is already decided. Getting a PhD will not change that. One should simply try to become Kṛṣṇa conscious. He mentioned that Mr. Modi, the founder of Modinagar, where we recently had our program, was not an educated man, but he had fifty thousand people working for him.

Girirāja told a similar story about Henry Ford. He had been criticized by a newspaper that he was an ignorant man. He brought a case against the paper, and in court the defense lawyer began asking him questions on science and history. At one point Henry Ford turned to the judge and said, "In my office I have a panel of buttons, and I can press any button and someone will come running to answer any of these questions. So am I ignorant?"

In the course of the walk, Prabhupāda also told us a couple of amusing stories. "When I was a child my father gave me one red gun; I was not more than eight years. Then, after getting one, I said, 'I must have another one.'

"Then father said, 'Why another one? You have got already one.'

"So I said, 'No, I have got two hands. I must have two guns.'

"Then my father, 'No, you are not ... I am not going ...'

"Then I made so much agitation, he was obliged to give me two guns."

We all laughed at his description as he told us that he was the "very pet child of my father and very pet son-in-law also." Then he added that he was the pet disciple of his guru also.

The other story he told illustrated how intelligence is superior to strength. "There was a lion in the forest, and he was disturbing all the animals. So there was a peace conference: 'Sir, you don't disturb every one of us. We shall come automatically.'

"So one day it was the turn of a rabbit. So he was a little late, so the lion said, 'Why you are late? My time is over.'

"'Yes sir, another lion on the way, he wanted to eat me. So I said, 'No, you cannot eat me. I will be eaten by such and such Mr. Lion.'

"So he became very angry. 'Who is that?'

"'Yes, come on. I will show you.' So he got him near a well, and he said that 'Here is the lion.'

"So immediately, 'Graww!'

Everyone laughed as Prabhupāda imitated the lion growling.

"And there was sound, 'Graww!' Then he saw the reflection and immediately jumped over.

"Buddhir yasya balaṁ tasya nirbuddhes tu kuto balaṁ paśya siṁha madonmataḥ śaśaḥ kena nipatata: A *śaśa,* the rabbit, killed a big lion by intelligence."

This story is from the *Hitopadesha.* Prabhupāda mentioned that Aesop's Fables, popular in the West, were actually derived from the *Hitopadesha.*

On the way into the temple grounds, Prabhupāda noticed a new minibus. It is for Acyutānanda Swami to tour South India in. When he heard that they are planning to have Rādhā and Kṛṣṇa installed in the bus, Prabhupāda suggested Gaura-Nitāi would be better. But on being informed that the people in South India like Rādhā-Kṛṣṇa and are not so familiar with

Gaura-Nitāi, he conceded.

As we walked on past the building site, Saurabha reported that work on the temple structure is going on smoothly and quickly. Only three stories remain to be built on the twin towers that will be the Guest House.

* * *

This morning's verse for class emphasized the necessity of studying the *Vedas* under the guidance of the guru. Prabhupāda explained that this does not mean everyone has to know Sanskrit. One simply has to hear and chant nicely; it isn't required that one be an erudite scholar. So the program he advised for the *gurukula* is for the students to attend *maṅgala-ārati* and *guru-pūjā,* and then *Śrīmad-Bhāgavatam* class. "So one should read or hear: *chandāṁsy adhīyeta guroḥ.* It is guru's duty. Transcendental knowledge, one should approach guru. So *gurukula* means "guru's place." So he keeps the disciples to learn the Vedic literature. This is *gurukula.*

"We are constructing such big, big houses. Why? We are inviting people to come here and live in this *gurukula* and learn Vedic literature. This is our purpose. Bombay is a very big city, people are rich, so we can give you nice room, nice *prasādam.* Come here, live here at least once in a week and learn Vedic literature, Vedic civilization. The essence of Vedic literature is *Śrīmad-Bhāgavatam.*

"Our mission is to invite people to take advantage of learning Vedic literature. And what is the ultimate goal of studying Vedic literature? To understand Kṛṣṇa. So therefore our Movement is known as Kṛṣṇa consciousness movement."

He also gave a practical example to show the nature of the exchange between guru and disciple. This is something that we on his personal party experience daily. "The son may be offender, but when he comes and offers his respect to the father, he [the father] forgets.

"So that should be done regularly, *suyantritaḥ,* just like machine. As soon as one sees guru, immediately he must offer obeisances. Beginning, end also. When he comes to see guru he must offer obeisances, and when he leaves that place he must offer obeisances. And in the inbetween, coming and going, he should learn from the guru Vedic understanding. This is the principle of living in *gurukula.* So our students, they are very obedient. And if our students see the guru hundred times, he practices this process, offering obeisances while meeting and while going. These things are to be practiced. Then he'll be self-controlled.

"Obedience is the first law of discipline. If there is no obedience there cannot be any discipline. And if there is no discipline you cannot manage anything. That is not possible. Therefore this is very essential, that the students should be very disciplined."

He told us how this idea of *gurukula* training had long been on his agenda, complaining again about the unfortunate mentality that has overtaken the people of India. "This is essential. To make the human life really civilized, the children should be sent to the *gurukula.* But there is no *gurukula* at the present moment. So we are starting. We have got some *gurukula* in the United States, Texas. We are starting another *gurukula* in Vṛndāvana, and we can start another *gurukula* here in Bombay to train the students.

"I wanted to start this *gurukula* long, long, ago before going to the USA, in 1960. Say '62, '61. But I approached so many gentlemen friends; they never agreed to give their sons to *gurukula.* They never agreed. Everyone said, 'Swamiji, what benefit there will be by training our students in the *gurukula* way? They have to earn their bread.' So that is India's position now. They do not care for their original culture. They are after money."

Prabhupāda emphasized that without proper training one is living a very risky life. There is danger of gliding down to become a cat or dog in one's next life. Therefore, this Kṛṣṇa consciousness movement is meant to remove that risk.

* * *

Jayapatāka Swami, Gopāla Kṛṣṇa, and Abhirām prabhus have come to Bombay to obtain Saurabha's plans for the development of the Māyāpur and Calcutta projects.

Our chances of actually getting the lake across the street from the temple in Calcutta are apparently growing. Now we must show our plans for development.

* * *

In his room in the afternoon Prabhupāda discussed the visa problems faced by our foreign devotees. Viśāla and his wife, Viśālinī, who were formerly living in Vṛndāvana, have just returned to India after having been forced by the government to go back to the West to renew their visas.

Prabhupāda suggested that ISKCON devotees should now lobby in Parliament for recognition of our true Vaiṣṇava status. We should state that we are coming here on pilgrimage. Why should we need visas, or even passports, he asked? Other religious pilgrims do not require to have visas in visiting Mecca or Jerusalem, etc. Why should we be put into difficulty? If this tactic fails, he suggested we approach the United Nations as well.

* * *

Since there were only a few visitors today, before taking his massage, Śrīla Prabhupāda replied a small amount of mail as he sat in his sitting room. He sent Akṣayānanda Mahārāja a letter informing him of Mr. Taparia's offer to let us use his house in Vṛndāvana. There are a dozen rooms there altogether, and he instructed that the householders could all move there and occupy the ten smaller ones. He suggested that the two large rooms might may be used as a temporary *gurukula.* Prabhupāda is so keen to end the regular commotion in the Guest House caused by having families living there as permanent residents that he told Akṣayānanda Mahārāja they can move onto the property even though the land is not ours. He said that later on we can negotiate to purchase it, or Mr. Taparia may even be willing to donate it.

Śruti Kīrti, who Prabhupāda wrote while we were in Māyāpur, is now in Boston with Ambarīṣa prabhu. Śruti Kīrti telephoned Puṣṭa Kṛṣṇa Swami the other day and reported that there is a good opportunity to begin a restaurant there. Ambarīṣa is prepared to invest a substantial amount, but there is a lack of manpower.

Therefore Śrīla Prabhupāda wrote to Hāsyapriya dāsa, the Los Angeles temple president, to suggest that perhaps eight devotees could go from there to work on the project. He said that it would also be a good opportunity for Hāsyapriya to learn how to run a restaurant, because Ambarīṣa and Śruti Kīrti have already successfully opened one in Hawaii.

Prabhupāda also read an advertising pamphlet distributed by one of his Vṛndāvana-based Godbrothers, Bon Mahārāja. It mentioned his life history and his preaching expeditions to the West: "following the tradition of Vivekananda, Rāma Tīrtha, and Rāma Kṛṣṇa *sannyāsīs.*" Prabhupāda shook his head disapprovingly, saying, "I had a little respect for him before, but now I can understand him. This means he is a *māyāvādī.* He is giving advertisement to Vivekananda."

The tract also described how Bon had spent four years undergoing penance in an underground cell, and when he came out he was inspired to start his college. It seemed it was meant to sound as if he had undergone great austerity and emerged at the end of it with a divinely inspired revelation.

Prabhupāda explained that Śrīla Bhaktisiddhānta had actually never liked this man. After His Divine Grace's departure one astrologer told Bon that he was an offender to his spiritual master. He was conscious of this, so the atonement was given that he should offer leaves of the *Bael* tree to Lord Śiva. Thus he went into his cell.

Prabhupāda told us that this also was a mundane attempt to rectify himself. He had planned to create a Vaiṣṇava University and worked very hard on the project, but it was never successful.

* * *

In the evenings Prabhupāda is enjoying the warm atmosphere by sitting out on the roof. We take up an *āsana* for him and pillows and mats for any guests that come. Generally there are only a few guests, so Prabhupāda has a chance to relax, although he is always keen to preach.

During this evening's session, Prabhupāda told a visitor that the potency of chanting done in the temple is increased a thousand times compared to that done elsewhere. Therefore so many people go to places like Vṛndāvana to chant.

April 15th, 1976

One of the memorable features of being in Bombay is waking up in the morning to the all-pervasive stench of an open sewer channel that runs right past our back boundary. It is enough to make you gag, and it seems all the worse to me because our quarters are at the back of the land. The smell only disappears once the sun comes up, so it is something of a relief to go down to the beach every day and breath some fresh air. It is an unfortunate blemish in an otherwise idyllic setting.

* * *

This morning's beach walk gave rise to a long and interesting conversation between Śrīla Prabhupāda and the barefoot Dr. Patel. Prabhupāda explained everything to him—from the uselessness of vegetarianism, to the perfection of Communism.

As far as being vegetarian goes, Prabhupāda told us about a Jain monk who came to meet him in Berkeley, America. When Prabhupāda had asked him what the results of his preaching were, the man replied that he had converted one million people to vegetarianism. But Prabhupāda didn't give him much credit for that. Although the Jains advocate nonviolence, Prabhupāda pointed out that being vegetarian is violence, since one has to kill the vegetables. Nor does being vegetarian or nonviolent mean one is on the spiritual platform. Garuḍa is the personal carrier of Lord Viṣṇu, yet he eats snakes; and Kṛṣṇa ordered Arjuna to kill his enemies. He said that the real point is to follow the order of Kṛṣṇa.

Dr. Patel interpreted the meaning of this as "feeling that one is doing every thing for Kṛṣṇa."

Prabhupāda responded that the orders are factual, not feelings. He also showed the vital role the spiritual master plays. "Not feel, but actually it's an order. Arjuna did not feel; he took order to kill. Not that you manufacture your idea. No. You take order directly and then do it—otherwise you'll be responsible. Therefore the guru is required to act as representative of Kṛṣṇa. If he says, 'Yes, it is all right,' then it is all right. Otherwise not. *Yasya prasādād bhagavat-prasādaḥ.* Otherwise why guru is required? We must take every moment order from him."

Prabhupāda told the doctor that simply by becoming Kṛṣṇa conscious one develops all good qualities, so there is no need for a separate endeavor to be vegetarian.

The discussion moved on to the topic of scientists, and Śrīla Prabhupāda highly praised his disciple Svarupa Dāmodara, for writing the book *Scientific Basis of Kṛṣṇa Consciousness.* "Dr. Svarūpa Dāmodara, PhD; you have read that book? It is first class. The scientist, so-called scientist, unless he is insane, he cannot say that there is no God. He has written so nice."

"But the real scientists are also God conscious," Dr. Patel interjected.

"That is all right. He [Svarūpa Dāmodara] is real scientist."

"You have been unfortunately against them," Dr. Patel argued, "but think of Albert Einstein. He was totally God conscious throughout his life."

"Yes," Prabhupāda agreed. "He is all right, but mostly they say, 'What is the use of God? Now science, everything science.' They say like that."

Dr. Patel protested. "You have been very harsh to the scientists."

"They are misleading," Prabhupāda said. "These rascals are misleading. That is the way."

"He was very God conscious when he made the atomic bomb," Puṣṭa Kṛṣṇa added sarcastically.

Dr. Patel found it disagreeable and bridled a bit at his junior's disrespect. "How many of us are scientists here? He might help you also!"

Prabhupāda gave the ultimate perspective to settle the issue. "We know a real scientist because we know the biggest scientist, Kṛṣṇa. Therefore we are scientists. Without Him we don't claim to be scientists—fools, rascals. He is everything. If you simply understand Kṛṣṇa, then you become scientist, philosopher. And I was never a scientist, so we challenge the scientists, and I have produced this scientist [Svarūpa Dāmodara] to challenge them. But I was never a scientist. That book is actually revolutionary amongst the scientists. *Scientific Basis,* you have read that? Very nicely he has written, very, very nicely, from all scientific... He has challenged the scientists. He has clearly declared, 'Darwin is wrong, and scientists, they do not know.'"

The conversation moved on to one of their favorite topics, Communism. But this time Prabhupāda offered a different perspective. He disagreed when Dr. Patel said that Communism is finished. He said that it simply needs the addition of Kṛṣṇa, then it has value. Like a zero with a one placed in front.

The Communists say that religion is the opiate of the people, but Prabhupāda pointed out that opium also has its proper medical use. It is poison undoubtedly, but if it is in the hand of a physician, it is nectarine. Dr. Patel agreed that opium is the first thing they use in heart-attack cases. Therefore, Prabhupāda said, whatever God has created has some use; one must simply know how to utilize everything properly. Thus Communism will become perfect, as soon as it is connected with Kṛṣṇa.

* * *

During class, which continued with the description of *brahmacārī* life, Prabhupāda explained the essential difference in attitude between the people of the East and West.

He said that human beings are thoughtful. We have developed consciousness, but when this is not applied to higher thoughts, or when there is no spiritual idea, it is misused to artificially increase the necessities of life. He said that nowadays even a simple action like shaving requires a machine. In the East, however, the mentality is to minimize everything.

"This is the distinction between East and West. The Eastern civilization is, 'If I can lie down on the floor, where is the necessity of a bedstead or a cot? If I can lie down, resting my head on the arms, why there is necessity of pillow? If I can, say, drink water with my palms like this, what is the use of any water pot?' Minimize. Minimize. Spiritual life does not mean artificially increasing the necessities of life."

Once again Prabhupāda expressed his strong disapproval of India's unfortunate plight and his sympathy for the young. "So the whole thing is topsy-turvied. We have given up our own culture and imitating the foreigners and the Western countries. That also we cannot do very properly because we are meant for a different purpose in India.

"In India, one who has taken birth in India, it is understood that in his previous birth he tried to cultivate spiritual culture; therefore he has been given the opportunity to take birth in India. India is so fortunate. But as soon as he takes birth, the rascal leader spoils him. The rascal father spoils him. The rascal teacher spoils him.

"So what can they do, the poor younger generation? They are being taught that 'The spiritual culture is useless. Because we are so much spiritually inclined, the foreigners came and they ruled over us. Now give up all this nonsense. Become technologist.' This is going on. So this will not make us happy."

* * *

Prabhupāda has been taking his noon massage sitting on the tiny balcony between his bedroom and the kitchen. When we began today, I slipped the Hare Kṛṣṇa ring from his finger. He has been wearing it continuously since it was given to him in Māyāpur, but because it is a little loose I usually take it off to massage his hand.

Prabhupāda looked at it when it came off. Then he looked at me and said, "It is loose? So, now you try it."

Surprised, but very eager, I put it on the little finger of my left hand, but it was a bit slack.

He said, "Oh, too big?"

Not wanting to lose the opportunity, I didn't reply but quickly tried it on the little finger of my right hand, and it fit nicely.

"All right," he smiled, "you can have it!"

I immediately offered him my obeisances and very gratefully tucked it into the fold of my *gamsha.*

Prabhupāda doesn't give away such items often, so I was in ecstasy to get this special gift from him without any prompting and for no apparent reason.

April 16th, 1976

On today's walk along the beach, Prabhupāda continued his discussions with Dr. Patel, focusing again on the topic of scientists.

Dr. Patel predictably took a contrary view but, as always, submitted to Śrīla Prabhupāda's superior reasoning. Being a doctor, he often gives credit to the scientists' progress, yet he accepts the limitedness of material science, and his conviction ultimately lies in spiritual knowledge.

Prabhupāda had him laughing today when he called the scientists "double *mūḍhas.*"

* * *

Today's *Śrīmad-Bhāgavatam* verse continued to elaborate on the life of *brahmacārya.* One responsibility is to go out morning and evening and collect alms on behalf of the spiritual master. Whatever a *brahmacārī* does must be for the benefit of the guru.

Prabhupāda told us that this is the standard he has in mind for the new *gurukula* here. "A small collection, it is going to the temple for offering *prasādam* to the Lord and *prasādam* to the Vaiṣṇavas, *brāhmaṇas.* Therefore something must be given. If we open this *gurukula* as we are contemplating, the students should be trained up to go house to house and take little alms. It doesn't matter one has to give one kilogram, no. Whatever you can, you must give. This is the system all over India still.

"So here it is said that *sāyaṁ prātaś cared bhaikṣyam.* Twice in a day the *brahmacārīs* should be trained up to collect alms, in the morning, in the evening. And whatever collection is there, it should be offered to the guru. Not that something kept for my own purpose. No. Everything should be offered, whatever you collect. You cannot keep, because everything in the *gurukula* or in the temple, it is for the interest of the guru."

He did, however, recognize that in this age of *Kali-yuga* many of the standards mentioned in these verses are extremely difficult to follow.

He therefore quoted from the Twelfth Canto of *Śrīmad-Bhāgavatam,* explaining that the essence of everything is the holy names.

"So these things as far as possible we shall introduce, but our main principle is chant. If the *brahmacārīs* are trained up to rise early in the morning and chant Hare Kṛṣṇa, attend *maṅgala-ārati,* then go to the sea for taking bath and again come and again attend *vaidhika* school. And *veda-vyāsa* ... *Veda-vyāsa* means to study Kṛṣṇa literature. Because nowadays it is not possible that the students, especially foreign students, they will be very much inclined to read from *Sāma-Veda, Yajur-Veda, Ṛg-Veda,*

Atharva-Veda, or pronounce the *Upaniṣad, Brahma-sūtra.* The time is changed. As far as possible ... But there is essence of all these Vedic literature. *Bhāṣyayam brahma-sūtrānāṁ vedārtha-paribṛṁhitam.* This *Bhāgavata,* this is the essence of *Brahma-sūtra.*

"So we are contemplating to start this *brahmacārī āśrama,* so these things should be followed, that a *brahmacārī* should always remain dedicated to the guru. Whatever collection he makes, he should offer to the spiritual master, and spiritual master will ask him, 'My dear such and such, my dear son, please come and take your *prasādam.*' If he forgets, then we should not go personally. And we should wait, or we shall fast. These are the some of the rules and regulations as far as possible."

* * *

Kiśorī dasi arrived from Vṛndāvana today. She was in quite a disturbed state. She has come to see Śrīla Prabhupāda to complain that her son was mistreated at the *gurukula.* She said that he had been hit, and therefore she had taken him out of school.

Prabhupāda was very upset to hear that a young boy was hit by a teacher. He emphasized very strongly that this should not be done for any reason. "If a teacher hits a child he should not just be sent away, he should be hanged! He should be hanged! He should be hanged!" he declared, stabbing his right index finger in the air for emphasis.

Later, Gopāla Kṛṣṇa discounted Kiśorī's claim and said that her son is quite incorrigible and has caused considerable disturbance at the school. Contrary to Kiśorī's assertion that she is keeping him away, he said the teachers are not allowing him to attend.

Despite this, Prabhupāda continued to stress the point that teachers must be very kind and loving with the children, as well as strict.

April 17th, 1976

We took our last walk along Juhu Beach this morning, as Śrīla Prabhupāda will be leaving tomorrow to begin his world tour. The conversation took up from yesterday's discussion about science. Dr. Patel began by stating that the scientists of *aparā vidyā*, or material knowledge, and those with *parā vidyā*, or superior spiritual knowledge, like Śrīla Prabhupāda, must not have any quarrel.

Prabhupāda's response was frank. "No, there is no quarrel, but we say that these are for the rascals. Yes. *Aparā vidyā* is for the rascals." Unless one comes to the point of understanding Kṛṣṇa, he said, he is still in the *aparā vidyā* and is therefore less intelligent.

Dr. Patel was firm in his belief that although we are spirit soul, *aparā vidyā* is necessary since we have a body.

Again Prabhupāda disagreed. "No, no. No. That is to make the best use of a bad bargain, how to use the body best to perfect *parā vidyā*. That is intelligence. Just like you have a car. A car is not neglected. We don't kick out the car, but it must be used for spreading Kṛṣṇa consciousness."

"That is what I say, sir, that you must have the knowledge of car, and that knowledge of car is *aparā vidyā*.

"No. No. No. There is no need of. You have the car, you can go from this place to that place very quickly, so utilize it for Kṛṣṇa conscious."

"They must know how to drive it. That is knowledge. Why do you say no?" Dr. Patel protested.

"That automatically comes," Prabhupāda said.

"How can automatically? Nothing can come automatically."

Prabhupāda explained. "You'll see many drivers. They do not know about mechanics, but they are very first-class driver."

"Well, learning driving is a knowledge of driving," Dr. Patel said.

"You are a physician," Śrīla said. "You are not a motor mechanic, but you know how to drive. That is not very difficult thing."

Gurudāsa Mahārāja grasped Śrīla Prabhupāda's point. "Isn't it when you drive for Kṛṣṇa, doesn't it become *parā vidyā* then?"

"Yes," Prabhupāda answered. "Everything is done for Kṛṣṇa, that is *parā vidyā*."

Dr. Patel clearly likes to think of himself as an appreciator of both disciplines. He seemed intent on proving that scientists are not as bad as Prabhupāda makes them out to be. This is probably because, as a doctor, he considered himself something of a scientist. In his opinion, if they studied Kṛṣṇa's energy, in one sense they are connected to Kṛṣṇa. He obviously felt that this study was necessary in order to come to higher spiritual knowledge.

Śrīla Prabhupāda pointed out, though, that the intentions of the scientists are not as noble as the doctor likes to think. "Now scientists say that 'Now we are advanced. We don't require God.' There is a book. Yes. 'We don't require God. Now we shall adjust. We shall create human beings according to our necessity.'"

Dr. Patel conceded the point, yet persisted in trying to defend the scientists. But as we walked steadily across the sand, occasional jets booming overhead and the docile sea waves continuously breaking along the shore, Śrīla Prabhupāda repeatedly reduced his arguments, and he gradually began to let down his defense.

Prabhupāda's playful criticisms of Dr. Patel's arguments often make us laugh. But for Dr. Patel, being constantly defeated in front of Prabhupāda's young disciples is sometimes a little hard to take, as he wants us to show him respect. Today he took it all good naturedly because he actually has great appreciation for Śrīla Prabhupāda. "So I look a fool and they'll become wise, all of them, eh?" he said.

Without irony, Prabhupāda immediately reassured him. "Oh, yes. You are wise."

"They want that I should say something, and then you call me a rascal, and they take pleasure in it."

Gurudāsa Mahārāja assured him that although we may laugh, we do not do it out of envy, or pleasure in seeing him discomforted. "No, no. *Para-duḥkhī.* A Vaiṣṇava is not happy in someone else's misery."

Śrīla Prabhupāda encouraged him that actually he should associate more with the devotees [*sat-saṇga*]. "Amongst devotees, if you remain, then *Kṛṣṇa-kathā* will be so pleasing, *rasāyana kathā.*"

"Even good literature *saṇga* is also *sat-saṇga,* is it not?" Dr. Patel asked Prabhupāda.

"Yes. Yes."

"So in the morning I do your *sat-saṇga,* and afterwards I do the *sat-saṇga* of *Bhāgavata* and *Bhagavad-gītā.* So it is a continuous *sat-saṇga.* So don't say I am not doing it," Dr. Patel laughed.

"No, no, I don't say that you are rascal," Prabhupāda humbly said. "Rather, I think myself rascal because I could not draw you in my temple." Everyone laughed at this.

Dr. Patel was immediately appreciative and reciprocated the sentiment. "You have drawn me lot, but still, you are dragging me by leg nowadays. I think I am not fit to be with you, so far I consider myself. I must correct myself and all my defects. Otherwise I would pollute you."

It was a pleasant exchange. Dr. Patel was encouraged, and he gave Prabhupāda his assurance that he intends to fully dedicate himself to spiritual life. "I will become after sixty-five."

Prabhupāda laughed. "You are fifteen years late already!"

* * *

For his final class in Bombay, Śrīla Prabhupāda elaborated upon some of the qualities of a *brahmacārī* described by Nārada Muni.

One of these qualities is *dakṣa,* or expert. He gave the example of Ragunātha dāsa Gosvāmī who was completely disinterested in material affairs. Yet when it was required, he rescued his uncle from a difficult situation by expert political dealings. Prabhupāda said that being a devotee does not mean we cannot do anything else.

"This is called *dakṣa.*" Not that because he has become Kṛṣṇa conscious and *Vaiṣṇava,* he is unable to do anything of this material world. No. One who is Kṛṣṇa conscious, he is conscious of everything, and he knows how to deal with them. That is called *dakṣa;* not that 'Because I have become Kṛṣṇa conscious I have no knowledge in other things.' No. That is intelligence, to know something of everything and to know everything of something. That is wanted. You may be expert, a devotee.

You know everything of devotional service, but you should not be callous. You know something of everything."

Another quality he described was *śraddadhānaḥ*, being fully faithful to the words of one's spiritual master. Of course, Śrīla Prabhupāda is the epitome of this quality. He told us that when he read a purport on a verse in *Bhagavad-gītā* by Śrīla Viśvanātha Cakravartī Ṭhākura, he realized the importance of his Guru Mahārāja's instruction to him to preach in the English language.

He urged us to take particular note of the Ṭhākura's advice. "*śraddadhānaḥ*, faithful. Faithful to whom? To the spiritual master. Whatever he says, the *brahmacārī* should take it: 'Yes, it is my life and soul.' That is the explanation given by Viśvanātha Cakravartī Ṭhākura. He is explaining with reference to the verse *vyavasāyātmikā buddhir ekeha kuru-nandana.* He very nicely explains. You have perhaps read it. Viśvanātha Cakravartī Ṭhākura has taught very, very nicely about guru. Therefore he has written in *Gurv-aṣṭaka*, '*yasya prasādad bhagavat-prasādah.*'

"He is the practical example of *guru-bhakti,* Viśvanātha Cakravartī Ṭhākura. He accepted his guru, Narottama dāsa Ṭhākura. So he said, 'I am not interested for my salvation or going back to Godhead. I am not interested. Interested means it may come; it may not come. That I don't mind. But I am interested only with the words of my guru. That is my life. Whether I will be successful or not successful, it doesn't matter. I must take the words of my Guru Mahārāja as my life and soul.'

"Actually that is the secret of success. *Yasya deve parā bhaktir yathā deve tathā gurau, tasyaite kathitā hy arthāḥ prakāśante mahātmanaḥ*. So that is the secret of success, *śraddadhānaḥ,* to accept the words of guru very, very faithfully."

Śrīla Prabhupāda's words had all the more impact because he is the embodiment of faith in guru. With nothing more than faith in the words of his spiritual master, he struggled for thirty years to preach in India before Kṛṣṇa rewarded his efforts with the phenomenal success of his worldwide ISKCON society. It is evident that all the secrets of Vedic knowledge have been revealed to Prabhupāda, and now he is revealing his secret of success to us.

* * *

Some film producers came to see Prabhupāda during the evening *darśana* on the roof. Midst the swaying fronds of the coconut trees and as a cooling breeze gently blew, Prabhupāda sat comfortably on his *āsana* and preached to the guests until 9:00 p.m.

They spoke briefly about the guru who advertises 'TM', or 'Transcendental Meditation.' When Śrīla Prabhupāda asked what the purpose of this process was, one of the visitors said that it pacifies the mind, and that also helps to relieve high blood pressure.

Prabhupāda had me look up the meaning of 'transcendental' in the dictionary. It was given as 'going above the mind.' So Prabhupāda asked, if transcendental means 'above the mind,' why is this guru calling his system 'Transcendental Meditation' when it deals on the level of the mind's activities? It is simply cheating, he told them.

April 18th, 1976

Prabhupāda took his massage at 5:00 a.m. after which he bathed.

I had been rushing about since 3:30 a.m. preparing for the trip. First I packed Prabhupāda's suitcase, then my own. After that I massaged Śrīla Prabhupāda, and while he bathed, I put away his dirty cloth, set out a clean set and then changed into my clean clothes. After I packed the massage paraphernalia, I set up his *tilaka* in his room. As he sat at his desk to apply it, I rushed to pack his bathing gear. And after he had finished his *tilaka,* I hurried back to complete the packing of his desk items.

When I came to his room at 7:00 a.m. with everything packed and ready to go, he was ready to leave and noted that I was also. But he didn't budge. Instead, he looked at me, tipped his head up slightly, and said, "So, you have something?" I could not think what he was alluding to; perhaps I had forgotten something.

With a slight upward gesture of his eyebrows he indicated my vest pocket, and it suddenly dawned on me what he was referring to. Last night, at the end of the evening *darśana,* I had picked up a ten-rupee note that one of his guests had placed at the foot of his *āsana*. Usually, Prabhupāda immediately puts such *dakṣiṇā* in his desk drawer or his red bag, and later it is deposited in some account, such as the Māyāpur-Vṛndāvana Trust. This time, however, I had slipped it into my pocket, thinking to give it to him later. But I had forgotten about it. I took it out of my pocket, and he called Girirāja in, handed over the note, and told him to deposit it. That matter settled, he then headed out the door.

Prabhupāda does not overlook the slightest detail. He is always very, very careful to see that whatever anyone gives him is used in Kṛṣṇa's service and not wasted. He is exact down to the last rupee. Being such an conscientious manager, I can understand why he becomes upset at wasteful and careless disciples for whom, in the Western countries, money is so easily available.

Finally, at 7:10 a.m., together with Puṣṭa Kṛṣṇa Swami and myself, he left for the airport to begin the long journey to Melbourne, via Colombo and Singapore.

Within a short while we were seated on the plane, on our way to Australia. Śrīla Prabhupāda and I were seated in first class, and Puṣṭa Kṛṣṇa Mahārāja sat in the economy section. As we took off, I glanced out the window for a last look at Bombay. We won't return until August.

As soon as we were airborne, Prabhupāda had his breakfast. I set out each of the four circular, stainless-steel containers and filled them with whatever Prabhupāda indicated from his well-packed tiffin box. From the multi-tiered container he ate *sabjis, puris,* rice, some fried savories, *vaḍa,* and *samosa,* as well as some fruit and *sandeśa.* I served him very carefully, much to the interest of the other passengers.

As he does wherever and whenever he travels, Prabhupāda maintained his regular eating schedule. Knowing this I was well equipped for the journey, and I am by now well-versed in all the items that Prabhupāda requires when traveling. On planes he never accepts anything provided by the airlines, because they handle meat. He doesn't even use the utensils like knives, forks, and spoons, because generally the metal ones have already been used. He will use new plastic ones though. He won't eat anything touched by *karmīs*. He will not even accept the salt that they provide. So in addition to the *prasādam*, I carried small packets of salt, pepper, and ginger.

Generally he eats alone, but on the plane this was not possible. Unperturbed by his surroundings and the curiosity of the passengers, he simply continued following his daily schedule. He ate very slowly and carefully. By watching Prabhupāda take *prasādam* it was easy to understand that the Lord's mercy, *prasādam*, is to be rendered service by the devotee. *Prasādam* should be eaten as humbly as one performs other forms of devotional service. Completely free from lust and other mundane attributes, Śrīla Prabhupāda's devotion was apparent even in the most basic activity of eating.

When he finished his meal, Prabhupāda told me to call Puṣṭa Kṛṣṇa Mahārāja. Together, we shared whatever was left over. I always feel a little uncomfortable eating in Prabhupāda's presence, thinking that it may offend him. But he always insists that his servants take *prasādam* whenever he does, and he is concerned to see we are taken care of. Some of the passengers saw us eating the remnants of Prabhupāda's half-chewed *puris*, and I think they were a little shocked. But, of course, in Prabhupāda's association we were unaffected by their mundane opinions.

At the end of his meal, Prabhupāda very carefully cleaned his mouth with a toothpick, then poured a little water on his hand to cleanse it, before drinking from the cup. He first swilled his mouth out and then drank, and thereafter he completed his ablutions in the bathroom. By the time he returned, I had cleared everything away.

Prabhupāda spent the rest of the time before our arrival in Colombo silently chanting *japa*.

The plane landed in Colombo at 10:30 a.m. As we waited on the tarmac, Prabhupāda recalled his first trip there in 1965 aboard the *Jaladuta*, bound for the USA. Because he had never been to Śrī Lanka before, the captain of the ship very kindly arranged for a car to take him around the city to show him the sights.

On the two-hour leg to Singapore he read the typed manuscript entitled *Matter Comes from Life,* sent to him by Mādhava dāsa, one of our scientist devotees.

I moved to an empty seat nearby to give him some room and privacy, and also to nap and chant my rounds.

The plane touched down in Singapore at 5:00 p.m. for a four-hour transit stop. Because Prabhupāda and I were in first class, he decided to use the first-class lounge to rest in. However, it was located inside the airport, and to get to it we had to pass through immigration.

As soon as the officials saw our shaved heads and robes they refused us entry. I felt angry to see these mundane men obstruct the entry of a pure devotee, yet sad that they were guaranteeing their stay in the material world by their offense. Prabhupāda is undergoing so much trouble, with no personal motive whatever, simply to do good for others, yet they were such rascals that they wanted to obstruct him.

Puṣṭa Kṛṣṇa Swami argued with them for nearly fifteen minutes before they agreed to let us through. They gave us a special pass, and we proceeded to the lounge, which turned out to be a public bar. It was closed when we first walked in, so Śrīla Prabhupāda sat at one of the tables and took his lunch. Afterward, he lay down on one of the seats to nap.

But before long the bar was opened, and the place soon filled up with noisy drinkers and smokers. Prabhupāda went out to sit—for what turned out to be several hours—on the uncomfortable molded-plastic seats in the terminal.

The plane was due to begin boarding at 8:15 p.m. for a 10:00 p.m. departure to Australia, but some mechanism on the plane required attention, and we boarded an hour late. There were further delays, and we had to sit on the aircraft for another three hours. To keep everybody happy, the crew handed out free drinks to the passengers. Consequently everyone became very noisy and boisterous. Prabhupāda sat patiently through the ordeal without complaining. It was not until 12:30 a.m. that the Qantas flight took off.

Flying in the first-class section offered more sitting room but little facility for lying down. So after a short while in the air,

Prabhupāda went back into the economy section and lay across an empty row of seats until about 3:30 a.m.

Our seats were directly in front of the movie screen, and when Prabhupāda returned there was a war movie playing. Without headphones, we both watched as the hero, David Niven, ran up a mountain side, got shot, then blown up, and then again began fighting in hand-to-hand combat.

Prabhupāda looked for a couple of minutes and then turned to me with mock surprise. "Still alive?" he said, and laughed. With the sound turned off the movie looked like what it was, a silly make-believe, the epitome of the material world. Prabhupāda turned away and chanted *japa.*

Although he tolerated everything without complaint, the unbroken, seven-hour flight to Australia, plus the long delay in Singapore, was very difficult for him. He mentioned that any trip longer than three to four hours is a strain. Nevertheless, for preaching he is prepared to accept any difficulty; his own personal comfort is his last consideration.

CHART OF THE DAYS OF THE WEEK

English days of the week	Name of Demigods		Bhagavatam list of planets		Sanskrit day of the week
	Teutonic	Roman	English	Sanskrit	
Sunday	Sun		Sun	Ravi	Ravi-bara
Monday	Moon		Moon	Soma	Soma-bara
Tuesday	Tiw	Mars	Venus	Sukra-graha	Mangal-bara
Wednesday	Woden	Mercury	Mercury	Budha-graha	Budha-bara
Thursday	Thor	Jupiter	Mars	Angaraka-graha	Brhaspati-bara
Friday	Freya	Venus	Jupiter	Brhaspati-graha	Sukra-bara
Saturday		Saturn	Saturn	Sanaiscar-graha	Sani-bara

Appendix A

ABOUT THE AUTHOR

Hari-śauri dāsa was born in England on November 17th, 1950. In May 1971 he emigrated to Australia where, on the second day of arrival, he met the members of the newly-emerging Kṛṣṇa consciousness movement. He was duly accepted as an initiated disciple by His Divine Grace A. C. Bhaktivedanta Swami Prabhupāda on April 9th, 1972 in Sydney.

In August of 1975 he moved to the newly-opened ISKCON Krishna-Balaram temple in Vṛndāvana, India, where he served as temple commander. In November of the same year, he joined Śrīla Prabhupāda's personal entourage, remaining as His Divine Grace's servant for sixteen months.

In March of 1977 Śrīla Prabhupāda appointed him ISKCON's Governing Body Commissioner for Australia, New Zealand and Indonesia, a service he performed for over seven years. During that period he oversaw the growth of the ISKCON society in the South Seas from four temples and *āśramas,* to seventeen, including four farming communities, two schools and several restaurants. He was also instrumental in establishing branches of the Bhaktivedanta Book Trust in Australia and Indonesia.

In 1986 he began the work of transforming the diary he kept while traveling with Śrīla Prabhupāda into a book.

In 1990 he moved to America and worked as publisher for *Back to Godhead* magazine, the Kṛṣṇa consciousness movement's spiritual periodical, for a year.

He is currently living in the United States with his wife Śītala dāsī and daughter Rasarāṇī, writing the remaining volumes of *A Transcendental Diary.*

GLOSSARY

A

Abhiṣeka—a bathing ceremony, particularly for the coronation of a king or the installation of the Lord's Deity form.
Absolute—Truth the ultimate source of all energies.
Ācārya—an ideal teacher, who teaches by his personal example; a spiritual master.
Acintya-bhedābheda-tattva—Lord Caitanya's doctrine of the "inconceivable oneness and difference" of God and His energies.
Adharma—irreligion.
Advaita Prabhu—an incarnation of Viṣṇu who appeared as a principal associate of Lord Caitanya Mahāprabhu.
Ahaṁ brahmāsmi—the Vedic aphorism "I am spirit."
Ahaṅkāra—false ego, by which the soul misidentifies with the material body.
Ahiṁsā—nonviolence.
Ajāmila—a fallen *brāhmaṇa* who was saved from hell by chanting the name of Lord Nārāyaṇa at the time of death.
Ajñāta-sukṛti—pious or devotional activity performed accidentally, without knowledge of its effect.
Ānanda—spiritual bliss.
Ananta Śeṣa—the Lord's thousand-headed serpent incarnation, who serves as the bed of Viṣṇu and sustains the planets on His hoods.
Aparā-prakṛti—the inferior, material energy of the Lord (matter).
Ārati—a ceremony for greeting the Lord with chanting and offerings of food, lamps, fans, flowers and incense.
Arjuna—one of the five Pāṇḍava brothers. Kṛṣṇa became his chariot driver and spoke the *Bhagavad-gītā* to him.
Āsana—sitting place
Āśramas—the four spiritual orders according to the Vedic social system: *brahmacārya* (student life), *gṛhastha* (householder life), *vānaprastha* (retirement) and *sannyāsa* (renunciation).
Asura—a person opposed to the service of the Lord.
Atharva Veda—one of the four *Vedas*, the original revealed scriptures spoken by the Lord Himself.
Ātma—the self (the body, the mind, the intellect, the Supersoul or the individual soul).
Avaiṣṇava—a nondevotee.
Avatāra—a descent, or incarnation, of the Supreme Lord.
Āyur-veda—the Vedic scriptures containing medical science.

B

Bābājī—a person who dwells alone in one place and leads a life of meditation, penance and austerity.
Baladeva—See: Balarāma.
Balarāma (Baladeva)—the first plenary expansion of Lord Kṛṣṇa. He appeared as the son of Rohiṇī.
Battle of Kurukṣetra—a battle between the Kurus and the Pāṇḍavas, which took place five thousand years ago and before which Lord Kṛṣṇa spoke *Bhagavad-gītā* to Arjuna.
Bhagavad-gītā—the discourse between the Supreme Lord, Kṛṣṇa, and His devotee Arjuna epounding devotional service as both the principal means and the ultimate end of spiritual perfection.
Bhagavān—the Supreme Lord, who possesses all opulences in full.
Bhāgavata Purāṇa—See: *Śrīmad-Bhāgavatam.*
Bhāgavata-vidhi—the devotional process of serving pure devotees and preaching *Śrīmad-Bhāgavatam.*
Bhajana—any of various practices of direct worship of the Lord, especially hearing and chanting (or singing) His glories.
Bhakta—a devotee of the Supreme Lord.
Bhakti—devotional service to the Supreme Lord.
Bhakti-rasāmṛta-sindhu—Rūpa Gosvāmī's definitive explanation of the science of devotional service.
Bhaktisiddhānta Sarasvatī Ṭhākura—(1874-1937) the spiritual master of Śrīla A. C. Bhaktivedānta Swami Prabhupāda, and thus the spiritual grandfather of the present-day Kṛṣṇa consciousness movement. A powerful preacher, he founded sixty-four *maṭhas* (temple-*āśramas*) throughout India and abroad.
Bhaktivedāntas—advanced transcendentalists who have realized the conclusion of the *Vedas* through devotional service.
Bhaktivinoda Ṭhākura—(1838-1915) the great-grandfather of the present-day Kṛṣṇa consciousness movement. He was the spiritual master of Śrīla Gaurakiśora dāsa Bābājī and father of Śrīla Bhaktisiddhānta Sarasvatī.
Bhakti-yoga—linking with the Supreme Lord through devotional service.
Bhārata Mahārāja—an ancient king of India from whom the Pāṇḍavas descended. A great devotee of the Lord, he developed an attachment causing him to take birth as a deer. In his next life, as the brāhmaṇa Jada Bharata, he attained spiritual perfection.
Bhārata-varṣa—India, named after King Bhārata.
Bhāva—the preliminary stage of ecstatic love of God.
Bhogī—sense gratifier
Bhukti—material enjoyment.
Brahmā—the first created living being and secondary creator of the material universe.

Brahmacārī—one in the first order of spiritual life; a celibate student of a spiritual master.
Brahmacārya—celibate student life; the first order of Vedic spiritual life.
Brahmajyoti—the spiritual effulgence emanating from the transcendental body of Lord Kṛṣṇa and illuminating the spiritual world.
Brahman—(1) the individual soul; (2) the impersonal, all-pervasive aspect of the Supreme; (3) the Supreme Personality of Godhead ; (4) the *mahat-tattva*, or total material substance.
Brāhmaṇa—a person wise in Vedic knowledge, fixed in goodness and knowledgeable of Brahman, the Absolute Truth; a member of the first Vedic social order.
Brāhmaṇa thread—a multistranded thread worn by *brāhmaṇas* across the left shoulder and chest.
Brahma-saṁhitā—a very ancient Sanskrit scripture recording the prayers of Brahmā to the Supreme Lord, Govinda.
Brajbhāṣaḥ—dialect of Hindi spoken in the Vṛndāvana area.
Brijvāsī—inhabitant of Vṛndāvana See also: Vrajavasi
Buddha—an incarnation of the Supreme Lord who, by bewildering the atheists stopped them from misusing the *Vedas*.

C

Caitanya-caritāmṛta—a biography of Śrī Caitanya Mahāprabhu composed in Bengali in the late sixteenth century by Śrīla Kṛṣṇadāsa Kavirāja.
Caitanya Mahāprabhu—(1486-1534) the Supreme Lord appearing as His own greatest devotee to teach love of God, especially through the process of congregational chanting of His holy names.
Caitya-guru—Lord Kṛṣṇa personally giving guidance as a spiritual master from within the heart of an advanced devotee.
Cāṇakya—the prime minister of King Candragupta. His aphorisms are still famous throughout India.
Candana—a cosmetic paste prepared from sandalwood. It is used in Deity worship.
Capāti—a flat bread made from whole-wheat flour.
Chonki—a low wooden table.
Crore—ten million; one hundred *lakhs*.

D

Dāl—dried beans such as urad or mung or the soup made therefrom.
Dakṣiṇa—a disciple's gift to his spiritual master, collected by begging and given as a token of gratitude.
Dāmodara—Lord Kṛṣṇa in His pastime of being bound by mother Yaśodā.
Daṇḍa—a staff carried by those in the renounced order of life.
Daṇḍavats—respectful obeisances, falling flat like a rod.

Daridra-nārāyaṇa—"poor Nārāyaṇa," an offensive term used by Māyāvādīs to equate poor men with the Supreme Lord.
Deity of the Lord—the authorized form of Kṛṣṇa worshiped in temples.
Demigods—universal controllers and residents of the higher planets.
Demons—impious beings who do not follow the instructions of the Lord.
Deva—a demigod or godly person.
Devakī—the wife of Vasudeva and mother of Lord Kṛṣṇa.
Devotional service—the process of worshiping Lord Kṛṣṇa by dedicating one's thoughts, words and actions to Him with love.
Dhāma—abode, place of residence. The term usually refers to the Lord's abodes.
Dharma—religion; duty, especially everyone's eternal service nature.
Dhotī—a simple garment worn by men in Vedic culture.
Dhruva Mahārāja—a great devotee who as a child performed severe austerities to meet the Lord and get the kingdom denied him. He received an entire planet the Pole Star and God realization as well.
Durgā—the personified material energy and the wife of Lord Śiva.
Duryodhana—the eldest son of Dhṛtarāṣṭra and chief rival of the Pāṇḍavas.
Dvādaśī—the twelfth day after the full or new moon, thus the day after Ekādaśī.
Dvārakā—the offshore-island kingdom of Lord Kṛṣṇa, where He performed pastimes five thousand years ago in India.

E

Ekādaśī—a special day for increased remembrance of Kṛṣṇa that comes on the eleventh day after both the full and new moon. Abstinence from grains and beans is prescribed.

F

False ego—the conception that "I am this material body."

G

Gamchā—a item of cloth, worn casually, usually around the waist.
Gandharvas—demigod singers and musicians.
Gaṅgā—the Ganges River.
Gañja—marijuana.
Garbhodakaśayī Viṣṇu—the second Viṣṇu expansion, who enters each universe and from whose navel grows a lotus upon which Lord Brahmā appears.
Gauḍīya-Mādhva-sampradāya—the Vaiṣṇava disciplic succession of bona fide spiritual masters coming through Śrīla Mādhvācārya and Śrī

Caitanya Mahāprabhu; the followers in that tradition.

Gaudiya Matha—the institution founded by Śrīla Bhaktisiddhānta Sarasvatī Ṭhākura.

Gaurakiśora dāsa Bābājī—the disciple of Śrīla Bhaktivinoda Ṭhākura who was the spiritual master of Śrīla Bhaktisiddhānta Sarasvatī Ṭhākura.

Gaura Pūrṇimā—the appearance day of Lord Caitanya.

Gāyatrī-mantra—the Vedic prayer chanted silently by *brāhmaṇas* at sunrise, noon and sunset.

Ghee—clarified butter.

Godhead—the ultimate source of all energies.

Goloka Vṛndāvana (Kṛṣṇaloka)—the highest spiritual planet, Lord Kṛṣṇa's personal abode.

Gopāla—the Supreme Lord, Kṛṣṇa, who protects the cows.

Gopī-jana-vallabha—the Supreme Lord, Kṛṣṇa, who is dear to the *gopīs.*

Gopīs—Kṛṣṇa's cowherd girl friends, who are His most surrendered and confidential devotees.

Gosvāmī—a controller of the mind and senses; the title of one in the renounced, or *sannyāsa,* order.

Govinda—the Supreme Lord, Kṛṣṇa, who gives pleasure to the land, the senses, and the cows.

Gṛhamedhī—a materialistic householder.

Gṛhastha—regulated householder life; the second order of Vedic spiritual life; one in that order.

Gūnas—the three modes, or qualities, of material nature: goodness, passion and ignorance.

Guru-kula—a school of Vedic learning. Boys begin at age five and live as celibate students, guided by a spiritual master.

Guru-pūjā—worship of the spiritual master.

H

Hanuman—the great monkey servitor of Lord Rāmacandra.

Hare—See: Rādhā(rāṇī)

Hare Kṛṣṇa mantra—the great chant for deliverance: Hare Kṛṣṇa, Hare Kṛṣṇa, Kṛṣṇa Kṛṣṇa, Hare Hare, Hare Rāma, Hare Rāma, Rāma Rāma, Hare Hare.

Hari—the Supreme Lord, who removes all obstacles to spiritual progress.

Hari-bhakti-vilāsa—Sanātana Gosvāmī's book on the rules and regulations of Vaiṣṇava life.

Haridāsa Ṭhākura—a great devotee and associate of Lord Caitanya Mahāprabhu who chanted three hundred thousand names of God a day.

Hari-nāma-saṅkīrtana—congregational chanting of the holy names of the Supreme Lord.

Haṭha-yoga—the practice of postures and breathing exercises for achieving purification and sense control.

Heavenly planets—the higher planets of the universe, residences of the demigods.
Hell—hellish planets within this universe meant for the punishment and rectification of the sinful.
Hindu—a newly-concocted name for members of various social and religious groups of India. The term has no spiritual significance.
Hiraṇyakaśipū—a powerful demon who tormented his son Prahlāda, a great devotee, and was slain by Lord Nṛsiṁhadeva.
Hṛṣīkeśa—the Supreme Lord, the supreme master of everyone's senses.

I

ISKCON—the International Society for Krishna Consciousness.
Īśopaniṣad—one of the principal Upaniṣads.
Īśvara—the Supreme Lord, who is the supreme controller.

J

Jagāi and Mādhāi—two great debauchees whom Lord Nityānanda converted into Vaiṣṇavas.
Jagannātha—the Supreme Lord, who is Lord of the universe; the particular Deity form of that Lord at Purī, Orissa.
Jagat—the material universe.
Janmāṣṭamī—the celebration of Lord Kṛṣṇa's appearance in the material world.
Japa—soft recitation of the Lord's holy names as private meditation.
Jaya—an exclamation meaning "All victory to you!" or "All glories to you!"
Jīva (jīvātmā)—the living entity, who is an eternal individual soul, part and parcel of the Supreme Lord.
Jīva Gosvāmī—one of the six Vaiṣṇava spiritual masters who directly followed Lord Caitanya Mahāprabhu and systematically presented His teachings.

K

Kāla—time
Kālī—See: Durgā
Kali, age of—See: Kali-yuga.
Kāliya—the many-headed serpent chastised by Lord Kṛṣṇa for poisoning a section of the Yamunā River.
Kali-yuga (Age of Kali)—the present age, characterized by quarrel. It is last in the cycle of four ages and began five thousand years ago.
Kāma—lust.
Kaniṣtha-adhikārī—a neophyte devotee.

Kapha—mucus, one of the three main elements of the body.
Kapila—the incarnation of the Supreme Lord who appeared as the son of Kardama Muni and Devahūti and taught the Kṛṣṇa conscious Sāṅkhya philosophy.
Karaṇa Ocean—the corner of the spiritual universe in which Lord Mahā-Viṣṇu lies down to create all the material universes.
Karaṇodakaśayī Viṣṇu—Mahā-Viṣṇu, the expansion of the Supreme Lord from whom all material universes emanate.
Karatālas—hand cymbals used in *kīrtana.*
Karma—material, fruitive activity and its reactions; also, fruitive actions performed in accordance with Vedic injunctions.
Karma-yoga—the path of God realization through dedicating the fruits of one's work to God..
Karmī—one engaged in karma, fruitive activity; a materialist.
Katyāyanī—the material energy personified. She is also known as Durgā.
Kauravas—the descendants of Kuru who fought against the Pāṇḍavas in the Battle of Kurukṣetra.
Kīrtana—the devotional process of chanting the names and glories of the Supreme Lord.
Kṛpā-siddhi—perfection attained simply by the blessings of a great devotee or transcendentalist.
Kṛṣṇa—the original, two-armed form of the Supreme Personality of Godhead.
Kṛṣṇa-prasādam—See: *Prasādam.*
Kṣatriya—a warrior or administrator; the second Vedic social order.
Kṣīrodakaśayī Viṣṇu—the expansion of the Supreme Lord who enters the heart of every living being as the Supersoul.
Kumāras—four learned ascetic sons of Lord Brahmā appearing eternally as children.
Kumkum—a red cosmetic powder.
Kurukṣetra—a place of pilgrimage held sacred since ancient times and the site of a great war fought five thousand years ago; located near New Delhi, India.
Kuvera—the treasurer of the demigods.

L

Lakh—one hundred thousand
Lakṣmī—the goddess of fortune and eternal consort of Lord Nārāyaṇa.
Lakṣmi-Nārāyaṇa—the transcendental couple of Lord Kṛṣṇa in His four-armed form and the goddess of fortune, Lakṣmī.
Liberation—freedom from the material concept of life; being situated in one's constitutional position as an eternal servant of God.
Līlā—pastimes.
Loka—a planet.

M

Mādhvācārya—a great thirteenth-century Vaiṣṇava spiritual master who preached the theistic philosophy of pure dualism.
Mahābhārata—Vyāsadeva's epic history of greater India, which includes the events of the Kurukṣetra war and the narration of *Bhagavad-gītā.*
Mahājanas—great self-realized souls, authorities on the science of Kṛṣṇa consciousness.
Mahā-mantra—the great chant for deliverance: Hare Kṛṣṇa, Hare Kṛṣṇa, Kṛṣṇa Kṛṣṇa, Hare Hare/ Hare Rāma, Hare Rāma, Rāma Rāma, Hare Hare.
Mahāmāyā—the illusory, material energy of the Supreme Lord.
Maha-prasādam—the remnants of food directly offered to the Deity of Lord Kṛṣṇa.
Mahārāja—a title for a great king or sage.
Mahātmā—a "great soul," an exalted devotee of Lord Kṛṣṇa.
Mahā-Viṣṇu—the expansion of the Supreme Lord from whom all material universes emanate.
Maṅgala-ārati—the daily predawn worship ceremony knowing the Deity of the Supreme Lord.
Mantra—a transcendental sound or Vedic hymn that can deliver the mind from illusion.
Maṭha—a monastery.
Mathurā—Lord Kṛṣṇa's abode, surrounding Vṛndāvana, where He took birth and to which He later returned after performing His child hood pastimes in Vṛndāvana.
Matsya—the fish incarnation of the Supreme Lord.
Māyā—the inferior, illusory energy of the Supreme Lord, which rules over this material creation; also, forgetfulness of one's relationship with Kṛṣṇa.
Māyāvādī—an impersonalist philosopher who conceives of the Absolute as ultimately formless and the living entity as equal to God.
Mlecchas—uncivilized humans, outside the Vedic system of society, who are generally meat-eaters.
Mokṣa—liberation from material bondage.
Mṛdaṅga—a clay drum used in congregational chanting.
Mūḍha—a foolish, asslike person.
Mukti—liberation from material bondage.
Mukunda—the Supreme Lord, who is the giver of liberation.
Muni—a sage.

N

Naiṣṭhika-brahmacārī—one who has been celibate since birth.
Nāma-aparādha—an offense against the holy name of the Lord.

Nanda Mahārāja—the king of Vraja and foster father of Lord Kṛṣṇa.
Nārada Muni—a pure devotee of the Lord who travels throughout the universes in his eternal body, glorifying devotional service.
Nārada-pañcarātra—Nārada Muni's book on the processes of Deity worship and *mantra* meditation.
Nārāyaṇa, Lord—the Supreme Lord in His majestic, four-armed form. An expansion of Kṛṣṇa, He presides over the Vaikuṇṭha planets.
Navadvīpa—the place where Lord Caitanya appeared in this world.
Nityānanda Prabhu—the incarnation of Lord Balarāma who appeared as the principal associate of Lord Caitanya Mahāprabhu.
Nivṛtti-mārga—the path of renunciation, which leads to liberation.
Nṛsiṁhadeva—the half-man, half-lion incarnation of the Supreme Lord, who protected Prahlāda and killed the demon Hiraṇyakaśipū.
Nyāya—logic.

O

Oṁ (Omkara)—the sacred syllable that begins many Vedic *mantras* and that represents the Supreme Lord.

P

Pādayātrā—a journey or pilgrimage undertaken on foot.
Pāṇḍavas—sons of Pāṇḍu; Yudhiṣṭhira, Bhīma, Arjuna, Nakula and Sahadeva, the five warrior-brothers who were intimate friends and devotees of Lord Kṛṣṇa.
Paṇḍita—a scholar.
Parā—transcendental.
Paramahaṁsa—a topmost, swanlike devotee of the Supreme Lord; the highest stage of *sannyāsa.*
Paramātmā—the Supersoul, a Viṣṇu expansion of the Supreme Lord residing in the heart of each embodied living entity and pervading all of material nature.
Paramparā—a disciplic succession.
Parā prakṛti—the superior energy of the Supreme Lord.
Parivrājakācārya—the third stage of *sannyāsa,* wherein the devotee constantly travels and preaches.
Prabhu—master.
Prabhupāda, Śrīla—the founder and spiritual preceptor of the Hare Kṛṣṇa movement.
Prabodhānanda Sarasvatī—a great Vaiṣṇava poet-philosopher and devotee of Lord Caitanya Mahāprabhu.
Prahlāda Mahārāja—a devotee persecuted as a child by his demoniac father Hiraṇyakaśipū but protected and saved by the Lord in the form of Nṛsiṁhadeva.

Prakṛta-sahajiyās—pseudodevotees of Kṛṣṇa.
Prakṛti— the energy of the Supreme; the female principle enjoyed by the male *puruṣa.*
Prasādam—the Lord's mercy; food or other items spiritualized by being first offered to the Supreme Lord.
Prāyaścitta—atonement for sinful acts.
Prema—pure love of God, the highest stage in the progressive development of devotional service.
Purāṇas—eighteen literary supplements to the *Vedas.*
Puruṣa—the enjoyer, or male; the living entity or the Supreme Lord.

R

Rādhārāṇī—Lord Kṛṣṇa's most intimate consort, who is the personification of His internal, spiritual potency.
Rajas—the material mode of passion.
Rāmacandra—an incarnation of the Supreme Lord as the perfect king.
Rāmāyaṇa—the epic history about Lord Rāmacandra, originally written by Vālmīki Muni.
Rasas—the loving moods or mellows relished in the exchange of love with the Supreme Lord.
Ratha-yātrā—an annual festival in which Deities of the Supreme Lord are drawn in procession upon huge, gaily decorated, canopied chariots.
Rāvaṇa—a demoniac ruler who was killed by Lord Rāmacandra.
Ṛg Veda—one of the four *Vedas,* the original scriptures spoken by the Lord Himself.
Ṛṣabhādeva—an incarnation of the Supreme Lord as a devotee king who, after instructing his sons in spiritual life, renounced His kingdom for a life of austerity.
Ṛṣi—a sage.
Rukmiṇī-Dvārakādhiśa—the transcendental couple manifested as Kṛṣṇa, the Lord of Dvārakā, and His queen Rukmiṇī; name of the Deities of ISKCON Los Angeles.
Rūpa Gosvāmī—the chief of the six Vaiṣṇava spiritual masters who directly followed Lord Caitanya Mahāprabhu and systematically presented His teachings.

S

Sacred thread—a thread worn by persons initiated into the chanting of the Gāyatrī *mantra.*
Sādhana—the beginning phase of devotional service, consisting of regulated practice.
Sādhu—a saintly person.
Sādhu-saṅga—the association of saintly persons.

Sahajiyā—an offensive, immature devotee who does not follow proper devotional regulations.
Śalagrama-śilā—a Deity incarnation of the Supreme Lord in the form of a stone.
Samādhi—trance; complete absorption in God consciousness.
Sāmhitās—supplementary Vedic literatures expressing the conclusions of particular self-realized authorities.
Sanātana Gosvāmī—one of the six Vaiṣṇava spiritual masters who directly followed Lord Caitanya Mahāprabhu and systematically presented His teachings.
Sāṅkhya—analytical discrimination between spirit and matter;
Saṅkīrtana—congregational glorification of the Supreme Lord, Kṛṣṇa, especially through chanting of the His holy names.
Sannyāsa—renounced life; the fourth order of Vedic spiritual life.
Sannyāsī—one in the *sannyāsa* (renounced) order.
Sari—Vedic women's dress.
Śāstra—revealed scripture, such as the Vedic literature.
Sat—eternal.
Sattva-guṇa—the material mode of goodness.
Sevā—devotional service.
Sevaka—a servant.
Sevya—one who is served.
Siddha—a perfected person, or mystic; a demigod from Siddhaloka.
Siddhi—mystic power or perfection acquired through yoga practice.
Śikṣāṣṭaka—eight verses by Lord Caitanya Mahāprabhu glorifying the chanting of the Lord's holy name.
Sītā—the eternal consort of Lord Rāmacandra.
Śiva—a special incarnation of the Lord as the demigod in charge of the mode of ignorance and the destruction of the material manifestation.
Śloka—a Sanskrit verse.
Soul—the eternal living entity who is the marginal energy, eternally part and parcel of the Supreme Lord.
Śrīdhara Svāmī—the author of the earliest extant Vaiṣṇava commentaries on *Bhagavad-gītā* and *Śrīmad-Bhāgavatam.*
Śrīla—a title indicating possession of exceptional spiritual qualities.
Śrīmad-Bhāgavatam—the Purāṇa, or history, written by Śrīla Vyāsadeva specifically give a deep understanding of Lord Kṛṣṇa, His devotees and devotional service.
Śūdra—a laborer; the fourth of the Vedic social orders.
Śukadeva Gosvāmī—the great devotee sage who spoke *Śrīmad-Bhāgavatam* to King Parīkṣit just prior to the King's death.
Supersoul—See: Paramātma.
Suras—demigods or devotees.
Svāmī—a controller of the mind and senses; the title of one in the renounced, or *sannyāsa*, order.

Śyāmasundara—the Supreme Personality of Godhead, Kṛṣṇa, who is blackish and very beautiful.

T

Tamo-guṇa—the mode of ignorance.
Tapasya—austerity; accepting some voluntary inconvenience for a higher purpose.
Tilaka—auspicious clay markings placed by devotees on the forehead and other parts of the body.
Tri-daṇḍa—a staff, made of three rods, carried by *sannyāsīs* who are devotees of Lord Kṛṣṇa, signifying service with mind, body and words.
Tulasī—a sacred plant dear to Lord Kṛṣṇa and worshiped by His devotees.

U

Upadeśāmṛta—a short Sanskrit work by Rūpa Gosvāmī containing important instructions about devotional service to Lord Kṛṣṇa.
Upaniṣads—108 philosophical works that appear within the *Vedas.*

V

Vaikuṇṭha—the spiritual world, where there is no anxiety.
Vairāgya—renunciation.
Vaiṣṇava—a devotee of Lord Viṣṇu, or Kṛṣṇa.
Vaiṣṇava-aparādha—an offense to a devotee of the Lord.
Vaiśya—a farmer or merchant; the third Vedic social order.
Varāha—the incarnation of the Supreme Lord as a boar.
Varṇas—the four Vedic social-occupational divisions of society, distinguished by quality of work and situation in the modes of nature (*guṇas*). See also: *Brāhmaṇa*; *Kṣatriya*; *Vaiśya* and *Śūdra.*
Varṇa-saṅkara—children conceived without regard for Vedic religious principles; thus, unwanted population.
Varṇāśrama-dharma—the Vedic social system of four social and four spiritual orders. See also: *Varṇa*; *Āśrama*
Vedānta—the philosophy of the *Vedānta-sūtra* of Śrīla Vyāsadeva. It contains a conclusive summary of Vedic philosophical knowledge and shows Kṛṣṇa as the goal.
Vedas—the four original revealed scriptures (*Ṛg, Sāma, Atharva* and *Yajur*).
Vedic—pertaining to a culture in which all aspects of human life are under the guidance of the Vedas.
Vidyā—knowledge.
Vidyadharas—a race of celestial beings who possess material knowledge.

Vijñāna—realized or practical knowledge.
Vimūḍhas—foolish rascals.
Viṣṇu—the Supreme Lord; Lord Kṛṣṇa's expansions in Vaikuṇṭha and for the creation and maintenance of the material universes.
Viśvanātha Cakravartī Ṭhākura—a great Vaiṣṇava spiritual master in the line of Lord Caitanya Mahāprabhu, and a commentator on *Śrīmad-Bhāgavatam* and *Bhagavad-gītā.*
Vivasvān—the demigod in charge of the sun.
Vraja(bhūmi)—See: Vṛndāvana
Vrajavāsī—inhabitant of Vṛndāvana See: Brijvasi
Vṛndāvana—Kṛṣṇa's eternal abode, where He fully manifests His quality of sweetness; the village on this earth in which He enacted His childhood pastimes five thousand years ago.
Vyāsa-pūjā—worship of the compiler of the Vedas, Vyāsadeva; worship of the bona fide spiritual master as the representative of Vyāsadeva.
Vyāsadeva—the incarnation of Lord Kṛṣṇa who gave the *Vedas, Purāṇas, Vedānta-sūtra* and *Mahābhārata* to mankind.

Y

Yajña—a Vedic sacrifice; also, the Supreme Lord, the goal and enjoyer of all sacrifices.
Yajur Veda—one of the four *Vedas,* the original revealed scriptures spoken by the Lord Himself.
Yamarāja—the demigod who punishes the sinful after death.
Yamunācārya—a great Vaiṣṇava spiritual master of the Śrī-sampradāya.
Yaśodā—the foster mother of Kṛṣṇa, who was the Queen of Vraja and wife of Mahārāja Nanda.
Yātrā—journey.
Yavana—a low-class person, generally a meat-eater; a barbarian.
Yoga—spiritual discipline undergone to link oneself with the Supreme.
Yogī—a transcendentalist striving for union with the Supreme.
Yoginī—a female yogī.
Yugas—ages in the life of the universe, occurring in a repeated cycle of four.
Yuga-dharma—the religion for the age.

A

Aṣṭāṅga-yoga, 64
Abhirām dāsa, 484, 549
Abortion, 75, 202, 419
Acyutānanda Swami
  Bhaktisiddhānta glorified by, 365
  cited on Communists, 224
  foundation-stone ceremony and, 209
  impersonalism and, 138, 204
  kīrtana led by, 177, 367
  Life Members and, 212
  moderator role by, 187
  Rama Krishna Mission and, 183
  South Indian preaching and, 62, 138, 212-13, 332, 359, 546-48
  thief impersonates, 311-12
  Vṛndāvana guests and, 524-25
Ādi Keśava Swami, 466
Aditya dāsī, 322
Admar Matha, 138
Advaita Ācārya, 283, 329, 340
Aesop's Fables, 547
Africa, 347-48
Agarwal (the thief), 311
Agarwal, Laxman S., 488, 495, 497-98, 501
Agni-pok germ, 122
Ahaṁ tvāṁ sarva-pāpebhyo, 294
Ahaṅkāra-vimūḍhātmā, 177-78
Ahmedabad, 122, 172
Ahobalam, 532
Aja dāsa, 62
Ajñāta-sukṛti, 375, 447-49
Akṣayānanda Swami
  ācārya's qualification and, 87
  cow protection and, 76
  japa standards and, 94-95
  Kanpur preaching by, 228
  Pagal Baba and, 49
  Prabhupāda chastises, 67
  Pṛthu Putra and, 39
  Vṛndāvana management and, 45, 403
Alanātha dāsa, 47, 74, 85-86, 417
Aligarh, 503
Allahabad, 344
Ambarīṣa dāsa, 15, 18, 451, 550
Amogha dāsa, 361
Ānakadundubhi dāsa, 303, 309
Analogy
  cannon and Freudism, 139
  chicken's mouth and sacrifice, 224
  cloud and Indian culture, 449
  coconut's covering and material body, 164-65
  decorating face and satisfying Kṛṣṇa, 360
  Duryodhana and scientists, 399
  electricity and Kṛṣṇa, 513-14
  elephant and sinner-atoner, 222
  finger and living entity, 188
  fingernail and matter, 359, 410
  flowers and men, 90
  flower without smell and man without education, 136
  fog and sinful desires, 230
  full moon and Caitanya, 364
  Hanuman and Prabhupāda, 391
  human body & social body, 89-90
  Kṛṣṇa and Prabhupāda, 205
  Kṛṣṇa's energy and ISKCON, 205
  leaves and women, 90
  mason and scientist, 399
  match and pure devotee, 435
  Matsya and ISKCON, 467-68
  Prahlāda and Prabhupāda, 95-96
  python and Prabhupāda, 529
  skin and spirit, 359, 410
  sparrows and materialists, 313-14
  state laws and Kṛṣṇa consciousness, 178
  stool analyzation and scientific discovery, 169
  sun and devotional service, 230
  toilet and material world, 385
  tree and planetary system, 471
  water and spiritual deviation, 435-36
  wood and conditioned soul, 435
Ananta Śeṣa, 220

Ansal, Susil, 9
Arcana-paddhati, 245
Arjuna, 26, 88, 136, 552
Arundhatī dāsī, 446, 543
Arya Samaja, 504
Asat saṅga tyāga, 526
Asher, R. E., 444
Aspiran Gardens, 243
Astrology, 78
Astronomy, Vedic, 121
Atlanta airport, 253
Atreya Ṛṣi dāsa, 413, 417
Attachment, material, 101, 229
Audalomi dāsa, 321
Aurobindo, 382, 477
Austerity, 222
Australia, 173

B

Back to Godhead, 81, 129, 197, 250, 254, 282, 438
Badruka, Hari Prasād, 442
Bahubhir militvā kīrtayeti, 468
Bahūdaka dāsa, 250-51
Balarāma, Lord, 27, 340
Balarāma dāsa, 499
Balarāma Rāsayātrā, 545
Balavanta dāsa, 330, 417
Bāṇāsura, 148
Bangalore, 511
Bangladesh, 201, 328
Bannerji, Surendranath, 382
Battle of Kurukṣetra, 207
Bavala, Gujarat, 169
Bengal, 382
Bengali Market, 500
Bengali sayings, 74, 164, 271, 424, 472, 520, 542
Bengali Sweet Shop, 14
Besant, Annie, 183-84
Bhagatjī, 25, 65, 70, 102, 161-62, 508, 528-29
Bhagavad-gītā
  authorized presentation of, 132
  Christian and, 184
  Gandhi and, 133, 233-34
  in college courses, 288
  in Dutch, 346
  as English-Sanskrit textbook, 541
  misinterpretation of, 184-85
  Prabhupāda's presentation of, 56, 132, 133, 157, 442, 477, 478
  scientists take copies of, 358
  site of, 26, 28
  source of hearing, 544
  symbolism and, 24
  understanding, 143
  universality of, 223
  violence and, 234
Bhagavad-gītā As It Is, 21, 444, 477-78
Bhagavad-gītā cited/quoted
  on birth as spiritual qualification, 159
  on charity, 241
  on divine and demonic, 145
  on falldown, 107, 232
  on Kurukṣetra, 544
  on material elements, 358
  on meditation, 214-15
  on sacrifice to Kṛṣṇa, 290
  on surrender to Lord, 427
  on tolerance, 222
  on work, 270, 276, 427
  on yogi, 440
  See also specific Sanskrit quotes
Bhagavad-gītā Como Ele E, 209
Bhagavad-gītā Tal Como Es, 77
Bhagavān dāsa, 346-47
Bhagavat Āśraya dāsa, 31, 78
Bhāgavat Darśana, 349-50
Bhagavat dāsa, 112, 257
Bhai, Manical, 176, 185
Bhakti-dīpa Mahārāja, 525, 526, 527
Bhaktijana dāsa, 381
Bhakti-rasāmṛtasindhu, 29, 251, 436, 511
Bhakti-śāstrī exams, 217-18, 225-26, 236, 239, 245, 319-20
Bhaktisiddhānta Sarasvatī Ṭhākura
  astonomy and, 121
  appearance day of, 363-68

Bhaktivinoda and, 317, 337
Bon Mahārāja and, 551
book distribution and, 62, 343, 366-67, 496
book publication and, 210
brother of, 475-76
cited on scarcity, 465
cited on temple as business, 439
criticism of, 278
disappearance day of, 141-46
disciplic succesion and, 343
German disciple of, 162
intoxication and, 337
plot against, 337
Prabhupāda's writing and, 62
snake-killing and, 369
strictness of, 337
temples established by, 268
Tīrtha Mahārāja, and, 299
Bhaktivedanta Book Trust (BBT)
art department of, 218, 319
India project funding and, 311
Library Party of, 215-16, 254, 288, 443
Indian, 78-79
loans from, 247, 291
Mail Order Department of, 318, 478-79
remittances to, 77, 289, 334, 348
Spanish department of, 77, 210
trustees of, 420
See also Book...categories
Bhaktivedanta Institute, 342, 370
Bhaktivedanta Manor, 156, 386
Bhaktivedanta Swami, A.C., Prabhupāda. See Prabhupāda, Śrīla
Bhaktivinoda Ṭhākura
Bhaktisiddhānta and, 337
birthsite of, 476
Caitanya's birthsite and, 365
cited on recognizing devotee, 496
foriegners and, 266, 366
gṛhastha/sannyāsī controversy and, 454
Gaudiya Math Deity of, 317
parikrama to house of, 438
quoted on imitation devotee, 489
Bhaktyā mām abhijānāti, 494
Bhānu dāsa, 367
Bhārata bhūmite haila, 46
Bhāratavarṣa, 482
Bhārgava, Śrī R. N., 228
Bhārgava dāsa, 361
Bhāṣyayam brahma-sūtrānāṁ, 557
Bhāvabhūti dāsa, 176, 177, 207, 243, 310-11
Bhavānanda Swami, 270, 296, 300, 339-40, 412, 480
Bhṛgu Muni dāsa, 515
Bhūdevi, 220
Bhūmir apo 'nalo vāyuḥ, 187
Bilvamaṅgala dāsa, 382
Birla, Aśoka, 122, 125
Birla, Gopī Kumāra, 122
Blessing-seekers, 191-93
Body, material, suffering from, 125-26
Bombay, 136, 149, 247
Bonaparte, Napoleon, 201
Bon Mahārāja, 249, 282, 551
Book distribution
Bahūdaka and, 251
Bhagavān's report on, 346-47
Bhaktisiddhānta and, 62, 343, 366-67, 496
boat program and, 412-13
Bṛṣākapi's report on, 238
business and, 288-89, 290
competition and, 198
effect of, 130, 200, 318, 510
in Europe, 85-86
in Germany, 308
Hridayānanda's report on, 209
in India, 62, 161, 361-62, 372, 377
by India library party, 78-79
Jaśomatīnandana and, 349-50
Jayatīrtha's report on, 289
Kṛṣṇa remembered via, 510
by Library Party, 215-16, 288
Life Membership and, 372
opposition to, 82-83, 84, 130
in Poland, 386

by Prabhupāda's son, 341
Rāmeśvara's report on, 61-62, 81, 196-97, 253-54
by RDTSKP, 129
Rūpānuga's report on, 371
Satsvarūpa's report on, 288
Tamal Krishna's report on, 129, 175
Tuṣṭa Kṛṣṇa and, 246
Uttamaśloka's report on, 81-85
book printing, 81, 198, 217, 361
of *Gītar-gāna*, 257
Book production
Bhaktisiddhānta and, 210
book revision and, 218
of *Caitanya-cartāmṛta*, 218
Hridayānanda Goswami and, 209, 210
Prabhupāda's schedule and, 531
Prabhupāda's supervision of, 319
Pradyumna and, 543
Sixth Canto completion and, 376
in South America, 77
See also: Bhaktivedanta Book Trust
Book reviews, 216, 318-19, 320-21, 359, 378
quoted, 442, 443-46
book translation
by Dīna Dayal, 381-82
in Hindi, 7, 112-13, 505, 511
in Indian languages, 161-62
in Malayalam, 133
by Nirañjana, 511
in Oriyan, 344
by Prabhupāda, 66
in Telegu, 120
Bose, Lalitā, 261
Bose, Subhas Chandra, 261
Brahmā, Lord, 87, 91, 220
Brahmānanda Swami, 263-64, 334, 347-48, 468
Brāhmaṇas, Prabhupāda's standard for, 239
Brahmāṇda bhramite kona, 448
Brahma-saṁhitā, 515
Brahma-sarovara, 23, 27, 111
Brahma satya jagan mithyā, 179
Brahmeti paramātmeti, 179
Brazil, 209
Brilliant as the Sun, 434
Bṛṣākapi dāsa, 237-38, 371
Buddha Jayanti Commemorative Park, 497-98
Buddhimanta dāsa, 84
Buddhir yasya balaṁ tasya, 109, 547
Bulgaria, 418
Bureaucracy, 67
Burma, 396
Butler, Pennsylvania, 282

C

Caitanya Gaudiya Matha, 260, 317, 342, 404, 413
Caitanya Mahāprabhu
advent of, 462-463
appearance day of, 461-69
atonement for sins and, 211
Choṭa Haridāsa and, 436-37
compared to full moon, 364
cooperation and, 468
eating stricture by, 203
humility and, 464
Īśāna and, 533
mission of, 124
order by, 45-46, 241-42, 525
preaching by, 45-46, 120
prediction by, 230, 459, 495
process given by, 138, 160
quoted on devotee's desire, 297
as Rādhā-Kṛṣṇa, 482
Rāmānanda Rāya and, 189, 190
sannyāsa by, 45-46, 465, 466
as servant, 144
special blessing of, 138
training by, 476
understanding Kṛṣṇa and, 432
Vṛndāvana and, 80
Western countries and, 207
Caitanya-candrāmṛta, Śrī, 364
Caitanya-caritāmṛta, Śrī, 129, 218, 260, 341, 350

Caitanya-śikṣāmṛta, Śrī, 27, 496
Caitya-guru dāsa, 16, 27, 88-89, 287, 311, 535
Cakravartī dāsa, 37
Calcutta University, 341
Cāṇakya Paṇḍita, 68, 126, 136, 137, 301, 369-70, 411
Capitalism, 17, 274
Cārdeṣna dāsa, 253
Caru dāsa, 470
Caste system, 189
Causal Ocean, 431
Ceylon (Śrī Lanka), 510
Chanting Lord's holy name(s)
  atonement via, 211
  effect of, 167-68
  efficacy of, 211
  on Ekādaśī, 340-41
  environment for, 551
  in Hungary, 417-18
  in Kali-yuga, 138, 189-90
  Kṛṣṇa consciousness via, 37
  qualification for, 464
  by Sanand residents, 154
  sin eradicated via, 505
  sinning and, 69, 473
Charity, 241, 271-72
Chaudhuri, M. N., 293, 297, 314, 351, 362
Chayavana Swami, 334, 341, 374, 393, 487, 489, 499, 501-2
Chenique, Francois, 477-78
Chief Justice of Madras, 186
Chief Minister of Punjab, 510
China, 455, 456-57, 460
Chinmāyānanda, 319
Choṭa Haridāsa, 436-37, 479
Christianity, 249, 355, 524
CIA (Central Intelligence Agency), 261, 279-80, 526
Citsukhānanda dāsa, 501, 511
Cleanliness, 21, 272, 296, 330-31, 406-7
College preaching, 62-63, 250-51, 288, 289, 370, 371
Colombo, 564
Communism/Communists
  centralization and, 538
  exploitation and, 274
  food production and, 224
  future of, 17, 537-38, 554
  preaching to, 273-74, 418-19
  spiritual, 274, 537, 554
  thesis, antithesis, and synthesis and, 162-65
  wealth distribution and, 16-17, 392
Contraception, 75, 163, 202
Cow protection, 76

D

Dāmodara (child), 294-95
Dāmodara Mahārāja, 277-79
Darby, Mike, 350
Dayānanda dāsa, 315, 327, 359, 362, 405-6, 433
De, Vrindavan Chandra, 341, 363
Death, 33
Deity (Deities)
  in Agarwal home, 488
  of Alwars, 221
  of Bhaktivinoda, 317
  of Garbhodakaśayī Viṣṇu, 219, 220
  guide for worshiping, 245
  at ISKCON Washington, 238, 239
  Jagannātha, Balarāma, and Subhadrā, 256
  of Kṛṣṇa and Arjuna, 26
  of Lakṣmī, 219
  Māyāpur development plans and, 316
  of Nṛsiṁhadeva, in South India, 375
  Prabhupāda circumambulates, 295, 339
  Prabhupāda dances before, 450-51
  Prabhupāda greets, in Vṛndāvana, 513
  Prabhupāda's childhood, 485-86
  Prabhupāda's seat height and, 123
  of Rādhā, Rukmiṇī, and Kṛṣṇa, 233

of Raṅganātha, 219
of Raṅga-nāyakī-devi, 219
in Saigal home, 504
seeing Kṛṣṇa and, 440-41
as sensual, 264
for South Indian preaching, 547
Śrī Bālajī, 221, 223
Śrī Śālagrāma-śilā, 266
Śrī Śrī Gaura-Nitāi
for boat program, 257, 276, 324, 351
for village preaching, 116-17
for bus in Brazil, 143
college preaching and, 216, 217
Śrī Śrī Rādhā-Kṣīra-corā Gopīnātha, 248
Śrī Śrī Rādhā-Govinda, 256, 485-86, 487
Śrī Śrī Rādhā-Londonīśvara, 262
Śrī Śrī Rādhā-Mādhava, 264, 266
Śrī Śrī Rādhā-Madana Gopāla, 77
Śrī Śrī Rādhā-Pārtha-sārathī, 232, 536
Śrī Śrī Rādhā-Rasabihārī, 116, 119, 149
Śrī Śrī Rādhā-Vanabihārī, 247
Śrī Śrī Rādhā-Vṛndāvanacandra, 125
of Varāha Narasiṁha, 511-12
worship of, in home, 422-23
Department of Developing and Planning, 293
Detachment, 96-97
Devahūti dāsī, 34
Devotees of Lord
association with, 128, 376, 435-36, 559-60
fear by, 373-74
desire of, 297
as gentlemen, 523
imitation, 488-89
Lord serves, 534
mercy of, 492
pure 87, 167, 435-36
quality of, 523
relationships among, 236
sins by, 69, 393, 489
symptom of, 496
Devotional service
advancement in, 80
brahmacārya and, 538
falldown from, 232, 436-37
hearing from authority and, 230
material rewards from, 148
pure, 533-34
qualification for, 352, 357
scarcity and, 32-33
sinful activities and, 230
Dhanañjaya dāsa, 67, 497
Dhṛṣṭadyumna dāsa (Swami), 458, 460, 466
Dhruva Mahārāja, 140, 168, 517
Dialectic Spiritualism, 223
Dīkṣāvatī dāsī, 254
Dīna-dayal dāsa, 226-27, 381
Dīnatāriṇī dāsī, 247
Disciplic succession, continuance of, 38-39, 415-16, 423-24
Drama, 110
Dum Dum Airport, 255
Durgā, Goddess, 123, 231-32, 515
Dvādaśī, 258, 340
Dvārakā, 233
Dvārakā-*śīlā*, 223
Dvarakeśa dāsa, 273

E

East Germany, 418
Eastern Europe, 377
Easy Journey to Other Planets, 77, 282
Eclipse, 23, 27
Economic development, 110
Economy, 156, 160
Education, 136, 137, 546
See also: Gurukula
Einstien, Albert, 553
Ei ta eka kalir chelā, 489
Ekādaśī, 168, 257, 258, 340-41
Ekādaśī feast on Gaura Pūrṇimā, 461
Elements, material, 98
Elevation to Kṛṣṇa Consciousness, 77
Engels, Friedrich, 118, 224

Envy, 369-70
Exams on scripture, 217-18, 225-26, 236, 239, 245, 319-20

F

Faith, 44
Family life, 75, 96, 150, 229-30, 301, 532
Fasting, 168, 340, 461
Faultfinding, 205-6
Fire, life within, 122, 182
Fogal Asrama, 539
Ford, Henry, 546
Freud, Sigmund, 137, 138-39, 303

G

Gabhīra dāsa, 370
Gaja-Lakṣmī, 220
Gajendra, 351
Gandhi, Indira, 253, 261, 427, 445
Gandhi, Mohandās, 126-27, 132, 133, 229, 233-34, 477, 494, 540
Gangā-Sāgara-melā, 257, 259
Ganges River, 47, 257-58, 259, 292
Gañja smoking, 337
Garbhādhāna saṁskāra, 539
Gargamuni Swami
  Calcutta management by, 257
  father of, 96
  gṛhastha/sannyāsī controversy and, 402
  GBC responsibility for, 419-20
  preaching in India by, 78-79, 203, 354, 396-97
  Siddha Svarūpa and, 470
Garuḍa, 552
Gaudiya Math
  beginning of, 366
  Bhaktisiddhānta and, 343
  Governor visits, 364
  ISKCON's relations with, 299-300, 342-43, 368-69
  Krishna-Balaram Temple visited by, 529
  at Kurukṣetra, 23
  preaching success and, 215
Gauḍīya Pañjikā, 340
Gaura Govinda Swami, 78, 312, 344
Gaura Pūrṇimā, 340, 461-69
Gaurī dāsī, 254
GBC meetings
  gṛhastha/sannyāsī controversy and, 427-28, 452, 455
  GBC zones and, 416-17, 459
  gurukula and, 433
  resolution changing and, 438
  sannyāsa initiation and, 428
  temple presidents meeting and, 459-60
Gelade, Garry, 444
Ghanaśyāma dāsa, 443, 444
Ghosh, Aurobindo, 382
Ghosh, Tarun Kanti, 334-35
Ginsberg, Allen, 337, 431
Girirāja dāsa, 116, 119, 122, 125, 420, 546
Gītār-gāna, 257, 351, 375, 412-13, 446
Godruma-dvīpa, 438
Golden Avatar studio, 521
Gopāla Kṛṣṇa dāsa
  as BBT trustee, 420
  book distribution and, 377
  book printing in India and, 62, 361
  Delhi property and, 500
  Hari-śauri and, 86
  Nellore land donation and, 196
  Prabhupāda chastises, 67
  Russia and, 456
Gopavṛndāpāla dāsa, 254
Gopīnātha dāsa, 480
Gopīparanadhana dāsa, 27
Gopīs, 233
Governor of Pondicherri, 364
Governor of Tamil Nadu, 177
Govinda Bhavan, 485
Govinda Mahārāja, 404, 413
Guṇārṇava dāsa, 29, 31, 67, 79
Guru
  association with, 325
  bogus, 88, 139, 143, 318, 320, 542

bramacārya vow and devotion to, 539
disciple's relationship with, 52, 72, 548-49
duty of, 11, 525
expenditures for, 295
faith in, 561
hearing from, 414
ISKCON's future and, 38-39, 415-16, 423-24
necessity of accepting, 88, 139, 552
personal service to, 40-41
qualification of, 46, 87, 190
submission to, 139-40
worship of, 435
Gurudāsa Swami, 144, 474, 509
Gurukṛpa Swami
boat preaching and, 351, 357
China and, 457
GBC zone for, 459
gṛhastha/sannyāsī controversy and, 402
India funding by, 186, 332
Japan and, 185-86, 199, 355
Krishna-Balaram Temple and, 403
Trivikrama and, 185-86, 199, 355
Guru kṛṣṇa-kṛpayā, 140
Gurukula
Bhagatjī's donation for, 102
Bombay, 540, 546
Dallas, 70, 281, 290, 291, 404-6, 433
defined, 548
government regulation of, 70, 281, 291, 433
hitting by teacher in, 557
Māyāpur, 257
Nitāi and, 116
RDTSKP donations to, 129
support of, 290-92
training in, 50-51, 548-49, 556-57
Vṛndāvana, 50, 245, 328-29, 382
Guru-pūjā in Vṛndāvana, 54
Guruvayor temple, 132
Gurv-aṣṭaka, 561

H

Haihaya dāsa, 154
Hansadūta dāsa
Bavala reception and, 169-70
Dialectic Spiritualism and, 224
Germany and, 174, 308
Harrison and, 156-57
Marx and, 17
Prabhupāda's letters and, 36, 39
preaching expansion by, 20
Sanand *paṇḍalas* and, 168
sannyāsa initiation and, 48, 466
silverware gift by, 173-74
village preaching and, 116-17, 169, 174, 308, 354, 512
Hanuman, 74, 220
Hanuman Jayantī, 545
Harāv abhaktasya kuto, 100, 137
Hardwar, 348
Hare Kṛṣṇa Explosion, 378, 390-91
Hare Kṛṣṇa Land
description of, 115
development of, 129
medical facility at, 146
opposition to, 119
Prabhupāda returns to, 173
sewer problem at, 552
tenant laws and, 116
Harer nāma harer nāma, 189, 223
Hari-bhakti-vilāsa, 245
Haridāsa Ṭhākura, 425, 474, 510
Haridāspur, 474
Harikeśa dāsa (Swami)
argument with Tamal Krishna by, 306-7
Bhāgavatam class and, 55-56, 57-58
cooking instructions by, 325-27
duties of, 2, 35
guidance by, on serving Prabhupāda, 14
Hari-śauri's recruitment and, 1, 2, 8, 34, 86-87, 92
Hungary and, 377, 386, 417-18
illness by, 297, 312-13
intensity of, 196

jīvas' entering material world and, 91
King's son and, 170
Kurukṣetra and, 26
Marxism and, 16
materialistic philosophies and, 162-64
mistake by, 269
Nellore hosts and, 195-96, 203
Nellore reception and, 194
philosophy essay by, 223-24, 250
posing as materialist, 107, 108
Prabhupāda quoted on, 170-71
Prabhupāda's mail and, 27-28
sannyāsa initiation by, 314-16, 324, 325
science essay by, 69-70, 73, 97
scientists and, 15, 16, 169
Vedic cosmology and, 297-98
Hari-nāmāmṛta-vyakāraṇa, 541
Hari-śauri dāsa
ant-killing and, 345
attache case and, 255
Calcutta and, 86
cleanliness and, 330-31
cooking training for, 528-29
feelings of devotion by, 298-99
Indian boy and, 172-73
intelligence in Kṛṣṇa consciousness and, 48
mātajī approaches, 305
massage by, 4-7, 8, 305
mistake by, 12-13, 20-21, 166, 309-10
Patel restricted by, 142
Prabhupāda gives chaddar to, 117
Prabhupāda rebukes, 20-21, 166, 309-10
Prabhupāda's mail read by, 27-28
retention of, 20, 34, 86-87, 92
ring gift for, 555
sannyāsīs' requests and, 350
Śāstrī and, 518-19
saving food remnants and, 207-8
sevice demand on, 401
silk *dhoti* of, 263
tilak mirror gift by, 42
Harrison, George, 101, 156-57, 386
Harvard Unuversity, 359
Hāsyapriya dāsa, 254, 550-51
Hegel, Georg Wilhelm, 118
Himāvatī dāsī, 48, 512
Hippie lifestyle, 101
Hiraṇyakaśipu, 72, 95, 231, 309, 319, 369, 400, 415, 511
Hitler, Adolf, 201, 494
Hitopadesha, 547
Hoola Ghat, 276, 329
Hridayānanda Goswami
atheistic arguments by, 323, 324
Bangladesh and, 350
book distribution and, 209
book production and, 77, 209
book review and, 320-21
Gaudiya Matha and, 368
gṛhastha/sannyāsī controversy and, 402
Indian preaching and, 387
poem by, 143
sannyāsī assistants for, 317-18
sannyāsī-women contact and, 462
science theories by, 398
secretary service assumed by, 317
TSKP in Brazil and, 143
Humility, 14, 19
Hungary, 273, 274, 377, 386, 417-18

I

Impersonalism, 7, 138, 142-43, 179, 204, 213
India
birth in, 132, 135, 419, 554-55
book distribution in, 62, 161, 361-62, 372
book printing in, 361
British rule and, 136, 261
Gandhi's rule of, 253
government of, 111, 132
guru proliferation in, 93
land donations and, 228
materialism in, 549

piety in, 154
tenant laws in, 116
thievery in, 501
Western influence in, 392, 483, 554, 555
youth in, 544, 545, 555
See also: Preaching in India
India Gaura Pūrṇimā festival
accomodations for, 432
devotees arrive for, 432, 438
Gaura Pūrṇimā day attendance at, 466-67, 469
initiation ceremony at, 464-66
Māyāpur atmosphere at, 538-39
parikramas and, 438, 446, 509
project exhibition at, 432-33, 440, 442-46
Ingalls, Daniel H. H., 443
Initiation beads, 78
Intelligence, 48, 351-52, 547, 558
Iran, 515
Īśāna, 533
ISKCON (International Society for Krishna Consciousness)
Africa, 234-35, 347, 468, 516
Ahmedabad, 249
Amherst, 63, 371
Athens, 226-27, 381
Atlanta, 371
Australia, 285-86, 446
Bangladesh, 350-51
Belgium, 346
Berkeley, 216
Bhubaneswar, 344
Bombay. See Hare Kṛṣṇa Land
Boston, 62, 550
Brazil, 143
Calcutta, 78-79, 256-57, 484, 549
Caracas, 209
Chicago, 81
as CIA, 279-80
compared to Matsya, 467-68
Denver, 288
exports from India by, 373
Fiji, 235, 236-37, 276, 510
France, 346-47
Gainesville, 288
Gaudiya Matha cooperation with, 342-43, 368-69
Germany, 174, 308, 354
Hawaii, 551
Houston, 288
Hyderbad, 78, 120, 442
Indian government and, 426-27
Japan, 355
Kurukṣetra, 451
judge quoted on, 371
Kanpur donation and, 228
London, 262
as Lord's incarnation, 364
Los Angeles, 197
Māyāpur, 257, 264, 265-66, 267, 277, 466, 467
See also Māyāpur development
Mexico, 77
Miami, 288
Nellore, 194-95
New York, 75, 76, 126, 175, 263, 285, 371-72
New Vṛndāvana, 125, 446, 484-85
New Zealand, 245-46
opportunity via, 230, 375-76
opposition to, 251
Oregon, 247
Orissa, 78
overspending in, 335-36
Pennsylvania farm, 76
purpose of, 402-3, 432, 509, 548
relationships within, 235-36
swami denounces, 205, 206-7
Tennessee, 371
Toronto, 248
Vṛndāvana, 30-31, 97, 403, 540, 550
Washington, D.C., 237-38
wealth of, 391
See also: GBC meetings; under *Gurukula*; under Temple management; names of specific ISKCON members
ISKCON Food Relief, 129
Īśopaniṣad, Śrī, 120, 204
Īśvaraḥ paramaḥ kṛṣṇaḥ, 179

J

Jaduraṇī dāsī, 218, 254
Jagaddhatri dāsī, 84
Jagadiśa dāsa, 70, 210, 291, 404, 459
Jagāi and Mādhāi, 374
Jagannātha Purī, 348, 527
Jagannātha Suta dāsa, 438
Jagat Guru dāsa (Swami), 389-90, 466, 516
Jain monk, 552
Jains, 534
Jalāṅgī river, 438
Jananivāsa dāsa, 367-68
Janma karma ca me divyam, 178, 493
Japa, 94-95, 134, 272
Japan, 185-86, 205, 207
Jaśomatīnandana dāsa, 122, 153, 155, 158-59, 169, 249, 349
Jaya and Vijaya, 220
Jayadvaita dāsa, 454
Jayapatākā Swami
- boat program and, 375
- broken dioramas and, 271
- at Caitanya Maṭha, 260
- Chaudhuri and, 120, 297, 351, 362
- Ekādaśī and, 258
- Māyāpur Guest House and, 270, 276, 294
- Māyāpur report by, 257
- Prabhupāda praises, 469
- preaching at village āśrama, 482
- *sannyāsa* initiation and, 380
- Vedic Planetarium and, 388

Jayaśacīnandana dāsa, 101-2
Jayatīrtha dāsa, 197, 247, 281, 289-90, 452
Jerusalem, 550
Jesus Christ, 524
Jewelry business, 288-89
Jīva Gosvāmī, 523, 541
Jorbagh Colony, 9
Juhu Beach, 115
Jung, Carl, 357
Jyotisar, 26-27, 111

K

Kabul, 20
Kailash Temple, 228
Kali-yuga
- *brahmacārya* training in, 556
- Caitanya's process for, 222-23
- chanting Lord's names in, 138, 189-90
- Lord's advent in, 462-63
- strictness in, 430
- symptom of, 17-18, 170, 212, 431
- women and, 277
- See also: Modern civilization

Kallman, Alan, 492-93, 521
Kanpur, 78, 228
Kapila, Lord, 127
Kāraṇadakśāyī Viṣṇu, 431
Karoly, Dely, 418
Katri Corner, 228
Kattamanchi, Subhaprada, 194
Khānara Vacana, 288
Khāṇḍava fire, 49
Kiba śudra kiba vipra, 190
King of Sanand, 153
Kirāta hūṇāndhra pulinda, 159
Kīrtanānanda Swami, 125-26, 130, 148, 484-85
Kīrtirāja dāsa, 27, 36-37, 386, 392, 395
Kiśorī dāsī, 58, 65, 557
Knapp, Stephen, 130-31
Kokilanam svaro rūpām, 411
Kṛṣṇa, Lord
- advent of, 449, 462-63
- *ajñāta-sukṛti* and, 448-49
- attachment to, 91, 167
- attraction for, 131
- Banasura and, 148
- as *caitya-guru*, 352
- descent of, 159-60
- devotee served by, 534
- as doer, 44
- energy of, 187
- as everything, 513
- Gandhi and, 133

instructions by, 123-24. See also: *Bhagavad-gītā*
liberation awarded by, 69
as Pārtha-sārathī, 232-33
pervasiveness of, 513-15
potency of, 361
as proprietor, 361
as protector, 383
as provider, 32-33, 523
reciprocation by, 227, 352, 412, 489-90
remembrance of, 118
sacrifice to, 124
satisfaction of, 360
seeing, 528
as sensual, 264
sinful reactions and, 294
Śiśupāla and, 319
as source
of everything, 358, 359
of impersonal, 179
of incarnations, 188
of knowledge, 10, 181
surrender to, 170, 463-64, 490-91
understanding, 431-32, 493-94
Kṛṣṇa-Arjuna Temple, 111
Kṛṣṇa book, 175, 227, 254, 346
Kṛṣṇa consciousness
action as, 43-44
authenticity of, 36-37
birth and, 159
chanting Lord's names and, 37
efficacy of, 158
falldown from, 37
as higher pleasure, 57
as Indian birthright, 132
sectarian faith compared with, 178
varnāśrama system and, 188
Western acceptance of, 371
Kṛṣṇa Consciousness Movement Is Authorized, The, 253-55, 318-19, 478-79
Kṛṣṇa-janma-bhūmi, 531
Kṛṣṇa Kānti dāsa, 521
Kṛṣṇa nāma vinā ār, 100
Kṛṣṇa Rūpa dāsī, 453
Kṛṣṇa śakti vinā nahe, 278
Kumbha Melā, 344
Kurukṣetra, 18, 19, 22-23, 26, 111, 510, 544
Kurukṣetra University, 25
Kuruśreṣṭha dāsa, 289
Kuvera, 517

L

Lakśahīra, 56
Lakṣmī, Goddess, 123, 338
Lalitā Prasāda Ṭhākura, 475-76, 481
League of Nations, 392
Lenin, Vladimir, 224
Letters
from/to Acyutānanda and Yaśodśnandana, 138
from/to Aditya, 322
from/to Akṣayānanda Swami, 228-29, 550
from/to Ambarīṣa, 451
from/to Bahūdaka, 250-51
from/to Balavanta, 330
from/to Bhagavān, 346-47
from/to Bombay student, 543-45
from/to Brahmānanda, 234-35, 334, 347-48
from/to Bṛṣākapi, 237-39
from/to Cakravartī, 37
to Chaudhuri, 293
from/to Chāyāvana, 341, 393
from/to Citsukhānanda, 511
from/to Dīna-dayal, 226-28, 382
from/to Dwarakeśa, 273-74
from/to English brahmacārī, 63
to Gabhīra, 370
from/to Gaura Govinda, 344
from/to Gopāla Kṛṣṇa, 361
from Gopīparanadhana, 27
from/to Gurudāsa, 144
from/to Hansadūta, 308-9, 354-55, 512
from/to Harikeśa, 417-19
to Hāsyapriya, 550-51
from/to high school student, 350

from/to Hṛdayānanda, 143-44, 209-10
from/to Jagadiśa, 291-92
from/to Jaśomatīnandana, 249, 349-50
to Jayapatākā, 120
from/to Jayaśacīnandana, 101-2
from/to Jayatīrtha, 247-48, 281, 289-91
from/to Kīrtirāja, 27, 36-37
from/to Knapp, 130-32
from/to Kīrtanānanda, 484-85
from/to Kṛṣṇa Kānti, 521
from/to Mādhava, 357-59
from/to Madhudviṣa, 236-37
from/to Mahāṁsa, 120, 274
from/to Mukunda and Bhaja Hari, 386
from/to New Zealand *bhakta*, 237
from/to Nirañjana, 511
from/to Nitāi, 245, 382
from/to Phillips, 63-64
Prabhupāda's responses to, 36
from/to Prāṇada, 498-99
from/to Pṛthu Putra, 344
from/to Puṣṭa Kṛṣṇa, 27, 37, 295
from/to Puru, 520-21
from/to Rādhāballabha, 217-18, 319
from/to Rāmeśvara, 196-97, 253-54
from/to Raṇādhir, 478-79
from/to Raṇadhīr and Svarūpa, 318-19
from/to Rūpānuga, 370-72
to Saurabha, 344
from/to Śatadhanya, 355
from/to Sātsvarūpa, 215-17, 288-89, 319-20
from/to science student, 424-25
from/to Siddha Svarūpa, 470-71
from/to South Indian man, 198-99
from/to Śruta Kīrti, 451, 550
from Sudāmā Vipra, 470-71
from/to Svarūpa Dāmodara, 121-22, 342
from/to Tamal Krishna, 129-30
from/to Trivikrama, 199-200
from/to Tulasī, 132-33
from/to Tuṣṭa Kṛṣṇa, 38, 245-47
from/to Upendra, 235-36
from/to Viśvakarma, 248-49
from/to Yamunā, 247, 248, 372
from/to Yaśodānandana, 511-12
from/to Yogī Rāj Dev Svarūp, 64
Library Party, 215-16, 254, 288
Indian, 78-79
Living entities
Brahmā's position held by, 91
free will of, 447-48, 490
normal condition of, 188
on other planets, 97-98
pervasiveness of, 122, 182
Lloyds Bank, 373
Lokanātha dāsa (Swami), 39, 45, 146, 147, 149, 512
Loke vyavāyāmiṣa-madya, 145

M

MacGregor, Geddes, 442
Mādhava dāsa, 342, 357-59
Mādhava Mahārāja, 260
Madhudviṣa Swami
arrival of, in Calcutta, 260
Fiji management and, 236
GBC zone for, 459
gṛhastha/sannyāsī controversy and, 429
Melbourne Ratha-yātrā and, 173, 245
New York management and, 126, 263, 285, 372
philosophical contradiction and, 427
preaching in India and, 261
Siddha Svarūpa and, 420, 421, 470
Madhva-sampradāya, 359
Madras, 62, 182, 188-89
Māgh Melā, 344
Mahādevia, Kārttikeya, 153, 166, 169
Mahāmāyā dāsī, 305

Mahāṁsa Swami, 196, 213, 223, 241, 274, 303, 442
Mahātma dāsa, 254
Mahāvīra dāsa, 317, 346, 353, 360, 381, 388
Mahāvirya dāsa, 479
Mām ca yo 'vyabhicāreṇa, 189
Māṁ hi pārtha vyapāśritya, 159
Manava Dharma Trust, 23, 26
Mānipura, 122, 342
Manipur Gītā Mandal, 394-95
Mangalore, 138
Man-manā bhava mad-bhakto, 46, 214
Manu Samhitā, 109
Manusuta dāsa, 82, 84
Marina Beach, 182
Markine Bhagavāta-dharma, 332
Marx, Karl, 118
Marxism, 16, 17
Massachusetts Institute of Technology (MIT), 358
Matchless Gifts, 120
Material world, perceptions of, 374
Mathurā, 29-30, 531
Mātṛvat para-dāreṣu, 126, 137
Matsya incarnation, 467-68
Matter, spirit and, 357-58, 359, 410-11
Mauna vow, 507-8
Mauritius, 348
Māyā, 47, 148, 378, 396, 494
Māyāpur atmosphere, 268, 273, 292
Māyāpur development
  by Bhaktivinoda and Bhaktisiddhānta, 365-66
  Deities and, 316
  flooding and, 426
  Guest House and, 269-70, 355-56, 377, 400-401, 408-9
  land aquisition and, 362, 377, 378, 426
  overview of, 287
  Prabhupāda's enthusiasm for, 287, 365-66
  Vedic Planetarium and, 284, 287, 348-49, 387-88, 471-72
Māyāpur-Vṛndāvana Trust, 563
Mayā tatam idaṁ sarvaṁ, 179
Māyāvāda philosophy/ Impersonalism, 7, 138, 142-43, 179, 204, 213
Māyāvādī bhāṣya śunile, 542
Mecca, 550
Meditation, 214-15
Melbourne Ratha-yātrā, 173, 244, 245, 260
Menstruation, 35
Middle East, 413
Moda Place, 95
Modern civilization
  as animalistic, 108, 137, 302, 392
  Communist philosophers and, 118
  complicatedness of, 107
  destiny of, 18, 95, 541-42
  economic development and, 68, 107
  India and, 392
  killing in, 75
  material focus of, 133
  as pandemonium, 51
  security in, 108-9
  sin proliferation in, 374
  suffering in, 59-60
  women and children and, 475
Modinagar, 502-3, 546
Mohammedans, 328
Mohta, Brijratan, 125
Moon, 10, 24, 97-98, 121, 199, 358
Morning walk
  atmosphere of, 93
  in Buddha Jayanti Commemorative Park, 497-98
  in Calcutta, 257-58
    at Victoria Memorial, 262, 263
  controversial subjects at, 87
  in India, 99
  in Juhu, 117-18
  in Māyāpur, 306
    on Mandir roof, 345-46
  in Madras, 182
  in Nellore, 204
  in New Delhi, 107

in Sanand, 156
in Vṛndāvana, 54, 513
Mṛdaṅga, fiberglass, 293
Mṛgāri, 222, 345
Mukherjī, Aśutoṣa, 202
Mukunda dāsa, 386
Mulaprakṛti dāsī, 254
Mullik Gopīśvara, 486
Mullik, Kashinath, 485
Murāri Gupta, 460-61
Muslim League, 503
Mussolini, Benito, 201
Mysore, 138

N

Nāhaṁ prakāśaḥ sarvasya, 449
Nāma Haṭṭa party, 185-86, 355
Nāma rūpe kali kāle, 364
Nāmnād balād yasya, 69, 212, 232
Nanda, Gulzarilal, 18-19, 23-26, 111
Nanda Kumara Swami, 334, 347
Nanda Mahārāja, 91, 97
Nandarāṇī dāsī, 315, 327, 345
Nārada Muni, 222, 345
Nārada-pañcarātra, 499
Narottama dāsa Ṭhākura, 236, 340, 463, 540, 561
Na te viduḥ svārtha gatiṁ, 123
Navayogendra Swami, 334
Nawab Hussein Shah, 211
Nāyaṁ deho deha-bhājāṁ, 302
Nayanābhirāma dāsa, 107, 110
Nectar of Devotion, The, 29, 251, 436, 511
Nectar of Instruction, The, 175, 185, 217-18, 251, 505
Neem leaves, 545
Nehru, Jawaharlal, 127
Nellore, Andhra Pradesh, 191, 193
New Delhi, dilapidation in, 107
Nirañjana dāsa, 511
Nirjana-bhajana, 425
Nitāichand dāsa, 331
Nitāi dāsa, 2, 87, 92, 116, 218, 245, 328
Nitai Pada Kamala boat, 257, 276, 324, 329, 351
Nityānanda, Lord, 340, 344
Nobel prize, 216
Nṛsiṁha, Lord, 338, 340, 369, 373, 375, 511, 522, 532
Nṛsiṁha Vallabha Gosvāmī, 250, 278
Nūnaṁ pramattaḥ kurute, 9

O

Oxford University, 359

P

Pādayātrā, 543, 544
Pagal Baba, 49
Pañca Draviḍa Swami, 417
Pañcatattva dāsa, 129
Pāṇḍavas, 482
Pāṇḍu dāsa, 415, 472
Paṅkajaṅghri dāsa, 367-68
Paramahaṁsa Swami, 321
Paraṁ vijāyate śrī-kṛṣṇa-saṇkīrtanam, 167
Parasya śaktir vividhaiva, 187
Parīkṣit Mahārāja, 482
Park Circus, 259
Patel, Chaturbhai P.
acceptance of Prabhupāda by, 118, 127, 136-37, 559
Communism and, 118, 537-38
Gandhi and, 127, 253
Hari-śauri restricts, 142
Indian birth and, 135
inguiries by
on guru, 140
on cutlure and education 136-37
manner of, 118, 136, 252, 253
medical science and, 252
medical service by, 141
morning walk boycott by, 147
ownership and, 538
pūjārīs and, 118-19
Prabhupāda cited on, 253
Prabhupāda teases, 134-35

Prabhupāda's disciples and, 119, 559
Prabhupāda's tolerance and, 252
quoted on Nehru, 127
quoted on Prabhupāda's preaching, 128
Sanskrit teaching by, 540-41
sat-saṅga and, 560
scientists and, 553, 555-56, 558, 559
temple construction and, 129
theistic views of, 252
Patience, 22
Pejavara Math, 138, 510
Perfection of Yoga, 120
Phillips, Mark, 63
Pisimā, 363, 389, 397-98
Poland, 27, 36, 386, 392, 395
Pole Star, 298, 471
Polygamy, 277
Portugal, 209
Prabhodānanda Sarasvatī Ṭhākura, 364-65
Prāṇada dāsa, 498
Prabhupāda, Śrīla
acceptance of disciples by, 37-38
adversity and, 86
aetheism refuted by, 323-24
alertness by, 562-63
in Aligarh, 503-5
anecdote by, 184
anger by, 309-10, 458, 536
appreciation of devotion by, 98-99
arrival in Vṛndāvana by, 31
association with, via books, 130
association with disciples by, 210
bābājī initiation and, 479
Bangladesh property and, 351
Bhagatjī and, 70, 102, 161-62
Bhaktisiddhānta's disappearrance day and, 141-42, 144, 145-46
Bhaktivinoda deity and, 317
birth information on, 78
blessing-seekers and, 191-93
boat inspection by, 276
bogus gurus and, 318-19
Bombay quarters of, 133-34
Bombay-to-Melbourne flight and, 563-66
book distribution and, 81-82, 85, 129, 161, 175, 198, 347, 372
book production and, 218, 319
book profits and, 198
book reviews and, 216, 318-319, 359, 378, 442-46
breakfast for, 58-59
broken dioramas and, 271
Caitanya Matha visited by, 413
Calcutta audience and, 259
car accident and, 535-36
chanting Rādhā-Mādhava, 55
Chaudhuri and, 115, 120, 314
Chāyāvana and, 334, 501-2
childhood neighborhood visited by, 485-87
children and, 295
China and, 456-58
cleanliness and, 272, 296, 406-7
in Colombo, 564
compassion of, 110, 111
compromise and, 385-86
cooking lesson by, 545
cooperation and, 186, 199
cow protection and, 76
daily schedule of, 52-53
dakṣiṇa from Australia for, 446
Dallas gurukula and, 404-6, 433
dancing before Deities, 450-51
darśana adjustment by, 353-54
dealings with disciples by, 441
Deity greeting by, in Vṛndāvana, 513
departing Madras, 191
departing Vṛndāvana, 105
detachment by, 97
deviant disciples and, 321-22
devotees' material welfare and, 73, 258-59, 437
drama and, 110
dream by, 328
eating strictness by, 563-64
effulgence of, 298

English usage by, 51
evening snack by, 65-66
example set by, 41
faith in guru by, 561
family members of, 255-56, 259, 341, 363, 447
festival exhibition and, 440, 442-46
fiberglass *mṛdaṅga* and, 293
with film producers, 562
Fogal Asrama aquisition and, 539-40
foundation-stone ceremony by, 208-9
gṛhastha/sannyāsī controversy and, 402-4, 414, 428, 429-31, 452-56
Gandhi cited on, 261
Gaudiya Math members visit, 368
GBC resolutions and, 438
Godbrothers of, 93-94, 277-79, 434-35
See also: Gaudiya Math; names of specific Godbrothers
government intervention and, 223
Governor of Tamil Nadu and, 177
Govinda Mahārāja and, 404
Guest House drainage and, 79
guru-disciple relationship and, 72
Hare Kṛṣṇa Explosion and, 390-91
Hare Kṛṣṇa Land development and, 119, 129, 146, 148-49
in Haridāspur, 474
Hari-śauri reprimanded by, 20-21, 166, 309-10
Hari-śauri's Deity photo button and, 172-73
Hari-śauri's japa and, 134
Hari-śauri's first mistake and, 12-13
Hari-śauri's retention and, 92
Harikeśa rebuked by, 269
Harikeśa-Tamal Krishna argument and, 307
Hindi translators and, 7, 112-13
hot water shortage and, 67
humility of, 19, 131, 278, 560
illness by, 139, 140-41, 168, 173, 250, 282, 332, 373, 389, 176
impersonalism defeated by, 142-43, 213
Indian exports and, 373
Indian translators and, 161-62
injury by, 500
ISKCON expenditures and, 335-36
ISKCON manpower in India and, 174
itinerary of, 499, 531
Jagat Guru and donation to, 389-90
Jain monk and, 552
joking with bank manager, 517-18
at Jorbagh Colony, 9-12
journey to America by, 282
Kallman and, 492-93
kindness of, 117, 141, 243, 304
King's son and, 171-72
Kurukṣetra temple sites and, 26-27
Lalitā Prasāda and, 481
leadership appointments by, 419-20
Life Member-*brahmacārī* and, 393-94
London Deities and, 262
lunch for, 13
Mahāvīra and, 388
management by, 42-43, 61, 68, 174, 293, 322, 395, 563
massaged by Hari-śauri, 4-7, 8
massaged by Upendra, 1-3
materialistic philosophies defeated by, 162-65, 166
Māyāpur atmosphere and, 292, 331
Māyāpur *gurukula* students and, 306
Māyāpur inspection by, 269, 270-72, 276
Māyāpur management and, 346, 352-53, 367
Māyāpur quarters of, 267, 268
meal privacy by, 171
Melbourne Ratha-yātrā and, 244, 245
Mercedes limousine of, 405, 406, 535-36
mercy of, 60-61
Middle East preaching and, 413
at Modinagar, 502-3

movie director and, 247, 250
Nandajī and, 18-19, 23-26, 111
Nectar of Instruction and, 217
Nellore hosts and, 195-96, 202-3, 243
Nellore land donation and, 239-41, 274, 294, 303, 310-11
new centers and, 78
New Delhi apartment of, 4
newly published books and, 175
objectivity by, 127
partiality by, 28
Dr. Patel and. See: Patel, Chaturbhai P.
patience of, 22
personal association with, 19-20, 40-41
personal possessions of, 34-35
pilot and, 255
Pisimā and, 397-98
poem glorifying, 130-31, 518-19
as "Poet," 62, 257
poster of, 521-22
Pradyumna's assistance to, 543
prasādam distribution and, 14, 65, 156, 161, 469
prasādam taking by, 60-61, 564
preaching expertise by, 25, 56, 93, 123, 165
preaching spirit of, 166, 169, 245, 497
predictions on, 283
press conference by, 176, 233-34, 498, 502
protectiveness by, 93-94, 305
qualities of, 41, 72, 77, 181-82, 210, 252, 284, 298, 305, 375, 396
questioners challenge, 180
with Rādhā-Dāmodara TSKP, 467-68
at Raṅganātha Temple, 218-21
rāsa-līlā discussions and, 185
reception of
at Ahmedabad, 172
at Bavala, 169-70
at Bombay, 537
at Māyāpur, 265-66
at Madras airport, 176
at Nellore, 193-94
at Raṅganātha Temple, 219, 435
at Sanand, 153-55
relaxed mood of, during massage, 306
ring gift for, 480
sannyāsa initiation and, 39, 45-48, 112, 322, 324, 360, 379-80
sannyāsī-women contact and, 462
Sanskrit school and, 540-41
Śāstrī and, 535
śāstric vision of, 288, 327, 351
scientists and, 69-70, 73-74, 95, 97, 99
scriptural knowledge of, 411
secretary's duties for, 35
servant expenditures and, 116
servant's duties for, 35
Sharma and, 425
Siddha Svarūpa and, 409-10, 420-23
śilā worship and, 223
sleeping by, 65
smile of, 60
in South Africa, 516
spiritual identification by, 72, 447
with Śrīdhara Mahārāja, 459
Sudāmā Vipra and, 373, 379, 381
thief and, 312
Tīrtha Mahārāja and, 283
Thursday afternoon travel and, 244
tolerance by, 21, 565-66
toothpaste recipe of, 147
translating work by, 66
Tulasī Devi and, 461
two-year-old boy and, 294-95
Vedic Planetarium and, 284, 287, 387-88
village preaching by, 169, 400, 474
villagers entertain, 413
Viśāla chastised by, 43
Vṛndāvana bank branch and, 376, 517-18
Vṛndāvana *gurukula* and, 328-29

Vṛndāvana vendor and, 517
Viṣṇujana's disappearance and, 479
waste and, 128-29
Western appreciation of, 316-17, 442-43
woman approaching Hari-śauri and, 305
writing by, 62, 257
Yogashakti Ma and, 384-85
See also: Letters; Morning walks; Prabhupāda cited; Prabhupāda quoted; Preaching engagements; specific subject matter
Prabhupāda cited
on animal mentality, 108
on atheistic mentality, 264
on atonement for sins, 211
on Aurobindo, 382
on authority, acceptance of, 9-10
on *baḍa*-making, 264
on Bengali culture, 382
on *Bhagavad-gītā*, 24
on Bhaktisiddhānta, 337-38, 343
on "big, big monkey...," 74
on bodily discomfort, 125-26
on Bombay gurukula, 546
on Bon Mahārāja, 249
on book distribution, effect of, 318
on Brahmā, 91
on *brahmacārya*, 538, 541
on bread made by nondevotees, 330
on British rule, 261, 275
on business, 289
on Caitanya, 482, 533
on chanting Lord's names, 211, 505, 511
on character development, 542
on charity, 243
on Choṭa Haridāsa, 436-37
on cleanliness, 331
on Communism, 392, 418-19, 554
on cooperation, 421-22, 429, 454-55
on culture, 15
on Dallas gurukula, 70
on debt and laziness, 390
on Deity thread remnants, 519
on Deity worship in home, 422-23
on desire to be master, 402
on *dharma*, 186-87, 188
on donor selling meat and liquor, 276
on Durgā, 515
on Fifth Canto production, 298
on Ekādaśī, 168
on enthusiasm, 416
on extended selfishness, 531-32
on family life, 75, 301
on farm projects, 371
on fast days, 340
on fear by devotees, 373-74
on flying a plane, 255
on Freud, 138-39
on *gañja* smoking, 337
on Gandhi, 229, 233-34
on Gangā-Sāgara mela, 258
on garland *prasādam*, 58
on GBC zones, 286
on Godbrother(s), 215, 260, 316, 342-43, 426
on Gopāla Kṛṣṇa, 377
on government, 275
on guru
association with, 325
bogus, 88, 139, 143, 320
disciples as, 415-16, 423-24
expenditures for, 295
hearing from, 414
worship of, 435
on Harikeśa, 386
on harmonium, 251
on health, 313
on hearing from authority, 230
on himself
1950s, 169
1958-65, 282-83
Bhaktisiddhānta and, 338
childhood of, 487
early days in America by, 395-96, 440

father's desire for, 336
preaching life of, 280
previous life of, 460-61
success by, 525
on hippies, 44-45, 475
on hippie tendencies, 520
on Hiraṇyakaśipu, 415
on humility, 307
on impersonalism, 252
on Indian climate, 20
on Indian leaders, 18, 483, 529
on initiation beads, 78
on intelligence, 351-52
on ISKCON-Gaudiya Matha cooperation, 368
on ISKCON gurus, 415-16, 423-24
on ISKCON Japan, 355
on *jīvas* entering material world, 91
on jealousy, 278
on Kṛṣṇa
advent of, 449
Deity as, 504
as everything, 513
as provider, 523
reciprocation by, 489-90
satisfaction of, 360
understanding, 88
on Kṛṣṇa conscious action, 43-44
on Kṛṣṇa consciousness movement, 32
on land prices, 276
on Life Membership, 394
on life on other planets, 98
on Madras preaching engagements, 190
on *magha-melā* dances, 110
on Mahā-Viṣṇu, 431
on managcment, 221
on marriage, 333
on material activities in Vṛndāvana, 75-76
on material attachment, 101, 229
on materialists, 314
on matter as spirit, 410-11
on *māya*, 396
on Māyāpur Guest House, 438
on medicine, modern, 141
on modern civilization, 51, 59-60, 75, 302-3
on modern economic system, 156
on modern education, 281
on Moscow visit, 392
on Ph.D.s, 370
on pilgrim, 258
on Prahlāda, 32, 338, 415
on *prasādam*, 307
on preaching effectively, 111-12, 495-96
on preaching in India, 116-17
on proprietorship, 538
on pure devotion, 167, 230
on Rāmacandra *mantra*, 531
on rain, 323
on *rasgulla-making*, 332
on reading his books, 225
on renunciates, false, 79-80
on *sambandha, abhidheya* and *prayojana*, 50
on *sannyāsa* order, 45, 47, 374
on Sanskrit recitation, 126
on saving money, 529-30
on scientists, 162, 399
on security via education, 546
on servant expenditures, 78
on sex, 400, 404, 539
on Sharma's renunciation, 380, 381
on shaving head, 359
on silence, 507-8
on sins by devotees, 393
on source of knowledge, 186
on *Śrīmad-Bhāgavatam*, 212
on Sudāmā, 257
on sun, 99
on sweet shop sweets, 14
on teacher-student relations, 557
on train travel, 191
on Trancendental Meditation, 562
on *tulasī* tea, 330
on *vānaprastha*, 428
on *varṇāśrama* in ISKCON, 333
on Vedic cosmology, 298

on Vedic culture, 259, 300-301, 522, 522, 538
on Vedic study, 540, 548
on vegetarianism, 552, 553
on village people, 155
on village preaching, 151, 166-67, 169
on visa problems, 550
on Vṛndāvana, 32
on women, 277, 283-84, 286, 419
on work, 287
Prabhupāda quoted
on abortion, 202
on activity by Lord, 323
on Ahmedabad aquisition, 249
on *ajñāta-sukṛti*, 447-48
on association with devotees, 128, 376, 559-60
on atomic theory, 398-99
on attachment, material, 90-91
on attachment to Kṛṣṇa, 91, 167, 168
on attraction for Kṛṣṇa, 131
on attraction to wife, 301-2
on Authorized pamphlet, 254-55
on beauty, 411
on Besant, 184
on *bhakti* for material reward, 148
on Bhaktisiddhānta, 366
on Bhaktivinoda, 266
on Bhāratavarṣa, 482
on *bhāva*, 450
on bicycles, 95
on birth in India, 419
on birth qualification, 159, 524
on Bon Mahārāja, 551
on book distribution
Bhaktisiddhānta and, 62, 198, 366-67
book prices and, 198
Christmas marathon and, 254
competition on, 198
effect of, 510
by Gargamuni, 79
government restiction of, 86
by himself, 62
importance of, 289, 364
in India, 62
Kṛṣṇa pleased by, 85
Kṛṣṇa remembered via, 510
Prabhupāda obliged by, 362
pressure for, 246
result of, 129-30, 217, 362
on book distributors, 85
on book printing, 198
on book production, 77
on Brahmā, 87
on *brahmacārya* qualities, 560-61
on *brāhmaṇa* initiates, 239
on Bṛṣākapi's inheritance, 371
on bullock cart preaching, 120
on bureaucracy, 67
on business, 290-91, 434-35
on Caitanya Mahāprabhu
advent of, 463
desire of, 366
mission of, 46, 241-42, 515-16
order of, 45-47
preaching by, 120
prediction by, 230, 207
process given by, 160, 189-90, 222-23
Rāmānanda Rāya and, 190
on cash crops, 160
on chance, 17
on change, tendency for, 102, 109
on chanting Lord's names, 167-68, 189-90, 464, 473
on charity, 271-72
on Christianity, 249, 297, 524
on CIA issue, 279-80, 526
on civilization, origin of, 121
on cleanliness, 21, 272
on Communism, 538
on cooperation, 216-17, 430, 468
on cow, 76, 356
on culture, 137-38
on *dakṣaḥ*, 560
on death, 33
on Deities for ISKCON Washington, 239
on Deity donations, 439-40

on Deity worship, 440-41
on Delhi dilapidation, 107
on devotee relationships, 236
on devotional service, 131-32, 352, 357
on Dhruva, 140
on disciplic succession, continuance of, 38-39
on divine and demonic, 145
on Durgā, 123, 232
on *durgā*, 389
on East-West distinction, 554
on eating outside temple, 363
on economic development, 110
on education, 126-27, 137
on effective preaching, 157
on Ekādaśī, 258, 341
on elements, generation of, 98
on energy, 187
on faith, 44
on falldown, 37, 232, 436, 437
on faultfinding, 205-6
on form and formlessness, 179
on *gṛhasthas* preaching programs, 511
on Gandhi, I., 253
on Gandhi, M., 126-27, 133, 477, 540
on GBC, 235, 458
on glorifying him, 165-66
on Godbrothers, 279, 300
on government, 109
on grain production, 224
on guru
  bogus, 112, 157-58, 233, 542
  disciples as, 38-39
  disciple's relationship with, 52, 548-49
  duty of, 525
  necessity of, 88, 139, 552
  qualification of, 46, 190, 465
  submission to, 139-40
on *gurukula*, 50-51, 281, 290-92, 548-49, 556-57
on happiness, 108
on Harikeśa's preaching, 170-71
on Harrison, 156-57
on haunted house, 275
on hearing from authority, 544
on hippie lifestyle, 101
on Hiraṇyakaśipu, 231, 511
on himself
  childhood of, 485-86, 546-47
  disciples of, 279, 526-27
  early days in New York and, 75, 431
  expectations by, 1965, 527
  father of, 517
  retirement of, 269
  sannyāsa acceptance by, 398
  success of, 477, 526
on hitting gurukula student, 557
on horses, 263
on Hridayānanda's poem, 143-44
on human mission, 11-12, 71-72, 75, 177-78
on humility, 307-8, 464
on imitation, 383, 488-89
on impersonal interpretation of *Īśopaniṣad*, 204-5
on independence, 201-2, 530
on India, 387, 549, 554
on Indian youth, 545, 555
on initiation, 37, 516
on intelligence, 352, 547, 558
on ISKCON
  achievement of, 267
  Fiji, 237
  as Lord's incarnation, 364
  Māyāpur, 266
  mission of, 548
  opportunity via, 230
  opposition to, 251
  purpose of, 402-3, 432, 509
  wealth of, 391
on *japa* standard, 94-95
on jealousy, 369-70
on Jīva Gosvāmī, 523
on Kṛṣṇa
  advent of, 159-60
  as doer, 44
  mercy of, 168

pervasiveness of, 513-15
as proprietor, 361
protection by, 459
as provider, 32-33
reciprocation by, 352, 412
sacrifice to, 124
seeing, 440-41, 528
sinful reactions and, 294
Śiśupāla and, 319
as source, 181, 188, 358, 359
surrender to, 459, 463-64, 490-91
ten hands of, 336
as ultimate goal, 427
understanding, 431-32, 493-94
on Kṛṣṇa consciousness and sectarian faith, 178, 180
on Kali-yuga, 17-18, 170, 189, 430, 431
on Kanpur land donation, 228-29
on knowledge, 558
on *kṛpa siddhi*, 491
on Kurukṣetra development, 27
on Lalitā Prasāda, 476
on Life Membership, 372
on life's mission, 10, 542
on management, 353, 405
on marriage, 63, 302
on Marxism, 16
on material enjoyment, 56-57, 163
on material facility for preaching, 534
on materialistic mentality, 99-100
on materialistic philosophers, 224
on matter's relation to spirit, 357-58, 359
on *mauna*, 508
on *māyā*, 47, 148, 378
on Māyāpur development, 365-66
on Māyāpur *pūjārīs*, 367-68
on meat-eating, 356
on medical service, 146-47
on meditation, 214-15
on mind, 358
on modern civilization
as animalistic, 108, 137, 392
destiny of, 18, 95, 541-42
economic development and, 68, 107, 133
exploitation in, 231
security in, 108-9
on modern education, 63
on money and Americans, 368
on moon, 358
on moon landing, 199
on mosquitos, 303
on Nectar of Instruction, 217-18
on *nirjana-bhajana*, 425
on Nṛsiṁha, 532
on offering fruit, 426
on *pādayātrā*, 544
on parents, responsibility of, 291-92
on politics, 111
on Prahlāda, 11, 72, 319, 402, 407
on preaching
in America, 81
to Communists, 273-74, 419
as life, 516
sannyāsa initiation and, 38
success of, 215, 228, 477
to youth, 63
on pride, 339
on proprietorship, 285, 361
on protection, 383-84
on publishing disciples' books, 342
on pure devotion, 533-34
on qualities of nature, 407-8
on qualities of nondevotee, 523-24
on quality of devotees, 523
on Rādhā-Kṛṣṇa-Rukmiṇī Deities, 233
on Rādhārāṇī, 123
on rain, 288
on Rāmacandra, 49
on reading his books, 217
on Ṛṣabhadeva's instructions, 9
on Rūpa GosvāmI, 523, 533-34
on *sādhu*, 183
on Sanātana, 533-34
on *sāṅkhya* philosophy, 127
on *saṅkīrtana*, 138

on *sannyāsa* initiation, 339, 381, 465-66, 502
by women, 322
on *sannyāsīs,* respect for, 78
on Sanskrit textbook, 541
on Śāstrī's poem, 296-97
on saving food remnants, 208
on scientists, 556
atheism by, 303, 559
civilization's origin and, 121
creation theory by, 159
defeat of, 424-25
foolishness of, 169
ISKCON's challenge to, 553-54
knowledge source for, 98, 122
life's origin and, 121-22
moon landing and, 199
preaching to, 128
promises by, 15
on self-interest, 123
on service compared with mercy, 491
on sex, 107-8, 149-50
on Siddha Svarūpa, 237
on sinful activities, 69, 121, 170, 473
on sinful reactions, 230
on snakes, 369-70
on social welfare, 213-14
on soul's freedom, 490
on soul's origin, 542
on sour cream, 521
on South Americans, 210
on speculative mentality, 87, 88
on spiritual advancement, 80
on spiritual culture, decline of, 136
on spiritual relationships, 72-73
on spiritual strength, 215, 249-50
on spiritual subject matter, 128
on *śraddadhānaḥ,* 561
on stealing, 502
on studio recording, 521
on successful life, 13-24
on suffering, 230
on suicide, 436, 437
on sun, 349
on *svadharma,* 188
on Svarūpa Dāmodara, 121, 553
on Śyāmasundara, 110, 111
on Tamal Krishna, 456
on *Tantra śāstras,* 499
on *tapasya,* 222
on temple management, 229
on temple *prasādam,* 203-4
on temples, opportunity via, 375-76
on thesis, antithesis, and synthesis, 162-65
on time, 68-69
on Tīrtha Mahārāja, 299-300
on truth via experimentation, 149
on Tuṣṭa Kṛṣṇa, 237
on understanding *Bhagavad-gītā,* 143
on *vairāgya,* 73, 96-97
on *varnāśrama* system, 188, 189
on Vedic Planetarium, 348-49
on vegetarianism, 246
on Viśvanātha Cakravartī, 561
on village preaching, 354-55
on Vrajavāsīs, 527-28
on Vṛndāvana, 80, 97, 281
on war, 60, 112
on Western disciples, 212
on widows, 372
on women, 89 90, 453
ISKCON project by, 248
on work, 270-71, 528
on Yamunā's singing, 102
on yoga practice, modern, 64
on yoga *siddhas,* 348-49
on yogis in West, 530
See also specific Sanskrit quotes
Pradyumna dāsa, 446-47, 510, 543
Praghoṣa dāsa, 82, 84
Prahlāda Mahārāja
authority of, 32, 63
birth qualification and, 32
cited on material aspiration, 399-400
cited on protection, 383
compassion of, 495

Hiraṇyakaśipu's death and, 369
Hiraṇyakaśipu's position and, 415
humility of, 407
life's purpose and, 11, 71
Lord benedicts, 522
Lord pacified by, 338
Lord rescues, 511
material advancement and, 231
mauna and, 507, 508
modern society and, 68
Prabhupāda compared to, 95-96
Prabhupāda inspired by, 72, 95
prayers to Nṛsiṁha by, 373
pure devotion of, 533
as servant, 402, 414
wealth and, 101
Pramāṇa Swami, 466
Prasādam distribution
at Gaura Purnimā festival, 466
in Hungary, 417
Indian preaching and, 161, 167
by Indian temples, 203-4
in Māyāpur, 271
Prabhupāda's concern for, 65, 156, 469
Pratāparudra Mahārāja, 190
Pravṛttiṁ ca nivṛttiṁ ca, 100
Prayer to the Lotus Feet of Kṛṣṇa, 332
Preaching engagements
at Agarwal paṇḍala, 501
in Bavala, 169
at Birla estate, 122-25
with Bombay Life Member, 140
at Delhi Rotary Club, 493-94
in Gujarati village, 166-67
at India Press Colony Grounds, 505
in Madras hall, 176-81, 186-90
in Mathurā, 531
in Nellore, 210-11, 221-23, 230-31
Rotary Club, 241-42
at Rām Līlā grounds, 497, 502
at Sanand paṇḍala, 155, 158, 167, 170, 171
with scientists, 128
Preaching in India
by Acyutānanda, 212-13, 332, 359, 546-8
boat program and, 324, 351, 375, 412-13
by bullock cart, 120, 469
Deities and, 547-48
educated Indians and, 132-33
Gargamuni and, 397
by Hansadūta, 116-17, 168, 169, 174, 308, 354, 512
importance of, 387
Jaśomatīnandana and, 169, 349
large-scale plans for, 261
Madhudviṣa and, 261
manpower shortage and, 512
Tamal Krishna and, 262
village-to-village, 151, 156-57, 166-67, 169, 308, 354, 400, 512
by Yaśodānandana, 212-13, 332, 359, 375, 511
Premananda, Punjabi, 543-44
Preraka dāsa, 84
Prostitutes, 283
Pṛthivīte āche yata, 207, 266, 515-16
Pṛthu Putra dāsa (Swami), 33-34, 39, 45, 344, 400
Puṁsaḥ striyā mithunībhāvam, 150
Punar mūṣika bhava, 541
Punja, Deoji, 236, 276, 283, 510
Punja, Karṣanjī, 237
Punjab National Bank, 162, 376, 517
Purāṇas, 56
Pure devotional service, Rūpa-Sanātana story and, 533-34
Puru dāsa, 520-21
Puṣṭa Kṛṣṇa Swami, 37
car accident by, 535-36
competence of, 425
gṛhastha/sannyāsī controversy and, 429, 430
Mercedes limousine and, 27, 295, 405, 406, 535-36
secretary position assumed by, 405
Singapore officials and, 565

R

Rādhāballabha dāsa, 150, 217
Rādhā-Dāmodara TSKP
  Bhaktivedānta Institute and, 342
  book distribution by, 81, 129, 197
  darśana with Prabhupāda by, 467-68
  expansion of, 315, 467
  gṛhastha/sannyāsī controversy and, 454
  Harikeśa and, 315
  India remittances by, 311
  Madhudviṣa and, 459
  Pṛthu Putra and, 39
Rādhākrishna, 477
Rādhā-kuṇḍa, 93, 425
Rādhārāṇī, Śrīmatī, 91, 123, 232-33, 340, 534
Raghunātha dāsa Gosvāmī, 560
Rajasthan, 258
Rājavidyā, 120
Rājeśvarī Kalyāna Maṇḍapam, 176
Rāmacandra, Lord, 16, 49, 50, 74, 238, 340, 530-31
Rama Krishna, 551
Rama Krishna Mission, 183, 478
Rāmānanda Rāya, 189, 190
Rāma-navami, 529
Rāman-reti, 79, 516
Rāmānujācārya, 219, 221, 543
Rāmānuja-sampradāya, 359
Rāma Tīrtha, 505, 551
Rāma Tīrtha Mission, 505
Rāmeśvara dāsa (Swami)
  book distribution report by, 61-62, 81, 161, 196
  GBC zone for, 417
  Nectar of Instruction and, 175
  Prabhupāda poster and, 521-22
  preaching report by, 161
  sannyāsa initiation and, 452, 466
  Uttamaśloka's book distribution report and, 85
Rāmeśvaram, 348
Raṇadhir dāsa, 318, 478-79
Rānaghāṭa, 265
Ranga Gardens, 519
Raṅganātha dāsa, 84
Raṅganātha Temple, 218-21
Rasajñā dāsa, 426
Rāsa-līlā dance, 170, 185
Ratha-yātrā festival, 129, 131, 173, 244, 245, 260, 486
Rāvaṇa, 16
Ravīndra Svarūpa dāsa, 342, 370, 480
Ṛddha dāsa, 499, 501
Rebala, Sujathamma, 194
Reddy, B. Gopāla, 208-9, 213
Reddy, Kalaprapurna, 211
Reddy, G. Gopāla, 241
Regulative principles, 49, 145
Rehman, Mujibul, 201
Reincarnation, 11
Restaurants, 451, 550-51
Ṛkṣarāja dāsa, 374-75
Rohiṇī Kumāra dāsa, 381
Romania, 418
Romapāda dāsa, 84
Ṛṣabhadeva, Lord, 9, 11
Ṛṣi Kumāra dāsa, 502
Rukmiṇī, Śrīmatī, 233
Rūpa Gosvāmī, 29, 30, 79, 88, 96, 371, 523, 533-34
Rūpānuga dāsa, 76, 285, 342, 370-72, 459
Russia, 16, 456

S

Sadāpūta dāsa, 342
Ṣaḍbhuja dāsī, 84
Sahib, Yuvrāj Ṭhākura, 153, 171-72
Saigal, Surendra Kumar, 9, 499, 503
Śālagrāma-śilā, 223
Salvation Army, 282
Sanand, Gujarat, 153-55
Sanand, King of, 122
Sanand Palace, 155
Sanātana Gosvāmī, 30, 96, 245, 533-34
Sanat-sujāta, 356
Sāṅkhya philosophy, 127

Sāṅkhya-pūrvaka-nāma, 94
Sannyāsa initiation
Bhagavāt and, 112
by Caitanya, 45-46, 465, 466
ceremony for, 45-47, 464-66
GBC resolutions on, 428
Hansadūta and, 48
Harikeśa and, 314-16, 324, 325
Mahāvīra and, 317-18, 360, 381
necessity of, 339, 374
Pṛthu Putra and, 39, 45-47
preaching and, 38, 45
qualification for, 379, 380
Rāmeśvara and, 452
requests for, 47, 322, 380
Ṛkṣarāja and, 374
Tatpur and, 465
Viraha and, 317-18, 324-25
women and, 322
Sannyāsa order, respect for, 78
Santa Cruz, California, 216, 290
Sarasvatī, Goddess, 26
Sarva-dharmān parityajya, 463
Sarvopādhi vinirmuktaṁ, 90
Śāstrī, Anantarāma, 273-74, 296, 480, 509, 518-19, 535
Śatadhanya dāsa (Swami), 355, 466
Satsvarūpa Gosvāmī, 215-16, 254, 288-89, 319-20
Saurabha dāsa, 67, 68, 79, 129, 149, 281, 287, 344
Schloss Retterschof, 37
Science, modern, 69-70, 95
Scientific Basis of Kṛṣṇa Consciousness, The, 62, 553
scientists, 556
analogies on, 399
atomic theory and, 398-99
authority of, 9-10, 98, 99, 121-22
cosmology and, 471
creation of life by, 73-74, 303
Harikeśa instructed on, 169
in ISKCON, 359
ISKCON's challenge to, 74, 553-54
life's origin and, 97
moon and, 97-98
Patel defends, 559
Prabhupāda's challenge to, 472
preaching to, 74
promises by, 15
Russian, 537
"scissor philosophy" and, 470
Vedic Planetarium and, 471-72
Sex attraction, 149-50, 539
Sex enjoyment, 107-8, 163, 400, 404
Sharma, Veni Śaṅkara, 183
Sharma dāsa, 380, 381, 425, 510
Shenai band, 435, 438-39
Siddhaloka, 348-49
Siddha Svarūpānanda Goswami, 38, 237, 373, 405, 409-10, 420-23, 470-71
Simhachalam, 511
Siṁha Giri, 511
Sinful activities
atonement for, 211, 222
chanting and committing, 69, 473
by devotees, 393, 489
in Kali-yuga, 170
modern society and, 374
offense via, 212
uprooting of, 230
Śiśupāla, 319
Sītā-devi, 283
Śiva, Lord, 148, 551
Six Gosvāmīs, 30, 80, 455
Social welfare, 213-14
Sour cream, 520-21
South Africa, 27
South America, 77
Soviet Union, 111, 377
Spanish BBT, 77, 210
Spiritual master. See: Guru
Spiritual world, *māyā* reflection of, 148
Śravaṇānanda dāsa, 135, 176, 177, 243, 244, 310-11
Śrīdevi, 22
Śrīdhara dāsa (Swami), 39, 45, 257
Śrīdhar Mahārāja, 317, 410, 459
Śrīmad Bhāgavatam
civilization's origin and, 121
detachment and, 97
French edition of, 347
modern astronomy and, 121

newly published volumes of, 175
Prabhupāda begins, 282
Prabhupāda finds, in America, 282
Prabhupāda's translating of, 66
printing of, 81, 217
production of, 150-51
stories in, 212
Śrīmad Bhāgavatam cited
on atom, 399
on *brahmacārya*, 556
on guru, 88
on holy names, 556
on impersonal conception, 179
on Kali-yuga, 17-18
on madness, 9
on planetary system, 471
on sun and moon, 10
Śrīmad Bhāgavatam quoted
on atonement for sins, 222
on birth as spiritual qualification, 159
on devotional service, 230
on family attachment, 96
on hearing about Kṛṣṇa, 189
on Lord as everything, 410
on Lord's advent, 462-63
on Prahlāda's compassion, 495
on sinful desires, 230
on wealth, 101
Śrīpati, 82, 84
Śrī Rebala Lakshminarasa Reddy Public Hall, 210
Śrī Vaiṣṇava-sampradāya, 220
Śrī-vigrahārādhana-nitya-, 272, 514
Śrī Viśvambhara Dayal, 65
Śruta Kīrti dāsa, 451, 550
Subala dāsa, 396
Subhadrā, 27
Subhāga dāsa, 331, 350
Śubhānanda dāsa, 342
Sucandra dāsa, 47
Śuci haya muci haya, 159
Sudāmā Swami, 47, 257, 324, 329
Sudāmā Vipra Swami, 373, 379, 381, 405, 470
Suez Canal, 282
Suffering, 101, 125-26, 202, 230, 490, 496
Suicide, 436
Śukadeva Gosvāmī, 138, 175
Sukla, V. N., 504-5
Sun, 10, 24, 95, 98, 99, 121, 298, 349
Sun god, 24
Supreme Lord. See Caitanya Mahāprabhu; Kṛṣṇa, Lord; specific forms of Lord
Sva-karmaṇā tam abhyarcya, 270
Svami Nārāyaṇa Temple, 170
Svarūpa Dāmodara dāsa, 62, 121, 553
Svarūpa dāsa, 318
Svarūpa, Prabhu, 474
Swarūp, Yogī Rāj Dev, 64
Sweden, 74, 482
Śyāmasundara dāsa, 110-11, 234
Sylvania Light Company, 488

T

Tagore, Ravīndranath, 382
Tamal Krishna Goswami
argument with Harikeśa by, 306-7
arrival of, in India, 175
as BBT trustee, 420
bee and, 346
blessing-seekers and, 191
book distribution competition and, 197, 198
at Caitanya Maṭha, 260
China and, 455-58, 460
cited on Africa, 234-35
cited on Andra Pradesh government, 221
cited on new devotees, 284
cited on Prabhupāda in London, 262
gṛhastha/sannyāsī controversy and, 427-28, 429, 430, 452-53, 454, 455
massage by, 262-63
Nellore hosts and, 203
preaching in India and, 262
quoted on book distribution, 200

quoted on falldown, 232
quoted on temple facility, 204
RDTSKP report by, 129
scriptural exams and, 225-26
women's issue and, 286
Tantra śāstras, 498-99
Taparia, Kanailal, 539, 550
Tata Iron Factory, 99
Tatpur dāsa, 388, 465
Tejīyas dāsa, 14, 15, 107, 110
Temple management
Bhavānanda and, 339
Calcutta and, 256-57
of Kṛṣṇa-Balarāma Temple, 45, 68, 102-3, 403
Māyāpur and, 267, 346, 352-53, 440, 367
Madhudviṣa and, 263
Mahāvīra and, 353
New York and, 126
Raṅganātha Temple and, 221, 229
Tiger Lock Company, 9, 499
Ṭime, value of, 68-69
Tīrtha Mahārāja, 283, 299-300, 343
Tirupati temple, 221, 223
Titanic, 384
Titikṣavaḥ kāruṇikāḥ, 118
Transcendental Meditation, 562
Transmigration of soul, Christian and, 184
Tripurāri Swami, 82, 84, 253
Triveri, Keśavalal, 204, 205, 206-7
Trivikrama Swami, 186, 199, 355, 456
Tṛṇād api sunīcena, 127, 464, 483
Truth, experimentation and, 149
Tulasī dāsa, 254
Tulasī tea, 330
Tulasī tree, 98-99, 203, 240, 461
Tuṣṭa Kṛṣṇa Swami, 38, 237, 245-46
Tyaktvā dehaṁ punar janma, 213

U

United Nations, 266, 392, 550
University of Copenhagen, 64
Upadeśāmṛta, Śrī, 175, 185, 217-18, 251
Upaniṣads, 56
Upendra dāsa, 1-3, 235-36, 510
Uttamaśloka dāsa, 81-85

V

Vaiṣṇave jati-buddhih, 206
Vajpeye, Kailash, 444-46
Vallabhācārya-sampradāya, 176, 389-90
Varāha, Lord, 340, 342
Varṇāśrama system, 188, 189, 333
Varnāśrama University, 18
Vedānta-sāra, 543
Vedic culture, 96-97, 283-84, 522, 538
Vedic knowledge as perfect, 122
Vedic University, 246
Vegetarianism, 552, 553
Veiga, Robert, 424
Viraha dāsa, 317
Viraha Prakāśa Swami, 324-25
Viśāla dāsa, 43, 550
Viśālinī dāsī, 550
Viṣṇu, Lord, 148, 552
Viṣṇujana Swami, 286, 436, 479
Viṣṇu Purāṇa, 511
Viśvakarma dāsa, 248
Viśvanātha Cakravartī Ṭhākura, 561
Vivasvān, 24
Vivekānanda, 183, 443, 551
Voltaire, Francois, 470
Vrinda Books, 341
Vṛndāvana
attachment to Kṛṣṇa in, 91
Durgā deity in, 515
material activities in, 75-76
Prabhupāda departs, 105
residing in, 80, 281, 527
sin and, 69
spiritual atmosphere of, 29-30, 97
value of, 32
Vyāsadeva, 17
Vyavasāyātmikā buddhir, 561

W

War, 18, 59-60, 109, 112
Wealth, 101
Women
equality of, 88-90
marriage of, 277
as mother, 137
service by, 453
Tamal Krishna and, 286
Vedic culture and, 283-84
World Council of Churches, 444
World's Parliament of Religions, 443
World War II, 134, 261
World Yoga and Peace Conference, 384

Y

Yadubara dāsa, 488
Ya idaṁ paramaṁ ghuyaṁ, 214
Yamarāja, 100
Yamunā dāsī, 101-2, 144, 247-48, 372
Yamunā River, 29, 30
Yāre dekha tāre kaha, 46, 128, 242, 477
Yaśodā, Mother, 91, 97
Yaśodānandana Swami
as BBT trustee, 420
Dvārakā-*śilā* and, 223
gṛhastha/sannyāsī controversy and, 402
impersonalism and, 138
Nāma Haṭṭa party and, 185
quoted on food shortage, 231
quoted on Varāha Narasiṁha, 511-12
Ramakrishna Mission and, 183
South Indian preaching by, 62, 138, 212-13, 332, 359, 375, 511
Yasya deve parā bhaktir, 561
Yasyāsti bhaktir bhagavaty, 137-38
Yat karoṣi yad aśnāsi, 290
Yei kṛṣṇa-tattva-vettā, 454, 465
Ye 'nye 'ravindākṣa, 179
Yogashakti Ma, 384-85
Yogeścandra dāsa, 72